Mum
eratum.

BUSH

Verbena bidens. Lag
Verbena thymifolia
(thebula)

MATA NEGRA

A solid tuft of flowers
No scent.

Nierembergia patagonica Speg

Oenothera Odordin.

Alstroemeria
patagonica Phil.

Solanum triflorum Nutt.

Mimulus glaucaris H.B.K.

Califol·

berris buxifolia

Adesmia boronioides
Hook fil

Calligraya vilagerina

Lady's Slipper
calceolaria polyrrhiza (smooth leaf)
C. lanceolata (hairy leaf).

A Story of Patagonia

A Story of Patagonia

John Locke Blake

The Book Guild Ltd
Sussex, England

First published in Great Britain in 2003 by
The Book Guild Ltd
25 High Street
Lewes, East Sussex
BN7 2LU

Typesetting in England by MRM Graphics Ltd.

Printed in England by SRP Ltd.

A catalogue record for this book is available from
The British Library.

ISBN 1 85776 678 4

Contents

Foreword   ix

Preface   xi

Acknowledgement   xiii

Maps   xiv

1   Beware of Britons   1
    Conquest by Spain
    English pirates
    Other expeditions
    The English invasions
    First feet in Patagonia
    The *gauchos*

2   A Whole New Country   21
    New Argentines
    The *Beagle* and her Channel
    Straits settlement
    Camwy Colony
    Traders on the coast
    Settlers by invitation

3   Somerset to South Atlantic   40
    The early Blakes
    Falkland Islands
    Hill Cove
    The drovers
    Partnership

4   Port San Julian   60
    Estancia Coronel
    The company
    Uncle Robert
    The new farm
    Robert and Edith

5   Robert and Arthur   **77**
     War service
     The Intervention
     The strike
     The town
     Dipping

6   Arthur and Millicent   **95**
     Home and marriage
     Life in the camp
     Up to the Big House
     Hotel Miramar
     The nursery

7   To School and Back   **114**
     Snow and show
     Schooling
     The 'phoney' war
     Transatlantic dash

8   Growing Up   **131**
     Interlude at home
     The Grange
     Farm holidays
     School leaver

9   To the Falklands   **151**
     Fox Bay West
     Hill Cove
     Shearing
     Stanley Sports
     'Westfield'

10   Home in England   **168**
     Army service
     Cambridge
     Gaviota
     Graduation
     Patagonia revisited

11   Monica and John   **191**
     Deck tennis
     Down to work

Winter alone
Newly wed

12   Home in the Falklands   **210**
The bungalow
First UK leave
Royal visit
Move to Condor
The golden years

13   Junior Management   **227**
Estancia Condor
Setting up house
The old ways
Rebuilding

14   Senior Management   **248**
April Fool's Day
The new ways
Sandy Point
Farm merger

15   Cormo Argentino   **270**
Three-quarter bred
Round the world
Green pastures
Boarding schools
Back to college
Oil and gas

16   The 'Queen's Farm'   **293**
Cañadon Condor
The dirty war
Scab in the south
Cordoba Hills
Letter to Perón

17   The Family's Farm   **315**
Ganadera Coronel SA
Summer holidays
Diagonal Norte 547
Storm clouds
Sale of Coronel

18   Our Own Farm   **338**
     Last Christmas together
     Community relations
     Killik Aike Norte
     Beach cottage
     New Year's honours

19   South Atlantic Tragedy   **360**
     Vernet and the *gauchos*
     The inconvenient colony
     Galtieri and the marines
     The forgotten community
     Post-war repercussions

20   A New Day Dawns   **382**
     Down to basics
     The Lady Friend
     'Keoken'
     Centenaries
     Congresses
     Artic to Antartic
     Academy recognition

21   Modern Patagonia   **405**
     Retirement
     Benetton
     Moving house
     The snow of the century
     Gathering the roots

Appendix 1:   ***Early History of the Falkland Islands***   **428**

Appendix 2:   ***Technical Aspects of Sheep Production***   **432**

Appendix 3:   ***Bibliography***   **440**

Appendix 4:   ***Family Trees***   **443**

Index   **448**

Foreword

A Story of Patagonia follows the lives of generations of distinguished Anglo-Argentine farming families in Patagonia, set in the context of Argentina's history. Aficionados of travel, biography, history and geography – not to mention farming and South America – will be among those who find much of interest in these pages.

Readers will live, as it were, with the families on the farms, looking out over the windy expanses of Patagonia, smelling the deliciously sizzling grills at *asados*, riding with the shepherds and perhaps joining in songs at haunts like the Miramar hotel in San Julian (the words are provided). They will also learn something about gaucho lore and a lot about sheep and their husbandry. They will travel on journeys which seem formidable but which were a normal part of life. Particularly evocative for me were the train journey to school in Chile over the Andes from Argentina and the frightening voyage of a young boy returning home from England in 1940, on an unprotected ship across the Atlantic at the height of war.

The historical background to the settlement of Argentina is vividly described. Magellan, Drake, San Martin, Rosas, Darwin, Pinochet, Peron and Evita will all be encountered, together with Chileans, Falkland Islanders and the Welsh community of Patagonia. There will even be cameo appearances by Butch Cassidy, St Exupery and Tarquin the Bull.

As the narrative unfolds it reveals wider issues underlying the history. Some of these, such as the fate of the Tehuelche and other 'Indian' people are briefly exposed. Others, including Argentina's difficulty in achieving consistent democratic prosperity and the differences between Argentina and Britain over the South Atlantic, are discussed in more depth. On certain historical episodes, notably the dreadful 'dirty war', opinions are offered and those of readers may differ with them. However there would surely be wide support for the implication throughout the book that Britain and Argentina should succeed in creating a more constructive relationship in respect of the Falklands than has been the case at times in the past.

A Story of Patagonia paints a detailed picture of the lives and livelihoods of the Anglo-Argentines. They represent now a very small proportion of the population (less than one per cent); yet, as the book shows, they played a crucial role in developing the very successful Argentine economy of the late 19th and early 20th centuries. Their institutions, as well as their community spirit and individual sacrifices in two world wars, are well described. Certain of the institutions, such as the excellent secondary schools and the British Hospital, flourish now as true Argentine assets. It would be good to think that for the future the skills of the 'Anglos', not least in building trust and making institutions work, will be put to the service of Argentina as a whole.

I hope, too, that John Blake's book will inspire people to visit Patagonia for themselves. There they will be able to experience and enjoy spectacular scenery, remarkable natural sights such as the Moreno glacier, the national parks and the wonderful wildlife, like that in the estuary at Puerto Deseado and in the seas around Puerto Madryn when the whales return to rear their young. Estancias like those in *A Story of Patagonia* will welcome the visitor. And if you have read this book you will be mightily well prepared.

William Marsden CMG, British Ambassador to Argentina 1997-2000

Preface

Calafate is a shrub which grows all over Patagonia. There are in fact several species, but they all have in common hard spiky thorns, bright yellow flowers and sweet purple berries. Because Patagonia is a land of contrasts, the wild arid steppes setting off the green watered valleys, imposing mountains giving way to flat unending pampas, howling gales alternating with soft spring breezes, calafate has become a symbol of this land of extremes. Few people are indifferent to Patagonia – either you love it or you hate it. But local tradition says that if you have eaten the fruit of the calafate then you will always come back.

This book is about people – real people and what they did. Those who went and settled in Patagonia a hundred and more years ago had to adjust to a new and exacting environment, meeting conditions very different from those prevailing in their countries of origin. As time went by, changes took place both in Patagonia and in the rest of the world, requiring adjustments of all sorts. But even though such changes have been accompanied by progress in transport, communications and related technology, the basic thorny character of the region remains. This creates situations and requirements not often met with elsewhere, the resolution of which requires dedication and originality. This poses a challenge which can provide great satisfaction and a sense of achievement to the doers, which is why there are still people who must have eaten calafate berries, as they return time and again.

Most of the people we are going to hear about had one thing in common: their lives revolved around, and depended upon, the ***sheep***. This humble animal, in all its shapes, sizes, colours and breeds, has provided food, clothing and wealth for man for thousands of years. It has provided the basis for whole cultures and ways of life, and Patagonia – which is the real subject of all these musings – would not have been settled at all were it not for the sheep.

Nowadays there are other productive activities in Patagonia, but they could not have begun without the basis of settlement and civic infrastructure which was created, maintained and developed for nearly a century by people who were concerned, directly or indirectly, with sheep.

This is the story of some of them.

Acknowledgements

This is a true story – about things which happened and about real people. Where we are concerned with recorded history I have quoted the proper sources, but much has been gathered directly from the people concerned with the story, their relatives and descendants and has never been published. I have tried to get it right, but if there is the occasional date, name or place which is not quite correct then please forgive me – the overall story is there just the same. Thank you all for your help.

Particular thanks are due to Norberto Bentivoglio whose original drawings decorate and add atmosphere to the chapter headings and endings, to my brother Hugh who drew the maps and assembled the family trees, and to Jane Cameron in Port Stanley, Osvaldo Topcic in Rio Gallegos and John Wilson in Windsor, Nova Scotia, for research into archives to find relationships and other historical details. The watercolours of Patagonian wild flowers which decorate the endpapers were painted by my mother, Millicent Blake, between 1924 and 1939.

But it is my immediate family whom I must thank especially, for unfailing advice and even more importantly, criticism and suggestions, and most especially my wife, Monica, who has shared in all the experiences related and to whom the book is fondly dedicated.

Map 1: Argentina

Main Map

70 65 60 55 50

La Quiaca
JUJUY

Antofagasta
Humahuaca

PARAGUAY

R. Pilcomayo

GRAN CHACO

SALTA

R. Paraguay

25

Atacama
Desert

FORMOSA

Asuncion

R. Parana

BRAZIL

2

Bay of
Santa
Caterin.

CATAMARCA

TUCUMAN

SANTIAGO
DEL
ESTERO

CHACO

Corrientes

MISIONES

LA
RIOJA

CORRIENTES

Coquimbo

ARGENTINA

SANTA
FE

R. Parana

30

SAN
JUAN

La Cumbre
Cordoba

CORDOBA HILLS

Concordia

R. Uruguay

3

CHILE

CORDOBA

ENTRE
RIOS

Salto

Uspallata Pass
Vina del Mar
Valparaiso

M.Aconcagua

Venado
Tuerto

Rosario

Paysandu

URUGUAY

Santiago

Mendoza

SAN
LUIS

Zarate

Colonia

M. Tupungato

MENDOZA

Buenos Aires

Montevideo

Solis
Maldonado

35

Curico

Gen.Pico

La Plata

Punta del Este

Concepcion

Quemu-Quemu

**BUENOS
AIRES**

Chascomus

Rio de la Plata (River Plate)

3

LA PAMPA

Coronel
Pringles

C. San
Antonio

Samborombon Bay

Bahia
Blanca

Necochea

Miles 0 120 240 360 480

N

NEUQUEN

Choele-
Choel

Km 0 200 400 600 80

R. Bio-bio

Zapala

R. Limay

R. Negro

Conesa

40

Junin

San Martin

RIO NEGRO

Carmen de
Patagones

4

Puerto
Montt

Viedma

Bariloche

PATAGONIA

Peninsula
Valdes

Maiten
Leleque

Madryn

Isla de
Chiloé

Esquel

Trelew

Golfo Nuevo

Trevelin

R. Chubut

Rawson

Tecka

Camarones

Chonos
Archipelago

CHUBUT

45

45

M. Hudson

Comodoro
Rivadavia

L. Buenos
Aires

Los Antiguos

R. Deseado

Deseado

L. Pueyrredon

R. Baker

Lago
Posadas

**SANTA
CRUZ**

50

San Julian

R. Santa Cruz

Santa Cruz

**Falkland Islands
(Islas Malvinas)**

50

Lat Hope
Inlet

Rio Gallegos

Puerto
Natales

Cape Virgins

Straits of Magellan

Punta
Arenas

Tierra
del Fuego

Straits of Le Maire

55

Ushuaia

55

Beagle Channel

Cape Horn

75 70 65 60

Inset Map: South America

75 60 45

PANAMA

Maracaibo

VENEZUELA

COLOMBIA

River Amazon

0

ECUADOR

Galapagos
Islands

Payta

46° 37'

BRAZIL

PERU

Lima

Arequipa

La Paz

Mollendo

BOLIVIA

15

Sao
Paolo

Rio de
Janeiro

**Tropic of
Capricorn**

Iquique

CORDILLERA DE LOS ANDES

CHILE

PARAGUAY

30

Santiago

URUGUAY

SOUTH

**Is de Juan
Fernandez**

Buenos Aires

Montevideo

River Plate

ATLANTIC

ARGENTINA

OCEAN

PACIFIC

45

OCEAN

**Falkland Islands
(Islas Malvinas)**

South
Georgi.

75 Drake Passage 60 45

Map 1: Argentina

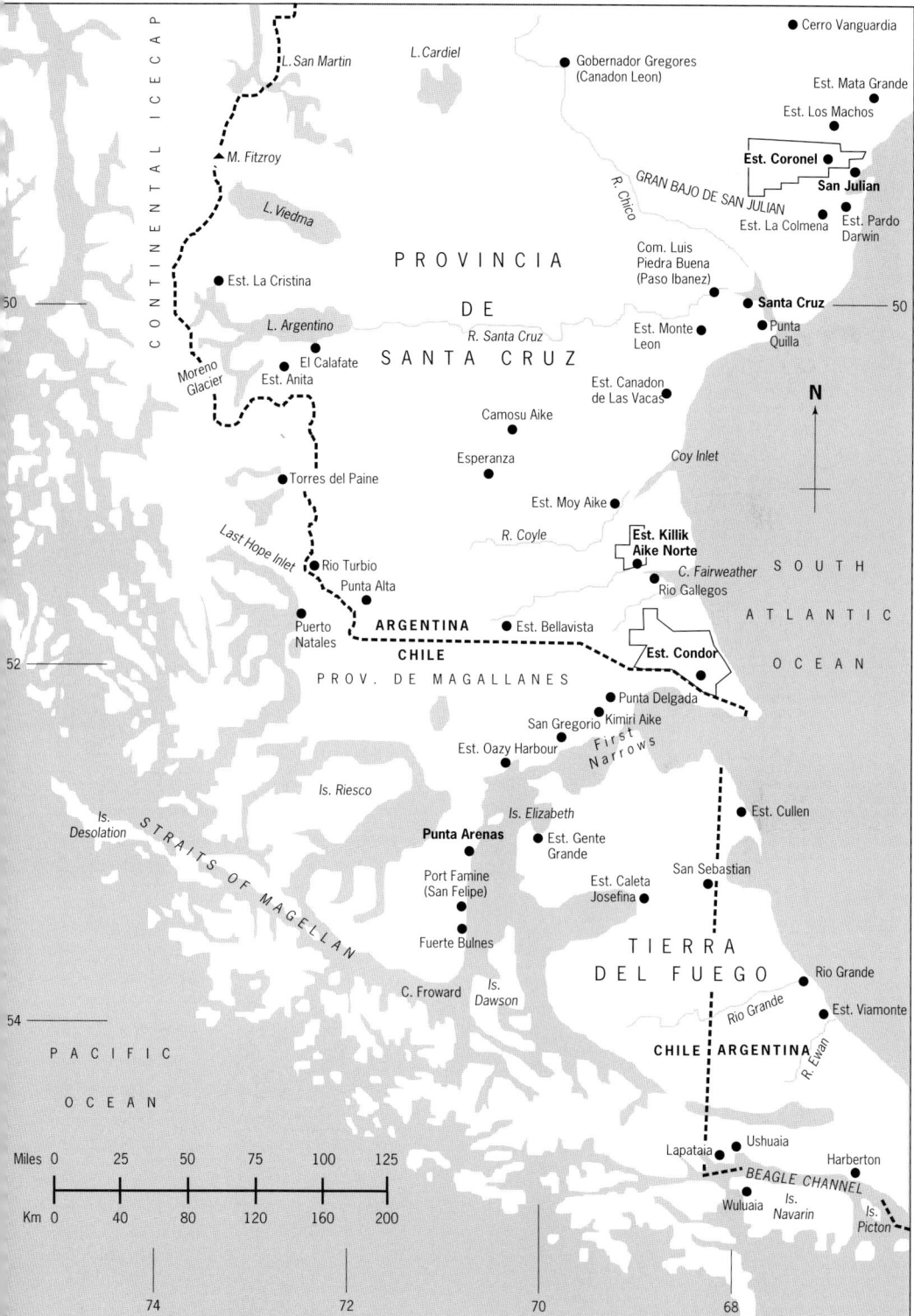

Map 2: Southern Patagonia

CONTINENTAL ICECAP

L. San Martin
L. Cardiel
● Cerro Vanguardia
● Gobernador Gregores
(Canadon Leon)
● Est. Mata Grande
● Est. Los Machos
Est. Coronel ●
▲ M. Fitzroy
R. Chico
GRAN BAJO DE SAN JULIAN
San Julian
● Est. La Colmena
● Est. Pardo
Darwin
L. Viedma
PROVINCIA
DE
● Est. La Cristina
L. Argentino
Com. Luis
Piedra Buena
(Paso Ibanez)
● **Santa Cruz**
50
50
SANTA CRUZ
R. Santa Cruz
Est. Monte
Leon ●
● Punta
Quilla
Moreno
Glacier
El Calafate
Est. Anita
Est. Canadon
de Las Vacas ●
● Camosu Aike
Coy Inlet
N
● Esperanza
● Torres del Paine
Est. Moy Aike ●
**Est. Killik
Aike Norte**
R. Coyle
C. Fairweather
SOUTH
Last Hope Inlet
● Rio Turbio
Rio Gallegos
ATLANTIC
● Punta Alta
Puerto
Natales
ARGENTINA
● Est. Bellavista
Est. Condor
OCEAN
52
CHILE
PROV. DE MAGALLANES
● Punta Delgada
San Gregorio ● Kimiri Aike
First Narrows
● Est. Cullen
Est. Oazy Harbour ●
Is. Riesco
Is. Elizabeth
Punta Arenas ●
● Est. Gente
Grande
San Sebastian ●
Is.
Desolation
STRAITS OF MAGELLAN
Port Famine
(San Felipe)
Est. Caleta
Josefina ●
TIERRA
DEL FUEGO
● Rio Grande
Fuerte Bulnes
Rio Grande
● Est. Viamonte
54
C. Froward
Is.
Dawson
CHILE ARGENTINA
R. Ewan
PACIFIC
OCEAN
● Ushuaia
Lapataia ●
Harberton ●
BEAGLE CHANNEL
Wuluaia ●
Is.
Navarin
Is.
Picton

Miles	0	25	50	75	100	125
Km	0	40	80	120	160	200

74
72
70
68

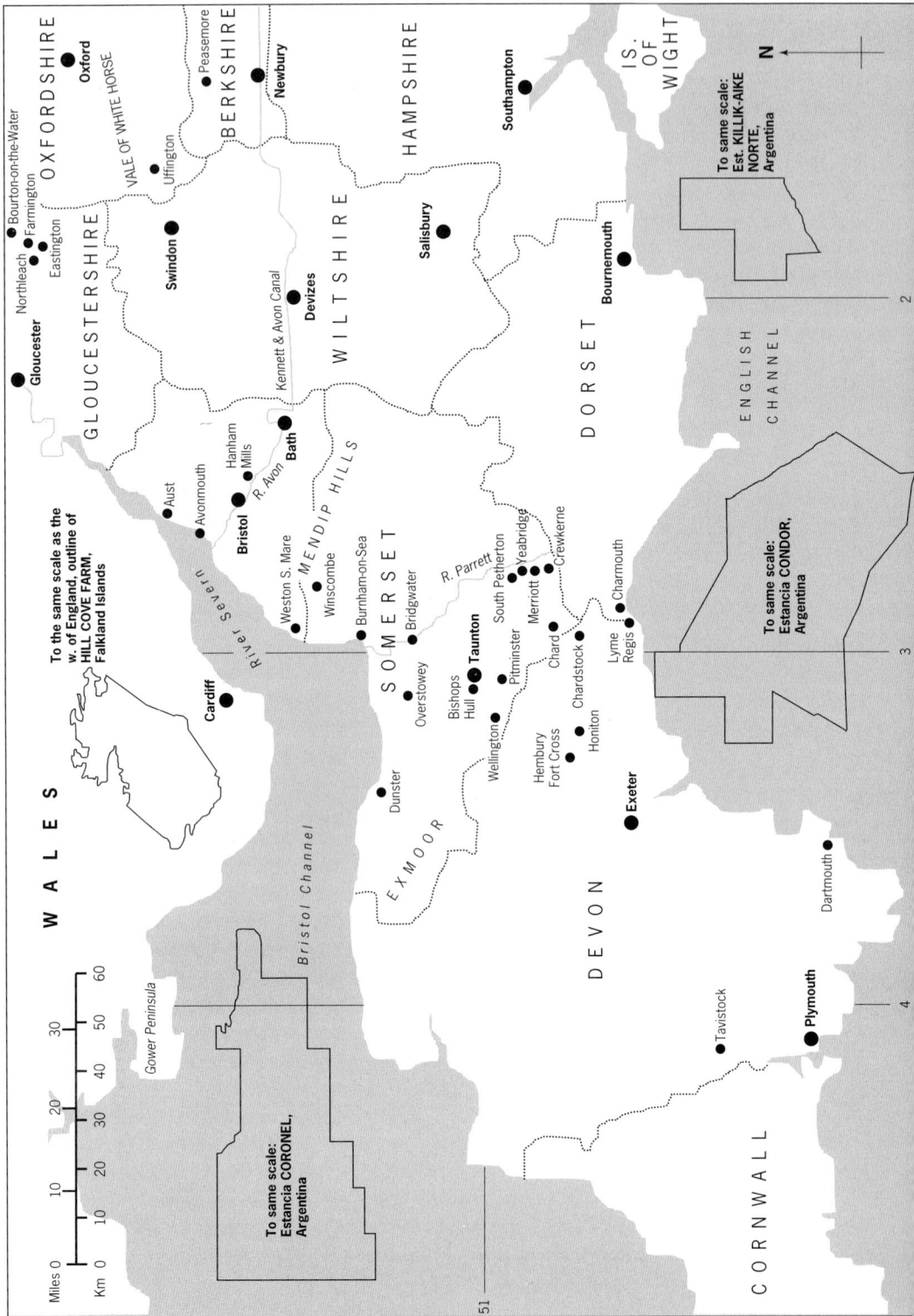

Map 3: The West of England

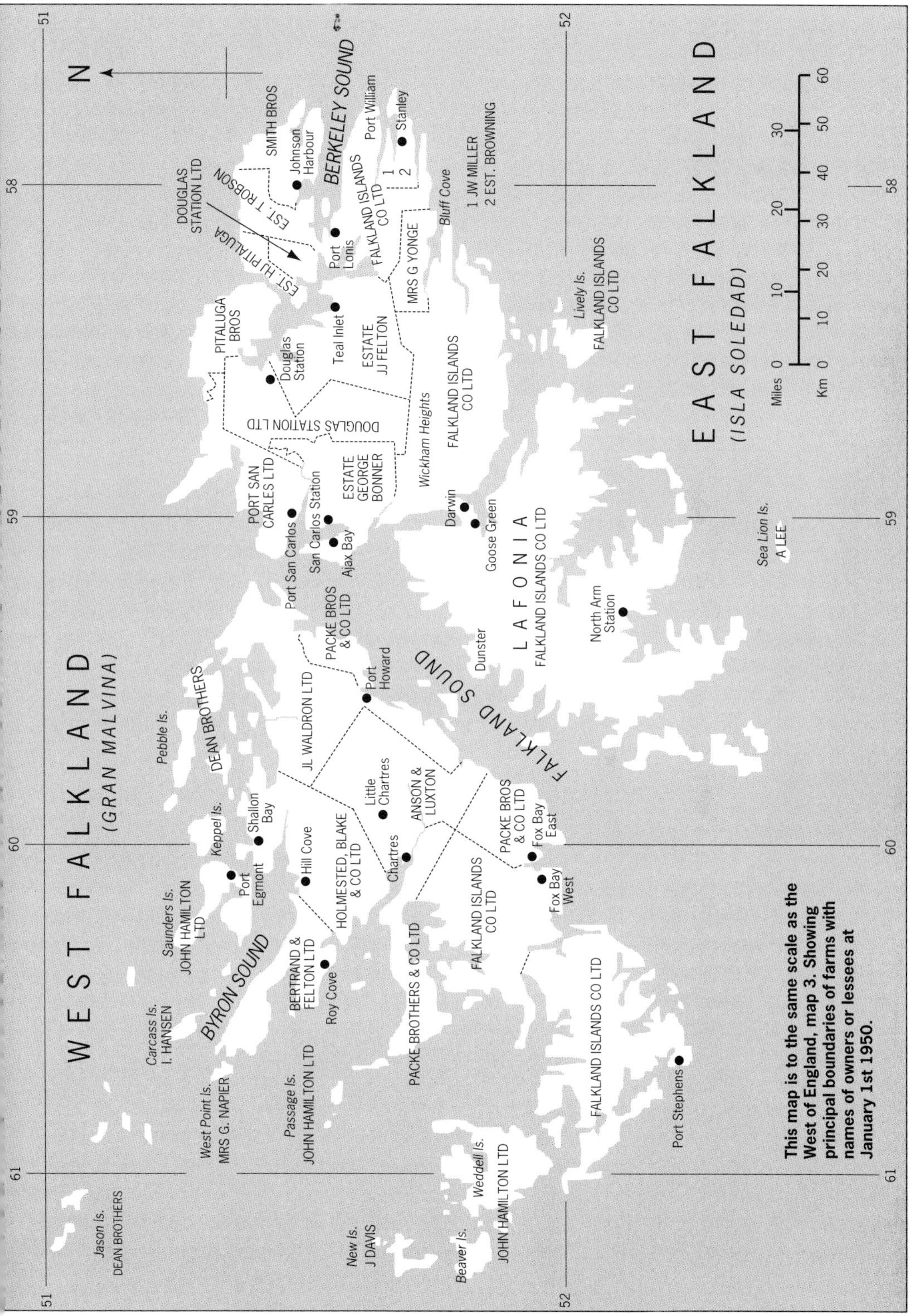

Map 4: The Falkland Islands (Islas Malvinas)

This map is to the same scale as the West of England, map 3. Showing principal boundaries of farms with names of owners or lessees at January 1st 1950.

WEST FALKLAND
(GRAN MALVINA)

EAST FALKLAND
(ISLA SOLEDAD)

N

BERKELEY SOUND

SMITH BROS

Johnson Harbour

DOUGLAS STATION LTD

EST. T ROBSON

EST. HJ PITALUGA

Port Louis

Port William

Stanley

1 JW MILLER
2 EST. BROWNING

FALKLAND ISLANDS CO LTD

1
2

Bluff Cove

MRS G YONGE

PITALUGA BROS

Teal Inlet

ESTATE JJ FELTON

Douglas Station

Lively Is.
FALKLAND ISLANDS CO LTD

DOUGLAS STATION LTD

Wickham Heights

PORT SAN CARLES LTD

Port San Carlos

ESTATE GEORGE BONNER

FALKLAND ISLANDS CO LTD

San Carlos Station

Ajax Bay

Darwin

Goose Green

LAFONIA

FALKLAND ISLANDS CO LTD

Sea Lion Is.
A LEE

PACKE BROS & CO LTD

Pebble Is.

DEAN BROTHERS

JL WALDRON LTD

Port Howard

Dunster

North Arm Station

FALKLAND SOUND

Keppel Is.

Shallon Bay

Little Chartres

ANSON & LUXTON

Saunders Is.
JOHN HAMILTON LTD

Port Egmont

Hill Cove

Chartres

PACKE BROS & CO LTD

Fox Bay East

Carcass Is.
I. HANSEN

BYRON SOUND

HOLMESTED, BLAKE & CO LTD

Fox Bay West

West Point Is.
MRS G. NAPIER

BERTRAND & FELTON LTD

Roy Cove

FALKLAND ISLANDS CO LTD

Passage Is.
JOHN HAMILTON LTD

PACKE BROTHERS & CO LTD

Jason Is.
DEAN BROTHERS

New Is.
J DAVIS

Weddell Is.
JOHN HAMILTON LTD

Beaver Is.

FALKLAND ISLANDS CO LTD

Port Stephens

Miles 0   10   20   30   40   50   60

Km 0   10   20   30   40   50   60

51

58

59

60

61

52

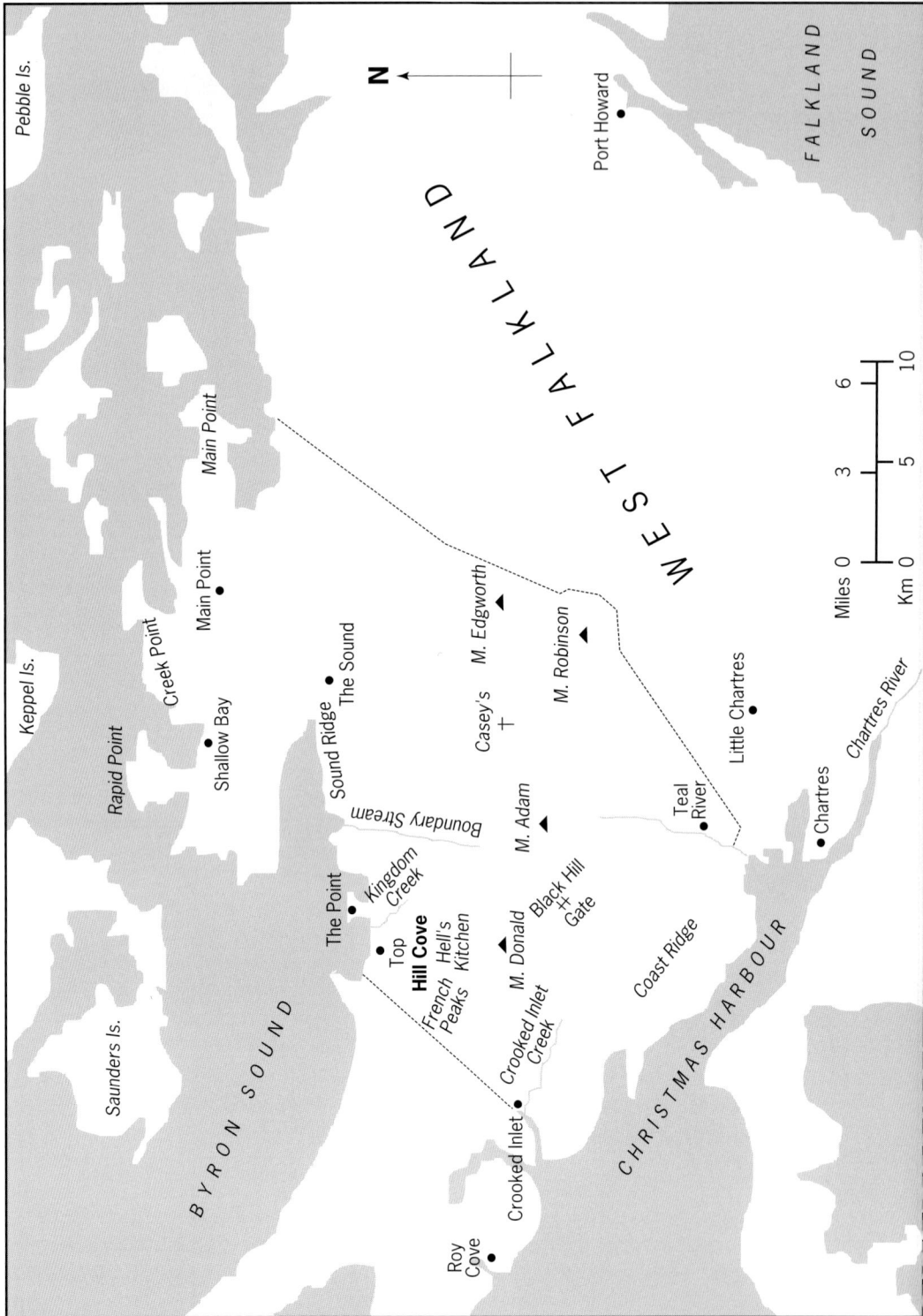

Map 5: Hill Cove Station

Pebble Is.

Keppel Is.

Saunders Is.

Rapid Point

Creek Point

Main Point

Main Point

Shallow Bay

Sound Ridge

The Sound

The Point

Top

Kingdom Creek

Hill Cove

Hell's Kitchen

French Peaks

Boundary Stream

Casey's

M. Edgworth

M. Robinson

M. Adam

M. Donald

Black Hill Gate

Crooked Inlet Creek

Crooked Inlet

Roy Cove

Coast Ridge

Teal River

Little Chartres

Chartres

Chartres River

Port Howard

WEST FALKLAND

FALKLAND SOUND

BYRON SOUND

CHRISTMAS HARBOUR

N

Miles   0   3   6

Km   0   5   10

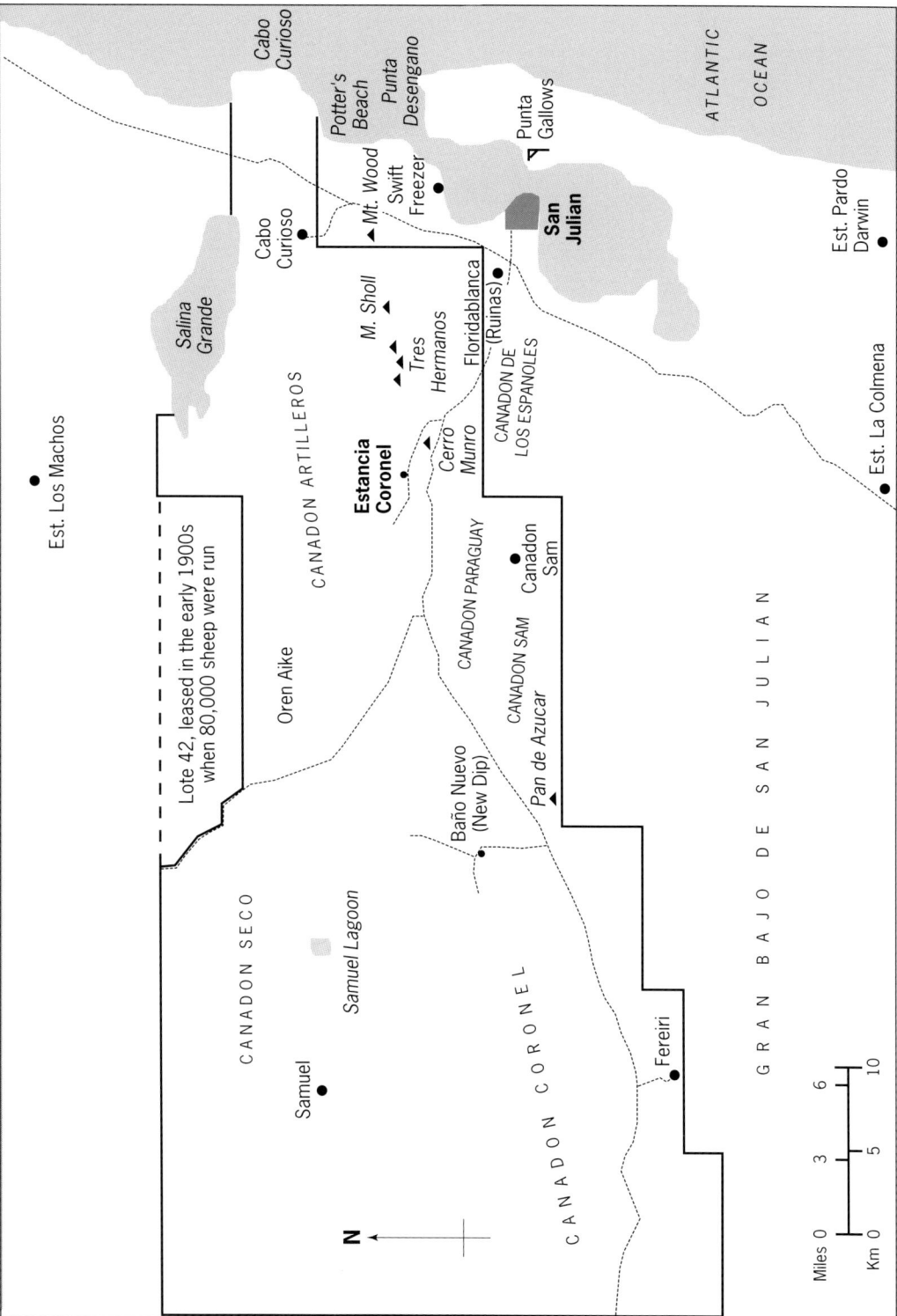

Map 6: Estancia Coronel

Est. Los Machos

Salina Grande

Cabo Curioso

Cabo Curioso

Potter's Beach

Punta Desengano

Mt. Wood

Swift Freezer

Punta Gallows

San Julian

ATLANTIC OCEAN

Est. Pardo Darwin

M. Sholl

Tres Hermanos

Floridablanca (Ruinas)

CAÑADON ARTILLEROS

Estancia Coronel

Cerro Munro

CAÑADON DE LOS ESPAÑOLES

Est. La Colmena

Oren Aike

CAÑADON PARAGUAY

Cañadon Sam

CAÑADON SAM

Pan de Azucar

Lote 42, leased in the early 1900s when 80,000 sheep were run

Baño Nuevo (New Dip)

CAÑADON SECO

Samuel Lagoon

Samuel

CAÑADON CORONEL

GRAN BAJO DE SAN JULIAN

Fereiri

N

Miles 0   3   6
Km 0   5   10

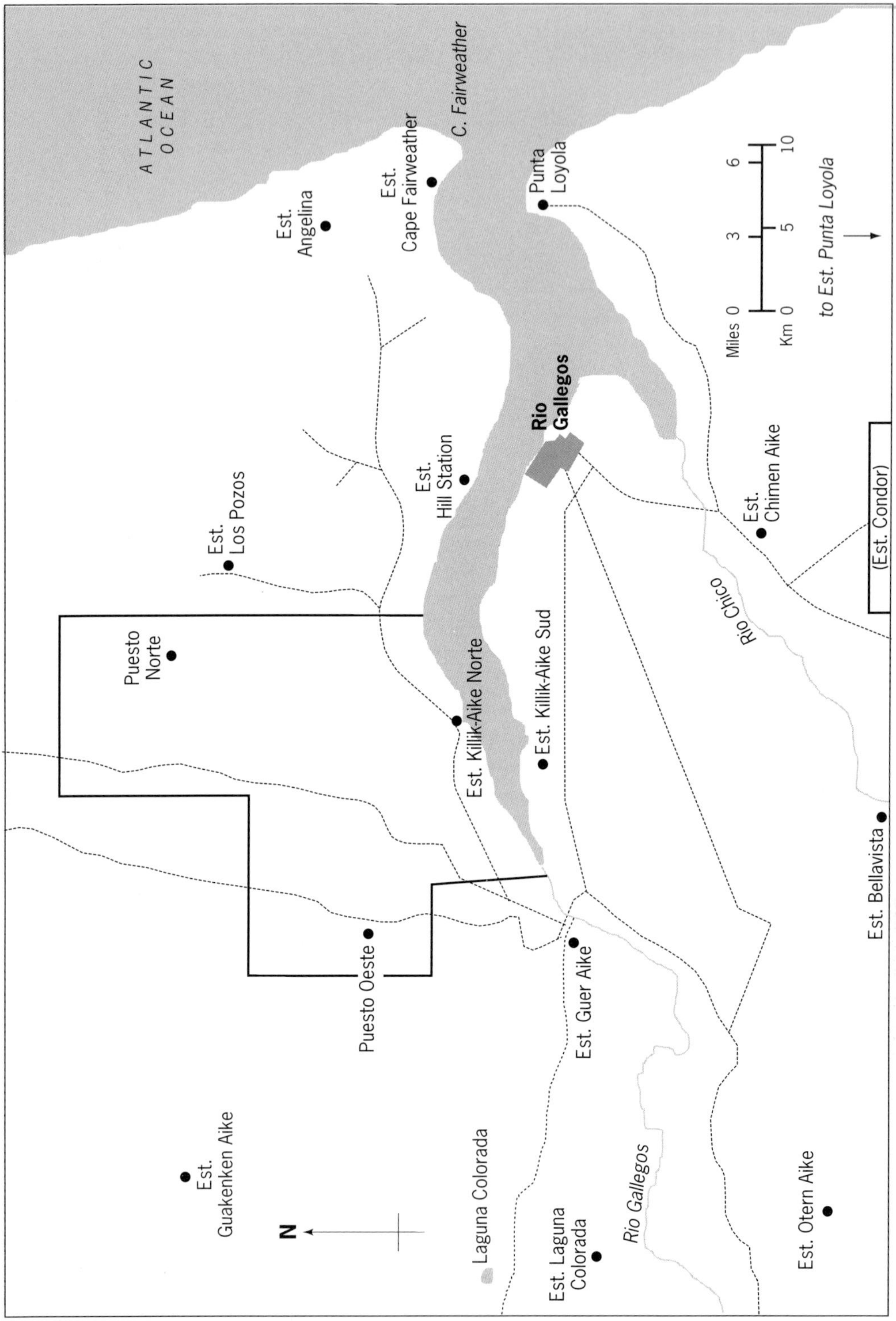

Map 7: Estancia Killik Aike Norte

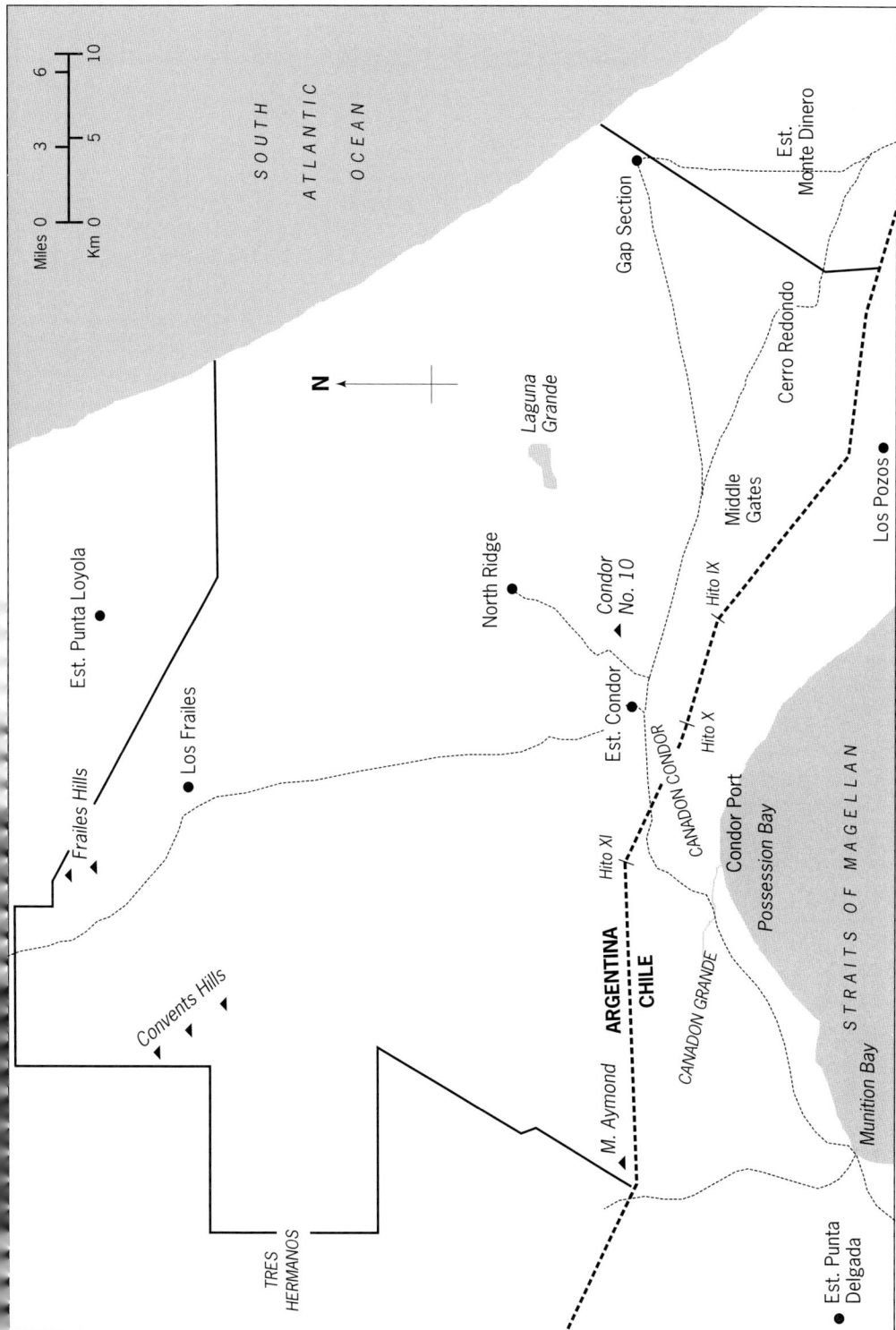

Map 8: Estancia Condor

1

Beware of Britons

Conquest by Spain

It all started of course with Columbus discovering America in 1492, followed by the conquest of much of South America by Spain. Buenos Aires was first named by Juan Díaz de Solís in 1515, but was not finally settled until 1580, by Juan de Garay. After this, lines of communication and outposts were extended north-west towards the gold and silver mines of the Andes, giving rise to the name *Rio de la Plata* (River of Silver), anglicised as 'River Plate'. On the Pacific side, the Spanish conquest spread down from the isthmus of Panama to Peru. From there they pushed eastwards across the Andes and Bolivia into what is today north-western Argentina, setting up trade routes down and out to the River Plate. Following down the Pacific coast, the Conquistadores continued as far as southern Chile, but were halted at the Bío-Bío River by the Araucanians. This was later to have far-reaching consequences for sovereignty issues in southern Argentina.

The Portuguese in the meantime had tended to voyage eastwards, following the discovery of the Cape of Good Hope by Bartolomé Dias in 1488, but they also voyaged westwards (from Lusitania) and this soon brought trouble with Spain, who considered America their own stamping ground. The Pope, as so often, had to pour oil on the dispute which was resolved by the Treaty of Tordesillas in 1494. In this it was agreed that all new discoveries east of a meridian defined as '370 leagues west of Cape Verde' would belong to Portugal and those west of this line would belong to Spain. The Pope's intention was clearly to leave America to Spain, but eventually the 370 leagues was found to coincide with the meridian 46°37' west of Greenwich which runs from the mouth of the Amazon down roughly to Porto Alegre, which is why Brazil got to be settled by the Portuguese.

Magellan, on his voyage of discovery, headed south-west from the Brazilian coast, across the stormy bay of Santa Catarina, but being Portuguese was not concerned with the River Plate as such, although he crossed its mouth near enough to the north shore to see the *cerro* (hill) of present-day Montevideo, which he named accordingly: *'monte video'*, meaning 'I see a hill' in Latin. Continuing south without landing, they reached the sheltered waters of San Julian Bay in March 1520, where in thanksgiving for their safe arrival they celebrated Mass for the first time on Patagonian soil. Here also they recorded the first encounter with the natives (Tehuelche) who appeared to the fearful mariners to be of enormous stature. Modern ethnic studies have indicated that they were in fact some 10cm taller than the Spaniards and Portuguese of the time, but their use of loosely-wrapped skins by way of footwear left very large footprints. Whatever their stature, it was these footprints which caused the newly-discovered land to be described in the chronicles of the time as *Tierra de los Patagones* or Patagonia, from the Spanish *pata* (foot) and *-gón* = large. (1) Following the Spanish introduction of horses to America by Juan de Garay, most native nations including the Tehuelche soon became magnificent horsemen, thus starting the still surviving Patagonian custom of not walking anywhere if you can possibly ride, be it on a horse or in a vehicle! But in Magellan's day the Tehuelche still walked on their own two feet, whatever size they may have been.

While at San Julian, Magellan had to deal with a mutiny, which was put down and the ringleaders beheaded on what is still known as Isla de la Justicia (Island of Justice). (In medieval Spain, *justicia* meant not only justice as such, but the carrying out of a sentence – usually execution!) He then continued south to the Santa Cruz river, and then to the Gallegos, named after one of the sailing masters of the expedition and not, as is often thought, after the inhabitants of the Spanish province of Galicia, many of whom later settled in this area. From there he continued south to Cape (of the eleven thousand) Virgins, discovered on Saint Ursula's day, and into the straits which bear his name. In spite of the limitations of the ships of the day with their elementary rigging, which made beating up against the prevailing south-westerly winds difficult, Magellan was able to get through the straits and so on into the Pacific and round the world.

English pirates

Spain did not at first take much interest in Magellan's discoveries, until the escapades of English seafarers obliged her to devote great importance and considerable outlay to the setting up of outposts and to fortify the region against the 'English pirates'. This was not without good reason, since the Elizabethan captains, many of them veterans of the defeat of the Spanish Armada in 1588, achieved considerable success in raiding the Spanish Main (the mainland of Central America) and taking treasure galleons, not always under a clearly defined state of war. Queen Elizabeth I, whose diplomacy often blew hot and cold relative to Spain, used to issue Letters of Marque to her trusted captains. This was an accepted practice at sea right up to the mid-nineteenth century, whereby one country, by issuing such documents, would authorise the bearers, known as 'privateers', to attack the shipping of one or more other countries (specified) with whom the issuing monarch was possibly at loggerheads but not actually at war. Pirates, on the other hand, were ship-borne thieves and brigands of any nationality (often many) who preyed on whoever they could catch. The difference between pirates and privateers was not always obvious to the victims.

The first and most spectacular *pirata inglés* was Sir Francis Drake, who following Magellan's route in 1578 made a landfall at San Julian, where he also beheaded two mutineers. He was unable to negotiate the Magellan Straits, but steered well south of Cape Horn, which had been discovered by the Dutch, Schouten and Le Maire, in 1516, reaching the Pacific via Drake Passage which separates the American continent from Antarctica. After causing the Spanish Main considerable distress by raiding the relatively undefended Pacific side, he eventually crossed the Pacific to circumnavigate the globe.

Hawkins was another voyager, and probably the first Englishman to sight some islands out there which he did not explore, but named 'Hawkins' Maidenland' in honour of Elizabeth I, the 'Virgin Queen', who no doubt had contributed financially to the expedition, and later profited by it. Elizabeth was no fool when it came to business. This land was the Falkland Islands, subsequently discovered by Davis in the *Desire*, on Cavendish's second expedition in 1592. No attempt was made at this stage to land, although as a matter of principle Davis claimed it for England.

In 1581, after Drake's resounding voyage, Spain sent out an expedition under Pedro Sarmiento de Gamboa with the logical purpose of fortifying the Straits of Magellan against further incursions by the English. Sixteen ships with some 2,000 sailors, soldiers, priests and settlers, including women, set forth from Cadiz. Dissent among the fleet reduced it to five ships, which reached Cape Virgins and founded the fort, 'Nombre de Jesús', in 1584. Four of them returned to Spain, leaving Sarmiento with some 277 colonists

3

Entrance to Port San Julian, Mt Wood on right. From Charles Darwin's Beagle Diary, 1834

and only one small vessel, the *María*. They soon realised that it would be impossible to survive at that exposed site, so with the *María* going ahead to explore, they trekked west, round the north shore of the straits, to a point some 50km south of what today is Punta Arenas. There they founded 'Ciudad de San Felipe'. Sarmiento saw to the building of houses and the church, and then returned to Spain to fetch supplies, but was captured by the dastardly English and never returned. In spite of the new fort being in a more sheltered position, they all perished except for one survivor who was found in 1586 by Cavendish, who had watered at Puerto Deseado (Port Desire), thought to be named after his flagship, the *Desire*. San Felipe today is known as Puerto Hambre (Port Famine).

Inevitably, Spain would refer to all English privateers as *piratas*, whether they carried Letters of Marque or not. The 'English pirates' tradition became so strong in Argentina that during the South Atlantic War some traditional names for food items such as *sopa Inglesa* (trifle) or *Salsa Inglesa* (Worcester Sauce) appeared on restaurant menus in Buenos Aires as *sopa pirata* and *Salsa pirata*. Admittedly the picture was complicated by the activities of the likes of Henry Morgan who in the seventeenth century started his career as a pirate, and carried out a number of operations against the Spaniards, including the sack of Maracaibo, with and without Letters of Marque. He amassed a large fortune (still not found, it is said) and then 'turned honest' and was knighted by the newly-restored King Charles II, becoming vice-governor of Jamaica, possibly on the basis that an ex-buccaneer was the best person to keep order in the turbulent Caribbean.

After the English Civil War the Spanish Crown was reluctant to recognise the Commonwealth, and gave some succour to the Royalist ships of Prince Rupert. This produced yet another situation of semi-hostilities, whereby in 1655 Cromwell first sent out his 'general-at-sea', Admiral Robert Blake (2) to show the flag and generally point out to the Spaniards the error of their ways. This proved to be a wearisome campaign involving long periods at sea, watching and waiting, and solving problems of victualling the increasingly crank ships. It finally culminated in the Tenerife Raid of 1657, in the course of which Blake captured twelve galleons of the Spanish Treasure Fleet homeward bound from Panama, thus adding his name to the illustrious roll of *pirata inglés*, even though the Commonwealth government had attempted to save their puritan conscience by declaring war on Spain in 1656, just before they actually ordered Blake to seize the treasure fleet.

Other expeditions

The only English expedition in the seventeenth century not considered hostile by Spain was that of John Narborough (1669–71) who did much exploring and surveying of the Patagonian coast south of Puerto Deseado, and made some contact with the aboriginals. His boatswain, John Wood, while exploring inland from San Julian, left his name incised on the rocks of what is still known as 'Mount Wood'.

Commodore George Anson (1740–44) was not a pirate or even a privateer, as England was genuinely at war with Spain at the time, engaged in the little-known 'War of Jenkins' Ear'. His fleet of seven ships was ordered out by Whitehall in 1740 with the specific purpose of raiding or even capturing the Spanish possessions on the Pacific coast, complete with a train of artillery for the purpose. After much initial delay over fitting out, victualling and crewing, the expedition suffered incredible hardships including the wreck of the *Wager* on a remote island off the rocky coast of southern Chile.(3) Anson, with three ships, managed to reach Juan Fernández (Robinson Crusoe's) Island, where his depleted crews were able to recover from scurvy. Continuing north with 335 men out of the original 961 who had left England in these ships, they proceeded to sack the port of Payta and later capture the '*Manila Galleon*', full of treasure from the then Spanish Philippines, *en route* for Acapulco. Anson then continued on westwards round the world, like Drake before him, arriving back at Falmouth after a voyage of four years. Among the survivors of the *Wager* (from scurvy, exposure, mutiny and murder) was the Hon. John Byron, then still a midshipman. Known later as 'Foul-weather Jack', as Admiral Byron he also explored these same waters, discovering and naming a number of features including 'Sandy Point' (Punta Arenas), and in 1764 set up the first British settlement in the Falkland Islands, at Port Egmont on Byron Sound, in West Falkland waters. His grandson, the poet Lord George Byron, drew on the wreck of the *Wager* for his shipwreck scene in *Don Juan*.

A number of voyages by Spanish explorers were carried out in the first half of the eighteenth century, some of them by Jesuit priests (Mascardi, Stroebel, Cardiel, Falkner) in attempts to evangelise the natives. Many geographical features were discovered during this period, but they had little success in converting the heathen. No successful attempts were made at settlement, but legend has it that a group of Jesuit missionaries crossed the Andes from Chile into the eastern foothills of the upper Limay Valley (now Neuquén) bringing many European plants including apple trees. The missionaries did not survive but the apples did, becoming wild and giving their name to the 'Manzanero' tribe of warlike Indians, a branch of the Mapuche nation.

The Falkland Islands, in spite of having been sighted by Davis in 1592 among others, were first visited by the French expedition of Louis de Bougainville in 1764. He named the islands 'Malouines' (he and many of his men came from the port of St Malo) and founded the French settlement of Port Louis. The British were not far behind them, with the occupation the next year by Admiral Byron of Port Egmont in the West Falkland, so the Spanish crown became seriously concerned about all these incursions into what they considered their sphere of influence. They had been able to purchase Port Louis from the French in 1766 and, were in deep and secret negotiations with Britain over the Falkland Islands which resulted in the eventual abandonment by Britain of Port Egmont in 1774, but the real concern of Spain was directed to the mainland of South America.

Attention had been drawn to non-Spanish America by the American Declaration of Independence in 1776 and, with the ever-increasing amount of ships of all nations, not only English, capable of crossing the Atlantic, Spain was finally obliged to do more with its New World possessions than just mine gold and silver using the indigenous slave labour. 'Operation Patagonia' (4) was set up in 1778 by a Royal Order from King Carlos III, with the stated object of 'impeding the English or their insurgent colonists' from getting there first and setting up their own trading posts *(factorías)*. In the latter context it is perhaps ironic to observe that in fact it was citizens and ships of the United States who were responsible both for the Falklands denouement of 1833 and the ensuing occupation of the islands by the British. In fact, English and Dutch ships were already operating out of Puerto Deseado, taking seal and penguins for oil, for some time before the Spaniards got there.

The first result of the Royal Order was an expedition of four ships with 232 people on board, sent out from Corunna under the command of various people of whom Antonio de Viedma emerges as the final leader – he founded Carmen de Patagones *(Colonia de Nuestra Señora del Carmen)* at the mouth of the Rio Negro in 1779. Viedma continued down to San Julian where he founded the town of 'Floridablanca' in 1780, some ten miles inland from the bay. He then travelled inland as far as the lake which bears his name, before returning to Carmen de Patagones.

Spain continued to send out ship after ship with colonists intended to expand and reinforce the early settlements. These expeditions are well documented, and included genuine emigrants with families, farm and household supplies, as well as soldiers, sailors and gaol sweepings, all intended to settle Patagonia. Some ships were never seen again, a few managed to reach their intended destinations, but many were able to make a landfall at Maldonado near the mouth of the River Plate, where their crews and passengers were either unable or unwilling to voyage any further under incredibly hard conditions, and so settled right there in Uruguay, thus providing many of the earliest settlers in that country.

It proved impossible to maintain Floridablanca, which was abandoned in 1783. A second settlement was made in 1790, at Puerto Deseado this time, but this could not be maintained either and was finally abandoned in 1807. Thus, when independence was declared in Buenos Aires in 1810, there was no effective Spanish presence on the continent of America proper, south of Carmen de Patagones on the Atlantic side and the Bío-Bío River on the Pacific side.

The English invasions

If the English caused Spain concern over the security of her River Plate colonies, they also had a great deal to do with her eventually losing them. In 1806 a fleet commanded by Admiral Sir Home Popham, carrying several British regiments under Sir David Baird was sent out to South Africa where it proceeded to retake the Cape of Good Hope settlement from the Dutch. At this point, news of the defeat of the French and Spanish at Trafalgar reached the cape, so, reasoning that his force could be spared from returning to European waters to pursue the struggle against Napoleon, Popham took off on his own. He persuaded Baird to give him the 71st (Highland) Regiment of Foot, commanded by the fiery Colonel (later Major General Sir) Denys Pack, and further troops including a squadron of the 20th Light Dragoons and some artillery as well as a detachment of the 88th Foot (Connaught Rangers). Recruited from the wilder parts of Ireland, neither they nor the Highlanders owed particular allegiance to the English Crown as such, but fought valiantly in all the wars that the British Empire engaged in during the seventeenth and nineteenth centuries.

This force amounted to some 1,600 men, and was commanded by Brigadier-General William Carr Beresford. It is fairly certain that this part of the venture was undertaken without any orders from Whitehall, although Popham had certainly been recommending an expedition of this sort before leaving England for the cape.

Popham proceeded direct to Buenos Aires, landed his troops right at the port and Beresford easily took possession of the town, which was defended

The concept of Patagonia as a separate country or region, to the south of the Bío-Bío, Limay and Negro rivers, as expressed in an early map (1813).

8

only by a reduced detachment of Spanish troops. The main fighting took place near the Convent of Santo Domingo, from where the 71st Regiment moved some 300 metres north along the present 'Defensa' (defence) street to the present Plaza de Mayo, capturing the Cabildo, where among the colonial archives Beresford recovered the lead plaque that the English had left at Port Egmont on the West Falkland in 1774 when they withdrew after negotiation with Spain.

With the limited force at his disposal, Beresford was unable to consolidate his victory and could only hold the town for some six weeks. The Spanish viceroy of the River Plate, Sobremonte, was unable to cope with the situation, but Santiago de Liniers, a French Post Captain serving with the Spanish Navy, rallied the mixed Spanish and local forces outside the town and re-attacked on the line of the present-day 'Reconquista' (recapture) street. The Highlanders, although valiant (and there is local evidence to this effect), were not trained in what today would be called urban guerrilla combat, and had to surrender, Beresford and many others being taken prisoner. The table on which he signed the capitulation can still be seen in the Dominican Convent, together with the captured colours of the 71st Regiment.

By this time Whitehall had to take notice. Popham had not been the only one casting an eye at the River Plate, and important commercial interests were already in play. Some 5,000 men under the command of Sir Samuel Auchmuty, intended as a reinforcement for Beresford, left Portsmouth in October 1806. This force included the second battalion of the 71st Highlanders, the 40th Regiment (5) and some Light Infantry among whom was the young Harry Smith of the 95th Rifles, later Major General Sir Harry Smith. After a distinguished army career he became Governor General of South Africa, where the town of Ladysmith was named after his wife, Juana, whom he had married after the siege of Badajoz in romantic circumstances.

By the time this contingent reached the Plate, Beresford had been forced to surrender so Auchmuty landed at Maldonado, an excellent anchorage some sixty miles east of Montevideo, on the east bank (*la banda oriental*) of the River Plate and then still part of the viceroyalty of Buenos Aires. From here he proceeded to storm and capture Montevideo, where they remained for some seven months.

Further troops were assembled, at sea and on land, until the final force amounted to some 10,000 men, and included several crack infantry regiments such as the 36th (Worcestershire), the 38th (South Staffs), the 87th (Royal Irish Fusiliers), the 88th (Connaught Rangers), the 9th Dragoons, detachments of artillery and two battalions of the 95th Rifles, later the Rifle Brigade. The latter was part of the Light Division created by Sir John Moore, founder of the light infantry concept of individual initiative and marksmanship, and was under the command of the redoubtable General 'Black Bob' Craufurd. The fact that a force of this magnitude was sent to the River Plate is a measure of the importance given to this venture by the British Government. The quality of the troops sent out was to be equalled only by the Falklands Task Force of 1982, which as well as commandos and paratroops included two Guards battalions – the only time the Brigade of Guards has sent troops for active service in America.

Part of General Craufurd's force had in fact been dispatched from the Cape of Good Hope in April 1807 with the little-known objective of taking possession of Chile, but when Whitehall received news of Beresford's defeat, a fast frigate was sent off to order this fleet into the River Plate. Further reinforcements came out directly, under the command of Admiral Murray who was to replace Popham. A fourth fleet was now sent out, bringing the total number of ships to over a hundred. Such a force was clearly a senior officer's command, and this was given to Lieutenant-General John Whitelocke.

Argentine history tends to refer to the first and second English Invasions, but as far as the British were concerned it was a single campaign. (6) Unfortunately the second expedition was also a failure. Having occupied Montevideo, Auchmuty sent a force under Pack (who, with Beresford, had managed to escape from their captors) upstream to take Colonia del Sacramento, just across the river from Buenos Aires. In spite of this auspicious beginning, the eventual landing took place south of the city at Ensenada de Barragón, near present-day La Plata and some 56km from the Riachuelo River which bounds the federal capital in the south. Whitelocke was by now in overall command, and by all accounts the action was a disaster. The first attack, headed by the Rifle Brigade under Craufurd was unable to make progress in the narrow streets in spite of the best efforts of the riflemen, who were more accustomed to skirmishing and using their initiative than the line regiments. The main body of the force, under Major-General Leveson-Gower did not come up, the artillery could not get over the Riachuelo and the reserve was not sent up by Whitelocke until it was too late. The British were driven off with casualties and many prisoners were taken. Craufurd is said to have urged his men to 'shoot the scoundrel' (meaning Whitelocke), but the battle was lost and the expedition withdrew to Montevideo to bargain with the Spaniards for the exchange of prisoners.

Whitelocke was court-martialled and cashiered for his failure, although Popham seems to have escaped censure, and Harry Smith put the blame on Leveson-Gower. Beresford, Pack, Craufurd, Smith and many others later went on to see distinguished service in the Peninsular War under Wellington, as did the regiments mentioned. There is evidence, however, that many of the rank and file remained, particularly a number of the 71st who had been taken inland after the first battle. Having been well treated by their *Criollo* captors, they preferred the rough freedom of life on the pampas to the harsh

Estancia *Los Yngleses*, founded by the Gibson brothers in 1823 in Indian territory, only 140 kilometres from Buenos Aires. [Photo from Gibson, *Sheep Farming in the Argentine Republic*, 1893]

discipline of the regular armies of the day. William Lawrence says he was offered 'a fortune – and his daughter' by a gentleman in Montevideo if he would desert and remain in the country, which he did not take up – however, he quotes others who did. Some officers were also tempted – Harry Smith was wounded and says that the lady of the house where he was billeted as a prisoner offered him 'her daughter in marriage and 20,000 dollars, with as many thousand oxen as I wished, and she would build me a house in the country upon any plan I chose to devise'. He must have been able to get out to see the country, as in his autobiography he describes it very favourably and indeed accurately. He did not take up the offer but there were others who stayed on and took to civil life in Buenos Aires, such as the Pipe Major of the 71st who became a well-known music teacher to a number of patrician families.

These expeditions were not just wildcat attempts at adding more pink to the map of the British Empire, but part of a policy over the balance of power in the Atlantic Basin, whose leading exponents were Lord Castlereagh and George Canning. They were concerned with the clearly upcoming power of the United States, with that of Latin America as a whole, and the possibility of Britain replacing Spain as a colonial power was clearly a strong one. The French aspirations in North America had been more or less contained so a strong British presence either in the River Plate or in the Caribbean would have provided an important

11

balance.

The second expedition having failed, a third was planned, this time to Venezuela where a nationalist movement was already underway, eventually to surface under Simon Bolivar. To this end an imposing force of some 9,000 men was assembled in Cork in June 1908, under the command of Sir Arthur Wellesley, the future Duke of Wellington. Before it could sail, however, Napoleon deposed King Ferdinand IV of Spain and installed his brother Joseph as 'king'. The Spanish people rose against the French invaders and asked Britain for help. So the expeditionary force intended to invade South America was sent to Portugal instead, to start the series of campaigns known as the Peninsular War which was to drive the French back over the Pyrenees. It might be observed here that there are not a few present-day Argentine citizens who, seeing the degree of development and prosperity achieved by comparable ex-colonial territories such as the Dominions of Canada and Australia, express some degree of regret that the 'English invasions' did not succeed !

The successful defence of Buenos Aires was mainly due to the efforts of the locally-born settlers (known as *Criollos*) who rallied to the help of the Spanish troops. It was this success in defeating the *Ingleses* which, added to the continuing disorganisation of government in Spain and the ineptitude of the viceroy, inspired the *Criollos* to start a movement towards self-govern-ment. On 25 May 1810, at a public meeting (*Cabildo Abierto*) in Buenos Aires, the first step was taken by declaring the colony to hold no allegiance to France. This was followed on 9 July 1816 by the Declaration of Independence of the 'United Provinces of the River Plate' (later the Argentine Republic or Argentina).

The word 'Argentina', by the way, is a Spanish adjective meaning 'of or pertaining to silver'. So we have in Spanish *La República Argentina* or *La* (understood) *Argentina, los (ciudadanos) Argentinos*, etc. It therefore follows that in English, the citizens of Argentina are **Argentines** and not, please, 'Argentinians'.

Following the initiative of the citizens of Buenos Aires in 1810, the general move towards independence of the present South American nations from Spain started, involving a great deal of history which is not really part of this story. The movement in general received tacit support from Britain, who could hardly help openly, being nominally allied with Spain. On the other hand she refused to actively help Spain to put down the insurgents, and with the British Navy controlling the Atlantic would not allow other European powers to intervene on her behalf. So the *Criollos* had to pursue their own destiny, which they achieved by and large without overseas help, a circumstance which served to enhance their already fiercely independent nature.

The Argentine national hero was, and is, José de San Martín. Although born in Yapeyú Corrientes, his father, a serving Spanish officer, returned to Spain with his family when José was only eight. Following the family tradition of a military career, he received a Spanish commission and saw service against the Bonapartes during the Peninsular War, both in combat and staff appointments. Returning to Argentina in 1812 he joined the Patriot (*Criollo*) forces and managed to survive an action when his horse fell and he was saved from the Spanish Lancers by the prompt intervention of one of his NCO's.(7)

The independence movement was gaining momentum, and he was asked to raise and lead an army over the Andes to join the Chileans and drive the Spanish forces out of Chile and indeed, South America. This extraordinary feat was duly carried out, and his successful crossing in 1817 through the mounting passes with some 4,800 infantry, 1,600 cavalry and 22 guns (which had to be carried on mule-back), and the 10,600 mules and pack animals to carry supplies, can be compared with that only of Hannibal crossing the Alps. Joining forces with General Bernardo O'Higgins (the leader of the Chilean independence movement and the first Head of State), they successfully defeated the Spanish at the battles of Chacabuco (1817) and Maipú (1818).

After Waterloo (1815) the armies of both San Martín in Argentina and Bolivar in Venezuela were greatly strengthened by veteran soldiers, officers and men, who had fought both for and against Napoleon. These included Lord Alexander Cochrane, who after a number of escapades as a dashing frigate captain in the British Navy (and a notorious lawsuit at the bar of the Guildhall for alleged fraud) fought for both Chile and Peru in the Pacific, and General William Miller who had served with Wellington's artillery in the Peninsula, came to Buenos Aires in 1817 and joined San Martín in Chile just after the Battle of Chacabuco. He commanded both artillery and cavalry under San Martín, and was entrusted by O'Higgins with founding and organising a force of marines for the Chilean Navy, which he later led in several engagements. A true professional soldier, Miller fought both on sea and land during the subsequent campaigns in Chile and Peru which finally liberated these countries from Spain. Gradually the various nations were formed, which together comprise present-day Latin America.

The subsequent shape, boundaries and sovereignty in general of the emerging South American countries followed in the main those of the former Spanish colonies, at least initially or until modified by subsequent events. It must be borne in mind that at the time when Argentina broke away from Spain, there was *no* Spanish presence on the Atlantic seaboard south of Carmen de Patagones, nor was there in Chile south of the Bío-Bío River. This was to bring not only the sovereignty of the Falkland Islands into question, but also that of the whole of Patagonia from the Atlantic to the Pacific. There are indeed old maps of South America showing a supposed

The Tehuelche Indians had tents, or *toldos*, made from *guanaco* hides sewn together with sinews from the powerful leg tendons of ostriches, as were the robes or *quillangos* which, before the coming of white man, were their only clothing.

'country' called Patagonia, extending right across from the Pacific to the Atlantic, with a northern boundary following the Bio-Bio, Limay and Negro Rivers.

First feet in Patagonia

We must now go back some time in the history of man, and look at the original inhabitants of southern South America. They were called 'Indians' only because Columbus originally thought he had reached the *eastern* Indies, but the name stuck and, even today, people from Spain who went out to America (and by definition had made their fortunes there) are referred to in Spain as *Indianos*. The Spaniards found a variety of nations, from the Aztecs in Central America to the Quichua and other tribes of the Peruvian and Bolivian highlands, often wrongly called 'Incas'. (The Incas were the kings or chieftains, not the people.) Some of these had reached a very high degree of civilisation, but were ruthlessly exploited by the Spanish Conquistadores for the extraction and processing of gold and silver. Pushing on down through Chile, however, the Spaniards soon came into contact with a much tougher proposition – the Araucanians *(Araucanos)* who inhabited most of the southern half of Chile. This warrior nation successfully resisted further penetration, although it is possible that the Spanish advance may have lost momentum when it was realised that southern Chile held no mineral wealth to speak of. Be that as it may, the Spanish advance was halted at the Bió-Bió River. The Araucanian nation comprised several more or less warlike tribes (Pehuenche, Mapuche, Manzanero) with lifestyles varying from sedentary (the Pehuenche lived off the nuts of the Pehuen, a tree of the genus *Araucaria*) through the herding of flocks to hunting the abundant wild game and predatory raiding of other tribes, including white settlers once these started to appear. Some tribes had spread over the Andes, and inhabited the eastern slopes, relying for subsistence on the abundant wildlife. Once horses (introduced by the Spaniards) spread and became abundant, the Mapuche ranged right across the central pampas to what is today the Province of Buenos Aires.

South of the 'Mapuche Belt' there were more peaceable and marginally more primitive peoples: the Chilotes on the Pacific side, mainly in the islands of Chiloe and surrounding areas, living mostly on fish and the cultivation of potatoes; and the Tehuelche all over the present-day Argentine Patagonia, from the Negro River down as far as the Straits of Magellan. They were completely nomadic hunters, living almost entirely off the *guanaco*. *(Llama guanicos* is the largest and widest-spread of the South American *camelidae* (8) and can be found from northwest Argentina right down to and including Tierra del Fuego). Further south again, and each tribe progressively more primitive, were the Alacaluf or Canoe Indians living mostly on fish, in the maze of ocean channels to the south and south-west of the continent proper. Then came the Ona on Tierra del Fuego, who lived, like the Tehuelche, off the guanaco, and finally the Yaghans, the most primitive of all, who lived *in* their dugout canoes around the Beagle Channel and nearby waters.

The Yahgans had somewhere acquired knowledge of the use and bene-fits of fire, but found it easier to carry it round with them rather than to kindle it as required. So there was a fire pot in every canoe, tended by the grandmother of the family. It was the spectacle of these little fires in hun-dreds of canoes, flocking to see the strange foreign ships, that caused the region to be called 'Land of Fire' (*Tierra del Fuego)* by Magellan.

The Tehuelche on the mainland, notwithstanding the fears of the early mariners, were a peaceable folk who did not regard the white man as an enemy, not having a warrior/raiding tradition as did the Mapuche and Manzanero tribes further north. Apart from the occasional Jesuit mission-ary, the '*Aónikenk*' ('southern people' as they called themselves in their own language) did not seriously come into contact with white men until the Welsh landed in Chubut in 1865. Being also peaceable, the Welsh took good care to get on with the Tehuelche; indeed it is probable that they would not have survived without them. The Tehuelche did not take readily to regular work 'white man style' any more than the Australian Aboriginals, although they did become shearers and were already magnificent horsemen. Their women and families never got a chance to leave their guanaco-skin tents (*toldos*) and become 'domesticated'. Tragically, it was the missionaries (both Anglican and Catholic) who were responsible for their disappearance, more so even than the traders in rot-gut booze or the indian-hunters at a pound a nose. The latter were confined mostly to Tierra del Fuego, and their activities have been much exaggerated, but sadly they did indeed operate, just as they did in North America. The missions, in their attempts to evangelise and clothe the heathen, collected cast-off clothing in Europe, full of the germs of white men's diseases. Medical knowledge of general hygiene and epidemiology was, sadly, not up to recognising the risk of infecting a susceptible indigenous population, so the always pacific Tehuelche died in their *toldos* of measles, diphtheria, whooping cough and tuberculosis. A reservation for them was set up, at Camosu Aike in southern Santa Cruz, where the very few survivors have assembled. Most of the people there today, however, are of mixed blood with Chilean surnames, but there are British surnames there also.

The *gauchos*

Harry Smith was not the only Englishman to observe the fertile lands on both sides of the River Plate. We have seen how by the early 1800s there were already powerful British commercial interests in play, sufficient to persuade the government in Whitehall to send out the powerful military expedition of 1807. Under Spanish colonial rule, no foreigner could own real estate but in 1810 there were said to be 124 British persons legally resident in Buenos Aires. Leading members of the 'British Commercial Rooms', founded in 1809, were certainly involved in the events of that year, and a squadron of four British men-of-war were at anchor in the River Plate with most of their crews on shore leave during the week of 25 May 1810. When the assembled townspeople declared their break in allegiance to Spain, the ships fired a formal salute in honour of the occasion, an event missed by many history books.

Once the republic finally declared its independence in 1816, a trickle of Scots and English settlers started to find their way over, engage in trade and banking and take up land. (9) John Miller, from Elgin near Aberdeen, had arrived in 1810 and was a member of the Commercial Rooms. He married Dolores Balbastro, joined the Roman Catholic faith in order to do so, and in 1812 was declared 'citizen of Buenos Aires' by government decree. He later acquired several important properties (*estancias*) and imported 'Tarquin' the first Shorthorn bull to be imported from England. The Gibsons came

Estancia *Curumalan* in Buenos Aires Province was one of the first to install machine shears, before 1890. [Gibson, 1893]

out in 1818 and by 1825 had acquired five *estancias* including Estancia 'Los Yngleses'(*sic*) on the south side of Samboronbon Bay, near Cape San Antonio. The Parish Robertson brothers owned land in Corrientes before 1810, and it was William Parish Robertson who was appointed first British consul in Buenos Aires in 1824 by George Canning, and was largely responsible for bringing over the first organised colony of European settlers.

This was a group of Scots who came out in the barque *Simplicity* in 1825 and settled near Monte Grande on land formerly owned by Gibson. Names like Dodds, Bell, Mackinley and Rodgers appear among the earliest title deeds. William Henry Hudson, the novelist, was born in 1841 at Estancia

'Veinticinco Ombúes' near Quilmes, where his father (from Devon) had settled in 1832. Richard Blake Newton, Gibson's manager at 'Los Yngleses' in the early days, settled land of his own in 1844 and was the first to enclose his property behind fences. [There are a number of Blake families in Argentina, most of Irish descent, with no connection with the Blakes of Somerset.] Samuel Fisher Lafone was another early settler, owning land on the Atlantic coast near Gibson, but he later sold up and transferred to Uruguay. Others came to join the already influential group of families settled in Buenos Aires and Montevideo, mostly in trade and shipping. The 'third English invasion' – a pacific one which was to continue for well over a century – had begun.

They were not, of course, alone. Like Harry Smith's hostess, Spanish people already resident on the banks of the River Plate could see the rich land just there for the taking, and they were followed by the first government-sponsored settlement of land by immigrants, which took place in 1857. As relative political stability succeeded the colonial era and land formerly owned only by the Spanish Crown became available for settlement, there were plenty of takers. The first fifty years or so of the infant nation's history were characterised by much squabbling among different factions for power in government, but the process of amassing wealth first by investment in the land and then by the sale of its abundant produce, once started, continued and flourished for over 150 years.

But to own land was one thing – to farm it was quite another and here we must introduce the *gauchos*. In the early days of the Spanish colonies, the pampas were roamed exclusively by the various nations of native Argentines. Both horses and cattle had been released by the earliest Spaniards and the Indians soon became excellent horsemen. With abundant wild cattle available for the next meal, they saw no point in joining the infant townships which in any case were inhabited by *huincas* (palefaces). On the other hand, there came to be many of the latter, of Spanish or other European descent including British, who were equally attracted by the free and easy life at large on the pampas. It was only too easy for a man, having perhaps committed some misdemeanour in the city, to saddle up and ride away into the interior, far away from the reach of such little law as there was. The *gauchos* were a law unto themselves, and soon became an important element situated, in effect, midway between the white settlers in the towns (and increasingly in the surrounding lands), and the native tribes proper. They seldom actually lived with the tribes or otherwise took entirely to native ways, although a certain amount of miscegenation inevitably took place, and they remained part of the rural scene on the fringes of the settled lands.

The Indians, not unnaturally, objected to the *huincas* occupying the plains that they had roamed from time immemorial and soon enclosing them with wire fences, although they were very happy to continue raiding the flocks and herds the land had been stocked with. The 'frontier' of settled Argentina at that time was nowhere near the Andes, but just a few days' ride from Buenos Aires, and meant a roughly defined area beyond which it was unsafe for whites to go, often deeply breached by raiding parties of Manzanero and Mapuche Indians. 'Los Yngleses' was initially far beyond the frontier and was provided with a fort complete with cannon firing stone balls, and this seems to have been enough to deter the war parties of *malones* (literally 'big bad ones'). In a series of campaigns over a period of some forty years, the Indians were gradually pushed back to the Andes and finally kept there, and the '*gaucho* cavalry' played an important role both in the armies of Rosas (1832–52) and of Roca's desert campaign of the late 1870s which finally defeated the Indians.

Once the marauding tribes were 'pacified' and the land became safe for settlement and farming, the *gauchos* were most reluctant to dismount and perform any kind of manual labour. They were fine at working cattle and their descendants continue doing so to this day, but to till the soil and unlock the real wealth of the pampas, the early landowners either had to do it themselves or look for another source of labour. Fortunately, this became available relatively quickly.

Notes

1 Some writers have disagreed with the origin of the name 'Patagonia' as expressed here. From other authorities we find that although there is indeed no proven version, most historians go along with the *'Patagón'* version as expressed by Pigafetta, the chronicler of Magellan's expedition, so we are doing the same.

2 For the admiral's life see *Robert Blake, General at Sea* by J.R. Powell.

3 An excellent description of this harrowing voyage and others, including those of Magellan, Drake and Sarmiento de Gamboa may be found in *The Blind Horn's Hate* by Richard Hough.

4 *Operativo Patagonia* by Juan Apolant traces the origins of many of the Spanish families who settled in Uruguay, often recruited originally for settlement in Patagonia

5 Originally the 2nd Somersetshire Regiment of Foot, renumbered 40th Foot and later the Lancashire Regiment. When Sergeant William Lawrence joined just before the River Plate campaign, the regimental depot was at Taunton. The original 1st Somersetshire became the 13th Foot and later the Somerset Light Infantry. See Chapter 5.

6 Much fascinating detail can be found in *A Dorset Soldier* by Sergeant William Lawrence of the 40th Regiment, and *A Soldier of the Seventy-first*, edited by Christopher Hibbert. For a good account of the Argentine point of view, see Felix Luna's *Historia Integral de la Argentina* and Jorge Castelli's *El Delicado Umbral de la Tempestad (The Delicate Threshold of the Storm)*.

7 The 'combat' of San Lorenzo, in which Sergeant Cabral saved San Martín's life at the cost of his own, has been immortalized in Argentina. It was not, however, a major action. The Spanish forces were concentrated in Chile and Perú, under command of the Viceroy in Lima, and after the initial uprisings in those countries had been put down (known as the Reconquista), the independance movement had to set up a major campaign which eventually would defeat the Spaniards.

8 The llama, the alpaca and the vicuña are found further north, in the Andean regions from mid-Argentina (Catamarca, La Rioja) right up to Bolivia and the Peruvian highlands known as the *Altiplano*. The guanaco occurs from there right down to and including Tierra del Fuego, and ranges across to the Atlantic coast.

9 *The Forgotten Colony* by Andrew Graham-Yooll provides much historical detail about the early British entrepreneurs in trade and on the land.

2

A Whole New Country

New Argentines

Europe in general throughout most of the nineteenth century was not a happy place for many humble people. Religious and political persecutions, economic and social stresses such as those created by the Industrial Revolution, land enclosures and other destabilising influences, coupled with the availability of cheap steerage passages in the new steamships, caused many to cross both the North and South Atlantic in search of a new life. The majority came to Argentina from Spain and Italy, but almost every European country was represented. Some came as defined ethnic or religious groups, and settled as such, often setting up self-contained communities which persist today. Others just came to seek their fortunes, and eventually most found them, although in many cases not without years of hard work and making their way.

Prior to 1856 hardly any grain was grown, and almost all food supplies other than the (wild) beef had to be imported. Four thousand people arrived in 1857, and by 1863 some 8,000 hectares were under cultivation. The trickle of immigrants soon grew to a flood, and by the end of the century over 100,000 per year were coming in. The new arrivals provided the needed workforce, and soon found their way into productive activities on the land. In addition to hands-on labour as such, they also brought much farming expertise which was soon put to good use. Money was always in short supply, so a variety of share-cropping systems and of barter in kind were developed. Usually the landowners would hand over sections of land to applicants (known as *colonos* regardless of where they came from), who would fence it and build a dwelling, and then till the virgin soil, planting wheat and maize mostly but virtually anything can be grown on what is termed the 'humid pampa' – to distinguish it from the deserts which bound it to the west and south. Rent was paid in kind – i.e. returning a percentage, usually half, of the crops harvested.

Crop yields were such that this arrangement provided wealth for both owner and *colono*, and with the passage of time many of the latter were able to buy freehold title to the land. Another common arrangement was to hand over the land for cultivation over a fixed number of years after which the *colono* would return it sown down to alfalfa, thus creating pasture for the beef herds which were starting to be bred behind wire, replacing the former *baguales* (wild cattle) which had roamed the unfenced pampas for nearly 200 years.

There was scope also for the small business, and many a village shop-keeper from Galicia or the mountains of Asturias would sell up, bring his small capital over and start again in one of the infant townships that sprang up in the wake of the railways. It was the building of these, though, which really started to open up and develop the resources of the interior of the country, and this can be considered the fourth English invasion. The first train in Buenos Aires ran for 10 kilometres from what is now Plaza Lavalle, by the Colón Theatre, out to Palermo, which at that time was 'out in the country'. It was drawn by a Stephenson locomotive called *La Porteña*, on track laid in 1857 by William Wheelwright, an American entrepreneur who also laid the first railway in Chile, and was a promoter of several of the Argentine railway companies. He later became a prominent ship owner and founder of the Pacific Steam Navigation Company which was to provide passenger and freight services to the west coast until well after the Second World War.

From this small beginning the government had the vision to see that here, at last, lay the means to open up, settle and develop the immense, undeveloped interior. Railway companies were floated in London, and the risk capital put up by the City was further helped by the land grant system. Concessions of 1 league (5 kilometres) of land each side of the projected lines were granted to the railway companies as well as other areas, currently valueless for lack of settlement but potentially productive. Once the tracks were built, or even before, the value of land rose accordingly and it could be sold off, thus creating new capital which in turn served to drive the permanent way further inland and open a new cycle of development.

So the lines started to be laid: iron rails shipped from Manchester and Glasgow were spiked to *quebracho* sleepers from the Chaco, cut in the Misiones jungle and rafted down the rivers. *Quebracho* wood (literally 'break-

Quemú-Quemú, a typical small country town on the former Central Argentine railway, in a grain-growing district.

axe') is very hard and impervious to soil-borne rot so the tracks could be laid directly on the soil *in situ* and not ballasted in rock chips, so reducing construction costs enormously. Stations were sited at due intervals, around which land was taken up and settled, and there the townships grew, attracting urban settlement by immigrants who had been small traders back home or artisans with other skills than farming. The general store would usually be the first business to appear, with its *pulpería* or wine counter along the side, but soon someone would set up a bakery with a wood-fired mud oven. Soon other crafts came: carpenters, blacksmiths, farriers and wheelwrights. Carts and sulkies carried goods and people out to the farms which, with an established supply base, could now be sited even further inland.

It was the railways, then, that opened up the 'humid pampa' – the Southern in 1865 and the Central Argentine in 1866 linked first the precariously settled land west and south from Buenos Aires, and then continued out towards the 'frontier' which was still a long way from the Andes. Meantime, the Central Cordoba ran to Rosario on the Paraná River, and then on, linking up with the old Spanish cities of Cordoba and Tucuman, and further north-west to Salta and Jujuy, and eventually to Bolivia. Thus the old trade route along which Spanish pack trains brought the gold and silver mined in the Andes down to the River Plate, was re-established in reverse. Crossing the Paraná by train ferry at Zárate (the entire train was shunted on board and rolled off again the other side, at Ibicuy), the lines continued up across Entre Ríos to Corrientes and Misiones.

As early as 1871 a link across the Andes in the wake of San Martín's expedition was being planned by President Domingo Faustino Sarmiento, a renowned educationalist and far-seeing statesman, who laid the foundation of much of present-day Argentina, and a loan was put up by Baring Brothers in London. The surveying expedition of that year under Robert Crawford ranks as one of the earliest documented crossings of the Andes, still very much Indian territory. They had first to ride all the way to Mendoza (some 1000 kilometres or 600 miles). Then, on mule-back, well armed and escorted by a detachment of soldiers, the engineers proceeded up the Uspallata Pass, over the watershed and down the Grande and Tordillo Rivers to Curicó in Chile. Crawford himself had a near escape when his mule fell off a mountain ledge, fortunately he was leading it at the time and not mounted. In addition to surveying equipment they carried an inflatable boat in which they could cross the rivers when there were not trees available for bridging or rafting. By way of sport they shot *guanaco* by stalking them just like deer. One Scottish engineer got separated from the main party, together with fourteen mules, but met up with a relief party of soldiers and rejoined eight days later. A further twenty mules were lost when a puma, attracted by the smell of roasting meat from the campfire, crept close and they stampeded from fright. When bathing in the ice-cold streams they were bothered by leeches, one of which attached itself to the leg of the expedition doctor, causing Crawford to remark that it was no doubt attracted 'to a professional colleague'. Small wonder that once they reached Curicó five months after leaving Mendoza, the innkeeper was amazed at the frequency with which they took hot baths!

Work on the Pacific Railway started in 1873, driving westwards from Buenos Aires across to San Luis and reached Mendoza in 1885 and finally over the Andes to Chile in 1891 – no mean feat, as we will see in Chapter 8. By 1891 there were 10,000 kilometres of track, and nearly double this by the end of the century. The total length of railways in Argentina would eventually reach some 42,000 kilometres, roughly the same as Australia and only exceeded by India, Canada, Russia and the USA.

So first the grain started to flow back down the railways to feed the cities, and soon there was plenty for export. This was followed by cattle, first for canning and extraction at the Bovril and Liebig Extract of Meat plants on the Uruguay river, and at Fray Bentos in Uruguay proper – i.e. on the east bank. After refrigeration came into use in 1874 the vast trade in chilled beef began, from the freezing works of Swift, Armour, Anglo and many others. To carry all this food to Europe called for considerable shipping, most of it British.

From the British Isles also, along with all this activity and investment, came the people – mostly with drive and acumen and in particular many skills which were in short supply. They came from all walks of life: engineers to survey, build and operate the railways; drivers, fitters, signalmen, telegraphists, linesmen and platform staff to run the trains; staff for the meatworks and the many, many businesses and service activities which grew up to supply both farming and industry. As the children grew, schools were started – St Andrew's Scots School in 1838 was the first and others followed. The British Hospital was founded in 1843 to tend the sick, and sporting and social clubs began to flourish, often sited in suburbs with names like Banfield, Temperley, Hurlingham, Wilde, City Bell, Ranelagh and Claypole.

Sport was always important to the British, and most of the major sports practised in Argentina today were first introduced by the 'mad English'. Many sporting terms passed into the vernacular such as *gol, orsai* (offside), *referí, foul, fixture, hooker* and *scrum*. There is no doubt that the greatest contribution made by the British to Argentine culture was the introduction of Association Football (*futbol*) which has become a (if not *the*) national passion. Leading professional football clubs with names like 'River Plate', 'Boca Juniors' and 'Newell's Old Boys' recall those early players who worked during the week on the mainline trains running out of Retiro (River Plate), in the workshops and marshalling yards and meatpacking plants along the Riachuelo (Boca Juniors) and in the port of Rosario with its own goods yards and meatworks (Newell's Old Boys). In other divisions we have clubs like 'Chacarita Juniors', 'Racing', 'All Boys', 'Wanderers' and 'Chaco For Ever'.

The *Beagle* and her Channel

True to the tradition that 'Britain ruled the waves' which prevailed during most of the eighteenth and nineteenth centuries, the Admiralty sent out a number of surveying ventures into the southern hemisphere. In the wake of Anson, Narborough and Byron came James Cook who made a number of observations in Falkland and Fuegian waters on his way to the Pacific to observe the transit of Venus in Polynesia in 1769, and again on his second voyage in 1772.

Cook was followed by HMS *Beagle*, a ten-gun brig of 242 tons purchased and fitted out for the specific purpose of surveying and charting all the South American coast from the River Plate down to the Straits of Magellan and round into the mass of islands and fjords on the Pacific side. This monumental task was to employ the ship for nine years, during which she made several voyages. Leaving Deptford in 1826, under the command of Commander Pringle Stokes, she spent two years surveying the Atlantic seaboard until in 1828 Stokes, worn out by incessant toil, took his own life.

The cross of Commander Stokes of the *Beagle*, near Cape Froward, the southernmost tip of the American continent proper. The other graves, presumably also of Royal Navy personnel, are unmarked.

The voyage was completed and the ship brought back to England by the first lieutenant, Philip Parker King.

Stokes' grave can be visited south of Punta Arenas at Bahía San Juan, just to the east of Cape Froward. The tiny graveyard and the white cross erected by HMS *Challenger* look out over the bleak waters. The site is carefully and respectfully tended by the Chilean Navy. Another casualty of this voyage was the second officer, Lieutenant Sholl, who died at sea and lies buried on a headland overlooking the bay of San Julian. His name has been given to a nearby hill and to the beach below his grave.

Both Stokes and King were professional seamen, into whose ken swam almost anything going and whose interests ranged far wider than just marine hydrography. In addition to surveying, they observed the new regions, described them, drew or often painted them in exquisite watercolours, and collected specimens. There are, in the herbarium at Kew Gardens, for example, botanical specimens gathered at San Julian by Parker King all those years ago.

For her second voyage in 1829, the *Beagle* was commanded by Captain Robert Fitzroy, an officer of a very different cast. He was a post captain from a well-connected naval family who would become admiral in the fullness of time. In the course of nearly two years off the Patagonian and Fuegian coasts, the *Beagle* made some contact with the Yaghans, who lived in their canoes in and around the aptly named Beagle Channel, which bounds Tierra del Fuego proper on the south and separates it from Navarin Island. When they returned to Britain in 1831, they brought three young Yaghans with them. In Fitzroy's eyes they were 'specimens' in the zoological or possibly anthropological sense. There were few ethnic groups in the world as remote as the Yaghans, and the idea was to study these people's reaction to 'English civilisation'. It was also hoped that, after clothing, educating and in particular catechising the no doubt unwilling and confused hostages, they might – on being returned to their native habitat – be able to spread enlightenment in these matters to their naked heathen brethren.

After a complete refit, the next task for the *Beagle* was to first complete the survey of the Patagonian coast and then to continue into the Pacific and on round the world so as to complete the observations through 360° of longitude. Conscientious and responsible as the naval officers were in recording their discoveries, the Admiralty had also taken to sending naturalists on some of the more important voyages, starting with Sir Joseph Banks who had accompanied Cook to Polynesia. The naturalist appointed for the monumental enterprise of the *Beagle* was Charles Darwin, only 22 when they left Plymouth on 27 December 1831. The voyage was to take nearly five years, and Darwin spent many years thereafter writing up his copious notes and evolving his theory of the origin of the species.

Both the voyage and its outcome have been well chronicled elsewhere, (1) so all we will mention here is that while the *Beagle* was being beached for repairs at Santa Cruz, Fitzroy, with a party including Darwin, attempted to travel up the river by longboat. This meant long stretches of hauling the boat from the bank by ropes against the strong current when the wind was (usually) against them, and although they did sight the main Andean chain and named its principal peak Mount Fitzroy, they had to turn back exhausted and so failed to reach the lake which, fed by numerous glaciers, overflows into the Santa Cruz River. According to Skottsberg(2) this was discovered in 1867 by an English engineer, H. Gardiner but he does not say what he was doing there. Most Argentine historians say it was discovered and named 'Lago Argentino' in 1873 by Valentin Feilberg, a junior officer of the Argentine naval sloop 'Chubut', which was commanded by a Captain Lawrence and whose boatswain was George Stephens and the quartermaster William Jacobs.(3)

Darwin must have eaten calafate berries when in Patagonia, as in spite of its 'negative characters, being without habitation, without water, without trees, without mountains, supporting merely a few dwarf plants', he admits to being deeply impressed and even if his body did not return his thoughts certainly did. It was here that he first started to find fossilised marine specimens on the tops of hills, and began to ponder deeply on the origins of both the earth and the creatures which inhabit it.

Fitzroy duly returned his Yaghans to their native habitat, together with a missionary named Matthews who proposed to continue the work of education and evangelisation, but the experiment was a sad failure. Returning over a year later just before setting off into the Pacific on the second part of the voyage, they were found to have reverted completely to their former primitive state, and Matthews was only too glad to be taken off.

This first attempt to evangelise the Yaghans was followed by Allen Gardiner, who had founded the Patagonian Missionary Society in 1850, and with six companions and two 7-metre decked boats, had himself and his party landed at Banner Cove. They were no more successful in resisting the importunities of the Yaghans, especially when it was discovered that their reserve supply of ammunition had not been landed from their transport vessel. To avoid the Yaghans, they moved camp to a very exposed site, where they all perished from exposure, scurvy and starvation. Gardiner, the last to go, left clear suggestions in writing as to how the evangelical work he had attempted could be carried out.

The mantle then fell on the Rev. George Pakenham Despard, at the time vicar of Lenton, Nottinghamshire and secretary of the Society which in 1864 became the South American Missionary Society. Its activities were later extended to the native inhabitants of the Paraguayan Chaco, where it continues its good works today. Despard had previously been the vicar of St Nicholas' Church in Bristol, hard by Bristol Bridge. One winter's night, so the story goes, a baby wrapped in fine linen was found on the bridge and brought to the church where the little boy was adopted by the vicar, who christened the foundling Thomas, and for want of a surname, Bridges because of the bridge or possibly as the name of the architect who built both the Georgian bridge in 1768 and the nave of St Nicholas' church was James Bridges.

On hearing of the fate of Gardiner and his party, Despard threw himself wholeheartedly into the breach. Funds were raised, and the Society was able to build and equip its own ship, named *Allen Gardiner*. Following Gardiner's posthumous recommendations, a lease was taken up of 5,000 acres on Keppel Island off the West Falkland, which would be used as a base to which, hopefully, Yaghans could be taken and taught the elements of civilised life.After a first voyage in 1854 to set up the Keppel settlement, the *Allen Gardiner* set sail from Bristol carrying the Rev. Despard, his wife and family including young Thomas Bridges, then only 13.

Over the next five years Despard was able to get on friendly terms with the natives, and indeed he persuaded a number to go over to Keppel. But it was a slow process. The first attempt at a Fuegian settlement at Wulaia was a disaster, resulting in the massacre of eight of the ship's crew and passengers, and the little schooner was stripped of everything moveable. Despard returned to England in despair, but Thomas Bridges, by now 18, insisted in staying on Keppel to continue his study of the Yaghan language, which he was convinced was the key to getting to know the people. In 1863 the Rev. (later Bishop) Whait H. Stirling came out to take charge of the project, and after first sending young Thomas home to take Holy Orders, finally set up the mission at Ushuaia, on the main island of Tierra del Fuego in 1869. A house was erected, gardens dug, and in 1870 Stirling and the *Allen Gardiner* sailed away leaving the young Bridges, now married, in sole charge. This time the settlement was successful, and we can read all about it in his son Lucas' excellent book, *Uttermost Part of the Earth*.

Argentine naval expeditions had been probing further and further south along the Atlantic coast, but no attempt had been made at any settlement south of the Santa Cruz River where in 1854 Comandante Luis Piedra Buena had set up a trading post. In 1878 a squadron under Comodoro Luis Py had gone as far as Santa Cruz to show the flag, followed by another under Piedra Buena, by now an authority on the South Atlantic, in 1882. Rio Gallegos would not be founded until 1885, and Cape Virgins was only reached in 1887 by an overland expedition led by Captain Teófilo de Loqui. He reported that gold had been discovered near there, by a native called Lukatche or Lucacho, and adventurers of various sorts started to appear.

Meanwhile in 1884, a small squadron headed by the historic naval transport *Villarino* (4) commanded by Captain Federico Spurr and Colonel Augusto Lasserre in the gunboat *Paraná* sailed up the Beagle Channel and, somewhat to their surprise, found the by now flourishing mission well established at Ushuaia. Bridges had always been conscious of where he was, and took care that the flag which flew from the mission flagstaff was an innocuous one portending no nationality in particular. With great respect and considerable ceremony, this flag was lowered and the Argentine ensign raised instead. Bridges was later rewarded for his settlement of the area on behalf of Argentina by the grant of a very important tract of land on Tierra del Fuego, known as Estancia 'Viamonte'.

Bridges and the mission did valuable work in teaching the Yaghans something of human values as understood in other parts of the world, although as late as 1895 the 'Canoe Indians' as they had become known were still prone to begging and stealing from passing ships, who to them were nothing more than a source of food and of fascinating objects. When Joshua Slocum passed through in that year in his single-handed *Spray*, (5) he was seriously threatened, in spite of having firearms. He hit on the brilliant idea of scattering tin-tacks over his decks, which deterred the barefooted savages in a humane but most effective manner!

Straits settlement

Meanwhile, not far to the west, at the southernmost end of the American continent proper, Chile had taken possession of the Straits of Magellan as long ago as 1843, when Captain Juan Williams of the Chilean Navy had landed first at what later became Fuerte Bulnes, just south of Sarmiento de Gamboa's ill-fated *Ciudad de San Felipe*. In 1849 the settlement was moved some 75 kilometres further north to the much more suitable Punta Arenas (the 'Sandy Point' of Byron's surveying expedition of 1764). This port, due to its location in very sheltered but deep waters soon became a vital trading and supply point for ships trading between both seaboards of the American continent. Period prints show more than fifty sailing ships anchored out in the roads. Sheep were first introduced to the Straits of Magellan in 1876 by Henry Reynard, an English trader in Punta Arenas who brought them over from the Falklands and ran them on Elizabeth Island, a small island in the Magellan Straits, where they duly multiplied and soon spread to the mainland of what is today Magallanes province of Chile, and also to the island of Tierra del Fuego proper. Reynard leased and settled Estancia 'Oazy Harbour' on the mainland but did not purchase it and later moved north into Argentina where he founded Estancia 'Cañadón de las Vacas', one of the principal properties in Santa Cruz district and still farmed today by his descendants. Reynard was soon followed by others, one of the earliest being Ernest Hobbs. He was a nephew of Ernest Holmested, who together with Robert Blake had settled Hill Cove on the West Falkland (Chapter 3) and had spent two years with them before going over to the Chilean part of Tierra del Fuego in the early 1880s with 750 sheep. There he founded Estancia 'Gente Grande', which grew into one of the big sheep farming companies in the area. Don Ernesto had a distinguished career on and off the 'island', as Tierra del Fuego is often termed locally, including becoming *alcalde* (mayor) of Punta Arenas where he formed the trading partnership of

The windjammer *Talisman* dismasted off Cape Horn and repaired in Port Stanley around 1900.

Hobbs and Stubenrauch, into which family he married. His second child Ethel was the first white child to have been born in the Chilean part of Tierra del Fuego.

Other settlers started to appear, spreading northwards first into the Chilean province of Magallanes, and then across the border (real, but as yet undefined) into Argentine territory of what is today the province of Santa Cruz. Up until this time there had been no effective settlement of southern Argentina beyond a line halfway across the present province of Buenos Aires. The marauding Indians who controlled the central pampas (La Pampa, Rio Negro and Neuquén) were not 'pacified' until General Roca's expedition to the desert of 1879, when the tribes were pushed right back to the Andes and firmly kept there. There are many similarities to the 'conquest' of the North American West. The territories of Chubut and Santa Cruz were only added after negotiation with Chile. The latter had an arguable claim east of the Andes and extending right across to the Atlantic coast, based on the former occupation by tribes of the Mapuche nation, and the absence of either Spanish or earlier Argentine settlement.

This enormous area, roughly the size of Western Europe, had not as yet been settled at all (by the white man), except for the tiny Welsh colony in the Chubut Valley, which by 1880 had spread from the first settlement in the

31

lower valley across to the Andes, and founded the towns of Esquel and Trevelin. Much land in that area was already being farmed. The Welsh were granted the extraordinary privilege of choosing whether they wished to belong to Chile or to Argentina, and a plebiscite was held at Trevelin in 1880 at which they voted to be Argentine. Chile was rather flexing its muscles after defeating Peru in the 'War of 1879' over bits of the northern, nitrate-rich Atacama Desert, and nearly went to war with Argentina over Patagonia. Fortunately statesmanship and good manners prevailed and following further negotiations between the two countries Chile formally withdrew any claim it might have had to lands east of the Andes, in return for access to the Atlantic via the Straits of Magellan. A treaty was signed in 1881, laying down the principles defining the boundary between Argentina and Chile in the region, although tensions continued until in 1898 Presidents Roca and Errázuriz, aboard the Chilean battleship *O'Higgins* moored in the Straits embraced in a historic gesture (*el Abrazo del Estrecho)* and swore eternal friendship.

The Andes proper divide south of Lago Argentino, the main chain continuing south to Last Hope Inlet and the mass of islands ending in Isla Riesco, while a string of volcanic craters stretches east along what was to become the southern boundary of Argentina, nearly as far as Cañadon Condor (Chapter 16). There are valleys there where one can see quite clearly where the lava flow, millions of years ago, halted and cooled forming a low bluff which would eventually become covered with soil, and the basalt boulders shelter good pasture and, eventually, sheep.

The trouble had arisen over the interpretation of the treaty, which stated that the frontier should follow the Andes mountains along a line joining the 'highest peaks of the watershed' (*altas cumbres que dividen aguas)*. It was soon found that quite often the watershed lay many miles distant from the highest peaks, so finally the two countries appealed to the British Crown to settle the dispute. King Edward VII ruled that a boundary commission should survey the disputed border and interpret the terms of the 1881 treaty on the ground. Under the command of Colonel Thomas Holdich, (6) a party of British and Norwegian surveyors and engineers was appointed, and in 1903 started on their Herculean task of surveying the frontier. This often involved fixing an arbitrary (but duly arbitrated) point midway between two irreconcilable positions. Considering the logistical difficulties involved in hauling first surveying equipment and then boundary pylons (metal structures set in concrete) to the tops of peaks in the Andes in the year 1903, using only animal (and human) transport, it is remarkable that only some twenty-odd points of dispute were left to be sorted out in the twentieth century. Two of these, the Beagle Channel and Lago del Desierto were only resolved in our time and the final one, the division of the continental icecap, is still in dispute.

Camwy Colony

The Welsh colony has played a very important part in the early settlement of Patagonia. The original group of settlers came from the mountains of North Wales and the Lleyn peninsula where, following the construction of railways first to Liverpool and then into Wales itself, driving the tracks across to Holyhead in order to have better communication with Ireland, they could see that their centuries-long semi-isolation from the English, whom they regarded with some justification as invaders, would not be long in coming to an end. With the idea of getting away from it all and being able to live peaceably with only their own language, customs and religion, they negotiated with the Argentine Government who, having as yet no settlement in Patagonia at all, was only too glad to have them. The first settlers arrived on the '*Mimosa*' in July 1865, and made a landfall in sheltered waters in the Bay of Nymphs (Golfo Nuevo), soon to become Port Madryn, named after Madryn Castle whose owner Sir Love Jones Parry had been an important contributor to the venture and a signatory to the contract with the Argentine Foreign Minister, Guillermo Rawson, together with D.G.Whalley MP and David Williams, Sheriff of Merioneth.

To the newly arrived colonists the country was far more inhospitable than they had been prepared for by the very optimistic, not to say misleading, reports taken back to Wales by the delegation who had made the original arrangements with the minister of the interior, Guillermo Rawson. So they trekked over the semi-desert to the valley of the Chubut River (from the Tehuelche *Chapat* – the Welsh called it '*Camwy*') where they found an irrigable floodplain which they could farm much as in Britain. Here they founded the City of Lewis, or Trelew, and around it over the ensuing years the colony grew and spread slowly upriver.

First they grew subsistence crops, vegetables and fruit, then grain which was harvested first by hand until they could afford threshing machines driven by steam traction engines. Wheat from Trelew won prizes at exhibitions as far afield as Chicago. At an early stage they made contact with the Tehuelche, with whom they were always on good terms, and from whom they picked up all the *gaucho* lore and horse-riding skills, from which it was but a short step to running sheep on the pampas and soon wool as well as wheat was being exported out of Port Madryn.

Thrusting further inland, first exploring parties and then settlers pushed in as far as the Andes where at last they found good, well-watered country where almost anything would grow, sheep and cattle fatten and the hard-working farmers prosper. They founded Trevelin (City of the Mill) and Esquel, in whose streets today you can still hear Welsh voices, often as not raised in song. (7)

The early settlers had a very tough time indeed, but managed to survive,

Threshing machinery in the Chubut Valley before World War One.

eventually prosper and in the main achieve their aims. Although they had in the end to accept the Spanish language and Argentine civic culture instead of the English ones they had sought to escape, this did not happen for a further two generations, during which time they were trusted by the Argentine government to organise and administer their communities. They were even allowed to dispense their own justice, a privilege enjoyed by no other immigrant group. Today, after four or five generations, English as a second language to Welsh has given way to Welsh being a second language to Spanish, but otherwise they still preserve their own customs, religion and culture.

Traders on the coast

White settlement in the south of Argentina proper had begun in 1859, when Commander Luis Piedra Buena set up a small dwelling and store on an island in the Santa Cruz River called Isla Pavón. This became a trading post or *factoría*, first exchanging goods and supplies for pelts brought in by the Tehuelche, and soon providing supplies for ships of all flags which scoured the South Atlantic at that time, taking fur and other seal for their pelts and also boiling both them and penguins down for oil. Piedra Buena engaged as his agent one William Clark, who had first come to these waters as mate (chief officer) on a ship, the '*Snow Squall*' from Salem, Massachusetts, which had been chased off the Cape of Good Hope by the Confederate warship

'*Alabama*' during the Civil War. Clark later took up land near the headwaters of the Coyle River, and his descendants are still around. By the time Musters (8) passed through in 1869 the trading post had expanded to three buildings.

Further downriver, both Anglican and Catholic missionaries had made contact with the Tehuelche at Cañadón de los Misioneros on the south bank, and although these attempts at evangelisation failed, the site proved highly suitable for settlement, being an excellent anchorage for shipping, and the town of Santa Cruz was founded there in 1872 with the arrival of the *Roebuck*, a chartered vessel bringing settlers from Buenos Aires. This venture was set up by a Frenchman, Ernesto Rouquaud, who had dealt in tallow and animal oils in Buenos Aires for some thirty years. Seeing the possibility of extending his business into the southern fisheries, he obtained a grant of 70 square leagues of land from President Sarmiento, and chartered the barque for two voyages, bringing supplies and followers to set up an onshore fish-processing plant as well as horses and goats (there is no mention of sheep) to stock the land. A Spanish league is 5 kilometres (about 3 miles) so a square league is 2,500 hectares (about 6,250 acres). Seventy square leagues was therefore 175,000 hectares or about 480 square miles – a very considerable extent of land.

The Rouquaud venture was not very successful, but a start had been made and other settlers followed. Following the appointment of Captain Carlos María Moyano as governor of the territory of Santa Cruz in 1875, followed a few years later by the appointment of a justice of the peace, Don Juan Richmond, Santa Cruz became the first administrative capital of the territory. The Santa Cruz River rises in Lago Argentino and carries a considerable body of water, being the third largest in the country (after the Paraná and the Uruguay, which together form the River Plate). The sheltered, deep-water anchorage at its mouth was to be the principal port for the region for many years, even after the seat of government was transferred to Rio Gallegos in 1888 because of sabre-rattling by Chile.

The river was still crossed at Isla Pavón however, opposite which land had been taken up on the north bank by one Gregorio Ibañez whose wife ran a *boliche* (liquor store) there. A rowing boat was used to provide the ferry service in those days, and horses would be swum across. Northbound travellers arriving at the south side would light a fire and brew up a few *mates* (9) until somebody over in the *boliche* saw the smoke and was sober enough to pull across the fast, swirling current to fetch them. A cable ferry driven by the current took the place of the rowboat in the 1920s. The crossing was known as 'Paso Ibañez' or just 'The Paso' until the eventual town was dignified by the name of Comandante Luis Piedra Buena in 1934. After the Second World War a 'Bailey' bridge was built by army engineers several

Droving sheep.

miles upstream, which carried road traffic until the present main road bridge was built in 1984 at Isla Pavón.

Although the main function of a *boliche* was the sale of liquor, they were also meeting-places and you could both eat (a cut off the communal roast) or sleep there (on the dirt floor, rolled up in your poncho). Ned Chace, whom we will meet in Chapter 4, gives a graphic description of his first night in one after he jumped ship in Santa Cruz in 1897.

There were a lot of rough-looking fellows squatting on the dirt floor about the fireplace at cards . . . not a bench or a table to be seen. There was gear piled along the walls, and six-litre Spanish leather bottles (*botas*) hung on pegs, brought in by the carters for refilling with the red wine of Mendoza. There was a big iron pot on the fire, and macaroni and pound chunks of mutton stewing in it, *puchero* they called it, for them that wanted it, and there were *galletas* – big fat biscuits of white flour, hard as a stone, bags (*maletas*), skewered it on iron rods they carried with them, and stabbed these into the dirt floor before the fire, and sat drinking *mate* while the meat roasted . . . In a little barroom that opened off the big room, men threw dice for wine and hard liquor, and talked gossip and politics with the *patrona* . . . Eventually everybody, drunk or sober, got to sleep on the floor, wrapped in his *capa* – guanaco blankets, that old hands use with the fur outside, the way the guanaco does . . . A good few would always go outside to sleep, never consenting to a roof at night.

Settlers by invitation

Argentina, having established sovereignty over this enormous area quite empty of the white man, urgently needed to settle it. President Roca was a pragmatist as well as a statesman, and realised that he needed to attract settlers from the colder climates of Northern Europe, rather than from Spain

An early Falkland hand shearer before 1900.

and the Mediterranean. So a general invitation was extended, by publicity and embassy representations in various countries, 'to the peoples of the world' to come and settle in southern Argentina. More directly, the governor of Santa Cruz Territory, Carlos Maria Moyano, had been given specific orders to encourage such settlement, particularly including people from the Falkland Islands. Not for the last time, the sovereignty issue of the Malvinas was temporarily set aside when more practical and economic factors were at stake.

Moyano duly went over to Port Stanley and carried out his mission to such good effect that he proceeded to marry a Falkland Islands girl, Ethel Turner. (10) He was able to interest a number of potential settlers, since by that time most of the available land in the Islands had been taken up, so the possibility of virtually unlimited freehold land on the coast at a very low purchase price was attractive. The Halliday brothers (1884), Rudd and McCall (1885), Herbert Felton (1887), John Hamilton (1887) and the Smith brothers (1889) were among the first to pack up their belongings and move over to settle in Santa Cruz Territory, although they were forestalled by Germans from Silesia like Eberhardt (1883), Bitsch (1884), Kark and Osnabruck.

Soon the commercial possibilities of wool-growing in the region became evident and capital started to flow from other sources. The Waldrons, well-to-do farmers in Berkshire with considerable resources who had already settled land on the West Falkland, were already leasing enormous areas both on Tierra del Fuego and on the Chilean mainland before 1880, together with their cousins Wood and Wales, and settled Estancia Condor on the north shore of the Magellan Straits in 1886. Prior to the boundary settlement in 1903, their letterhead 'Condor, Straits of Magellan' and the telegraphic address registered in 1901 was 'Condor, Cabo de las Virgenes', no country was specified in either case. Other interests from Europe as well as local entrepreneurs like José Menéndez and Moritz Braun were laying the foundations of the many large sheep farming companies which were started before the turn of the century. Wool-growing in Patagonia had become a sound and lucrative business.

Notes

1 In addition to Darwin's own *Voyage of the Beagle*, *Darwin and the Beagle* by Alan Moorehead is one of the best.

2 Carl Scottsberg D. Sc – 'The Wilds of Patagonia'. Edward Arnold, London 1911

3 Lenzi, *Historia de Santa Cruz*.

4 The steamer *Villarino* plied the Patagonian coasts for many years, being first employed in ferrying troops from Buenos Aires to the Rio Negro in the late 1870s for General Roca's desert campaign. She was still going in 1898 when Professor Hatcher from Princeton University came to Rio Gallegos seeking fossils (see Chapter 18), but later ran aground on a reef near Camarones, according to Hatcher because everybody on board was celebrating the successful birth of a child to one of the passengers.

5 See *Sailing Alone Around the World* by Joshua Slocum.

6 Later Sir Thomas Hungerford Holdich KCMG, vice-president of the Royal Geographical Society and author of *The Countries of the King's Award*.

7 Richard Llewellyn's novels *Up, Into the Singing Mountain* and *Down where the Moon is Small* provide a brilliant picture of early life in the colony.

8 George Chaworth Musters, an early traveller and author of *At Home with the Patagonians*.

9 *Mate* (pronounced 'máttey') is a herbal infusion made from *Yerba Mate* (Paraguayan tea), widely drunk throughout Argentina, Paraguay, Uruguay and southern Brazil.

10 The grandson of Carlos María Moyano and Ethel Turner de Moyano was Carlos Moyano Lerena, who became a well-known figure in government and minister of economy in our time. He represented Argentina several times at talks on the Falkland Islands at the United Nations, where he always put the Argentine case with prudence and sensitivity.

3

Somerset to South Atlantic

The early Blakes

We have seen how the first settlers on Patagonian soil came from varying origins and for a variety of reasons. Some were purely adventurers, looking for excitement or maybe running away from it, others had worked for employers elsewhere and, having saved their money, were looking for land of their own to settle down. Yet others, starting from existing farming enterprises elsewhere, whether in the Old World or in the Falkland Islands, were attracted by the opportunities which the new land was offering. Among the latter was Robert Blake, one of the earlier settlers in the Falklands. How did he get there?

For a full story, we need to go back to Somerset, where there had been Blakes since at least the sixteenth century. They were mostly country folk, yeomen and gentlemen, farmers of their own land and traders, living either in towns like Bridgwater or Taunton, or on their modest country properties. Some went to the universities and became doctors, lawyers and ministers of religion. Staunchly nonconformist, parliamentarian and God-fearing, it is no surprise to find some of them, if not actually on the *Mayflower*, then certainly among the earlier settlers in New England.

Let us start, however, with Humphrey Blake (d. 1558) of Plainsfield, Overstowey, who was a man of substance and the founder of a dynasty. From his son and heir, John Blake 'The Elder', are descended not only the main line of Somerset Blakes, but at least seven families who emigrated to

40

New England between 1630 and 1640. Between them, the Blake, Wolcott, Richards and Torrey families have today over 1,700 traceable descendants in the USA. Humphrey's third son Robert (d. 1592) moved to Bridgwater, then an important port on the River Parrett, where he set up as a merchant and purchased the house in Blake Street (formerly Mill Lane) which is today the Blake Museum. The business prospered and by the time his son Humphrey (1563–1625) took over they were into shipping, owned at least four ships and had sent out several important (and lucrative) trading ventures.

This Humphrey Blake had fourteen children, of whom the eldest was Admiral Robert Blake (1598–1657). He went to Wadham College, Oxford from where he graduated as a BA in 1618, but much of his early life is unknown. Undoubtedly he was concerned, together with his brother Humphrey, with the family trading business after their father's death in 1625, but it is remarkable that there is no record of him in Bridgwater until he was elected Member of the Short Parliament in 1640. Possibly he was away at sea on their trading ships, an experience which would have stood him in good stead later in life. He first gained recognition on land during the Civil War for his spirited and inspiring activity during the defence of Bristol for the Parliament in 1643, followed by similar actions at Dunster, Taunton and Lyme. During the Commonwealth, he was made 'general at sea' and was largely responsible for the reorganisation of the Navy which had not changed much since the days of the Spanish Armada.

Blake and his colleagues realised that ships had become platforms of floating artillery, rather than bearers of troops, and that the best way to fight them was in line astern rather than abreast, as in Drake's time. They organised victualling, crewing and many other aspects of fleet management, which were to continue with little change right through to Nelson's day and beyond. Following his defeat of the Dutch in the Channel and North Sea during the First and Second Dutch Wars, Blake was sent in 1655 with a powerful fleet to negotiate with the King of Spain who was sheltering a Royalist fleet under Prince Rupert. His final action was to capture twelve galleons of the Spanish treasure fleet from Havana, at Tenerife in 1657. He died at sea while returning from this exploit, almost within sight of his native land, and received a state burial in Westminster Abbey. Admiral Blake has since been recognised as the founder of naval organisation and of combat under sail, which was eventually to be honed to a fine pitch by Nelson.

The present Blake story which concerns us may be said to have started with Rev. William Blake (1773–1821), who like his father (also Rev. William) was the Presbyterian minister in Crewkerne and descended directly from John Blake 'The Elder' of Plainsfield. Six generations had gone by, all living in or near Pitminster, Wellington, Taunton and Crewkerne. His older brother, Dr Malachi Blake (1771–1843) had studied medicine at Edinburgh,

John and Monica Blake in 2000 by the statue to Admiral Blake in the centre of Bridgwater.

and returned to Somerset to practise in Taunton, where he founded the Taunton Hospital. Malachi married Mary Locke, daughter of John Locke of Pitminster whose first wife was Mary Jarman, niece of John and Elizabeth (Wyersdale) Jarman. There had been Blakes at Pitminster since about 1617, some of whom emigrated to America, but there does not seem to be have been any previous blood connection with the Lockes. Clearly all these North Somerset families, of similar standing in the community, would be closely acquainted if not actually related.

The Farewell family on the other hand, whose estate and manor house at Bishop's Hull near Taunton had been held by them since the reign of Henry VII, were major landowners and connected by marriage to many leading families in the West Country, such as Dyer, Parker, Montague and the Seymours, Dukes of Somerset, who had been granted the 'Royal Augmentation' to their armorial bearings following the marriage of Henry VIII to Lady Jane Seymour.

Sir George Farewell (d. 1647) who was knighted in 1609, had married Mary Seymour and they had twenty children. One of their sons, John, was a barrister at the Inner Temple and he married Dorothy Routh, the heiress of a substantial property known as Brenley near Faversham, Kent, which thus became part of the Farewell estates. However, the family died out in the male line and the last Farewell of Bishop's Hull was Anne (d. 1757) who married Nathaniel Wyersdale, a wealthy Bristol merchant. Their daughter Sarah married John Jarman, and both the Bishop's Hull and Brenley estates, by now augmented from both Wyersdale and Jarman trading enterprises, were inherited by their granddaughters Hannah and Elizabeth. This is where the Blakes come onto the scene, because the second Rev. William Blake of Crewkerne (1773–1821) married first Hannah Jarman, who died in childbirth, and then her sister Elizabeth who was thus the sole residuary heiress to the Bishops Hull estate.

On the death of Rev. William and Elizabeth (Jarman) Blake, their eldest son, also William (1815–1901), inherited from his mother the former Farewell properties at Bishop's Hull and Brenley. He had married Fanny Follett Osler Browne, whose mother Mary Osler came from the Birmingham family of that name, and they lived comfortably in the manor house at Bishop's Hull, where eight out of their nine children were born.

William then became the beneficiary under the will of a Miss Elizabeth Eason, who left him the charming small manor house of Bridge, which takes its name from Petherton Bridge, where the Fosse Way crosses the River Parrett near South Petherton, and which had been the scene of a skirmish during the Civil War. Miss Eason, a much respected spinster, lived in South Petherton and seems to have left the property to William Blake for no better reason than that he was a well-respected neighbour who would take good and responsible care of the Bridge estate, which she had inherited from her brother. He had lived there all his life, and left it to his sister with the proviso that the eventual heritor had to live on the property or else forfeit the inheritance.

So the William Blakes moved to South Petherton, but with eight children (the ninth, Arnold, was the only one born at Bridge) the old Elizabethan farm house dating from about 1590 was too small for such a large family, so in order to comply with the conditions of the will he sold the properties of both Bishops Hull and Brenley and built a new mansion on the Bridge estate. This was completed in 1860 and called Bridge House, being sited just up the hill, some 180 metres away from the smaller house, which was from then on known as Old Bridge. (1)

William and Fanny lived at Bridge in some style, and pursued active family, social and public lives, typical of their time. As Lawson-Clarke in his book *The Blakes of South Petherton* points out, they 'were not aristocrats but members of a landed gentry whose birthright was the gift of authority and they were trained to accept it naturally'. He might have added that they did not assume an attitude of 'privilege', but dispensed their authority with the responsibility and humanity which their deep roots in the country and its people had created over the centuries, and which was to be carried on both in England and overseas by the generations to come.

William was a Justice of the Peace, one of the longest-serving magistrates in Somerset, active in the Liberal Party and was appointed high sheriff of the county and deputy lieutenant in 1869. He had attended Manchester College, a Dissenting Academy then in York (later moved to Oxford), and also University College London, and saw to it that his sons received a similar education. His daughters were also well educated, though in that generation women did not attend university.

The eldest son of William and Fanny was William Farewell (b.1846) who would inherit the estate. Their second son was called Malachi Locke in memory of Dr Malachi and his wife Mary Locke. The name 'Locke' has been continued through later generations right down to the present day. Uncle Locke became a serious farmer who had taken the trouble to spend two years as a farm pupil in Norfolk, where the tradition of Coke of Holkham and other improving farmers of the eighteenth century was still very much in evidence. One of Locke's early comments was that 'the big farmers in Norfolk were gentlemen', by which he meant well educated, wealthy, 'hands-on' farmers operating their own estates of considerable acreage, rather than titled aristocrats who ran their 'place in the country' through an agent or manager. Returning to Bridge full of new farming ideas, Uncle Locke was soon managing the Bridge farm of 400 acres for his father, and he continued to do so all his life.

The third son and fifth child of William and Fanny was my grandfather, Robert Blake, born in 1851 at Bishop's Hull, but for him home was always Bridge. Like his brothers, Robert went first to Dr Hudson's Unitarian boarding school in Bristol, then to a school in Hampstead run by a Dr Case, and from there to Munich University where he studied engineering until the outbreak of the Franco-Prussian War obliged him to return home. He then went to study mechanical engineering 'hands on' at Galloway's Carriage Works in Manchester, staying at first with the Herford family. W.H. Herford, an old family friend and the founder of Ladybarn House school, was an advanced educationalist and practitioner of the Froebel method for teaching young children. But Robert was not happy with city life, and returned to South Petherton. Galloway's had given him valuable experience, but as a younger son he could expect little from the estate beyond a close and loving family and he had not yet found his true vocation. Being of an original and adventurous disposition he was naturally intrigued by the arrival of Frederick Edward Cobb in 1873 to marry his sister Emily.

Port Stanley Harbour veiwed through the Narrows, circa 1886 [photo A.F. Cobb].

Falkland Islands

Fred Cobb was the colonial manager of the Falkland Islands Company, incorporated by Royal Charter in 1851. Britain had annexed the Islands in 1833, the last of a series of confusing events following their occupation by Argentina in 1823, which we will describe more fully in Chapter 19. When the British took over the only settlement was at Port Louis (*Puerto Soledad* in Spanish). The colony was administered by naval officers until the appointment of the first colonial governor, Richard Moody, in 1841. Moody moved the settlement to its present site at Port Stanley in 1843, both location and harbour being far better both for locating a town and as an anchorage for shipping than Port Louis.

In 1844, Samuel Fisher Lafone appeared on the scene. Born in Liverpool in 1805, this enterprising businessman had at one time owned a considerable extent of land in Argentina, and had been engaged in trade in Buenos Aires since 1825. A staunch Anglican, he had in 1832 married a Roman Catholic heiress, María Quevedo de Alsina, whose family objected to what they considered a *mésalliance*, and in the ensuing furore Lafone was banished from Argentina and his bride and her mother sentenced by the court to spend a month in a convent. They were later pardoned and the marriage registered, but in the meantime Lafone had transferred his assets and business to Uruguay. He was engaged in the export of cattle hides to Europe, the only exportable product from the vast semi-wild cattle herds on the pampas until the advent of refrigeration in about 1878.

He also dealt in sealskins. The steam-powered industrial revolution in the British Isles had created a considerable demand for leather, which was an essential material for making sealings and packings used in all sorts of machinery. These were made mostly from cattle hide, but it seems that leather made from the skins of the larger species of seal was particularly suitable for this purpose and therefore was much sought after. It is quite possible that the seal poachers whose depredations in effect started the 'Falkland Islands Incident' of 1833 were not only after fur seal as is generally supposed, but also elephant seal and other large pelagic mammals.

Lafone negotiated the purchase of an enormous tract of the East Falkland still known today as 'Lafonia', where there were already large numbers of cattle running in a semi-wild state similar to the pampas of Argentina and Uruguay at the time. He set up a considerable enterprise to exploit them, bringing in both more cattle and the *gauchos* to hunt them and slaughter them for their hides. This enterprise as such was not very successful and in 1851 he negotiated with financial and shipping interests in London to form the Falkland Islands Co. (FIC).

It would seem to have become evident that some other form of production was needed, and that the example of extensive grazing of natural grassland with sheep, being actively pursued in Australia and New Zealand about this time, might be followed. Cobb therefore had been given the dual task of reorganising the exploitation of the company's lands, involving the introduction of sheep as the main line of production, and also encouraging other people to go out and settle the large areas of land not taken up by the FIC.

It must have sounded fascinating to the young Robert Blake, only 22 and ready for adventure, so he jumped at Cobb's suggestion that he go with them to the Islands to 'have a look', and they sailed for the Falklands in May 1873. Blake first went to Darwin, the principal FIC station on Lafonia, to learn something about sheep farming. After he had been there for about three months he heard that one Ernest Holmested was looking for a new partner for his venture at Shallow Bay on the West Falkland, known at the time as 'Adelaide Station', so he jumped on a coasting schooner and went off to see what the possibilities might be.

Settlement on the West Falkland had followed a different pattern. In 1867 a ship, the *Diane*, was chartered by a group of settlers headed by James Lovegrove Waldron, a wealthy farmer from Peasemore, near Newbury,

Berkshire and loaded with the 'necessaries of life for years to come'. The Waldrons took up land on the eastern side of the mountains which divide the island, with their main settlement at Port Howard, on the Falkland Sound. Holmested was English, but had come from New Zealand together with William Wickham Bertrand, on an adventurous journey across the Pacific, over the Andes on muleback and eventually, after several months on the Argentine and Uruguayan pampas, to the Falklands. (2) Here in 1868 they took up land on the western slopes of the mountains of the West Falkland, fronting onto Byron Sound, and started making their settlement at Shallow Bay, together with one John Switzer who had joined the pair while in Uruguay.

Bertrand however soon became engaged to marry Kate Felton, daughter of Henry Felton, one of the earlier settlers on the East Falkland. A Sergeant-Major in the 2nd Life Guards, Felton had been the second in command of a detachment of 30-odd Greenwich and Chelsea pensioners who were sent out in 1849 to defend the Islands. With typical Whitehall parsimony it was hoped that they might also settle there once their turn of duty was over, which indeed several including the Felton family did. Henry became the proprietor of 'The Queen's Arms' pub in Stanley and his son John James settled the Teal Inlet property on the East Falkland. The young Bertrands lived first at Shallow Bay, where their first two children were born, but Bertrand soon separated from his partners and went over to found Roy Cove Station (Bertrand and Felton), which comprises the western end of the island adjoining the Holmested and Blake property. Holmested in the meanwhile, while on a visit to England in 1872, had met one Rees who had capital and wanted to emigrate, so he joined the partnership in place of Switzer who had had to return to New Zealand to face legal charges.

Rees was not a success as a partner, so Holmested was looking around for someone else when Robert Blake arrived in the Islands, and after that first visit joined him in 1874. They got on well together, and eventually Blake's father advanced him the money to buy out Rees, and so the partnership of Homested and Blake was started. Early days at Shallow Bay were pretty rough, and the young Robert soon found plenty to get his energetic teeth into: buildings to be erected, fences strung, and the first wool clips harvested and sold to provide funds which were immediately ploughed back into the property. Their land included the mountains which form the backbone of the West Falkland, Mounts Adam, Donald, Robinson and Edgeworth, as well as important grazings on the 'South Side' (of the mountains) running down to Christmas Harbour at the mouth of the Chartres River (pronounced 'Charters' in the Falklands).

Stanley House, the residence of the Colonial Manager of the Falkland Islands Company, circa 1870 [photo A.F. Cobb].

Hill Cove

According to farm legend, the new stone house at Shallow Bay was built in 1880 for Robert Blake who had returned to the UK in 1878 and while there had become engaged to be married to Dorothea Herford (always known as Dora), daughter of W.H. Herford of Manchester, with whose family he had stayed while at Galloways. However, before he returned home after a further three years to get married, Holmested went on leave and returned unexpectedly with a wife – so it was he who took over the new house. Understandably, this caused a considerable rift and Blake proceeded to build his own house over at the other end of the farm, at Hill Cove. This is a deep water bay on Byron Sound, nestling in the shelter of Mounts Adam and Donald from the south. There was nothing there at all – no buildings, no paddocks, no yards, no installations for working sheep. But Robert Blake, with his vision and acumen now sharpened by seven years at Shallow Bay, could see that Hill Cove was a more central point from where to manage the property as a whole, including the considerable extent of land to the south of the mountains.

So, just below the pass over the mountains known as 'Hell's Kitchen' with the main riding track to Teal River and on eastwards to Chartres and Fox Bay (the track to Roy Cove ran up over the French Peaks in a westerly direction), the first building was erected. This, which survives today as 'the carpenter's shop', had a small room tacked on where Robert slept; heating and cooking and boiling up the glue pot all being carried out on the small woodstove in the shop proper. This was knocked up in a few days, after which a modest house of more commodious proportions was constructed nearby. This would later become a shepherd's house but for now, in November 1881, it became Robert and Dora's first home.

Work soon began on the big house proper, and other buildings were added over the years until the 'Top Settlement' as it came to be called comprised the store, barn, stables, cowshed and two houses for shepherds. The shearing shed and cookhouse for single men, however, were built down at the 'Point Rincon' (3) or simply 'The Point' where the water was deeper and in future years a jetty would be built which allowed quite large ships to come alongside. Every farm in the Falklands had to be its own port for shipping out the wool, and Hill Cove was one of the best and most sheltered.

The farm was virtually divided between the two partners at 'Boundary Stream' some 3 kilometres to the north of Hill Cove. No actual separation of property was carried out however, and the partners soon found it possible to work together while living apart – one family at Hill Cove and the other at Shallow Bay. Blake gradually emerged as the more energetic partner, and by 1884 was running the place from Hill Cove, which was situated more centrally than Shallow Bay, and enjoying his growing family. Holmested continued to live at Shallow Bay for some years, but finally removed to England in 1889. Holmested, Blake & Co. Ltd (H&B) was formed in 1890, and it is worthy of note that the two families continued in close and amicable partnership throughout the life of the company, and it would be the granddaughter of Ernest Holmested, Bettye Stronach, who was in the chair of the board of directors which wound up the company nearly a hundred years later.

Life was still pretty rough, however. We cannot do better than quote Robert Blake's own words, from a letter to his brother Edward (4) in August 1884, which carries a note at the top: 'This is the worst winter known since 1868':

Robert and Dorothea Blake soon after their marriage in 1881.

My dear Edward,

'Coals on fire' on my head aren't a patch to the letters you write me. Somehow I have not fulfilled my promise lately. I should like to give you my sentiments on snow, and particularly on Falkland snow, but as proba- bly others may see or hear what I write, I refrain, if I once began I should swear such a volley of oaths as would astonish even Cousin Arthur. (5) If I had a gift at composition, writing etc. I would spin you a good letter, or rather I would send the account to some magazine or paper, as it would probably amuse a good many people.

The *gauchos* have been working the Mt Edgeworth camp for the last three weeks, and have taken off between 80 and 90 hides there. At the end of last week I sent for them, and they came here on Saturday with Napper and their horses. On Sunday I left with them for Teal River after breakfast. The snow everywhere lay about six inches deep and in the drifts was any depth up to twenty feet. Besides the horse I rode I took two spare ones, and all told we drove 28 horses in front of us. It was slow work, often we could not go faster than a walk owing to the drift snow.

We reached the *gauchos'* house about two, and of course the first thing was to light a fire, the house by the way is about 14ft by 11ft 6in, furniture there is none, with the exception of one stool, which when turned upside down serves as a boot jack. They have three cups, so the fourth person in our party had to wait until somebody was 'through' with his cup. They have picked up somewhere an old oil tin . . . and cut it off [at the top], the upper part has a cork driven in the mouth and is used as a washing basin, both for body purposes and for washing the crockery, the lower part is the water bucket, and in this too they mix their bread. Any towel that is handiest is used for drying the crockery. There are no knives and only one three-prong fork and the prongs all turn different ways – I used it once. Everybody uses his skinning knife, and this if more dirty than pleasant is easily cleaned – just push it in the ground and wipe on your trousers. As soon as the fire was started, one went away to shoot a goose, in order to get a wing which was wanted for a brush, to sweep the floor etc., (6) and the others had a mouse hunt with knives among the sheepskins on which we had to sleep – we cut down two. A small round hole has been cut in the top of the stool, and in this the neck of the washing basin fits. There is a small table, on which stands a bag of sugar . . . the large iron spoon is kept in the sugar bag, another sack is nailed to the wall, in which the biscuit or bread is kept, and the mice hold revels continually in this bag, as long as there is anything to eat. There are two bunks, or rather one long bunk 11ft 6in by 6ft – I had one end of it, Louis and Napper slept in the other end while Peter (7) had a couple of sheepskins on the floor.

None of this would have been thought out-of-the-way by camp-dwellers in Patagonia. After breakfast (bread, cold mutton and black coffee) Robert continues:

By eight we are in the saddle, all armed with breechloaders, and away. Louis, as boss, takes the lead. Today superiority has its drawbacks – he, as leader, finds out all the holes and we carefully avoid them.

We rode for the foot of Mt Robinson, where from the shanty with glasses we could see cattle. When we drew near the two *gauchos* made a wide cast to get well round a flock [*sic*] and Napper and I stayed behind. We killed twelve out of this lot and 'skint' them; 'skint' in the camp is the past or perfect tense of 'to skin'. Cold work it was too, freezing like mad all the time.

This alone was no mean feat, but the hunt continued:

In about two minutes a flock of over 20 appeared with Louis behind them. As soon as they were well started with heads downhill we all start, Louis and Peter were at the bottom as soon as the bullocks; not so your brother. Peter came down over a place which I have named and probably for ever will be known as 'Peter's Cliff' – a fearful place . . . We killed 18 out of this flock – the last only half a mile from the shanty. It is the biggest kill, 30, we have ever made in one day. If I had not imported breechloaders, we should never have killed the cattle as we have done. As compared with the lasso they are so quick. The men shoot with one hand, holding the gun like a pistol and often never stopping the horse when a flock is running. I am awfully thankful we have so few left to annoy the sheep during this bad snow.

Other hazards were not lacking:

There is no candlestick of course [in the shanty], and the candle was stuck into a gunpowder flask. We were smoking and yarning when an awful noise was heard and the room was filled with smell and smoke – the candle had burnt down and slipped into the flask. Luckily it was nearly empty . . .

By 1888 they were shearing 25,000 sheep, and an important mileage of fencing had been erected. At Hill Cove proper the shearing shed had been erected in 1882 and equipped with a hand-operated hydraulic wool press. Sheep were shorn with hand shears, and continued to be so until the 1960s. Improving rams were imported from Kent (Romney Marsh) and Hill Cove-bred rams were sought after by other Falkland farms. Wool was the main product, with a secondary trade in sheepskins. In 1890 a try-works was installed, for boiling down surplus sheep to extract their tallow which was in demand for soap-making – in those days whaling was in its infancy and vegetable oils were almost non-existent. Ever innovative, Robert Blake had sown down a number of paddocks with English grasses for hay, and had planted several acres of trees. The Hill Cove 'forest' was, and still is, unique in the Islands.

The flocks multiplied further, and soon Hill Cove was running 30–32,000 sheep. Some sale of ewes to other growers was still possible, but in spite of the try-works the disposal of surplus stock started to be a problem. Ever conscious of the dangers of overstocking, in 1890 Robert wrote to his brother Edward: 'this year I must get rid of 10,000 sheep' – a far cry from the modest beginnings of sixteen years before. So, like a number of others in the 1880s, Robert started looking towards 'the Coast', a term generally used in the Falklands to refer to the mainland of Patagonia, both Argentine and Chilean, including Tierra del Fuego.

The drovers

The Governor of Santa Cruz Territory in southern Argentina, Carlos María Moyano, had been appointed by President Roca in 1880 with the specific objective of bringing about settlement of this enormous and hitherto unoccupied region. Moyano had already carried out considerable inland exploration in southern Santa Cruz, in conjunction first with Piedra Buena and later with 'Perito' Moreno, (8) and further undertook an expedition in 1881 from Isla Pavón on the Santa Cruz River northwards to Carmen de Patagones, scouting out an overland route along which livestock could be driven down from the Rio Negro Territory, at that time the furthest extent of farm settlement southwards from the Buenos Aires pampas. A small drove of cattle had been brought down from the Rio Negro in 1878 to the Santa Cruz by one Cipriano García, who also acted as guide to Moyano's expedition. The first drove of sheep was undertaken by Laciar and Guillaume in 1885, who brought down 2,500 Merinos from Conesa, Rio Negro, to the River Deseado, where a sprinkling of settlers had already started to take up land.

South of the Gallegos, settlement had spread north from the Straits of Magellan, and in 1884 William Halliday bought sheep in Chile from Menendez's 'San Gregorio', and took out a lease on Hill Station, on the North Bank just opposite the town of Rio Gallegos which at that time consisted of just two houses. Before bringing the sheep up he returned to the

Shepherds setting out for a gathering operation at Bleaker Island, East Falklands, around 1900.

Falklands to fetch his family. Together with his wife, father-in-law McCall (9) and seven children they landed in Rio Gallegos off the SS *Ranee*, Captain Winther, in July 1885. They had brought building materials, all their household goods and stores for a year. A storm got up while they were unloading and ferrying everything over to the other side, but by dint of superhuman effort they were able to salvage most of their belongings. Exhausted, they flopped down to sleep in the rough shelter of tarpaulins draped over the bushes, not yet knowing that the Gallegos had the third highest tides in the world.

In the morning they woke to find snow on the ground, and everything that floated had been carried away, all their belongings and the timber intended for their house. Only a chest of tools, a few cooking pots and the cast iron Singer sewing machine were left. They had to live off the country, herding their sheep until they could shear the first wool clip, sell it in Punta Arenas and finally purchase materials for a first house. They were hard times.

The first drove from the Rio Negro to reach the Gallegos was carried out by the brothers John (Jack) and William Rudd in 1886. Their father John Rudd hailed originally from Exmoor, the 'Lorna Doone' country, and may well have been related to 'gert (great) Jan (John) Ridd' or Rudd, hero of the novel by R.D. Blackmore. He had left his native Devon in 1850 on a ship bound for Madras, but storms overtook the vessel and they ended up in Port Stanley. Rudd remained there and with his Exmoor background must have been a competent sheep man as in 1861 he was appointed manager of Darwin Station for the Falkland Islands Company, where in 1864 he was assaulted and killed by an aggrieved worker, said to be 'a half-bred Indian named Gill'. He had married Ellen Roach, the daughter of one of the pensioners who came out in 1849 and his son Jack had married one of the McCall girls, sister of Mary Halliday. Seeing like the Hallidays the possibilities of farming on the coast, and the Falklands by then being almost wholly taken up, they came across in their wake.

The Rudds bought sheep from around Bahia Blanca. The number is not recorded but was said to be 'an important' amount of sheep, which was just as well since they had a lot of losses, arriving with only two thirds of the original flock, with which they proceeded to stock their property at Cape Fairweather on the north bank of the Gallegos River.

In 1888 a group of Scots, who had taken up land in the Rio Gallegos district following in the steps of the Hallidays, got together to bring down sheep to stock their holdings. George MacGeorge had also come from the Falklands and taken up land 'Guakenken Aike'; Henry Jamieson had come from Australia and settled at 'Moy Aike'; John Hamilton and his partner William Saunders had come from Scotland via the Falklands, where they had taken up Weddell, Beaver, Saunders and Keppel Islands adjacent to the West Falkland, and on the coast had settled 'Punta Loyola' on the south bank of the Gallegos. The fifth partner was Jack Maclean, from the Outer Isles. MacGeorge had to some degree pioneered the route by bringing down a troop of mares two years previously and he, together with Jamieson, seem to have been the leaders. These experienced stockmen first took ship to Buenos Aires, where they arranged the finance to purchase livestock, then travelled on the brand-new Southern Railway to Bahía Blanca, where they purchased stores and the wagons to carry them in. They were joined by Alexander Denholm, who with his brother Walter had come out from Scotland in 1860 and settled near Paysandú, in the north of Uruguay and still Indian country. They seem to have suffered from raiding, so they moved to Chascomús in Argentina. This was still 'frontier country' so, liking the sound of Patagonia where by all accounts the natives were at least peaceable, Alexander and his nephew Tom, only 16, joined the partners and the group set about buying horses.

They roamed around from Curumalán to Sierra de la Ventana to Necochea, collecting some five hundred in all including riding horses, brood mares and stallions. They then swam the Negro River at Choele-Choel and started to assemble their sheep, buying from the established sheep farmers in Rio Negro until they had got together some 5,000 ewes, and presumably the sheepdogs with which to handle them. The sheep were said to be 'locally bred, somewhat crossed with Merino'.

This considerable mob left the Rio Negro in September 1888, and took two years to reach the Coyle. They took it slowly, grazing the virgin grasslands, proceeding from water to water, swimming the rivers as they came to them. When the cold weather set in, they holed up for the winter and were in no hurry to move on in the spring, but let the ewes lamb down, sheared the flock and continued when the lambs were big enough to travel. For quite long stretches they divided the flock into two, under MacGeorge and Jamieson, so as to spread the grazing and make better use of the waterholes, which were often separated by considerable distances. By the time they reached 'Jamieson's Water', just south of the *Gran Bajo* of San Julian, Maclean took his share of sheep and settled right there. He did not take out a settler's lease but just squatted, and after a couple of years he sold out to Hope. The rest continued south and eventually arrived at the Coyle with their flock increased and wool (i.e. saleable produce) in hand.

This was the biggest and most famous of the drives, but there were others. In 1891 William Hope brought a 'few hundred' down from the Rio Negro to San Julian, and settled Estancia 'La Colmena' with these added to those which he had bought from Maclean. A *colmena* is a beehive, and takes its name from the adobe hut shaped like an igloo that Hope put up there, to live in with his wife, Annie Kyle. She later died in childbirth, all alone while her husband was riding desperately to Santa Cruz in search of medical aid. She is buried there, and this sad little tale has been remembered in a local folk song. Hope, broken - hearted, sold out to Jack Frazer, a schoolmaster from the Falkland Islands.

The early drovers needed shepherds to help with the work. They took their pay once the drove was over but did not necessarily take up land themselves at the time. William Wallace and Andrew Kyle, for example, had left their families in the Falklands to come over and take part in the 1889 drive. Wallace then brought his family over to San Julian, but died before he could settle a property. With his savings however, his widow was able to open the Hotel Miramar in 1901. Andrew Kyle also brought his family over, and settled 'Darwin Station', (10) on the coast just south of La Colmena.

Then there were the Smith brothers, John and Peter, who had left the family holding at Johnson's Harbour on the East Falkland and taken up land at Coy Inlet, the mouth of the Coyle River. They arrived a bit later, and were able to buy sheep from the Welsh colonists in the lower Chubut, near Trelew, which they drove down in 1892 to stock their property. The name 'Coyle' for the river, by the way, comes from the Tehuelche 'Cuheyli' (so spelt by Musters) and adapted by the early English navigators into 'Coy Inlet'. The Spanish tongue is unable to cope with this phrase, and turns it into something sounding like 'Co' í'le' or Coyle, and so it appears on all the maps from about the turn of the century.

Partnership

All this new settlement in southern Patagonia had created a considerable demand for sheep, and Robert Blake was at first content with supplying this demand by selling sheep off Hill Cove for shipment to the coast, but at the same time he arranged for two shepherds to go over to have a look at the country. Donald Munro and John McAskill had come out from the Island of Lewis in the Hebrides on contract to Hill Cove, and when this was up, rather than return to Scotland they thought they would try their luck 'over on the coast'. They took ship from the Falklands to Santa Cruz in 1889 or early 1890 and started scouting around, but by then most of the best land on the coast and within easy reach of a workable bay or port had been taken up, particularly south of the Santa Cruz River. So they looked further north, no doubt met and talked with people like Hope, Jamieson and MacGeorge who had crossed the pampas, grazed their droves there and found many of the waterholes. There seemed to be excellent grazing land, well watered, just west of San Julian, so in June 1890 Munro sat down in Doña Gregoria's *boliche* at the Paso, and penned off a letter to Robert Blake at Hill Cove, proposing a joint venture to take up land there.

Robert Blake and the Hill Cove shearing gang, taken around 1890. Robert Blake is on the right, with pipe, next to him is Sydney Miller.

There were ships available to carry his letter across from Santa Cruz to the Falklands, and Robert immediately replied suggesting that Munro go over to Hill Cove and work out further details of the agreement. In a letter to his brother Edward, Robert tells of this visit, describing the proposed venture as an 'investment', and eulogising on its possibilities.

June 23 1891.....The '*Rippling Wave*' has just sailed to Patagonia with another load of sheep, the last I shall send this year. *Munro* the man I have gone into partnership with in *San Julian* came across in her to see me. We are starting over there with three times as many sheep as there were here, when Rees sold out, & I firmly believe this speculation will turn out a good investment unless Munro is a liar which I don't think he is. We have 95,000 acres of land taken out on the coast of Port San Julian, with a water frontage to the sea of 12 miles (20km). The land on this square block which is rather over 12 miles square, Munro tells me is well watered throughout and has good sheltered valleys. The block next it is not very good but beyond that again, the land is as good as that he now occupies. I have commissioned him to take up this last-mentioned block of about 95,000 acres (11) & advanced the rent money, which is for the first ten years L32 per year, with the right to buy, or renew the lease at the expiration of the ten years.

During the first half of 1891 the first sheep were sent across in the schooner the *Rippling Wave* – two voyages at least, to be followed by Robert in person later in the year. Munro had applied for the land, but it was Blake who was putting up the capital so he had to formalise the leases and as soon as possible acquire the freehold. Besides, it was up to him to organise the operation which would become in due course over twice the size of Hill Cove. Once Patagonia became settled and equipped with telegraphs, a postal service and law and order (they arrived more or less in that sequence), followed by banks, shipping and general trade, it soon became better sheep country than the Falklands could ever be. Heavier clips of finer and therefore more valuable wool could be grown, lambing rates were far higher and once the frozen meat trade got going after the First World War there was an important outlet for surplus livestock, all of which factors still apply to the present day.

For Robert Blake it was a brilliant opportunity to expand, coming just at a time when his own family commitments were growing. He and Dora now had five children, and the older ones, Elsie and Robert Junior, were already at school in England. The possibility of the family removing to England was starting to loom, although it was not to happen for another seven years and after three more children. Well-farmed and go-ahead as Hill Cove might be, it seemed unlikely to be able to be improved further, a possibility that two of Robert's sons and three of his grandsons worried away at for the next ninety years or so. Robert Blake had the vision, the business acumen and the courage to see the possibilities of enlarging his interests in this way, and the San Julian venture would prove in fact to be the best investment he ever made. He was also the only settler on the coast with his own source of sheep back on the Islands, apart from the Waldrons with their much greater financial resources. He could thus at one stroke relieve Hill Cove of surplus stock and with it settle the new venture without having to go out and buy livestock, so directing his resources to the purchase of land and equipping it with buildings and installations. The first of several shipments of sheep carried by the *Rippling Wave* heralded the partnership of Munro and Blake. The shipping mark for wool from the new enterprise was, and still is, 'MB'.

Notes

1 For a full account of the Eason inheritance, and much fascinating detail about country life of the time, see *The Blakes of South Petherton* by Peter Lawson-Clarke.

2 An account of Ernest Holmested's voyage, written up from his diaries, may be found in *Falkland Heritage* by Mary Trehearne. Daughter of Robert Blake's eldest son Robert, in this and its sequel *Patagonian Harvest* she relates the lives of two generations living and rearing families in this remote corner of the world.

3 A *rincón* (Spanish for 'corner') in Patagonian parlance means a promontory jutting out to sea, usually joined to the mainland by a narrow spit of land.

4 Edward Jarman Blake was the family solicitor and founder of the Crewkerne firm of Sparks & Blake. The brothers were next in age, and very close.

5 'Cousin Arthur' would be Arthur Frederick Cobb, son of Fred Cobb and Emily Blake and father of John Cobb, sometime racing motorist and director of the Falkland Islands Company.

6 Goose wings are still widely used in the Islands, particularly for sweeping up peat ash round fireplaces.

7 'Louis' and 'Peter' were probably Luis Alazia and Pedro Llamosa, *gauchos* from the Port Louis settlement, whose descendants with the same surnames may be found on the West Falkland today. I do not know who Napper was.

8 Dr Francisco Pascasio Moreno explored much of the southern Andes and was the leading geographical authority in Argentina. Together with his Chilean counterpart Dr Diego Barros Arana, he was instrumental in settling the frontier dispute with Chile in 1881. He was appointed consultant and expert (*perito*) on behalf of Argentina to the boundary commission set up by the British Crown in 1901.

9 William MacCall was a Scottish shepherd, who upon his wife's death was left with several children including four daughters. He was recruited by Fred Cobb in 1873 for the Falklands and given a job, a house and free passage for the entire family. His daughters married Halliday, Rudd, Cameron and Fell, all of whom would in time find their way over to the coast.

10 Not to be confused with 'Darwin Station' in Lafonia, on the East Falkland. The farm at San Julian, being sited in 'Cañadón Pardo' was later named 'Pardo Darwin' and I have subsequently used this version.

11 95,000 acres was 40,000 hectares or 16 square leagues of 2500 hectares each. The total extent of the Company's freehold would eventually amount to 175,000 hectares.

4

Port San Julian

Estancia Coronel

San Julian Bay is a landlocked cove, sheltered from the violent South Atlantic winds, as the early navigators in sail knew very well. No river flows into it, but it forms the mouth of a great natural depression known as the *Gran Bajo de San Julián*, some of which is below sea level, extending 75 kilometres or more in a direction slightly south of west from the head of the bay. North of the *Bajo* and west of the bay the land rises sharply to form a low plateau 200 metres or so above sea level, which stretches away for hundreds of miles inland. This is known to English and Spanish speakers alike as the '(*la*) pampa', not to be confused with the pampas (in the plural) which are flattish rolling plains in central Argentina inhabited by cattle and *gauchos*. The Patagonian pampa is inhabited only by sheep, wildlife and sheep farmers.

At intervals the Pampa is broken by steep-sided valleys running mostly in an easterly direction towards the sea, caused by glacial and water erosion and of a characteristic shape, with a marked change in slope at the edge of the horizontal ground; quite different to the rolling hills of older formations. These in Spanish (and English) are known as *cañadones*, as distinct from *valles* (valleys), meaning smoother, more gradual depressions usually with a stream or river at the bottom. The sloping side of a *cañadon* is called a *faldeo*, a Patagonian term derived from *falda* (skirt).

Water is, of course a key factor in a semi-arid climate where annual rainfall is seldom more than 25cm, often less. There is beautiful country watered by streams along the eastern foothills of the Andes but it is a long way between there and the coast, and the rivers are far apart. We now know that a sub-artesian aquifer extends across much of the Patagonian pampa, fed by the Andean glaciers, so that water can be found almost anywhere by boring to depths between 50 and 200 metres. But for the indigenous peoples and early settlers alike, places where such water came to the surface naturally at springs were clearly of vital importance. The word *aike* which forms part of many place-names means in the Tehuelche language 'water' or 'watering place', and from there by association a place where people may camp or live.

Donald Munro and John McAskill had set up a precarious settlement in a well watered *cañadón*, one of several which break up the pampa escarpment some 32 kilometres to the west of Port San Julian, and which have abundant springs. In those early days there was a stream flowing down the valley, fed from springs further up which were tapped in later years to supply the settlement with running water. Munro and McAskill had applied for the first lease of land adjoining the bay, a block of four square leagues of 'camp'. *Campo* means 'country' or 'countryside' – or more specifically in modern times, 'non-urban land'. A league is 5 kilometres or roughly 3 miles, so a 4-league block was 10,000 hectares – i.e. about 25,000 acres. In a letter to his brother Edward, Robert Blake enthuses about the convenience of this land, its water supply and its proximity to the port.

Having decided on the venture, Blake set about organising it and carrying it out. As mentioned in Chapter 3, the first shipments of sheep from Hill Cove were sent over in 1891, in the schooner *Rippling Wave*. This historic vessel, which carried more sheep destined to settle the newly-inhabited lands of southern Patagonia than any other ship, belonged to the shipping firm of Braun & Blanchard of Punta Arenas and therefore flew the Chilean flag. She seems to have been fitted with 'tween-decks and pens specifically for the carrying of sheep, and to have been used almost exclusively for this purpose for a number of years. Chace (see below, page 64) says that she was registered in Boston, and as a New Englander himself he ought to know. One can picture a trim but aged Yankee schooner, pining away at her moorings in a Boston shipyard and being bought up cheap by Moritz Braun for a risky venture in the South Atlantic. Robert Blake describes how the 500 or so sheep on board were watered daily, a bottle being given to each, one by one, and had bundles of tussac grass (*Poa flabellata*, a very nutritious grass found only in the Falkland Islands) hung from the deckhead for them to help themselves. On most voyages with favourable winds and calm seas only a few might die during the two- to three-day voyage, but in bad weather it was much more risky. One shipment consigned to Herbert Felton (1) managed to make Punta Arenas after a week of storms, but with only 150 sheep left alive.

Robert Blake had better luck and following the first sheep came cargoes of goods from Britain – building materials, provisions, clothing, baling and fencing materials, sheep dip – the lists went on and on. One can picture Robert writing late into the night at Hill Cove, with his pipe of plug tobacco and his cups of strong tea, making out the lists and sending off the orders to Spearing and Waldron in London. The Waldrons were wealthy farmers in Berkshire, and like José Menéndez and his associates, could see the importance of tying up the trade and shipping with that of primary wool production in the newly-settled territories. They had taken over the business carried out until 1889 by Townsend and Spearing in providing goods, services and even personnel for the new and upcoming sheep ventures in the South Atlantic and the shipping to carry it. Many provisions were shipped by Messrs Thom and Cameron of Glasgow in their brig *Cross Owen* direct to the ports of Santa Cruz or San Julian, and dumped on the beach for the settlers to collect in their carts as and when they could.

To organise all this on site, and to purchase the land and so consolidate the original leases that Munro had taken out, Robert Blake first went across in April 1892, leaving Dora to travel to England with their five children and put the eldest (Elsie and Robert Junior) into school. He joined them in England in June, having visited San Julian and Buenos Aires in order to get

Robert Senior (left) with Dora, Elsie and Robert Junior at Bridge House in 1892. Robert had just returned from San Julian and the two children started going to boarding school.

the land purchases under way. Further materials for building and fencing were ordered in London, as well as two bloodhounds for hunting pumas. Robert then returned, first to the Falklands for six weeks and then in November to Punta Arenas where he was met by Donald Munro with a *tropilla* or troop of twenty-four horses. They rode up to San Julian in eight days, sleeping mostly at farms along the way, but out on the pampa when there was no farm or shanty to be found.

The site chosen by Munro for a settlement seemed a good place to Blake, and the *Cross Owen* having arrived with her first cargo, they set to and started to put up the timber and corrugated iron buildings: a dwelling house for the staff, a bunkhouse for the men, a cookhouse for all. Fences came later – the sheep were herded on the open pampas at first, the shepherds sleeping behind calafate or incienso bushes until shanties could be built for them.

Robert Blake had a knockdown prefabricated hut for himself shipped by Messrs Sparrow of Martock, which still survives after being used by two generations of children as 'The Playhouse'. Writing from this little hut with the wind whistling round, he was not greatly taken with the country, but he continued to appreciate its possibilities. So he consolidated the leases which Munro had applied for, and put his energy, leadership and construction skills into building a shearing shed, a dipping bath and a warehouse just up from the beach at San Julian – the first building to be erected at the port. (2) This was a plain wood-framed shed, clad in galvanized corrugated iron just like those in the Falklands, which served to hold stores and materials unloaded from the ships, before they were carted out to the farm, and wool bales going the other way, pending shipment, saving both from being just dumped on the beach.

Robert Blake's description of this job gives some idea of the conditions the early pioneers lived and worked in. The timber and other materials were all there lying on the beach, where the *Cross Owen* had offloaded them, and Robert and his two companions slept in the open, sheltered from the wind by some scrubby bushes. They lay on their sheepskins, with a loaded revolver close to hand in case of marauding pumas. Meals were mutton and ship's biscuit, and their water supply was brought down daily in a bullock-drawn water cart from the farm settlement (San Julian has no fresh water – then nor now). On one occasion the water cart failed to arrive, and they went four days without washing and twenty-four hours without any water. Blake says:

> I never knew what real thirst was until then. Still we none of us slacked, only eyes were lifted continually to see if the cart was coming. It came at last, but so late that I had quite made up my mind we would have no water that night. It was nobody's fault, only the bullock was lost. I had one wash in eight days, and when I came home here I had three or four the first day. The skin seemed to want water, and I watered it accordingly.

63

Munro and McAskill were primarily stockmen, so they tended the sheep while Blake set about organising the farm. He had other help, of course – there was the German carpenter, Ernest Behm, who had helped put up the shed at the port and afterwards became foreman; and later there was Ned Chace, the 'Yankee'. Chace was from New England, and in 1897 had shipped before the mast as carpenter on a Boston schooner, but jumped ship at Santa Cruz to escape from a drunken, bullying captain. (3) He had a varied and wide-ranging life in Patagonia which fortunately has been written up and provides an excellent picture of the early settlement days, when Patagonia was all wide open and not unlike the North American West of the time. Chace spent some time on the new sheep station at San Julian with Munro, with whom he became quite friendly, and put up many of the shepherds' shanties, other buildings and fences, following up the work started by Blake who in fact only spent one winter there in 1893. He soon picked up the many skills needed by a 'camp' man, and tried his hand at most things, from fencing through shearing to droving and hunting wild cattle round Lago San Martín. He ended up as manager at Estancia 'Anita', one of the big Menéndez outfits on the border south of Lago Argentino, where he was discovered by the Barretts who were visiting the area (on horseback) in 1927. Their Yankee accent and speech made him homesick, so he returned to New England where they were able to extract his stories and ghost them up into *A Yankee in Patagonia*, one of the most readable and true-to-life books about early days in that region.

The property was named 'Estancia Coronel', (4) and although we as a family have always referred to it as a 'farm' it would be more correct to talk about a 'ranch', 'sheep station' or *estancia* when referring to an operation of this size and complexity, having very little in common with the Old World notion of farming. It is in fact an extensive and exacting operation, grazing sheep in large numbers for the production of wool and sheep meats on the native pastures. The origin of the name *'Coronel'* (Spanish for 'colonel') for the *estancia* is obscure. There is a valley on the property called Cañadón Coronel, and there was an Argentine *gaucho* around in the early days called Juan Coronel who took up with a Tehuelche squaw and had a large family.(5) Chace mentions an important tribe whose chief *(cacique)* was called 'Ferrero', from whom undoubtedly the 'Fereiri' section gets its name, so possibly Ms Coronel was from this tribe and they camped in a nearby *cañadón* . . .

Then there is the Cañadón Artilleros, whose name must have had to do with the mutiny in Punta Arenas of the garrison artillery in 1851, whose participants fled into Argentina hotly pursued by both Chilean and Argentine police who caught up with them somewhere north of the Santa Cruz river – Chace says he saw skulls rolling on the pampa, and there is a story about boots having been found 'sticking up out of the graves'. We never found any skulls but certainly in our time a rusty cavalry sabre was found in this *cañadón*.

The company

President Roca's policy to attract settlers was successful, and from 1894 the Argentine government started issuing freehold title deeds for the initial leases, and selling further grants of freehold land. Robert Blake continued to purchase tracts on this basis, extending west and north from San Julian Bay, until the property amounted to 175,000 hectares (437,000 acres, nearly the size of the county of Worcestershire). But further capital was also needed to put up buildings, fences and sheep-working installations such as yards and dips. The best way to provide increased capital for development was to float a company and sell its shares, so the San Julian Sheep Farming Company Ltd was incorporated in 1900. Other British owners were doing much the same at about the same time, and there was much interchange of shares on a 'friends and neighbours' basis.

Port San Julian around 1893, showing the Company's bale shed, and the *Rippling Wave* (left) and *Cross Owen* beached for unloading.

Among the first shareholders we find Edmund J. Mathews, the manager of Port Howard for J.L.Waldron Ltd, and A.E. Bell and Hilary.W. Jacomb of the wool-broking firm Jacomb Hoare and Company, who were also directors. Another important shareholder was Moritz Braun, whose Estancia 'Oren Aike' became part of the company's land. It is thought that Oren Aike was originally settled by one Heysen for whom Chace first went to work, and who like many early settlers could not make a go of it so the farm was taken over for debt by Braun & Blanchard, the shipping agents in Punta Arenas who later became part of the Braun/Menéndez group of interests known as the 'Anónima'. Certainly the only Argentine resident capital in the original San Julian Sheep Farming Company was the 30 per cent Braun holding.

One name missing from the list of shareholders was that of Donald Munro. From 1897 onwards, we start picking up from Robert Blake's letters that he was not happy with Munro's handling of the local business aspect of the partnership. Munro's share in this amounted to one third of the total capital, and he had been receiving dividends on this basis, although it is also understood that he was using company funds locally, for his own benefit. He invested first in the town of San Julian, buying up the original *boliche* (basically an eating and drinking shop) set up by one Reid, possibly with Munro's help in the first place. Then he branched out into a general store in Punta Arenas. Sadly, he was no businessman and when his partner Lippert got into financial difficulties he had to go down there to sort things out. On the long ride home in early 1900 he got caught in a storm, slept out wet on the pampa, caught pneumonia and died.

Munro's untimely death leaving debts and no will was to cause the company and the Blake family great trouble for many years to come. However, the most immediate requirement was to arrange for the running of the farm. McAskill by that time was a sick man, having treatment in Buenos Aires where he later died. Robert Blake went out and arranged for Robert Patterson to take over the management. The four Patterson brothers (Robert, Jim, George and Will) were Falkland-born, their father having come out from Scotland before 1864. They came over in 1892 to join Hope who had settled 'La Colmena' to the south of the *Gran Bajo*, and looked after the place for him while he returned to Port Stanley to marry his bride, Annie Kyle (see page 55). However they were looking for a place of their own and by 1897 had taken up land immediately north of the Munro Blake tracts, forming Estancia 'Mata Grande'. There were by this time a number of other British settlers round San Julian, such as Hope. Andrew Kyle had brought his family over in the wake of his daughter, and settled 'Pardo Darwin'. The Denholms had squatted at 'Jamieson's Water', and in due course took out leases on other properties such as 'Miramar', later to become part of 'Darwin'.

They were joined soon after the turn of the century by John Scott, also from Dumfries, who had settled first 'Bellavista' south of the Gallegos on the Chilean border. Here he had very heavy losses of sheep from the disastrous snowfall of 1904, so moved further north to San Julian and settled 'Los Machos' which adjoined Munro Blake on the northern side, to the west of Mata Grande. Other early British settlers who took up land included Kemp, MacDonald, Cameron, Finlayson, Anderson and in the town there were Englishmen like Steve Alder from Wiltshire who had gone to the Falklands in 1882 at the age of 18, and later worked at Condor, Sydney Saxby (1895) who appears on the books at Killik Aike Norte and Irish Tommy Quigley who had landed in Bahía Blanca in 1888 aged 18 and come down with one of the epic droves.

Nearly all the first settlers round San Julian were British, except for a few Germans like Mackeprang and Veley. Not until after the town was officially founded in 1901 did other nationalities start to come in: Spaniards, Italians, Greeks, Croatians, Russians, mostly starting work on the existing farms and later setting up their trades in the port. Some took up land, but not all of them took out the freehold of the land they were occupying. Unlike the Rio Gallegos district, there seemed to be more than enough land available, fiscal leases were easy to get and cost nothing, so a large number of settlers did not acquire the freehold, and others including 'the Company' expanded out from a central block to occupy neighbouring leasehold.

Uncle Robert

Meanwhile, the younger generation was coming along. Robert and Dora Blake had moved back to Somerset in 1898, after their youngest child Norman was born, leaving Hill Cove in the capable hands of Sydney Miller who had been assistant to Robert for eight years. They leased 'Yeabridge', a charming small country house quite near to Bridge House, from where their eight children continued their schooling. Uncle Robert (the eldest son, Robert Blake Junior, 1884–1965) had been at school in England from the age of 8, first at Ladybarn House and then at Sedbergh. On leaving school, he went out to Buenos Aires with his father in September 1903, and from there to San Julian to learn the job under Robert Patterson. He spent most of the next eighteen months there, fitting in two quick trips to the Falklands from Punta Arenas. In the course of these he visited the Chilean part of Tierra del Fuego, meeting such pioneers as A.A. Cameron and Ernest Hobbs, and visited other farms in the Rio Gallegos district including Estancia 'Condor'. This property of 200,000 hectares (500,000 acres, 550 square miles) had been settled on the north shore of the Magellan Straits in 1885 by the Waldrons and their Wood cousins and is today the largest sheep ranching operation in the world run as a single unit. Larger properties may be found in northern Australia, but they run cattle only.

After a visit home to Somerset, in 1905 Robert went to Australia and spent eighteen months there, mainly on Quambone Station near Coonamble in north-western New South Wales. This is located far into the outback and at that time was reached by an overnight train from Sydney. We read that it was 64 kilometres (a 15-hour ride) from Haddon Rig, which is still famous today as a Merino stud. As a 'jackaroo' (Jack of all trades) Robert had to turn his hand to anything that came along, from mustering to riding bore drains and fighting bush fires. He also fitted in a couple of months in New Zealand, mostly in South Island where he visited a number of properties including 'Hui-Hui', where he met James Little (founder of the Corriedale breed of sheep). He quotes a Mr Smith of Morven Hills who 'believes Corriedale to be the sheep of the future'. Uncle Robert's diaries reveal an intense and single-minded dedication to 'learning the job' as a jackaroo, both while on his travels and back at San Julian.

Robert spent his days in the saddle herding, gathering and droving sheep;

Robert Blake Senior and Junior at San Julian, probably in 1907.

in the yards, working, drafting and dipping the flocks, and hours on the wool table rolling newly-shorn fleeces ready for baling. On returning to San Julian in 1907 (with his father and sister Violet), he was already on a par with Patterson and by early 1908, at the age of 24, had taken over the management. In 1909 a new house was built for the manager. It was known, as all such houses are on Patagonian farms, as the 'Big House' (*Casa Grande*). It was very like the Hill Cove house to look at, and was presumably ready for the visit by Robert's parents in October 1909, when he observed: 'drove up Mother in coach'. This was the first of Dora Blake's two visits to San Julian, and she recorded it in an exquisite set of small watercolours of all the ports visited on the voyage, which now hangs at Killik Aike. The coach trip clearly was of momentous import, as indeed must have been the impact of 'Mrs Blake' on this small, tightly-knit, largely male community. For weeks beforehand we read 'exercised horses in coach', a task clearly undertaken by Robert in person and not entrusted to the Chilean carters.

Another laconic entry in June 1909 reads 'took on Mathews'. This was John (Jack) Mathews, son of Edmund J. Mathews who, as the manager for James Lovegrove Waldron of the 'Port Howard' property on the West Falkland, was a good friend and neighbour to Robert Blake Senior at Hill Cove. Mathews Senior had been a great support to him in the early years at San Julian, paying several visits to help and advise, and indeed putting in capital – we find in the lands office registry that several of the original tracts of land were taken out in his name. Jack Mathews continued as cadet and assistant to Uncle Robert until the outbreak of the First World War, and would have succeeded him as manager, but he felt it his duty to return to England to fight in the war, which sadly he did not survive. The link with the Mathews continued for many years however, in the person of Jack's younger brother, Edward Gray (Ted) Mathews. Their mother had been a Waldron, so Ted soon became an important figure in the boardrooms of sheep farming companies operating in Patagonia and the Falkland Islands, including both Condor and Coronel, and we will meet him again later on.

The new farm

If it was Robert Blake Senior who founded the farm and got it going initially, it was Uncle Robert who really developed it into a thriving enterprise and business. He had the knack of picking up from his varied and wide-ranging travels as a very young man anything and everything that might be of use at San Julian. He did not allow himself to be limited, as so many other settlers did (and still do!) to what their own forebears had done, either there or someplace else. In a new country, farming customs and methods as found in Scotland, Somerset, Spain or even the Falkland Islands were not necessarily the best – there were new ways to be found, introduced, adapted or invented. It was true pioneering, as there were important aspects of climate, ecology, human resources and communications (or lack of) which differed both from the Falklands and from Australia – the only places in the world where sheep production was (and still is today) carried out on a similar scale.

In 1903, when Robert first arrived as a very young man, there was just the one settlement, started in Munro's time, in the valley west of San Julian. Its shearing shed and dip had been built by Robert Blake Senior ten years before, and a number of shepherds' houses or 'shanties' (*puestos* in Patagonian Spanish) scattered over some 800 square kilometres. In those days of inland haulage by cumbersome horse or bullock carts, it was clearly more efficient for the sheep to carry their own fleeces to a point close to a port. Consequently all the early farm settlements, with shearing shed, were sited either on the sea as their own port (as in the Falklands, Tierra del Fuego and Straits of Magellan) or close to one. For other operations, however, including the interminable dipping against sheep scab, such a large area soon became divided into subdivisions or 'sections'. In Patagonia this term came to be applied to the settlement or headquarters from which such subdivisions were run. The first and main section of the settlement west of San Julian was known as the 'New Dip' (*Baño Nuevo)* from the dipping bath installed there in about 1904, and was sited roughly in the centre of the property (see map). Then there was the 'Fereiri' section towards the south-west corner, which took its name from a Tehuelche chief (*cacique)* called 'Ferrero', whose tribe roamed the area in the early days. There was also the 'Samuel' section (always pronounced 'Sam-well' in the Spanish way) in the north-western part. As there was also a '*Cañadon* Sam' shanty there must have been someone called 'Samuel' around but it is not known who he was or if it was the same person. However, on one of the epic drives, possibly the Jamieson-MacGeorge expedition of 1889–90, there was an English shepherd called Samuel. A letter of his survives, written to his brother and sister in London in 1891 but quoting no surname, saying how he was then working in Chile for Hamilton and Saunders (who were also on that drive). Maybe he knocked around San Julian for a while before drifting south. There was another shanty in the next valley, the *Cañadon* 'Paraguay', which according to Chace is named after an old Indian shepherd of that name.

At each section there was a cookhouse, where food was prepared on a wood-burning range and served in an adjacent dining room with long wooden tables and benches. The men slept in wooden bunks on sheepskins by way of a mattress, either in the same building or in separate bunkhouses. In the early days the itinerant shearing gangs would have slept on the floor of the shearing or any other shed or behind a bush, and on some *estancias* still do. Most however put in separate bunkhouses and cooking facilities for the shearers. A separate washhouse held a boiler or copper, usually lit on Sundays for the weekly wash, both of persons and of their clothes. A 'little house' or privy would be lurking round the back, with one or more seats according to the size of the gang. Apart from the installation of piped running water in the inter-war years there has been little change in these living conditions until the present day. If to modern urban readers they sound very basic, if not primitive, it must be borne in mind that they were (and are) a great advance over the facilities available in peasant shacks or shantytowns back home wherever the labour hailed from originally, be it the Balkans, Chile or the Western Isles.

The main settlement also boasted a staff house, built in Munro's time, where the manager, foreman, bookkeeper and others in responsible jobs could live and sleep. At the beginning, and for many years at the sections, they would eat in the cookhouse in a separate *comedor chico* or small dining room apart from the men. The first married woman to live on an early farm such as this would have been the wife (or equivalent) of the bookkeeper, and she would cook for the staff. After the Big House was built in 1909, other houses for married men followed.

The farm office, with store attached, was a fairly early building. In Munro's day the only store was part of the staff house, and bookkeeping such as it was happened there also. But quite early on a resident bookkeeper was employed, as the office and support services which eventually became available in the town of San Julian were not yet available.

Other buildings and installations were scattered around. Adjacent to the shearing shed and dip, and integrated with them, were the 'corrals' or sheep-working pens and yards, covering over an acre. The horse corrals, two or three interconnecting enclosures some 15 metres in diameter with sides 2 metres high and open-boarded with planks could hold between forty and fifty horses and were in daily use. The horses grazed in nearby paddocks, and would be rounded up at the crack of dawn by the wranglers or *campañistas*. Up to twenty-four cart-horses and fifteen or more riding horses could be needed every day. When the Big House was built it was sited so that Uncle Robert could see the troop come into the horse corrals from his chair at the head of the table in the dining room, while he was having breakfast.

The dog kennels were equally essential: each regular shepherd might own ten to twelve working sheepdogs, so at any time there might be sixty or more dogs in residence. Dog discipline was, and still is, firm. During the day a shepherd will take out for use the dogs he needs, usually two or three. The remainder stay shut up in their kennels enclosed behind high railings. In the evenings, however, they are all let out for a run which usually takes the form of what the Scots called 'daft-racing', all streaking across the settlement, barking and racketing, to the other side and back. As small children we used

The daily morning routine. The saddles are the Argentine *bastos*, with no wooden tree, and all the other gear is made of rawhide.

to be terrified of this daily routine and took good care to be safely behind a garden fence.

To feed some sixty humans and maybe the same number of dogs requires a fair amount of meat – mutton of course – amounting to around twelve sheep per day and double that during shearing. The butchery, usually called the 'killing shed', was sited adjacent to the sheep pens and handy to the shearing shed where the sheepskins could be hung on wires to dry in the shade. The annual production of 2,000–3000 air-dried sheepskins was a not unimportant sideline.

The stable for the horses, near the corrals, provided storage for the cart gear as well as everybody's saddles – in those days fifteen or more horses might be saddled daily – and there was trough room for feeding riding horses during the winter. Then there were the workshops – a carpenter's shop, a wood store and, adjoining the shearing shed and housing the shearing engines and press pumps, the mechanic's shop, which also handled the maintenance of the windmills (more correctly wind pumps) installed around the property to supplement the natural springs for watering the livestock.

Following his father's visit in 1909, Robert set about putting into practice all he had seen on his travels. His aim was to create a productive enterprise in this remote location. The overland telegraph had been installed in 1901, and the port of San Julian officially founded that same year, but virtually all supplies were still shipped out from the UK, although direct shipment in chartered sailing ships like the *Cross Owen* had been largely replaced by an increasing flow of goods to Punta Arenas and onward from there in local coasting steamers, mostly owned by Braun & Blanchard. Don Elías Braun was a Russian Jew who with his family had fled from a pogrom in 1874 and set up a general store in Punta Arenas, where the family prospered and his son Moritz married Josefina, daughter of José Menéndez, while his daughter Sara married José Nogueira, another trader and one of the few Portuguese to reach these shores. By the turn of the century the joint Braun and Menéndez trading and shipping interests had spread all over Patagonia. The 'Anónima' (*Sociedad Anónima Importadora y Exportadora de la Patagonia*) was formed in Buenos Aires in 1908, and from there their ships carried on a coastal freight and passenger service which was to continue until the 1950s. They also set up their stores and warehouses in all the new ports and townships, so that provisions and supplies of all sorts could be obtained locally.

Robert and Edith

From his earliest days, Uncle Robert put a lot of thought and hard work into wool growth and production as an enterprise. The earliest sheep, descendants of those shipped over on the *Rippling Wave* were of somewhat mixed descent, in which the English Romney Marsh (Kent) breed predominated. These had proved reasonably suitable for the peat-boggy Falkland Islands but on the dry pampas of Santa Cruz Territory the coarse and open fleeces let in a lot of dust. Some attempt was made to correct this by crossing with Merino rams, but it was the introduction of the Corriedale breed from New Zealand which solved the problem. (6) The historic first shipment of rams of this then relatively new breed into Argentine Patagonia was imported by the Blakes in 1908, soon to be followed by others, and the company was to dominate the local breeding scene for the next sixty years. To transfer this improving blood from a handful of imported pedigree rams to tens of thousands of commercial sheep was a major breeding operation, in which Robert's Australian experience stood him in good stead.

Then there was the installation of machinery. In Munro's day, sheep were still shorn using hand shears, but machine shears had been in use on the great *estancias* in Buenos Aires province like 'Los Yngleses' (Gibson Bros) and 'Curumalán'(7) since 1893. The first in Patagonia had been installed at Condor in 1898, and other leading company farms like Coronel soon followed. A transmission system for sixteen shears driven by a Fairbanks-Morse petrol engine was installed in 1904, but the flocks grew to 80,000 sheep and the wool cut rose as the new Corriedale breed took hold – first to 3 kilos per head and later to 4. So in 1913 the first hydraulic wool press, made by John Shaw at Salford, Manchester was installed, together with the great 24hp Blackstone kerosene engine which took four men to start up, by rotating its massive 2-metre flywheel manually. Its exhaust going 'chunk, chunk, kerchunk, chunk' could be heard all over the settlement – I can hear it still.

In 1911 Robert went home on leave, joining the family at Yeabridge. His younger sisters Bridget and Violet had gone to Clifton High School, a pioneer establishment which from 1878 was providing 'thorough and comprehensive education for women', and there became friendly with Edith Wedderburn, daughter of Dr Maclagan-Wedderburn of Edinburgh. A leading and much respected medical practitioner, he had attended Lady Strathmore at the birth of Lady Elizabeth Bowes-Lyon, later the Queen Mother. Other Wedderburns had also become eminent in the medical and legal professions in Scotland.

Bright and lively, Edith had become a good friend to the Blake sisters and often visited them at home in South Petherton. Now, with Robert expected for one of the few gatherings of Robert Senior and Dora together with all their eight children, Bridget wrote to invite her to stay with them. In spite of being used to dealing with some very tough characters in Patagonia, Robert was really quite shy and introverted, certainly where young women were concerned.

Nevertheless he managed to propose, and after a whirlwind courtship of two months they were married in August 1911 and embarked after a fortnight's honeymoon for Buenos Aires and San Julian.

Robert and Edith's engagement, taken in the garden at Mark's Barn, 1911. Seated, left to right: Robert, Dora, Violet. Edith and Bridget below. Standing: Dorothy and Robert Junior.

74

Dainty and petite, intelligent and well-educated, Edith had that core of steel that all pioneer women must have if they are to be able to provide the support and encouragement that their husbands need, while making a home for them and bearing their children under primitive conditions. The Big House at Coronel may have been larger and more comfortable than the staff house, but although Edith had been able to put pictures on the bare wooden walls, rugs on the linoleum-covered wood floors and soften it all with curtains and covers, it still had no conveniences of any sort. In 1912 she described the joy of having water piped into the house, and of a run-away drain replacing former buckets in and out, but running hot water was not installed until 1919. The Blakes had rather puritan concepts about not attending too much to creature comforts at the expense of work – some still do!

Robert and Edith's first home leave, in 1914, with baby Edie, was overshadowed by the gathering clouds of war, but there were 80,000 sheep and around sixty people to be looked after, so in early September they took ship again for Punta Arenas and thence back to San Julian, to be met by the farm coach for the dusty journey up the *Cañadón de los Españoles*, past the ruins of Floridablanca, the old Spanish colony, past the Sierra Munro, to the estancia settlement, now home, nestling at the foot of the Stony Hill. They were not to return to England for another seven years, after three more children, the Great War, and some very trying times for them, as for all of Patagonia.

Notes

1 Herbert Felton was a younger brother of J.J. Felton of Teal Inlet, East Falkland. He was settling Killik Aike Norte on the north bank of the Gallegos river at about this time. See Chapter 18.

2 The town of San Julian was officially founded on 17 September 1901 when a map of the town layout was ordered by President Roca, accepting the fact that there were already settlers there requiring services and infrastructure. Blake's warehouse was followed by others and by 1896 there were two *viviendas* (dwellings). In 1897 Reed's *boliche* appeared and was later bought by Lippert and Munro. These beginnings were fully recognised and honoured at the centenary celebrations in September 2001.

3 See *A Yankee in Patagonia* by Katharine and Robert Barrett.

4 The name 'Estancia Coronel' was not much used in San Julian. People referred to 'the Company's', *'la compañía* or *la chifarmi* (for sheep-farming).

5 See *Historia de la Provincia de Santa Cruz*, by Osvaldo Topcic.

6 The Corriedale breed was developed in New Zealand by crossing Merino with Lincoln and other English longwools, mainly by James Little at 'Hui-Hui'. It was to become, and still is, the major breed in Patagonia south of Latitude 46°. See p.8 above, also Chapter 15.

7 'Curumalán' was the greatest Argentine *estancia* ever to be operated. In its heyday it carried 300,000 sheep, 50,000 head of cattle and 18,000 head of horses on some 280,000 hectares (700,000 acres). Originally a government concession designed to open up the south of Buenos Aires province, it was settled originally by Edward Casey and partners but later acquired by Houlder Brothers who had important shipping interests in the River Plate.

5

Robert and Arthur

War service

Arthur Locke Blake, my father, was born at Hill Cove in the Falkland Islands on 1 May 1885, the seventh child and third son of Robert Blake Senior and Dorothea (née Herford). Ten years younger than his brother Robert, he was only three when the family moved back to England to live at Yeabridge, near South Petherton. He went to school first at Ladybarn House, like his brothers, but then was sent to Boxgrove, a preparatory school near Guildford, and from there to Uppingham. At all of these he won prizes, both in the classroom and for sports, and at Uppingham he became captain of the school, already showing a facility for leadership. On leaving there in the summer of 1914, at the outbreak of war, like most of his contemporaries he joined up. Most boys at public schools at that time belonged to an in-school cadet force known as the OTC (Officers Training Corps), and following the Wellington tradition of drawing almost exclusively on the public schools for officer material, any school-leaver who had been in the OTC automatically received a commission. In the Army, that is. The Navy required its officers to have entered the Royal Naval College at Dartmouth at the age of 12. Arthur's elder brother, Willie, had done this and saw service in both world wars before going down with the ship he commanded at Narvik in 1940.

So Arthur joined the Somerset Light Infantry, together with his younger brother Norman and his first cousin Humphrey, (1) was gazetted second lieutenant and sent off to India to join the 5th (Territorial) Battalion in training

Captain Arthur Blake with the cable wagons of the 14th Signals Company, 35th Infantry Brigade, Mesopotamia, 1917.

at Ambala in the Punjab. After a period of general service, his knack for organisation and things mechanical got him moved sideways into the newly-formed Signals section and he became battalion signals officer. Wireless telegraphy was still in its infancy and mostly confined to shipping, so communication on land was usually by wire, using either a telegraph in Morse code, or by speaking on a magneto telephone, or else by visual methods such as flags, semaphore or heliograph. The latter used mirrors to reflect the light of the sun and transmit in Morse just like a shutter-operated signalling lamp at sea, and was much used in India and Mesopotamia where the sun was seldom inconveniently obscured by cloud as it was in Flanders. In January 1917, after more training on the North West Frontier, the 5th Somersets were sent to Palestine to become part of the 233rd Infantry Brigade in the 75th Division, and they took part in the Mesopotamia campaign against the Turks. Arthur was posted to the 14th Signals Company in the 35th Brigade, and was later awarded the OBE(Mil) and was mentioned in despatches, the citation for the latter being signed by Winston Churchill, then Secretary for War. We could never get him to tell us just what he actually did to earn these decorations.

Before joining up in 1914, Arthur had thought of engineering as a career, and had applied to Pembroke College, Cambridge. However, on being demobilised in 1919, his father put it to him that brother Robert needed some assistance and support out at San Julian, especially since his erstwhile assistant Jack Mathews had been killed on active service. Wool prices were high, business was booming and the farm, by now well organised, was doing well, but labour activists had been stirring up trouble all throughout the war, so Uncle Robert felt he could not yet leave his post to take some well-earned leave with his family. So Arthur duly took ship for Buenos Aires, and reached San Julian in December 1919. But instead of embarking on the usual apprentice-like period of learning the basic skills and practices of sheep farming, he was to be tipped off the deep end of responsibility in no uncertain manner.

The Intervention

Donald Munro had died intestate in the eyes of Argentine law, leaving no visible direct heirs by marriage, descent or legacy. His estate, if he had any,

Cable wagons on the march.

would have therefore been forfeit to the state for the benefit of the ministry of education and earmarked for the education of poor and needy children in remote areas. Santa Cruz at that time was a territory administered by governors who were appointed by the federal government in Buenos Aires. The path of any supposed funds from their source to the needy children was long and left plenty of scope for the skimming off of fees and similar along the way, so when the federal judge in Rio Gallegos, Dr Ismael P. Viñas (qualified lawyers in Argentina are dignified with the title of 'Doctor'), found what he considered a flaw in the affairs of this prosperous farm, second in size in the territory, he thought he had a good thing going.

Robert Blake Senior had taken good care when setting up the San Julian Company in 1900 to not only pay off all Munro's personal debts (some £7,000 – a lot of money in those days) but also to buy out the latter's share of the former partnership by payments to his relations in the Hebrides. The new company had been duly registered as owner of the land both in the Lands Office and in the Property Office but these being federal they were sited at that time in Buenos Aires and the judge in Rio Gallegos may not have been in full possession of the facts. Alternatively, he may have chosen to ignore them in the hope that he could stampede the company, in the person of its manager Robert Junior, into some kind of out-of-court settlement or even an *ex-gratia* payment in his favour. Viñas had misjudged, however, the character and tenacity of his opponent. Notice was served on the company in December 1919, intimating that unless immediate reparation was made the farm would be 'intervened' (*intervenido*). This process means appointing a federal trustee or *interventor* to oversee the affairs of a company or other entity, take over the property (supposedly under inventory), and operate it until such time as the legal process is finally defined. Normally the *interventor* acts as a sort of bailiff, seeing that all is in order and protecting the interests of both sides.

Given the somewhat Wild West character of Santa Cruz still prevailing into the 1920s, the reality was rather different. Knowing the claim to be quite unfounded, Robert ignored it. The judge ordered the intervention to proceed, and to impose it he sent the secretary of the *Juzgado*. This was not a clerical post but an administrative one, being the judge's second-in-command and therefore the official responsible for the implementation of judicial orders. The secretary, Dr Rillo, found it necessary to take along not only the *interventor*, Rodríguez, but the chief of police of the territory, the local *comisario* (chief of police of San Julian) and five policemen armed with rifles in addition to their regulation issue revolvers.

This formidable party appeared at the farm on 12 February 1920, and after considerable argument arrested Robert who was taken away to Rio Gallegos, leaving Edith, their nursemaid and four children alone in the Big House. When it became clear that the official party expected to lodge and be fed there also, Edith was obliged to threaten them at rifle-point in order to restrict their movements to the ground floor. Arthur in the meantime, while all the discussion was going on, had managed to slip away to the port and warn people there, before returning to the farm where he was able to keep Edith and the family company until the next day, when they were taken down to the port and lodged with the Potter family at the Swift freezing plant, who had children much the same age and with whom they had as a family become good friends. (2)

Robert was taken to spend the night at the Hotel Miramar, then the meeting-place for the British farming community and town people associated with it. As he was escorted, handcuffed, into the hotel and across the saloon bar to a room, he was able to declaim in a loud voice what was going on and that he had been unjustly arrested without being charged. The next day he was taken to Rio Gallegos and kept in jail, not actually in the criminal cells but in better quarters reserved for 'political' prisoners. Edith was allowed to pack their personal belongings, into which with Scottish prudence she was able to stuff the family silver, and was driven with Arthur to the port and out to the freezer near the mouth of the bay, where the Potters made a home for them. Arthur was not allowed to set foot on the property, but had managed to arrange to meet some of the stalwart Scots shepherds like 'Chico' Macleod and Alec Kennedy on the boundaries, so that he could keep abreast with what was going on, and hopefully arrange discreet movements of sheep to avoid undue losses. The *interventor* had been joined by his brother Rafael, but they made no attempt to operate the farm, beyond ordering sheep to be killed for meat as and when required. The nearest and fattest were the Corriedale pedigree ewes and many of these were killed for this purpose. Interestingly, most of the Chilean *peones* left, as they could see that they were unlikely to get paid by the new bosses.

Julio Aloyz, the farm agent in San Julian (see page 101), together with the company's local lawyer, Dr Miguel Segovia, had in the meantime been sending almost daily telegrams to Buenos Aires, where the company's representatives, Waldron and Wood (3) and their lawyers had started court proceedings to regain possession. In Rio Gallegos, Judge Viñas on reviewing the case found that while in his view the company's right to the land was at least in doubt if not faulty, there was no case personally against Robert, who was released on 11 March after 31 days under arrest. Looking at this again in the light of present-day knowledge of Argentine and especially Patagonian 'mores', it seems to indicate that perhaps Viñas was not the real instigator of the plot, but that he had been put up to it by others.

Edith had been able to leave the children with the Potters and join Robert in Rio Gallegos for the last three weeks of his detention, and on returning to San Julian they all travelled to Buenos Aires, leaving Arthur to continue to keep an eye on the farm as well as he could. Robert saw his family safely embarked on board a ship bound for England and his parents at Marks Barn and then returned to the Phoenix Hotel to eat his heart out, waiting for the court to decide in the company's favour, and even longer to arrange to carry it out which would involve reversing Viñas' judicial orders. There was not a great deal he could personally do, as the affair was already in the hands of good Buenos Aires lawyers.

There was, in fact, no fault to be found with the title to the land, as evidenced by the speed with the federal appeals court in La Plata found in the company's favour, and by the fact that the case did not go higher, maybe right up to the supreme court as has been the case with other tricky lands cases in Santa Cruz. Once the proper documentation, including affidavits from the Munro relations in the Outer Isles had been assembled, Viñas' findings were quashed and he was ordered to return possession of the farm. But the wheels of justice grind slowly: here 'speedily' meant not within weeks but within months, or even years. It was therefore some time before the court produced its verdict, but finally it was formally published, confirming in every respect the San Julian Sheep Farming Company's full and legal ownership of the land in freehold and all the livestock, movables and improvements on it. The farm in fact was to be returned to its rightful owners.

In order to carry out this verdict, the federal judge for the territory of Chubut, Dr Borelli, (4) was ordered to proceed to Santa Cruz and apply the court's overruling of Judge Viñas' action. This is of interest, as it shows that the appeals court considered it a domestic territorial matter, rather than a real federal case. Had the latter been so, they would have had to send down a senior official from the ministry of justice who would outrank Viñas, rather than sending his colleague Borelli from the next territory.

The Big House at Coronel, built in 1909 for the manager and his family.

Although the verdict was not officially announced until 16th July 1920, Robert had been advised of the court's decision and was able to embark in the *Asturiano* on 25 June, still champing at the bit in view of reports from Arthur on how badly the *interventor* was running the farm (or as he put it, *not* running it), allowing the sheep to lose condition and die off for lack of water. After picking up Judge Borelli at Madryn, the port for the city of Rawson, capital of Chubut Territory and the seat of its judiciary, they proceeded to San Julian where they arrived on 3 July to be met by Arthur and Julio Aloyz with further harrowing tales of the state of things on the farm.

In a letter to his mother, written on 9th July 1920 [Argentine Independence Day], Arthur describes Robert's arrival:

Dear Mother,

Well – well – well, here we are again, and very nice too!! It is almost worth it all just to enjoy being back again. We arrived up here last Saturday afternoon, some five hours after Robert landed off the boat from BA I did not recognise him at first as he was wearing a brand new Homburg hat – a thing quite unprecedented , so we might have known that something unusual was about to take place. . .

Borelli had intended to continue first to Rio Gallegos, and only order the farm to be handed back after doing the paperwork with Viñas. However the Blakes, backed up by the always loquacious Don Julio and Dr Segovia, persuaded him that it was more urgent to retake possession of the farm so as to avoid further losses of livestock, it now of course being midwinter. While the above discussion was going on, Arthur and Macleod rattled round town borrowing cars to transport the official party out to the farm. The judge was unwilling to go without an armed police escort, whether in fear of possible resistance by the occupants or in order to embellish his august office, history does not relate. However the Rodríguez brothers withdrew peaceably enough, and the long process of checking the inventories and counting the sheep could begin.

This involved gathering all the flocks, amounting at that time to some 84,000 sheep, and counting them in the presence of the judge or one of his officials, all in midwinter. Robert laconically remarked that they were 'fortunate in the weather', which was dry and frosty, and they got this heroic task completed in just twelve days. Nine thousand sheep were found to be missing – in fact dead from thirst or starvation due to not having been shepherded properly or indeed worked at all for the past four months. Neither had they been dipped, and it is remarkable that scab, although present, was not rampant. The figures sound horrific, but in point of fact a loss of less than 10 per cent was a reasonable one under the circumstances. That it was not greater was a measure of the devotion of foreman Macleod, Kennedy and the other shepherds out at the sections.

Once the farm had been formally returned and the inventory signed, Robert left Arthur and his assistants to carry out the much-needed dipping and returned to Buenos Aires to tie up the legal position once and for all. Even so, in order to avoid the risk of any similar problem arising at a future date, it was thought advisable to retain a legal firm on a watching brief, which was kept for nearly fifty years until the San Julian Sheep Farming Company was wound up in 1964.

Although his family was still in England and had been increased by the birth of Mary, Robert returned to San Julian where shearing time was rapidly approaching, to continue the work cycle for most of the season. Only in April 1921 did he feel he could be spared to take ship and rejoin his family for a much-needed summer holiday far from the stresses of Patagonia. By the time they had all returned to the *Casa Grande* in late 1921, the farm was reasonably back to normal and lamb-marking and shearing started in the usual way in December. An unexpected number of men taken on during the intervention opted to stay on – perhaps not so surprising in view of subsequent events.

The strike

The availability of labour has always been a problem in Patagonia since the earliest days. The native Tehuelche did not take kindly to the regular routine spelled out by the cookhouse bell of well-organised farms, although they were excellent horsemen and did become tamers of horses and shearers of

Rio Gallegos in winter, 1905, looking westwards along Avenida Roca. It would have looked little different in 1920.

sheep. Sadly, however, they did not survive the spread of the white man and his diseases, ranging from measles to tuberculosis to venereal disease and aided by traders' strong drink. Perhaps we should add here that the hunting of Indians at a pound a nose, which has been greatly exaggerated by the misinformed, took place on Tierra del Fuego and did not affect the Tehuelche.

Their place was taken in the main by the Chilotes, the inhabitants of Chiloé and adjacent islands in southern Chile, who tended to carry out the pick-and-shovel jobs, (5) but many were also carters (horse and bullock) and with their peaceable temperament soon became good shepherds. There was also a considerable number of Europeans from widely differing back-grounds. Skilled workers of any sort had to be imported, as nobody from Buenos Aires and environs would dream of going south where it was cold and there were still Indians. Some immigrants were taken out by the earlier settlers, particularly the companies. They were mainly shepherds but also men with other trades, mostly Scots but also English and Spaniards. These we might say were 'pulled' by proper recruitment and working contracts, but others were 'pushed' out by varying circumstances back home. Social and political upheavals in various countries caused people to emigrate, and while they were mainly hard-working folk who only wanted to try to better their estate in the New World, they did include a proportion of hard cases and political misfits whose erstwhile homeland was only too glad to see go.

Among the latter were a small group, usually referred to as anarchists, led by a Spaniard, Antonio Soto. Arriving in Buenos Aires in 1912, Soto found little scope for his doctrines, as although labour conditions were not good to present-day eyes, they were vastly superior to those the mass of European migrants had left back home. There was work, there was opportunity, and most important there was cheap food. So Soto, like other misfits before and since, found his way down to Rio Gallegos where he first organised a union among the port workers – the most important activity in town as all supplies came in by sea while the products (wool and frozen meat) went out the same way. The Swift freezer was an industrial plant but it only operated for three months a year using skilled staff brought down from the parent plant in La Plata, and local seasonal Chilean immigrant labour, none of whom were prepared to listen to the agitators. So Soto turned his attention to the rural workers out in camp, and mounted groups of 'strikers' started going from farm to farm intimidating or inducing the men to down tools. It is not very clear just what they were striking about. Even José María Borrero, the author of *La Patagonia Trágica* and one of the most bitter writers on the subject, who had no love for landowners, puts on the cover of his book: 'An unprecedented strike. The workers are not asking for a rise in wages nor a reduction of working hours. What is it they are seeking?'

There was a lot of talk about living conditions, which has been taken out of context in modern times by authors with sociological axes to grind such as Borrero and Barbería. But realistically, both pay and living conditions were no worse than those most of the workers had left back home, and on the well-organised company and privately-owned farms owned and/or operated by people of British descent, considerably better. The Menéndez/Braun interests, who have often been vilified in this connection, in fact would employ British managers whenever they could get them and the working conditions were perfectly good. The Chilotes in particular, who came over to earn cash wages not available in their native islands, desperately needed the work which by their standards was well paid, and did not want to strike at all.

Despite all this, Soto and his 'heavies' found a limited following among the malcontents and misfits always present in the early years and whose numbers were increased after the war by emigrants, mainly from the Balkans. It was easy for the smooth-talking Spanish professional agitators to sway both the easy-going Chileans and the Yugoslav immigrants, many of whom may not have understood much Spanish in any case. The more peaceable men were cowed into support, although it is doubtful how many of them actually joined the mounted bands who started to roam the area north of the Gallegos River, demanding that the farm gangs join the strike even to the extent of suspending shearing. There were a number of cases of owners or managers and their families being maltreated and locked up, and several woolsheds were burned down, but there were no murders, rapes or bloodshed.

Word of all this had reached San Julian, so when a band of strikers was reported to have crossed the Santa Cruz River at the Paso Ibañez heading north, it was time for dispositions to be made. War surplus Lee-Enfield and Martini-Henry rifles were readily available, so a stock of guns and ammunition was discreetly laid in. Horses were being taken by the strikers, often the only damage done, so when they reached Estancia Colmena and took all the horses there, most of the company's horses were sent up to the New Dip section out of the way. After a number of alarms and excursions in the district, including burning the woolshed at Mata Grande, a body of mounted strikers set out for the Company's farm. This being the principal farm in the district, the strikers presumably supposed that if they could get support from the workers there, then other local farms might be expected to follow suit. It was, in effect, a key operation.

At Estancia Coronel shearing was under way, being carried out by a contract gang from La Pampa who had no interest in these, to them, wild local ideas. Like the Chilotes, they came to earn good money and take it home. Robert is said to have called all the men on the farm together, and offered to pay off with no hard feelings anybody who felt like joining the strikers. There were no takers. In addition to Arthur, there were a number of other British ex-servicemen among the men, as well as the Scots shepherds. There were plenty of wool bales available, and these were laid out as breastworks at both ends of the settlement, particularly on the side facing the port, which is at the top of a small slope – a natural defensive position.

Farm legend has it that Robert walked unarmed down to the front gate to ask the riders their business and inform them that no worker employed on the farm wished to join them, but that they were welcome to send a representative up to the settlement to talk to the men and check on this. The strikers, doubtless observing the parapet of wool bales lined by armed Brits (who were probably longing to have a go!), meekly declined the offer and returned to San Julian. This was, in fact, the beginning of the end of the strike. Government troops from Buenos Aires had already reached Rio Gallegos and begun the process of putting down what was considered by the central government to be an insurrection, Santa Cruz being at that time a federal territory and not an autonomous province. The severity of this process, which ended with the shooting of some 160 men including all the ringleaders at Estancia Anita near Lago Argentino on 11 November 1921 has been much criticised since, but it is difficult today to separate the historical facts from the idealistic, not to say tendentious, fiction which has since been published on the subject. Even the historians differ in their interpretation of the events. (6)

The rifles purchased by Estancia Coronel during the disturbances of 1920–21 were carefully locked away together with their ammunition in a special cupboard known as the 'magazine', tucked away discreetly at the back of the tool store rather than in the more obvious office and store building, or in the manager's house. There they remained untouched for over half a century. During the troubled times of the early 1970s, first the 'dirty war' and then the Cepernic provincial administration which threatened to expropriate the larger farms including Coronel, the manager, Lionel Pickering, removed them and buried them in a remote spot. Lionel died in 1995 without revealing their whereabouts.

The town

Port San Julian (*Puerto San Julian*) had been officially founded in 1901, ten years after the earliest settlers had begun to put up store sheds like Robert Blake had in 1891, followed by dwellings and the first small businesses. In the National Census of 1895 there were already 84 inhabitants in the district (together with 46,100 sheep, 2,665 horses and 1,375 head of cattle), and in 1897 Reed opened his *boliche*, quoted by Chace, although it was bought out a year later by Lippert and Munro. This was no doubt also a general store, similar to the *pulperías* in the humid pampa, and was followed by another owned by Juan Rivero who for many years carried the mails (on horseback) to Santa Cruz and later to Rio Gallegos. Other communications

The original Hotel Miramar built by Janet Wallace near the beach. Peter Bedatou later built the new hotel close by, replacing this one.

were effected by carrier pigeons, run by the army, and the *Palomar militar* (army pigeon loft) appears on the early maps. It was soon superseded however by the overland telegraph connecting Buenos Aires with Cape Virgins, one of President Roca's great achievements, which opened in 1901, and the San Julian postal and telegraph office in 1902.

Right from the beginning, the Port provided a base for the vast hinterland of extensive sheep farming which was eventually to extend all the way to the Andes and even beyond, since there was an important extent of rich pasture land on the Chilean side west of lakes Posadas and Pueyrredón which had no outlet to the Pacific. So there was an early demand for lodgings for travellers and the first hotel was put up by the widow Wallace in 1901 (page 102) although one could doss down at any *boliche* such as Reed's. Other traders followed, of many nationalities including German (Müller), Spanish (Tresguerres), Croatian (Bucic), Greek (Michudis) and others. Like the townships on the pampas, in came the baker, the carpenters, the blacksmith and many other trades. Police were an early requirement, and in 1899 a group of settlers including Munro, Frazer, Kyle and Patterson applied to the Governor of the Territory for the appointment of Mateo Gebhard, known as the '*Comisario Chico*' from his low stature. As a young man he had served in the Austrian army before emigrating, and his original methods of imposing law and order were suited to this rough and ready community. Chace tells the story of how he ordered Henry Perkins to be given twelve *planazos* (strokes applied with the flat of a cavalry sabre) for insolence, only to find that Perkins, who had been in the Royal Navy, had been flogged before and knew how to hunch his back so as to avoid the worst of the blows . . . Perkins was a cook, who worked on most of local farms with his wife Emma, and had a numerous family. His death of a heart attack in the Hotel Miramar in

1903 is the first entry in the new town's Register of Deaths. There being as yet no doctor in town either to save the patient or to certify his demise, the death certificate is signed by local citizens.

The dusty, windy and somewhat ramshackle town was always short of water, as Robert Blake has described, and Darwin tells of being sent off towards a lagoon that had been sighted, only to find it full of salt. There were wells out beyond the freezer, to the north, but the best source of fresh water were the springs in the 'Company's Cañadon'. A subartesian aquifer flows beneath the *Meseta central* (central tableland) which stretches away inland, and near the coast it breaks out into spring lines along the *faldeos* or sides of the valleys. The main road inland at that time wound up past the main settlement of Estancia Coronel, to some strong springs near which a family of Russians, Volonski, rented a few hectares from the Company and operated a market garden and raised chickens. From here, for forty years and more, virtually all the drinking water for the town was carted in tankers, first horse-drawn and later by lorries.

The *aguateros* (water carriers) were a feature of life when I was a boy. They trundled daily up and down the 25 kilometres or so in their elderly lorries, usually carrying two square 1000 litre water tanks which could sit safely on the flat bed of the truck. In town every house had both a drinking water tank into which the precious carted water (which had to be paid for) was kept, and a rainwater tank or *aljibe* collected such rain as fell. Household linen was bundled off by ship to Santa Cruz once or twice a month to be laundered. Baths were therefore a luxury and other sanitation provided by the 'little house' at the back end of the patio. The drivers were a cheerful crew, their doyen one Nicanor Hernández, and they were always ready to help a stranded car or give farm people a lift into town. Although the extra traffic did the quite unimproved track no good, especially after wet weather, the supply of water was of importance to the town so that the Municipality kept an eye on the matter and would send out working parties and in the latter years a grader to keep the track in a passable condition.

As the years went by, the water supply for the town was to become an increasing headache for the farm. Although in 1940 the springs in all the principal *cañadons* were measured by the Public Works department and found to be insufficient for a town of 2000 inhabitants, in the late fifties Provincial Legislation was passed which obliged the Company to cede water and allow access to its land. Collection works were built and water piped to town, and some of the best grazing land in the district began to dry up.

Dipping

In addition to the events just described, the grim years between the wars were filled with other worries, arising this time out of the sheep husbandry aspect rather than the human relations one. We have referred earlier to dip, (7) dips and dipping, which are concerned with the control of sheep scab. This is caused by a mite which burrows under the skin and causes intense itching and distress to the animal, resulting in loss of condition and in extreme cases shedding of the wool. It was at that time endemic to all sheep-raising areas of South America, having been brought over from Spain on the earliest sheep in colonial days. It is extremely contagious and can spread very quickly given the right conditions.

From the earliest years scab was a problem. Chace describes in some detail the difficulty of spotting it in the early stages; it takes a trained eye to spot that little bit of taggety wool along the side, lighter in colour where the sheep had been biting at the itch. It was only the leading hands and foremen, Scots mostly, who could be trusted with the job of spotting it in the yards or out in camp, and Chace himself developed something of an eye for it and would be sent out to roam the flocks to see if any sheep were scratching. Any suspect flock would be immediately gathered up for closer inspection, and if there was any doubt it would be dipped.

To cure the affliction several insecticides were used, such as arsenic, tobacco and various proprietary products such as Cooper's or Little's, but the most efficient preparation for killing the scab mites was known as 'lime and sulphur'. Big farms like Coronel had installed boilers and plant for

The main shearing shed at Coronel, built by Robert Blake in 1893-4, with the dip alongside. The pipes on the right convey the dipping fluid from the plant where it was made, or 'cooked'.

preparing the mixture – known as 'cooking dip'. This was a smelly and laborious process which involved first slaking the lime in a large wooden box or tray, then putting it into cast iron vats or 'pots' of about 1,500 litres capacity with water and sulphur. Steam was then run through from the boiler so as to boil up the mixture for an hour, stirring the whole time. The resultant noisome liquid, smelling strongly of rotten eggs due to chemicals called polysulphides, was then run into the dip with further water. When freshly made, lime-sulphur dip was totally efficient at curing scab – i.e. killing both the live mites and, more importantly, their eggs (dormant pupae).

The process consisted of swimming the sheep through a bath some 30 metres long, during which their heads were ducked twice by men wielding implements called 'crooks' in Britain but 'crutches' in Patagonia. (8) Dipping was very hard on the sheep, and took place whenever necessary, often as much as four times a year including during the winter with consequent losses. Chace tells of one harrowing winter when it came on to snow the very night dipping finished and continued for two weeks. When it melted and they got around to skinning the carcasses, over 5,000 sheep had died.

Mysteriously though, in spite of all efforts, scab would recur and the whole laborious process would have to begin again. The fastest it is possible to pass sheep through a swim dip is about 600 per hour, but if they are stubborn and your gang not well trained, only half this rate can be achieved. With pauses to refill, count out and so forth, in a good day's work some 2,000 or so sheep can be dipped. Allowing for Sundays off and other non-dipping days spent in mustering, drafting, cooking dip etc., to dip all 60,000 or so sheep might take from four to six weeks, four times a year. The process would always take longer in winter because of the shorter days, pipes freezing up and so forth. The process was therefore an enormous drain on labour resources, and had a high cost in terms of losses of sheep and wear and tear on the manager responsible for it all. Arthur used to make up verses, most of which followed the metre of well-known tunes and so could be readily sung, often in the car on long trips. His 'Ballad of Dipping' brings home some of the frustration of dipping, and the patience needed to deal with it.

Ballad of Dipping -

Arthur Blake
Tune: Camptown Races

The farmer woke from a gentle sleep,
    Doodah, Doodah
And said to the *capataz:* 'dip the sheep!',
    Oh, Doodah Day.
'Gwine to dip all night, gwine to dip all day;
'There´s only a million more, my boys, finish on the Judgement Day.'

Verses

The farmer stood by the cookhouse door,
  And said to the *capataz:* 'dip once more,'

The farmer stood by the dripping stage,
  'Dip the blighters *otra vez !*'

The farmer wielded a hefty crutch,
  'One more dipping won't hurt them –much,'

The farmer sweated in the forcing pen
  Dipping his sheep all over again,

The farmer drowned himself in the dip,
  Too much dipping had given him the pip.

Capataz: foreman.
Dripping stage: where the dipped sheep drain off.
Otra vez: once again.
Crutch: dipping crook, for dunking sheep.
Forcing pen: the pen just before the 'chucking-in pen', where most of the hard work was done.

William Cooper and Nephews, recognising that their in-house product was less efficient than lime and sulphur, had put a lot of research into the matter at their own research station at Berkhamstead, and came up with a small testing kit which could be used on the spot to check the concentration of polysulphides in the wash, and Arthur undertook to test this out for them at Coronel. The idea was to check on the concentration of the farm-produced fluid, given the somewhat primitive nature of its preparation.

The testing kit appeared in the 1940s, during the Second World War, and hit the nail on the head, revealing a phenomenon that nobody had as yet thought of. While freshly-prepared dip was perfectly good and efficient, samples taken from the used wash after several thousand animals had swum through showed that its concentration had dropped to a degree where it was no longer effective, even though wash used for replacement was perfectly up to strength. Why did the used fluid lose its strength? After much thought and further testing over several seasons, Cooper's and Arthur together came up with the answer.

On reaching the end of their swim, the sheep climb out onto the dripping stage, which has a concrete floor. Here they stand for a while to allow surplus dipping fluid to drain off them and run back into the dipping bath proper, which is by now further contaminated by dust, faeces and urine. Each animal will retain anything up to 5 litres of fluid according to the length of the wool, but in addition the fleece acts as a strainer, retaining the active ingredients so that the recycled fluid becomes progressively weaker until it fails to kill the pupae present on the fleece, which then hatch out ten days later and you get a fresh outbreak.

This process is known as stripping. Once it was discovered and understood, it was an easy matter to bring the over-diluted wash back to strength by judicious reinforcements when refilling the dip, and immediately the plague of scab began to be brought under control and life became very much easier. If I have wearied the reader with the details, how much more wearisome must it have been to the participants, as Arthur's ballad demonstrates. In later years, more efficient chemicals, easier on the sheep and simpler and safer to use, were to be introduced, but the real problem – the stripping process – had been broken for ever. Scab had been dominated, and as the technique spread to other properties the risk of reinfestation became almost nil. Any sheep from surrounding properties were suspect until they in turn became 'clean' and before very long large areas of Santa Cruz were

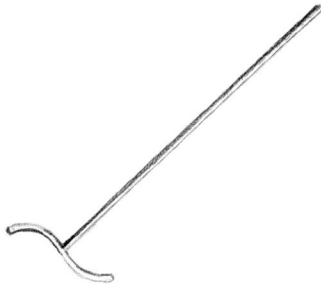

quite free from scab, as they still are today.

Notes

1 The life of John Humphrey Blake, who died three months before his hundredth birthday, has been written by his son Christopher in *Times and Seasons*.

2 The freezer had been put up by Swift of Chicago in 1912, and was sited at the mouth of the bay, some distance out of town. One of the Potter sons, Clifford, later became a correspondent for the *Buenos Aires Herald* on farming matters, especially Patagonian ones. A nice beach between the freezer and Cabo Curioso is still known as 'Potter's Beach'.

3 The firm of Waldron, Wood & Co had been set up just after the Great War by George Wood, to look after the affairs of the Waldron interests, and soon came to represent other British companies in Patagonia and elsewhere.

4 Judge Borelli was no relation to Dr Pablo Jacinto Borrelli, medical practitioner in Rio Gallegos in our time, who was to bring all our own children except Alison into the world.

5 No true *gaucho* will demean himself by doing manual labour off his horse. In the humid pampas of central Argentina the soil was tilled and worked by immigrants.

6 For further reading on this painful subject see *Historia de Santa Cruz* by Juan Hilarion Lenzi, *La Patagonia Argentina* by Edelmiro Correa Falcón, *Los Vengadores de la Patagonia Trágica* by Osvaldo Bayer, *La Patagonia Trágica* by José María Borrero and *Los Dueños de la Tierra en la Patagonia Austral, 1880–1920* by Elsa Mabel Barbería.

7 The word is used equally for the process, the bath and the wash. You dip sheep in the dip which is full of dip.

8 There is a rich vein of colloquial Spanish used only in southern Patagonia, which has firmly embedded in it Anglicisms such as *croche* (crutch), *guipe* (whip), *guachiman* (watchman), *queque* (cake), *cuqui* (cook) and *guaipe* (cotton waste or rags for wiping grease off hands).

6

Arthur and Millicent

Home and marriage

After the trials of the intervention and the strike, Arthur was more than ready for his first leave in 1922, returning to the bosom of his parents and sisters. The Robert Blakes (Senior), finding Yeabridge a bit cramped for a family which had now grown into young people rather than children, and helped by the financial success of the San Julian venture, had in 1916 purchased the much larger Mark's Barn near Merriott. The relaxed life of an English summer in a large country house in the 1920s, set among the green Somerset fields, was such a wonderful contrast to dry and dusty Patagonia. Tennis parties, croquet on the lawn, strawberries and cream and social activities of all sorts were the order of the day. Relations also came to stay, and one day the Philip John Worsley family arrived. They were distant cousins from Birmingham related to the Blakes through Arthur's grandmother, Fanny Follett Osler Blake of Bridge House. Their daughter, Millicent, had been educated at Roedean at a time when not every young lady received a serious education, and had met there one of Arthur's sisters, Dorothy. Through this connection it had been suggested that Millicent's younger brother Philip, who had just left school, might start a farming career by going out as a cadet to Hill Cove, so Robert Blake naturally invited them to come and stay and talk the matter over.

They were duly met at Martock railway station and driven to Mark's Barn where, so the story goes, the door was opened to them by a 'white-haired

Millicent as a young girl.

young man', this being Arthur. Millicent never knew him without white hair, which was already starting to go grey when he returned from war service in Mesopotamia in 1919. The visit was followed by others of Arthur to Birmingham, where one day they went out for a drive with Philip. The driver of a car in those days was often separated from the passengers, so Arthur took advantage of the occasion to 'pop the question'. Family legend has it that at this point the horn stuck fast, so announcing to all and sundry the confusion of the passengers. But the answer was 'yes' and Arthur returned to San Julian at the end of his leave engaged to be married. Philip did indeed go to Hill Cove where he spent two seasons with Mr Miller, and then a further season at San Julian before going on to New Zealand.

The Worsleys were a well-connected family with branches in London and Yorkshire, related also to the Taylors of Norfolk, John Taylor having been an eminent engineer. Several generations back, a Worsley had gone into trade by joining the brewing firm of Whitbreads in London, and one of this

branch, Philip Worsley, was my great-grandfather. He set up a manufactur-
ing chemist business in Bristol, and lived at Rodney Lodge on Clifton Down.
Millicent's father, Philip John Worsley, was an engineer in Guest, Keen and
Nettlefold in Birmingham, and through her mother, Muriel Howard Smith,
she was related to other Unitarian and Quaker families in the Midlands
such as the Oslers, Cadburys and Darbys.

Like the Blakes, the Worsley family had strong liberal and non-conform-
ist religious roots, and I remember Grandfather Philip being among several
of the Lewin's Mead (Bristol) Unitarian congregation who would not bow
their heads before their Maker, so therefore always stood up to pray. The
two families, in addition to being connected through the Oslers, had a great
deal in common as to religion, background and general liberal and puritan
principles.

Aunt Edith had married Robert within three months of their meeting,
and accompanied him to a *very* primitive establishment with little more than
her own good Scottish sense to guide her. Millicent on the other hand had
two years in which to prepare for marriage. Among other things, she was
advised to learn how to bake bread, how to cut her husband's hair, and if
she wished to take out her piano, how to tune it. She did all these, and
married Arthur in 1924 at the Church of the Messiah in Birmingham. After
spending their honeymoon in Scotland, they duly embarked for Buenos
Aires and so to San Julian, where they started married life in the small house
that had been built for them, just at the end of the garden, beyond the Big
House.

Life in the camp

'Camp', from the Spanish *campo* means the countryside or anywhere outside
a town, but with fairly outback connotations. Life on a farm in Patagonia in
the 1920s, if much better than when Edith went out in 1911, was still primitive for an educated girl from Birmingham. Cooking was done on a closed
stove, burning firewood cut on the property, which was also used in the
sitting-room grate and to heat the copper for washing clothes outside in the
washhouse. Baths were taken in a galvanized bathtub on the bedroom floor,
having heated the water on the kitchen stove. Other needs were catered for
by chamber pots and an outside earth closet. In Patagonian English, the
latter convenience is always known as the 'líttlehouse', as opposed to 'little
house' or small dwelling.

There would have been fifty to sixty people living on the farm at this time,
but there were only two houses for families other than Robert and Arthur's,
all the rest being single men. As time went by houses for married people
were added, until by the late 1930s there were five families. The foreman

(Alec Mann), the mechanic (Bob Rolfe), the stud stockman (John Mackay) and the shepherds (Alec Kennedy and Tommy Affleck) all had children. Rolfe was English but all the rest were Scots, as were a number of the single men on this and other farms in the district. Quite half the labour force – i.e. the foremen and charge hands, shepherds and shantymen, were English-speaking. Roughly half the remainder were Chilean, and the rest were a wide range of European nationalities: Croats, Spaniards, Basques, Germans, Russians and Greeks. Uncle Robert said that in the early days he had men of up to fourteen nationalities on the place. In the vernacular used in Patagonia they were grouped more simply: *gringos* (1) were English speakers, of whatever origin; *austríacos* included Croats, Yugoslavs, Austrians and Germans (i.e. people from the Austro-Hungarian Empire); *rusos* were all Slavs and eastern europeans including Finns; *turcos* meant anyone from the eastern Mediterranean except Jews. I never heard of a Jew in camp, but there are a few long-settled families in trade in the towns. Spanish of course was the lingua franca, but English was widely used. Gaelic-speakers from the remoter parts of the Highlands or the Outer Isles (the Hebrides) learnt both their Spanish and their English in Patagonia. Argentine-born workmen from further north were a rarity, as there was no shortage of work available in the more hospitable climate of the humid pampas and therefore little inducement for them to come south. (The *pampa húmeda* comprises the provinces of Buenos Aires, eastern La Pampa, Santa Fé and southern Córdoba).

Before the coming of radio, for relaxation after the day's work people turned to books and music. Arthur and Millicent had taken out their own considerable library, and Estancia Coronel like many other company farms employing a considerable number of English speakers had its own library. Illustrated and other magazines were subscribed to, but mail came by sea, and took a month from England, with luck. Millicent had taken out her piano (and tuned it!), and their 'Aeolian Vocalion' record player (78rpm, hand wound), a wedding present. It is still in the family. Broadcast radio appeared in the 1930s, both from the BBC Overseas Service and from local long-wave stations, and was probably the most important step forward in amenities for these far-flung communities since the advent of the automobile.

There was also gardening. A big farm like Coronel, with sixty-odd mouths to feed (twice that number during shearing) employed a full-time gardener, and extra labour at that time was relatively cheap. During Arthur and Millicent's time many fruit trees were planted, the gardens were extended and modestly landscaped, and the Big House came to be pleasantly surrounded by lawns and flower beds, providing a soothing contrast to the surrounding arid native pasture. My sister Rosemary's poem at the end of the next chapter brings out this contrast, so typical of Patagonia.

Arthur and Millicent having a picnic.

Up to the Big House

The first years soon sped by, Arthur busy catching up with the basic aspects of sheep work, and learning from his elder brother the ins and outs of management; Millicent busy learning Spanish and coming to grips with the realities of life in Patagonia. Their newly-built small house, in many ways more comfortable than the Big House was just a few hundred yards further up the garden and was ideal for them. Robert was due to hand over the management of the farm to Arthur in 1928 and return to England with all his family, partly for the children's education but also because his father was getting elderly and was by now confined to his wheelchair with arthritis. An indefatigable letter writer to the end, he never complained about his infirmity, which he correctly attributed to many years of hard living under rough conditions in his youth.

First however Arthur and Millicent were due for leave (which was usually taken three-yearly) in 1927. The clouds of the intervention and the strike were behind them, and although wool prices were low the new Corriedale sheep were growing more wool than any sheep before them, and more than it was possible to grow in the Falklands. The Swift freezer was taking all surplus animals to slaughter for export, so the sheep farming business in Patagonia was proving a very good investment. The vision and foresight of Robert Blake (Senior) were coming to fruition.

In April of that year they took ship for a joyful summer in Somerset with both the Blake and Worsley families. Philip Worsley had taken early retirement from Guest Keen and Nettlefold in 1924, as a result of the Depression, and settled in Winscombe, just 15 miles south of Bristol, nestling in rolling country just beside the Mendip Hills. Their big stone house, 'Westfield' stood on an old bridleway called 'The Lynch', at that time still completely rural. That first leave was a happy affair, with their time divided between Mark's Barn and Winscombe. Not very long after returning to San Julian, Millicent found that she was expecting her first child, and so she was faced with the choice of having the baby on the farm with the local midwife (as Edith had done), or travelling either to Buenos Aires or Punta Arenas where there were good medical services, but no friends or relatives to rally round. In the event she and Arthur, after much heart-searching and practical consideration, decided it was best for her to return to England, so Millicent travelled back to Britain in March 1928, followed only a month or two later by Robert, Edith and their younger children, leaving Arthur to hold the fort alone on the farm.

So I was born at Westfield, Winscombe on 14 July 1928, attended by Dr Cooper who had not long moved in just up the Lynch, and was to be family GP for many years. In due course I reached San Julian in November when I was 4 months' old, my mother being accompanied by Aunt Dorothy who, as yet unmarried, was to keep us all company and help Arthur and Millicent into the Big House now that Robert, Edith and family had left. She stayed on for some months, before returning to England where she married Wyndham Carles, a settler in Kenya, and went off to make a home on their farm near Nanyuki, in the White Highlands.

Arthur's job, even then, was very different to what Robert's had been. The farm was well organised, up and running, but the town of San Julian had grown considerably as the settlement of land for sheep raising stretched further and further inland, requiring the provision of supplies and services for a very large area, stretching right across to the Andes. There were already important stores such as the Anónima, two banks (Banco Nación and the Bank of London and South America), and a doctor. A postal service, telegraphs and police had been there since the first years of the century, and the farm had its agent, Julio Aloyz. Don Julio was a Ukrainian Jew who in 1903 after a pogrom had made his way to Odessa, aged 15, looking for a ship going anywhere as long as it was away from Russia. It happened to be going to Chile, where he had an uncle. After a few years there he found his way over to Buenos Aires, from where he drifted fairly pennilessly southwards as far as San Julian, where he got taken on as a foot *peón* at Coronel . His greenness made him a natural butt for the experienced Scots shepherds who used to pull his leg unmercifully but he stuck it out and, being intelligent, learnt both English and Spanish. Uncle Robert promoted him to storekeeper, and later the company set him up in his own office in the port, adjacent to the warehouse that Robert Blake (Senior) had put up in 1893. Julio was devoted to the Blakes all his life, and sent his daughter Raquel to Northlands School in Buenos Aires to learn English, in which she became a qualified teacher in due course.

Raquel often went out to the farm to keep Millicent company when we children were very small and Arthur was often away at the sections for weeks on end for the interminable dipping. She later made a name as a writer, and in her *Raigambres Sureñas* (*Southern Roots*), published in 1984, there is the poem 'Patagonian Shadows', which is reproduced here in the original English in which it was written.

Raquel Aloyz

Patagonian Shadows

Walking alone,
Through coarse grass and rugged bushes,
Stepping on stones and dust,
Climbing up a wind-worn Patagonian hill
I've seen the shadows,
The shadows of the smallest
Particle of sand,
The tiniest blade.
Heart-rending, wind-swept
Patagonian soil –
I've felt your shadows
Closing around, nailing me down
To this, your arid beloved ground.

There is also an essay entitled 'Millicent' in which she describes her as a 'lady' in the cultural sense. Raquel clearly saw how an educated woman needs on occasion to be able to talk with others of a similar cultural level, as a change from the worthy salt-of-the earth women who most of the other farmers' wives were. There was at least one owner's wife and matriarch,

101

founder of a dynasty, who could neither read nor write. Millicent would often go to the port to have tea with the wives of the doctor, the bank manager or the notary, who were educated Argentine women, not just to practise her Spanish but also to have an informed conversation on wider-ranging topics than babies and sheep. When John Scott (Senior) over at Los Machos lost his first wife, he married an educated businesswoman from Dumfries. This was Evelyn, known to us as 'Scottie', and she became a very good friend to Millicent and a sort of aunt to all of us.

A charming meeting with Raquel occurred years later. In 1980 I had gone with our four eldest children and a team of rams to the Comodoro Stock Show, they acting as my *cabañeros* to handle the sheep, lead them into the show ring and so forth. One evening, with a group of youngsters they all went off together and were having a drink at a *confitería* in nearby Rada Tilly when they observed that the lady of the house kept looking hard at them, until she finally came over and said in English, 'Surely you are Blakes?' This was, of course, Raquel who had seen the family resemblance, particularly in Alison, then aged 22.

Hotel Miramar

With a doctor resident in San Julian, Millicent was happy to stay at home for her next-born, so Hugh Worsley Blake was born on 13 June 1930 on the farm, although he was actually brought into the world by the local midwife, Sara 'Mamita' Bedatou, wife of Peter Bedatou who in his early days had been a carting and labour contractor. Her father, Walter Wallace had been one of the early drovers (1892–93) and brought his family over from the Falklands soon after. In 1901 his widow put up the first Hotel Miramar right on the beach, and in 1909 Peter contracted two carpenters, Tommy Quigley and Sydney Saxby to build a new hotel to replace the former. Like her mother before her, Sara acted as midwife and general wise-woman to the district. Of French descent, both Peter's English and Spanish were a bit shaky, and with some pride and considerable accuracy he would boast that he ran 'the worst hotel in the world'.

The Hotel Miramar (literally 'Sea View Hotel') was built practically on the waterfront, so passengers landing from the lighters of the coasting steamers could just walk up to the hotel carrying their bags. It was the first hotel as such – i.e. where travellers could sleep in a room of their own instead of on a communal floor in a *boliche* such as Reid's, described by Chance. In spite of the free and easy ways of the hotel as suggested in the ballad below, which are all quite true, Peter gave his three daughters a good education at boarding schools in Buenos Aires, so he can't really have done too badly.

Ballad of Peter's Bar

Arthur Blake
Tune: 'So Early in the Morning'

When we're dry and want a drink
When our tums begin to shrink,
Where do we go? Where do you think –
We all go round to Peter's.

Chorus
We all go round to Peter's
We all go round to Peter's
We all go round to Peter's
To Peter and his bar.[Last time: 'To the Hotel Miramar']

If the barman isn't there
You help yourself without a care
It's such a free and easy air
That we all go round to Peter's.

Our Peter has the silent touch,
He talks with smiles and winks and such,
But he hears a lot and sees too much,
So we all go round to Peter's.

He likes it when there's no one in,
An empty house it makes him grin,
He thinks to take your cash a sin,
So we all go round to Peter's.

He doesn't often go to jail,
And when he does it makes us pale,
But 'spite of rain and snow and hail
We'll all go round to Peter's.

So here's a health to Peter B,
A better man you'll never see,
Which is the very reason we –
We all go round to Peter's.

By the early 1930s a number of commercial enterprises were installed in the town, and their number would be swelled by commercial travellers coming down from Buenos Aires during the season. There were the wool buyers, of course, the dip salesmen headed by Cooper's, the bank boys, the freezer staff and others. Most would be English-speaking if not indeed

British and they all went to the Hotel Miramar. The hotel became such an institution that no attempt was made to form a British club, even though there were sufficient Brits to support one, until after the Second World War when the Miramar burned down.

The first branch of the Bank of London and Tarapacá had been opened in Rio Gallegos in 1899, and was soon renamed the Anglo South American Bank. Branches were later set up in Santa Cruz, San Julian and Deseado, and the 'London Bank' (later the Bank of London and South America and today Lloyds Bank) has been a feature of life since the earliest days. The senior staff at the bank were mostly British, and there were always young men out from Britain as bank trainees, known as the 'bank boys'.

The first manager of the London Bank in Rio Gallegos (2) was Don Francisco Campos Torreblanca, a Spaniard of *hidalgo* blood who was to marry a daughter of José Menéndez and found the Campos Menéndez family, who were always very Anglophile. In 1905 the Rio Gallegos bank was the scene of a celebrated robbery, when outlaws from the American West held it up and got clean away with no bloodshed but considerable booty. These were Butch Cassidy and the Sundance Kid, aided by their 'Moll', Ella Place. (Sundance is a town in Wyoming where the Kid, otherwise known as Harry Longabaugh, hailed from) Following an important train robbery at Wagner, Montana on 3 July 1901, they had left North America just ahead of the sheriff, in true Western fashion. The law did not, for the time being, pursue them to Argentina. They settled in the upper Chubut region, bought a farm at Epuyen, near Esquel, and became respected local citizens. After carrying out the Rio Gallegos foray they built a store on their property and continued to live quietly. But old habits die hard and they heard of a convoy of gold to be shipped over from Chile to the mint in Buenos Aires. The bullion was taken by pack train across the Andes to Mendoza, and put on a train, but this was held up in desert country east of Mendoza and gold ingots amounting to 672 troy pounds (about 250 kilos) were removed and loaded into saddle-bags. Eight armed men were seen riding south across the Rio Colorado, the boundary between Mendoza and Neuquén provinces, and near the Cassidy ranch they hid the booty in a remote ravine. Suspicion fell on the *estancieros yanquis* and the Pinkerton Agency was brought in, but the outlaws had the local *comisario*, one David Humphries under their control as they had discovered he was running a nice sideline in contraband liquor. Humphries tipped them off and they fled to Chile. The hidden bullion has not, as far as we know, ever been found.

When we were little we seldom went into town, although at least one of the erstwhile shop assistants at the Anónima, Tommy Quigley's daughter Agnes (later Mrs Rodríguez), remembers me 'running along the counter top' which had to have been when parents were not looking.

When the Aeroposta Air Service started in 1930, the flight from Buenos Aires arrived on Sundays (back on Mondays) so it became usual to collect the mail that day, the post office opening especially for this important weekly event. I can remember being stuck on the track in the dark, with mechanical trouble to the Ford Model A car, my father and another man talking about the 'nut' and me being intrigued because of course nuts grew on trees and there were no trees in Patagonia . . .

In the summer we would often go for picnics to some fresh water ponds in the Number 1 paddock to sail home-made boats. Arthur always insisted on boiling a 'billy' can for tea instead of a kettle, a habit picked up no doubt from Anzac diggers during the war. An empty half-pound Players tobacco tin was fitted with a bit of wire for a handle, and it was fun to collect twigs of *Mata negra* (*Verbena tridens*) for the fire.

Other expeditions included walks with Millicent, which involved collecting wild flowers. The wild flowers in spring can be spectacular, particularly after a snowy winter, which seems to stimulate them. Perhaps as a natural reaction to the high winds and scarcity of pollinating insects, they bloom profusely and many have a strong scent. The unimpressive white or mauve flowers of the ubiquitous *Mata negra* can perfume leagues and leagues of camp, while the dull pampa is waving with white 'pale maidens', also highly scented, interspersed with masses of flat pink 'scurvy grass' and bunches of yellow nodding 'lady's slippers'. Many native flowers have English names. The most spectacular is no doubt the 'flame bush' (*Anarthrophyllum desideratum*) which grows in clumps which are profusely covered with orange-coloured flowers. The effect from a distance is that the whole hillside is in flames.

Then there was 'poison bush' (*Colliguaya integerrima*) whose attractive bright green foliage contains an alkaloid capable of killing a horse. Locally-bred animals avoided it, but occasionally drovers with horses from other disticts had to be careful. Incienso or Molle (*Schinus dependens*) has fearsome spines which no herbivore will touch, and grows to two metres or more in height. Its hard red wood is valuable for firing, and the horse carts used to spend long weeks hauling firewood in from the remoter camps.

The quality of life continued to improve, with the installation of telephone lines to the port and to the sections during the 1920s. Arthur could now ring Don Julio daily, from his own house, and organise his section foremen. The daily telephone session in the evenings, after other work was over and therefore everybody back at home, became part of every manager's life, and still is. Other developments followed. One of these was the gradual spread of motor transport. Cars, in particular Model 'T' Fords, had started to appear after the war, and during the 1930s lorries began to replace the cumbersome horse carts that had been such a feature of life in the early days, used for hauling the wool to port and stores everywhere.

One of the two daily loads leaving the farm for the port. This wagon has 25 bales on board, some 5000 kilos (5 tons) of wool, and is being pulled by 18 horses. Two spare horses follow behind.

These were large four-wheeled wagons known as *chatas*, capable of carrying five tons or more and drawn by anything from six horses to a dozen or more. The shaft horse or *varero* had full harness, collar and breeching and was usually a heavy animal, capable of sitting back on his heels to supplement the brakes when going downhill. The leader, or *cadenero*, pulled in front with collar and chains and was trained to steer the equipage by throwing his weight to one side or the other. Four *laderos*, two each side, also pulled in collar and chains on the front axle, and this basic group of six had to be properly tamed. They were supplemented by other horses, each haltered to the next on the inside and wearing the simple criollo saddle or *bastos* fastened firmly on by a cinch, which in turn was fastened by a rawhide rope to a big chain running along the side of the body of the cart. The driver sat perched up on a seat which projected forward from the body of the cart, and controlled the team by reins to the leader and shafter, and by a long whip and much invective to the rest. The cinch horses were not necessarily tamed, and were often hard cases given up by the riding tamers, but a trip or two to port pulling five tons of wool bales soon took the 'mickey' out of them.

I was too young to remember, but old hands have told me that getting the two daily carts off with wool to the port was quite a spectacle. The carts would have been backed up to the loading platform the night before, and the wheels taken off and put in the dip so as to avoid the wood shrinking. First thing in the morning the wheels were put back on, and the cart was then loaded while the horses were harnessed and tied in – often an exhila-

106

rating process on a cold morning. When all was ready the driver would climb up, release the brakes and off they went, often at a gallop until the wilder elements of the team settled down. Chace says that some drivers tied themselves down to the seat, but this added to the risk of serious injury as if the cart turned over they would not be thrown clear. Like horse tamers, few carters failed to pick up a few broken bones in their time.

Patagonia was growing, becoming more businesslike and, at long last, more civilised. Whereas in Robert and Edith's first years the farm demanded their full attention and housekeeping was a matter of basic survival, now Arthur could give more attention to the affairs of the company, involving relations with government officials, on-farm entertaining, more frequent trips to the port on business in spite of the telephone, and visits to other farms both near San Julian and further south.

Regular visitors included the Lucas Bridges family from the 'Baker'. Following his youth in Tierra del Fuego, (3) on returning from the war Lucas had been offered the job of managing the Baker Company's farm in northwestern Santa Cruz. The Baker River actually flows into the Pacific and most of the land lay in Chile, although the estancia headquarters was in Argentina, alongside Lago Posadas. The property had been settled at the beginning of the century and stocked with 20,000 ewes purchased from Estancia Condor in 1907 (see Chapter 17), whose drive across country, mentioned by Chace, was legendary. Their nearest port and source of supplies however, was San Julian, over 500km away to the east, there being no outlet to the Pacific. Lucas spent much time on several hair-raising canoeing expeditions down the Baker River aimed at trying to open an outlet to the Pacific. On one of these occasions he got gangrene in his fingers, so handing the axe to one of his companions said 'Chop!' The man had the guts to do so, thereby saving Lucas's life minus two fingers.

Don Lucas was known throughout Patagonia for his stories. I can remember as a small boy sitting literally at his feet listening, while he lay on my mother's sofa at Coronel, no doubt recovering from one of his forays.

The nursery

Having moved into the Big House, our parents soon found that, with the general expansion of commercial and other activities all over Patagonia, a big farm like Coronel required more attention from the manager than just organising the work. There were public and business relations to be attended to, which involved entertaining at home, plus visiting in San Julian and six other families on the place all requiring attention. On their next leave in 1931, with two bouncing boys in tow, Arthur and Millicent decided to engage a nanny so that Millicent would be able to give more of her atten-

Hugh's christening at Rodney Lodge, 1931. From left to right: Isobel Worsley, Philip Worsley Senior, Katherine Worsley (hidden), Granny Muriel Worsley, Bessie Cook, Mary Worsley, Violet Blake, Millicent, Arthur A Worsley, Philip Worsley Junior, Alice Worsley. Below, left to right: Susan Worsley, Arthur, John, Hugh, Bridget Blake.

tion to helping her husband with the affairs of the farm, and to the welfare of the other families living on the place. So Bessie Cook joined the family and I say she was part of the family advisedly. I do not really remember early childhood without Bessie, who presided over the nursery with the help of Joey the canary who sang for hours and hours in his cage hung in a sunny corner. I have a vague recollection of playing under the kitchen table, so must have been pretty small at the time. Millicent always had local British or Falkland Island girls to help in the house, in particular Mary Middleton who later married the mechanic, Carlos Agustin, and Ethel Martin who used to take turns with Bessie to take us out for walks.

I have a vivid picture of going for walks down in the Number 4 paddock with Ethel and being greeted every afternoon by Alec Kennedy, one of the shepherds, who would conveniently be riding back that way from his rounds of the paddocks. Their wedding duly took place in the Big House garden, and they then lived at the Cabo Curioso shanty where they had two daughters. I used to go and stay with them occasionally. The Kennedys stayed on in the company's service until after the Second World War, when they returned to Scotland. Many years later, when cousins Seymour and Daphne Blake were touring in the Highlands, they came across a cottage offering Bed and Breakfast, called 'Patagonia'. This was, of course, Ethel, now widowed and delighted to meet some Blake cousins. Doing much the same ourselves in 1987 with Stuart and Frances, we again found Ethel, by then over 80, who gave us all coffee in her little parlour surrounded by photos and mementoes of San Julian and of the farm. It was interesting how many of the reminiscences of her husband, as she related them to us then, had to do with the tensions of the Intervention.

Life in the Big House took on the aspect of any middle- or professional-class household in England of that time. Our life revolved around the nursery with Bessie, although once we were big enough we lunched with our parents in the dining room, and the threat of being banished to the nursery was enough to cope with most misdemeanours such as refusing to eat one's pudding. After nursery tea, we would join our parents in the sitting room for a jolly period of games before early bed. Outside the house, however, the differences began. There was a yard boy who chopped the firewood, fed the chickens and milked the goats. The woodpile was of considerable size, handily placed behind the wash house, near the chicken run, and sometimes provided a refuge for skunks, who are partial to barnyard fowls. Traps were set, and I remember once getting too near a trapped skunk out of curiosity, so of course it 'fired' at me. Luckily only my clothes were affected, as apart from the strong smell, skunk's 'ammunition' contains formic and other acids which can damage your eyes, and eat into clothes so that they have to be thrown away.

The goats were there because the Blakes reckoned that there was not enough grass in the nearby paddocks to support cows, which may well have been the case in those days of having to feed hundreds of cart and riding horses. There would be a flock of twenty or thirty goats of all ages and varying colours, although our parents had taken the trouble to bring down well-bred Toggenburgs and Saanens to improve the milk supply. Goats have an amazing capacity for finding open gates – the garden was surrounded by a paling fence, but you only had to leave a gate open, with not a goat in sight, for them to sense it and in half an hour they would be inside. The gardener in the 1930s was a German called Schaer, whom I used to follow like a little dog, and he would often have to chase the goats out of the garden, waving a rake and uttering incomprehensible German oaths. Schaer was an excellent gardener who was mainly responsible for creating a veritable oasis there, and it was with real regret that Arthur had to ask him to leave on the outbreak of war.

War of a more peaceable sort, within the settlement, used to occur over the water supply. This was piped down from some springs up in the Number 6 paddock, and the main line ran through the garden, supplying the house, and on 'down below' to the rest of the settlement, in particular the dip, which used a lot of water. If the latter was in operation, there would not be enough pressure to send water up to the header tank in the two-storeyed house. On Mondays (wash day), this could cause really serious problems. If it came to the point, dipping had to come first but considerable management planning went into trying to see that this did not happen! When a flush lavatory was finally installed in the 1930s, it was advisable to check on the fullness of the tank before using the adjacent convenience.

Much of this would have been strange to Bessie, but she was always calm and peaceable and nursery life flowed its tranquil way. It was no trouble therefore for her to look after us on the farm when the next baby came along, and Millicent and Arthur left for Buenos Aires. The *José Menéndez* coasting steamer on which they were to travel was delayed, so they switched to the new Aeroposta Argentina, a private company with French capital which had grown out of the early pioneering flights of Jean Mermoz, Saint Exupery (4) and others. The first commercial flight from Rio Gallegos to Buenos Aires had taken place in 1930, using a French Latécoère single-engined aircraft carrying six passengers, captained by St Exupery, and the service was extended to Tierra del Fuego and grew slowly from there. By 1932 there was a regular service, and there is a story that on one occasion Mrs Jannette Bridges, Don Lucas's wife, struck a very bumpy flight and as she was obviously about to be unwell, one of the other passengers, a naval officer and evident gentleman, whipped off his uniform cap and offered it, with an 'allow me, madam!'

Possibly in some doubt as to the relative stability of the sea compared to the air, Millicent and Arthur duly flew to Buenos Aires without incident, and Eleanor Muriel was born in the British Hospital on 16 August 1932.

As I grew older, Millicent started to give me lessons. She was already teaching the other children on the farm, and school took place daily in the *galería*. A *galería* or conservatory is an essential part of any house in Patagonia and the Falklands, being a well-glassed sun-room tacked onto the northern side. Although plants are usually grown there, that is not the main purpose, which is to trap sun and its heat for the house as a whole and provide extra living space sheltered from the elements. The *galería* at Coronel led out from the nursery, becoming an extension of this. There were shelves for geraniums round under the windows, a door out into the garden, cupboards for toys and games, and a no-nonsense wooden floor which could be scrubbed.

Christmas was always a family celebration, possibly more so because our parents tended to feel their expatriate state much more than we did a generation later. It was, of course, summer, which in latitude 49°S meant it was light at 4 a.m. We would hang up our stockings, which performed their designed task of keeping the little horrors quiet in bed when they (inevitably) woke up at the crack of dawn, and Santa Claus had his ritual to perform when filling them – small presents, of course, to be opened, including comestibles to assuage the pre-breakfast pangs of hunger, ending with an orange in the toe and the whole topped by a balloon. Getting through that

The Big House, tennis court and pre-war buildings, looking towards the settlement and Cerro Munro in 1939.

lot allowed our parents to sleep on a bit as of course it was shearing time when work started at 6 a.m. daily so the one-day holiday for Christmas was very welcome. After breakfast would come the opening of 'proper' presents downstairs – parcels sent weeks beforehand by grandparents having been secreted away until the day.

Christmas trees were not usually set up, live trees being too precious to cut down, although I do remember one year there was a children's party in the dining room with a real tree and real flaming candles. Trees with real candles in a wooden house were, perhaps, not the best thing to have and a wet sponge on a stick was on hand in case of emergency. Another time, around 1934 or 1935, a large packing case from Gath y Chaves department store in Buenos Aires arrived, and on Christmas morning we came downstairs to find in the *galería* a doll's pram (for Eleanor), a pedal car (for Hugh) and a 'fairy cycle' for me! We never had 'Christmas dinner' as such, it was far too hot, but there would usually be an *asado*, sometimes a big one with all the neighbours coming over for the day, and tennis would be played. *Asado* means roast meat in Argentina and by association, a social event at which the principal viand is meat (in Patagonia a lamb, or several if the gathering is numerous), roasted whole on a vertical spit or *asador* in front of a large fire, in the open air.

A concrete tennis court had been built in Uncle Robert's time, and the high fence around it served equally to keep balls and children in. Grandfather Robert's hut, known as the 'playhouse' had been put in one corner of the enclosure, and was children's territory. Many, many activities other than tennis could of course be pursued there – we used to ride our bicycle and pedal car round and round and round for hours, ditto roller skates after we came back in 1940. The car would be washed there, but the only other time I can remember a vehicle coming in was a pickup being backed up to the front door of the house to load the luggage for an imminent voyage, to Buenos Aires or to England.

We had a fair amount of freedom, especially during shearing when we could go 'down below' – that is to say out of the garden into the working part of the settlement. One went 'up' to the Big House and 'down' to everywhere else. There we would watch or even join in some of the work, such as helping to 'yard' the incoming flocks of sheep which had been driven in down the Stony Hill.

Notes

1 'Gringos' really meant foreigners. There is much controversy over the origin of the word, which some say goes back to the private soldiers from the English invasions who took to the pampas, among whose songs was 'Green Grow the Rushes, Ho'. In central Argentina it is also used to mean any European, mainly Italians, but in Patagonia refers only to the British.

2 Banco de la Nación Argentina first opened in Rio Gallegos in 1900, in Deseado in 1917 and in San Julian and Santa Cruz in 1921, in each case following the London Bank. Until the Banco de la Provincia de Santa Cruz opened in 1958, they were the only banks operating in the territory.

3 See *Uttermost Part of the Earth*, by Lucas Bridges, which tells the story of the Ushuaia Mission (see Chapter 2) and his youth there. It has become a classic which every Patagonia-watcher should read, and is a unique record of the indigenous Fuegians (now sadly extinct), among whom Lucas lived and into whose tribal customs he was accepted. His later exploits at the Baker and elsewhere, often the subject of his many stories, have not so far been published.

4 Antoine de Saint Exupery, author of *Wind, Sand and Stars, Southern Mail, Night Flight* and other works. Pioneered many air routes in North Africa and Patagonia.

7

To School and Back

Snow and show

In 1934, Jubilee year, we all went on leave, including Bessie. I remember it chiefly because in preparation for the sea voyage we were taken to Gath y Chaves department store in Buenos Aires and fancy dress costumes were purchased, a quite unheard of luxury as normally any kind of 'dressing up' meant home-made costumes. There was an 'acting box' at home, containing all sorts of cast-off clothing in which on long winter afternoons we used to dress up. One winter, Millicent put on a pantomime, acted by the children of her school. Duncan Mann and I being the smallest (we were about 6 then) were the hind and front ends respectively of the donkey, whose costume was got up on the farm, made from wire and hessian. It was still in the attic thirty years later . . . Our costumes in 1934 were a cowboy outfit for me, a French policeman's uniform for Hugh, and a Dutch girl's costume for Eleanor. We wore these not only for the fancy-dress parties on board ship coming and going, but also for the Jubilee Parade in Winscombe. This had been largely organised by Grandfather Worsley (known as 'Par-Par'). It started at the church hall and processed, complete with band, through the village to the recreation ground which had been donated by the local community as a war memorial instead of the usual monument. Par-Par had a flagpole at Westfield, on which he would fly either the Union Jack or a large bright-coloured Japanese paper fish according to the occasion. The arrival of the Blake family from Patagonia was considered to merit the Union Jack.

Our youngest sister, Rosemary Joy, was born in the British Hospital in Buenos Aires on 7 July 1935, we three older ones having stayed on the farm with Bessie. Fortunately Arthur, Millicent and the new baby arrived back (both ways by air) in San Julian before the snow fell, as it turned out to be one of the severest snows of the century, only exceeded, as far as we can determine, by the snows of 1904 and 1973. It fell in early August, when the steamer *José Menéndez* was in San Julian, taking on passengers en route for Buenos Aires. Among these were two bank boys who had come out to the farm to say goodbye. Other 'passengers' included six show rams being sent by the company to the Palermo Show in Buenos Aires. Something like a metre of snow having fallen overnight, the only way to get them all down to the port to board the steamer was for the men to ride, and a sledge was rapidly put together to convey the rams. A troop of thirty horses was driven in front to 'break snow' – i.e. trample down the drifts to produce something like a packed surface which could be ridden over, then the riders on shod horses accompanied the horse-drawn sledge carrying the precious rams. Horses in Patagonia are not normally shod, except in winter when the ground is frozen. They are then fitted with shoes with spiked heels which will grip on ice. To us children, of course, snow was fun. The picture of the three of us on a toboggan on unbroken snow, was taken at a spot where in

Winter fun after the heavy snow fall of 1935. The snow was at least 1 metre deep at this point.

summer there were bushes of about a metre in height. These were snowed over enough to walk on or sleigh over.

The shipment of rams to the Palermo Show was somewhat of a milestone in the progress and development of the Company in general and a considerable personal achievement for Arthur. The original importation in 1909 of Corriedale rams from New Zealand had been followed soon by pedigree ewes, and Uncle Robert had continued breeding them as a stud flock. In 1927 the *Sociedad Rural Argentina* started a registered pedigree flock book for the breed, and the Coronel flock was registered as Number 9. Pedigree breeding takes time, but gradually the Company's sheep acquired quality and renown up and down Patagonia. Stock shows started to be held in the mid-1920s, and we read in Edith's memoirs of a trip to the Deseado Show, and the success there of the Company's rams. Ably assisted by stud stockman John Mackay, this was followed by other successes, until finally Arthur took the plunge and went for the grand accolade of the Palermo Show in Buenos Aires, which at that time was one of the four (1) most important stock shows in the world as far as sires (rams and bulls) were concerned. The first rams sent there were those sent in 1935, through the snow and they won gratifying ribbons but no major prizes. But in 1937 and again in 1939, Coronel rams went on to win the supreme achievement of the grand championship.

Competing at stock shows in those pre-war days was related to serious production and the prize-winning rams or bulls were those showing real commercial advantages. But as the years went by, other factors relating to what one can only call 'beauty' crept in, so the magnificent champions in the ring were not necessarily the progenitors of the most productive animals out on the pampas. New breeders appeared whose sole object was the show ring and the sale of prize winners, rather than the commercial production of wool, lamb or beef. In Corriedales, for example, wool was allowed to grow on the face to the extent that many animals became 'wool blind' and unable to fend for themselves in a natural state. Arthur never allowed this problem to develop at Coronel. Another problem was lack of body size – there was a tendency for the show ring to favour 'small but beautiful' sheep. The Blakes reckoned that sheep needed long legs and a stout constitution to range leagues over the pampas in search of food and water, so size was actually very important in the 'real world'.

Arthur was very much an instinctive breeder – he just had a 'feel' for the right sort of animal to aim for, and working back from this aim, he knew just what sort or type of animal to use to get there. By the 1940s he was selecting his pedigree rams on fleece weight (by weighing the newly-shorn fleece) and attempting to relate it to the bodyweight of the shorn animal. He had a concept of 'balance' – in order to grow and carry a heavy fleece (we are talking about 5 kilos or more) the sheep had also to be large – say 50 kilos live weight. His concept, twenty years later, proved to be correct but at the time nobody had yet worked out the genetic aspects of all this. It was not until the post-war period that research in other countries started to come up with some of the answers, which we will look at in Chapter 15.

Family life on any farm is directly affected by the activities and problems of the paterfamilias, and in Patagonia to a greater extent than most other environments. The demands and stresses of shearing, for example, are perhaps comparable to those which occur during any harvesting activity elsewhere. Later on, I was to see something of this during harvest at Uncle Philip Worsley's farming operation on the Cotswolds (see Chapter 10), where the pressures were not dissimilar. Much the same occurs on extensive sheep operations during lamb-marking, which is another form of harvest. During these periods the family reverts to its supportive role towards its head, as his time is not his own, but this is understood because it is what we are all here for. What is much more trying is the worry and demand on time for weeks on end, produced by the eternal dipping against sheep scab. We have covered the practical aspects of this in Chapter 5, but it is difficult to convey the enormous amount of work involved in dipping, and the degree in which it affected everybody's life.

Shearing was (and is) different, again like any harvest. Once the last sheep is shorn and the last fleece baled up, that's the end of it until the same time next year. But scab could break out any time, and the whole backbreaking process had to begin again.

By the late 1930s, the British community in San Julian had reached quite important proportions. English was spoken freely round town, and not a few farmers' wives could not speak Spanish at all, beyond the most elementary household terms. I remember much later, in 1953, being surprised that the former Mrs Rolfe, who had married Dan Fraser when Rolfe died and who had lived at the 'Company's' all her married life did not know what a *tortilla* (omelette) was. Considering that eggs of both hens and ostrich were much used for making omelettes as a change from the eternal mutton, one would have thought she would, as a housewife, have known this word. Eggs of the ostrich, more properly the rhea, are relatively easy to find, and were particularly valued for making cakes, as the white is stiff and holds up a batter easily.

Rhea darwini is the Patagonian species of rhea – rather smaller than the 'Ñandú' or *Rhea americana* which is found all over the humid pampas and north-eastern Argentina – but both species have the same breeding habits, in that it is the male that rears the family. He will first put together a 'harem' of females, like many other feral males, and it is he who selects the family nest. Any convenient depression in the ground is suitable, providing it is about a metre across. The females then proceed to lay their eggs, one by one, until the nest is full, at which point the male takes over and sits down (literally) to hatch out the brood. If a female rhea is headed towards the nest in order to lay, but it is occupied by another and she can't wait, or if the nest is already full, then she lays her egg alone on the pampa some distance away, but always pointed towards the nest. So if you followed one in the right direction you would come across some fifteen to twenty or more large green eggs, each equal to about six hen's eggs.

There is a story about Don Julio Aloyz as a young and very green *peón* out gathering the Cañadon Seco camp, a particularly large one, with Alec Mann and other Scots. Julio came across an ostrich nest with twenty or more eggs, so having no saddle-bags (*maletas*) rolled his poncho into a sort of tube with the eggs inside it, and slung it across himself like a bandolier. But it was a hot day, and the sheep were stubborn, and Don Julio had to gallop about in order to turn them, with disastrous results to the eggs . . .

The male having hatched out his brood of, perhaps twelve to fifteen chicks, may feel its size is not a credit to his male rhea-hood, so he will then fight other males for the possession of theirs, much as he fought them for the females in the first place. So by midsummer you may see 'families' of thirty to forty chicks all running together.

Schooling

I can remember feeling embarrassed whenever some Brit (2) farmer insisted in talking in English in front of a non-English speaker such as the manager of the Anónima. Our parents were always very insistent on this point of good manners. There was an English School in San Julian, funded I believe partly by the Anglican Church but mainly by the settlers themselves, and

The staff and pupils of the English School in San Julian, on a visit to the farm about 1937. Miss Vernham at centre of seated row, on her right (with glasses) is Cathy Mann.

run by Miss Vernham. She was a minute lady who wore long Edwardian dresses and sported pince-nez. All the local boys and girls in town of British descent went there, and a surprising number of others as well. I remember a large party held for the Coronation of King George VI, at which we were all given souvenir spoons and china mugs.

Quite soon the problem of our own education reared its head, always one of the biggest problems for families living on the land in Patagonia, as indeed it still is today. As well as the little English school and a German school, a public primary school had existed in the town of San Julian since 1908, but the logistics of getting children living on the farm to school in town (about 20km away) daily were not to be tackled for another twenty years. The state school naturally taught the Argentine primary curriculum in Spanish, and in the mid-1930s there were still many English-speaking families on the farms who did not really mind which language their children used. It was only in the next generation, when secondary education became available, that all children went to the Argentine schools in the towns and spoken English started to disappear. There were four other families living at the 'Company's', one of them (the Mann family) with nine children, so Millicent set up her own school on the farm, and taught them all to read, write and do sums (in English), us included. In this she was much helped by Aunt Bridget, who would send out 'child education' books and other material designed for teaching at a distance.

But for us I don't think there was ever any real doubt – sooner or later we would go to an English boarding school (first 'prep' then 'public') just as Uncle Robert had gone to Sedbergh, Arthur to Uppingham and their sisters to Clifton and Roedean. We certainly learned to read, write and do sums with Millicent, in preparation for this important step. Our next home leave was due in 1937, and it had been decided that Hugh and I were to go to prep school in England and board there when the rest of the family returned to Patagonia. The idea of boarding school was so much a part of life at that time for people of our background and upbringing that the fact of extra distance did not seem to matter. There were, after all, plenty of families living out in India and other parts of the British Empire in exactly the same situation. Our parents must have been very torn over it all themselves, but I cannot tell or remember, now, if they took any especial care to prepare us for the event, (on the whole I doubt it), or whether it just happened. Life, in any case, was full of adventure so this was just one more.

So Hugh and I went in 1937, aged 7 and 9, to Lambrook school, which was in Bracknell, Berkshire. We had been preceded there by both Uncle Robert's sons, Bob and Bill, although by then they had progressed to Uppingham and Eton respectively. Lambrook seems to have had something of a reputation for 'bringing out the best in boys' (to quote from a letter from Robert Blake Senior to his son Arthur), and possibly in the private school field of the 1930s it would have been known to advanced educationalists such as the Herfords. Certainly there were a number of boys there whose parents were also overseas. Don Lucas Bridges had sent his youngest son David there, a year ahead of us, and there were many other boys with parents in the Army or Navy or the Colonial Service out in various corners of the British Empire.

It was all new – first came the sea voyage, then the summer at Westfield with a family holiday by the sea at Crantock in between, then the excitement of buying school outfits which involved going to London because the outfitter's was Gieves. Thus there were visits to London Zoo and the changing of the guard at Buckingham Palace to enjoy as well.

After Hugh and I went to boarding school, Bessie Cook did not return to San Julian with the family. Our parents kept in touch with her for many years, and before she died Hugh (living in Bristol) had the opportunity to visit her and reminisce.

So a new life started at Lambrook, for which I at least, aged 9, was ready. Aunt Edith used to say that I was an 'impossible little boy' when I first went to stay with them at Hembury Fort Cross, – perhaps I already needed the wider scope of life away from home. Lambrook was a private preparatory school, one of many in the Windsor-Epsom-Virginia Water area against whom we competed in games, and was owned and run by A.H. ('Archie') Forbes and his wife. It was, I am sure, far harder for Arthur and Millicent to leave us than it was for us to enter this completely new world, and I realise now that it was very much the Forbes' doing that we were in fact kept busy and occupied, with little or no time for homesickness. I can only remember feeling homesick once or twice at Lambrook, when in bed with some sickness and therefore feeling depressed or possibly bored with being in the sanatorium. Not at other times, though – there was too much going on.

The curriculum was broad, aimed at getting everybody into a public school via at least the Common Entrance exam, but there was also a lengthy roll of scholarships available – my cousin Bill had got one to Eton some eight years previously, and I had started to work towards that level, with Greek added to the obligatory Latin. Music figured largely, both personal (we both learned piano there) and choral. The school of course had its own chapel where Archie Forbes played the organ, the air for which had to be pumped up or 'blown' manually by two boys who heaved up and down on a lever in a little cubby-hole behind a door next to the console. I remember one service when at a critical point in the sung responses there was no air forthcoming and Archie, very red in the face, was banging furiously on the door to wake the blowers up! I was at that time a bit shaky at holding a tune vocally, and so later on became a blower which we thought was great because we did not have to attend choir practice!

Thirty-five years later, together with my daughter Alison, I revisited

Lambrook (which looked much the same). We found Mrs Forbes living in retirement in a cottage in the grounds. On my tentatively intruding with the words 'Excuse me, er, my name is Blake . . .', she came right back, quick as a flash, with: 'Bob, Bill, John or Hugh?' I learned a lot at Lambrook, not all of it in the classroom.

The 'phoney' war

To two small boys at a boarding school in England, in early 1940, the reality of war was not yet apparent. My brother Hugh and I had, it is true, heard Mr Chamberlain broadcasting the Declaration of War in September 1939, while we were staying with our grandparents towards the end of the summer holidays, and had seen air-raid shelters being dug on Bedminster Down in Bristol. Back at school in Berkshire, we had been issued with gas masks, and had been shown how to walk down to the cellars in an orderly fashion if there was an air raid. But although we had seen an anti-aircraft gun while on our walks to the woods nearby, we did not know what an air-raid was. The more immediate demands of the classroom, the playing fields, the Scouts and other aspects of normal life at a well-run prep school filled our days, as they had for the past three years.

Our mother had taught us to read and write to such good effect that we were able to adjust to school classes at once – indeed I was moved up two classes after the first term, in spite of coping with Latin, and later Greek. All sports were of course new to us, so they were fun to learn although neither of us particularly excelled, then or later. Wolf Cubs, and later Scouts, related much more to our rather pioneering existence in Patagonia and we avidly learned how to light a fire with one match, boil up nettles for stew and to build bridges tied together with rope.

In the holidays we would visit our Worsley grandparents at Winscombe, Somerset, and our guardians Uncle Robert and Aunt Edith Blake at Hembury Fort Cross, near Honiton in Devon, but most of our time was spent at a splendid rambling farmhouse with riding stables not far from Chard, where Captain and Mrs Shields took in children for the holidays, most of them like us with parents abroad. With their three daughters of about our age there were always a dozen or so youngsters for the holidays, and there was riding every day. Back at home on the farm in Patagonia we had ridden since an early age. I remember well looking out of my bedroom window on the morning of my birthday, I think my fifth, and seeing a man leading a small black horse (a mare, actually). This turned out to be 'Beauty' on whose broad and stable back we learned to ride, sitting at first on a sheepskin only. One was not allowed to use stirrups until one could ride without, and all horses in Patagonia are reined 'Spanish' – i.e. steered by

John and Hugh on Beauty, with Millicent, San Julian, 1935.

lateral pressure of the rein on the neck, but in fact greatly assisted by the rider moving his or her weight. I did graduate to stirrups at about 8, before leaving for boarding school. At the Shields' we were well taught, and once we had mastered the smooth English saddle and the strange way of steering the horse by the mouth, we were away. We soon learned how to jump, which led to Pony Club activities at shows and gymkhanas in summer, and hunting in winter.

Hembury Fort Cross was also a large house, with spacious grounds including a sort of wilderness with a pond and a punt in it. Our cousins were all much older so we didn't see much of them, but I remember Bill one day taking us off in the car to the top of Hembury Fort, a Roman encampment, and letting us drive on the empty road up there. Another time a village cricket match was coming up, at which I had been asked to keep wicket – indeed I actually had the gloves ready, so it was a great disappointment when we could not in the end play, having come down with measles – or it may have been mumps . . .

We did not spend much time at Winscombe itself, but would join gatherings of Worsleys when they happened, mainly seaside holidays at St David's in Pembrokeshire, Wales with Grannie and Par-Par Worsley and their sons and families as they came along. I also particularly remember the festivities one Christmas at Rodney Lodge. This considerable mansion on Clifton Down, Bristol, had been the home of Great-grandfather Worsley, who was extremely well off, and at the time it was the home of 'the aunts' – the five maiden sisters of Grandfather Philip. One never went to Bristol without calling at Rodney Lodge, which was a perfect model of 'the old ways' when household and garden staff were employed and everything was done most beautifully. All that, of course, was to change with the war but I am very pleased that I was able to see it, and remember how it all was.

That Christmas we were allowed to stay up and join the grown-ups for dinner, which took place in all its glory and with all the trimmings, served by the maids at the (so it seemed) enormous dining-room table – there had to have been fifteen to twenty people there if I count them all up, which I won't do here as we will meet them all later on. What I do remember particularly is liqueurs being served in some very special small silver goblets with three handles, and then later we all adjourned to the drawing-room which could be enlarged into a sort of small ballroom, to play things like charades and dumb crambo. Earlier in the evening, of course, we would have gone to the Christmas service at Lewins Mead Unitarian Chapel, which was an important part of the Worsley's lives, and I mention it here as it was at Lewins Mead on 3 September 1939 that we heard Mr Chamberlain's broadcast announcing that Britain was at war. It was when we were driving back to Winscombe with our grandparents that we saw air-raid shelters being dug on Bedminster Down, and Par-Par told us what they were used for . . .

There were other relations not far away. Cousins Humphrey and Amy Blake were at Chardstock near Crewkerne. Their third son Martin was about my age and we often met up at Pony Club and other social events in the neighbourhood. I can remember going to dances – not that we danced much at that age but there were usually parlour games also. Uncle Norman and family were at South Harp, near South Petherton, which was not too far. In London, there was Aunt V (my father's elder sister Violet) who lived at Golders Green and was *always* there to ferry small boys from Waterloo to Paddington or wherever, often via London Zoo or the Science Museum.

All that being as it may, it was still a turning point in my life when without any previous warning, one day in June 1940, Archie Forbes called us both out of school and said: 'Blake brothers, you are going back to Patagonia – Matron is packing your bags and we are putting you on the 4.45 train to London, where you will join your parents.'

And so it was. It is all a bit hazy now, but we were met at Waterloo by Aunt V, taken to Euston where we joined our parents, who with Eleanor and Rosemary had come up from Bristol in the meantime, and that same evening found ourselves all together on a crowded, blacked-out boat train heading for an unknown destination. This turned out to be Gourock on the Clyde, and the ship RMS *Highland Brigade*.

'I never thought I would see the dear old Stony Hill again,' was my comment.

The eight children of Robert and Dora Blake at a family gathering in 1937. From left: Norman, Dorothy, Elsie, Robert, Bridget, Willy, Violet and Arthur.

Transatlantic dash

Only in later years did we gather all that had gone on in the preceding months. My father, like most managers of farming companies in South America, was on a three-yearly leave cycle. Having last come home when we first went to boarding school in 1937, his next leave was due in 1940. So as to see more of us at Lambrook, Millicent and the girls had preceded him by several months and we had spent the Easter holidays with them at Westfield, and there was talk of renting a house in Winscombe for the summer – we actually went to see it and were looking forward to it. But after the fall of Dunkirk in May 1940, everything became very much grimmer, so Arthur, with an OBE and a mention in despatches on his record from the First World War, offered his services as soon as he arrived in England. Predictably, he was told to get right back to Patagonia and continue producing wool and mutton for shipment to Britain. There was also the matter of the administration of a British asset, since the San Julian Sheep Farming Company was

At Captain and Mrs Shields' holiday home in Somerset, 1939. John, second from right, looking down, Hugh just behind.

one of eight UK-registered farming companies operating in the territory of Santa Cruz at that time. (3)

So we found ourselves outward bound on the *Highland Brigade*, one of the Royal Mail Line's fleet of fast passenger/cargo liners designed for the chilled-beef trade from the River Plate. In peacetime, they did the Buenos Aires–London run in eighteen days, and were therefore supposedly fast enough to outrun a surfaced submarine. There was a 3-inch gun on the poop, and all the male passengers over the age of 15 formed a roster of lookout watches in addition to those kept by the crew, to increase the number of eyes looking out for periscope wakes or torpedo tracks.

The ship, of course, was packed – even the second-class accommodation, which usually carried immigrants from Spain. There were some forty unaccompanied children on board, and one did not move outside one's cabin, even to meals, without taking both one's lifebelt and an 'abandon-ship' bag, carefully packed for emergencies. Being only 12, I did not have to stand a watch, but on the second day out our mother brought us sharply down to earth (up to then it all seemed a bit of a lark) by getting out the Berlitz language books and we had to sit down seriously and learn Spanish. When we were little, with an English nanny and Falkland Island or Scots domestic staff in the kitchen, only English was spoken in the house. Even out of it, we were not allowed to mix with the mainly Chilean *peones*, and only had contact with the shepherds and other skilled hands who were all British, mostly Scots. Most other farming settlers whom one was likely to meet on farming or social occasions were also of British origin, so it was hardly necessary for the women and children to speak Spanish at all – indeed there were many who could not do so. But in 1940 Millicent could see that this was coming to an end, that we were living in a Spanish-speaking country, were going to have to go to school there and so we had better start learning the language!

On leaving the Clyde, it got colder for two days as we headed north-west in convoy well out into the Atlantic so as to avoid the 'Western Approaches' and the risk of U-boats. Then the ship turned away from the convoy, increased engine revolutions and headed south alone. She would zig-zag during the day, but at dusk you could hear the engine beat increase and the wake would straighten out as she went flat out so as to make as much southing as possible during the hours of darkness. The voyage was uneventful and we were not, in the event, chased by anything, possibly to the disappointment of the half-dozen or so Royal Artillery gunners who would carry out gun drill daily at the 3-inch gun mounted on the poop. But a sister ship, the *Highland Chieftain*, was later attacked and managed to outrun the submarine, at the expense of all the crockery in the second-class accommodation.

It was interesting on arrival in Rio to see interned German ships anchored out in the roads, while the Red Ensign moved in and out freely. Brazil was always more pro-Allies than Argentina. We duly reached Buenos Aires and put up at the Phoenix Hotel, the traditional modestly-priced hostelry on San Martín street, much used by Patagonian Brits as it was close to the sea passenger terminal at the North Basin. It was also handy for shopping, with Harrods just round the corner and Gath y Chaves and the cinemas a short walk up Florida.

After a week or two we took ship again, this time in the SS *Asturiano*, one of the fleet of coasting vessels operated by the *Sociedad Anónima Importadora y Exportadora de la Patagonia*, universally known as *La Anónima* and part of the trading empire put together by Don José Menéndez (who hailed from Asturias in Spain) and his descendants. No Patagonian can fail to have had contact with this family at some time or other, and we will meet them many times in these pages. They had set up trading houses from the beginning of the century in every port along the coast, and supplied provisions, materials and general goods to the settlers. They also invested in land, and were not above taking over a settler's land for debt, when he was unable to pay his overdue bills for supplies. In fairness to them, it must be said that they also financed many early settlers, allowing a great deal of supplies to be taken on credit, and only foreclosing when it was terminal and unavoidable. The Menéndez family as a whole was known to irreverent British Patagonians as the 'royal family', mainly because they lived in considerable style and did not mind visibly splashing their considerable wealth about.

One of the (to us) unpleasant things about travelling by ship, was the awful taste of the reconstituted powdered milk. The 'royal family' would get around this one by shipping their own cow with its cowherd – not only on their own coasting steamers but on liners to Europe as well!

Most of my memories of Patagonian sea voyages stem from that trip on the *Asturiano* when I was 12, although some come from further back. I remember the first part downriver, the water still muddy and the lounge full of ladies sitting around discussing in loud Argentine voices their oncoming symptoms of '*mal-de-mer*', and the lounge gradually emptying as blue water was reached and the ship started to move. Then from earlier voyages, because of Bessie Cook being there, I have a clear recollection of her horror at the 'unsuitable' (for English children) food offered in the dining saloon, full of garlic, oil and other delicious 'native' seasonings never then used in British households, dear me no. The menu offered consisted of a single list of eight or nine dishes (cold starter, soup, fish, pasta, vegetable dish, made-up meat dish, roast or grilled meat, pudding and dessert) which were served one by one in due order, and you either ate them as they came or waited for the next one. Some gentlemen were quite capable of ploughing solemnly through the whole menu, dish by dish . . . If wine was being drunk by the adults, and the bottle was unfinished, the level was carefully marked in pencil before leaving the table to avoid it being lowered by the kitchen staff before the next meal . . .

The cabins were quite small, with upper and lower bunks, and I naturally shared with Hugh, who grabbed the top one. Millicent had put her fur coat on a hanger, on a hook on the wall at the foot of the bunks, the cabin being panelled in vertical tongue-and-grooved boards. When rough weather later confined us to our bunks, we could measure the degree of rolling by counting the number of planks by which coat swung back and forth. This finally produced the undoing of Hugh, but I managed to scoot out of my bunk in time!

At the ports we would watch with fascination the unloading of cargo and of passengers. Madryn was the only port with a quay to which a ship could go alongside, and I remember we took a run ashore and drove over to Trelew to visit the British school there. At all the other ports the ship anchored off and lowered the boats which it carried for the purpose. These consisted of a flush-decked steam tug and two 'scows' or 'lighters'. The tug really fascinated us. It was handled by a coxswain who stood up at the back steering with a long tiller, and a deckhand (known to us children as 'the poor man in the launch') who hopped around in sou'wester and full oilskins as he was frequently drenched by white or green seas. Presumably there was also an engineer or stoker below, shovelling in the coal. Passengers had to climb down the gangway and into one of the scows – which if it was wet or stormy might have had a tarpaulin drawn over the top – and just stand there holding on as best they could. Once towed to the shore the scow would be beached on the shingle and a single wobbly gangplank extended for us to walk down. The sailors, who were mostly Spanish, Galician or Basque, dressed in waders and oilskins and would extend a helping hand – small children and pretty young ladies were usually carried to shore in their brawny arms!

So, after ten days or so we arrived back at San Julian where the ship anchored and lowered its boats, just like Magellan, Drake, Anson, Fitzroy, Piedra Buena and many others had done before it. From the top deck I could see the Hotel Miramar, the Anónima warehouse and general store, the Company's wool store, the Banco Nación, the parish church and other important buildings ranging away from the bay along the gravelled main street. The latter was a good 100 metres wide so as to allow a wagon with its twelve- to sixteen-horse team to turn round after unloading its cargo of wool bales on the beach, above the high water mark. This area, when we arrived that time in spring, would have been fairly clear, but later in the season it became covered with stacks of bales awaiting shipment. In the distance I could see, stretching away into the purple-blue distance, the escarpment behind the farm, with landmarks like the Cerro Munro, the Pan de Azucar and the Tres Hermanos Hills showing up clearly against the westering sun.

We duly climbed down the gangway into the lighter, were towed by the steam tug to shore, and so processed across the gangplank onto the gravelly beach. The farm car was waiting, with cousin Bob come to meet us, and a pickup truck for the luggage, and soon we were bouncing along the dusty track, back to our childhood home, nestling at the foot of the Stony Hill.

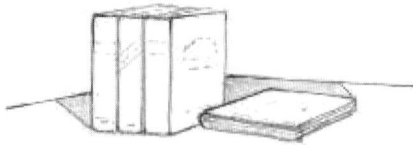

Patagonia   by Rosemary Goring

Line upon endless line of barren hills,
Brown, barren, flat-topped hills, fading away
Into immense purple distances
Beyond the bleak horizon. A windmill stands
Stark skeleton, against the hard sapphire sky.
And wind: the never-ceasing hard, dry wind,
Rustling the stiff bristly tussocks of stinging grass,
Quivering the gnarled, crabby-fingered bushes,
Whipping up eddies of dust which spinningly stagger
Down the valley. Out of the wind-battered silence
Spirals the thin solitary baa
Of a single sheep, lonely in the vast
wilderness . . .
The peewits' piercing panic-stricken cries
Burst from the ground with the black-white liveried birds,
And a hare breaks cover close by, racing hard,
Ears flat, up the black-bush-dotted slope.
A pale brown ribbon, linking hills together –
The track: and on it, one black beetle crawling –
A car, dwarfed by the hills' encircling hugeness
Startles a herd of guanaco, poised on the skyline,
Who lollop lazily off, sailing easily over
The fence, thin line that straggles on forever . . .
Smooth round sea-worn pebbles, scant dry grass,
A threadbare garment for the arid earth:
An endless empty land; dry desolation . . .
But lo! In the valley, a thick green carpet spread,
And trees, willows and poplars, gracefully bending,
Red roofs, and running water, sweet spring water,
And Eden blooming in the wilderness!

Note: Rosemary left San Julian in 1947 at the age of 11, and wrote this some two years later. In a heading to the poem, published in 1993, she observes, 'I was born in Argentina, and some years after our return to England, I recalled the land where I had been brought up. It was not an easy land to inhabit.'

Notes

1 The other leading shows were the English Royal Show, Sydney (Australia) and Christchurch (New Zealand). I would hesitate to rank them in order of importance.
2 'Brit' is a modern term of, I believe, American origin. At the time we are writing about, 'Britisher' was usually used, at least in Patagonia, to denote a person of British origin or descent.
3 There were at least thirty British-owned lands or farming companies operating in Argentina at the beginning of the Second World War. Some of them, such as Bovril, Liebigs or the Argentine Southern Land Company, were of considerable size.

8

GrowingUp

Interlude at home

The Stony Hill that I had once thought I would never see again was an area of hill-side some 25 hectares in extent, hard by the Big House garden. This had been the first paddock enclosed by Munro in 1891 to hold the flocks of sheep brought in from the as yet unfenced grazing lands, prior to being shorn or dipped as the case may be. Thousands and thousands of hooves over half a century had eroded all the topsoil from this area, leaving virtually nothing but round shingly stones, making the hill, which was quite steep, difficult to climb. But you could get a splendid view from the top of the whole settlement spread out below, and the valley stretching away to the low ground towards San Julian, the town and the sea in the distance. Another favourite walk was to the Cerro Munro, always called (wrongly) 'Sierra Munro'. This was a round hill some 6km down the valley towards San Julian, actually no higher than the surrounding pampa, but seen from below it seemed more prominent. Traditionally one was supposed to carry a stone from the bottom to the top of the Sierra Munro, for luck, and over the years quite a cairn had been collected there.

So we landed in early September 1940, to be met by our cousin, Bob (Robert Blake III, Uncle Robert's eldest son), who had been in charge of the farm in Arthur's absence. Bob had gone on from Lambrook to Uppingham, and on leaving there in 1936 returned to Argentina, where as an Argentine-born he had to do military service. Possibly because he knew how to ride, he was drafted to the crack Horse Grenadiers Regiment, stationed then, as now, in the Palermo Cavalry barracks in central Buenos Aires. The *Granaderos* are the Argentine equivalent of the Household Cavalry, providing the daily dismounted guards at the Casa Rosada, (1) as well as presidential escorts on state occasions. I remember Bob coming to our hotel in uniform, it must have been when we were on our way to England in 1937 to go to school, and being impressed by the fact that he was wearing a revolver. After his service he went down to San Julian where he worked first as a cadet and then as assistant and understudy to his uncle Arthur, much as Arthur and Robert had done in their day. Hugh remembers the wooden 'knife' that Bob carved for him, and helping me paint Bob's bedroom blue.

In 1940, however, Bob was only waiting for Arthur to come back and resume the management, so that he could return to Britain and join the Royal Air Force. I remember a big *asado* being held to wish him and a number of other local young men and young women farewell on their way to the war. Sadly, a number of those present on that occasion did not return, among them Bob, who was killed in an air crash while training in Canada. Another group of volunteers from Argentina, including Bob Patterson from Mata Grande, son of the erstwhile manager of Coronel when Munro died, and Ronnie and Nora Frazer of La Colmena, the oldest estancia in the district, were lost when the *Avila Star* was torpedoed *en route* for England – a sad loss for San Julian.

Arthur, however, although he had stalwart foremen like Alec Mann, John MacKay, Tommy Affleck, Alec Kennedy and Archie MacDonald, still needed a young, active assistant to replace Bob. Casting around, he heard of a likely young man currently running a small farm inland from Deseado, entirely alone, but who had been a cadet under Mr Cullen at Estancia Monte Dinero down at the very tip of the continent. This was Lionel Pickering, who came to join the management at Coronel, where he soon proved himself a capable assistant. But he also felt the need to serve in the war to which so many young persons of British descent had gone, so after little more than a year on the farm he was able to arrange for his younger brother Tom to take his place. Tom was only 18 when he came, but was to stay with the company for the rest of his active life.

The next thing for us, of course, was school. This naturally meant boarding school, somewhere away from San Julian, and our parents must have had a hard time working this one out, although after having us on the other side of the Atlantic it would be nothing at all for us to be a mere 2,000 or so miles away. Or even further. The premier English-language boarding school for boys in Buenos Aires at the time was St George's College, Quilmes. As a member of the Headmasters' Conference of English Public Schools, it was in theory a Public School outside England, although it did provide the full Argentine primary and secondary curriculum for those not

Bob punting at Oxford with Uncle Robert, before leaving for training in Canada.

intending to proceed to Public School in Britain, as well as Common Entrance for those who did. All we were told was that we would not be going there, as it was full up as a result of the war (as we know, there had been some forty unaccompanied children on the *Highland Brigade* rejoining their families in Argentina), but possibly there were other reasons and our parents may not have been too happy with what the college had to offer. Luckily for all concerned, a number of families of British descent in southern Chile, as also our old friends the Lucas Bridges, were sending their sons to a relatively new school, The Grange School, in Santiago, Chile. So after several months of idyllic family existence on the farm, in March 1941 we set off with our mother, first to Buenos Aires to buy school clothes.

This meant our first trip in an aeroplane, courtesy of Aeroposta Argentina, who by 1940 were operating Junkers JU52s – three-engined transport planes much used by the Germans for troop-carrying. The civil version carried sixteen passengers and trundled majestically and noisily at 240kph, vibrating with the effort and with the wingtips flapping, taking twelve hours for the 2,000km trip from San Julian to Buenos Aires, fourteen hours from Rio Gallegos. It stopped at every town on the way for refuelling both aircraft and passengers, so inevitably became known as 'the milk run'. Veteran pilots, becoming bored by the long flight, would often come down low enough to amuse themselves if not the passengers by chasing sheep. It was only many years later that I discovered that the height above which sheep will take no notice of aircraft is only about 200 feet (60 metres) – not very high for a passenger-carrying aeroplane. At the time we schoolboys just enjoyed the fun! Present-day jet aircraft of Aerolineas Argentinas fly from Rio Gallegos to Buenos Aires in three hours and do not go chasing sheep.

From Buenos Aires to Santiago, that first time, we went by train – no doubt because of having to take our school trunks. At Retiro station we boarded the Transandino (Trans-Andean) train run by the Buenos Aires Pacific Railway, which was British owned and run, as were all the railways in Argentina at that time. In comfortable sleeping compartments we travelled overnight to Mendoza, where we arrived next morning to discover that the track had been destroyed by an avalanche in the Uspallata Pass. The railway company had laid on a fleet of cars (for first class passengers) and buses (for second class) to convey everybody to Las Cuevas where the train from the Chilean side was waiting.

The rest of the trip was quite spectacular, involving ascending some sections with the help of a rack-and-pinion device under the engine, to help pull the train uphill in the event of ice on the rails. In other sections the train would reverse to proceed in a zig-zag fashion back and forth as the steep slope did not permit the construction of hairpin bends. And then there were the snow sheds. These were a sort of roof stuck onto the side of the mountain and sloping out over the track, to protect the latter from avalanches of snow and rocks. To passengers it seemed little different from a series of rather boring tunnels, until you happened to look out in the gaps between the snow sheds and see the simple and apparently unprotected ledge along the side of the mountain on which the track ran. One is tempted to quote Kipling, whose 'If' hung in every classroom at The Grange, for the Transandino railway was one of the great feats of British railway engineering. (2) 'The eagles is screamin' around us, the river's a-moaning below', from his poem 'The Screw Guns' might equally be applied to the Andes as to the Himalayas.

The Grange

So in due course we arrived at Mapocho station in Santiago at about midnight, to be met by John A.S. Jackson, the headmaster, and Olive Hobbs. The Hobbs family were, like the Bridges, old Patagonian friends from way back. They all went to school in England, and would often spend holidays with the Blakes at Mark's Barn. Olive was single and lived in Santiago, as did Nona, who was married to Humphrey Bloomer, whose son was also at The Grange. Olive was our guardian as well as that of David Bridges who

The new Grange School buildings situated in Tobalaba, Santiago, Chile, with the Andes towering behind.

had been at Lambrook with us and had preceded us to The Grange by a year.

The Grange had been started some twelve years previously by 'Johnny' Jackson and his assistant and partner Captain Graham Balfour, with their wives and Jackson's sister Mrs Scott, whose husband was the bursar. From a small school of a few boys in a private house, it had grown by 1940 into a flourishing establishment of 450 boys, 150 of them boarders, in purpose-built new buildings in Tobalaba. This at the time was right on the outskirts of Santiago, and still surrounded by farmland. I remember maize being grown just across the road. The Prince of Wales Country Club was right next door and we shared their playing fields and swimming pool. Santiago had not then developed the smog problem which affects it today, and one could see clearly across and up to the mountains towering above. 'The school 'neath the Andean range' is a phrase in the school song, and we would watch the snowline creep down and up as the seasons progressed.

It was at that time a truly bilingual establishment – all boys spoke English, classes were in Spanish or English as required, and everybody emerged with a Chilean University Entrance Level *(Bachiller de Humanidades)* and a perfect knowledge of English, even those from wholly Chilean homes. Most of the boys were, naturally, of non-British descent, especially the 300 or so day boys, and most of the 150 boarders were from families in Santiago and so went home every weekend. From further afield, nearly all were British – there was a strong contingent from Concepción in the mid-south who might go home at long weekends, but a hard core of about twenty, including us, came from Argentina, Peru, Bolivia or even further, as well as from Punta Arenas in the far south or Iquique in the far north of Chile. Not more than about 20 per cent of the boys in the school came from English-speaking families – nevertheless everybody spoke English all the time and speaking Spanish was a misdemeanour punishable by both staff and prefects. The usual punishments were 'walking' and 'detention'. The former consisted of spending one's break between classes simply walking round and round the quadrangle, thereby missing whatever fun activities might have been going on elsewhere, or often, and more effectively, being unable to have a quick brush-up to some subject coming up in the next class period! For the occasional severe misbehaviour the cane could be applied, always by Johnny Jackson in person so that the solemnity of being called out of class to go to the headmaster's study was probably a bigger deterrent than the very few strokes actually applied! This regime was fully accepted even by the Chilean parents and nobody thought twice about it.

I was placed, presumably based on reports from Lambrook where I had just started to work towards a scholarship examination for a Public School, in the third year class among boys mostly a year older than me. The Spanish secondary course was called *Humanidades*, lasting six years and giving an entrance qualification for all South American and many North American universities. As I had not done the first two years of the course, I had to sit a special exam covering all the subjects done in the first and second years. Plus of course working up my still shaky Spanish. The teachers there were really first class, both on the English side as well as the Spanish, and I was able to make the grades required. Classes in English covered various subjects, and a high level was achieved, but the only other course available was a special Common Entrance class preparing boys for entry to English Public Schools.

Most of the leading families in Chile were sending some if not all of their sons to The Grange, although the strongly Catholic families would send them to the Jesuit college, the 'Sagrados Corazones', against whom we competed in sport. There were two other British boys' schools near Viña del Mar. Sport figured largely in school life, of course, and The Grange was largely responsible for introducing Rugby football to Chile. The 'OGs' Club (Old Grangeonians Rugby Football Club) is still one of the leading Rugby Union clubs in the country.

Jackson and Balfour had not fallen into the trap of trying to imitate an English Public School. Instead they created something original, both academically and business-wise, which was to prove more stable in the non-English environment. In order to get together capital with which to put up the new buildings, a company had been floated and every parent sending a boy there had to buy a share. In theory they could sell it again when the boy(s) left, but this was considered 'not done', and so before long the school became financially self-sufficient and thus bypassed the problems which bedevil so many private schools when the original principal(s) die or otherwise cease to influence the school.

The company nowadays is run by a board of directors consisting mainly of former pupils, who keep a firm grasp on policy, maintaining the Jackson tradition, and can afford to headhunt excellent staff from Britain as required, while at the same time adapting to local changes – be they educational, social or political. This enabled them to survive the communist regime of the 1960s and the political upheavals which led up to it, so that with the return first to organised government and then to democracy they were able to consolidate, absorbing staff and resources from other private schools which had not been able to withstand the pressure. The Grange today is probably the finest bilingual and coeducational private school in South America.

For the first two years that we were there, the school had three terms, after the English custom, so we did not return to Argentina until the end of the year for the long summer holidays of three months, December to March. For the mid-year holidays we went to a boarding house with a big garden at Peñablanca, midway between Santiago and Valparaiso, run by the Misses Douglas who had two nephews at the school.

At weekends, long and short, there was always a group of boys who did not go out. Being almost all English speakers, they regarded themselves with some degree of accuracy as 'the backbone of the school'. The duty staff was always there to organise special activities, sporting or otherwise. There was a flourishing hiking club at the school, and we would go off camping at weekends, up into the mountains, finding quite unspoilt country just a bus ride away from the capital city.

So the first year at The Grange came to an end and, as on our later trips to and from Santiago, we flew back to Buenos Aires by Panamerican Grace Airways (Panagra) in a Douglas DC3. These luxurious aircraft (compared to a Junkers) actually carried stewardesses on board who served meals in flight and attended to airsick and short-of-breath passengers. The cabins were not pressurised, of course, but beside every seat was an oxygen supply which you could suck through a sterilised mouthpiece as required. Panagra were very proud of their safety record, which was just as well because on most flights one flew *through* the Uspallata Pass, looking *up* at Mount Aconcagua (7,000 metres!), so perfect weather was clearly required! On a few occasions the perfect weather was to be found above a cloud layer which covered the peaks, so one flew unpressurised at about 7,500 metres. I do not remember ever taking oxygen, being young and fit, but plenty of the other passengers did. In my fifteen crossings of the Andes by air, I only remember one which was at all dicey, when we went some distance further south to look for a safe pass to go through, taking three hours instead of one to fly from Mendoza to Santiago.

Farm holidays

Summer holidays at San Julian were a sheer delight for us. Shearing would be under way when we arrived back in mid-December – a very busy time for Arthur and his staff with plenty going on for us to join in. We had our own troop of horses which we had to look after ourselves, and used to spend a lot of time working in the sheep corrals. We had a weekly allowance of pocket money, but at a very early stage we started to earn extra cash at 20 cents an hour (about 35 US cents today) which was at the time the wage of a *peón* – *provided* we were actually doing something which really saved the farm a man. We kept our own accounts and soon learned the value of money in terms of work. 'Fun' work like riding out to help with droving, gathering the flocks or chasing in the half-wild breeding herds of horses did not count, but fairly serious jobs of maintenance and carpentry did. I remember renewing sash cords in the windows for the princely sum of 5 pesos each. We had .22 rifles, and most of our earnings went on buying bullets to shoot foxes and other vermin (for which the farm paid a bounty), hares for their pelts or ostriches for their feathers, which could be sold to dealers at the port. It was then the custom of the big provision stores like the Anónima to give Christmas boxes of goodies to important clients; we boys thought all this wine and nougat stuff was rather a waste of good free giving, so one year Hugh took the box back and negotiated for a free box of .22 bullets from the manager, much to the latter's amusement.

The *Rhea darwini* is a fairly common inhabitant of the Patagonian

John and Hugh with a champion Coronel ram at the San Julian show, 1943. The judges are Dr Lopez Arias (left) and Dr Speroni, of the Ministry of Agriculture.

Hill Cove 'Top settlement', showing Big House with Mt Donald in the background, and the 'forest'.
Watercolour, Dorothea Blake, 1889

Big House, Hill Cove with the French Peaks in the background and the old carpenter's shop at far left.
Watercolour, Dorothea Blake, 1886

'Yeabridge', South Petherton   Watercolour, Dorothea Blake, 1903

Blake children at Hill Cove, with 'Snipe' in old garden, later the cemetery. Looking across the Point Rincon, to Saunders Island on left, Keppel Island in the distance. From left: Violet, Willy, Bridget, Dorothy.   Watercolour, Dorothea Blake, circa 1896

The Point settlement, West Lagoons hills beyond.   Watercolour, Millicent Blake, February 1959

'Loanda', full rigged ship built in 1881 by Bennett Smith, Windsor, Nova Scotia.
Commanded by Capt. Henry Charles Moore Almon from 1889 to 1893.

Oil Painting by Edouard Adams c. 1890. By kind permission of Catherine Coates

Estancia Coronel with Cerro Munro, and San Julian bay in distance.

Watercolour, Millicent Blake, circa 1936

Moreno glacier, Lago Argentino

Photo: J.L. Blake

pampas, and its wing feathers are widely used in Argentina for making feather dusters or *plumeros*. European or Belgian hares had been introduced into Argentina in the very early days, and are common all over the humid pampa and Patagonia. They should not be confused with the so-called 'Patagonian hare' or *mara* (*Dolichotis patagonica*) which is not a hare at all. These animals are not very common in the south, although Hudson (3) saw them often in Rio Negro. They tame very easily and used to wander loose along the paths of the zoo in Buenos Aires, mixing quite freely with the visitors.

Vermin proper – i.e. damaging to the sheep – had been mainly reduced to the birds by our time. Pumas had been driven back to the cordillera by then, although we remember Robert Blake importing bloodhounds to deal with them and Chace had some hair-raising stories about hunting them in caves along Cañadón Paraguay and the Bajo Grande. The large red fox, which can measure 2 metres from nose to the tip of its tail was kept well under control and the little grey fox, 'Don Juan', so called because of its curiosity and the sound of its bark, was too small to bother sheep. Inquisitive and crafty, grey foxes will chew up your rawhide gear during the night unless you bring it into the tent with you, and I have seen one steal an ostrich egg from a pile near a shepherd's *puesto*, roll it down the slope to a fence post and knock it against the wood to break the shell and get at the yolk!

But the carrion birds, the land-born *carancho* or *caracara*, and the seagulls, mainly the southern black-backed or Dominican gull, were the real pests, and still are today. Squeamish readers may now jump a paragraph. These carrion birds will attack a sheep which is 'down', even a perfectly fit one which has fallen or lain awkwardly and cannot get up again because of a heavy fleece, rough terrain or advanced pregnancy. The bird will start its meal usually with the eyes, followed by the tongue. If the sheep is not found by the shepherd at an early stage and helped to her feet, all he can do when he finally gets to the unfortunate animal is to put it out of its misery, whereupon the skinned carcass is promptly polished off by the birds and grey foxes.

The farm paid a princely 30 cents per *carancho* beak (or egg if you found a nest in the spring), but there was nothing anyone could do about the gulls. These birds are even more cruel than the *carancho*, and fly in from the ocean in their hundreds. You could always tell it was killing (mutton) day on a farm, from the cloud of gulls milling round waiting for the offal to be thrown out from the killing shed.

The Belgian hare was also considered a pest, as it abounded and competed with the sheep for the scanty native forage, and more importantly for alfalfa where this had been sown in enclosed paddocks for cutting to make hay. The farm paid 20 cents for a pair of hare's ears and you could sell the dried pelts to fur dealers in the port. Hare stew was always tasty. The older farm boys, who did not go away to boarding school and so had more time, especially in spring, had become expert hunters and trappers and from them I learned how to set snares for hares round the edges of the alfalfa fields. I never got into trapping, always a more skilled operation, but some of the older boys got together sufficient pelts of the wild cat or *gato montés* (*Felis geof-froyi*) to have tanned and made up into a pram rug which they presented to our mother by way of thanks for teaching them to read and write. I can remember Rosemary as a baby sleeping under the nice, warm, black-and-white spotted fur cover.

One of the characteristic sounds of Patagonia is the 'tuky-tuk, tuky-tuk' grunts of the *Tuco tuco* (*Ctenomys magellanica*), a small rodent that burrows beneath bushes, easily heard but not easy to see. There was a large incienso bush, more than 2 metres high and twice that in length near the settlement on the track towards the port, where they abounded. The bush was known to us, inevitably, as the 'tuky-tuk bush' and was a convenient distance for walks. Then there were the *pichis* or small armadillos (*Tatusia hybrida*) and the larger *peludo*, both of which perform a useful ecological function by burying such dead bodies of animals as come their way. The former makes very good eating for humans when roasted in its shell, and has flesh very like that of a sucking pig.

By the age of 14 I was driving, first a tractor (an early Fordson with coil ignition and steel wheels which was best driven standing up), and then the car – a 1939 Ford – on trips into San Julian with the family, conscientiously handing over the wheel to an adult at the town boundary. By the time I was old enough to get a driving licence I had been driving for two years. No test of course – the first driving test I ever took was in Weston-Super-Mare in 1947, and I failed it because of 'over-confidence' and parking too far from the kerb, being used to the wider American vehicles! Once I had a licence I was allowed to drive a pickup truck alone, doing odd jobs, and by my last summer holidays I was driving a lorry.

Boating was an early enthusiasm also, which has never been far in the background – perhaps the tradition of the admiral is in there somewhere. Our first craft was a raft of wood floating on empty dip drums, but it did have a mast and a sail. I was allowed the run of the carpenter's shop when a bit older, and built a canvas canoe called the *Jolly Roger*. There was a big freshwater lagoon up in the Samuel section which never dried out in our time, but it was a long way from any settlement. To sail there thus involved loading raft, tent and camping gear onto the farm lorry and setting off for two or three days. Arthur wisely let us go off under the wing of Alec Mann, the foreman, whose son Duncan, who was about my age, would also be of the party. Perhaps the big attraction of these expeditions was that they involved camping out away from home, and we learned much Patagonian lore from Don Alec. The lagoon was something of a wildlife sanctuary, full

John, Hugh (left) and Eleanor with *Jolly Roger* on the Samuel Lagoon, 1945.

of duck, geese, black-necked swans and the rarer white coscoroba swan, flamingos and other smaller migrants. In 1933 my parents found flamingo nesting there, which had never happened that far south; nor has it happened since.

There was not much social life away from the farm, which we did not mind at all after being away at school all year. We just wanted to be with our own family. Most of the English-speaking families in the district lived, of course, on the farms, and so during much of the summer they were busy with the sheep work just as we were. There might be the occasional *asado* at one or other of the neighbouring farms, with a number of families attending and maybe a bit of tennis, but it would take several hours drive to get there over bumpy dirt roads so such gatherings only tended to happen on special occasions like Christmas or New Year. More usually one would meet people on visits to the port, maybe two or three times a month.

Towards the end of February, however, once shearing was over, there was a bit of a lull in the work so everybody would down tools and head to the port for the annual stock show. Here the leading breeders in the district would exhibit their carefully fed, tended and pampered show rams, competing for prizes and hopefully a final accolade in the form of a handsome price when they were offered for sale on the closing day. The Company was at that time one of the principal Corriedale studs in the Santa Cruz

Territory, so this was for all of us an important event. We would help lead the Company's rams round the ring, but were too young to participate in the various social events which took place at the same time, and would be firmly bundled off back to the farm in the evenings, when there would be dances in the hall of the *Asociación Española de Socorros Mutuos*. (4) For many settlers from further inland, the show was the only annual event of a getting-together nature so there was inevitably a fair amount of celebration. I remember one of our Scots shepherds donning his kilt, plaid, sporran and all, and parading with his bagpipes up and down the main street, full of good imported Scotch and oblivious to the world, followed by a charmed train of town children.

But the Scots were not the only Celts to have taken their culture to Patagonia with them. The *Gallegos* or inhabitants of Galicia in Spain are also Celts, and so have many customs and traditions in common with the Irish, Welsh and Scots. While it is true that they do not wear the kilt, they all shear sheep by tying up the legs (the Highland way, untied, is of Pictish – i.e. Scandinavian – origin and not Celtic), and they play the bagpipes. I can remember the Galician pipes (*gaita Gallega*) being played at San Julian and elsewhere, and young folk in traditional dress dancing the folk dances from the old country.

Music, which was to be important to us all when we were older, did not as yet figure much at home. We had 'done' piano at Lambrook, and Hugh had continued it at The Grange, but I had to give it up due to the pressure of other work. Millicent had most of the Gilbert and Sullivan operetta scores, and we would sing them and other English songs, clustered round the piano, even attempting some part singing. There were a few 78rpm records for the Aeolian Vocalion gramophone, which we sometimes played on wet days (there are few of these in Patagonia!) The radio was a serious thing: it was driven by an accumulator and lived in the sitting room (i.e. parental domain). It was used only to listen to the BBC news and 'Radio Newsreel'. There was, after all, a war on.

The war as such did not impinge much on our adolescent lives, but our parents were extremely involved. The Anglo-Argentine business community had instituted a blacklist of commercial firms with German capital or backing, some of which were important in Patagonia. They were firmly boy-cotted, even though lack of supplies or services at that particular moment made farm operations difficult. The firm of Waldron and Wood who repre-sented in Buenos Aires many of the British-owned farming companies including the San Julian Sheep Farming Company, acquired a private air-craft ostensibly to be able to visit their clients in the south. These included both Condor and Cullen Station on Tierra del Fuego. This plane came and went quite freely, and nothing was ever said, at least in our hearing, but we did observe that visiting company directors or businessmen known to us

142

Aircraft totally subscribed for by the British community of Rio Gallegos, 1914-1918.

San Julian tinsmith 'Freddy' Gibbs with some of the scrap metal collected in and around San Julian, the largest amount of all British communities in Argentina 1939-45.

143

would often be accompanied by other gentlemen, said to be from the British Embassy, who would visit once, presumably saw what they came to see or met who they had to meet, and then were never seen again . . .

The British community of the River Plate contributed a great deal to the Allied war effort. At least 2,000 young men and over 500 women from Argentina and Uruguay went off to serve in the forces, and some 200 made the supreme sacrifice. Serious money was also raised and sent to Britain to purchase fighter aircraft for the RAF. In the Great War the British community of Rio Gallegos alone had donated two DH4 aircraft to the war effort, but now fundraising was organised on a wider basis from Buenos Aires. The 'Fellowship of the Bellows' was dreamed up and from business firms and private contributors raised quite important sums of money. Spitfires for the Battle of Britain at first, then a whole squadron of Typhoons and later a Mosquito bomber were all subscribed by the 'Bellows'.

Money was further contributed and garments knitted by the women for the comfort of the troops, all of which was channelled through the Red Cross. Scrap metal and other second-hand materials were also collected and sold. The local handyman and tinsmith, Freddy Gibbs, a pure-bred Cockney from Bow, collected an impressive amount for the war effort. Fundraising activities of all sorts took place, including fêtes and *asados*, popular gatherings hosted by the British at which the non-British locals always contributed generously.

This seems a good place to quote another of Arthur's Ballads, written about this time. The people it refers to were all in and around San Julian in the early 1940s. Jack Clarke was the manager of the Swift freezer and the others were all farmers, 'Patt' being short for Patterson. Arthur used to keep a mouth-organ in the glove box of the car, and would bring it out to while away the time on long trips when somebody else was driving.

San Julian Fair

Arthur Blake
Tune: Widdecombe Fair

Jack Clarke, Jack Clarke, lend me your old car,

All along, down along, out a long lea,

For I want for to go to Hotel Miramar,

Wi' Bob Patt, Johnny Scott, Ronnie Fraser, Ronald Lambert, Tommy Kyle, Charlie Kemp, Old Uncle Jack Frazer and all,
Old Uncle Jack Fraser and all.

And when shall I see again my old car?   All along, etc.
By Friday soon or Saturday noon,   Wi' Bob Patt, etc.

But Friday came, and Saturday noon,
And Jack Clarke his old car had not yet rattled home,

So Jack he climbed up to the top of Mount Wood,
And he see'd his old car down a-bogged deep and good,

Now Jack Clarke's poor old car her just faded and died,
And Jack he sat sat down on a bush and he cried,

But this isn't the end of this shocking affair,
Nor though they be tight, of the horrid career, of Bob Patt,

When the wind whistles cold on the pampa at night,
Jack Clarke's old car doth appear ghastly white,

And all the night long be heard groaning and jolts,
From Jack Clarke's old car and her rattling bolts, and Bob Patt, etc.

Note: Mount Wood was a prominent hill just behind the freezer, not far from the mouth of the bay. It was named after John Wood, boatswain of Narborough's expedition of 1670, whose name can still be seen carved in the rock.

School leaver

At the beginning of March each year, Hugh and I would return to school – first by Aeroposta to Buenos Aires, where we would be met by Frank Matthews of Waldron and Wood, and were put up by kind friends of our parents while we were shepherded through travel document processes. Both Argentina and Chile at that time were rather particular on the subject – the latter-day easing of border crossing had not yet taken place. Then we would board the luxurious Panagra DC3 for the six-hour flight to Los Cerrillos airport in Santiago.

If at Lambrook we learned much, at The Grange we filled out both in the classroom and out. I coped with the transition to Spanish for most classes and enjoyed the other aspects of life, which were many. Virtually all sports were played, and there was a first class physical training and athletics instructor who had represented Chile at the Olympic Games. Every end of year there was big PT display put on, with the entire school of 450 marching and countermarching to a regimental band, with more complicated exercises like handsprings and back-flips by the initiated.

The school was, inevitably, much integrated with the local British community and joined with it for various events connected with the war effort. I can remember a large group of us singing 'Land of Hope and Glory' with great emotion at the Caupolicán Theatre. Once a year the school lent its premises for a British community fête. Worthy Brits came and put up stands – a coconut shy, tombola, Aunt Sally etc. – and we boys were in demand to help man the stalls. We were happy to do this for a while, as it saved any temptation to spend our own pocket money, but we would soon sneak away to the assembly hall, where a real live band was playing for dancing with *real girls*. People brought their sisters, and the girls' schools Dunalastair and Santiago College came *en masse* so it was usually possible to get introduced to a dancing partner who patiently put up with our quite untutored steps. I remember one girl remarking conversationally, 'A bit tricky, these sambas, aren't they?', charmingly glossing over the fact that I clearly did not know how to dance a samba!

I duly finished the prescribed *bachillerato* course in December 1944, but before this both my parents and I had had to do some hard thinking. With the end of the war more or less in sight, a return to England was at least foreseeable and the question of university arose. Not all the Somerset Blakes (being Dissenters) had gone to university, although there was a link with Wadham College, Oxford, from where the admiral had graduated in 1618 and to which others including cousin Humphrey had gone in more recent times. The Worsleys on the other hand had gone to Cambridge – my grand-father, Philip, his brother, Uncle Arthur and both my uncles, Edgar and Francis, had all been to Emmanuel College and there were other family con-nections. My father himself would probably have gone to Pembroke were it not for the First World War, and he felt keenly his own lack of scientific training. He was far ahead of his time in the sheep-ranching world, having jointly with William Cooper and Nephews, the leading manufacturers of sheep dip at the time, more or less broken the back of the interminable war against scab (Chapter 5). Reading widely, he had cautiously ventured into sowing exotic (to Patagonia) seeds to see if the native pastures could be improved, and was attempting to breed stud sheep using selection methods whose genetics had not yet been fully researched at that time. Much of this, of course, rubbed off onto me and by the time I went back to The Grange at the beginning of 1944 I had committed myself to a farming career.

Edgar Worsley had been in touch with Emmanuel College, where his former tutor, Edward Welbourne, was now senior tutor and largely respon-sible for admissions – at that time still very much a matter for the colleges. Although the Chilean *bachillerato* would give me entry to most universities in America, North and South, Cambridge still required Latin and we were advised that if I sat the Overseas School Certificate and obtained a sufficient number of passes with credit, I would be able to enter without having to sit an entry examination on arrival in Britain. So I went back to The Grange in 1945 for an extra year. Johnny Jackson took me on as a pupil-teacher, and I helped out with staff duties part of the time while studying for the School Certificate, together with a classmate, John Street, who had one of those razor-sharp brains which always put him top of the class without seeming to open a book. For Latin I went to a brilliant Jesuit priest downtown at the

Sagrados Corazones school. He made the language all so clear and alive –
I remember reading about Hannibal crossing the Alps in the original Latin,
with as much enjoyment as one might read in English about Wellington's
Peninsular War exploits.

As pupil-teachers we were 'staff' and so had much more freedom than the
boys, even the prefects. The Prince of Wales Country Club just next door
across the playing fields filled up at weekends with families and on Saturday
nights dancing took place to a gramophone. We soon joined a pleasant
group of boys and girls of our own age, and were also asked to birthday and
similar parties at people's homes. I was also asked to a very different party:
the golden wedding of Don Ernesto Hobbs and señora, which took place at
Olive's house in Providencia. When I walked in, I was greeted by a loud and
shrill female voice: 'Oh, there is a young man I have always wanted to
meet!', which made me want to sink through the floor, as I was really quite
shy socially at that time. This was Ethel Hobbs, the eldest daughter, who had
spent many school holidays at Mark's Barn, and wanted to catch up with the
Blakes.

Soon it was exam time again, and we duly sat the Overseas School
Certificate without difficulty. But exam results were one thing, and actual
places at college were another. Although we heard back at San Julian some
weeks later that I had made the grade, John Street and I obtaining the
highest marks in the overseas examinations of that year, we were advised
that the war now being over, the demand for places was such that I could
not hope for an actual vacancy for another two years. So while Hugh
returned to The Grange in March 1946 for his final year, I put in useful
work on the farm.

We had always ridden and helped generally in the work, but now I
learned the thrill and wonder of working a good sheepdog – one that had
been Bob's. Coached patiently by some of the shepherds, particularly one
Angel Domínguez, I learned other 'camp' skills such as how to stay on a
tricky horse, how to repair (and later make) my own rawhide riding gear and
how to throw the *bolas*. These are three stone balls encased in rawhide and
fastened by twisted thongs to a central point. If whirled around and thrown
(usually at full gallop) they will entangle the legs of any prey and bring it
down. Many shepherds still carry a small set for catching ostrich or baby
guanaco. A full-sized set of *bolas* can bring down a horse, and was still used
at that time for wild horses. The breeding herds on Coronel amounted to
some two to three hundred head: stallions, mares, foals and yearlings all ran
together and bringing them in once a year was an exhilarating process.
Sometimes some crafty old mare would refuse to be rounded up and kept
breaking away, followed by others, until finally the foreman in charge of the
round-up would order, 'Ball her!' whereupon the most skilled riders would
shake out their *bolas* to entangle her front legs and bring her down with a

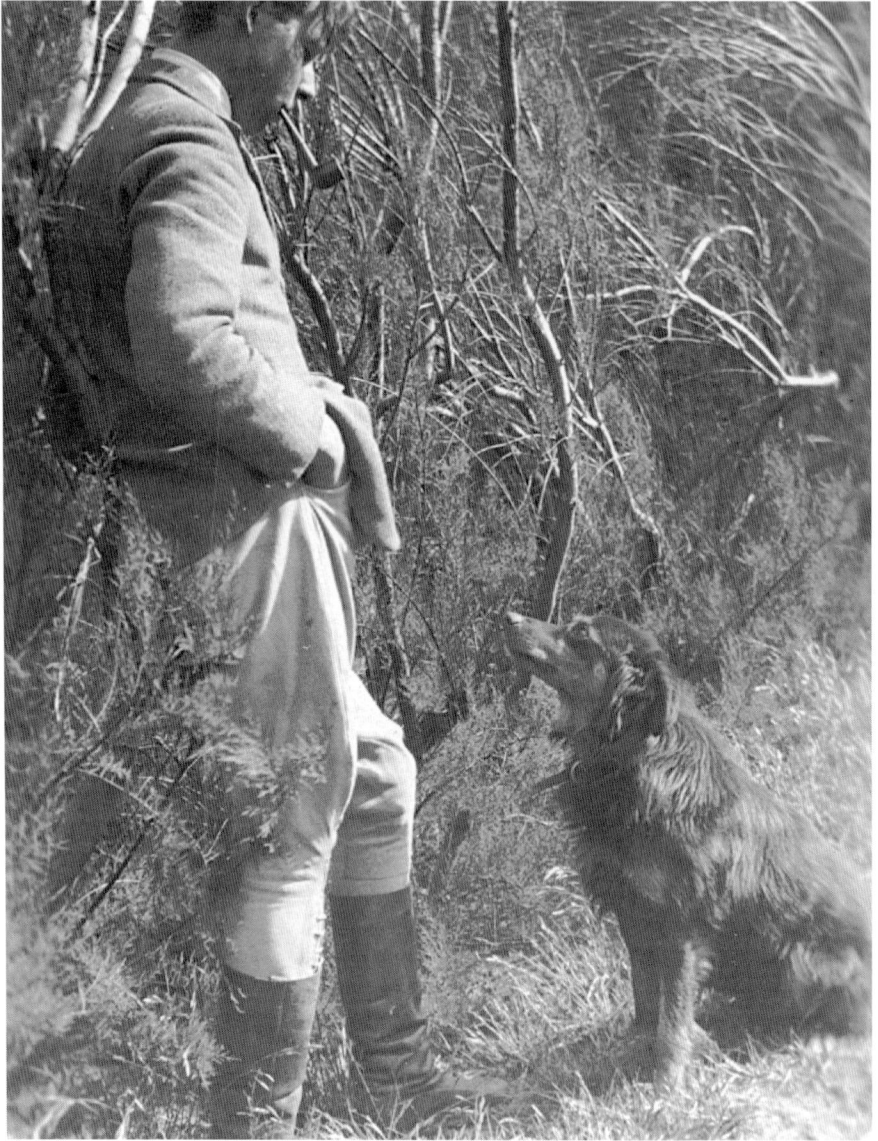

Robert Blake III with Toby, his favourite working sheepdog at San Julian, 1939.

thump. Once untangled, she would usually rise meekly and look around for the safety of the herd. I never saw a horse that needed balling twice, nor any horse nor man injured.

The animal psychology aspect of all this was of course to teach the errant beast that it was not safe to break away on its own, that it was much more comfortable tucked into a herd with the others and that man (or rather the man/horse animal) was the boss. The principle applies to all 'domesticated' livestock and we will meet it again concerning cattle in Chapter 17. In spite of the thrills, however, we found chasing and balling not really practical and more risky than we youngsters cared to admit at the time, and the process was already under way to detect the wilder mares and give them a short taming course to calm them down, after which bringing in the breeding herds became a dull affair conducted at a smart trot, rather than at a gallop!

Arthur also insisted that I learn 'the other side of sheep farming', meaning the meat trade as opposed to the wool, so I worked at the San Julian freezer, which was run by the Swift Meat Packing Company, for the killing season from March to May. It was indeed valuable experience and has stood me in good stead since then.

In May, things on the farm became very much easier for Arthur with the return of Lionel Pickering from the war. His younger brother Tom had been filling in adequately but Alec Mann, the foreman, was due for retirement, the Kennedy family at the Cabo Curioso shanty had returned to Britain at the end of the war and others like Archie Macdonald, who had come from the Western Isles and learned both his Spanish and his English in Patagonia, were getting on in years. Lionel had gone first into the Tank Corps, but found he suffered from claustrophobia when shut up inside a tank so to get out of there he had volunteered for the Paratroops. He dropped at Arnhem and was taken prisoner, and spent the rest of the war in a German POW camp. On repatriation after VE Day in 1945, most South American volunteers were demobilised fairly quickly, so Lionel soon arrived back at San Julian. He had been engaged to be married to Mary Mann before leaving for the war, so this wedding took place in April 1946, followed shortly by the marriage of Tom Pickering to Lydia Mann. These two families were to form the backbone of Coronel for the next thirty-two years.

Since our second year at The Grange, when the school went over to the general local custom of having only two terms in the school year, separated by a three- or four-week holiday in July, we had been returning to Argentina for the winter holidays. Eleanor had started boarding at St Hilda's school at Hurlingham in 1943 and Rosemary in 1945, so our parents would come up to Buenos Aires and we would all have a holiday together at an original (for that time) sort of guest-estancia or dude ranch called 'La Quebrada' on the western side of the Cordoba Hills. Although in later years the area became a favourite one for semi-retired Brits to build retirement homes in, at that time it was fairly out in the sticks, although it combined all the amenities of an estancia with hotel comforts. There would always be other families holidaying with youngsters, and both St George's and Northlands schools from Buenos Aires would send any boys and girls respectively who were unable to return to their homes. The latter were firmly chaperoned by their head-mistress, the (to us) formidable Miss Winifred Brightman, whom her girls adored, much to our surprise. Among the boys was Christopher Bonner, whose father Jack Bonner was the owner of San Carlos station on the East Falkland; Michael Weaver whose father, like Arthur, was manager of a large sheep property in Patagonia; and others who we were to meet at different times later in life.

Our last holiday together at La Quebrada was in July 1946, after which we went our several ways: Arthur and Millicent to the farm at San Julian; Eleanor and Rosemary to St Hilda's; Hugh back to The Grange for his final year there; and I to Montevideo to catch the *Fitzroy* for the Falklands, where I was to spend a year at Hill Cove before continuing on to England.

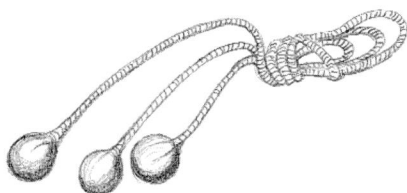

Notes

1 The *Casa Rosada* is the seat of the executive power, situated in the historic *Plaza de Mayo,* and both symbolically and in practice the centre of government, like the White House in Washington. The president has an official residence in Olivos, known as the *Quinta Presidencial.*
2 Built in 1891, the Trans-Andean Railway was surveyed in 1871 by Robert Crawford, itself no mean feat, which he wrote up in his book *Across the Pampas and the Andes.*
3 See *Idle days in Patagonia* by William Henry Hudson.
4 'Spanish Mutual Aid Society'. The Spanish communities in many towns in Argentina were originally better organised and more integrated than the British, although later they became much divided by the political tensions which had given rise to the Spanish Civil War.

9

To the Falklands

Fox Bay West

The SS *Fitzroy* belonged to the Falkland Islands Company and was a tiny
vessel of some 500 tons, carrying passengers and cargo on a regular service
between Port Stanley and Montevideo, enlivened by occasional trips round
the Islands and, roughly once a year, a trip to Punta Arenas. She enjoyed the
rather doubtful distinction of being the only ship trading out of Montevideo
to board which you went *down* the gangplank instead of up. She was commanded at that time by Captain Bill Johnson, a jovial Irishman, and crewed
mainly by Falkland Islanders headed by Billy Goss, the first officer.

Due to the Argentine sovereignty claim, no ship carrying a foreign flag
was allowed to trade between two Argentine ports, so the Falkland Islands
trade was ostensibly carried on with Montevideo rather than Buenos Aires.
This did not however interfere with Argentine firms selling goods for hard
sterling cash, so most of the bulk provisions for the Islands in fact came from
Buenos Aires, after first being shipped over to Montevideo.

Passenger accommodation on the *Fitzroy* consisted of a cluster of three-
berth cabins at the foot of an internal stairwell known as the 'Snake Pit',
although on that first trip I was allotted the only single-berth cabin, a sort of
box up on the boat deck. On the main deck there was a small saloon for
sitting in on one side, and on the other the dining saloon presided over by
the Chilean steward, 'Johnny' Baldrini. I am a reasonably good sailor, so was
able to partake of most meals, and the four-day voyage went by quietly

enough watching dolphins, whales and penguins and playing cards with a group of Royal Navy telegraphists who were going down to man the signals station. In these days of satellite communications it is as well to recall the former vital importance of the transatlantic (north and south) submarine cables. Some of these had been laid right at the beginning of the century, but the cable ships run by the Western Telegraph Co. (later Cable and Wireless) continued to operate right through the Second World War and after. The South Atlantic cable did not end in the River Plate, but continued down to Port Stanley. By the Second World War, most shipping, naval and mercantile, had direct radio communications with UK, Germany or wherever, but for business and trade the telegraph was universally used. Most commercial firms, including all sheep farms, would have a copy of the Bentley five-letter code, and such important operations as selling the wool would be carried out by coded telegraph. With a bit of practice it was possible to compress several lines of argument or discussion into a few groups of code, and every firm would have a telegraphic address.

So we duly arrrived at Port Stanley and steamed in, past Sparrow Cove with the hulk of the *Great Britain* lying at anchor, through the Narrows and into Stanley Harbour, with two other demasted sailing ship hulks at anchor in the bay, now used for storing wool bales. We tied up at West Jetty and I was met by Captain Roberts, colonial manager of the Falkland Islands Co. (FIC), who kindly put me up at Stanley House.

When Robert Blake Senior removed with his family to Yeabridge in 1898

SS *Fitzroy* leaving Montevideo for Port Stanley.

he handed over the management of Hill Cove to Sydney Miller, who had already been assisting him there for eight years. Miller had first worked for Wickham Bertrand over at Roy Cove, but they were not temperamentally suited and the story goes that one day after a heated discussion Miller sat Mr Bertrand on a hot stove, saddled his horse and set out for Hill Cove. Mr Blake was busy at the time laying rocks to provide a hard causeway across Kingdom Creek, between Hill Cove settlement proper and the Point, when Miller rode up to ask for a job. Blake said, 'Let me see your hands', and observing that said hands were properly calloused, took him on on the spot.

Miller managed Hill Cove for thirty-one years and in his turn became an almost legendary figure. On his death in 1929 he was succeeded by his son Syd, who only stayed for two years as having married Bet Felton he was required to move over to Roy Cove as manager for the firm of Bertrand and Felton, on the death of old Wickham Bertrand. To fill the Hill Cove job, Holmested, Blake & Co. Ltd took on Hugh Harding who had worked hitherto mainly for the FIC as manager of their North Arm station on the East Falkland, and he continued as manager until his retirement in 1952.

Captain Roberts informed me that, as the Hardings were away on UK leave, I was to go to Fox Bay West for a couple of months until their return. So as the *Fitzroy* was calling at Fox Bay on her very next trip, after only a couple of days in Stanley we sailed again for this port, the communications and government centre for the West Falkland which has no town as such, only the various farm settlements, each being its own port. Fox Bay however, in addition to two farms – Fox Bay East (Packe Bros) and Fox Bay West (FIC) – had a government wireless station from where telegrams could be sent all over the world, and a doctor who had his house there and prescribed mostly over the telephone, but had his own troop of horses and a guide. Some of his calls could involve a ride of eight or more hours to distant farms, being re-horsed along the way from shepherd's house to shepherd's house. There was not then, nor would there be for another ten years, any form of cross-island motorised transport.

The settlements of sheep farms in the Falklands bore a general resemblance to those found on the coast, comprising a shearing shed, dip, sheep yards, a cookhouse for the single men, a manager's house, store and office and a varying number of houses for families. The main difference was that in the Islands the shearing shed and maybe a bale store would be sited near the beach with access to a jetty, most of which were provided with a small set of rails down which bale-carrying trolleys would be run when loading wool. Not all farm ports had enough depth of water to allow a ship even the size of the *Fitzroy* to tie up alongside, but there were several smaller vessels around which carried much of the inter-island traffic.

Fox Bay West had been settled originally by Baillon and Stickney who had shared the chartering of the bark 'Diane' in 1867 with James Lovegrove

Waldron, but had later sold out to the FIC. The manager was C.H. 'Charlie' Robertson, whose father James had been brought over from New Zealand in 1895 as Assistant Government Stock Inspector with the specific mission of ridding the islands of sheep scab. The Chief Inspector, J. I. Mowat, returned to New Zealand once scab had indeed been wiped out, but James Robertson married Theresa Carey and stayed on, becoming manager of Port Stephens which bounds with Fox Bay West at the south end of the West Falkland. Charlie had spent some time in Australia as a young man and his wife Anne was Australian. I lodged with them in the Big House, but had my meals with the foreman, Bob Pearson and his wife.

It was September, early spring, which is a time of little activity on sheep farms. The ewes were heavy in lamb, and indeed began to drop the new crop towards the end of the month, so the main activity of the shepherds consisted of riding round the flocks daily, picking up ewes who had fallen on their backs or into streams, and generally making sure all was well. This activity is known to Patagonians and Kelpers alike as 'running camp' (*recorriendo campo*). 'Kelpers' are Falkland Islanders born and bred, but there has been so much contact with the coast over the years that a very large number of Spanish terms are in common use. These mostly relate to horses, their gear and colours, and sheep and their working. Among purely English (or Scottish) terms we find that a dog by definition means a canine used for working sheep, usually a Border or Welsh collie although an Australian Kelpie would also qualify as a dog. All other dogs, however, from Alsatians and Great Danes to Pekinese and Yorkshire terriers, are 'poodles', or more likely 'bloody poodles'.

Hill Cove

At Fox Bay I had been employed as a cadet and got landed with all the odd and supposedly unskilled jobs. The fact that my Uncle Robert was at that time a director of the FIC in no way altered this, indeed the opposite approach was more usual and I was expected to work and behave just the same as everyone else. Personally I had no problem with any of this, having learned at an early age at San Julian that being the son of the boss conferred no privilege whatever. I had not yet heard the story of Blake, Miller and the calloused hands, but was perfectly happy working as builder's labourer to an old mason, laying the foundations for a new house. It was dry stone work so I learned how to build a dry stone wall!

I had, of course, brought my own saddle and riding gear, and was able to pick up a dog called 'Queen' so when in October lamb-marking time came along I was ready to join in. This operation, one of the key ones in the sheep year, involves gathering the ewes and lambs together in order to put an own-

John on Betty.

ership and age mark into their ears, castrate the males and cut off all the tails. The lambs are quite small, mostly four- to six-weeks old, but many are younger and quite unused to being handled. The ewes, like all females with small young, are nervous and touchy. This makes for an extremely tricky operation which can test the shepherding skills of all concerned, and the leadership of the man in charge even more so. No attempt is made to bring the flock into the main yards, but special sets of lamb-marking pens are built at strategic sites, towards which the sheep are gathered, slowly and quietly. If all goes well, not too many ewes will have become separated from their lambs, and there will be one or more at the front, either without a lamb or with her own at her side who will step out firmly and lead the flock in between the wide-open wings of the yard. At this point the boss gives the word, everybody dismounts and nets are spread out behind the flock so that any panic-stricken lambs who have lost their mothers can be physically restrained, and so the whole flock is firmly shut in behind the gates of the pens. Sometimes things go wrong – ewes lose their lambs before getting to the pens, and before you know it there are fifty or more motherless lambs chasing round wildly, the same number of ewes ditto, losing all respect for man or dog and it only takes one lamb to break through the encircling but not yet closed ring for it to be followed by others and you have a 'lamb-break'. Lambs and ewes scatter to the horizon and there is scant chance of getting them back that day.

Once the flock is safely penned up, everybody can relax as they have been out since before daybreak some three to four hours previously. Horses are tethered or hobbled, gear loosened, and all hands settle down to eat their sandwiches and drink tea which has been brewed up nearby by the 'net boy'. That year at Fox Bay, this was my job. The nets, kettle etc. were carried by a packhorse or *carguero* so I added to my rapidly expanding camp expertise the art of loading a pack saddle. I was tutored in this by one of the shepherds, Charlie Poole. His father had been a legendary figure, sailing his own cutter round the Islands. He was reputed to have been somewhat of a pirate, and was certainly a very tough character who, having fallen overboard in an advanced state of drunkenness, was shot in the water by his own crew. Charlie, by contrast, was a peaceable soul, although his daughter Emmy, who cooked for Mrs Robertson at the Big House, was a hard-boiled young lady whose forthright speech doubtless came from her grandfather.

The actual work consisted of catching the lambs, putting in the earmarks, castrating the males, cutting off the tails and letting the lambs go outside the pens. Meantime, the ewes were counted and let go to find their own lambs. If the job of gathering is done properly the ewes will have become separated from their young not far away, but it is usual to have a man out on horseback with a quiet dog to keep the ewes from straying too far, and the pens have to be sited near good feed and water. We will see later the vital importance of lambing percentage (number of lambs produced per hundred ewes) for the viability of a sheep ranching enterprise. In the Falklands, lambing rates tend to be on the low side for a variety of reasons so every effort is made to avoid lamb loss of any sort.

Soon after the end of lamb-marking at Fox Bay West, word came down from Hill Cove that Mr and Mrs Harding had returned and I should get over there to join them. This involved a ride across country, and Dave Mackay from the Teal River shepherd's house came down with horses to get me. Knowing that I would have to ride up sooner or later, I had spent some of my spare time at Fox Bay stitching myself a pair of travelling saddle-bags so as to carry my essential clothes and belongings. My suitcase got itself to Hill Cove by some convenient ship several weeks later. It was about 50km across country from Fox Bay to Hill Cove, and this could be done non-stop in about eight hours, changing horses *en route*. On this occasion however I was let off lightly, as the first day we only rode as far as Teal River. The next day we were to help gather Mount Donald camp, along the south side of the mountains, a more useful occupation than just travelling from Teal River to Hill Cove.

Dave Mackay was one of the few Falkland Island shepherds who had put in a serious amount of time working on farms on the coast, and he knew Patagonian lore and customs better than most. Although much of the farming ways are similar both sides of the water, often I would find that the

Island ways had got stuck, whereas on the coast we had found a better way. Later on I would be in a position to put new ways into practice, but that first season I was very junior and just observed and kept quiet. Starting with Dave and his wife Rosie, and continuing with most of the other people at Hill Cove, I found a new attitude towards myself. At Fox Bay I had been just a junior cadet; at Hill Cove as far as work was concerned I still was, but because I was a Blake there was something different in the relationship. Most called me 'Mr John', but there was nothing subservient about it – on the contrary the fact of being one of the owner's family made it even more incumbent on me to buckle down and learn all there was to learn, which was plenty.

So we spent a night at Teal River, and I got my first introduction to the etiquette of putting up at shepherds' houses, although I was already *au fait* with most of the customs after having had my meals with the Pearsons at Fox Bay. But at Teal River, on being asked what kind of eggs one liked for breakfast, instead of boiled, scrambled etc. the choice was hen, duck, tame goose, wild goose, mollymauk (albatross) or gentoo (penguin). All these eggs (and others) were to be found for the collecting, and the thrifty shepherds' wives always had plenty stored away.

The next day we helped to gather Mount Donald camp (1) and drive the assembled flock up over Hell's Kitchen and down to paddocks near Hill

Hill Cove, 1947, viewed from Kingdom Creek, looking towards the French Peaks with the road to the Point between gorse hedges in the foreground.

Cove proper for shearing during the coming week. 'The Kitchen' was so named, not for being particularly hot, but for being difficult to cross through the abundant peat bogs. It was, however, the only convenient pass over the mountain chain which divides the Hill Cove property, and indeed the West Falkland Island. I was made welcome by Hugh Harding and his wife Beat, who put me up with them at the Big House. This was as comfortable as the San Julian house, with all mod cons except electricity, 'Aladdin' incandescent mantle kerosene lamps being used for lighting. Peat was the only fuel used for cooking and heating throughout the Islands, and its cutting, carting and handling took up a lot of time and labour. Indeed, although life was fairly comfortable, it was all done with a great deal of effort.

Beat had two maids in the kitchen, a cowman-gardener to milk the cows and tend the garden (what you didn't grow you didn't have) and a peat boy to chop up the day's supply of peat – say six to ten buckets-full – into 'nublings' or pieces just the right size for burning in the open-front 'Stanley' range, and carry away the ashes the maids put outside the back door (good peat can give out plenty of heat, but leaves a lot of ash). Open-fronted peat grates heated the living and dining rooms, and the water heater in the bathroom was lit every day during shearing, and twice a week during the rest of the year. Running water was piped in from a stream, and like everywhere else in the Islands was brown in colour, usually about that of whisky and water, but after heavy rain it could be much darker so that you could hardly see yourself in the bath. Rainwater ('white' water) from the roofs was caught and carefully stored in barrels or tanks for washing clothes. This took place every Monday, when the peat boy would light the fire under the copper out in the wash house and lunch was always cold mutton.

Hill Cove was unique in having two settlements: at the Top Settlement there was the Big House, houses for the cowman-gardener and a shepherd, the farm store, a carpenter's shop and a farm office adjoining the Big House. Near the Top Settlement but separate from it was the dip with its yards, which was supplied with water from a stream running down from the French Peaks. Some 2.5km away was the Point, which as its name implies was beside the sea with a jetty at the end of it. Backing up from the jetty were the bale store, skin shed, try-works, killing shed and shearing shed with its yards. The cookhouse housed and fed the single men, and at that time there were three other houses, one for the foreman, one for the head navvy and one for a shepherd. A cart track ran from top to Point, across Kingdom Creek over the rocked causeway built by Robert Blake and Sydney Miller all those years ago. Apart from Teal River, there were shepherds' houses at Crooked Inlet, Byron Sound, Shallow Bay and Main Point (see map), bringing the number of men employed to fifteen or sixteen counting the manager and the cook. At that time, on the coast, it was usual to reckon one man per thousand sheep as well as bringing in contract labour to do the shearing. Hill

Cove was running about 28–30,000 sheep – i.e. about 2,000 per man, and that included doing the shearing.

Shearing

With a workforce of this size everybody had to hop around to get all the work done. It was not possible to gather and drive in the flocks one after the other so as to keep the shearing and pressing going continuously, as I had been accustomed to at San Julian, even though the Falkland Islanders were generally, man for man, far more skilled and productive than the labour on the coast. So we would all go out and gather in several flocks, hold them in nearby paddocks, then set to and shear them. Hand shears (blades) were used, as they leave slightly more wool than machine shears on the shorn animal which affords a bit of protection in the event of cold, wet weather. There were eight stands or shearing positions in the shed, so the eight best shearers (shepherds usually) clipped the wool off while the younger boys picked up the fleeces and threw them onto slatted tables. I was given the job of skirting and rolling the fleeces, which were then classed by the foreman and put into quite large bins. Once the flocks in hand had been shorn, shearing would stop, the accumulated wool was pressed up by the navvy boss and his gang of three or four while the shepherd gang set about returning the shorn sheep to their camps and bringing in more.

My 'mate' on the rolling table was 'Old Ted' Johnson, the retired foreman. He had been brought out from Somerset by Robert Blake Senior many years before, had worked all his life at Hill Cove and his family was still very much integrated with it. His eldest son, Eric, had succeeded him as foreman; another, Alfie, was shepherd at the Top Settlement while a third, Les, had completed the circle by returning to South Petherton and was cowman for Uncle Norman Blake at his farm at South Harp. Old Ted lived in Stanley, but came out every year to help with shearing.

The wool bales were stored under cover until a ship came to collect them. This might be the *Fitzroy* or the *Philomel*, a small coasting steamer owned by the government. When this happened, everybody dropped their usual occupation and became a stevedore. First the incoming cargo was offloaded, and was either piled on the jetty or stowed away by the farm men in the sheds. Then the wool bales were rolled onto a trolley which ran on its track downhill and out along the jetty to the ship's side, where the bales were loaded by the ship's derricks and stowed by its crew. Hours of working were dictated by the tides, and the process often continued well into the night. If the ship was the *Fitzroy* doing a trip round the islands, there would be passengers as well who would visit either Big House or other houses and it all became quite a social occasion.

Hill Cove shearers at the beginning of the century. The scene would have been similar in 1946.

Social events otherwise were few and far between. At Christmas on the farms it was usual to string together Christmas Day, Boxing Day, Falkland Islands Day (theoretically 8 December) with the nearest weekend so as to obtain the 'Christmas holiday'. Shearing was suspended, and one or other of neighbouring farms would play host to the rest. My first Falkland Christmas was at Port Howard, where I met the local gentry. Beat was the sister of Keith Luxton of Chartres (Anson and Luxton), and their sister Babs was married to 'Wick' Clements, the manager of Fox Bay East (Packe Bros) and nephew of old Wickham Bertrand. The Luxton's mother had died quite young, and Mr Luxton (Senior) married again, this time to Connie Miller, Syd's sister, who was widowed by the time I got to know them all. Beat and Connie were firm friends, neither had children and both were magnificent horsewomen. We will meet them again later on. Connie lived in Stanley, but would come out to the West, where she kept her own troop of horses, from time to time to visit her friends and relations on the various farms.

Our hosts at Port Howard were Mr and Mrs Pole Evans, one of the few Falklands families I had met previously. Mrs Orissa Evans was the sister of Frank Lewis of Port Santa Cruz, their father having been a missionary with Thomas Bridges both at Ushuaia and on Keppel Island. (2) The Lewis family had also settled several properties near Santa Cruz, and we had met them all at the Phoenix Hotel in Buenos Aires the previous winter. A cousin, Maurice Lewis, was at that time managing Douglas station on the East Falkland. Mr Evans was called 'Old Pole' to distinguish him from his son Douglas, then not long married to Mary Woodgate, who came from a Buenos Aires family.

The houses at the host farm were bursting at the seams of course, the Big House included, and people slept in dormitories according to sex, many of the men on the floor. One day was spent riding there and another getting home, and the remainder in sleeping, eating and drinking (usually in that order). In the evenings dances took place in the cookhouse. These were lively affairs directed by a master of ceremonies. Recorded music was scorned, and anybody who could play an accordion or maybe a violin would play for the reels, country and old-fashioned dances which were the order of the day. There was a fair amount of drinking, but seldom any unpleasantness and anybody who got out of hand would be quietly bundled away by older and wiser heads. A married man was allowed one bottle of spirits per week, and a single man half a bottle, either good imported duty-free Scotch or navy rum from the West Indies. Beer was sold freely, but was expensive as it was imported, bottled, from Uruguay. A surprising amount of fizzy lemonade, concocted and bottled in Stanley, was also consumed.

Among the visitors was Mr Ted Mathews, out on a directorial visit as he was on the boards of both the Port Howard and Hill Cove companies. He had a bed in our room (with half a dozen others), and I achieved notoriety when I fired a pillow at him one night when he was snoring rather loudly. Fortunately it was taken in good part, as indeed intended, and did not affect my future career. Looking back now, it might even have helped it, as ten years later it was Ted Mathews who offered me the job of manager of Condor.

We will meet most of the other 'Westers' (inhabitants of the West Falkland) later on in this narrative, so for the time being let us return to Hill Cove. Shearing continued well into January, and was followed by a number of jobs such as haymaking and peat carting. Robert Blake Senior had sown down several paddocks round the top settlement with improved English grasses, so the hay from these had to be cut, dried and carried to the barn where it was stacked ready for the winter, to be used for feeding the working (riding) horses. Horse-drawn equipment was used, except for one paddock which was too steep for a mower so had to be cut with a scythe. Thus I learned how to use a scythe.

Peat being the only domestic fuel available in the Islands at that time, its cutting, drying and collection were of vital importance. Peat bogs conveniently near to the settlements were used, and the actual cutting was a skilled operation carried out by the navvies on piece-work. Using a specially sharpened spade, the peat would be cut into sods – 15 centimetre cubes – and thrown up onto the 'bank' (the former grass level) to dry. At this stage the peat is quite wet, about the consistency of fresh cheese, but after a couple of months or so it is be dry enough to be handled, and is piled up for further drying. This work was often done by the women and children, stacking the peat up into 'rickles' to dry until next year. Then it would be carted and piled into big stacks behind every house. Haulage off the peat bogs was tricky due to the soft, wet nature of the ground. Hill Cove had just acquired a small Caterpillar tractor, which was used to cart peat at the Point, but at the top I was put onto carting, using a one-horse cart with a tipping body, identical to those still in use in Somerset at that time for muck-spreading. The carthorses were of mainly Percheron blood, slow and plodding and quite unlike those used for carting on the coast, which were nearly all rejects from the riding troop.

All the farm settlements and most of the shepherds' houses were connected by party telephone lines. The main lines ran from Roy Cove to Fox Bay with a branch to Port Howard at Little Chartres house, where the shepherd's wife, Mrs McAskill, acted as a sort of exchange. To call up you turned a handle, driving a magneto to generate ringing, and each house or settlement had its own code of rings. If for any reason the rings could not reach their intended destination, you would ring 'Mrs Mac' and get her to put you through. The party phone was an important feature of farm life, and at certain times of day conversation groups would get on the line, the wives during the afternoon, the managers in the evening, for example. Anyone could listen in, of course, and it was quite a usual thing for the isolated shepherds, once the evening radio news broadcasts from the BBC and Stanley were over, to 'have a listen' for whatever gossip might be going on. If too many receivers were lifted at the same time, this absorbed the energy of a ringing call and made it too weak to reach its destination, so if such a call was urgent, like calling Fox Bay for the doctor, it was quite in order to tell people to 'get off the line' and hear half a dozen clicks as they hung up. Once the call was answered, however, they would all listen in again to find out what was going on!

Stanley Sports

In February, after all the farms had finished shearing, came another interlude before getting down to the autumn work. Much as the farming people on the coast downed tools and headed for the local stock shows, in the Falklands they would get together for the sports or race meetings. Usually there would be one in Stanley and another on the West Falkland, the principal farms taking it in turn to host the events. However, 1947 was the first year since the war when a gathering could be held, so only the one meeting was held in Stanley and most people from the West Falkland went in for the occasion. The FIC had just bought a second ship, the 1,200-ton *Lafonia* to supplement the *Fitzroy*, so both ships went around the Islands collecting up passengers from key ports. There was no hotel as such in Stanley at that time, so as on the farms at Christmas all the houses expanded to receive the visitors. I again stayed at Stanley House, but slept along with Chris Bonner on mattresses in the sitting room, there being at least ten other people, all farmers, in the house. The other larger houses like Malvina House, Stanley Cottage, Sulivan House (where the colonial secretary lived) and Government House itself were all bursting at the seams with visitors from 'the camp'.

Racing took place daily on the racecourse, complete with tote (but not bookmakers) for betting. Most of the horses were Falkland bred, and indeed several had been shipped over from the West Falkland along with us passengers, although some imported horses with longer legs from Punta Arenas (where there was a flourishing racecourse) were much fancied. One day was devoted to foot races for people of all ages. In the evenings dances took place in the town hall. These were very similar to the cookhouse dances

Hill Cove from the air, taken from the seaplane of HMS *Ajax* in March 1938. Big House at centre right with garden and further right sheep yards and dip, the lower slopes of Mount Donald beyond.

except that the music was better with several players amounting to a band.

Soon it was time to board the steamer again and return to the West Falkland and to work. This now consisted mainly of dipping. Scab had been eradicated from the Islands before the end of the century, but the sheep ked (known incorrectly as 'tick') was a nuisance even if kept reasonably under control by one annual dip. The vital point was to make sure that every single sheep got dipped, which started with gathering the camps without leaving any animals behind. Unlike coast sheep who could walk or even run freely for vast distances, some Falkland sheep would not go very far before flopping down apparently exhausted, known as 'squatting'. This was not limited to the thinnest or the fattest, and was clearly a nutritional or behavioural phenomenon which was not yet understood (see Chapter 11). The fact was that if a sheep squatted on your beat, you had to kill and skin it on the spot if it was a gather for dipping, or shear it if for shearing. To the latter end all hands carried shears and a pair of wool *maletas* – large hessian saddlebags capable of carrying four fleeces. I had learned how to skin a sheep at San Julian, but now I had to add shearing to my newly acquired skills. A good blade shearer can take a fleece off in two or three minutes in the shed, maybe five out in camp, but I was happy if I took under twenty!

The season proper continued into May, by which time the dipping was finished, surplus sheep if any disposed of, all the flocks sorted out ready for the winter and finally the rams let go with the ewes for service, thus in effect starting the new breeding cycle. Winter was relatively quiet, mainly used for maintenance jobs and enlivened by pulling sheep out of ditches, leading on into September and the new lambing.

Before the end of April, however, I had to be on my way, *en route* for England this time. Passenger shipping to the UK was still scarce in the post-war years, and the *Lafonia*, with much better accommodation than the *Fitzroy* had been acquired partly for this reason. She was to make the full trip from Stanley to Tilbury and I had a passage on her. This took four weeks, enlivened by the refrigeration breaking down off the Brazilian coast. Although not a refrigerated cargo ship, she was carrying a full supply of good Falklands beef and mutton for the voyage, all of which had to go overboard to feed the sharks – quite a spectacle! We put into Pernambuco for repairs and to restock with some rather tough tropical beef in lieu.

In due course we docked at Tilbury, and entrained to London for our various destinations. I remember one Falkland Island couple, in their mid-forties maybe, for whom it was their first ride in a train, and they were just like children about it. I was little more than a child myself, of course, and was able to share their enjoyment.

So to Paddington, and onto the Great Western Railway. My train was drawn by a Castle class express steam locomotive, which took me to Bristol Temple Meads where the rest of the family was on the platform waiting for

Eleanor, Hugh and Rosemary about the embark SS *Asturiano* in March 1947. Agnes Mann on left.

me. It was just seven years since we had boarded the boat train to Gourock, returning to San Julian because of the war.

'Westfield'

The year 1947 was one of general family movements. At San Julian, Arthur was preparing to hand over management of the farm to Lionel Pickering, who in turn, recently returned from his war service and not long married, was only too ready to take over. Hugh had finished his *bachillerato* course at The Grange, and wanted to study architecture in England. Eleanor and Rosemary, aged 14 and 11 respectively, would continue their schooling in Britain, where they would follow their mother and grandmother to Roedean.

Passenger traffic from the River Plate to England had not yet fully got going again after the war, so available passages were at a premium. I was away in the Falklands, but the rest of the family travelled once again on the old *Asturiano* to Buenos Aires, where Arthur and Hugh got berths on the *Fresno Star*, a small refrigerated ship which did not usually carry passengers but fitted a few in under the circumstances. They took the luggage while Millicent and the girls flew by air, all the way. British South American Airways (BSAA) had just started their service to Buenos Aires, flying Avro Lancastrians (3) which were a civilian version of the four-engined Lancaster bombers, but quite luxurious compared with the Junkers JU52's of

Aeroposta. I travelled later on the *Lafonia* as we have seen, being the last to arrive in England in May 1947.

Grandfather Worsley had died in 1946, so Grannie Worsley was only too glad for us to make our home with her at 'Westfield', a big stone house with a large garden and a tennis court, which was to be our home for the next twenty-five years or so. It was then virtually in the country, on the outskirts of Winscombe, nestling at the foot of the Mendip Hills and within easy reach of Bristol by road, bus or train, although at that time it was still just outside the range of daily commuters.

The Worsley family had been in the habit, before the war, of having summer holidays together by the sea, and I remember going on one such, to St David's in Pembrokeshire. By now my uncles were all married and had families, so in 1947 the practice was restarted. Our youngest uncle, Frances (known as Sam), had a very young family and did not go, but even so what with ourselves, Grannie Worsley, the Philips and the Edgars we took up an entire boarding house on the seafront at Aberdovey, and it was great fun – even getting there was an adventure. Grannie now had Arthur to drive her pre-war Flying Standard saloon car on the lengthy journey from Winscombe to the Aust ferry across the Bristol Channel, then across the wilds of Wales to Aberdovey. Hugh and I had been given bicycles on returning to England, so we loaded these onto a train and went as far as Builth Wells in mid-Wales, then bicycled to Aberdovey from there, mostly downhill.

Each of the Worsley uncles had three sons, all younger than us, Millicent having the only girls, but the balance was somewhat redressed by the presence of Nancy Summerhayes with her daughters Peggy and Dinny. Nancy was a first cousin of Millicent, and being the only girls in their generation they had always been close, and had been at school at Roedean together. Her husband Christopher had pursued a distinguished career in the Diplomatic Corps and was later knighted, his final post being that of ambassador to Nepal in 1953 when the British expedition led by Sir John Hunt climbed Everest for the first time. Their eldest son David was also in the Foreign Service and was later to do valuable work in the British Embassy in Buenos Aires, while their younger son Bobs went up to Emmanuel at the same time as I did.

Notes

1 As on the coast, a large fenced enclosure where sheep grazed most of the year was known as a 'camp' (*campo*), probably several thousand hectares in extent. A 'paddock' (*potrero*) was smaller, usually less than 1,000 hectares.
2 See *Uttermost Part of the Earth*, by Lucas Bridges.
3 British South American was less fortunate than Panagra. In August 1947 a BSAA Lancastrian crashed in a snowstorm on the top of Mount Tupungato in the high Andes, with the loss of all on board. The site of the crash was not discovered for fifty years.

10

Home in England

Army service

It transpired that I would not be able to enter Cambridge for another two years, so Arthur suggested I go into the Army. As an overseas resident, strictly speaking I was not liable for call-up under the Emergency Act (1939), which was still in force, but my father with his own personal experiences well in mind pointed out that it would be 'a good chance to learn about handling men', especially if I were to get an officer's commission. This proved to be excellent advice and I have always valued my army training and experience.

So I duly registered, and in September 1947 reported to Taunton barracks for primary training. This was run by the Somerset Light Infantry and we received basic infantry training, but the main object of going there was to be sorted out according to educational levels, previous skills if any and general aptitudes, before being sent to other more specialised training units.

September was the time when boys who had left school at the end of the summer term were called up, so there were a number of public school leavers with me, and together with several others from Somerset families we were sent to join the Royal Artillery (RA), at the 17th Training Regiment RA at Larkhill on Salisbury Plain. There we learned how to do gun drill on 25-pounder field guns, a process of some six weeks during which those of us considered potential officer material were put through various further examinations and tests. The winter of 1947/48 was extremely severe, especially on top of the Plain, just opposite Stonehenge, and gun drill on the packed snow of the parade ground was no joke. We all got a chance to thaw out in November, celebrating Princess Elizabeth's wedding.

From Larkhill we would get weekend leave, and it was quite easy for me to get home, due west across the Plain by bus or maybe hitchhiking to Bristol and down to Winscombe. Hugh had started on a secretarial course at Clark's College in Bristol, living during the week in digs, and the girls were at Roedean so only came home for school holidays. At Hill Cove I had earned my own money for the first time, and the first thing I bought was a piano accordion. I had always regretted having had to give up music at The Grange, and observing the players in the Falklands had thought the accordion would be a very easy instrument to play – the piano keyboard for the right hand I could manage and it seemed that all you had to do with the left was to press a few buttons! It was not, inevitably, quite as easy as all that but I found it very satisfying and used to practise a lot at weekends.

Soon after the New Year 1948 we came to the end of our training at Larkhill, and together with Ted Jones and Ricky Cooper from Somerset and a few others, I was posted to the Basic Officer Cadet Training Unit in Aldershot. Here we had our first experience of really tough drill sergeants from the Foot Guards, mindless spit and polish, and being thoroughly chased around. It was all modelled on the way of life at the Royal Military Academy, Sandhurst, the general idea being that if you stuck it out and did not let it get you down, then you were possessed of sufficient spirit and stamina to become an officer. So we spat on our already gleaming boots, stiffened our already erect spines, and loosened the bolts of our rifles so that they 'crashed' loudly on presenting arms. (It was advisable to reverse the process if you were actually required to fire the weapon.) We finally went on a battle course near Okehampton down on Dartmoor where real ammunition was flung around, although the only casualty we actually saw (on a stretcher) was one of the permanent staff who had been so remiss as to allow a thunder-flash to go off in his hand.

Most of us duly passed this stage all right, and we gunners moved on to Mons barracks, Aldershot, for specific artillery training. Gunnery at junior officer level requires rather more brains than some other forms of soldiering, so we were treated more like human beings as we were taught how to handle the mathematics and physics and other aspects of the job. We were not let off gun drill, however, which – because we were potential officers – had to be more perfect than ever before. But we survived that too, and after actually firing our pieces down on the Brecon Beacons in Wales we received His Majesty's commission and were gazetted second lieutenants RA.

Many of my companions, having been enclosed in the British Isles all their lives, were keen to go abroad and what with occupied Germany, India and the Colonies there was still plenty of abroad to go to. But I, having been abroad, just wanted to be near my family in England so I asked for a home

169

Gunner Blake, J.L.

posting and was sent to the 68th Training Regiment RA, at Oswestry, Shropshire, near the Welsh border. The National Service Act had by then been passed, and was to come into force on 1 January 1948, so the Army was reorganising its training system for peacetime conscription. The 68th (formerly a Light Anti-Aircraft unit with honourable service in North Africa and Italy) formed part of the 18th Training Brigade, and we shared the officers' mess with our old friend the 17th TRRA, which had moved up from Larkhill to become one of the four regiments in the Brigade. Our job was to receive the recruits on call-up, kit them out and teach them a few rudiments of drill and army ways, while the specialised personnel selection staff sorted them out according to their educational and other skills. It was much as we had experienced ourselves at Taunton, except that the process had been cut down from six to two weeks. One would receive a new draft every fortnight, which gave no time to get to know any of them personally at all, and could have been rather soul destroying, but as the succeeding drafts came from different parts of the country it was fascinating to observe British youth in the mass, as it were.

As a new second lieutenant, even if RA, I was still a very junior form of life. I had charge of a squad of thirty recruits, but their life in turn was ruled not by me but by the squad sergeant who kept them on the go from reveille to lights out, assisted by a bombardier (corporal, RA). My sergeant, Arthur Pilkington, even though he chased the boys around adequately, was mild and soft-spoken and had been on active service in Italy with the regiment when it was still a light anti-aircraft unit. My troop commander was a senior lieutenant called Dick Ward-Best, who with Sergeant Pilkington took me gently in hand and continued to make an officer out of me. Dick was a regular, and because the world is just so big and no more, was appointed some years later as the full-time regular officer attached to the North Somerset Yeomanry, a territorial (part-time) unit which early in the war had lost its horses and become a mechanised artillery regiment, among whose officers was my cousin, Seymour. I took over command of the troop when Dick was promoted, and sure enough I learned a great deal about handling men. I also went on a methods of instruction course and learned how to give lectures and get information across to an audience.

In September, we received an intake with a number of public school leavers, just like those I had coincided with a year before. Among them was my brother Hugh, although he was not posted to the 68th but to our sister regiment the 67th over on the other side of the lines where they shared a mess with the 64th TRRA who did arms training like the 17th. Eventually all the OR1s [potential officers] of that year ended up as a single squad in the 64th, and I remember going over to see my brother and having the barrack room leap to attention at the appearance of this visiting troop commander from the 68th! One of their number was Kemble Croft, who later joined Hugh at the Royal West of England School of Architecture and they became lifelong friends. It was not for many years that I learned that Kemble had been in my squad in the 68th , and that I had been a bit of a bore in matters like keeping things tidy, squared off, shining, polished and in order, known in the Army (and elsewhere) as 'bull'. Hugh was commissioned in due course and was posted to the 4th Regiment RHA (Royal Horse Artillery) where he became Assistant Adjutant, a job he always described as 'a sort of up-market military clerk'. The RHA bears much the same relationship to ordinary gunners as the cavalry to the infantry.

We had learned how to ride a motorcycle as part of our officer training, so now that I was living for free at His Majesty's expense, and even getting paid for it, I bought one of my own, a 350cc AJS which was a great joy. Life at Oswestry was not too exacting, there was a regimental horse that one could ride, and it was a delightful area to explore, with Llangollen just over the border (I went to one of the first international choral Eisteddfods there). Chester not too far away one way and Shrewsbury was fairly close in the other direction. Some of us used to follow the Border Counties Otter Hounds, a form of hunting countenanced in those days due to the damage otters did to poor unfortunate trout and salmon. We shamelessly used Army 'recreational' transport to go to the meets and then hop from river to river or from pub to pub as the case may be. I also pursued my accordion practice, which was soon discovered by the battery commander who made me play for sing-songs at jolly get-togethers at the end of each course before our recruits, now instant soldiers and boon companions, went their several ways.

Many of the senior officers, captains and majors, were married and lived in the nearby villages, often giving hospitality to us juniors, and through them one thus got to know other local, non-army people. One such was a character called Thurlow Craig, whom I visited a number of times. As a young man, he had roamed all over north-eastern Argentina and spent some time in the Paraguayan Chaco. He had written a book which had been one of my teenage sources of *gaucho* lore. (1) Thurlow affected *gaucho* dress even in Shropshire, *bombachas* and all, and was delighted to offer me *mate* to drink. He rather revelled in shocking the Salopians by larding his speech with rude Argentine expressions, most of them fortunately not really understandable other than by a fellow Argentine. He was, however, fully conversant with all the big cattle ranching companies such as Bovril or Liebig's, and could be quite entertaining when telling about the mores not to say scandals of some leading families in what was still virtually British Argentina.

Cambridge

After about a year at Oswestry, with duty alternating with leave which allowed me to have Christmas at home and summer holidays at Aberdovey, the matter of going up to Cambridge started to rear its head and I was delighted to discover first that there was a thing called a Class B release which allowed servicemen to be demobilised early in order to join university courses at the beginning of the academic year, in October, and secondly that I could obtain an ex-service student grant. This perhaps was more important to my father, who still had the two girls at Roedean and Hugh would not qualify for a grant having gone into the army under the 1948 National Service Act. I was 21 by then, and he gave me some share certificates whose income, added to my ex-service grant, provided enough for my fees, living and so forth at Cambridge, and I have been financially independent ever since.

So in September 1949 I went up to Emmanuel College, following the footsteps of my grandfather, Philip, my great-uncle Arthur and my uncles Edgar and Francis Worsley. Edward Welbourne, who as Senior Tutor had been influential in my gaining entry to the college, would be elected Master the following year, on the retirement of Dr 'Timmy' Hele. Welbourne was one of the Cambridge 'greats' and his forward thinking and often unconventional approach was influential on Emmanuel for at least thirty years. Another, though more distant, connection was the Senior Fellow Philip Worsley Wood, a distinguished mathematician who had been a Fellow for fifty years. He had been Senior Tutor in Edgar's day and may also have had a say in my admission. His mother, Katharine Worsley, came from the Isle of Wight branch of the Worsleys, who were descended from Sir Edward Worsley, a devoted Royalist who was rewarded by King Charles II for his spirited defence of Carisbrooke Castle during the Civil War by the gift of a watch, still preserved in the family.

Also up at Emmanuel at this time was 'Bobs' Summerhayes, brother of Peggy and Dinny. Their eldest brother David was a graduate of Emmanuel, and by then in the Foreign Service following the footsteps of father Christopher – yet another Emmanuel man. In our last year we were joined family-wise at Cambridge by Alan Carles, son of Aunt Dorothy Blake who had married Wyndham Carles and made their home in Kenya. Alan was a member of the first course to be taught by the new Cambridge School of Veterinary Medicine which only in 1951 had been hived off from the Faculty of Agriculture. Another relative who came up that year was Veronica Cadbury at Newnham. Bobs and I held a graduation party in our last term for all our several parents, and many good friends.

But we are leaping ahead. I arrived by train complete with suitcase, trunk, accordion and bicycle and found I was lodged for my first year in digs in Warkworth Street, just five minutes cycle ride away from college. Housing was in short supply in those post-war years, and food rationing was still in force. Meals were served in hall, attendance at lunch and dinner being obligatory, although you could 'sign out' for a limited number of meals per term. College was more one's life than the university proper in many ways, and actual residence or 'keeping' was just as, or maybe even more, important than passing such exams as might come one's way. The rules for being awarded a BA degree by the university were to have kept nine full university terms (i.e. three years) – there was no mention of exams. Even more oddly, you 'proceeded' to an MA degree six years after your BA, again without any further study or even residence. These curious facts are little known to the outside world. Of course, once you actually left ('went down') and started looking for a job, well that was another matter – potential employers started asking questions about exams passed, although in London at least those who had gained a 'Blue' by having played for the university at a major sport could still usually get a job on the strength of it.

The courses of instruction, lectures, laboratories etc. were organised by the various university Faculties but tuition proper was run by the colleges. Your tutor was *in loco parentis* and therefore responsible for your well-being and behaviour, but not your studies unless these happened to be in his own subject. Study would otherwise be guided by a director of studies, and overseen in more detail by supervisors. My tutor was Peter Hunter Blair, later Professor of Anglo-Saxon Studies. He would become Senior Tutor after Welbourne. My director of studies was 'Jimmy' Line, the college bursar at the time but also a lecturer at the School of Agriculture. Academic excellence was very much sought after by the colleges, even more so than sporting prowess in many of them, so good care was taken that exams were, in fact, passed.

I had registered for the general agriculture course, lasting three years and leading to a BA degree and a Certificate of Proficiency in Agriculture. Most of the lectures took place at the School of Agriculture, in the teaching complex known as the Downing Street site, within easy walking distance from Emmanuel, and the laboratories were there also. I found Chris Bonner there on the same course, and also Steve Leach from Salta and his cousin Gerry Capes, plus Donald Sword from Entre Ríos. There were a number of other students from all over the world, and the Professor of Agriculture, Sir F.S. Engledow, made it quite clear in his address of welcome to the new students that the university did not try to teach any particular sort of farming, but attempted to instil the principles for graduates to take home and apply there. 'Farming, gentlemen, is an art, a science, a business and a way of life, and a combination of all four – don't think you know it all just because you have been to university,' was his advice, and how true it has proved.

We were lucky in having as lecturers a number of eminent scientists who had done fundamental research, some of it of world renown, into farming-related subjects before and during the war. Professor Engledow himself was very much of a theorist, but Drs H.E. Woodman and R. Evans, who taught us animal nutrition, had researched into basal metabolism (i.e. how much did the body, animal or human, really need to eat in order to live) for the wartime Ministry of Food. This was pretty strategic stuff, leading to top-level government decisions on designing the ration system for the armed forces and the civilian population, and from there the organisation of supplies, distribution and rationing of food during the war.

Then there was Sir John Hammond, who had done classical work before the war in animal breeding, and pioneered the earliest artificial insemination both live and *in vitro*, and even transatlantic fertilisation of ova, embryo transfers and the like. His lectures were aimed at a wider audience than our course, and took place weekly in the Faculty of Natural Science. They were always packed, Sir John being one of those outstanding men who, in addition to being a brilliant scientist, could also be most entertaining on such subjects as transatlantic insemination of rabbits.

Lectures took up all weekday mornings, practical work in the laboratories occurred three afternoons a week and on Saturday mornings we would cycle out to the university farm along the Girton Road clad in duffle coats, wellington boots and 'gorblimey' caps to tramp over the stubbles and learn about gault clay, sugar beet and mangold-wurzels. The university did not, like some, require us to do any actual 'hands-on' farming work during term, arguing I think correctly that our time in residence was better spent in absorbing learning in lecture rooms and laboratories. We were, however, required to do serious farming work during the summer vacation, which lasted nearly four months.

All this did not leave a great deal of time for sport, but I played Rugby with the college third fifteen. This was a delightful team, composed of some who, like me, were not really good enough for a higher team, but also of some really good players whose study load did not permit them to keep up a more intense sports routine. We played two or three afternoons per week against other college teams, which one did or did not attend according to the laboratory work schedules, and on Saturdays we would play away matches against local clubs in the district. Some of these led to notable 'third halves' in the village pubs!

When the summer term came along, together with a number of other rugby players, I turned to rowing. We were coached with great patience by one of the senior oarsmen, it being said that if you could only get a rugger 'eight' to pull together properly, they had the power to move very fast. We duly rowed in the May races, or 'bumps'. The River Cam (like the Isis over at 'the other place') is too narrow for two eights to race side by side, so you race one behind the other, and attempt to 'bump', literally, the boat in front. When this happens both boats pull over to the bank to allow the ones behind to pass, and for the next race they change places. Racing takes place for four 'nights'(afternoons actually) running and an eight achieving four bumps is allowed to keep their oars. We narrowly missed this in my second year. Being a very powerful and by now experienced crew, on the first night we were just about to bump when the boat in front bumped the next ahead. Denied our prey, we piled it on in an attempt to bump the third boat ahead (known as an 'over-bump' which, if successful, would have shot us up three places instead of one). But although we caught them up and indeed overlapped, their cox was too skilful with his rudder and was able to 'wash us off' so that we did not actually bump them. We bumped on all three other nights, though, and always considered that we had made a 'moral' over-bump.

By this time I had acquired reasonable proficiency on the accordion, which I had upgraded to a 120-bass model on which I used to practise assid-uously. The two other students in the same digs nobly put up with this, and one of them put me in touch with an old Etonian pal of his who was getting together musicians to form a Scottish dance band. Tony Reid was a brilliant

Emmanuel College VII boat, crewed by powerful rugby players at the May races, 1951. John Blake at number 7.

accordionist, and had got together a pianist, a drummer and one other 'box' (for squeeze-box) apart from myself. I was the only Sassenach. We used to practise in the drummer's digs over on Chesterton Road and eventually played for Scottish dancing events. Our *tour de force* came in my second year, when Tony managed to get the band engaged for the annual university Highland Ball, held at the Dorothy Ballroom. This has a sprung floor and tall mirrors around the walls, and I shall never forget the spectacle of several hundred dancers all 'setting' together, with the floor bouncing and the mirrors actually bending at the middle, to *our* music. This is one of the great satisfactions of music – playing for the enjoyment of others.

Other musical events came from quite another direction. In April of my first year I was invited by Chris Bonner to the (then) annual Cambridge dinner of former pupils of St George's College, Quilmes, Buenos Aires. I became acquainted with other old Georgians and they in turn realised that there were others, like me, up from the River Plate who had attended lesser institutions than St George's. So we got together and founded the 'Criollo Club', composed of undergraduates who had come from the River Plate region of South America, about a dozen in all. We used to meet at irregular intervals to chat and drink *mate* and wine instead of beer, and soon to sing, as one of the leading members was Barney Miller. A natural musician

176

with a perfect ear for harmony as well as melody, Barney was for ever getting up musical and other shows. I learned to strum the guitar reasonably in tune, and we used to play at various events. Our outstanding achievement was when Barney wangled us onto the programme of a Spanish Society concert which took place at Girton College. Julian Bream, I remember, was on the programme among other fairly serious presentations, and to this august audience appeared the Criollo Club, fairly well primed, singing popular songs from the River Plate, fortunately in key!

Music at this time filled much of my life. At home at Westfield, the four of us had started playing together for fun (the piano had long since been moved from the drawing room to a side room). Eleanor had taken piano tuition both at St Hilda's and at Roedean and could play almost anything by sight, Hugh more or less ditto but he had also learned the guitar and the accordion, and Rosemary had taken up the violin although at the beginning she was more or less bullied into playing the drums. We called ourselves the 'Westfield Band' and used to take on engagements like local village 'hops' and cousins' twenty-first birthday parties.

For my second year at Emmanuel I was given a room in college, in North Court which is reached by a subway under Emmanuel Street. The set of rooms just above me was occupied by Mr (later Professor) 'Freddie' Odgers, a descendant of Dr William Blake Odgers KC, former Recorder of the City of Bristol and therefore distantly related to us, but I did not realise this at the

Playing accordion with Hugh's South American band, *Los Sambreros*, Bristol 1952. Left to right: Dick, Pete, Alan, John, Mike Pebody (behind), Hugh at piano.

time. I promptly hired a piano, which Mr Odgers did not seem to mind, and spent many hours which should doubtless have been spent in study in arranging scores, mostly for the Westfield Band, as well as composing some original songs. Two of these I later entered for the 'Write-a-song' contest run by Radio Luxembourg, without success.

For my third year, I had been asked to captain the Third Fifteen. This was a great honour, especially as it proved to be a historic year for rugby football at the college, and the First Fifteen won the 'Cuppers' (university intercollegiate cup) for the first time *ever*. For the actual final match, almost the whole college turned out in support, most in fancy dress, and the rejoicing afterwards was spectacular. Among the regular players in my team was David (later Sir D.G.T) Williams who had a distinguished career at Cambridge, becoming professor of English law and President (Master) of Wolfson College before being elected the first full-time Vice-Chancellor of the University (1989–96). I remember David as a small, nippy scrum half. Then there was Chris (later Sir Christopher) Collett, a hard-working forward who would later become Lord Mayor of London and together with Sir Adrian Cadbury was instrumental in founding the Cambridge Society.

The agricultural course, even if it did not include hands-on activities during term, required us to do some serious farming work during the long vacation, and to bring back a report at the beginning of the Michaelmas term. I did most of this with Uncle Philip Worsley at his farm in the Cotswolds. After spending two years as a cadet at Hill Cove with Mr Miller, a season at San Julian and then some time in New Zealand, Philip had returned to England and bought a farm of about 350 acres at Farmington, near Northleach, Gloucestershire, called 'Starvall'. Not put off by the name, he had renamed it 'Grove Farm' and with his wife Peggy (Sale) set out to improve the very light soil by intensive folding of chickens in portable runs, and also folded sheep, so manuring the land *in situ*. The build-up of soil fertility so achieved, allowed them to grow wheat very successfully when the war came along and every acre that could be ploughed up was of value. Philip was able to expand his holding, and also rent further land from the Farmington estate, so that by the late 1940s he was farming nearly 1,000 acres.

I did two harvests with Uncle Philip, for the first one lodging with one of his tractor drivers in Farmington, and for the other living with them at Hampnett House, where the Westfield Band also played for his eldest son James's twenty-first birthday party. Nearly all aspects of haymaking and harvesting came my way, the latter mostly bagging grain off the combine but some corn was still cut with a binder and stooked, then carted and piled into ricks for threshing out during the winter. So I learned how to stack corn as well as hay. Part of Uncle Philip's land ran up to the A40 at Eastington, and bounded with that of a Mr Lawrence, whose red combine we would often see in operation from the other side of a deep valley known as 'Rotten Pot', but we never actually met Mr Lawrence or his family during those years.

Gaviota

The urge to go boating was still niggling away, and Hugh and I cast around for ways and means. During the Easter vacation of 1950, we found a 17-foot clinker-built open dinghy going cheap, and were able to pick up an almost-new British Anzani outboard motor, with which we motored shakily through the port of Bristol and up the Avon to Hanham Mills, where there was a boatyard, a pub, room to pitch a tent and easy cross-country road access from Winscombe without having to go through Bristol. Here we converted the boat to a small cabin cruiser which we called *Gaviota*. Our financial resources were limited, which fitted in fine with the time factor as we were both working hard at our respective studies, so the job had to be strung out over the various holidays. By August she was ready. There were only three berths, two in the cabin and one on the floor of the cockpit, which had a removable canopy to keep out the weather, so we could take only one crew-person – usually one of our sisters.

Rosemary, Hugh and John at Hanham Mills on the River Avon, near Bristol.

Our first venture was up the Avon to Bath and across Wiltshire on the Kennet and Avon Canal, the idea being to get as far as we could and then return. The canals at that time still belonged to the railway companies, and the surge of popularity of the canals as leisure resources which has led to their wide-spread restoration had not yet started. Locks and other installations were in poor repair, but there was still a sturdy human resource in the form of the 'length men' (each in charge of a length of canal) who were only too glad to see a boat come along and actually use their locks. To go up the flight of twenty-nine locks at Devizes – which took all day – we were assisted by three length men, who stuffed up the leaky gates with weed and jiggled the water levels so as to float us through. We did in fact get as far as Newbury, but could not get any further as the River Kennet connecting with the Thames was closed to all traffic by the Canal Authority, so we returned to Hanham.

The following August (1951) we embarked on a more ambitious trip, starting with a tow from an oil tanker from Avonmouth out into the Bristol Channel and up to Gloucester, then up the Severn to Worcester, where we locked up into Diglis Basin and on along the Worcester and Birmingham Canal, climbing steadily as far as Gas Street Basin, Birmingham. Edgar and Vida Worsley lived at that time in nearby Edgbaston, and this was a necessary stop for baths as our on-board washing facilities consisted of a small enamel basin. From there we carried on eastwards to the Grand Union Canal, with a short side trip as far as Rugby for another ablutions stop with Uncle Sam (Francis) and Aunt Mary Worsley, then on down the River Nene Navigation past Oundle and so down to Peterborough. From there it was a fascinating journey across the Fens, joining the River Ouse at Denver Sluice, near Downham Market, and so upriver to join the Cam and on to Cambridge. During my final year I took the boat out on various excursions, ending with a grand May Races with *Gaviota* dressed overall with suitably gay bunting.

In June 1952, accompanied by 'Bobs' Summerhayes and another Emmanuel man, Colin Herridge, I took *Gaviota* through the Bedford Levels across the Fens back to Peterborough. Changing crew, we proceeded on up the Nene to rejoin the Grand Union Canal, turned left and so proceeded down to London, into tide water at Brentford and then up through Teddington Lock into the Thames. When we had left Bristol the year before we had some hopes of the Kennet and Avon Canal being reopened so as to complete the circuit back to Bristol. But it was not to be, so we travelled slowly up the Thames, stopping at Weybridge where old Patagonian friends like the Bill Waldrons and Dick Buxtons were living, then on to Oxford where we left *Gaviota* moored, thinking maybe the trip could be completed another year. But family and personal plans moved on, and in the end Hugh sold her there. I wrote *Gaviota* Song to a more or less original tune by way of a memento, and the four of us recorded it for posterity. This was long before the days of tape recorders, so it meant going to a proper studio and recording live onto a master disc, from which copies could be made. We also recorded some of the Westfield Band's repertoire, and the historic 78 rpm recordings are still extant.

Gaviota Song

John Blake
Tune: Original, Calypso rhythm.

Now, *Gaviota* was her name,
she never made no pretence to fame;
Over eight hundred miles and not a plank went wrong,
so to remember her we sing this song.

Chorus: Let's sing of *Gaviota*,
happy little boat-a,
how she like to float-a 'pon the sea

Her maiden trip was to Newbury,
  as trying a trip as a trip could be;
The weed was long and the water low,
  so when the motor stop we had to tow.
Just abreast of Seend, where we stuck once more,
  was a gang of children, ages eight to four;
'Give us your rope', they shouted with a smile,
  and then they towed us nearly half a mile.

On summit level the rain was teeming,
  that didn't bother our Able Seaman,
In mackintosh and gumboots she felt quite hot,
  and so she took a plunge and soaked the lot.
Next summer came, and we were off once more,
  waving goodbye to the Avon shore,
Up Severn, Worcester and Birmingham,
  and down Grand Union, Nene, Fen, Ouse and Cam.

At Irthlingboro' de dawn did burgeon,
  no cover near, but de need was urgen',
We lifted canopy, struts and all,
  and we planted him upon the shore!
Oundle schoolboy sculling by,
  from Able Seaman – the gladsome eye!
Handsome sixth-former turns around
  to have a look and runs his skiff right hard aground.

Down Grand Union cut and up Thames so broad,
in Oxford waters we left her moored.
'Adios, *Gaviota*, you've done us well –
and that, my friends, is all I have to tell.'

181

Graduation

Meantime at Cambridge, the final examinations were soon upon us and I got a '2:1' [Cambridge exam results are graded into four levels, described with inscrutable logic as first, second (1), second (2) and third] Perhaps if I had not spent so much time playing the accordion and indulging in other pastimes I might have got a first, but I was not going to be a scientist anyway, and I have never regretted the time and activities spent outside the lecture rooms. So I duly graduated BA with Certificate of Proficiency in Agriculture.

Before going down from Cambridge, Barney Miller had asked me to join him and a few others to form a dance band which he was going to take out to Majorca to play in the hotels during the summer season. My father, however, doubtless with visions of all sorts of sinful life floating around, put his foot down, a fact I have always slightly regretted, even though years later Barney told me that the tour was a bit of disaster – but it would have been yet another experience!

However it was now time to seriously consider a career and a future. Although I had looked at other forms of farming while up at Cambridge, and discussed it at length with friends like Chris Bonner and Steve Leach, when it came to the crunch, for all of us, our roots exerted their pull. Chris duly returned to the Falklands, and Steve returned to north-western Argentina, where 'Leach's Argentine Estates' were still a power in the land. I had always felt the attraction of Patagonia, but when I broached the idea at home, my father suggested going back to Hill Cove, where my cousin Bill was shortly to take over as manager.

Bill had been a scholar of Eton and Trinity, and served in the Colonial Service during the war. Uncle Robert, no doubt feeling the loss of his elder son Bob, suggested he take over the management of Hill Cove where Hugh Harding was coming up for retirement. So Bill went out in 1949 with his wife Doreen to learn the job as understudy to Hugh Harding. A small house known as 'the bungalow' was built for them, where they lived for three years, before moving up to the Big House in 1952 when the Hardings retired. It was now suggested that I go out to San Julian for one season to let Bill find his feet as manager, and then join him as assistant manager in the spring of 1953.

Only many years later did I learn from Aunt Edith that there was much more to this that met the eye at the time. Bill had left San Julian as a boy of 6 and had never been back, so he had not had the chance of picking up the basic skills in his teens like I had, and both Robert and Arthur were well aware that there were many working practices which had been developed on the coast, as well as basic breeding techniques, which were as yet unknown in the islands. So I was to spend a season at San Julian first, to brush all this up, before going to Hill Cove and hopefully put it into practice. One of the problems (and there are many) of sheep raising in the Falklands is that no single breed of sheep found elsewhere is suitable for modern commercial production under the prevailing climatic and other features of the Islands. The breed used mostly in Robert Blake Senior's day was the English Romney Marsh, or Kent. This was perhaps the most suitable for the wet, marshy conditions of the peat bogs, but was less hardy for the mountain grazings and the Blakes felt that more and better wool could be grown.

Hill Cove had a small flock of pedigree Corriedale ewes (from San Julian), and Cheviot rams from the Scottish Borders had been tried with some success, particularly the 'North Country Cheviot' strain which was said to have better wool than most. Both Arthur and Uncle Robert thought this would be just what Hill Cove needed, but none of the parties concerned had the genetic know-how to put it all together. Nor, as it turned out, did I at that time, but our seniors fondly hoped that I might.

So I found myself in June 1952 in the Scottish Border country near

John Blake's graduation.

Langholm, on the property of one Andrew Beatty who was a leading breeder of this type of Cheviots, giving a hand with the shearing or 'clupping' as they say in those parts. I stayed with Beatty in his house in the valley, and every day we would go up 'on the hill' to attend whichever flock or 'hirsel' was being clipped that day. This was a great social event for the herds (shepherds) as the labour was provided by all the other herds including the neighbours, who shore the sheep with blades on a rick sheet or large tarpaulin laid out on the ground, while the womenfolk prepared food for all concerned.

My job was to pick up and roll the fleeces, which were then stuffed into a 'sheet' which was a sort of flat woolpack suspended between two posts. On about the fourth day the foreman asked if I would like to have a go with the shears, which I did, using the style of shearing that I had learned in the Falklands. Inevitably I was the last to finish, and heard the comment, 'Och, that's the Hieland way'.

Neither style tied the sheep's legs, but the Lowlanders basically kept the animal in the same position and moved themselves round it, whereas the Highlanders stayed put and moved the sheep around their person to get at the difficult bits. As it was mostly Scots from the Highlands who went out to Patagonia (and Australia, New Zealand and elsewhere) taking their way of shearing with them, when machine shears came in, (2) it was the Highland way which got adapted to having the hand-piece tied to the wall with a down-tube, and the other styles faded out. For the record, I found the Lowland way to be easier if you are using blades, and adopted it when I went back to the Falklands.

Patagonia revisited

By September 1952, passenger shipping to the River Plate had resumed its pre-war regularity – a vital element of the chilled beef trade from Montevideo and Buenos Aires to London. Chilled quarters of beef have a refrigerated life of twenty-one days, so if you send them on a ship taking just eighteen days for the voyage, they arrive just in time for immediate sale to the best and highest-priced hotel and restaurant trade in London. To avoid delays, particularly in the Brazilian ports, the beef was shipped in passenger liners which also carried the mail. As a result they had to keep to a schedule which was respected by the port authorities, and the ships were allotted berths alongside and were not subject to wharf-side delays. The shipping lines were thus able to offer first-class stateroom passages at a fairly reasonable price, and for two generations and more this had been the way to travel for administrative and managerial staff employed by the many British firms in trade, banking or farming in South America. For all such firms and their employees, 'UK leave' every three years or so meant not only maintaining family and cultural ties but also maintaining a closer relationship between the boardroom in London and the overseas staff. It had been part of the pattern of my parents' life and was now to become part of mine also.

The vessels of the Royal Mail Line had survived the war and I had a passage on the *Highland Monarch*, the sister ship of the *Highland Brigade*. In peacetime these ships carried about a hundred first-class passengers from Tilbury, and picked up some 200 mostly Spanish emigrants in Vigo, who berthed aft in second class.

Having left Argentina as a callow youth of 18, I now came in contact with other British Argentines on board and continued to enlarge my education as most of them were either from Buenos Aires or the central and northern provinces. Not having been to school in Buenos Aires, my only contact with non-Patagonians had been those brief holidays in the Cordoba Hills. Among the passengers was Basil Thompson, a journalist and columnist for the *Buenos Aires Herald* newspaper. For years he had written a small column entitled 'Ramón writes', most amusingly in pure 'Spanglish'. This is a variety of English commonly found in Latin America but only really appreciated by truly bilingual English/Spanish speakers, and has several degrees. The most basic form is, when stuck for the correct word in English, to use its Spanish equivalent in a more or less Anglicised sort of way such as 'acercate yourself' (come nearer) from *acercar*. More subtly, a real English word meaning something quite different is used in a context where the sense is really Spanish – i.e. 'creature' for *criatura* (a baby or infant). To properly appreciate 'pure' Spanglish you really have to be perfectly fluent in both languages!

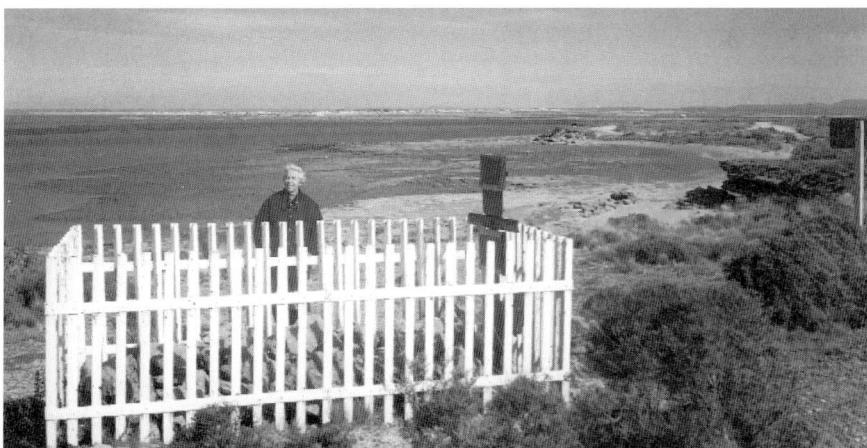

San Julian bay and town at Centenary, September 2001. Monica by the grave of Lt Sholl, of HMS *Beagle*

[Photo JLB]

So it was back to Buenos Aires, and then to San Julian. Aeroposta had been nationalised by Perón soon after the war and become Aerolineas Argentinas, and was now flying Douglas DC3s (the 'Dakota', a flying workhorse which had been widely used during the war), still on a milk run basis from port to port down the coast, but the trip now took six hours instead of twelve. At the Company's, Lionel and Mary were by now living in the Big House with their four children, and I lived there also. Lionel was the hands-on manager, assisted by his brother Tom who had married Mary's younger sister Lydia, but Arthur continued to fly out every year during shearing and was very much in control of the operation. Lionel and Tom had proved apt pupils and working alongside them that one season I was able to bring my practical knowledge of sheep farm operation up-to-date.

The overall principles were commercial, but Arthur had a broader view than most and some of his ideas were thought original if not indeed unconventional by other farming operators in the south. This applied both to general working procedures as well as to breeding. Coronel had one of the oldest pedigree flocks of the Corriedale breed in the country, and was at that time one of the four leading stud farms in Santa Cruz province. Corriedale breeding in Patagonia in later years was to become unduly influenced by the show ring, to the extent of sacrificing productive characters for 'beauty in the ring'. At the time, however, the half-dozen or so major studs, mostly company-owned, were conducting their breeding according to commercial productive values. I was fortunate in getting alongside this aspect at this moment in time, and to participate in its development over the ensuing three decades.

I was able to take time off to visit other farms, notably Condor, south of Rio Gallegos, then as now the largest estancia in Santa Cruz both in acreage (500,000) and number of sheep (100,000). The Blakes had of course known the Waldron family, the principal owners, since the early days of settlement on the West Falkland, and personally we had known Bill Waldron, the then general manager and his wife Jean for many years, their daughters Fay and Pamela being about my age. We also knew the manager, Eric Davies, who had visited Coronel and bought stud rams for Condor, and had sent his eldest son Richard to The Grange in my last year there. I do not recall seeing anything particularly new at Condor at that time, and little did I imagine then the extent to which my future life would be bound up with it.

On another visit south, I made my first acquaintance with the 'collar-and-tie manager' syndrome. The British community in and around San Julian was still important and cohesive, and used to run an annual fête or *kermesse* to raise funds for community charities. One of the money spinners was the sale of beef, which was not often to be found locally. I, in my capacity of cadet and general dogsbody at Coronel, had taken the farm lorry down to Rio Gallegos to collect sides of beef which had been donated by farms down there. At one of these, I duly arrived and backed my lorry up to the ramp to load the beef and then, being the driver, made to lend a hand to lift and stow the cargo. The manager – who indeed was wearing a tie – restrained me with the words 'Leave it to the *peons*'. This was very far from the Blake/Miller/calloused-hands tradition, and a considerable eye-opener for me.

There was also time to see some other types of farming in Argentina, so I took up the invitations of other fellow passengers on the boat trip out. One of these was Guillermo Edwards, recently retired from managing 'Saucemelú', which belonged to Garovaglio & Zorraquín, one of the leading Hereford studs in the country, near Daireaux, some 360km south-west from Buenos Aires. This was top bull-breeding country and the Edwards had the *entrée* to all the showplaces and took me to several. These were, and are still, country mansions set in imposing parks, at that time often with the owners in residence. They were all Anglophile, to the extent of finding bound volumes of *Punch* or the *Illustrated London News* lining the walls of libraries or parlours which would not have been out of place in Hertfordshire, Hereford or Hampshire. Outside, one saw the famous bulls, fed and pampered, and the equally famous alfalfa pastures on which they were bred.

Another trip was to Entre Ríos, by Sunderland flying boat from Buenos Aires to Concordia, on the Uruguay River, where I was met by Bob Sword and we drove to their property, 'Buena Esperanza' at Los Conquistadores some 100km to the north. His father Ronald Sword had come originally from Somerset, and had several times travelled to Britain on leave trips on the same ship as my own parents. His brother Donald had been at Cambridge with us, and Bob, his wife Pat and baby Rupert had also been on board ship with me on the trip out. This was, to me, tropical country full of snakes and bugs, and it was fairly hot. Everyone took a siesta between the hours of one and four, in spite of all this they ran beef cattle and also sheep.

It was also *mate* country, so let us digress a bit to discuss the national beverage, widely used also in Uruguay and Paraguay and to a lesser extent in Brazil. *Ilex paraguayensis* or *yerba mate* grows freely in the natural region known as the Chaco, a tropical rainforest environment shared by Argentina, Paraguay and Brazil. The process of harvesting the bushes and chopping up the dried leaves (and stalks) is not unlike that of tea, which also grows in the region, but much less delicate and demanding. It is mainly drunk as an infusion, out of a hollow gourd known as a *mate*, into which the dried *yerba* is first poured, followed by hand-hot water, and is then sucked up through a metal pipe known as a *bombilla*. The drink has a bitter taste, refreshing even if hot, and contains when freshly brewed a powerful stimulant (*matein*, related to caffeine). It has strong laxative, diuretic and hunger-depressing effects. It is also full of vitamins and minerals. The old-time *gauchos* used to exist almost entirely on a meat diet, with only occasionally some hard bread (*galleta*), similar to ship's biscuit, and never a fruit or a vegetable from one year's end to the next. But they never got scurvy, beri-beri or other nutritional disorders as their *mate* provided the necessary balance to their diet.

There is considerable etiquette involved in drinking *mate* in groups of two or more. The server (*cebador*) always passes the *mate* gourd with his right hand (to show that he does not have a knife in it), and the drinker returns it in the same way, and so on round the circle, usually counter-clockwise. Only a greenhorn (or a *gringo* – same thing !) will say 'thank you' when returning the gourd for refilling. After innumerable rounds, when he is quite full and wishes to be left out of the round, he says '*gracias*', and the server will solemnly say '*buen provecho*' (good health). The person serving is usually the host (rarely hostess) but at Buena Esperanza I found the older custom of *mate* being served by a *criada* or maidservant. With some formality, in the afternoon after the siesta Bob would repair to the farm office to discuss the morning's events and the plans for tomorrow's work with the foreman, who would stand properly at ease and all present (including visitors) were served *mate* by a girl who kept very much in the background and took no part in any conversation.

After a few pleasant days with the Swords I returned to Buenos Aires, where I stayed rather anxiously at the Hotel Nogaró, as Eva Perón was dying and the Ministry of Labour and Social Service close by was always the centre of mob demonstrations and the like. Consequently it was advisable to go into the streets as little as possible. So after only a few cautious days in Buenos Aires I took ship again, this time on the *Highland Patriot*, back to England, having brought up from San Julian my saddle and other farm gear, ready to go out to the Falklands in September.

The Peróns – namely General Juan Domingo, his first wife Evita and his second wife Isabelita – have influenced Argentine life for over half a century and nobody connected with Argentina can fail to have been affected. Even today, years after Isabelita was belatedly removed from power in 1976, their influence lingers on. It has always been difficult to explain the 'mystique' of peronism to people with no experience of South America, particularly in Britain. Perón was an absolute dictator, more in the Italian model than the German, but with popularist concepts which no true right-wing autocrat would pay attention to. The key to peronism lies in the very word – of or pertaining to Perón. He did not pursue a fascist or a national socialist policy, nor did he, as did Pinochet in Chile in the 1970s, seek the support of the right-wing business establishment but rather went out of his way to antagonise it. Even the 'social justice' doctrine (*justicialismo*) which purports today to define peronist ideals does not tell the full story.

Peronism, purely and simply, meant *for Perón*. Where he saw a national need which could be turned in his favour or to his political or personal advantage, regardless of where it came from, he would take it up and put it through as his own. Evita and many others saw this, and climbed into his bed or onto his bandwagon. Social security and trade unionism for the hitherto unprotected lower urban working class (the *descamisados* (3)) would have arrived anyway in a post-war era, as they did in Europe. But Perón saw to it that they occurred, and took the credit. Women's suffrage was also likely to have occurred naturally, but Evita saw to it that it was introduced, took the credit and has been virtually deified by women nationwide as a result. A dictatorship is clearly right wing, but some of Perón's policies so courted the lower working classes as to appear as left wing – however, in spite of much lip-service to democracy there was little doubt as to who had the mailed fist.

Perón was not so successful, inevitably, in finding and selecting his advisers, particularly in the field of finance and economics. Post-war Argentina was rich, having supplied grain, meat and other primary produce to both sides during the war and after it to the groggy ex-combatants shored up by the Marshall plan. It had not as yet developed its own heavy industry and apart from banking and trade in general the country's wealth lay essentially in the land. Most of this was naturally in the hands either of small to medium owners or else of corporate enterprises, many of them British, but much was in the hands of patrician families who also owned property in or near Buenos Aires, such as those I had visited round Daireaux. These people were the natural enemies of the upstart Peróns, and were outspoken enough to become the targets of government harassment. It is not statistically true to say, as Perón tried to imply, that *all* land was in the hands of bullying landlords such as those who had been beastly to Evita as a young girl, but it was easy to see where the animosity came from. (4)

Had Perón been more of a statesman, and based the much-needed industrialisation process on maintaining the existing rural prosperity and starting from there, instead of taxing and otherwise downgrading the latter in order to finance the former, he might have created a really powerful economy. More importantly, he would have secured the political support of a much wider spread of national interests. This is more or less what Pinochet was to do successfully in Chile twenty-five years later, but neither Perón nor his advisers were able to take their hands out of the national till for long enough to make use of the opportunity. The tradition continues right up to and very much including the present day. The Peróns are no more but their followers continue to preach 'social justice' to the masses while still keeping their fingers firmly on the strings both of power and of the economy. Sadly no opposition party has as yet arisen with any better ideas, or the political guts to carry them out.

Not much of this, however, affected Patagonia. When Perón launched his presidential campaign of 1948 with the slogan 'The land for those who work it', agrarian reform was widely spoken of. This meant expropriation or compulsory purchase of the land, with little or no compensation to the former owners, and settlement supposedly by workers – but all too often by beneficiaries of political trade-offs. It had happened in several Latin American countries, particularly in southern Chile, just over the border. The Menéndez interests are supposed to have approached Perón to negotiate the possibility of 'land reform' being applied to certain lands only, and for the rest to be left alone. They were told, however: 'Don't worry, gentlemen, this is not actually going to happen'. The election was duly won by the Perón ticket, and the feared land expropriations did not, in fact, take place.

Patagonia at that time was divided into the territories of Rio Negro, Neuquén, Chubut, Santa Cruz and Tierra del Fuego. This system was a form of colonial-like organisation administered directly by the federal government. The territories were only granted the status of autonomous federal provinces (like the older provinces of Santa Fé, Cordoba etc.) in 1956/57 after constitutional government had been reinstalled following the overthrow of Perón in September 1955. We will come across the Perón story again, later on in these pages.

Notes

1 See *A Rebel for a Horse* by C. Thurlow Craig, a belly-to-ground description of his experiences during the Brazilian Revolution of 1932.

2 For the layman, the shearing hand-piece drives a cutter which oscillates at 3000 rpm across a lower cutter, or comb. It is driven from overhead shafting via a gut core which revolves within a vertical tube. This is firmly attached to the wall so the shearer has to bring the sheep to the cutter rather than 'follow' the hand shears round the sheep.

3 Literally 'the shirtless', so called from the common habit (in a warm climate) of removing the shirt, often winding it round the head in an unmistakeable way reminiscent of a Moorish turban, particularly when indulging in public disturbances.

  They were (and are still) usually unemployed, often recruited (and therefore paid) to come in from the shantytowns and demonstrate in central Buenos Aires. Perón extended the term to include broadly all the working class.

4 Those who have seen the musical *Evita*, or the more recent film starring Madonna, will have seen a remarkably true picture of the Perón story.

11

Monica and John

Deck tennis

My departure from England in 1953 was different from all the others that went before. I was at long last going out into the world, with my brand-new degree, two languages, a little but not much practical farming and other experience, a sure job to go to and a loving family back at home in support – what young man could wish for more? I was on a three-year contract to Holmested, Blake & Co. Ltd (H&B), which meant home leave after three years and then we'll see. At that time three years stretched way out into the misty future and that was as far as it went.

I was all equipped, having brought my saddle and gear from San Julian, and had no problem with customs coming or going. As I was going abroad for an indeterminate period, I had also updated my Settimio Soprani accordion, which had done me well with Tony Reid's band and elsewhere, but had been fairly old originally. So one day Hugh and I went into Brown's of Bristol, musical instrument suppliers who alas are no more, to see what they had. In the window was a gorgeous brand-new Hohner instrument with about six registers (sets of reeds making different sorts of noise), but way out of my price range and we did not think much of Hohners anyway. After a while, and having tried a few others, Mr Brown said, 'Would you like to try the best accordion in the shop?' Thinking he was referring to the Hohner, I thought I might as well see it at least, so said yes. But out from the back came a second-hand 'Odeon Stage'. Mr Brown said it was the best accordion

Frontalini ever made. Well, sure enough I bought it and it is still with me. It has three registers and enormous power. In those pre-amplifier days, to play to a hall full of people, even from a raised stage, the musician had to exert great wind or muscle power to get enough volume out of his instrument for the sound to carry to the back of the hall. I have played other people's accordions and been quite stiff about the shoulders after an hour or two. With the Frontalini you can just lean into it and out comes the most gorgeous volume of sound, and the tone is superb.

When we got on board the *Highland Chieftain* at Tilbury, we found the voyage was going to take a few days longer than scheduled as we were to put into Bilbao in Spain to load potatoes. Usually the cargo was cars and manufactured goods from the UK so the ships left Tilbury already loaded, dead on time. I was given a cabin to share with George Goodall, who came from an established farming family at Hereford near Venado Tuerto. This area, surrounded by fabulous alfalfa/cattle camps, was known as the 'Western Camps' and had a lot of farms owned by families of British descent, often for several generations. George and his brother had not long inherited the property.

The *Highland* boats were fairly large, over 100,000 tons, and had a lot of passenger public rooms and plenty of deck space for games. A few days out, the Bay of Biscay settled down, the sun came out and those people who had hitherto been confined to their bunks began to appear on deck and the general social round began. We started playing games and getting to know the other passengers. In my first two trips I had become quite good at deck tennis, and had won the men's singles on my previous voyage. One morning, while making up four for a game of mixed doubles, a young couple from Montevideo called Patching produced a girl who I had not seen before (she had, it turned out, indeed been confined to her bunk), and introduced me to Monica Lawrence. My fatuous opening remark was, 'I see you've played this game before!' as we threw the quoit back and forth across the net. And so it all started . . .

The social round on board a passenger liner was considerable, with games of all sorts during the day, interrupted for meals and general chit-chat, and a full programme of events every evening once Spain was left behind, several of them such as the initial captain's cocktail party being *de rigueur* black tie. There was dancing most nights. The ship did not boast a live band, so the main music was from records but you cannot keep an accordion hidden for long, and so mine was soon in demand for eightsome reels and the like.

There was a nice group of eight to ten young people on board, and we soon got to know each other and spend most of our time together – playing deck games, board games, liar dice, whatever. After lunch, most would gradually disappear for a siesta, and Monica and I just naturally happened to

On the *Highland Chieftain*, 1953. Left to right: George Goodall, David Fuller, Jean Hunter, Paddy (Second Officer), Monica, John, Ann Keen.

remain together in the lounge, talking. And talking and talking, and the hours went by and all of a sudden it was teatime and we were still there talking. If there is such a thing as love at first sight, then this was it – no blinding flash perhaps, but in those hours of getting to know each other we each realised that we had met somebody extremely special, and by the time we reached Montevideo we were both certain of it, although we were not quite ready to reveal our feelings.

Quite early on, of course, we had discovered the extraordinary coincidence that the Mr Lawrence, who farmed at Eastington next to Uncle Philip, and whose red combine I had often seen, was in fact Monica's Uncle Norman, and that she and her parents had spent much of the previous two months there! The Lawrence family has deep roots in the Vale of the White Horse on the Berkshire Downs, which go back hundreds of years in farming and country-related professions, much like the Blakes in Somerset. Monica's father, Herbert Beaven Lawrence, was born at Bourton-on-the-Water where his father, Sydney Herbert Lawrence, was branch manager of Lloyds Bank. After seeing service in Flanders with the Gloucestershire Regiment, Beaven joined the Bank of London and South America and went out to

Montevideo. There he married Monica's mother, Violet Sophie Almon, whose family was long established in the River Plate. Their two elder daughters, Pam and Joan, were born in Montevideo, but in 1931 Beaven was appointed manager of the bank's branch in Salto, Uruguay, where Monica was born in 1934 and the family lived until being moved back to Montevideo in 1943 for him to take over a more senior post. At the time we met he was just a few years off retirement.

The Almons came from Nova Scotia, and the family goes back to the eighteenth century when one James Almon, a ship owner living in Genoa, moved over to New Jersey as a young man, but died sometime before 1767. His widow Ruth (Hollowood) and son William James Almon were among the loyalist refugees who accompanied General Howe to Halifax following the evacuation of Boston in the spring of 1776. William married Rebecca, daughter of the Reverend Mather Byles, another loyalist who had sailed on the Howe fleet with his five motherless children, and from them the Almon family is descended. Later alliances with the leading Nova Scotia families include DeWolfe, Hensley and Smith. (1)

They were (and are) a family of position and property in shipping and the timber business, also in medicine, law and the clergy. Henry Charles Moore Almon was however of a more adventurous and restless nature so when his father died he took his inheritance and purchased a share in a ship. This was the three-masted barque *Loanda*, owned by Bennett Smith and his son Charles DeWolfe Smith of Windsor, Nova Scotia to whom he was related. It was quite usual for the master to take out an important share in the vessel and its cargo, although Almon was only 25 when he received his Master's Certificate in 1889. In early 1890 he sailed to the River Plate, where he met and married Matilde Woods, whose father had been one of the early railwaymen and had gone out from Bristol, with Matilde as a baby, in about 1870. She travelled on board with him on his voyaging, so that their children were born in various places round the world. Their first-born died in 1881 on a voyage to Batavia and was buried in the Java Sea, and Charlie was born in 1892 on a voyage from Philadelphia to Britain (his birth is registered in Avonmouth, and he retained British citizenship until he became a naturalised Uruguayan in 1930).

Family tradition has it that at this point Matilde said 'never again at sea', so the next voyage of the *Loanda* was to the River Plate, where Almon handed over command of the vessel (2) and settled in Quilmes, now part of Buenos Aires but then a small port and rural town, where Violet was born in 1894. He seems to have set up at first as a merchant or trader, and the family appears on the Quilmes roll of the 1895 census. They then moved to Montevideo, where Captain Almon became Lloyds' representative and Bertie and Gladys (the youngest) were born. Charlie and Bertie had a stevedoring business in Montevideo, while Gladys married Ernest Woodward, a senior cable engineer in Western Telegraph (later Cable and Wireless) who ran the cable ships which laid and maintained the transatlantic cables before and during the Second World War. They lived in Rio de Janeiro in Niteroi, near the beach, from where Uncle Ernest could supervise the transatlantic cable which came ashore there, and also go to sea to supervise operations. In these days of bouncing signals off satellites we sometime forget how vital those undersea cables were, but in the Second World War they were of the utmost importance. Despite this, the cable ships usually went about their work unescorted..

Having moved down to Montevideo at the age of 9, Monica had gone to the British Schools, an outstanding coeducational day school of which Violet Almon had been a founder pupil in her day. Always referred to in the plural, the 'British' was the top private school in Uruguay, and rather like The Grange both the British community and very many leading Uruguayan families sent their children there. Uruguay has always been more pro-British than Argentina. Monica in due course became head girl and captain of hockey, and then went to the Crandon Institute, an American foundation where she took a three-year executive secretarial course. On graduating from Crandon she got a job first with Balfour Williamson and then with the Montevideo branch of Chiclets Adams, the American chewing-gum manu-facturers, where at that time she was private secretary to the manager, a con-tract appointee sent down from the parent company in the USA. Completely bilingual and bicultural, she was quite capable of holding down this formidable job at the age of 19, indeed they had some difficulty replac-ing her in the fullness of time.

I did not get the chance to meet Monica's family when we got to

Salto, Uruguay, 1930s. Wagons such as these were used all over the Pampas until replaced by the railways and eventually motorised road transport.

Montevideo, apart from her sister Joan and Joan's husband John Coates who came down to meet the ship. Due to the delay in calling at Bilbao we were two days late and the *Fitzroy* was waiting for the mail and passengers off the *Chieftain*. The latter docked in the next berth along, whereby the difference in size of the ships was never more apparent. The *Chieftain* was not leaving for Buenos Aires until the next day, so I was allowed to spend the night on board, and the *Fitzroy* sailed in the morning. Monica came down to see us all off, very smartly dressed in her secretarial suiting, and although it was all very stiff-upper-lipped I think that it was this that clinched it as far as we were both concerned, as within a few days we were writing reciprocal impassioned letters . . .

Down to work

Arriving in Port Stanley, I came down to earth with a bump. This was after all my future career seriously beginning, and the pink clouds that had been floating up there for the past three weeks gave way to the highly variable Falklands weather. What was the colony like, five years after I had last been there? Port Stanley, for a start, looked exactly the same as we steamed in through Port William and tied up at the west jetty, with the FIC's store just behind, the Front Road edging away westwards, past the Jubilee Villas, Stanley House, the Globe Store, Malvina House, the cathedral, the Ship Inn, the town hall with the hospital behind, Sulivan House and finally Government House. Past this there were a few new houses for government families and then the road, by now an unpaved track, ended at the race-course – and that was it. No road or even a track which could take a motor vehicle, led further inland.

But there had been changes since 1947. The colony's resources at that time were sheep farming with wool as the only product, and whaling. The latter took place in the Southern Ocean far down in the dependencies and into the Weddell Sea, by pelagic factory/catcher fleets (3) who seldom if ever called in at the Falklands proper, but important dues were paid to the Falkland Islands government, much like the deep-sea fishing fleets do today. The European countries, although rapidly recovering from the war, still needed proteins and oils and had not yet developed the various alternatives to woollen clothing which were to come in time from North Sea gas and other fossil sources. Sadly, there is nothing like a war to stimulate the use of wool for uniforms, and due to the Korean War the demand for wool was good and prices were high.

So both the colony as such, and the farms which comprised it, were in need of re-equipment, changes and new investment and had the money flowing in to do it with. The two most important changes were the Falkland

Islands Government Air Service (FIGAS) and the radio telephone service, also run by government. All farm settlements now had transmitter/receivers and a central operator in Port Stanley called everyone up daily, normally at fixed times as the farm sets were battery-operated so could not be left on listening watch unless there was something important going on, such as a medical emergency. The Air Service had started with a tiny Auster which landed on paddocks or hayfields, but had soon graduated to Beaver float planes which landed on water, every farm being its own port. Falklands weather can of course be extremely tricky, so that although flight schedules were drawn up, virtually every day was different and flying took place as and when it could. The morning weather information on the radio telephone from outlying farms was very important, and usually the day's flights were only confirmed once the weather reports were in. A simple chart was used whereby the farm operator, probably the manager's wife, could look out at the sea, interpret the amount of 'white horses' on the waves and report the estimated wind speed accordingly. The critical difference was between 25 knots (few 'white horses' to the waves – just flyable) and 30 knots (lots of white – not flyable). Passengers often had to wait days, even weeks, for suitable weather in which to be flown to an outlying farm.

I was fortunate on this occasion. The weather was good so I was able to be flown out to Hill Cove within about three or four days, so did not have very long in Stanley – just enough to get my bearings, which included a more or less *de rigueur* invitation to dinner at Government House. The governor at that time was Sir Miles Clifford, in his last year of office. Dinners were, of course, black tie and I remember being invited to the colonial secretary's home, Sulivan House, for a drink before going along to Government House for dinner. I was introduced to several people including Don Ernesto Rowe, who owned and ran the Globe Store and other assets of the Louis Williams estate and was the only Argentine in the islands at that time. All the men, of course, were in dinner jackets and when some of us left to go on up to Government House I put my still rather green foot in it by saying to Mr Rowe, 'See you later' or similar, assuming that he was also dining at Government House. But no, it seemed that Mr Rowe always dressed for dinner at his own house . . .

A couple of days later, the weather being fine, I was picked up by a Land Rover and taken to the Air Service jetty, a small structure towards the western end of town, out of the way of shipping, where the Beavers were kept, fuelled and serviced. Pilot Jim Kerr said it was fine to go, so off we went. The Beaver normally took four passengers, with one up in front beside the pilot, although sometimes a fifth could be squeezed in if one or more were children. When mail had to delivered, as on that occasion, only a few days after the *Fitzroy* had come in, it would be dropped in sacks to farms where no landing was required, so a typical day's flight might involve coming down at two or three farms to land or pick up passengers, and according to the route between these, flying over several others to drop the mail. This process could hardly be simpler – the bags were on the floor, clearly labelled, and either the front passenger or the pilot just opened the door and shoved them out, while the plane was doing a low-level 'buzz' over the settlement. At Hill Cove we landed in the sheltered bay – it was one of the easier farms to fly to – and taxied up to the buoy where the farm rowboat was waiting. It used to be said that 'all Kelpers have webbed feet' which is hardly fair nor indeed correct, as virtually nobody could actually swim. What it really means is that they are equally at home on the water in a boat, large or small, as on land. On land, like all Patagonians to whom many are closely related, they really prefer to ride rather than walk.

Hill Cove being the proud possessor of a couple of miles of driveable track between the Point and Top settlements, had by now acquired a Land Rover, so Bill duly met me at the jetty and we drove up to the Top with my suitcase in the back, instead of on horseback with belongings in saddle-bags, although the latter way was still how you went to other farms, or out to the shepherds' houses. There had been little change in the buildings since my last visit, although there was a rebuilding programme about to be started. Eric Johnson was still foreman, the Dave Mackays had moved from Teal River to Shallow Bay and a number of the same men were there – we will meet these as we go along. Bill and Doreen made me welcome, and I took up my duties as assistant manager.

SS *Fitzroy* tied up at Hill Cove jetty for unloading.

My first requirement was a dog. I had left Queen with Hugh Harding to pass on to Bill, but she was too old for work by now and Bill had his own dogs. Among other recent farm improvements, H&B had had the brilliant idea of importing a top championship-winning Border collie from Wales to be used for breeding and generally improving the local working dogs. This was Glen, who had not long arrived and was being temporarily cared for by Norman Morrison, the cowman-gardener, but somebody had to be his master and handler so he was given to me. Glen had arrived, of course, with his passport and other import documents and among these was a small paper which listed about half dozen commands to be uttered by the handler, with the corresponding interpretation of what the dog was supposed to do for each. So with this in hand, we started to learn how to work sheep together. Fortunately Glen was far more intelligent than I, so we got on fine. He often had his own ideas about how certain operations should be carried out, such as from which side to approach a gate with a small group of sheep, and it was often a real battle of wills to get him to do it any other way, until I found that usually his way was the better one in the first place! Both in Patagonia and the Falklands dogs are trained to follow the handler's hand signals, or the turning of his horse one way or the other to indicate which way to go. They are more usually worked by the whistle as the sound carries further than the voice, so there being no whistle signals in the instructions we worked out a few together, and after four years together I could almost talk to that dog.

I was also assigned my troop of horses. Most horses were imported from Punta Arenas, but Hill Cove also had a small number of brood mares which were served by a Welsh cob stallion to produce 'mountain' horses – a very necessary requirement as the Hill Cove camps included the main chain of mountains on the West Falkland. A 'mountain horse' does not mean one which leaps from crag to crag, but one that has a special gait suitable for ploughing through wet peat without getting bogged down, the bogs found in the mountains being more extensive, wetter and boggier than others. Horses from the coast panic when they feel the peat giving way, and a terrified bogged horse is an awful sight and not easy to get out. The few cases I witnessed were all got out by much expertise on the part of the shepherds, but one heard of others where the horse had to be put down. In your troop, then, would be one or two 'mountain' horses, and among the rest probably one or two 'track' horses. These were animals with an easy gait and a long stride, suitable for covering the many miles along the riding tracks between one settlement and the next. A good track horse like my Hazel also knew the way to most places, so once she realised where you were going to you could forget about steering and even go to sleep until your steed pulled up at the next gate requiring opening.

So spring and lambing came and went, along with lamb-marking as described in Chapter 9 – except that I was no longer a net boy but a full gatherer. I only took one dog, which once the sheep were shut in and the marking was going on, usually slept quietly by his master's saddle. Occasionally an unmarked lamb might jump out of the pen, but Glen was always on the watch for this and would go after the long-tailer and work it and work it until he got it into a corner where somebody could catch it.

Shearing was soon upon us, requiring much the same routine as before, except that while Hugh Harding and I used to amble daily down to the Point on two old plugs, Cherry and Fairy, Bill and I could now drive down in the Land Rover. But we still had our midday meal in the small Nissen hut near the cookhouse, the cook hurrying over with the food when he saw us walking up from the shearing shed. I spent much of the time in the yards rather than the shed proper. We had all (Bill, Robert, Arthur and I) been giving a lot of thought to sheep husbandry, and in particular the problem of worm control as also that of 'squatting' while sheep were being moved. This condition is, as far as I know, peculiar to the Falklands. Sheep in perfectly strong condition, neither too fat nor too weak, after a few miles will just flop on their bellies and there is no moving them. It had been suggested that this might be due to a deficiency of cobalt in the pastures, so we were dosing the just-shorn sheep with a cobalt supplement, and it fell to me to carry this out, including designing the pens to do it in. I made other alterations to the yards in general, starting to apply some of the coast practices which is what I had gone there for. At San Julian we had gone fairly deeply into the design of working yards for easy handling and saving of stress to both sheep and man to say nothing of man-hours, and in my time at Hill Cove we more or less rebuilt most of the main sets of yards.

All this time of course, Monica and I were writing to each other, and I was telling her all about this farm life, so different from any other, as well as filling out further as to ourselves and our families. In my first letter home to England after leaving Montevideo I had put my own family into the picture, and my father on his annual trip out to San Julian had stopped off in Montevideo to get acquainted with the Lawrences. Because the world is so small, among the passengers on the *Highland Chieftain* were a couple called Watson, the husband (known always as 'Wattie') having been one of those bank boys at San Julian who had to ride through the snow way back in 1935, so through the Bank Beaven was able to place us (the Blakes) in both Patagonian and Falkland contexts. Arthur called in at Montevideo on his annual trip to San Julian, and Uncle Robert and Aunt Edith came out to the Falklands and Hill Cove that season, so by the time they all returned to England the idea had been mooted for Monica to come on a visit to the Islands and Hill Cove and see it all for herself. Nothing could happen too quickly, of course, so we had to possess our souls in patience, but Bill and Doreen were to go on UK leave that winter (1954) leaving me in charge of the farm, and on their return Monica would travel down with them and come out to Hill Cove for a visit, returning to Montevideo on the next Fitzroy. So with this to look forward to we started to wind down the farming season towards the winter.

Autumn was dipping time, for which all the flocks had to be gathered, including those in the mountains. Hill Cove could put large numbers of sheep – virtually all its adult ewes and wethers (castrated males) – up onto the mountains for the summer, with consequent saving of the lower coastal camps for wintering. The biggest mountain camp was Mount Adam, which required all the available gatherers – some from Teal River to do the south side, the rest from the north side. In addition to the peat bogs, the steep mountain valleys were blocked in some places by 'stone runs' – accumulations of granite boulders whose origin has given rise to scientific discussion which we won't go into here. (4) They are uncrossable by sheep or horse, so the gathering involved a prearranged plan and interconnection of 'beats', mostly long established by custom. Some of the stone runs had had causeways made by filling the gaps between large stones with smaller ones, so you could lead a horse across. One beat involved leaving your horse in a small stone enclosure called the stable and covering an area of mountainside on foot, with your dogs. Meanwhile the next man down collected your horse and led it round by another way, until you met up at a certain spot a couple of hours later. Another beat was known as 'Casey's' or 'going up over Casey'. Ned Casey had been a carpenter back in Mr Miller's day, who

A stone run in Hill Cove camp, below Mount Adam, the highest mountain in the islands.

having finished a job out at Shallow Bay and possibly following a liquor-induced discussion with the shepherd there, had set out for Hill Cove settlement on foot and never arrived. In bad weather he had found his way right up to one of the shoulders of Mount Adam before finally lying down for good, and his body was only found some two years later by, I believe, Ted Johnson. I never got the Casey beat so could not point out the dread spot, which even the phlegmatic Kelpers would pass by on the other side of the valley. No Chilote would have gone anywhere near.

Another enthralling activity at the beginning of winter was 'putting the horses on the islands'. Hill Cove possessed two small islands off Rapid Point and Creek Point respectively, which were covered with tussac grass. *Poa flabellata* grows at certain places round the coasts, but can easily be eaten out by animals and is much prized as a feed if it is duly protected – on small islands, for example. The farm troop would be gone through –each shepherd would keep two horses and the navvys and bosses one each, which were fed daily in the settlements for the rest of the winter mostly on farm-grown hay. All the rest would be turned out to distant paddocks, and two lots put on the islands. The horses for each island would be driven out to the end of the point just opposite, and then stampeded down the beach with a lot of yelling and shouting, and with a bit of luck, and if the horses had been well chosen so as to include some who knew the ropes, some of the latter would lead off into the water and swim across, followed by the others. At Rapid Point a boat was kept in a boathouse and if the horses would not go on their own two would be caught and towed across behind the boat, with the rest of the men chasing the other horses in after them. It could be quite an exciting and wet-making operation, and when successfully concluded was always rewarded with medicinal tots of rum, the only occasion apart from lamb-marking when the farm provided the bottle . . .

Winter alone

Bill and Doreen duly left on their leave, and I continued at the Big House, looked after by Doreen's cook, Bella Butler and a housemaid, Glor (Gloria) Goodwin – whose father Dave Goodwin was the resident shepherd at the Top. Bella was engaged to, and later married, Richie McKay, Dave McKay's youngest son. Another son, Davy, was married and had the Sound shepherd's house. Richie was a bit of a madcap, and had gone off whaling for a season, coming home with a pocketful of money which he invested in a car – the only car on the West Falkland. It allowed him to go courting Bella in some style although usually he rode up to the top like anyone else. Richie was the farm rough rider, old Dave having been a horse tamer on the coast in his time, so it ran in the family. Norman Morrison and family lived in the other house up at the top. Norman had a terrible stutter but was the soul of kindness as indeed were all his family. He was however not at all well, suffering from something bronchial or cardiac, and one night after supper his son Billy came running over to ask me to send for the doctor as his father was 'took bad'. So I rang the doctor at Fox Bay, and he agreed that he would start out on the eight-hour ride at once. It was, of course, raining cats and dogs and I had to order people out into the muck, it being my job to stay by the telephone. So I first rang the foreman down at the Point: this was now Keith Betts, Eric Johnson having left to become manager at Douglas station on the East Island. Keith said that rather than turn anybody out in such weather he would go himself. So then I rang Chartres farm to tell them the doctor was coming through, and that the Teal River shepherd, Les Halliday, should go and meet him coming up from Chartres and bring him on to the Black Hill Gate to meet Keith coming down from Hill Cove.

No sooner was all this was set up, than there was a knock at the front door, and there was Keith Betts – I can see him still – in thornproofs, (5) his horses tied to the rail all ready to go, rain pouring off his sou'wester but with a big grin on his face, asking if there was any more news or orders, before he took his lonely way off in the dark, up over Hell's Kitchen and along Mount Donald to the Black Hill Gate and the rendezvous with the doctor.

Having set all this in motion, there was little I could do but build up the sitting-room fire and wait. Reports of the doctor and his progress from guide to guide came in over the phone through the night – Fox Bay, Little Chartres, Chartres, Teal River. The maids had inevitably got wind of the goings on, so the fire in the kitchen stove was also kept up, cocoa was produced about midnight, and when Dr Geoff Greenaway finally arrived about 5.30 a.m., we could offer him coffee to warm up. But only I drank it – Keith Betts duly came to report that they had arrived, but the doctor, after a gruelling ride of some eight hours on four changes of horses, had gone coffeeless straight to the Morrison house to see to his patient. To some avail, let us say right away – Norman was indeed in a bad way but the doctor had arrived in time and in due course all was well.

I have told this episode in some detail, not only because clearly it made an impression on me, but also because it is so typical of how people can rise to occasions and rally round, when somebody is sick or needing help. Keith was perhaps not quite right in his assessment of the men – if he had gone to the cookhouse to ask the single men for a volunteer for that ride, any of them would have gone and not thought twice about it.

Winter work was fairly routine. The farm ceased eating mutton at about the end of May and went onto beef, as it was difficult to keep a supply of mutton wethers fat through the winter. In any case they grew wool in the meantime which cattle do not. Now Falkland Island beef is different from any other. Most of the cattle-hunting by the *gauchos* brought in by the

Argentine settlers and later by Lafone, had happened on the East Falkland, but the range and climatic conditions are clearly no different on the West, and the cattle up on the mountains in our day were only slightly less wild than those hunted up and down Mount Donald by Robert Blake and the *gauchos* back in 1894. Now the bovine beast, through some difference in the bone/muscle structure in the hind legs, has no difficulty in ploughing through peat bogs such as the horse does. So they 'do' very well under semi-feral conditions, be it on the West (Hill Cove/Port Howard/Chartres) mountains, or on the Wickham Heights in Lafonia. The resultant beef, when you eventually get it onto a plate, is inevitably rather different from Argentine or Uruguayan alfalfa-fed steak. At first it is a welcome change from mutton, but after a few months we were glad to get back to mutton again.

One project I personally wanted to complete that winter was the road to the Point. The causeway across Kingdom Creek, filled with rock all those years ago by Grandfather Robert, was only negotiable (be it on horseback or in a Land Rover), at half tide or less. Otherwise you had to ride round the head of the creek – easy on horseback but sometimes requiring four-wheel drive and a fair amount of expertise in an off-road motor vehicle if the going was at all soft. With an important rebuilding programme ahead, we had invested in a stone crusher which, driven by a Fordson Major tractor, could reduce the abundant granite boulders from the stone runs to road metal or grit of varying sizes. So I set the gang to work, and in the course of that winter we converted the track round the creek into an all-weather road.

And so the winter passed, with letters from Monica arriving every mail drop. Soon the countdown started – from the day of the last trip of the *Fitzroy* bringing mail – because the next trip would bring the people! It was by now October, and the governor, Sir Miles Clifford having gone home, the new governor, Sir Raynor Arthur, had arrived and was starting a new era. A direct Churchill appointment, he clearly had specific instructions not only *vis-à-vis* Argentina but also within the colony. Looking back now with the advantage of hindsight, the message clearly was that if the colony was viable, socially and economically, then Her Majesty's Government would back it to the hilt, otherwise . . . who knows? Governor Arthur was clearly of the opinion that the colony was indeed viable, and put in train much to try to make it more so, and to improve its latent possibilities.

Lady Arthur did not choose to accompany her husband to these remote South Atlantic wastes, so the governor had provided himself with a very professional housekeeper, Mrs Pollitt, to run Government House. It was quite usual for farmers returning from leave to be invited to stay at Government House for the necessary few days at the whim of the weather and the FIGAS before they could be flown out to their farms. It also gave the governor the opportunity to get to know the people who were the back-

Daffodils have been naturalised in some of the Hill Cove paddocks, as here in November 1954.

bone of the colony, particularly those from the West Falkland who would otherwise come into Port Stanley only once or twice a year. So Bill and Doreen, accompanied by Miss Lawrence, stayed at Government House. The colony gossips, for all their almost journalistic expertise, did not quite know what to make of Miss Lawrence. Here was a young lady, clearly well educated, well dressed and of impeccable taste (as her purchases at the West Store, duly related round town, showed), staying up at Government House but nevertheless going off to the wilds of the West Falkland. Not that we were aware of all this at the time, nor cared then or later – the great thing was that she was coming!

So one cloudless day Monica came to Hill Cove. The Beaver plane touched down in the bay and together with Bill and Doreen she was rowed ashore by Keith Betts and Peter Duncan. It was early spring and serious work had not yet started, so there was plenty of time to show her most aspects of farm life and I was able to clothe some of the things reported by letter with reality, and we continued to talk and talk and talk. Finally, of course, down among the bushes near the shore, surrounded by daffodils (and probably dogs, although they may have realised the solemnity of the occasion and pushed off), I duly proposed and wonder of wonders, was accepted!

205

Newly wed

We were married on 14th September 1955 at Holy Trinity Church, Montevideo, down near the Rambla (Promenade) overlooking the river, by the Rev T. Isaacs. The original church had been built right on the water-front, but when the area was remodelled to accommodate vehicular traffic it was rebuilt on its present site, donated by Samuel Fisher Lafone together with the adjoining Lafone Hall. Monica's mother and sisters had all been married there, and she herself had sung in the choir for several years, so the links were strong. The reception was held at Bertie and Ethel Almon's house on Ellauri St in Pocitos, just a few doors down from the Lawrences' home. Arthur and Millicent had naturally come out for the occasion, and were my only actual relations present, but the event was well attended by friends of both families who comfortably filled both sides of the church. We went off for our honeymoon to the Hotel Nirvana at Colonia Suiza near Colonia, which was full of Argentine *emigrés* from Buenos Aires, and indeed our newly-wed bliss was somewhat interrupted by the news of the *coup d'état* which overthrew the Perón regime. The hotel manager spent two whole days glued to the radio, scanning both Argentine and Uruguayan stations and putting the bulletins out over the public address system, which most of the guests followed avidly. We were far too engrossed with each other to take more than general notice of an event which was to shape all our lives for years to come.

So we duly returned to Pocitos, and started packing up our wedding pres-ents for the long journey to Hill Cove. Meanwhile I continued to meet people. Apart from a few in shipping or trade, the British community in Montevideo had really very little contact with people from the Falklands. The better-off farm owners and their contract managers travelled regularly to the UK on leave but only spent a few days in Montevideo between ship and ship, getting to know very little about the place beyond the English Club and the Alhambra Hotel downtown. Other islanders did not travel at all, except for a few teenagers from Stanley who had won scholarships to the British Schools in Montevideo. There was as yet no full course of secondary education available in Stanley but the colonial government gave grants to perhaps half a dozen of the brighter children. Violet Lawrence was one of a group of enlightened matrons in Montevideo who would invite such youngsters to their homes to try to teach them a few social graces.

When it was known that Monica was marrying someone from the Falklands many were horrified and the suggestion was not un-seriously mooted that I might earn a better living by playing my accordion in the nightclubs of Montevideo! It was difficult for Monica, but with Beaven and Violet's solid support, for which I am eternally grateful, the long months between our engagement and the wedding became more bearable. She had

John and Monica's wedding, 14 September 1955. Left to right: Arthur, Millicent, John, Monica, Beaven, Violet.

her job, of course, which was very demanding, and now had the added burden of training up a replacement. Violet had also arranged with the British Hospital for Monica to be enrolled as a sort of auxiliary, to learn things like giving injections and delivering babies which, added to baking bread and cutting husband's hair, might prove useful to the young wife in the outback, which indeed in the fullness of time they all did.

The town of Salto where Monica spent her childhood years was, in the 1930s and 40s, still somewhat of an outpost. Situated on the Uruguay river and with both river and rail communication with Montevideo some 450km downstream, it was a supply base providing goods and services to a vast rural area stretching north and east into Paysandú and even southern Brazil. Thurlow Craig would have understood the life very well – it was said that you never asked a man who his grandfather was, as he might have started life as a cattle rustler or worse. Life for the bank manager's family in this small country town was not all that different from that of a farm manager's in Patagonia. There were servants to do the housework, and the manager, because of his job, had to be a model of discretion. This in turn laid firm rules on his wife and family. Their house was downtown, next to the bank, but Beaven had a special dispensation from the bank to own a *chacra* or smallholding on the outskirts, where vegetables were grown and a cow kept for the use of the house. The *chacarero* would ride into town daily to bring the milk and vegetables.

The girls had horses there, which they used to ride often, through the

Monica, Joan and Pam on their horses.

citrus groves where they would pick oranges standing on the horse's back to reach better, and along the driveways accompanying the droves of cattle on their way to the railhead for shipment to the *frigorífico* at Fray Bentos, just downriver. They had an amazing amount of freedom, really. Beaven insisted that they carried knives, just like everybody else did in the camp, but although some of the *troperos* must have been pretty rough characters they were also perfect gentlemen and never bothered the girls in any way. There were also visits to nearby estancias, particularly one belonging to the Rawlings family. Monica therefore already had a good deal of camp knowledge and experience on top of her English and Nova Scotian roots, and so to adapt to remote farm life was less of a jump into the blue for her than it would have been for a girl of fully urban upbringing. This was just as well, as our first few months at Hill Cove were not easy ones for a bride.

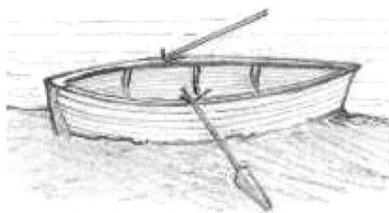

Notes

1 See 'The Almons of Halifax and their Descendants' by Heather Long, *Royal Nova Scotia Historical Society Journal*, 2 (1999) & 3 (2000).

2 'Loanda' continued trading, mostly across the North Atlantic, until in 1898, while at anchor in ballast in Bridgetown, Barbados, she was caught in a hurricane which blew her out to sea and right across to St Vincent, Cape Verde Is, where she became a total wreck. (Monica Lawrence)

3 An excellent account of post-war pelagic whaling may be found in *Of Whales and Men* by R.B. Robertson.

4 For the scientific aspect of stone runs, see J.R.F. Joyce, 'Stone Runs of the Falkland Islands', *Geological Magazine*, lxxxvii(2): 105–15.

5 The Falklands weather is so unpredictable that everybody carries on their saddles a full set of waterproof clothing which was usually made from Barbour's 'thornproof' oiled canvas.

12

Home in the Falklands

The bungalow

We made our home in a small house at the Top Settlement which had been built for Bill and Doreen when they went out in 1949 to understudy and in due course take over the management from Hugh and Beat Harding. Known as the 'Bungalow', it was sited on its own some distance away from the Big House, with a splendid view across to the Point Rincon with Byron Sound behind and across it to Saunders and Keppel Islands. The scenery in the Falklands is quite spectacular. Being a bit further away from the mountains than the Big House we had a better view of them also, looking up to the French Peaks and Hell's Kitchen, then Mt Donald stretching away towards Mt Adam, the highest peak in the Falklands. All the paddocks round the Top Settlement had been seeded to English grasses at one time or another, and were separated by thick gorse hedges which in spring and early summer were a mass of bright yellow blossom contrasting with the dark green foliage. The forest of course was another feature, and although all Falklands farm settlements are charmingly sited by the sea by virtue of being their own ports, we always felt that Hill Cove was particularly attractive.

Weddings and other mere human considerations had always to give way to the remorseless cycle of the farming season, so by the time we had returned to Stanley and gone out to Hill Cove, followed by our baggage on the *Philomel* coasting steamer, we had little time to settle into our home in the bungalow before lamb-marking was on us, with me away from pre-dawn to mid-afternoon every day. This was all right when I actually came home for the night but in order to work the northern part of the farm, where the best ewe camps were, Bill and I would spend several nights at Shallow Bay before returning home. Monica and I could phone each other nightly, of course, but no private conversation was possible given the party nature of the telephone system, with half the West Falkland listening avidly for gossip. We naïvely tried to avoid this at first by talking in Spanish, but this bounced back rather when the story came back down the grapevine that the new Mrs John was a 'native' – a term used in Falkland and Patagonian parlance of the time to refer to a Latin-American person of Spanish or other non-British descent.

H&B had re-equipped our house and furnished it from Heal's. A new Lister lighting plant had been installed by Bill and me during the winter, but this provided electric light for the Big House only so in the Bungalow we had to use oil lamps until the brighter but equally smelly Tilley pressure lanterns arrived. Unfortunately the modern solid-fuel cooker had not yet arrived either so Monica had to learn the hard way how to handle an open-fronted 'Stanley Range' which required not only stoking every twenty minutes or so, no matter how good the quality of the peat, but also a close watch on the dampers to avoid overheating, to say nothing of ash pervading the house from emptying the ashpan. It was also necessary to bank it down properly for the night by carefully piling on peat and closing the dampers, otherwise you came down in the morning to cold ashes instead of a nice bed of embers on which to boil the kettle for the first cup of tea of the day. Many a tear was shed before the efficient new Wellstood cooker was finally installed and it became possible for her to enjoy cooking and keep the house free from dust, even on windy days.

We discovered that domestic life, when living in such a tiny community, had its *rigueur* if not its etiquette. As assistant manager, I did not qualify for the services of the cowman-gardener, so had to dig my own garden, but my cows were milked by the shepherd, Dave Goodwin, and the milk brought over by our peat boy, young Leslie Morrison. On Mondays the copper in the wash house would be firmly lit for the weekly wash and filled with 'white' water (i.e. rainwater) for the linen and smalls. Regular water out of the taps came from a stream off the mountains and was at best a pale straw colour so could only be used to wash working clothes, of which there were also plenty. Monica had been used to washing being done any day, as the need arose, but it seemed to be 'not done' to hang out clothes to dry on any other day than Monday – on Sunday of course it was positively immoral! There was some vying among the women to see who got their washing hung out earliest on Monday mornings; indeed it was said that over at Port Howard old Mr Pole Evans had so disposed the houses as to be scattered enough so that the women could not see each other's washing lines.

Considering the smallness of the community however (four families at the Top and five at the Point) there was seldom if ever any serious squabbling or backbiting, and when there was any real need everyone would draw together round the family concerned, as we have seen in the case of Norman Morrison. Among other post-war amenities following the installation of electricity was a 16mm sound cine projector. The colonial education department organised the supply of films, good feature films mostly, and their exchange and distribution was almost as important as the mail drops. So most Saturday evenings we would fill the Land Rover with people from the Top and bucket off down to the Point for the weekly film show which took place in the cookhouse. This useful building had been purpose-built as a community centre, and several of the walls enclosing the dining room downstairs could be dismantled so as to form a large room like a village hall. Here the cookhouse dances were held, particularly in summer when the weather was fine for visitors to ride over from neighbouring farms. The

Monica and Jasper. I made her a full set of riding gear in stitched rawhide, bridle, halter and reins, as a wedding present. Jasper later won several races at the Hill Cove sports meeting.

nearest was Roy Cove, a mere two hours trot over 'hard camp' (i.e. no peat bogs to be avoided) as opposed to four hours to Chartres and five to Port Howard.

The cookhouse dances were lots of fun, and at the same time, period pieces. There was always a master of ceremonies (MC) who announced the dances (but did not 'call' them in the American fashion) and a good MC was essential to get it all going. The dances were almost all Old-fashioned (Veleta, St Bernard Waltz) or Scottish (Circassian Circle, Dashing White Sergeant, Gay Gordons) with a few modern introductions like the Palais Glide or the Hokey-Cokey. A slow foxtrot might send the men off, bored, to the bar but a good jazzed-up quickstep would usually bring them out again. All music was still live, so my accordion was welcome, and its repertoire of reels etc. from the Tony Reid days went down very well.

Among my jobs was responsibility for the farm store which was fully stocked not only with basic provisions but also a wide variety of 'amenity' stores such as confectionery and liquor. Hill Cove at that time did not subscribe to the rigid 'bottle a week per married man and half a bottle for bachelors' rule and we had no more trouble than any other farm. Families would put in their weekly store list, which we filled and then took the stores round in the Land Rover. During that first season we were very conscious that in February 1956 Hill Cove was due to host the annual West Falkland sports meeting, which involved considerable logistics and planning by the farm whose turn it was. I had been to the Port Howard sports the previous year and taken due note of all the arrangements.

The events consisted of horse racing, steer riding and foot sports, spread over three days with dances at night. For the latter the shearing shed was scrubbed out and tastefully decorated with baling hessian. For a couple of days beforehand, groups of riders with their best suits and long dresses in the saddle-bags, leading spare horses, racing or otherwise, would splash down over Hell's Kitchen or pound along the Sound Ridge from farms all over the West Falkland. The resident population of the two settlements of some 35 people was instantly expanded to 150 or more, so every house bulged at the seams, and the men slept in rows on the floor in the cookhouse. I had picked up some sort of bug, and spent most of the sports in bed, so Monica stood in for me at the store, filling orders like 'a bottle of rum, half a dozen of lemonade, a box of Black Magic chocolates and a packet of Aspros please, Mrs John'.

This was of course my third season as assistant manager, and I had by now got well on top of the routine aspects of the job, knew all the camps and most of the riding tracks and had started to work on newer and more exciting things. In the general climate of reinvestment and expansion prevailing, we had rebuilt the sheep yards at Shallow Bay and made important changes to the dipping yards at the Top settlement and the shearing yards down at the Point – all to basic principles learned at San Julian. We also ploughed up several paddocks and sowed them down to grass mixtures for hay, and were investigating continuously into the cobalt deficiency problem. Also during this time several of the houses for married families were rebuilt, as well as the jetty down at the Point. The old jetty had been demolished by the *Meres-N*, a ship contracted by the FIC to load wool bales in early 1954, which had been unable to put on the brakes by going full astern in time. So the new jetty was built, longer and stronger and at a better angle, converting Hill Cove into one of the best ports on the West Falkland, where nearly all ships could go alongside.

First UK leave

Having joined Holmsted, Blake & Co. in 1953, my first leave was therefore due in 1956 so much of the latter part of that season was spent in packing and preparations, and in mid-May off we went. That particular voyage to Montevideo in the *Fitzroy* was an unusually calm one. Poor Monica is very prone to seasickness and would usually disappear below decks for the voyage, but on that trip the weather was fine and sunny and we spent much time on deck with Norman and Ann Cameron, of Port San Carlos, and their children. There was no room for deck games, other than cockroach racing. For this exciting sport you first catch two or more of the abundant cockroaches and confine them under a tin on the deck, and then bet on which will first cross a chalked circle when the tin is removed.

Once we arrived in England, we proceeded to go the rounds of both the Blake/Worsley and the Lawrence/Beaven families respectively, based mainly at Winscombe with my family where Granny Worsley still presided. We were able to attend Hugh's wedding to Ruth Sleeman down in Tavistock, and Eleanor had become engaged to Christopher Davis, another architect (Hugh had graduated RIBA that year). Granny Worsley was thrilled by all this matrimonial activity and offered a prize (a toy white rabbit) for her first great-grandchild. This our Alison was to win in due course, although sadly Granny never got to see her. An early visit of course was to Eastington, near Northleach, to stay with Norman and Nina Lawrence and chuckle again over the red combine, and other coincidences. Beaven had always made a point of giving his daughters as much English culture as possible after all those years in Salto, so in 1947 had taken them over for a long visit, travelling on one of the first passenger ships available after the war, the *Javanese Prince*, together with Bill and Jean Waldron and their daughters. The Lawrences had spent Christmas 1947 at Eastington, so while I was doing gun drill on Salisbury Plain the girls were cycling up and down the Cotswolds. Now, Beaven and Violet were also on their way to

At Westfield on our first UK leave in 1956. Grannie Worsley seated at left, beside Monica.

England and arrived at Plymouth on the *Reina del Pacífico* later in the summer. Beaven hired a large car which I was very happy to drive for him, even in London and round Hyde Park Corner which was far less nerve-wracking than playing bridge with my mother-in-law who was a real expert.

From Eastington we drifted eastwards into the Vale of the White Horse, visiting other Lawrences and Beavens, in particular the village of Uffington where Tom Brown (he of the *Schooldays*) was born and Uncle Dick Lawrence still lived on the family farm with his son Jack. This was also the Waldron stamping grounds and we were invited to stay with the Ted Mathews' family at Pangbourne, Ted being a director of both Holmested, Blake & Co. and the San Julian company, and he seemed to have forgotten that I had once fired a pillow at him for snoring at Port Howard sports. Anyway, one day he took us off on a drive to see where the Waldrons originally came from, and this turned out to be Uffington and the Waldron and Lawrence families had known each other for generations! Indeed we heard later from the Lawrences that in the 1880s, when the coast and Straits of Magellan region was being opened up for settlement, Mr Waldron of Peasemore asked his good friend and neighbour Mr Lawrence of Uffington if maybe he had a promising young son or nephew who might like to go out to Patagonia. The Lawrences at that time were into serious breeding of the Berkshire breed of pigs with a ready export market to North America, so they did not take this one up.

At the same time, important events were brewing for us. One evening Ted Mathews asked me in his dry (but never pointless) way, if I had 'ever thought of joining the Patagonian Sheep Farming Company' (i.e. Estancia Condor).

215

My initial reaction was no, although I had visited there in 1952 and we knew both the Bill Waldrons and the Davies family from way back. It transpired that Eric Davies, the manager, was coming up for retirement in about four years' time and it was thought to need all of that in which to find, install and train up a replacement. We were very happy in our little house at Hill Cove and had not yet started to get itchy feet but, as Arthur put it when referred to: 'You make your name at Condor, my boy, and then the whole world will be open to you'. When we came to think of it seriously we felt that the professional possibilities in the Islands might in time become limited. The Ajax Bay freezer fiasco [page 225] was currently going on, which firmly put paid to the Islands ever developing a sheep meat trade, or any other serious change in farming. There was always more scope in farming, both business-wise and professionally, on the coast than in the Islands, which was of course why Grandfather Robert had gone to San Julian in the first place! Bill and I had worked well as a team together for three years, and had got a lot done, and there was still more to do, but clearly sooner or later we would catch up with ourselves and my position as junior manager would be phased out. We had as yet no children, but if we did, in the fullness of time there would be the question of education and we were well aware of the problems lying in wait.

So we accepted the Condor job, and it was arranged that we would return to Hill Cove for one more season, look after the farm for the winter while Bill and Doreen went on leave, pack up our stuff and leave after lamb-marking in November 1957. So three generations after the Lawrences' Berkshire pigs, it would be Monica who was to settle in Patagonia and her deep country roots would provide support and inner resources for all of us in the difficult times to come.

Royal visit

So with a new and exciting future looming ahead, we first of course had to return to Hill Cove and stand by H&B for just over another year. Our return voyage on the *Highland Princess* was not a good one – Monica was unwell much of the time and the ship's doctor was one of those elderly practitioners who had gone to sea for his health, so it was not until we got to Montevideo that we were able to confirm that she was in fact expecting, which great news soon dispelled any earlier anxiety! The Falklands at that time had an exceptionally well qualified and devoted medical team, and once we got home to Hill Cove the doctor on the West Falkland, our good friend Geoff Greenaway, soon took the patient(s!) in hand, and the weeks and months started to tick away.

We found the colony all steamed up over the approaching visit of Prince

The Royal visit by the Duke of Edinburgh in 1957.

Philip, Duke of Edinburgh, who having paid royal visits to Australia and New Zealand with the Queen, had chosen to return to Britain on HMS *Britannia* via the British Antarctic dependencies and the Falkland Islands. This took place in February 1957, and so that as many inhabitants as possible could take part, a combined sports meeting in Port Stanley had been arranged, much as in 1947, with both the *Fitzroy* and the Antarctic research ship *Shackleton* ferrying people from the West Falkland and other islands into Stanley. We were picked up at Hill Cove by the latter, and called at several other farms *en route* for Stanley, including San Carlos where my old friend Chris Bonner, who after leaving Cambridge had spent some years in New Zealand, had now returned with his bride Marguerite, to join his parents.

The royal yacht *Britannia* had left New Zealand some weeks previously and steamed across the lonely South Pacific, through Drake Passage and into the Weddell Sea, down to the British Antarctic Survey base at Deception Island – a trip not undertaken lightly even today by ships not especially strengthened to 'take the ice' as experienced mariners of the Southern Ocean would say. Deception lies off the northern tip of Grahamland, a peninsula which extends north of the Antarctic Circle proper into about 68°S and being relatively ice-free is a popular site for Antarctic bases. As well as the British one, there are those of Argentina and

Chile, both of whom claim sovereignty over superimposing sectors of the Antarctic cheese. In those years, it was said that once you crossed the Weddell Sea the importance of these national differences dwindled away and was replaced by a spirit of joint survival, genuine scientific research and comradeship between the crews of the various bases. On this occasion, the British base having laid on a guest night in honour of Prince Philip, invitations were duly sent to both the Chilean and the Argentine bases. The former accepted, but the latter, no doubt under pressure from a senior naval officer who had been sent down from Buenos Aires especially to make sure that all the correct attitudes were maintained, were obliged to decline. (No fraternising with the *piratas ingleses*!) However at this point Antarctic camaraderie took over, and a counter-invitation was leaked back for an informal get-together as long as it was 'unofficial'. So a group from *Britannia*, without the prince but headed by his ADC, Lieutenant Commander Parker, went up and by all accounts had a whale of a party, in true naval tradition.

So on the appointed day, from the upper deck of the *Shackleton* we watched *Britannia* enter Port Stanley harbour in proper naval fashion – the launches hanging from the davits splashed down together into the water only seconds after the anchor, and the royal salute was fired from the fore-shore by two 13-pounder field guns of First World War vintage which very few people knew existed. Soon the gleaming royal barge drew up to the jetty steps and Prince Philip stepped ashore, to be greeted by Governor Arthur in full dress uniform, plumed hat and all, and other leading citizens. It may be noted that the guard of honour drawn up at the head of the jetty was mounted by the Falkland Islands Defence Force, who also fired the salute, and not by the Royal Marines stationed in Stanley.

The three-day visit duly took its course and virtually the whole colony participated. Monica and I were on the general invitation list, so went to most functions including a cocktail party on board *Britannia*. In command of the royal yacht for this rather special round-the-globe trip was Admiral Sir Abel Conolly Abel-Smith, who had a daughter just Monica's age, also expecting, and he was very welcoming to us. It wasn't until several years later that we discovered that the Abel-Smiths lived at Fairford Court, not far from Eastington and the Norman Lawrences. Other events apart from the usual royal-style visits to the Stanley hospital, school and cathedral, included a demonstration of peat cutting out on the bogs behind Stanley, and sheep-dog trials on the racecourse. To see more of the farming side the prince was flown out to Fox Bay where practical sheep-working including shearing had been laid on, and an exhibition of sheep, fleeces and wool crafts was on show in Stanley town hall. Here Prince Philip, after examining a sheep exhibited by Port Howard, felt a tickle on the back of his hand and looked down to find a sheep tick [ked] crawling across it! This was promptly removed, and the manager of Port Howard, Douglas Pole Evans, managed to get hold of it and put it in a matchbox, to be exhibited throughout the week as the 'royal tick'.

A day of horse racing was also laid on, and predictably a cable had been received from *Britannia* a few days before, requesting horses for the prince and several of his staff. Equally predictably the prince was given probably the best horse, so assuring his win! Uncle Robert and Aunt Edith, out from Britain that year on a directorial visit, were presented to the prince on this occasion. Once *Britannia* had fired a 13-gun salute to the governor's flag, which was answered by a royal salute fired by the Falkland Islands Defence Force from the foreshore, she steamed out and headed back to Britain. We all returned home to East Falkland and West Falkland respectively to carry on the season.

Alison

Now we had to prepare for the birth of our first baby, due in mid-April. Due to the vagaries and risks of inter-island travel, by sea or by air, it was clearly advisable for any expectant mother to travel to Stanley not less than a month before the anticipated date; nor could she be expected to return before the baby was settled into a routine and there were no complications. No camp husband, be he navvy or boss, could afford to be away from his job on the farm during the working season, so not only were we having to contemplate a two or more month separation, but Monica faced having her first child quite alone, without either husband or any family relations in immediate support. However dear 'Auntie Connie' Luxton invited her to stay with her at Malvina House during this time. The daughter of old Sydney Miller, Connie had been born and brought up at Hill Cove, and later became the second wife (and by then widow) of old Mr Luxton of Chartres. Like her close friend Beat Harding, who although much the same age was in fact her step-daughter, she was an intrepid horsewoman and used to keep her own troop of track horses on the West Falkland where she spent much of her time. Connie was very good to us and especially to Monica and we held her in great affection – her staunch support and forthright advice on many matters were invaluable.

Invaluable also was the fact that the medical team at the hospital, headed by Dr Stuart Slessor and ably assisted by Sister Fleuret, was first class. It was a long and difficult birth, but finally all was well and Alison Jean was born on 17 April 1957. We were, of course, overjoyed even though it was to be another month before Dr Slessor would allow mother and baby to face the rigours of returning to Hill Cove. But one day the Beaver splashed down into the bay, and Monica and Alison were ceremoniously rowed ashore with wide grins on the faces of all hands. (It was customary in the camp for the proud father of a new baby to pass a bottle of rum around, a ceremony known as 'wetting the baby's head') It was a grand homecoming – Monica had said in her telegram to me that 'she looks just like you' which when faced with the reality I thought a bit optimistic; however I was converted instantly into a doting father.

We soon settled down into our new family routine, and rejoiced in our new baby, who soon started to show her (considerable) personality. When we first got married and set up house, the only one who was not sure about it all was my dog, Glen. He recognised Monica as belonging to the house, but rather on sufferance, and if I went away and did not take him he would sit outside the kitchen window with a big grin on his face, wagging his tail – but this was only his way of asking to be let into the porch, where he would tuck himself away under the geranium pots and growl if anyone except me tried to get him out. But the moment Alison appeared on the scene he seemed to realise what it was all about, and at once appointed himself pram guard. He allowed Monica or me to approach the baby, but nobody else could come near.

The winter of 1957 was particularly trying because the FIC, having commissioned a brand new ship, the *Darwin*, to replace the *Fitzroy*, had decided in their wisdom that the latter would be sailed back to Britain by her Falklander crew, who would then bring out the *Darwin*. Much as we all longed for a new vessel, this meant that the colony would left without a ship, mail or supplies for no less than six months. We were all assured that in any real emergency there was still the *Philomel* who could make it to Punta Arenas in perhaps three days with luck, and that the Beaver planes had sufficient fuel capacity to get there also, but of course they only had one engine with which to cross some 800km of sea . . . In the event neither of these was fortunately put to the test, but the lack of mail was keenly felt and we were very glad when finally in September the *Darwin* arrived in Stanley and the long-awaited mail drops could take place.

At Hill Cove, the winter passed uneventfully. Bill and Doreen had gone to England on leave, everything on the farm was well in hand and no emergencies reared their heads. We did however go into Stanley for the 'winter holiday' in July, when by common consent (there being little work to do in camp) farmers gathered in Stanley for things like meetings of the legislative council, the Sheep Owners' Association (SOA) and the 'agreements' – i.e. meetings between the SOA and the Labour Federation to agree upon wages and contract piece rates for shearing and peat cutting during the coming season. In short, the economic running of the colony, as far as it was determined locally rather than in Whitehall, was set out for another year.

Our flight into Stanley was not uneventful. The weather had turned nasty but the Beaver was on its way and duly landed at Hill Cove. The head pilot of the FIGAS, Jim Kerr, was at the controls. He was an expert if blasé pilot who remarked as we took off, headed directly *towards* the mountains, that it was just as well we were the only passengers because it meant he could make a short take-off! We then had to head out west a long way in order to get round the mountains, which by this time were well covered by thick cloud, and find a clear way which would lead to Stanley. Monica was well strapped into the front passenger seat, holding Alison to her lap as tight as she could (as airline regulations of the day laid down for the safe carriage of infants), but in an exceptionally deep air pocket there was an audible thump as the baby's head (luckily well clad in a thick woolly bonnet) hit the windscreen, fortunately with no damage to either . . .

Governor Arthur had been replaced by Sir Edwin Porter Arrowsmith, so he and his lady were entertaining at Government House and there was a fair amount of social activity. One's luggage, be it 'maletas' for horseback or a smallish suitcase for a floatplane, still had to contain 'black tie' and long dresses if you hadn't, as we had, parked them in a friend's house in Stanley. This for us, again, was Malvina House which was by now our second home, together with a whole crowd of other 'Westers'. One night after a big dinner to which the Arrowsmiths had been invited, most of the men started playing poker. Such is life, that when we finished I was the principal winner and the governor the heaviest loser! This caused great hilarity, especially when the next day I bought Monica a cashmere twin set with the proceeds, which was known thereafter as the 'governor's cardigan'.

Back at Hill Cove, with the coming of spring we could start to look forward and prepare for our forthcoming move over to the coast. The Top was not at that time a very happy place, as Bill's marriage was in the process of breaking up and we were really quite glad to be moving. Workwise, I had done the job I had been contracted to do, and with a new baby our outlook on the future was perhaps already changing. Although we did not have more than a glimmering of the exciting possibilities lying ahead, it was time to go. So we packed up our belongings and shipped them into Stanley on the *Philomel*. Meanwhile lamb-marking came and went and soon it was time to leave. We flew into Stanley in time to catch the *Darwin* bound for Montevideo in the first week of December, but there was one last thing to do before leaving the Falklands. Governor Arrowsmith had opined in my hearing that 'no good music could be played on an accordion', which stuck with me as a sort of challenge, so I had spent a lot of time playing at home during that last winter and worked up a programme which included a wide range of music from classical to light to reels. This I recorded in Stanley and it was broadcast over Stanley radio by way of bidding adieu to the Falklands. The accordion is very suitable for rendering bagpipe music, be it reels or laments, and I ended with that haunting lament 'The Green Hills of Tyrol'. The broadcast was, I learned later, also heard and appreciated by

Our baggage being loaded onto RMS *Darwin*, on leaving the Falklands for Condor.

Patagonian listeners many of whom, having family connections and other links with the Islands, would listen habitually to the Falkland's broadcasting station

The trip on the *Darwin* was positively luxurious because we had a cabin to ourselves, and we were welcomed in Montevideo by the Lawrence family. Beaven had by then retired from the bank, and he and Violet having sold their house in Pocitos were living out in Solís, near Punta del Este. Soon after moving back down to Montevideo from Salto, they had bought a house there, where they spent summers and weekends. Called 'Loanda' after Captain Almon's ship, this now became their home. Solis had excellent beaches, but had never become fashionable like Punta del Este and many families of British descent who preferred a quieter, less social holiday life had summer houses there.

On this occasion I did not spend very long with them as I had to get our baggage over to Buenos Aires and make arrangements for my family to follow once both I and our belongings had got to Condor. We were a little concerned about Alison having been born in the Falklands, but following the excellent advice of the Argentine consul in Montevideo we entered her birth in the Registry of Births in Rio Gallegos, from which flowed her Argentine papers in due course without ever a hitch.

For our baggage, I followed the equally excellent advice of Bishop Evans. The Anglican diocese of the Falkland Islands at that time included the

Argentine, Uruguay and Chile, and the cathedral was in Stanley, not in Buenos Aires. This enormous area was later divided into separate dioceses, and the Anglican diocese of Argentina (without the Falklands) now has its own cathedral of St John the Baptist on Viamonte Street in Buenos Aires. The good bishop used to travel frequently and when arriving in Buenos Aires would say to the customs officer, 'I have come from the Malvinas which you say are part of Argentina, therefore you have no right to open my bags'. I leavened this approach by also suggesting to the head customs man that I might send him up a gift of a lamb for his Sunday *asado*, and he in turn kept face by requiring that the luggage (some eighteen boxes and trunks) remain in bond until shipped south to Patagonia, which suited us fine as they were safer there than in a transport firm's warehouse. So after only a day or two in Buenos Aires I was ready to go south, and on the 19 December 1957 I flew to Rio Gallegos to start a completely new life.

The golden years

This seems a good point, having left the Islands for a new life, to look back on the period in which we had participated. The 1950s had ushered in a period of prosperity for farming in the Falklands, which had never been seen before, and which was to come to an end long before the South Atlantic War in 1982. Once the ravaged economies of Europe started to claw back to normality after the Second World War, all aspects of the textile trade were reactivated and there was a brisk demand for wool, soon to be accentuated by the Korean War. Wool, of course, is not just wool – there are many sorts as we will see in Chapter 15. For now let us just observe that Falkland wools were in good demand, and continued to be so for another twenty years. It was a period of reinvestment and re-equipment. Meanwhile living conditions on the farms improved immeasurably with the introduction of radio telephones, the Air Service, electricity and so on. New ideas, new techniques and the equipment to carry them out were starting to appear.

Motorised transport over land concerned us greatly at this time. The most vital tasks, such at hauling peat off the bogs or fencing materials out to the site were being done by small crawler tractors, but the new post-war wheeled tractors were starting to appear and I had been on courses both to Ferguson's at Coventry and Ford at Dagenham before leaving Britain. We found the New Fordson Major very satisfactory at Hill Cove, and equipped as it was with dual rear wheels was quite capable of haulage over peat. When H&B decided to rebuild the shepherd's house at Crooked Inlet (see map 5) Bill and I opted to haul all the materials over the French Peaks from Hill Cove, rather than have them landed by ship at the mouth of the Crooked Inlet creek. For this we had developed our own design of two-wheeled 'unboggable' trailer, embodying some of the principles of load transfer which had been pioneered by Harry Ferguson during and after the Second World War. By placing the axle of a two-wheeled trailer aft of centre, you transfer part of the load onto the rear wheels of the tractor, thus increasing the grip and avoiding wheel spin.

Several farms by now had Land Rovers, but there were hardly any roads to run them on. We could drive from Hill Cove to Roy Cove as the terrain crossed neither peat bogs nor streams, but that was about all. There were, however, a number of tractor tracks which could be negotiated, crossing the bogs with crawlers or dual rear wheels, and fording the streams at the passes. As long as it has both exhaust pipe and air intake placed vertically a diesel tractor can ford any stream even if the driver has to stand on the seat to keep his bottom out of the water. On representation to the government, grants were awarded for the construction of bridges over certain streams, and Hill Cove was among the first of the farms on the West Falkland to take this up. We then persuaded our neighbours to do the same, especially along routes required by the doctor.

I participated in the first operation in which the doctor was transported from Fox Bay to Hill Cove entirely by Land Rover. In much the same way as on horseback, he was driven first to Little Chartres by the government Rover kept at Fox Bay, then the Chartres one brought him on to Teal River where I met him. We had of necessity been obliged to route the track over hard camp which meant a longer distance than along the riding track. At one point we did in fact have to grind carefully out of a boggy bit, so I made Geoff Greenaway sit on the bonnet so as to give greater grip to the front wheels. We arrived safely, pretty late, and of course telephoned the news back down to all concerned. Such was the grapevine that by the time the news had made the rounds a second time and come back to us, the story was that we had been benighted and Geoff had had to sit on the bonnet holding a flashlight so as to spot holes to be avoided!

On the farms, attention was being paid to improving both the livestock and the conditions under which the sheep lived, pasture improvement, draining peat bogs, investigating things like the cobalt deficiency problem and internal parasites. Some attempt had been made to introduce a meat industry, but not enough farmers had the vision to keep up the pressure on the government to see it through, being quite happy with the ongoing high price of wool. There being no outlet for mutton other than home consumption, farms were so organised as to produce as little surplus sheep as possible, running the minimum number of ewes necessary for breeding up replacements, carrying large numbers of wethers and relying only on wool for income. It was clear however that if there were a market for sheep meat, those farms which had good lambing percentages could carry more ewes, and maybe the others might look at the problem more closely and eventu-

Beaven and Violet with their family. Pam on the left with Brian and Elaine, then Monica with Alison and Joan with Jimmy, Teddy (standing) and Cathy. At *Loanda*, Solis, December 1957.

ally get around to restructuring their flocks. During Governor Arthur's time, the Colonial Development Corporation (CDC) proceeded to erect a freezer at Ajax Bay, on Falkland Sound, well sited both to receive live sheep and to ship out the products. It was clear to anyone with a knowledge of practical sheep-rearing that it would have to operate at a loss – i.e. be subsidised by the government – for a number of years. Like farmers everywhere, most were reluctant to change the old, established ways and it would take time for them to first appreciate the commercial possibilities, and then to readjust both type and breeding of sheep to meet this new market. The Blakes and the Waldrons were among the few who could see this, but neither the government nor the CDC could, or were not prepared to do so, and after operating for only two seasons the Ajax Bay plant was put into liquidation.

Then there was the sheep breeding. It has always been a mystery to me that the Falkland Islands have never been able to develop their own breed of sheep, considering that no existing breed from elsewhere in the world is really suitable. There was a sort of basic local type, originating from English Kent (Romney Marsh) rams brought in by some of leading breeders in the early days, which then by local interchange of rams became widely spread. In the expansive post-war era people like the Waldrons and the Blakes were starting to look seriously into the matter, and other breeds such as Cheviot, Polwarth, New Zealand Romney and Corriedale had been cautiously tried, but none of them were fully successful on their own.

225

The Cheviot rams introduced at Hill Cove had done wonders to improve the lambings, being from their Border ancestry far more suited to wet, semi-mountain conditions than the essentially low-country Kents from the Romney Marshes, but had little wool and that of poor quality. Hill Cove had a small flock of pedigree Corriedale ewes from San Julian, and Port Howard had gone all out for Corriedales, but although their wool cut was far heavier and commanded better prices they were prone to foot rot and other problems associated with the wet and the bogs. At Arthur's instigation, at Hill Cove we crossed Corriedale with Cheviot, and the first cross (which was inevitably named 'Chevydale') was brilliant, being in effect a Cheviot with vastly improved wool on it, but in the event we left before the work came to fruition and I never really heard the end of the story.

During the 1970s things started to slide – wool prices fell away, and successive UK governments put differing emphases on the colony's problems, from the sovereignty issue to the economy. We will look at these later on in Chapter 19.

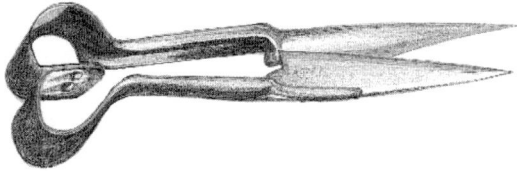

13

Junior Management

Estancia Condor

So what was this 'Condor' that was so famous but about which we as yet knew very little? That it ran 100,000 sheep on 200,000 hectares, the size of the then county of Oxfordshire, we all knew, together with a few of the many Condor myths which abounded. When I visited there in 1952 Bill Waldron was general manager, living in the Big House, and Eric Davies was the manager, living in the second or manager's house. I had also met the assistant manager or 'second', a New Zealander called John De la Tour who was at that time a bachelor and lived in the staff house. When Ted Mathews had offered me the job, I had of course gone up to London to meet the managing director of the Patagonian Sheep Farming Company (1908) Ltd. This was Maurice Waldron, one of the four sons of W.G. Waldron who were running the wide-ranging interests of the family in the current generation. Maurice lived in London and ran their farming and other companies' affairs from the office of Spearing and Waldron in Coleman Street. His brother Eric lived in Buenos Aires and ran the firm of Waldron and Wood. He and his wife Win were very good friends of my parents, and Hugh and I had often stayed with them at their house in Martinez on our way to and from The Grange. 'Bill' (Arthur Trengrouse) we have already met, but the fourth brother Trevennan, who lived in Rhodesia and attended to their interests in Africa, I never met.

Beyond confirming the possibility of my taking over the management from Davies in four years' time, I thought Maurice was not very precise as to what I actually had to do, or where we would live. It seemed that Bill had retired from day-to-day management and had moved down to Gap section as a resident director, while the Davies had moved up to the Big House so as to leave the second house free for De la Tour who had got married. His New Zealand wife however did not like living in Patagonia and so they had returned home. A new second, David Mackenzie, had been taken on but he was not considered future managerial material, and a new house was being built down at Gap, it not being very clear for whom. Maurice rambled on about how maybe I might be a sort of stud manager and technical adviser living down at Gap (where the stud flocks were), and his letter confirming the job refers to the need for studying ways to improve productivity, pasture improvement being specifically mentioned. The final decision was evidently left to the manager on the spot, Eric Davies.

So I landed in Rio Gallegos in December 1957 to be met by Duncan Pickering, brother of Lionel and Tom. In the post-war years, Waldron and Wood had expanded south and set up branch offices in all the main Patagonian towns, where they carried out services and represented the interests of their wool-growing clients much as Julio Aloyz had for Coronel. When I was in San Julian in 1952, Don Julio had retired and the business there was being done by Waldron and Wood, with Duncan Pickering as branch manager, so it was no surprise five years later to find him promoted to the more important Rio Gallegos branch. Duncan had married Ellen Macdonald whose parents had settled a farm in the San Julian district. Her elder sister Emily was a nursing sister, and later assistant matron, of the British Hospital in Montevideo. Duncan and I were to work together in harmony for thirty-five years.

Shearing at Condor was in full swing, so the farm driver, Ernesto Ojeda, had been sent in to fetch me. Eric and Joan Davies welcomed me to the Big House, and Eric lost no time in putting me into the picture. I was to assist him at Condor. There were no bones about it, Condor was where the work was and the Gap job would be subsidiary to it. This was to be David Mackenzie's responsibility, in spite of his alcohol problem, and it seemed he had already been told I was to be moved into Condor over the top of him. The snag was that the Mackenzies could not move out of the second house at Condor to make way for us, until the new house being built for them at Gap was ready, expected for 'after shearing' – i.e. perhaps at the end of January. In the meantime the Davies, whose children had all left home, would be happy to put us up at the Big House while the work was completed. So I made arrangements for Monica and Alison to travel down in the middle of January to join me.

I then set to as a sort of extra assistant, to find out just how this enormous farm was organised. It was twice the size of Coronel in terms of sheep carried, although only a bit larger in surface area. It required a labour force of over twice the size, employing at that time 120 men with a further 28 on contract when at full stretch during shearing, while Coronel never exceeded 40 men plus a shearing gang of 36. Apart from the Condor settlement, there were three sections: Gap, North Ridge and Frailes, each under a foreman responsible for camps running 30–35,000 sheep. Gap was on the Atlantic coast and had been run as a separate estancia for many years although the title deeds were never separated from the rest of the property.

The last manager of Gap station had retired in 1932, and all the sections by then being connected to Condor by telephone line, it had proved simpler and more economical to run Gap like the other sections under a foreman who received orders from the manager daily. It had by far the best land, and was a fully equipped working settlement with workshops, a shearing shed and a manager's house. The latter had recently been done up for Bill and Jean Waldron to live in, and the former was not currently in use although new machinery had been bought and was awaiting installation.

The Condor settlement and its surrounding camps were run by Ernest Speake, the general foreman, who had a certain amount of authority over the other foremen and was, quite plainly admitted to me by Mr Davies, 'the backbone of the farm, God knows what will happen when he goes!' Since his retirement would clearly happen in my time, I was most concerned, especially when I met him and he said quite plainly that he took his orders from the manager and never had any truck with seconds. Speake was English-born, his family had come out in the inter-war years when he was quite young, and he had knocked about a fair amount, droving and carting both with horses and bullocks (both of which were still in use at Condor at that time). He had known Ned Chace, Bill Downer, Jimmy Radboone and many of the other colourful characters abounding in the early days in southern Patagonia. Like Alec Mann, he was one of a select group of hard-working, honest, salt-of-the-earth Brits who never took up land of their own, preferring the security of working at good jobs for the leading companies, with a good pension at the end of it and care for the family in the meantime. I think I sized him up fairly well, and always treated him just as a junior subaltern treats the vastly more experienced sergeant-major. I always called him 'Mr Speake', he always called me 'Mr Blake' and we got on fine. Once he realised I knew my job there was never any problem about who gave the orders.

Shearing was in progress, and I began to learn the reality behind some of those Condor myths. It turned out to be quite true that the Big House was a whole kilometre away from the shearing shed, but not that its roof was made of Welsh slate, nor that the Queen of England's gardener came out every year to see to the gardens. To me at the time, Coronel was a 'big farm' and the way things were done there were the best in the business. But at

Carts like this, here hauling bales of wool to San Julian in the 1930s, were still in use at Condor until 1961.

Coronel there were a lot of personal relationships which acted in both directions between the owning family and the on-farm staff (at Hill Cove this had been even more marked). Condor on the other hand was a commercial company where the owning family was present in the boardroom but not much further, and so one came hard up against the company concept with a bump, where the orders and reason for doing things did not come from Arthur or Bill or Lionel who were real and visible people, but from the boss who, although just as real and visible, one knew very well was equally in thrall to the board back in London.

This went right down the line, and the manager's wife was also expected to toe the line and be at the beck and call of owners, directors and their wives. On the other side of the medal, a good board would be concerned about their managers' wives and their welfare, knowing the immense support they were required to give their husbands when out overseas, on the job, and the impact on family life that this inevitably produced. Further down in the pecking order, the farm staff were less associated with the planning and decision-making than I had been accustomed to. I remember being surprised once when I asked Speake why he had what I evidently felt was an unduly large number of horses on hand, being told 'in case it occurs to the boss to order a series of gathers'. At Coronel Alec Mann would have known what work was likely to be coming up, and would have been prepared for it.

At the other end of the labour force, I came for the first time in contact with the *jodéle al patrón* concept (1) from some of the men, which was much more vicious than the 'bother you, Jack, I'm all right' of the British workman and private soldier. Quite clearly, in the experience of many of the *peónes*, there were some horrible bosses out there who generally abused and took advantage of them, so by definition all bosses as a class were enemies to be hated and got back at by devious means. Only after months and even years of patient and fair treatment could one get over this barrier and establish the trust and mutual respect that is the basis of sound labour relationships. But (jumping ahead rather) I did find it possible and the resulting loyalty was well worth the hassle.

All the workmen lived 'down below' which at Condor meant beyond the store and office building, conveniently situated midway between the working area and the houses with families. There were bunkhouses for the men – three modern post-war masonry buildings with rooms for one or two men, which housed the more permanent staff, and two other buildings with dormitories for the less permanent personnel. The shepherds who were always an élite and in any case more or less lived together with their dogs, had a building to themselves. The cookhouse proper was an imposing building capable of feeding up to eighty men or so, with quarters for the two cooks, one baker and six galley boys, two coal-fired ships' ranges and a full-size masonry bake oven. In a roofed belfry outside was a large ship's bell which was rung for working and meal times and could be heard all over the settlement.

The bell had been salvaged from the wreck of the *Olympian*, a luxury paddle steamer which had been built in Troy, New York in 1875 (as per the inscription on the bell) for excursion trips on the Hudson River. Powered by a single-cylinder James Watt steam engine which drove the side-mounted paddle-wheels via a single crankshaft, she churned majestically between New York and Albany for twenty-odd years, before being caught up in the Gold Rush. Although not built for the open sea, she managed to steam all the way down to Punta Arenas and up to San Francisco and do two trips to the Klondyke goldfields with human and other cargo. Finally in 1901 she was sold for scrap, and was to be towed all the way back to New York for breaking up. Having left Punta Arenas eastbound through the straits, a gale got up which obliged the Dutch tug to let go the tow, and she beached in Munition Bay. Re-floated and patched up, they set off again, but the tow rope broke a second time and she went on the beach in Posession Bay for good.

The mists of history shroud the next stage, which is perhaps just as well since there is little doubt that some element of 'wrecking' went on. The ship was beached on the north shore of the straits, adjoining land owned at that time by Condor, and the local press say that the salvage rights were sold to the three neighbouring farms: Condor, Monte Dinero and Punta Delgada. Certainly the manager's house at Monte Dinero was constructed very largely from timbers removed from the vessel, and a number of cabin doors, bulwark railings and other identifiable elements were still to be seen at Condor in my time. The Waldrons always complained that the Explotadora

The largest shearing installation in continental Argentina, the iron shearing shed at Condor, built in 1911, had 28 stands and took 60 men to shear 3000 sheep per day and bale up about 15 tons of wool. It was indeed a factory.

Company (owners of Estancia 'Punta Delgada') had made off with the oak panelling from the main saloon and used it to line the walls of the living room of the general manager's house in Punta Arenas. The *Olympian* was a luxury excursion steamer, after all, and some of the stained-glass windows and the barbola-work decoration on the cabin doors could still be seen at Condor in 1995. When in my time as manager we rebuilt several of the old houses I insisted that the doors be reused. As ballast the *Olympian* apparently carried sledgehammer heads and iron bars suitable for forging into horse-shoes, all as equally usable in Patagonia as in the Klondyke. The horseshoes were used up long ago, but the sledgehammer heads in use at Condor in my time were of a pattern I have never seen elsewhere, before nor since.

Setting up house

The Condor settlement was arranged along what was virtually the village street, which began at the Big House and ended down below at the cook-house. The oldest house in the settlement, about halfway down, was the original shepherd's shanty built in 1886, and used at that time by the lorry driver, Ernesto Ojeda. Mr Speake and his wife lived in the foreman's house, the next house down the street after ours, and the accountant, Augusto Fleuret, and his family lived nearby. A smaller house was occupied by the Big House gardener, Ignacio Vivar, and his family. Then there was the staff house, always known as the *Comedor Chico*, (2) where the cadets and any unmarried foremen or other staff lived and were looked after by a married couple called Velazquez, whose daughter was married to Nicolas Pilic, the storekeeper. There were several cadets there at the time, who we will meet as we go along.

Continuing on down you came to the office and store, sited between the staff area and the men's quarters. If you proceeded on past the office, after passing the combined stables and cowshed (where in summer the cowman milked six to ten cows for the families and in winter the riding horses were stabled), you came to the police station, one of a network of such all over the territory, sited mostly on the bigger farms and staffed by a sergeant of the provincial police and a constable. The sergeant in my time was a first-class man from the Rio Negro, an expert *gaucho* and tracker who usually sloped around in *bombachas* (baggy trousers for riding) and *alpargatas* (rope-soled shoes), both traditional gaucho wear. But if one went down to the office first thing in the morning to find him waiting outside smartly dressed in full uniform, then there had probably been some form of disturbance and he had locked somebody up. The province did not actually provide a jail, but the farm had a concrete building used for storing stock feed which usually served the purpose – nobody troubled too much that it did not have any windows . . .

Meanwhile, up at the top end of the settlement in the Big House, our baggage had arrived safely by sea long since and was stacked in a shed, and we eagerly awaited 'after shearing' to be able to move into our own house. But it was not to be – we discovered that this hopeful phrase merely meant that once the all-pervading toil of shearing was over, then attention could start to be paid to other things. People did not, it seemed, tackle more than one thing at a time so we, who were later to tackle several lines of action as well as lines of thought all at the same time, just had to possess our souls in patience. The Davies family were very kind (it was not entirely their fault) and did their best to make us feel at home, but the house was not accustomed to a small baby and it was rather wearisome at times.

So the summer passed slowly, I still a supernumerary, and Monica living out of suitcases. I had had a specially large play-pen made, in which Alison played very happily, and during the summer the warm weather allowed mother and daughter to spend a lot of time out of doors. By April, however, Alison had learned to walk and she needed much close supervision to be kept out of mischief. She celebrated her first birthday still in the Big House, until finally the great day came – the new house at Gap was finally finished and the Mackenzies could move. By now it was 30 April and because Patagonia is like that, the first heavy frost of the winter fell that very day, and between the Mackenzies moving out at 11am and our moving in at 2pm, the water pipes froze up. Monica recalls that the very first thing she did was to go up into the attic and tie up a burst pipe with strips of inner tyre tube, to stop water coming through the ceiling into the dining room. We managed to thaw the pipes out without too many of them bursting, and at long last were able to unpack all our treasures and call a house our home.

Staff houses at Condor and most other farms at that time, particularly the larger company farms, had relatively modern 'conveniences', better than those of a generation before, but still lagging behind those regarded as usual in Buenos Aires, Montevideo or the UK. Cooking was done on hot-plate stoves fired by a kerosene drip feed, with a back boiler or side piping in the firebox which also heated running water. This was enough for washing the dishes and general use but for serious bathing in the Big House an auxiliary wood-fired boiler was lit on Wednesdays and Saturdays for baths and on Mondays to do the laundry. Flush lavatories there were, but only for the family; the servants still had to trot out to the Little House. Most of the plumbing had just 'grown' and was not necessarily proof against frosts of more than 5°C below zero without special precautions being taken. We did, however, have central heating (coal fired) in our house, but one night with the heating low was enough for any unprotected pipes to freeze up.

Electricity was supplied by a 110-volt DC battery plant of pre-war vintage which was just big enough to provide lighting for the existing houses and the farm office. The Big House and ourselves had recently acquired small imported washing machines, but these could only be used during the day when the generator was running to recharge the batteries and there was no drain on the lights. Still, for Monica it was a vast improvement over the peat-fired copper in the wash house, kerosene lamps and brown water in the Falklands. We did, however, have some help in the house, provided by the farm. This area was firmly defined according to seniority. The manager in the Big House had a married couple (cook and yardman) as well as a house-maid and a full-time gardener. We were entitled to a cook/maid and a gar-dener/yardman who also stoked the central heating. One must remember that life was still very basic: your meat was delivered (by the milkman) as a whole mutton carcass which had then to be cut up; stores were delivered to the door but you then had to bake your own bread; vegetables had first to be grown and then washed and cleaned; milk was delivered but if you wanted fresh butter you then had to make it.

During the autumn we had cast around and found that the farm carpen-ter, Miguel Oyarzo, was wanting to get married and bring his wife out to the farm, so when we finally moved in we installed Juana in the kitchen, the house having a servants' bedroom in the back. Neither were in their first youth: Oyarzo was quite a good carpenter, albeit desperately slow, which no doubt earned him his nickname *cangrejo* (crab). (3) Juana had worked as a cleaner/concierge at a country school back in Chiloe and had no domestic accomplishments at all, so Monica had to teach her everything including cooking and other home skills. To give them both their due, Juana very soon baked the best bread on the farm, although in other areas she was never better than a good plain cook – anything special had always to be made by the *señora*.

The weather that first winter was, after the initial sharp spell of frost, fairly mild and we could unpack and settle in without any great pressures from outside (those were to come later). I had sent for a few personal belongings from San Julian, particularly Millicent's desk and piano which now adorned our dining room. The house was rather larger than our bungalow at Hill Cove, and we could make a few alterations and redecorations, spread ourselves comfortably and have room for guests. The long winter evenings were whiled away listening to the radio. I had made sure we possessed a really good set, and from the BBC had received good advice about setting up a proper aerial, so we could get excellent reception pretty well worldwide. As well as the BBC, you could hear first-class concerts from Montevideo, even occasionally Radio Moscow or Peking. News, of course, came in both locally and from Buenos Aires – quite important really as although a newspaper was published in Rio Gallegos and the Buenos Aires papers were flown down daily, the frequency of trips to town varied from once a day during shearing to once a week or even less in winter, according to the state of the road. We also subscribed to monthly magazines, and Harrods in Buenos Aires at that time ran a lending library so you could get books sent down. The British Club in Rio Gallegos also had a library. But the radio was the main daily source of news, as well as of plays, features, and concerts from London, Buenos Aires or Montevideo which were enjoyed while we knitted or made gear respectively by our fireside, and Alison slept in her little room.

One evening in late winter, however, I observed that the knitting being set up in the other armchair was rather smaller than the by now usual Alison-sized garments – yes, thrill of thrills, a new baby was on the way! This was soon confirmed out by visits to the doctor in town. Rio Gallegos at that time had some 5,000 inhabitants and about half a dozen doctors, all GPs who were prepared to set their hand to anything that came along. There was a general public hospital funded by the government for charity patients, and two small private clinics. The first of these had not long been started by Dr Pablo Jacinto Borrelli, together with his recently qualified son Dr 'Tito' Borrelli and aided by his daughter Marta, who was a qualified medical administrator. His second wife Annie kept house for them all, the clinic initially being two rooms and a consulting room in their own house. Dr Borrelli was one of those dedicated GPs who looked after his patients in the widest sense and always gave the most stringent and pertinent advice on their health, often in the bluntest of terms. He was most particular on the subject of bringing up children in the rather extreme Patagonian conditions prevailing, then as indeed now, and was known affectionately to a generation of young parents like us as '*papi-abuelo*' ('daddy-grandpa'). So Monica started attending his clinic regularly and early February was suggested as a probable date.

Lamb-marking came and went, and shearing was upon us. Arthur and Millicent came out especially to join us for our first Christmas in our new home, and 'granny' stayed on with us into mid-January while Arthur went up to San Julian. Alison was a bundle of energy by now, and being quite at home up in the Big House where she had learned to walk and had her first birthday, thought nothing of taking herself off to go and visit them there. This was a bit worrying at times, if she was supposed to be playing quietly in the garden, so we had to put childproof latches on the gates!

We had made tentative arrangements for Monica to stay in town before and after the birth of the baby, which we were not very happy with as we did not know very many people locally as yet. In the event, on Sunday 1 February 1959, Monica woke me up and said, 'Maybe we had better go into town right away . . .' so I borrowed Mr Davies' car, fortunately a large and smooth-riding Chevrolet, and with Joan Davies, pillows and blankets etc. we set off on the hour and a half journey, and arrived safely and without incident at the clinic in time for Michael Locke to be born that same afternoon. He was duly bathed, clothed and tucked into his *moisés* [a warm, lined wicker basket like Moses used in the bulrushes, universally used in South America for small babies] and kept warm in the Borrelli's kitchen which was used at that time as a nursery for all newborn babies, being the warmest place in the house.

From the clinic, Monica and Michael went to stay with Pat and Jesse Aldridge in their house in town for a few days. Meanwhile Juana and I coped with Alison back at home. Although we had a telephone line from Condor to Rio Gallegos and so could ring the doctor at any time for advice, Dr Borrelli liked his patients who lived in camp to stay a week or so in town after leaving the clinic just to make sure all was well. Pat had been at St Hilda's in Eleanor's time, and was the daughter of Len Garrard, office manager of Gallie's office in Rio Gallegos, one of three or four such firms which, like Waldron and Wood, did the books and general representation for farms in the district. Jesse had been a farm manager, but was by then also with Gallie. He had two brothers in Punta Arenas, and they were closely related to the Aldridge family in the Falklands.

So after a week or so, Dr Borrelli having given his approval, we brought the new arrival home. Alison, of course, was thrilled to have a real little

Violet and Beaven visit us in the Second's house at Condor, here with Monica, Michael and Alison.

brother to 'help' mother look after, and there was no more running off to the Big House! Michael may have been in a hurry to enter the world, but once in it he became a calm, placid and very soon fat baby who slept the summer days away between feeds, tucked up in his pram in the garden, Alison and the dogs never far away. I had got Glen's son, Skip, sent over from Hill Cove on one of the *Darwin's* trips to Punta Arenas, and I had acquired another dog locally. Skip was never as good as his father at working sheep, but had a more tolerant disposition for small children, possibly more important at that moment in time!

News of Michael's birth, of course, was duly published in the press, both in Buenos Aires and in England. This produced some two or three months later a charming letter from a gentleman now retired and living in the West Indies, who had been in Rio Gallegos in the early days with the Bank of London and Tarapacá (later Bank of London and South America) and remembered a Mr Blake and his family passing through in a coach, *en route* for Punta Arenas and England. This of course was Grandfather Robert Blake Senior, presumably with Grandmother Dora (hence the coach – see page 69) and the year was 1910 or 1912, the only two occasions when Dora visited Patagonia.

The old ways

Meanwhile I had been getting into the work as second. Condor at that time was run in the old-fashioned way, with lots of labour and not too much attention given to its efficient use. Of the total payroll at that time four were English, six were Argentine born of British descent (all English speakers) one was Yugoslav (Croatian) and the rest were all Chilean. There were no other Argentines of any sort. A few of the Chileans were second-generation Croatian from Punta Arenas, but the vast majority were Chilotes from the islands of Chiloe.

These were regarded by their own compatriots as ethnically inferior, although they were treated with more respect by other Patagonians. They lived in some squalor at home in their islands eating the abundant fish and potatoes. So they fed all right, but when it came to earning money for other things they had to go away to earn it as there was at that time no local pro-ductive activity. Every spring the men would drift into Puerto Montt and crowd onto the decks of the *Navarino* coasting steamer for passage to Punta Arenas, where large numbers would be taken on by the big sheep farming operations, and the rest drifted over into Argentina. They were very good workers, and the majority quietly kept their money earned to take home at the end of the season and did not go boozing it away. Many would always return to the same farm year after year, which was welcomed by the hard-pressed managers as they knew the camps, knew the ways and often would return with a son or nephew in tow, and so farm/family relationships grew up, just as valid as if they were fully resident on the farms.

A lot of labour was required, as farm ways of working had altered very little since the beginning of the century, and I was to find that things we had taken for granted at San Julian had not yet entered anybody's head down here. The internal combustion engine had brought in lorries to haul the wool away, and pickups for the staff to get out to the sections, but there were no roads nor internal tracks and the 120 or so windmills were mostly tended on horseback. General carting was done by six-horse wagons, lighter and more versatile than the heavy *chatas* used for long-distance haulage, and bullock-carts were still used for some of the heavier work.

Lamb-marking was one of the most important annual tasks, just like any-where else. The Condor system required thirty-nine horsemen including the manager, the second and a third gang boss to gather and mark a flock of 3,500 to 5,000 ewes per day. Because of the lack of roads you slept out under canvas for the eighteen days or so required. The actual marking was done in permanent pens, strategically sited, as in the Falklands. To transport the camp, tents, stores and a mobile kitchen staffed by the head farm cook and four helpers took three bullock carts and two horse carts. All this required a minimum of fourteen or sixteen oxen, eighty riding horses and twenty-four carthorses, with a few extras amounting to 120 horses in all, which were herded by two horse tenders who brought them into camp every second day. It thus required fifty-one men in all to gather and work an average of say eighty ewes per man per day. At Coronel with roads to carry a motorised marking gang and portable pens, twenty men could handle nearly twice that number. However I had to accept that for roadless Condor at that moment in time the system was the best that could be devised.

After lamb-marking comes shearing. The main Condor shearing shed, where at the time all the sheep were shorn, had twenty-eight shearing stands and two hydraulic presses, and was run by the second. It turned out usually between 3,000 and 4,000 sheep (roughly one flock) per day. Most of the flocks took two days to gather and drive down, but from the more distant corners three or even four days driving were required. All this flock handling plus the return drives of shorn sheep required some forty men including the section foremen, and took considerable planning and coordination, so was organised by the manager. On arrival at the main yards every flock had to be drafted (parted) into its several sorts, and Eric Davies always supervised this himself, it being the only time in the year when he could personally see the results of the overall breeding programme that he was directing.

Shearing usually finished about the last week in January, and was followed by three or more wearisome months during which the lambs were taken from their mothers and put into separate camps, the ewes and other sheep were eyeclipped, dipped and reassembled into flocks for the winter, and the surplus sale sheep were sorted into lots for delivery to the Swift freezer in Rio Gallegos. This was a three-day drive, but by the time your shepherds had rested their horses, refreshed themselves in town and returned to the farm you were lucky to see them again inside a week. In between all this we had to find time to work the *manadas* or breeding herds of horses (Condor had 1,200 horses at that time, roughly half of them tamed), and to work all the 400 or so head of cattle, but somehow we never quite got around to handling them all and so built up a nice line in wild cattle which we didn't get under control for several years.

Mr Davies had never fully understood the negative aspects of wool blindness in sheep, and had allowed the Condor type of Corriedale to develop with far too much wool on their faces. About four months after being shorn or eyeclipped, a proportion of the flock would have enough new growth of wool obstructing their vision so as to interfere with their mobility and general well-being, so they would have to be clipped again. Lambs born in October could be quite blind by March, so at dipping time every sheep was eyeclipped. This job was at that time done manually: every man (including the second) was issued with a pair of shears and a hessian shoulder bag and you dived in among the sheep, grabbed one, upended it, cleared the wool off its face and forehead with half a dozen snips and stuffed the wool into your

The wearisome task of eyeclipping with hand shears would eventually be mechanised, although not for several years.

bag. Twelve energetic and well-trained men might clip a flock of 2,000 sheep in a day, after which you proceeded to dip them. Four to five months later they would all have to be clipped again, so virtually the whole winter was spent at this thankless task. As soon as dipping was finished and all the sheep disposed in their camps for the winter, and the rams joined to the flocks in May, we had to set to and go all round the flocks again.

My job basically was to understudy Mr Davies who did all the planning and coordinating of the often complicated sheep operations, and then Speake and I saw that they were carried out. Condor did not have a head shepherd as such, as did many farms, so I took charge of all the mustering operations, although Speake would detail the men to do them, and in our time this curious arrangement worked very well. At first glance it might seem rather a waste to have the assistant manager going out to camp gathering every day, but initially it was of great value to me for getting to know the geography of the farm and the different sorts of camp.

Much more fun was 'chasing horses'. There were some 1,200 horses on Condor, produced by four breeding herds in a well-planned system. One herd had a pure-bred Percheron stallion, one had a pure Criollo, (both high-priced animals bought at the Palermo Show), and two had half-bred stallions. The Argentine Criollo breed had arisen in central Argentina, descended from the original Spanish horses of the *conquistadores*, and spread all over the country. But it was essentially a cattle horse, and had been found too nervous and frisky for the more plodding sheep work. Crossed with something heavier, a large riding horse emerged, of a tranquil disposition,

240

capable of carrying an equally tranquil Chilote shepherd, his quite heavy saddle and maybe half a dozen sheepskins as well. Heavier horses went into the cart, and the lighter, more agile ones were used by people who wanted a more lively ride.

After weaning, the colts and young mares were kept in two large camps for two years or so until they were three years' old and ready for taming. Speake reckoned that it was necessary to tame fifty young horses per year to keep up regular replacements for both carting and riding. So each year they had to be rounded up for the three-year-olds to be taken off, and this involved some strenuous chases. We had no *gauchos* who could bring down the breakaways with the *bolas*, so the senior cadet, John Hewlett and I laid many crafty plans using a troop of tamed horses as decoys, and in the end got them all in, vowing to keep them in smaller camps next time!

Rebuilding

The general ways of working may not have changed much since the early days of the century, but other changes were in the wind and some already happening. The end of the Second World War had found the Peróns, Juan Domingo and Evita, firmly in control, with a lot of political verbiage flying around about 'the land for the workers' and threats of land reform – i.e. expropriation for subdivision of the larger farms with Condor at the top of the list. Consequently it was felt advisable to postpone any much-needed replacement of buildings, plant and machinery until greater financial and political security should arrive. Perón was overthrown in 1955, and the succeeding governments started to try and correct some of his mistakes.

To do this they wisely set about stimulating all forms of farm production (Argentina's wealth, then as now, lay in the land), and that included Patagonia. Among other incentives, vehicles, machinery and almost any item considered necessary for production were allowed to be imported tax free south of the 42nd parallel – i.e. in Chubut, Santa Cruz and Tierra del Fuego. The 'necessary for production' clause was subject to a very wide interpretation, with the result that a large variety of domestic goods including Scotch whisky were also brought in. It was only when a shipment of television sets reached Port Madryn, at a time when television was limited to the federal capital, that the import facilities were revoked.

Condor was thus able to start a building programme of which the new second's house at Gap was just the beginning. A steady programme of replacement as well as new building was undertaken, which was to continue for over ten years. Wool prices were high, and both the Argentine and British tax systems offered substantial rebates for reinvestment, so the farm was also able to renew all its vehicles, including three Land Rovers, tractors and farm equipment, new shearing machinery for Gap and much else. It fell to me to teach the head windmill mechanic how to drive a Land Rover, and to install the shearing and pressing machinery.

During our first years the drudgery of the interminable sheep work was thus relieved by all these renewals and the new ideas they generated, and in any case I had quite enough to get my teeth into, learning how it all worked, and how the manager set about organising it all, which I would be expected to do in a few years' time. I was also intrigued by the farming aspect and the relationships between the native grazings and the sheep products they grew. The camps seemed to be stocked in number and type of sheep according to long-established custom, and I had a feeling we could do better, but this obviously needed further investigation both on paper and in the field, so it would have to wait.

So we ticked over quietly in our little house. I would be away most days, but seldom for nights. We did not go into Rio Gallegos much ourselves, partly because all business matters were seen to by the manager, while it was my job to stay on the farm and run things in his absence. So the Davies might go about once a week, and we once a month, but our day there was our own for shopping and visiting friends and not filled with chores for the farm. The town office of Waldron & Co. run by Duncan Pickering in any case took care of most of these.

The Davies went home on leave in May 1959 in the traditional manner, after 'putting the rams out' (the manager's job as the person in charge of the breeding programme) and returned only in late October in time for lamb-marking. We were very happy to hold the fort in the meantime – the work was pretty routine and aided by Speake and John Hewlett, now installed as Gap second, and with Fleuret in the office it all went smoothly. This was the year we got the artificial insemination programme off the ground in Gap, with John as operator, but we will deal with the technical and breeding aspects later on in Chapter 15.

Those early winters were not uneventful, mostly due to the difficulty of getting around. This was not so much a problem of ice and snow, (4) as of mud and bogging down on the totally unimproved tracks, so that my experiences in haulage over soft peat at Hill Cove came in handy. In summer the drive to town took about an hour and a half, but the road was by no means all-weather and in winter could take twice as long, grinding all the way in four-wheel drive. Condor had invested in three Land Rovers, one of them a long-wheelbased model intended for the windmills, but in winter I kept it handy as it was by far the best for soft going. There were often thick fogs in autumn, due to the sea on one side and the Straits on the other. From Condor to Gap, and from there on to Monte Dinero, the track was quite unimproved and if wet quite dicey. There was a strict travel drill in place – you never left anywhere without ringing up your destination to advise of your departure, and anybody over an hour overdue would cause a rescue operation to be sent out.

The lighthouse down at Cape Virgins was manned by Navy personnel, and the officer in charge had married quarters and his family with him. One evening a call came through via Monte Dinero that their little girl was poorly with what sounded like appendicitis; they had been on the radio to Naval HQ in Rio Gallegos, who recommended instant evacuation of the patient. So they set off in their rather battered Navy jeep and reached Gap all right, from where John escorted them in the Gap Land Rover, while our mechanic, Roger Gleadell, went to meet them, the Condor-Gap stretch being too bad to risk alone. They reached Condor safely, and headed on to Rio Gallegos, a total of some nine hours on the track, and although it was indeed appendicitis the patient recovered fine. She later trained as a nurse, and was working in 1987 at the clinic into which over the years Borrelli's had developed when I had occasion to be admitted with a bout of pneumonia. She brought her daughters to meet Monica and recall that experience.

The Davies duly returned from leave in time for lamb-marking, by which time we were much more confident after seeing the winter through, and I started in a very small way to look at new ideas, and having spent much time during the winter reading and studying made a start on the matter of pasture improvement by sowing a small species trial of imported grasses. There were a few imported species to be found in the Condor valley so I used the 'acid test' approach and sited my trial plot up on top of the pampa at a very windy site on mediocre soil. The spring was late, dry and cold (it snowed the first night out under canvas for lamb-marking in November) so I didn't bother to go up to see my trial plots until Maurice Waldron came out for Christmas and asked what I had been doing in the matter. So up we went to look, and there were all the grasses growing nicely. This was the beginning of the pasture improvement work which was to end with Condor having ploughed and seeded half the cultivated area in the province of Santa Cruz. We will continue the story in Chapter 15.

Beaven and Violet Lawrence came to visit us early in the New Year and stayed on through January for Michael's birthday, which he celebrated by taking his first steps! 'Granfy' as my father had elected to be called by his grandchildren also came for a few days on his annual visit to San Julian. Then we were into dipping and the autumn sheep work. That winter it was to be our turn for leave, which we were looking forward to very much as we had not been back to Britain for four years, nor away from Patagonia for over two.

Much of the fun of long leaves is the making plans well ahead, so we started on this in good time, but before we left, with our trunks all ready packed, Monica found that our third child was on the way. The probable date was November, which gave us plenty of time to go to the UK and back,

A family gathering at Westfield, 1960. Left to right: Chris with Michael, Monica with Penny, Eleanor with Alison, Hugh holds Richard, Millicent holds John, Philip below, Rosemary holds Charlie, Arthur behind, Ruth.

although we all agreed that sea travel was not wise, and booked our passages by air. The South Atlantic was still crossed by piston-engined aircraft, so after spending a while in Solis with Violet and Beaven we boarded a four-engined Scandinavian Air Service DC 6B, which carried a plaque saying it was the actual aircraft which had pioneered the northern 'Great Circle' route between Europe and America via the Arctic Circle.

Back at Westfield, there were great family gettings together. Grannie Worsley had passed away in 1958, and Millicent and Arthur had plans for dividing the large house horizontally into two flats, which would make life very much easier for them and more flexible for coping with visiting families with small children, of which there were by now plenty. Hugh and Ruth were living in Bristol, and had Philip and Richard, while Eleanor had married Chris Davis in 1957 and they also lived in Bristol with Penny and baby John. Rosemary had according to Granfy Arthur failed to obtain a first at Cambridge (Girton) because she fell in love with Jeremy Goring (an Oxford PhD) in her last year. They were married in 1958 and now lived happily with their first baby Charlie in Lewisham, South London, where Jeremy was minister in the Unitarian Church, and also taught at Goldsmith's College.

We were also made most welcome by the Norman Lawrences at Eastington, with Aunt Margaret nearby in Church Cottage, Northleach and

Uncle Jack not far away at Stow-on-the-Wold, as well as the Philip Worsleys still at Hampnett House, Farmington. Slightly further away were Great Uncle Dick Lawrence at Idstone, and Great Aunts Mabel and Ida at Aldbourne.

Their gardener had worked for some years at Condor, the labour for which had been recruited in the early days from this part of the Berkshire Downs. This was also Waldron country which we were to get to know well on subsequent leaves. We hired a car from Clifford and Webb of Northleach, and engaged a nanny to help look after the children during all these family and other visits. This was Nanny Fraser who later became quite attached to the family and came back several times to help with the older children when the new babies came along. But most of the time we just relaxed at Westfield, playing with the children for whom Granfy had got a small paddling pool, slide and swing at the bottom of the garden. We discovered that Burnham-on-Sea has a lovely sand beach and was not much visited by holiday-makers who tended either to stop at Weston-Super-Mare or carry on down the A38 to Devon.

Leaves come to an end, and all too soon we were on our way to Heathrow to be cosseted by BSAA and shepherded on board their Comet IV – our first trip in a jet aircraft. All was fine until we landed in Dakar for refuelling in

Michael at Eastington.

245

the middle of the night, when we were informed that a mechanical hitch called for a twenty-four hour delay and we were all shuffled off to first-class hotels, the airline rather concerned over Monica's condition so we were looked after very well indeed.

The next night, after the due twenty-four hours, one of the jet engines failed to fire on start-up and a jet of burning kerosene was shot out onto the runway, for all the world like a Primus stove or blowtorch when you admit the air pressure without having heated it up properly. Fortunately nothing else untoward happened, but we were all offloaded while the plane was rechecked and the captain circulated among the passengers calming everybody down, much as a ship's captain does when the emergency signal has been blown.

The plane having been towed a few hundred metres away from the pool of unburnt fuel, we re-embarked, the engines started properly this time, and we trundled to the end of the airfield and began take-off. Halfway down the runway and already almost at take-off speed, the throttles were smartly shut down and we slowed, turned and taxied back to the terminal. By the time we got there several of the more nervous passengers were standing queued up at the exit doors with their coats and cabin baggage in their arms ready to get off. After a further delay it transpired that one of the air-speed indicator instruments (which could only be checked at speed) had acquired an insect during its stay on the ground and so could not register properly and the captain very properly was not going to fly the South Atlantic without it.

The rest of the trip went off without further incident, and after a few days in Solis and Buenos Aires we flew the final leg of some 2,800km (the same as from London to Moscow) back to Rio Gallegos. By now Aerolíneas Argentinas was operating Douglas DC4s which reduced the flight to eight hours. The following year they, also, acquired Comet IVs and Patagonia entered the jet age. I never heard of any similar series of events like that we had in Dakar.

Notes

1 'Let us annoy or otherwise molest the boss as he is going to persecute or mess about with us anyway'. In both languages *joder* (bugger) is used in this sense rather than any other.
2 '*Comedor chico*' means literally 'small dining room' – on farms (including Coronel) this was a room in the main cookhouse, separate from the men's dining room, where the same cook served meals to staff, cadets or even visiting managers.
3 Most of the staff and long-term employees had nicknames, some of them incredibly apt. I was known as *El Mister*, although I never knew whether I had another, less complimentary one, used behind my back!
4 The weather was not in the main all that cold – midwinter nightly temperatures might be from $-3°C$ to $-7°C$ but mostly rose during the day so that periods of solid freeze-ups were not common. Some snow fell most winters, but seldom lay for very long. On the other hand snap frosts of $-20°C$ or lower could occur, and snowfall has been recorded in every month of the year.

14

Senior Management

April Fool's Day

The rest of the 1960/61 season was concerned with working up to the handing over of the management, scheduled for 31 March 1961. Eric Davies was not at all well, and was only too glad for me to run the farm while referring back to him as needed, and I was equally glad to be able to get my hand in in this way. We even persuaded him not to go out under canvas for lamb-marking, a job he had never missed in his forty years at Condor. However, our third baby was due about then so we had to make a few preparations. Juana and 'Chau-Chau' (1) had asked us if they could bring their niece, María, then 18, down from Chiloe so we took her on as nursemaid and she continued with us for ten years. With Juana and María to look after Alison and Michael at home, I took Monica into town to stay with the Aldridges a fortnight or so ahead of the expected date.

In the meantime I started off on the three-weeks round of lamb-marking, with Eric Davies ready to come out to the camp to take over when any word came through from town. As it happened, one of the cadets had a transistor radio, then a very new item of technology and the first time a radio of any sort had been taken out under canvas. On this, one afternoon in the tents way out in the Convents, we heard a message that 'Mrs Blake had been admitted to the Clinic' so when Eric Davies turned up in his Land Rover to take over, I was all ready to leap into it and head for town and Borrelli's clinic. But Stephen Colin Lawrence Blake beat me to it, however, as I arrived in the evening in my working clothes straight from camp, to find Monica fine with this lovely new baby! It was the 13 of November, just when the apple blossom flowers. I could not stay on in town, however, as the lamb-marking operation was continuing its ponderous way and I had to return to Frailes to take over the work again from Eric. By the time lamb-marking was over, some two weeks later, I could bring them home to the farm to join the rest of the family.

Maurice Waldron, the chairman, came out with his wife Phyllis for Christmas and it was confirmed that Eric Davies would formally leave on 31 March and I would take over as manager as from 1 April 1961. Maurice's brother Bill lived in the Big House at Gap as a resident director, so he would continue to carry out some of the upper-echelon administrative functions as well as being on hand for consultations, leaving me to concentrate on running the farm. We had discovered that Eric and Joan Davies had never got to visit the Moreno Glacier near Calafate, nor Cape Virgins, in all those years, so we persuaded them to take time off during March to do so. Finally they left, not to proceed direct to England but on an extended trip to New Zealand and Australia, visiting Corriedale studs in both countries where Eric selected four stud rams for the company.

We then proceeded to move up to the Big House. This was not the most elegant nor best set out manager's house in the Straits of Magellan area, having been built in a hurry in 1911 to replace an earlier house which had burned down. Neither had it been intended for the general manager, for whom the much grander house over at Kimiri Aike (2) in Chile had been built, complete with minstrels' gallery, two staircases and *two bathrooms*! Condor lore had it that the Condor house had been designed by Arthur Waldron and built by Percival Masters, an English carpenter who worked at Condor for a number of years and later took himself off to settle Estancia 'Cristina' on the north shore of Lago Argentino – as far inland as you could go, and only accessible on horseback or by crossing the lake in the boat he had built. Mr and Mrs Masters would come down to Rio Gallegos every year or two, dressed in their best clothes, which dated from around 1910!

The Condor house had been much altered over the years, and both Bill and Jean Waldron and later the Davies had continued the process, but it still only had one bathroom for which the wood-fired water heater was lit on Wednesdays and Saturdays. We had already obtained the board's permission to update this state of affairs, so were able to put in a second bathroom and install gas-fired water heating.

The house was staffed by a married couple, Otilia and Erasmo Davet, and a housemaid who was married to a shepherd, but they had asked to be moved to the Comedor Chico, whose incumbents, the Velázquez family, were leaving to set up a hotel in Rio Gallegos. So we took María with us as combined house- and nursemaid. She could sleep near the children at the end of the long passage down at the bedroom end of the house, and we could entertain farm guests in the dining or living rooms some thirty-five metres away at the opposite end.

Otilia Davet was an Araucanian from Valdivia, and therefore looked down on all Chilotes, even if they comprised most of the workforce. She had come to Punta Arenas as a girl of 14, to be a scullerymaid or 'slavey' in the mansions of Don José Menéndez and other wealthy families. There were eight millionaires in Punta Arenas, each with his own mansion and all having made their fortunes out of wool. She worked her way up, picking up cooking from the French chefs who ruled those kitchens, and later worked for the Morrison family at Estancia 'Penitente', also in Chile, where she learned all the Scottish baking skills. She always weighed her ingredients in pounds, and if she had to follow a recipe, which was seldom, she was happier with a cookbook in English. She was quite capable of turning out a three-course meal at short notice if visitors arrived unexpectedly. Her husband Erasmo was of Swiss descent, from a group who came out to settle near Punta Arenas at the beginning of the century. He was a bit fond of the bottle, and his family in Punta Arenas considered that he had come down in the world. He washed up the dishes behind his wife, separated the milk and looked after the chickens, ducks, geese and turkeys. He was quite well educated and an excellent skater on ice in winter, and taught the children a lot, not only how to skate but he was also strict on table manners when meals were taken round the kitchen table. The Davets had come to Condor in 1945, and worked for the Davies family all the time until we took over. Erasmo died in 1979 but Otilia continued with us until the farm was sold in 1995, thereby completing fifty years of service. Nobody was ever able to get her to reveal a recipe!

We also had a full-time gardener, Ignacio Vivar, who had been with the Davies family for years and with them had been responsible for landscaping the gardens of both the second's and manager's houses. He was a very hard worker and had real green fingers, but was a bit shaky on the 'meum' and 'tuum'. Fortunately we discovered this quite early on, observing from the second's house bags of vegetables being loaded onto the wool lorry when the manager wasn't looking, and were able to set up an 'I know that you know that I know' situation which allowed us to continue retaining his otherwise competent services, and as far as I was ever able to ascertain not lose any more vegetables, neither side losing face in the process.

So, on 1 April 1961, I took over as manager of Condor. I can still remember the twinkle in Mr Speake's eye the first time he told some men to go and give me a hand to move our stuff: 'Off you go with the Boss . . .' Arthur in his inimitable way had summed it up: 'You'll find only about 20 per cent of your problems will have to do with sheep. Fifty per cent will have to do with the women on the place, and the rest will be things you never dreamed had anything to do with farming!' These remarks were not actually made to me, but have been much quoted over the years and how true they have proved to be!

Once we got the family reasonably settled into the Big House, or even before, the first problems started arising among the senior staff. The senior cadet since my arrival at Condor was John Hewlett. His father Rex had come out for the company as a young man in 1920 together with Eric Davies, and later married 'Tommy' Smith, whose father and uncle had settled Estancia 'Coy Inlet' (see Chapter 3), so Rex became their manager there. John's sister Ann had been at St Hilda's with Eleanor. John had been promoted to sub-manager in Gap when David Mackenzie finally drank himself out of the job, and was scheduled to move up to Condor to succeed me as second. He had married Mayo Mackenzie (no relation to David) while still at Gap, and their eldest child Leslie was born while they were there. But before they actually moved up to Condor in our wake he got offered the management of a small farm up country. This was a smaller job both in scope and in pay, but the social kudos of becoming a manager's wife rather than a mere second's was too much for Mayo so off they went. That 50 per cent again!

Our first winter in the Big House was cold and wet. Inside we had coal-fired central heating, but we had not yet put in hand the improvements we

Monica, Alison and Michael in the garden of Condor Big House, June 1961.

were able to do later. Three small children with Stephen a baby in nappies required lots of washing, and the wood-fired water heater was lit every day. Towards the end of May, Alison fell down and cut her lip, so we took her into town where she was duly stitched up by Dr Borrelli. The requisite number of days later we had to take her back to have the stitches out. The morning dawned wet and drizzly, so to make the trip I chose the Land Rover, thinking of soft going and four-wheel-drive stuff on the return trip. Leaving Michael and Stephen at home with Otilia and María, Alison, Monica and I set off. As soon as we got out of the settlement paddocks and up onto the higher ground, we found that the fog had turned to ice and the dirt track, usually affording reasonable grip due to its gravelly nature, was completely iced over.

We were not going fast, but the Land Rover got caught in a rut and slid slowly round on the ice, finally flipping over onto one side. There was a basket of eggs in the back and not one was broken, but Monica grabbed the child tight as we went over and so broke her own collarbone. We were perhaps 5 or 6km out, right up on top of the escarpment in a most exposed position, and the beautiful but empty pampa offered no shelter, so it was advisable to keep the circulation going by walking in the direction of home. Fortunately we had not gone far when we heard a vehicle coming and were picked up by an oil truck, which took us back down to the settlement. The truck left us at the bottom of the garden, but the freezing mist had now reached the valley, and all the paths were a sheet of ice, so we had to hand ourselves slowly and cautiously up to the kitchen door, holding onto the trees. Now, of course, we had two patients instead of one, so while we warmed up with hot coffee and a second breakfast I had the pickup got ready with wheel chains that would grip by biting into the ice. Then we set off again, this time without mishap.

The driver of the oil truck was one Joaquín Fernández, who we did not know personally at the time, but who was struck by the experience and it seems kept an interested eye on us for some twenty-odd years, following our doings and those of the children, before we met up again years later and put it all together. Of such experiences are human relationships formed, especially in Patagonia. It was to be another seven years (1968) before we got a road which could be considered passable in all weathers, winter included.

Having the vastly experienced Ernest Speake to run the main settlement, and me having only just moved up as manager, it did not matter too much for me not to have a second for a while. But it was necessary to have a competent foreman, so when the present one regretfully announced his impending retirement, that was serious, especially as he had important medical reasons and there was no chance of his staying on a bit longer. None of the three section foremen were up to the job, so we advertised seriously both in Rio Gallegos and in Punta Arenas, and were fortunate in securing the services of Pablo Peñaloza, who joined us in 1963 and continued to be my main assistant right up until his own retirement in 1985. His wife, Doña Luisa, was of German descent from southern Chile, a woman of the highest principles who was to prove a great support to Monica over the years.

The second's job was filled unexpectedly from London, where Peter Robertson walked into Maurice Waldron's office one day to ask for a job. Peter was the second son of Charlie Robertson, my erstwhile boss at Fox Bay West, had been to school at St George's in Buenos Aires and was just back from a spell in Australia looking up his roots. As he was of the right age and experience, after an exchange of cables he was taken on, and joined us in September 1961. Being Falkland-born, he had no difficulties in registering as an Argentine citizen (nor had my father Arthur in his day) and in pursuing a normal life. Rumours had abounded in the Islands about young men from there who had been 'caught' by the Argentine authorities and made to do military service, but I never heard of a substantiated case. Although he had no technical training, having worked on farms in Australia and so seen something of other farming scenes Peter was not limited by hidebound Patagonian or Falkand concepts and so became a very useful assistant. He later married Ann Chiswell, of an Anglo-Argentine family in Buenos Aires, and they had two children while at Condor.

The new ways

The farming scene I took over in 1961 had, broadly speaking, been going on with virtually no change since the early 1930s. Wool was shorn, baled up, hauled by motor transport over very indifferent roads to Rio Gallegos, piled up on the beach, and lightered into steamers bound for London (then the centre of world textile trading), where it was sold at auction by Jacomb Hoare and Company. Surplus sheep were driven on the hoof to the local Swift freezer, where they were slaughtered, frozen and lightered into steamers bound also for London, where the meat was distributed to chains of wholesalers supplying both the restaurant and retail trades. On company farms the financial aspect of all this was handled by the board, so the job of the on the spot manager was to plan and carry out the routine work, which took him most of his time, and to attend to the physical side of production in its two aspects: quantity and quality of the products; and cost of production. The first was a matter of carrying out a breeding policy, where the overall guidelines and policy were laid down by the board, but the manager had considerable freedom of action with which to carry the policy out, and this meant primarily the efficient use of labour and its application.

This was not so much a matter of wage levels as of man-time. Then, as now, farm workers were paid 'all found' – i.e. with full board and food supplied so that roughly half your labour cost came from fuel, food and the cost of supplying it. A skilled hand might receive, say, 20–30 per cent more money than an unskilled one, but they both cost the same to feed and board. So we started to look hard at productivity per man, particularly in the more labour-intensive jobs. The shearing operation itself was remarkably advanced, machine shears having been introduced in the 1890s and hydraulic presses as from 1903. Conveyor-belting had been tried and discarded and the only possible improvement pending was to increase the productivity per shearer. This was to come with the introduction of the newer shearing styles developed in Australia and New Zealand after the war (below). The very labour-intensive operations of lamb-marking, eyeclipping and dipping were however crying out for improvement.

Lamb-marking was intimately bound up with the husbandry system, and its form and timing was to change over time. However, for the time being we were stuck with it. With no internal roads available we could not use lorries like they did at Coronel, but with a bit of reorganising we could do away with the encampment and its very cumbersome haulage and portable cooking arrangements. This allowed us to sleep nightly at the sections where

Woolblind sheep will always be poor producers, even if eyeclipped four or more times a year. This genetic fault was not recognised as such for many years.

there were perfectly good buildings and cookhouse staff available, and the haulage of the men's bedding etc. was done by two tractor-trailer outfits. Some streamlining of the handling of the flocks further allowed us to reduce both the time taken overall and the number of men employed – all in all a considerable reduction in man-days per 1,000 ewes handled. Eventually changes in the nature of the freezer lamb trade brought about the possibility of integrating lamb-marking with shearing the ewes, producing an overall saving of 75 per cent in marking costs.

Tackling eyeclipping was a twofold process. In the longer term, breeding of an 'easy-care' type of sheep with little or no face wool was to me clearly necessary, but Eric Davies could never see this. So, in order to convince the board, I ran shearing trials which proved the superiority of an open-faced type both in wool growth and in body size. The breeding aspect in the event was overtaken by other factors as we will see in Chapter 15. More immediately, mechanisation came to the rescue when we designed tractor-driven portable shearing gear which could be taken to the sheep. Almost as important was the transport of the men. Formerly, to transport your gang of twenty or more hand shearers out to the yards where the work was to be done required fifty or more horses, as although a man worked five and a half days per week, each horse could only work two or three days if it was fed on native pasture. The tractor crew never exceeded eighteen men, could turn out at least 30 per cent more sheep per day, and was driven out on the tractor trailers. The latter were of a special design which Bill and I had developed at Hill Cove for hauling fencing and other materials across soft camp behind a wheeled tractor with differential lock or dual rear wheels.

The shearing process now came under inspection. In most of Argentina sheep were shorn with their legs tied, a style brought in by the immigrants from northern Spain, but the Chilean shearers who predominated in the south used the untied style brought from the Highlands by the Scots. In both cases the craft had been passed from man to man and when machine shears came in during the 1890s they adapted as best they could to the limitations imposed by the machinery (see page 184). During and just after the Second World War, however, over in New Zealand and Australia a new style had been developed as a result of shearing competitions, putting time-and-motion study to use with spectacular results. (3) I had seen Godfrey Bowen, the leading New Zealand exponent, demonstrate at the Royal Show in England, and in 1964 the Argentine Ministry of Agriculture contracted Bowen to come over and train instructors. The programme included demonstrations at a number of centres, including Rio Gallegos.

Condor had always provided half of its own shearers and contracted out for the rest. By so doing we could offer a very attractive package to the seasonal Chilote labour, and as a result be sure of employing serious, responsible and competent men. So when our contractor, Don Julio Corzar, passed away in 1963 I had take the plunge and instead of looking for another contractor we started employing all our shearers direct. Among the instructors trained at the main Bowen course at Balcarce was Oscar Vázquez from Santa Cruz, so I arranged the very next season for him to come and run a course at Condor, as a result of which we soon had a number of 'Bowen' shearers on the floor. In early January, a rattletrap jeep turned up with three men from Corrientes in northern Argentina where in spite of the hot weather a great number of sheep are reared. It seemed that there also a 'Bowen' instructor had been busy and these *correntinos*, hearing that we were doing likewise, had driven all the way down to Condor to see if they could get in some practice. They were José Giménez, son of a shearing contractor up there, and two of his shearers. We found room for them, the next year got four, and the year after the whole gang. They would drive all the way down in a specially designed lorry, sleeping in it or by the wayside. Don Isabelino, José's father, was something of a chieftain and father figure among his men and used to look after them accordingly.

The new style proved to be so efficient that we were able to reduce the number of men employed while still moving the flocks in and out at the same rate. The Condor shed was equipped with twenty-eight stands, or shearing positions, and in the Corzar days would turn out 3,000 to 3,500 sheep per day. Once we had the whole shed shearing Bowen style we could achieve this output with eighteen stands. The *correntinos* were always cheerful and a pleasure to have around, and our boys, now growing apace, always got on very well with them. 'Don Isa' was an expert butcher, and we used to arrange to kill a pig while they were with us, and enjoy *salames* and *chorizos* for months. When it was time to go, cakes were baked for them to take on the return journey. They also took with them their earnings in hard cash. When I suggested that sending the money by some other way might be less risky, Don Isabelino looked at me with a twinkle and said, 'I don't think anyone would dare to hold this lot up!' In true *gaucho* tradition, the *correntinos*, were renowned for their knives and their skill in using them. We also continued training local labour in the new shearing style, and often provided the sheep and facilities for courses run by Oscar Vázquez. The practice spread, and the older styles of shearing gradually began to be superseded.

Scab had been eradicated south of the SantaCruz river in the 1930s, but dipping against sheep keds was carried out yearly, in the months of March and April. Plunge dips were used – very cumbersome to our San Julian trained eyes and very demanding in labour. It took at least twelve men to put sheep through the dip: they had to be physically thrown in, a backbreaking job for which you changed the men hourly. Lambs and hoggetts were easy enough, but older sheep did not like being manhandled, first into the 'chucking-in' pen and from there into the dip. At San Julian Arthur had invented a layout whereby they passed through this pen freely at other times and so were fooled into losing their fear of the dip. Lambs with long wool, having swum the length of the dip (some 25 metres), arrived exhausted and unable to climb out, so you had to have two or three men there in waders to help them up the ramp.

Various forms of sheep showers and sprays had by this time been developed in New Zealand and Australia, and we kept a very close eye on this development. The method of application had to go hand-in-hand with the availability of suitable insecticides which in turn required Ministry of Agriculture approval. Eventually a run-through sprayer was put on the market in Argentina in the early 1960s (we later made our own improved version), and new synthetic chemicals started to appear. The spray-races which we use today can treat up to 2,000 sheep per hour (as fast as they will run through) whereas the fastest I have plunge-dipped sheep safely, with a well-trained gang and good installations, was 600 per hour.

The board had mooted the idea of concentrating all the stud work in Gap, mainly on the basis that this section had the best camp. Sheds to house the show rams and a set of yards for lambing the pedigree ewes were set up, and we all put a lot of work into the project during my time as second. But it proved impossible to lamb the ewes satisfactorily and one of the last things we did with Eric Davies before he left was to site a purpose-built *cabaña* for wintering young pedigree rams and feed, tend and titivate them for showing. We also put up a house for the *cabañero*, and a set of lambing yards, all handy to Condor but sited in a sheltered valley some distance away from the hurly-burly of the main settlement. Condor did not consider itself a showplace, and did not chase the big championships, but the sale of rams straight off the farm, up to 2,000 per year, was of some importance. Artificial insemination had been introduced into the district a few years before, Condor being the third farm to set up the necessary installations, which were down at Gap. It fell to me, however, to integrate the use of artificial insemination into the breeding system.

Finally we got round to tackling the cattle. There were thought to be about 500 head on the place but they had not been properly rounded up for years. Most of the big farms along the frontier ran cattle, mainly for the production of draught oxen. There is the famous story of a farm manager who sent up an order to Waldron and Wood to purchase a stud bull, presumably at the famous Palermo Stock Show where all the most blue-blooded cattle in Argentina could be found. Referring back to enquire which breed was in fact required, the answer was that he 'should have a good strong pair of horns' ! At that time the demand for beef in Rio Gallegos was negligible, so there was little sale and the beasts were allowed to run in a semi-wild state. At Condor, in addition, there was just not enough time – after shearing was over, it took you all your time, labour and resources to get all the sheep eye-clipped and dipped ready for mating in May, before the onset of winter. Any time left over was devoted first to the horse herds, so there were cattle out there which had not been rounded up for three years and in some cases more.

This caused a handling problem. Cattle can jump fences surprisingly well, which the locally bred horses could not, so it was quite usual to get your mob of cattle together in one place (which of itself had taken several hours of riding) only to have some old cow or wild bull take off, the herd following, and just pour over the fences like a pack of hounds. All the riders could do, after finding the nearest gate, was to re-muster and hope the cattle have run out of steam but very often the riding horses tired first. If the cattle tired first, they just stop, put their heads down and glare at the approaching rider and there will be no shifting them without aids. The principle of controlling the breakaways is just the same as balling horses (page 147) except that you cannot ball a cow, there is something about her gait which allows the *bolas* to just fall off. Cowboys light out after the leader and lasso her, then play her around a bit to teach her manners. Gauchos *rebenquear* them, i.e.. gallop alongside and hammer the hell out of them with their whip. In Australia they use dogs, 'Blue Heelers' who in spite of their name will also take a hold of the nose and swing on it, and a few dogs could be found in the Falklands who would do this.

We had none of these aids, but after studying the theory of cattle psychology in the 'Pastoral Review', decided to use the pickup trucks. One or two would follow the roundup at a discreet distance, and if a break occurred would step on the gas after the leader, pushing hard so as to catch them if possible across the hocks with your front bumper. When the beast got tired of this process it would turn round, lower its sharply horned head as before, but would see what was to him a bigger beast than himself coming on, so at that point would start to look for the mob and dive into its safety with a lesson learned. We got most of them in eventually, except for a number of really wild bulls which had to be shot. Once we put up a proper race and crush in the cattle and horse yards we could emphasise man's inescapable superiority, something not always present with inexpert wielders of the lasso, and begin to get them under control. In the mid-sixties well-bred beef began to be a saleable commodity, so we brought down Hereford cattle from Leleque who ran cattle more seriously and had good (and tamer) bloodlines.

It was a time of great activity and interest, and our home life had to adjust to it. The boards of big farms gave their managers comfortable living conditions and ample staff so that both the manager and his wife could devote all of his and much of her attention to the company's interests, although Condor was indeed modest in this respect. Just over the frontier at Estancia 'Punta Delgada' there was an indoor staff of six, and the meals were served with white gloves, even though there were HP Sauce bottles on the white tablecloth.

We were told we could do what we liked with the house, even to boarding our own guests, but there always had to be two double bedrooms available for farm guests. This all sounds very opulent, but we were still in the era when due to bad roads, long distances and poor communications in general, every farm had to be its own hotel. Directors on visits from London always came with their wives, and Condor was on the visiting list of embassies and other travelling dignitaries so the best attention had to be provided. Monica's own high standards were well up to all this, of course, and the children grew up into it. There was a big living room where we mainly lived as a family (a wonderful game of bears could be played under its full-sized billiard table), but when guests came, the children would disappear to the nursery while the gentlemen enjoyed their brandy, cigars and billiards and the ladies their gossip.

Christmases were particularly jolly. Bill and Jean Waldron always had a house party down at Gap, often with Bill's brothers Eric or Maurice and their wives, but always insisted that Christmas Eve dinner was eaten at Condor, often inviting the Fentons from Monte Dinero and of course the farm cadets, so there would be twenty or more guests, hot turkey, cold turkey, cold ham, flaming Christmas pudding, carol singing, the lot. The elder children were allowed to stay up until after dinner but then quietly disappeared to bed, although sometimes Monica and I had a job after the guests had all departed to get the stockings filled and hung up before somebody (usually Alison) started waking up again! All this, by the way, took place in the middle of shearing which continued over the New Year. It was the second's job to cope with any disturbances 'down below' – indeed in my day I remember being woken up early one Christmas morning by the police constable, rashly left in charge by his sergeant over the weekend, demanding transport to fetch reinforcements from the border police in order to quell the disorder.

It was a company rule that the manager never left the farm while the contract shearing gang (some fifty-six strong) was on it. This precluded us going to the New Year's Eve dance at the British Club in Rio Gallegos, which due to the strong element of Scottish descent took on a Hogmanay aspect. But we would go to other social events there, gradually getting to know people, puzzled at the beginning because we felt a coolness (I was after all from San Julian, practically a local), until we tumbled to it – it was because we had come over from the Falklands. Not because of the Argentine thing, but because many of the local families had close relations back there who had not, shall we say, made as good themselves, so they were afraid we would blurt out about their dear uncle who was cook on Weddell Island and got tight every weekend, or similar . . . We did in fact know some of these connections but kept our discreet counsel.

Sandy Point

In the early 1960s, Rio Gallegos was still very much a small town, with some 8,000 inhabitants, compared to Punta Arenas in Chile with ten times that number. Although the heyday of the latter came to an end with the opening of the Panama Canal in 1914, it was still an extremely key port as far as sea traffic in the South Atlantic was concerned. Goods were shipped out from Europe, and distributed to the many large and important farms running millions of sheep on both sides of the Straits of Magellan and in both countries. Braun & Blanchard ran a regular service for the 'ports of the Straits' which numbered about fifteen, as every major farm either was, or had, its own port. Condor, for example, in addition to operating Kimiri Aike near the first Narrows, had a ten hectares known as the 'Condor Port' on the beach near Cañadón Grande, where the coasting vessels beached at low tide for loading. Wool from these ports was transhipped in Punta Arenas on to larger vessels for the London auction sales. (4) Certainly up until the Second World War, most of the farms south of the Gallegos River looked towards Punta Arenas rather than Rio Gallegos for supplies, which were basically cheaper than goods from Buenos Aires. In our day a series of post-war

The Braun family house in Punta Arenas, today preserved as a museum.

Argentine import restrictions had cut out this source as far as main supplies were concerned, but Punta Arenas was still a source of imported consumer goods which you could bring back in your car.

So one went to Punta Arenas for the shopping. One could get all the English brands of clothes, toys, tricycles, Christmas decorations and goodies from Messrs Cadbury and Mackintosh. Scotch and other imported whiskies were cheap, although Rio Gallegos still had an ample supply left over from the duty-free days of the 1950s. Medical services were also better there. In the previous generation, whereas my mother had returned to England for her first-born, many British women living in southern Santa Cruz would go to Punta Arenas to have their babies, which if boys had the added advantage of not having to do military service in Argentina.

Tourism had not yet developed in any way, and in spite of its status as a port and trading centre, Punta Arenas was remarkably lacking in hotel accommodation. The only possible place to stay was the Hotel Cosmos, an venerable old-fashioned hostelry near the port, in fact not unlike the Hotel Miramar in San Julian but larger and with excellent service. On our first visit, with Alison, we made the mistake of bringing the remains of our lunch picnic (it was a full day's drive from Condor at that time), into our room, to the delight of the cockroaches and mice which could be heard rustling the paper in the middle of the night . . .

We had taken Alison because she had developed a deviation in one eye requiring specialist treatment. Fortunately, there was an outstanding eye specialist, Dr Borgoño, living in Punta Arenas for his health, rather than pursue a more lucrative practice in Santiago. His diagnosis, early treatment and advice were invaluable, and enabled her a few years later to be successfully operated upon and treated by Dr Malbrán in Buenos Aires, quite overcoming the problem.

One also went to Punta Arenas for the stock show. These shows, which we I mentioned briefly in Chapter 8, took place in all the coast towns at that time. San Julian, Deseado and Santa Cruz all had their shows, but the major ones were Comodoro Rivadavia, Rio Gallegos and Punta Arenas. Bill and Jean Waldron still related very much to the farming scene over the border in Magallanes, indeed Bill was farming in his own name the 'Los Pozos' camps which lay in the narrow strip of Chile between the Gap border and the Straits proper, which had been retained as Waldron property when the Kimiri Aike camps were sold to the Explotadora company in 1948.

There was a strong British expatriate presence in Punta Arenas at that time, with a British consul, an English club, two freezing companies and the Bank of London and South America. The powerful *Sociedad Explotadora de Tierra del Fuego* ran over a million sheep on both sides of the Straits and although registered in Santiago, its shareholders included a strong European element and its managers were all British – the general manager in Punta

Arenas being Bobby Huntley, who was married to Decima Hobbs, the youngest daughter of Don Ernesto, who had clearly run out of girls' names as he named his two youngest Nona and Decima. There were other large farming companies like Laguna Blanca and Rio Verde with British roots, some still strong with the owners coming out every year, and most of them had British managers. Several families had sent their sons to The Grange, and indeed I was to meet up again with several classmates.

The Menéndez-Braun family interests were another power in the land, with large holdings of their own as well as important shareholdings in the Explotadora and other trade and shipping enterprises such as the Anónima, as we have seen. Socially, Punta Arenas was where they gathered and three at least of the mansions were still kept open and used, at least at show time. Condor and the Waldrons were still very much a part of all this, having operated on both sides of the Straits in the early days, and for many years prior to 1947 having sent their considerable droves of surplus sheep to the freezing plants at Puerto Sara, Río Seco and Tres Puentes. As a leading Corriedale stud we also took rams for showing and were on the visiting list to the receptions and other social events. The last show to which we took rams was in 1967, by which time the Explotadora had opened the five-star Hotel Cabo de Hornos, still today the leading hotel in Punta Arenas. I remember a dinner party given by Don Carlos Menéndez, the last surviving son of José Menéndez, as well as a full-blown reception at the Braun

The Big House at Estancia San Gregorio in Magallanes, Chile. This was the first, and principal, farm founded by José Menéndez. The Menéndez-Braun holdings grew to over a million sheep before the family assets were subdivided in 1974.

Mansion (today preserved as a museum) with all the trimmings, and regard it as a privilege to be able to link back to those former times.

For the writing was even then on the wall for Chile, socially and politically, and the socialist pressure which was to end in the nadir of the communist government of Salvador Allende (1970–73) had already begun. Land reform was being mooted, a concept which received wide support from the middle strata of small businesses and tradesmen who loved the idea of 'having a bit of camp' but was not supported by the working-class people who, in theory, it was supposed to benefit. As early as 1960 the two largest properties on Tierra del Fuego, 'San Sebastián' and 'Caleta Josefina', running between them over 350,000 sheep, had been expropriated for sub-division. In all fairness, at this stage it was reasonably well run. There were little overt politics about the scheme, which was aimed at settling private operators on medium-sized, viable holdings, and the majority of the bene-ficiaries have since become successful farmers.

Farm merger

So the full months fled by, and soon we found another baby was on the way, expected early in the New Year of 1963, which would clearly be a busy time. Maurice and Phyllis Waldron were coming out that year and shearing was of course going on, including at the newly-refitted shearing shed down at Gap. We had managed to find Christine Hudson, an English girl teaching in Buenos Aires who was happy to come down and spend part of her summer holiday with us, helping Monica with the three children and teach-ing Alison, now 5, her first letters. All went well – at least by having babies in the summer you don't have to worry about the roads being impassable, so I took Monica in to stay with the Aldridges, and on 12 January 1963 our third son, Stuart, was born. We christened him John Stuart Beaven but the Spanish tongues in the kitchen, which had already some difficulty over his elder brother Stephen (so called him 'Chipi') were soon calling the new arrival 'Chacho' (short for *muchacho* – 'boy'), as he is still called to this day.

Alison was 6 in April, so the question of school had been in our minds for some time past. While we intended to give our children a sound bilingual education like we had both had, which would mean their going away to boarding school eventually, for the time being something closer at hand was needed. At that time there was no provision whatever for rural education of any sort – any family living in camp, boss or *peón*, had to send their children into the towns or have them stay unlettered. There were several other chil-dren of school age on the farm, so we approached the provincial education board and found them quite prepared to supply a (primary level) teacher as long as the farm provided a classroom and boarded the teacher. Our board

Condor School. Standing: Americo Moyano, Secretary of Education, Richard Lagiard, teacher, Emilio Garcia Pacheco, Inspector of Schools. Alison lower front, on right Ema Caram and Susana Penaloza.

in London, when applied to, agreed with me that to provide schooling as well as housing for families was good labour relations and a sound way of anchoring your key personnel. So Escuela Provincial No. 31 was founded in May 1963, the first school of its type for primary schooling outside of the scattered towns in Santa Cruz. It was later to be followed by eight others of a similar type. For that first year we were sent a young man as teacher, who boarded in the *comedor chico*, and a spare room in the basement of the accountant's house was used as a classroom.

1963 was a leave year for us, so in early June (after putting the rams out in May (i.e. supervising the mating process which set up the farming cycle for the coming year), we set forth, again by air. We had discovered that if you bought a through ticket from Buenos Aires to London, you could travel 'off-line' and visit, for example, Madrid or Rome for no extra cost in fares, only the hotels. So we blithely set off with Stuart, then 4 months old, in the carry-cot, and were only mildly put out when, on boarding the plane in Montevideo after a week at Solís with Monica's parents, the carefully-packed cabin bag for a sixteen-hour flight for four children under 5 got left behind. The cabin crew were marvellous, providing games and diverting paper towels from the loos to provide nappies for the baby. We spent three nights in Madrid seeing the sights, the Prado, Escorial and all. Our bag duly caught up with us and then we went on to Rome for a similar round of family sightseeing.

The Italians of course are nuts on *bambini* and I have the fondest recol-lection of leaving Stuart in his carry-cot under the safe eyes of the security guards in the Vatican Treasury while we looked around, and on a bus tour of the city putting the carry-cot on the luggage rack just beside the driver, who would waggle his fingers at the baby while shouting imprecations at the traffic out of the window. On arrival in the UK we discovered that near the then West London Air Terminal on Cromwell Road there were modest-priced family hotels which had Spanish maids who were always glad to babysit, so we spent a couple of nights there before proceeding down to Winscombe.

At Westfield Arthur had the flag up, and we settled into the upstairs flat with its separate entrance so we could be close to the grandparents but not on top of them. The large garden and tennis court allowed plenty of room for the children to run and play, and we entered Alison (6) and Michael (4) at 'The Chestnuts', a nursery school in the village which Hugh and I had attended in our day. Hugh and Ruth now had Thomas as well as Philip and Richard, and Jeremy and Rosemary had Charlie and George, but the family had been saddened by the death of Chris Davis, who had developed a cere-bral abscess and in spite of expert care and nursing in Frenchay Hospital, Bristol, passed away on 2 June 1963, leaving Eleanor with Penny and John as well as baby Robbie, born only two months before his father's death. We organised a joint seaside holiday at Charmouth down in Devon with all the families, a very small-persons' event as Alison at 6 was the eldest of eleven grandchildren! All our friends and cousins seemed to be having children and there were several family get-togethers, at one of which I rashly offered to roast an *asado* to solve the catering problem. It rained of course, but it was all good fun . . .

As before, I attended board meetings in London, including the Patagonian Sheep Farming Company's annual general meeting which was followed, as was the custom, by an elegant lunch at the Great Eastern Hotel. Here I found myself sitting next to a Mr Kenneth Suggett, chairman of the Argentine Southern Land Company (ASL), and learned that important changes were afoot. This was the biggest sheep operation in Argentina, an outfit operating several farms running a total of 125,000 sheep and 10,000 head of cattle in the foothills of the Andes in the upper Rio Negro and Chubut provinces from Bariloche down to Esquel. They ran Merino sheep and their main estancia, 'Leleque' was, at least until 1995 or so, *the* leading Merino stud in the Argentine. We knew a fair bit about them – Arthur had visited them at various times and Bob Blake had done two years as a cadet at Leleque. It seemed that a merger was being arranged between them and the Patagonian Sheep Farming Company. The latter was a private company but the ASL was public and the joint holding would be quoted on the Stock Exchange. It was, in the end, a true merger as although technically the

Patagonian Sheep Farming Company became a wholly-owned subsidiary of ASL, the final joint board had more ex-Patagonian Sheep Farming Company members than ASL members.

It was also a sound business venture – Condor had the leading Corriedale clip in the country while ASL had the top Merino one. The latter's head-quarters at Estancia 'Pilcañeu' near Bariloche was on the broad-gauge railway connected to the rest of central Argentina, so they could ship their store cattle by rail down to the province of Buenos Aires, where they oper-ated Estancia 'Adolfina' near Coronel Pringles, and could fatten them up for market. Each company had its own line of administration within Argentina, with separate firms doing their business in Buenos Aires, and this arrange-ment was continued so that taking into account the separate breeds, and the distance between the properties, in point of fact the two farming enterprises only met up in the boardroom in London.

On returning to Argentina I made it my business to visit the ASL farms. We had taken delivery in Buenos Aires of a new pickup for Condor, so leaving Monica and the children at Solís with Violet Lawrence, Beaven and I made the first of several trips south by road. In September 1963 there were no paved roads south of Bahia Blanca, and although the Argentine Automobile Club had set up a chain of service stations equipped with radio, it was still not easy to get information about the state of the roads. However, we followed the Rio Negro inland, crossed the Limay and arrived at Estancia Pilcañeu, picked up Route 40 south to Leleque, then headed south-east to the coast at Comodoro Rivadavia and then down Route 3 to Rio Gallegos and home. We only got bogged once, and were helped out by friendly truck drivers.

The following summer we were visited at Condor by the chairman of ASL, Kenneth Suggett and his wife, Nancy, and on that first visit they were accompanied by the general manager, Tim Paine, probably the most knowl-edgeable Merino breeder in the country at that time. They inspected our Corriedale sheep and Paine made the profound observation that 'merinos do not "do" where lichen grows on the fence posts' – meaning that they do not like wet, cold climates. Six years later when we were looking at alterna-tive breeds I remembered this remark and followed it up. No other member of the ASL staff ever came to see us. I thought their organisation extremely cumbersome and overstaffed, and their methods old-fashioned, but although we did in the end get to know our counterparts at Leleque and the other farms no integration ever took place and our lives were little changed.

Indeed, life at Condor had now settled down. A new house had been built for the foreman, so we were able to turn the one where the Speakes had lived (built before 1905) over to the exclusive use of the school. There was now room to house a married teacher, classroom and office, a *galería* for playing in on wet days and room upstairs to board a child or two from one or other of the sections, and this setup was to continue for over thirty years. It was also used as a sort of community centre – most of the public holidays happen during school term, so we would build a get-together and social gathering round a school function such as celebrating Independence Day. We always took great pains to integrate the school with the farm community and vice versa, as the latter grew in our time from five families with four children of school age to fifteen families and some thirty-five children under 14, although the number of pupils at the school seldom exceeded twelve at any one time. This was all part of company policy, to settle the best and more skilled men, the charge-hands and specialists, who being the more conscientious might push off to town so as to educate their children. It was backed up in due course by the company paying for boarding children in Rio Gallegos for secondary education.

The big farm social event was the children's party on Boxing Day, which we held at the Big House for all children and all wives whether they had children or not. The farm was of course shearing, and Boxing Day was not necessarily a holiday, but arrangements were always made to bring the families in from the sections. It was the event of the year for most of the wives. We had inherited from the Davies a Santa Claus suit, and a routine was soon established and firmly maintained by the older children for the delight of the younger, whereby 'Santy' appeared from the general direction of the hen run, was solemnly greeted by the *señora* and escorted to a chair on the lawn with his sack of presents for distribution. The first Santy was incarnated by Granfy Arthur who was out on his annual visit to Coronel; other years visiting grandfathers or uncles would be pressed into service, and our own boys took it over when they grew old enough.

The year 1964 was saddened by the unexpected death of my mother, Millicent, at her home at Westfield in December. We were busy in full season's swing, so there was nothing for it but to recall the many fond memories, and life just went on. Our children were now into horses and bicycles. Ponies as such are rare in Patagonia. Small horses known as *petisos* occasionally appear but are really dwarf versions of the prevailing breed so can be rather tricky. Consequently most children learn to ride on old nags. We had taken over a horse known as Sam, who was used by the windmill men to carry saddle-bags full of clunking tools. He was very tame but rather wily to catch in an open field. Monica (herself an expert horsewoman) and the two eldest had many an exasperating chase trying to catch him. Sam was soon joined by Pinocho, an enormous Percheron mare with perfect manners, who would allow a small person to get aboard by leaning a ladder against her side, climbing up and then kicking it away.

We never had an accident with horses, but one day the mechanic appeared up at the house in his truck, bringing with him a small inert body. Michael had fallen off his bicycle near the workshop and struck his head on a stone, causing mild concussion. We took him in to Dr Borrelli, who kept him in the clinic under observation while a full recovery took place. This did not take very long, but while still 'under' we heard Michael utter a remarkable display of swearwords in the vernacular. We realised that these must have been absorbed at a very early age, while lying in the pram for a siesta, or playing in the sand-pit at the bottom of the garden while shepherds passed by not too far away, shouting imprecations at their dogs, the sheep or anything else in like terms!

The trips to Punta Arenas with Alison continued, until Dr Borgoño advised us that the time had come for surgery, which he did not have the facilities for, and recommended us to Dr Malbrán in Buenos Aires – at that time the leading ophthalmic surgeon in southern South America. It was not just a question of the operation, but almost more importantly of the follow-up treatment and exercises, which could not be done in all Patagonia, but were available in Montevideo with occasional checkups at Malbrán's clinic in Buenos Aires. Monica's sister Joan was married to John (Chub) Coates, from an old-established family from the USA, one of the few to take root in the River Plate. Chub's grandfather, Herbert P Coates, founded the Rotary Club of Montevideo, from where the movement spread first to Buenos Aries and then to the rest of South America. The family business was refrigeration, an important one considering the extent of the chilled and frozen meat trade. Chub, however, was a textile engineer and managed the cloth mill of Fibratex in Montevideo, and I learned a great deal from him about the textile trade in general and the many differing ways in which wool can be integrated into it. Joan and Chub lived at Punta Gorda in Montevideo, and offered to have Alison to live with them and go to the British Schools in nearby Carrasco with their own children – the youngest, Cathy, being some twenty months older than Alison.

It was a hard decision to have to make at this moment in time, but Monica and I had already done our heartsearching on the subject of the children's education. Having been educated herself at an outstanding bilingual, coeducational day school, Monica was naturally not all that keen on boarding, but accepted the fact that our job at Condor was a sufficiently good one to be able to send them all to private schools, albeit boarding, and later to university. We had made up our minds that they should all grow up fully bilingual and bicultural, and obtain all the requisite qualifications up to university entrance. Not all parents even of our own generation took this view, and we were to run into limitations later on when it came to a choice of schools for the boys.

Alison had by now done two years of fairly basic classes at the little Condor primary school, with supplementary English at home with Monica. Maybe we might have kept her at home for a further year or two but would have had to send her away to a bilingual boarding school sooner or later.

Violet and Beaven Lawrence were not too far away at Solís, and Monica was able to visit them all during term, and take Alison over to Buenos Aires for periodical checkups as required. So by going to live with Joan, Alison was able to start good schooling away from home but without actually boarding.

Notes

1 *Chau* or *Ciao* in Argentina means ''bye for now, see you later' rather than 'Hi, how are you?' as it does in its original Italian. Juana's husband would always greet the children thus, so it stuck as a family nickname.

2 Kimiri Aike was situated south of Estancia 'Punta Delgada', some 40km down the road to Punta Arenas, and formerly owned by the Patagonian Sheep Farming Company. At the time the Big House there was built, around 1900, the affairs of the company were more concerned with Punta Arenas than Rio Gallegos, so it was there that the General Manager lived in the early days. (see Chapter 16).

3 For the layman, the advantages of the newer styles of shearing are: greater speed of operation through closer and more efficient passes of the cutter head across the skin; tidier harvesting of the wool with much less quantity of off-cuts and low grade pieces; and saving fatigue to the operator by teaching him how to hold the sheep easily and to care for and properly adjust his shearing equipment.

4 'Punta wools' is still a term used in the wool trade. It defines certain types of wool grown in the region roughly south of the Coyle River in Santa Cruz, including Magallanes (Chile) and all of Tierra del Fuego.

15

Cormo Argentino

Three-quarter bred

The fairly rapid expansion of large-scale sheep raising on both sides of the Magellan Straits, like that of the Falkland Islands some twenty or more years before, was fuelled primarily by the need for settling and stocking the land. Sheep were the medium necessary to convert the un-grazed, almost virgin pastures into wealth, which meant wool – any wool. It was more important for the early entrepreneurs to acquire more land than it was to concern themselves with what sort of sheep they stocked it with. In any case the only source of supply, initially, was to bring them over from the Falklands in vessels like the *Rippling Wave*. Those first importations very soon multiplied and by the time Condor was founded in 1886 a 'Straits of Magellan' type of sheep existed, based mostly on English Romney Marsh or Kent blood simply because that was the breed most suited to the Falklands. It was not, however, the breed most suited to Patagonia. Around the Straits proper, where the climate is wetter and many plants grow which are common to the Falklands, this type of sheep does well enough, but it is not suited to the drier ranges of continental Patagonia north of the Straits, as the Blakes had already realised.

None of the people involved in organising and operating the early properties were particularly good stockmen in the Munro tradition, apart from a few exceptions like Ernest Hobbs and the Morrisons who settled Estancia Penitente up inland on the border with Argentina near Last Hope Inlet. We know from the Condor stock books (which fortunately have survived complete) that Merinos were tried at the beginning of the century, that Romneys were also used and that Corriedale rams had been imported as from 1912, but Davies says (1) that the breeding in the 1920s was a mess and there is nothing in the stock books to disprove this. It seems to have been established quite early on that pure Merinos with their high-priced fine wool did not do well in the region but that Romneys which did well grew coarser, less valuable fleeces, so an attempt was made to keep the flocks (or rather the wool) somewhere in between these two extremes. This was done by various crosses or mixes, and when the Corriedale breed appeared on the scene it seemed to provide the answer.

Although the Blakes had been breeding Corriedales at San Julian since well before the Great War, it took a bit longer for Condor to get the message. Pedigree ewes had been imported from New Zealand and a small stud flock started soon after 1918, but the rams were only used for crossbreeding. In 1927 there was a board decision to henceforth breed only Corriedales, and Eric Davies, who took over as Condor manager that year had the job of building up the flock structure. The remarkable success of this operation, which was to come to fruition in the 1950s when the average cut per head reached first topped 5 kilos of a well-sought-after product, was entirely his doing.

Sheep breeding is a slow business, with one lambing per year. Young sheep, male and female, take between eighteen and twenty months to reach sexual maturity, so that if you arrange a creative mating in Year 1, you may shear the resulting animals in Year 2 but only mate them and breed the next generation in Year 3. Only then do you shear your first lambing as adults, so it takes four or even five years to make any impression upon the overall wool clip, in addition to which you probably spent a year or more planning the change and assembling the appropriate rams, as we will see below.

The classic breeding structure as found on all large farms in Patagonia in the 1960s consisted of a registered pedigree flock where both sires and dams were pedigreed – originally imported but soon locally bred. Due to the enormous numbers of commercial sheep, known usually as 'general flock' or *majada general*, the small pedigree flocks could never produce enough rams to service them all, so special ram-breeding flocks were set up, perhaps ten times the size of a pedigree flock. (2) These were serviced exclusively by pedigree rams, bearing in mind that while one ram is required for thirty ewes out in the open camp, if the flock is confined during mating to a smaller paddock the ratio can be increased to one to fifty or even more. Such flocks are generally referred to as *planteles*. On English-speaking farms the name for them varied: the term 'stud flock' is used in Australia and New Zealand for ram-breeding flocks regardless of size and whether registered or

Culverden Downs 353, the most important Corriedale sire ever imported by Condor, 1958. In one year alone 1300 ewes were inseminated by this ram.

not; at Coronel we also referred to the 'stud flock'; but at Condor they were called 'three-quarter bred'. This meant that the ewes in the flock were at least granddaughters of pedigree rams.

Eric Davies was an instinctive breeder like Robert and Arthur Blake, and they all had to work with flair and imagination, because the science of sheep breeding as such did not as yet exist. They had much the same idea of 'balance' – i.e. that to carry a heavy fleece plus a foetus over vast distances in search of food and water requires a stalwart body of fair size, with long legs well provided with muscle. This combined logically with meat production which by then had become second to wool in productive importance. Davies gave much importance not only to size but also to shape, and had special apparatus built to hold sheep in a natural upright position and rotate them in the horizontal plane so that the visual inspector or classer (i.e. himself) could judge and grade every one of the 3,000 or so three-quarter-bred ewes which made up the stud flocks, plus all the rams.

Every year he also personally graded every single ewe (35,000 at that time) and ewe hogget (10–12,000) in full wool when they came in for shearing, and for this he designed special equipment in the form of a raised, open-sided race along which the sheep passed. To the experienced classer's eye, any sheep lacking in visual qualities would be detected instantly and marked. This enormous task was justified by fact that the manager of a place as big as Condor had inevitably to spend most of his personal time in more general administrative duties, so that this yearly revision was the only time he could visually check up on the results of the breeding policy that he was responsible for carrying out. When my turn came, I also continued to inspect all 'my' ewes in this way for a number of years, until new techniques appeared.

I heard in later years that Uncle Robert used to say, 'When a manager starts to talk about "My Rams", then it is time to think about moving him on . . .' While indeed we have met managers with this proprietorial approach to their employers' property, after a lifetime in the profession I think it is fairer to say that to understand your owner's aims and identify yourself with them is, on the whole, a desirable trait.

Round the world

Back at Condor after our 1963 leave the renewals and renovations continued – we were to have builders on the place for another five years yet – and now there were glimmerings of really new and exciting developments over the horizon. I felt that I had so far made little use of my university training, and that having got the basic reorganisation going so as to equate Condor with known efficient ways of working, it was time to find out what was going on in the rest of the world. There had been an enormous amount of farming research put in hand at universities and experiment stations in the post-war years, much of it quite new and original. I had kept up with most of it by reading the Australian, New Zealand and American farming and technical journals, and was in touch with the Cambridge School of Agriculture library who would send me abstracts of important published work.

Technical contacts in Argentina came through the National Institute of Agrarian Technology (INTA), the official body for farming research. It was at that time funded almost entirely by a tax on farm products, and had managed to include among the staff very few unproductive government bureaucrats but a large number of devoted and often underpaid researchers among whom there was a strong *esprit de corps*. Although they had important research stations in the Pampa Húmeda, their only presence in Santa Cruz was a small station at Cañadón León (later Gobernador Gregores), some 200km inland from San Julian. I had visited it in 1952/53 and met the sole technician, Dr Cittadini, but by 1961 he had been replaced by Dalmiro Molina, a Peruvian agronomist with whom I worked very closely for twenty years or so, both at Coronel and at Condor.

The years 1959 to 1962 were all exceptionally dry, approaching drought conditions, and at Condor the first thing I had had to do on taking over the management in 1961 was to reduce the livestock by some 25 per cent. Concern was expressed in official circles about erosion, soil conservation and the like, and other INTA men started to come down, visit the area and come to Condor for a chat. Principal among these was Jorge Brun, who had got a MSc Degree at the University of Utah and whose later career took him into the upper echelons of INTA. Then there was Luis Iwan, a veteri-

273

narian of Welsh descent who knew Tierra del Fuego well and had also been to the USA and got an MSc at the University of Montana. Through them I started to get an inkling of the new knowledge and techniques which were starting to emerge from such sources, but which had not yet started to appear in the farming press. The Argentine government in the meantime had asked the Food and Agriculture Organisation of the United Nations (FAO) what could be done with Patagonia, and FAO as a first step sent down a team of experts to look into the matter, led by Dr Pat McMahon, Professor of Wool Technology at the University of New South Wales. They all came out to visit Condor, and I started to realise how much technology there was just lying out there ready to be gathered and put to practical use.

Eric Davies had done his round-the-world trip on retirement, but when I put it to Maurice Waldron that it would be of far more benefit to the company for me to do such a trip while I was still young and active he saw the point and we started to work on it, with the idea of combining it with our 1966 leave. At that time the only way to fly from Argentina to Australia was via San Francisco, so clearly a visit to the Western USA would come first, followed by New Zealand and Australia, in both of which I could usefully pursue company business by looking at and maybe buying stud rams.

Our children were by now 9, 7, 5 and 3, with the two eldest at school, Alison in Montevideo and Michael now attending the little Condor school. Clearly it was not practical for my wife and family to tag along on such a trip, so it was arranged that Monica and the children would first spend three weeks or so at Solis with the Lawrences, as Beaven was not at all well and he and Violet wanted to gather all their children together. Pam and Douglas had come down from Peru with their two children, Brian and Elaine, so all the grandchildren were there and I was the only son-in-law not present. In due course Monica and our four would be getting on the plane for Madrid, where I would meet them, having flown on round the world from Sydney via Hong Kong and Rome.

So having put Monica and the boys on the plane to Montevideo, I boarded mine for San Francisco en route for Salt Lake City, Utah where I was met by Selar Hutchings, a 'backsliding Mormon' (as he described himself) with the US Forest Service. This body controls all the grazing of the Rocky Mountains and with it the watersheds of the important rivers which go to form the upper Mississippi – in other words the movement of flood waters over enormous areas in central and western USA. I was already a disciple of Hugh Hammond Bennett, considered by many the father of soil conservation and related practices, whose book *Soil Conservation* had been used at San Julian by Arthur. The philosophy of range management – i.e. controlling the grazing animal (including man) so as to avoid deterioration of the native pastures – is clearly inherent to the conservation of both the water and vegetation resources.

My own reaction to the practices I saw in Utah was, 'Gee, this is just what we are (or should be) doing at home', and set about learning as much as possible about it. This involved visits to both desert and mountain grazings all over Utah, and meeting experts like Dr Wayne Cook at Utah State University. I saw their new breeds of sheep, the Columbia and Targhee, created at the US Sheep Breeding Station at Dubois, Idaho, and noted that it was possible to plan and create purpose-designed breeds. Then I moved north into Montana, and met Dr Leroy Van Horn at the University at Bozeman. I put in a quick visit to Yellowstone Park and again met with researchers in many subjects. I picked up the elements of pre-lamb shearing and shed lambing as applied in those extreme environments, always in the back of my mind looking for possible Patagonian applications.

My American friends were so efficient in arranging all these visits that it was clear I was going to finish ahead of time, so Van Horn suggested I see something of Wyoming, picked up the phone and called his old friend Paul Etchepare down at Cheyenne. So I flew down and spent a day with Paul, the principal owner of Warren Livestock Co., the biggest sheep outfit in the state. They had also created their own breed of sheep, and I was starting to form the concept that in large-scale sheep breeding, one did not need to keep slavishly to a 'breed standard' as expressed in the show ring.

So I went from Cheyenne to Denver, then to Honolulu and finally to Auckland, where I was met by the local man from Wright, Stephenson & Co., stock and station agents who arranged the export of stud rams for Condor and many others. Much of my time in New Zealand was taken up in visiting studs in the South Island, and indeed we arranged to buy two rams, one for Condor and one for Coronel, but I also went to both Massey and Lincoln Colleges and met leading sheep researchers like I.E. Coop, Henderson and A.L. Rae. Their most basic work had been on 'heritability' – i.e. to what extent will a visually superior ram pass on that superiority to his progeny – and on various aspects of growth and the negative effect of excessive growth of wool on the face. I was starting to get closer to the fundamentals.

I flew to Sydney, and put up at the Hotel Metropole, where Uncle Robert had stayed way back in 1905. My visits had been organised by Professor McMahon, and took in both Corriedale and Merino studs, as well as meeting leading scientists. Thanks to him I met Dr Helen Newton Turner, probably the most influential sheep geneticist of the century, and had a long talk in her office at Prospect.

I had three key questions which I had brought all the way over to ask. Which is more efficient, a large sheep or a small one, in terms of converting forage into wool and/or meat? Which is more efficient, to select your sheep on visual characteristics only or on measurable ones like fleece- or bodyweight? Why does excessive face cover reduce productivity? Helen packed me off to the Trangie experiment station of CSIRO (Commonwealth Scientific and Industrial Research Organisation), where men like Dun and Pattie were working on just these questions, and eventually the answers came back (large; measurable; hormonal imbalance).

After a swing south taking in Canberra, Melbourne and the Albury sheep show, I returned to Sydney where Professor McMahon greeted me with the news that the FAO had agreed to set up a research project in Patagonia and had appointed its leader, Dr Harry Carroll, who was in Sydney. Could we meet to discuss the project? He took the three of us off to spend the weekend in a cottage in the bush he had out in the Blue Mountains and we thrashed the matter out. I was not altogether in agreement with the FAO concept that they had to do research first, and then recommend such practices as might arise out of it. The leading growers (Condor *et al.*) were already using modern practices and what was needed was to build onto and expand them. McMahon, having been there, knew much of this but Carroll did not and was not prepared to be told. It was my first contact with the politicking which goes on in such organisations and allows scientists to make reputations. As so often, the eventual success of the project was only partial. Some good, even some vital work was done and we were able to pick up a few useful bits around the edges. Despite my plea for range management, this aspect was not addressed at all until far too late in the project and so was almost ineffectual.

Having written up my report for London and posted it, I boarded the plane for Hong Kong, Europe and the family. In Hong Kong I had arranged a sightseeing stopover, but a typhoon struck, and we were held up for twenty-four hours. My flights were Athens-Rome-Madrid, but when we landed in Greece the connection had departed and the only possible flight was by Ethiopian Airways. The Qantas transfer desk assured me that this airline was 'quite all right, really' so with some trepidation I boarded a gaily painted, elderly 707. All went well and I caught my connection in Rome all right, even getting to Madrid in time for a night's sleep in a hotel before meeting the family at Barajas airport next day.

I was allowed to go out on the tarmac to the foot of the gangway to greet the family, who piled off in good order and great excitement. To add to our adventurings, we had decided not to count on getting nice holiday beach weather in Britain, so had booked a fortnight in Tarragona, on the Mediterranean coast, which was just starting to become popular with the British for holidays. So we hopped onto a plane to Barcelona, and went from there by train to Tarragona where the Hotel Imperial Tárraco welcomed us to its comfortable bosom.

The gorgeous weather did not fail us, nor did it in Britain later. We spent another holiday at The Mumbles on the Gower Peninsula, where Hugh had

John, Monica and children at Westfield, Winscombe, 1966.

found a guest-house into which we all four families fitted, sadly without Chris Davis but Eleanor and her three joined us just the same. Westfield, also, was not the same without Millicent, but we settled in with Granfy downstairs and we spread ourselves out in the flat. Mrs Gatehouse, who had been in service with Granny Worsley, came in to 'do' for Granfy daily and would cook lunch for us most days.

While staying with Norman and Nina Lawrence at Eastington, they introduced us to their good friend and neighbour, Oscar Colburn, the leading sheep farmer in the district, who was engaged in 'making' a new breed of sheep. For this he was using no less than four existing breeds, each one chosen for a particular trait, and the breed was in due course recognised as such under the name of 'Colbred'. I remember being impressed with his courage as a breeder, little thinking I might be doing much the same a few years later.

Of more immediate application was a visit to Cambridge. Our first leave in 1956 had coincided with my MA degree, so I had taken Monica up for the event and subsequently I enjoyed returning to Emmanuel and dining at high table, as well as keeping in touch with the School of Agriculture. On this occasion I met Dr John Owen, a sheep-oriented geneticist who had worked closely with Australian and New Zealand workers in this field, and who was to be of great help to me over the next few years.

277

Although Michael had only just started school, we were already giving much thought to the boys' future education, and visited a number of possible schools, varying from Taunton to Uppingham, Marlborough, Stowe and Kings, Canterbury. We were not necessarily convinced about a public school education for him, even though the company would help with the fees and, if necessary, passages, but we felt all possibilities had to be explored.

With the routine work at Condor now going smoothly with the new ways and a trained staff, there was no need for the manager to return much before the end of October, so we had decided to return by sea. Michael and Alison at least were old enough to enjoy and remember sea travel, of which we both had fond memories. The *Highland* ships were no more, but their place had been taken by the post-war Blue Star liners, still carrying chilled beef from the River Plate, manufactures out from Britain and passengers both ways. The children were big enough to enjoy the deck games and swimming pool, and the three boys in particular developed a penchant for 'horse racing'. At these meetings 'horses' were bought, raced and betted on, and 'run' by jockeys who moved them along the track by throws of the dice. Our three little boys were much in demand as jockeys, especially as they won more often than not, and it was not until many years later that we discovered that there was more of a knack in throwing the dice than the angelic little faces ever let on at the time!

Green pastures

The next few years at Condor were given over in the main to putting into practice as much as possible of the new ideas and experience from elsewhere. We had however started cautiously into pasture improvement with species trials in 1960, and in 1961 sowed the first few hectares. Like every farm in Magallanes, Condor had grown oats for hay in days gone by, and like every farm in southern Argentina had sown alfalfa likewise. As with the early Romney Marsh sheep, neither were really suited to local conditions but nobody had yet thought up anything better so this was one of the things I had been contracted for. All the early work had been done with horses, of course, and there were tillage and haying implements to hand, indeed still plenty of draught horses. Among the equipment imported in the 'parallel 42' days were a Fordson Major and a Ferguson TE20 tractor, both with a range of equipment, so we had the tools and now needed to work out the know-how.

Hay was used mainly for feeding working horses in winter, and also for feeding a small number of pedigree rams being groomed for showing. At Coronel it was possible to stable the small number of riding horses and feed them a full working ration, but at Condor the need to mount some forty men daily for eyeclipping, plus draught horses for the carts meant that it was quite impossible to feed them all. This in turn meant a very heavy drain on native forage in the horse paddocks, and so forth. By mechanising the transport of personnel using tractor-trailer combinations we had already made important savings in this area.

Still, the first priority seemed to be to grow improved grass for hay, in the expectation of acquiring useful information and experience which would provide a basis for later work on a wider scale. The prime limiting factor was of course the low rainfall. Condor had pretty complete records going back to 1897 which gave a long-term average of 300mm per year although there was some indication that this average was not being kept. More important was the annual distribution which due to the sea masses in and around the Straits of Magellan was more constant and reliable than the continent proper, north of the Gallegos River. The soil seemed good, as flowers and vegetables grew happily in the gardens, and we had found white clover and ryegrass growing nearby, introduced some time in the past, in addition to the ubiquitous dandelion. I took soil samples from various places and had them analysed, using the laboratory service provided by the *Sociedad Rural Argentina* in Buenos Aires.

The fundamental conclusions drawn from those early samples, as well as others analysed out later by the FAO, were that in general Patagonian soils are fully fertile, well balanced in minerals and plant nutrients, and therefore capable of growing almost any crop compatible with the temperature range and latitude factor. The only limiting factor is the soil acidity (pH) which in some soils is mildly acid and therefore marginal for alfalfa, and this was the case at Condor.

In 1960 we had down trials of some twenty grasses and a few clovers, all selected 'on paper' – i.e. from their reported performance in similar situations in other parts of the world. We chose a dry, exposed site on the top of a hill, so as to submit them to as extreme conditions as possible. While waiting for the results we ploughed up a small paddock in the valley in front of the settlement, where there was a deep alluvial soil and a high water table, and sowed down a classical ley mixture of ryegrass, cocksfoot, timothy and white clover. When we cut this for hay in the following year we found that it produced more per hectare than the twenty-year old alfalfa patches, so we added further paddocks of this sort and it became the main source of hay for many years to come.

The winter of 1961, as we have seen, was a severe one. In winter temperatures usually go down to –3° to –7°C or so, with –10° being exceeded only once or twice in any winter. But that year we got –23°C and I remember the day well. Pipes were frozen and vehicles would not start, even inside garages. By midday one Land Rover had been started up, and this went round towing one after another to get them going. Meanwhile other people had been thawing out the pipes in several houses, and by the time the evening came we realised that the entire skilled resources of the farm had for the whole day been engaged solely in maintaining life.

When we came to look at our grass trials again they had stood two very dry summers, every wind going, and low temperatures of at least –20°C so we reckoned anything which grew up there would grow just about any-where, so we ploughed up some five hectares at Condor and sowed it with a mixture of the most likely species. This was followed by further species trials, plot grazing trials and gradual extension over the next few years of sown valley paddocks from 10 to 25 hectares in extent in the valleys surrounding the settlement at Condor, and also at the Gap, North Ridge and Frailes sec-tions. We had fairly well established that it was possible to reseed the native pastures economically; that there was no risk of wind or water erosion; and that the resulting pastures would carry two to three times the sheep than the native pastures they replaced.

So when the FAO (3) team headed by Dr Carroll finally arrived in early 1967, set up its headquarters in Bariloche and its experts in various fields (all Australian) started to come south, we already had some of our own answers. In the pasture area they repeated some of our work, ran fertiliser trials (which did not work) and helped solve the problem of implantation of clover.

Some of the other teams were more successful. There was a masterly survey of the internal parasites situation carried out by Dr Ian Johnstone, Associate Professor to Dr P. McMahon at the University of New South Wales, which is still the reference work on this subject. The team dedicated to sheep breeding and genetics was headed by our old friend Dr Luis Iwan and Brian T. Jefferies, a former livestock officer for the State of Tasmania. Their message and breeding doctrine was much what I had picked up on my trip, and together we were able to work out a practical way of selecting rams on fleece and body weight, which is just what my father Arthur had been trying to do twenty or more years earlier. We had to develop in-shed techniques for weighing large numbers of unidentified sheep, grading them on the spot and recording the results on charts. (4)

We also ran field trials in conjunction with the Bariloche project in several other areas, the principal one being research into the survival of new-born lambs related to their weights at birth. This was run by Dr Harry Carroll in person, and a lot of valuable information was obtained about pre-lamb nutrition and the timing of the drop relative to the availability of forage on the native grazings. As a result of these findings we shifted the Condor lambings back by a whole fortnight as a matter of policy.

Boarding schools

The children in the meantime continued to grow, and schooling gradually became a part of everybody's lives. Michael was already going to the little school on the farm, and Stephen started there also in March 1967. At the same time Alison, having left the British Schools in December, after the summer holidays started boarding at St Hilda's College in Hurlingham (Buenos Aires) where my sisters had gone twenty-odd years previously. Indeed the matron, Mrs Edwards, had been there since their time and remembered Eleanor and Rosemary perfectly. Nor had the school changed very much in that time either, and was held to be academically way behind Northlands, where Miss Brightman had long since retired but had been replaced by the equally outstanding Mrs Mary Parchewski. The head-mistress was said to be fond of her tot, but the board of governors had things well in hand and the following year took the unprecedented step of appointing a *headmaster* to a slightly old-fashioned girls' school. This was Norman Bisset, a brilliant Australian educationalist who pulled St Hilda's up to the point where the girls had no difficulty in later getting into British universities and teaching hospitals.

After taking Alison to St Hilda's in March 1967, Monica went over to visit her parents in Solis, where Beaven was ailing. Later in the year he was admitted to the British Hospital, Montevideo, where sadly he passed away on 30 October 1967, with his three daughters all present.

One of the things one has to put up with if you are going to be a professional sheep farm manager in Patagonia, apart from sending your children away to boarding schools, is that you can never, *ever* take a summer holiday in summer as that is the busy time on the farms. This was one reason, of course, for those long UK leaves and sea voyages. So summer holidays for the children meant picnics on the lawn or beside the swimming pool, an occasional trip to the beach on the Straits and days on the farm were filled with bicycles and horses. The elder ones had soon grown out of the old nags and on to more spirited mounts, and they had their own corral just outside the garden where they could run their troop in from the paddock. Soon there were dogs also, always sheepdogs of course, but Stephen had said he wanted a sausage dog, so one time we were up in Bariloche visiting the FAO setup as well as having a bit of a break, we saw an irresistible notice in a window: 'Dachshund puppies for sale'. We duly bought one, which being quite small and lonely, shared Monica's bed at the Hotel Colón in Comodoro on the journey home, and was welcomed with raptures by his new owner (whose bed he would quite often share). He was christened 'Oxford' ('Oxy' for short) after the sausage of that ilk.

I was vice-president of the Rio Gallegos *Sociedad Rural*, and therefore concerned with the annual stock show. With others on the committee we wanted to break out of the show being just a ram competition, and to make it a better attraction for townspeople. Several of us had children about the same age, so we started taking their horses into town to the show, to compete in ring events like we ourselves had done at Pony Club gymkhanas. On the Sunday it was usual for a group of farmers to attend the noon hoisting of the national flag at the centre of town, so we in some trepidation let the children parade solemnly to the ceremony. The horses of course were quite tame, but even so we made sure that every child had an adult horse-minder assigned, walking quietly nearby. This was just as well, because when the band struck up it was the tamest nag, Pinocho, who objected, so one of us whipped Chacho off his back while another grabbed the horse.

But they got their own back that afternoon, in the ring. A demonstration was given by an expert horseman, Willy Halliday, on how tame a horse could be, and he performed a number of tricks, ending up by crawling between its legs, which the horse, no doubt sensing that Don Willy was perhaps not as sober as he might have been, put up with amicably. (5) Not to be outdone, Chacho, aged 6, proceeded to run a figure of eight in and out of Pinocho's legs, which the crowd thought was great.

After several years of looking at schools for the boys, we had finally decided not to send them away to Britain, but to try to give them a dual education which would get them a full Argentine Secondary Certificate, but with the possibility of going on to universities in the UK or elsewhere. St George's was not really set up for this, being still concerned mainly with boys who proceeded from there to UK public schools. We had heard of a new school started in the Cordoba Hills which seemed to have a number of interesting features, and in fact my cousin Ann Wood (6) had sent her son Walter there.

A.H. (Bob) Thurn was a follower of the principle of combining classroom work with much sport and other outdoors activities as carried out at Gordonstoun and elsewhere. He had originally come out on contract for St Andrew's Scots School in Buenos Aires, and later set up St Paul's School. This was set in hilly country at Cruz Chica, just outside the modest town of La Cumbre, itself something of a holiday resort with a number of Brits retired there, a golf course and several large hotels. The school was run with a lot of outdoor features, camping just up on the hillside most weekends and lots of sport. In the early days the boys had helped to build much of the swimming pool and level the playing fields. We were much impressed when we went to visit it. On getting out of our truck in the front courtyard we were approached by a quite small boy, who asked us politely our business, and conducted us into the school to meet Mr Thurn. We liked the look of it all, and they must have liked the look of us because Michael was accepted on trust, without having to sit an entrance exam, as were his brothers in due course. Thirty-odd years later, it is fair to say that both sides in fact benefited

Michael, Stuart and Stephen sleighing on a frozen lagoon. The ice could usually support an adult with ease.

from the deal.

So Michael went to St Paul's in 1986. March was dipping time, so Monica again went up, and was joined by her mother in Buenos Aires for the trip to La Cumbre, our first introduction to long-distance bus travel in Argentina. The ONDA buses in Uruguay were like the famous Greyhound service in the USA, so the Lawrences were used to them. But on that trip a horrified Violet nudged Monica and said, 'Look, Monica, they changed drivers without stopping the bus!' Indeed, on the long, straight roads over the pampas, at night when you can see oncoming traffic for miles, it is easy for one driver to slide out one side of the seat and the other to slide in without stopping the bus!

Winter holidays had by now become a feature of life, and the great concern of all as the days passed and the arrival of those at boarding school approached was: would there be enough ice for skating? In most winters serious freezing (−3° to −10°C) usually started at the end of May and continued throughout June. Ice formed on any open water, and the lagoons round Condor would be covered with enough ice for an adult to skate on. There was never very much snow, so skiing was never a part of life, but ice could be enjoyed equally on skates, or on small sleighs on which small boys knelt and armed with two sticks carrying nails driven into the lower end, could propel themselves with amazing speed. Erasmo Davet was an expert skater, and legend had it that once, when the entire valley bottom was flooded over and iced up, Eric Davies had skated all the length of the settlement, over 1,000 metres, from the Big House to the shearing shed. But often in the second week or so of July the temperature would ease up and

When snow melts off frozenground, quite spectacular flooding can occur, crossable only by a tractor.

skating would become risky. The days were of course short, and the evenings long, so there was much family activity – making models, playing board and card games, with 'Racing Demon', 'Monopoly', 'mah-jong' and in due course 'Scrabble' the favourites. Television was still several years ahead.

Back to school again in August, and once spring was well under way that year (1968) we discovered to our joy that a fifth child, long awaited and much wanted, was on the way, some six years after Stuart. Dr Borrelli was now a minister in the provincial government but told Monica in his inimitable way that this would still be 'his' baby. It would also be the first time I would be able to be, if not actually present, at least pacing up and down in the waiting room. The baby was due about Easter, so we went into town in what seemed plenty of time, and put up at a hotel. Early on Easter Sunday morning, Monica suggested we had better get round to the clinic which we did, first ringing from the hotel for them to tell Dr Borrelli we were on our way. On arrival there, we found the night staff had not dared to wake him up but things were proceeding fast so this was soon done, and the good doctor appeared on the run, buttoning his white coat over his pyjamas and swearing at his staff. He managed to get there before the baby, but only just! So Frances Monica came into the world on April 9 1969, with no pacing up and down required of the proud and doting father, after all.

Back to college

We were due for UK leave in 1969, and had already started to face the fact that it would be the last one with all the children. Alison was now 12, and would enter secondary schooling the next year, which would require a fixed number of days' attendance at class, in addition to the work load of a dual curriculum heading towards both *bachillerato* and English university entrance level exams. Neither she nor her brothers in succession would be able to afford the time away from school. So we arranged again to fly over and return by ship, once more with a small baby in a carry-cot. We were welcomed by Granfy at Westfield and settled into the upstairs flat, assisted by a Norlands nanny who could take care of Frances when we wanted to travel afield with the elder children, although television having by now reached Somerset this was a popular pastime. Many a bottle was given to the baby while watching TV, and we all watched the historic landings on the moon in this way.

More ambitious expeditions were possible, and to 'go the rounds' of our friends and relations we assembled camping gear for a run which included the Davies near Norwich, a muddy field near Cambridge, Rosemary and family down in Sussex, Norman and Nina Lawrence now near Farmington, and ended up down in the New Forest. We also hired a boat on the Tewkesbury Avon.

In between family outings, I attended board meetings in London as before, and quite out of the blue the question was shot at me: 'Supposing we wished to grow significantly finer wool at Condor, how would you suggest we go about it?' Well, now, if they had asked me that while at Condor, with all my books to hand, maybe I could have answered right off the reel, but we were on holiday. So I wrote to Emmanuel to book a room (it was fortunately the long vacation) and went back to college for a whole week, mostly spent in the School of Agriculture library looking it all up. As an MA, I had my meals with the dons, of whom several were in residence, dined at high table, and it was easy to slip back into an academic routine.

The commercial aspect of the question was clear enough. Condor had bred up its Corriedale flocks to a very high level of productive potential, and in my time we had increased the overall carrying capacity, not so much by pasture improvement as originally expected, but by improving the watering facilities. Starting in 1963 we had been operating our own bulldozer to build dams for the collection of water. (7) These were sited at strategic points, so as to persuade the flocks to spread the grazing load over a wider area. By the time we had built some 135 water-holding structures we reckoned to have increased the carrying capacity of the property by some 20 per cent. It seemed unlikely that we could squeeze another kilo of wool off the land. The only way to significantly increase income, therefore, was to increase the value of the product – i.e. grow a finer type of wool.

Fortunately we had been testing (measuring) our wool since 1964, first in the Wool Testing Services laboratory in Wembley and later in the laboratory set up in Bariloche by the FAO/INTA project, and had started to get used to talking about microns to describe fibre diameter, instead of Bradford 'counts'. (8) There is a considerable variation in fineness in Corriedale wool, and it was known that in general the finer fleeces weighed less than the stronger ones. I now discovered why – there is a character for fibre density (number of fibres per unit of skin area) which is inherited independently from that for fibre diameter as such. Both factors are to some extent breed-related, with Merino sheep growing not only significantly finer wool but at a much higher density than Corriedale.

So why not change back to Merino, which after all had been run at the beginning of the century? First of all because this breed did not do well at latitudes higher than about 46°, anywhere in the world. Second because we were already getting an important income from sales of livestock for meat, which we were reluctant to give up. But it looked as if we might be able to do some form of crossbreeding in order to combine the positive aspects of both breeds.

Since meeting Oscar Colburn and admiring his project in 1963, I had met up with a number of geneticists worldwide, and was familiar with some of the schemes which had been carried out, particularly in the USA, to create new sheep breeds. The basic principle was simple: first you define

Alison with the first Corriedale sire bred on Condor with a really open face and high potential in other aspects. This basis became of great importance when creating the *Cormo Argentino* breed.

your objectives, the type of animal you wish to create. Then you find two or more suitable breeds (Colburn used four) which contain the characteristics you need, and mix them all together in a well-designed programme of crossing. It was Helen Newton Turner who made the analogy of the 'genetic pot' into which you tip all the ingredients and stir well. Finally you design a selection programme which will detect the right animals, where the genotypes (what they breed like) will produce phenotypes (what they look like) which contain the productive, measurable characters you are aiming for.

We had a number of advantages going for us. Condor had a solid genetic base of some 50,000 Corriedale ewes which had been bred up to a high level of productivity. I had been able to further add to Eric Davies' work by breeding much of the wool off the face, using fleece and body weighing to select improving rams, and we had a pretty good idea laboratory-wise about the fibre diameter story. Our association with the ASL meant that we had access to the very best Merino breeding stock in Argentina. So at the end of that week at Emmanuel I was able to advise the board that we could first out-cross with Merino, then back-cross to Corriedale carrying increased fibre density and fineness with us, thus creating a dual purpose breed with the meat potential of the latter but with much finer wool.

So I returned to the bosom of the family, but before our leave was over another surprise was in store. I took the three eldest children over the new Severn Bridge to Builth Wells in mid-Wales to the Royal Welsh Show for the day. There we ran into Harlan Greenshields, one of the owners of Douglas Station on the East Falkland. In conversation we got onto the subject of fine wool, and he told me he had read of a 'new' breed of sheep developed in Tasmania by crossing Corriedale with fine-woolled Merino, and that one of the people concerned with the project had been none other than Brian Jefferies, now with the FAO in Patagonia. This sounded promising, and could be followed up once we got back to the farm.

The return sea voyage was great fun, with the children that much older. Alison and Michael had quite serious homework to do, which they were consistent and responsible about and so were able to pick up their grades satisfactorily on return to school, but there was plenty of time for fun and games as well. On arrival in Buenos Aires, I took Michael back to St Paul's and was able to meet members of the staff and also a number of parents as it was just after the October exeat when the annual athletic sports were held. Michael had made friends with the McCallum boys, Peter and 'Tico', and had spent the May exeat with them, so I now met their parents. Mrs Kenneth McCallum looked kind of familiar, and turned out to be none other than Diana Davidson who had patiently put up with my untutored samba dancing back at The Grange when we were teenagers!

As soon as we got back to Condor I got in touch with Brian Jefferies, and learned that indeed a breed had been developed in Tasmania, by a Mr Ian

Downie at his Dungrove stud, called 'Cormo' (*Corriedade-merino*). At that time Australia had an export embargo in place on Merinos, but did allow the export of related breeds, so we proceeded to import seven Cormo rams from Dungrove, and at the same time brought down three top Merino sires from Leleque, so in May 1970 we started our fine-wool breeding programme, which may be found in Appendix II. The technical details of this have also been published, (9) so we won't go into it in detail here. In the fullness of time we had to put a name to our own breed, which differed somewhat from the original type bred by Downie, so we called it 'Cormo Argentino'.

Oil and gas

Drilling for oil had been going on in the Straits of Magellan region since the early 1950s, starting as so often in Chile. Wells were brought in on both sides of the water, and in due course the Chilean oil company ENAP leased an offshore rig from the USA and drilling was continued within the Straits proper. In 1959 the first geophysical survey was started in our part of Argentina (10) by the state oil company YPF (*Yacimientos Petrolíferos Fiscales*), and Condor had the doubtful privilege of being the first to be surveyed. It was several years before any drilling actually took place, but finally in January 1961 'Cerro Redondo No. 1' was drilled and oil discovered on our side of the frontier. The Cerro Redondo field is sited in the south-eastern part of Gap section, right on the Chilean border. Clearly the oil-bearing structures stretch below continental Argentina, Chile, the Straits proper and both countries' parts of Tierra del Fuego.

We were much concerned in the early stages with the risk of surface contamination and the matter of compensation for the use of the land in general. Mineral rights are vested in the state, so the landowner can only claim a sort of surface rent based on the productive use of the land at the time of entry. Over the years a whole set of rules for this was thrashed out, and I took part in many of the negotiations, ending up with a fair deal.

Drilling continued throughout the 1960s, and spread slowly westwards along the frontier camps towards the Condor settlement. The Cerro Redondo field proved to be mainly gas-bearing, with some very high-pressure wells indeed, while the Condor field had more heavy petroleum. Consequently the operational centre was sited in the latter, at a place known to us as 'Middle Gates', midway between Condor and Gap. Initially and for many years, the oil was pumped over the border into Chile and exploited jointly, while the gas wells were firmly screwed down closed, such gas as came up with the oil being burned off. The flares lit up the sky and could be seen from Rio Gallegos, 90km away.

Drilling rig with draw works, engine house, and derrick, pulling pipe, which is being stacked to the left of the platform. Most wells in the area were between 1800 and 2000 metres deep.

We found all this development quite fascinating, and not without excitement. From time to time a well would get out of control and, with gas rushing out at 150 times atmospheric pressure, some rare manoeuvres were indulged in. One, only 3km from the settlement, blew off for four days through a cracked valve head before the engineer in charge came to ask me for wool, which was injected into the well by the mud pumps and successfully blocked up the cracks. We only ever had one black gusher, which spouted up for three or four days, and we afterwards found oil on fence posts over 10km downwind.

But the prize was 'Condor 10'. During 1971 a 90cm gas pipeline had been built all the way from the Condor oil plant to Comodoro, from where there was already a pipeline northwards, so gradually all those gas wells started to be connected up and the gas to flow, eventually to Buenos Aires.

Condor 10 had been drilled some years back. It was only 5km away from the settlement, and was known to be a 'bastard', because it had very high pressure and was variable and unreliable. For this reason its rate of flow had not been properly measured. Operations were underway, when the column of mud holding the gas down started to rise, the automatic shutoff gear failed to operate in time, and with a whoosh she caught fire. Men were working away below the rig to try to close it off, when as one of them described it to me, there was a 'crack like a revolver' (from a stone striking a spark off the steel rig tower) and they knew they had just a few seconds to get the hell out of there, and in ten minutes the derrick was on the ground, a mass of twisted metal.

YPF decided to go it alone rather than bring down 'Red' Adair, the famous specialist who had snuffed out oil fires all over the Middle East. During the following month we got accustomed to the continuous roar which rattled the sash windows and the illumination of the burning gas which was bright enough to take photos by. During this time the wreckage was pulled away from the well-head. A 'turkey's nest' dam was built on the top of the nearest hill in which millions of litres of water was stored, pumped up from two lagoons down in the valley, and an impressive amount of equipment was assembled on site. Eight pump trucks were lined up, to draw water from the dam and emit it to fire nozzles. The pressure was too high to allow hand-held hoses to be used, so every line had to be screwed up in turn, taking about half an hour each. We were watching from across the valley, and as each additional nozzle came into play the height of the flame dropped by a metre or two. But by the end of the day it was clear that there was just not enough pumping capacity available. So the next day all stops were pulled out: at an early hour two large motorised pumps appeared through the frontier from Chile, and a drilling rig was stopped so as to add its pumps to the array. This time they succeeded and at about 4 p.m. the flame was snuffed out.

Now the really dangerous part began, as another spark could have set it off again. A massive 'Christmas tree' [oil jargon for the assembly of control valves, flange connectors and other devices which sits on the top of a well] was suspended from a crane and had to be lowered down over the well until the jet of gas issued up through the open stack of valves, which was then bolted down to the flanged base. The 20-ton structure bounced about like a ping-pong ball but was controlled by hauling on lateral tackles until it was positioned just so, with the gas flow rising through the open central hole. The water nozzles continued to drench the area but the risk of reignition was considerable. Ambulances, hitherto present but on one side, now backed up to the operations area, their attendants standing by with their stretchers out and on the ground, and two light aircraft were standing by for evacuation of casualties. But it went off without a hitch. The crane took the strain, and all available personnel manned the controlling tackles - roustabouts, drivers, firemen and most of the 40-odd journalists covering the event, who laid aside their cameras and notebooks and heaved away also, regardless of the cascading water. Slowly the monstrous mass of steel was coaxed into position, the waiting engineers slipped in the bolts and in a very short period the valves were being shut off.

We later learned, once the well had been properly tested and measured, that it was giving off rather more than 2 million cubic metres per day, *twice* the originally estimated figure. This was the reason why the first attempt had failed. The size of the gas reserves may be gauged from the fact that when the trunk gas pipeline started operating, 5 million cubic metres per day, about one third of the consumption of Greater Buenos Aires, was pushed up to Comodoro (about 1,000 kilometres) under well-head pressure alone. Over the ensuing twenty years or so, hooking up further areas in both countries and on Tierra del Fuego, plus the installation of pumping stations, has raised the flow to over 20 million cubic metres per day. Crude oil is now pumped through a pipeline laid, also in our time, from the Condor (Middle Gates) plant north to Punta Loyola at the mouth of the Gallegos River, where there is water enough for quite large tankers to berth alongside the jetty.

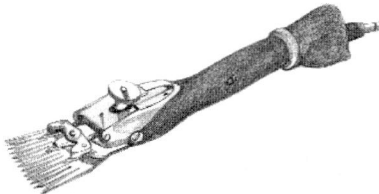

Notes

1 All my quotations from Eric Davies are personal communications, imparted mainly during the four years we worked together before his retirement. He himself did not publish anything beyond occasional articles in farming magazines such as the Australian *Pastoral Review*.

2 I use the term 'pedigree' throughout this book to signify sheep who are individually identified, with records kept of their parentage and descent, and also registered in a central flock book held by a responsible body. In Argentina this is the *Sociedad Rural Argentina*, whereas in other countries like Great Britain, New Zealand and Chile the Breed Society runs the flock book.

3 The project was run jointly with the Instituto Nacional de Tecnología Agropecuaria and therefore more correctly known as the INTA/FAO research project, FAO providing the team leaders or consultants.

4 Condor bred over 2,000 ram hoggetts annually, Coronel maybe half that number. The system of charts developed at this time was used by these and other studs for over twenty years, until on-farm computers could take over the statistics and number-crunching.

5 Chace quotes having seen frisky horses whose riders would have a job to stay aboard, becoming meek and mild when they sensed that the rider was 'under the weather' from drink.

6 Ann was the second daughter of Uncle Robert and Aunt Edith and my only relation in Argentina. She had married Jim Wood, son of George Wood who had founded the firm of Waldron and Wood (page 81 footnote 3) and they owned and lived on a farm called Estancia Huechahue near Junín de los Andes.

7 If snow or heavy rain fell onto frozen soil, this was unable to absorb the water so it would all run off, often creating quite spectacular flooding. Some of this ended up in lagoons, but most ran eventually into the sea, unless retained by manmade structures.

8 A Bradford count is the number of hanks of 540 yards of yarn which can be spun from a pound of wool which has been washed and combed ready for spinning – known as 'top'. Corriedale wools usually averaged a count of 56, merino 64 or so. The equivalent microns would be 27–28 and 20–21.

9 *Cormo Argentino – Development of a New breed for Wool and Meat Production in the Higher Latitudes* by J.L.Blake, VI World Congress on Animal Production, Helsinki 1988.

10 Oil had been first discovered in Comodoro Rivadavia in 1913, while drilling for water to supply the Boer settlers who had come over from South Africa. Drilling, both by YPF and private companies, had spread to nearby areas and into northern Santa Cruz, but the Straits of Magellan field was quite a new venture.

16

The 'Queen's Farm'

Cañadon Condor

The Waldron family from Berkshire were among the first to follow Henry Reynard and Ernest Hobbs into sheep raising on the Straits of Magellan. The Chilean government, having roughly defined their territorial claims in the region, had just as much need as the Argentine to get these claims substantiated by filling the land with settlers. So they offered enormous tracts for settlement on leasehold. The Waldrons took out leases on over a million acres (400,000 hectares – Estancias 'San Sebastian' and 'Caleta Josefina') on Tierra del Fuego, carrying some 300,000 sheep under the general management of their cousin Monty Wales. On the mainland their cousins Henry and Stanley Wood leased Merrick's (1) Valley, later known as Estancia 'Punta Delgada' where they ran a mere 140,000 sheep. This lease ran along the shore of the Straits, following Munition Bay, down to San Gregorio, some 60km inland, taking in the heights of Ci Aike and Dickie, and then about 30km along the Argentine border. The frontier had been agreed in principle by treaty in 1881 but had not yet been surveyed, although most people concerned had a pretty good idea where it was supposed to be.

In 1886 the Woods took out their first lease in Argentina, for 200,000 hectares adjoining the north shore of the Straits of Magellan right down to Cape Virgins and extending up the Atlantic coast, which was called Estancia 'Condor', taking its name from the wide, sheltered and well-watered valley in which they sited the first shepherd's house, and where later the main settlement was to develop. The origin of the name is unknown, maybe once a condor was seen by early riders, and this was such an event that the name *Cañadon del Condor*, which appears on the early maps, was adopted. Sheep were brought over from Merrick's Valley, and the first shearing of 4,882 sheep took place at Condor in December 1887. The old handwritten stock books survive, and chronicle the setting up of the flocks and the shepherds' houses at places with permanent spring water like the Gap, Los Pozos and Los Frailes (at first spelt 'Fryers', presumably for 'friars'). The names of the shepherds also appear, all British and almost certainly brought out from Berkshire.

In 1894 the Argentine government issued the first freehold title deed in respect of the concession hitherto leased. This historic document, the first one to be issued in Santa Cruz, has been preserved and can be seen in the National Historical Archives. It is remarkable in managing to define in perfect legal terms a tract of land whose southern border was as yet unknown. It says: 'from the Mount Aymond hill, a line direct to the Frailes Hill (*sic*), and from there to the Atlantic Ocean, which point to be adjusted North or South after eventual survey until an area of 200,000 hectares be enclosed'.

The Woods had been given much practical help and advice by Thomas Greenshields, a scion of the Greenshields family who had settled Douglas Station on the East Falkland. He had been knocking about the district since the early days of settlement and had a good idea where the best land was. He was appointed manager of Condor, and given one tenth share in the original Patagonian Sheep Farming Company when it was incorporated in London in 1895. (2) Greenshields married the formidable Louisa MacMunn, a lady whose early history is obscure but who appeared in Rio Gallegos in the early days, first married to a Mr Sparks. Greenshields then withdrew from the company, taking his tenth share in the form of the lands in the south-eastern corner, running down to Cape Virgins, known today as Estancia 'Monte Dinero'. At his death his widow then married Victor Fenton, whose brother, Dr Edward Fenton, was the first medical practitioner in Rio Gallegos.

In 1903 the Boundary Commission led by Colonel Holdich started its Herculean task of interpreting on the ground the delimitation of the frontier as agreed in the Treaty of 1881. (see Chapter 2, page 32). The Commission sited its first boundary marker (Hito I) on the foreshore at Cape Virgins, and proceeded in a westerly direction, placing its iron marker pylons on the tops of suitable hills more or less along the watershed in accordance with the Treaty. When they reached the Condor Valley, they found that their preliminary line would have placed the main settlement in Chile. The story goes that Arthur Waldron, on hearing about this, invited Colonel Holdich and his officers to dinner, at which lavish hospitality was dispensed and next day they went up and moved the markers X and XI to their present and permanent sites, leaving the settlement within Argentina. Certainly if you look at the map today, there is indeed a slight kink in the frontier . . .

The Chilean government in the meantime, having leased the land initially to settlers in much the same way, once sheep raising looked like becoming good business, in 1903 proceeded to sell it off to the highest bidders. The Waldrons did not pursue the matter on Tierra del Fuego, and vacated the leases. But the Woods were very keen to purchase Merrick's Valley on the mainland, right alongside Condor. Family legend has it that the Waldrons back in England were reluctant to release sufficient capital for the purpose, so the Woods went to the auction sale in Santiago with the funds they had. The sales had attracted a lot of potential risk capital, the prices soared and their resources only allowed them to buy two tracts: Kimiri Aike, fronting Munition Bay on the Straits, and a block of high land further in called Ci-Aike. These lands, plus those fronting the Straits alongside Condor comprised Estancia Kimiri Aike and were from then on run jointly with Condor.

Once the southern frontier was defined and marked out, it became clear that Condor did not in fact own or occupy the 200,000 hectares within Argentina to which it was entitled. It proved impossible to adjust the northern fence in accordance with the 1894 title deed, since the land on the other side was occupied by John Hamilton, (3) who flatly refused to give up any land to the Waldrons with whom at that time he was at loggerheads. By 1908 the frontier as set out by the Boundary Commission had been ratified, and the first survey carried out, so the Lands Office in Buenos Aires could now issue title deeds based on real surveys. Further capital was also needed for new buildings, fencing and other installations so a new company was formed, called the Patagonian Sheep Farming Co. (1908) Ltd. The new title deeds were therefore drawn up in the new company's name, with the Greenshields tract (4) excluded and the area of the original concession adjusted by adding further blocks of fiscal land westwards until the total land occupied was something near the 200,000 hectares of the original concession.

The southern cape at the mouth of the Gallegos river was named 'Punta Loyola' by Magellan. Its full name is Cabo San Ignacio de Loyola (the founder of the Jesuit order) and there is a group of small hills nearby clearly visible from the sea, which he named Cerros de los Frailes de Loyola, known today as the Frailes Hills. So there we have San Ignatius and his friars. A bit further inland another set of volcanic hills, known today as the 'Convents', are thought to have been so named by the irreverent and heretic British, presumably on the basis of the worthy friars needing female company . . .

Arthur Waldron continued to manage Condor until 1919, and his daughter Marjorie was the only Waldron to be born on the farm. After his retirement there seem to have been several unsatisfactory managements. According to Eric Davies, who arrived as a very junior cadet in 1920, during this time the farm was really run by the general foreman, Tom Sampson. Finally in 1921 the company headhunted Mr W.B. Rogers from the *Sociedad Explotadora de Tierra del Fuego* as general manager 'to put things in order', and much of the organisation and system related to stock-keeping and the like which I found in place when I joined the company stem from Rogers' days.

The Patagonian Sheep Farming Company also, as we have seen, owned Kimiri Aike in Chile, some 40km in from the frontier, and from there ran the 'Los Pozos' camps – that part of the original concession running along the north shore of the Straits of Magellan which found itself in Chile after the frontier was defined. They had also been granted a usufruct of 10 hectares running down to the beach of the Straits at the mouth of *Cañadon* Condor, where ships could be beached and loaded with wool. This was known as the 'Condor Port' and was provided with mooring chains, a large shed for storing the bales prior to shipment, and 'decauville' light railway tracks running down onto the beach. The wool would be brought down daily from Condor in bullock carts and stacked in the bale shed. Ernest Speake described to me how when the ship arrived more or less everybody would down tools at Condor, leap on a horse and ride out for the port, some 8km away, and become stevedores. Much as in the Falklands, the arrival of a ship was a welcome change in the farm routine, often enlivened by the odd

The manager's house at Gap, taken before 1932, when the last Gap manager retired and the house was then closed for twenty years.

bottle of liquor which ships always seem to carry . . . By the mid-1930s road transport by lorry to Rio Gallegos became possible and the route for wool to London via the latter became more convenient and cheaper than the Punta Arenas route.

Until 1932 Gap was run as a separate farm, so there were managers of Condor, Gap and Kimiri Aike farms, under the overall control of a general manager. In the Woods' days Punta Arenas was the key town for banking, shipping and supplies so they had built a mansion for the general manager at Kimiri Aike. In the days of horse-drawn transport and shipping from the Condor Port, this was perhaps a valid arrangement, but by the 1920s it was clear that the major part of the company's activities were in Argentina and therefore related to Rio Gallegos, so it became more practical for the general manager to live at Condor. (5) So a house was built in 1924 for the manager, at that time Jack Spooner, and Mr Rogers moved into the Condor Big House which had been hastily put up in 1911 to replace the original one built in 1904 which had been destroyed by fire. The telephone line from Punta Arenas to Kimiri Aike was extended to Condor, and remained in operation until the late 1950s. In 1930 Spooner was appointed manager of Cullen station, a closely allied Waldron farm in the Argentine part of Tierra del Fuego, and Eric Davies took over as manager of Condor. Mr Rogers retired the next year, and his place as general manager was taken by Arthur Trengrouse Waldron, known to all as 'Bill'.

Condor is nearly all good lambing camp, so from that modest beginning of 5,000 sheep, the flocks grew until they reached their maximum of 172,000 in 1907, after which stock numbers dropped back to around 120,000 sheep. Surplus ewes and wethers were initially sold off to other settlers, and many are the farms who started operations with Condor sheep. The best known was the sale in 1907 of 20,000 ewes to a group of entrepreneurs starting operations on the Baker River which drains Lago Buenos Aires into the Pacific. The estancia headquarters were in Argentina, at Lago Posadas in the north-west of Santa Cruz Territory, but the land was mostly in Chile. This was another epic drive, referred to by Chace who, no mean drover himself, knew several of the people concerned and says that they divided the mob into two flocks of 10,000 each 'for to handle them easier'. (6) The Baker farm is also of interest as after the Great War they engaged Lucas Bridges as manager, and he spent most of his working life there.

The first freezing plant on the Straits was built in 1912, and others followed, the Waldrons actively contributing and investing in this very important outlet for their production, as the sales of sheep to other settlers could clearly not go on for ever. With the Kimiri Aike set-up, a logical and well integrated system evolved, whereby all surplus sheep off the Condor property were moved into Chile once shorn, to be fattened on the high Ci Aike camps for two or three months and then moved on down, some to winter on

The Condor cookhouse.

the Kimiri camps and the rest to the Straits freezers. Even when Swift opened a freezer in Rio Gallegos in 1920, Condor sheep continued to travel over to Chile in this way.

In 1947 the Perón government closed the frontier to exports of sheep on the hoof, forcing farmers to send their surplus sheep to Rio Gallegos. The Kimiri Aike property, deprived of an annual input of sheep from Condor, proved unviable on its own, so was sold off in 1948, and from then on the Condor property was obliged to summer and fatten its own surplus sheep, so had to drop its numbers and could only shear 100,000 or so.

The Olympian bell.

Estancia Condor. Looking south towards the frontier and the Straits of Magellan. On left the shearing shed and yards, in centre the cookhouse and men's quarters, on right stables, office and staff houses extended along the 'village street', Big House in foreground.
Photo: Stephen Blake

Big house, Estancia Condor. Built in 1911, timber and corrugated iron
Photo: J.L. Blake

The whole family together, 1980. Stephen, Michael, Alison, Stuart. Below: John, Frances, Monica. In front garden of the Condor house.

Photo: J.L. Blake

Investiture,
Buckingham Palace
28th October 1981.
Stephen, Monica,
John, Alison.

Photo: Herald Photography

Killik Aike Norte. The owner's house in 2002. This had been rebuilt in 1944 on the site of the 1904 house.

Photo: J.L. Blake

Estancia Killik Aike Norte, general view of settlement, 2002

Photo: J.L. Blake

The fifth generation

Michael's children help bring in a point of sheep at Killik Aike, 2001

José González (head shepherd), Remigio Navarro (shepherd), Matthieu, Emilie.

Below: Matthieu Robert Locke Blake

The dirty war

On our periodic visits to the UK on leave during the 1950s and 60s, when catching up on things with our relatives and friends, we always found two aspects of life in South America which used to worry them: *de facto* governments and terrorism. With the Second World War still in quite recent memory, to the English any form of authoritarian government not freely elected was a dictatorship in the Hitler pattern. Democracy is much more than just having a vote – the electorate needs to be aware that it also has civic responsibilities such as respect for others, and more importantly the elected need to relate back to their roots or constituencies. Those elected must not, in effect, say 'You have elected me into office, now I will govern you as I please'. The idea that there are large areas in the world where the population are not ready, culturally and morally, to govern themselves, and that this might be better done by a firm hand, is of course anathema to the heirs of Magna Carta. So is the idea that there might be autocratic governments out there capable of governing without going to the extremes associated with Nazism. Several examples of both these situations have since appeared in various countries which were formerly part of the British Empire, but at that time most of these were continuing, albeit shakily, to practise the democratic system they had inherited.

Terrorism as such had not yet affected life in the UK, in spite of the already ongoing problems in Northern Ireland. In South America, however, one was much more in touch with the seamier side, and it started very close to home, in Uruguay, with the 'Tupamaros'. This urban guerrilla movement was fuelled from several sources, and was all the more curious in that Uruguay did not, then or ever, have a depressed social class in which the presence of real, grinding poverty provided a ready breeding ground for political doctrines – any doctrine – which might lead to alleviation of their lot. The Tupamaros were mainly of middle-class origin, and one source of indoctrination was certainly communist. The Russian embassy enclave in Montevideo (just a couple of blocks away from the Lawrences' house on Ellauri Street) was the second largest in all Latin America although sited in one of the smallest countries, and there is little doubt that training cadres were sent out from there. Another source came, sadly, from the Jesuit private schools teaching their pupils the same critical attitude to civil government which had got the order expelled from the Spanish Empire four centuries before. A third source was young men (and women) looking for thrills, again from the better-off families. In the previous generation, such youngsters looking for kicks might have gone to the war, on one side or the other, and many did. Those who returned had by then got it out of their system.

We would hear from the Lawrences and Coates that many families known to us were split right apart, with some of the younger generation having gone over to the Tupamaros while others, usually including the parents, had not. Monica paid several visits to Montevideo during 1970, where her mother Violet was not well – she passed away in September. Monica brought back quite rending stories about people we knew. In January 1971 the British ambassador to Uruguay, Sir Geoffrey Jackson, (7) was kidnapped and held incommunicado in an underground cell for nine months, often within a small cage and for long periods in total darkness. We have never heard what measures were taken by the British Government to obtain his release.

By this time the Tupamaros had got such a grip on the urban population that nobody dared to convey any information to the authorities about suspicious activities, houses known to harbour activists and the like, for fear of reprisals. This went on for several years, until the Uruguayan electorate were able to express their views via the anonymity of the ballot box in 1972. For the presidential elections the candidate for the Colorado party, having previously obtained the full support of the armed forces, ran on a 'No Tupamaros' ticket and was elected with a considerable majority. This was no coup, but a well-organised country setting its own affairs to rights within the law and framework of the constitution. Within a year the Tupamaro cells were disbanded, the disaffected youth fled to California, Mexico, Ibiza or London and most of the activists and trained cadre leaders sought other susceptible communities where their doctrines might prosper.

Many went to Chile, where the Marxist regime of Salvador Allende welcomed them openly. The communist penetration on the Pacific coast had begun with the infiltration of the Peruvian army, who overthrew the constitutional president Belaunde Terry and set up a dictatorship headed by General Velasco. Under this influence, Marxist principles spread south into Chile where the poorer classes hoped they might improve their lot. This led to the Communist Party under Allende being constitutionally elected in 1970, but it only had the real support of about 35 per cent of the population, less if you count non-voters. (8) Chile had thus become, technically, the world's first freely-elected Marxist state and therefore a model for communist doctrine.

From our vantage point just across the border, we watched it gradually fall to pieces, as all the classic weaknesses developed one by one. By and large Chile had always been self-sufficient in food, but with the introduction of land reform large estates were subdivided and given to the workers, who – however deserving – did not have the know-how to keep up modern levels of production, so output dropped. This was at first readily made up by importing grain from Argentina, but this had to be paid for. Economically, Chile had always lived off its mining resources, principally copper which was enjoying a world boom. So when Allende started trying to control copper exports experienced Chile-watchers said, 'Aha, this guy's had it'. He had also managed to fall foul of the heavy road transport unions, a powerful force in any modern country, so the supply and distribution of food broke down, and women took to the streets banging on their brandished cooking pots demanding food to feed their children.

So when a military junta headed by General Augusto Pinochet took over the reins of government in September 1972, it did so with the full support not only of the business, industrial and landowning communities in general, but also of large sectors of the populace including many who had voted for Allende originally. Such coups are usually bloodless, once both sides have displayed their cards, but on this occasion it was resisted by the communists and lives were lost, including that of Salvador Allende.

Under the presidency of Pinochet, the junta governed Chile for eighteen years, achieving an impressive economic recovery accompanied by the development of a thriving export trade mostly in fruit, wine and other food products. In this they were aided by a number of leading civilians, headed by the brilliant economist Hernán Büchi whose advice was later sought by Argentina after the final fall of the Peróns. Having achieved economic stability, Chile then set in motion a planned programme of 'return to democracy'. Parallels can be drawn with the withdrawal of British rule from several of the former colonies – first setting up an electoral system, then overseeing elections and finally handing over to the newly-elected representatives. In this case the programme was meticulously carried out, and in due course Pinochet handed over the presidential sash to the freely elected Patricio Aylwyn in 1989.

But we are not really concerned with Chilean history here except where it affects Argentina, and the first effect of the 1972 coup was that large numbers of citizens likely to be in trouble with established law and order, military or civil, found it expedient to hop over the border. These included both Chileans of Marxist or similar persuasions and ex-Tupamaros from Uruguay, and they mostly slipped in almost unnoticed as Argentina was having plenty of problems of its own. After the downfall of Perón there had followed a succession of both de facto and elected governments, for information on which I refer the reader to the history books. None were very successful as the Perónist Party continued to be proscribed, so internal unrest continued. Realising that the country had to get Perón out of its system one way or another, elections were held in 1971 in which the peronists were allowed to run, and inevitably won. The ensuing government of Hector Cámpora invited Perón to return from his exile in Madrid, which he did, to be greeted by ugly scenes including shooting on his arrival at Buenos Aires' Ezeiza Airport. It is still not clear just who was shooting at who. Cámpora soon resigned, and fresh elections were held in 1973, won by the Perón/Perón ticket – i.e. Juan Domingo with his second wife María Estela Martínez (known as 'Isabelita') as vice-president.

Throughout these unsettled years several clandestine groups had started to operate underground. Argentina was one of the food baskets of the world and there was enough food and work for everybody, so it was not a breeding ground for Marxism at working-class level. But middle-class extremism, which sprang from similar roots to the Tupamaros, arose just the same, and many of the latter having left Chile in a hurry had joined the ranks of organisations such as the ERP. (9) Its best-known exponent, Ernesto 'Ché' Guevara came from a middle-class family and held a university degree. Then there were the Montoneros who comprised the left-wing elements of the peronist party, and were always suspected of being the cause of the shootout at Ezeiza. Kidnappings of prominent businessmen for ransom became the order of the day, along with the murder of leading Argentines, such as General Aramburu, a level-headed leader who had been one of the prime movers in ousting Perón, and largely responsible for the post-Perón recovery of the country.

The campaign set up by the armed and security forces to combat this threat has become known as the 'Dirty War'. Latter-day media tend to imply or even state that it was carried out only by the de facto government which took over in 1976 (see below), and that it consisted of 'repression by the armed forces of innocent citizens'. Both these concepts are incorrect. It was certainly already underway in the late 1960s, and continued under the theoretically democratic governments of Cámpora and the Peróns. As in Uruguay, it was set up as a national security measure, with the armed forces acting in support of the civil power as is their proper function. Most of the citizens affected were anything but innocent, and the much publicised statistics of *desaparecidos* (people who disappeared without trace) include casualties of both sides. It is termed a 'war' because both sides were active and combatant. Wars also, sadly, tend to produce atrocities, again on both sides and this was no exception. The urban guerrilla cadres were mostly flushed out of Buenos Aires and other big cities, often leaving their young recruits dead behind them so they would tell no tales, and took refuge in the wilder parts of Tucumán. Special units of the army and of the marines were trained to tackle them, in the main successfully, the survivors mostly fleeing to Cuba (Guevara was among the first), Bolivia and Peru where, no doubt, many of them still are. From time to time persons have appeared in various countries, who on proper identification have turned out to have been on the list of *desaparecidos*, so one wonders how many more there are out there, terrorists or not, who would rather not be found . . .

Scab in the south

In Patagonia, however, neither politics nor terrorism had as yet arrived. A large number of Chileans of doubtful antecedents appeared in Rio Gallegos

The Shaw wool press, installed at Condor in 1913. An identical press was delivered by Shaw that same year to the San Julian Sheep Farming Co.

after the fall of Allende in 1972, but they were careful to keep their heads down. We were more concerned with business. Argentina in the 1960s still lived largely off the land, so to fill the fiscal coffers a form of tax known as 'export retentions' was invented. All primary exportable produce had a percentage of its value deducted (wool 8 per cent), which the grower never saw. There was an further deduction of 5 per cent to finance agricultural research, and most provinces had by then introduced a 'gross profits' tax, paid on all sales regardless of whether the farm made a profit or not, so direct taxation of this sort came to about 20 per cent in all. Those who ran their farming operations more or less efficiently, with good lambings and reasonable sales of livestock, could absorb this level of tax but there were plenty who could not make ends meet, particularly in areas unsuited to production of saleable animals for meat and so they relied almost entirely on wool.

I had been elected to the committee of the Rio Gallegos *Sociedad Rural* quite early on in my time as manager, and served two terms as vice-president. I declined becoming president, partly because I thought this post should be filled by a native Argentine, and partly because I did not really have enough time to do the job properly. Attending committee meetings was one thing, but the presidency demanded a lot of dedication. However, in 1971 I accepted the post of president of the *Federación de Instituciones Agropecuarias de la Provincia de Santa Cruz* (FIAS) which grouped together all the

303

rural societies in the province. Meetings were held in turn at all the different towns, and I enjoyed getting to know farmers all over Santa Cruz, and meeting those from other provinces in Buenos Aires and elsewhere. (10) In May 1971 a seminar was held in Bariloche by the FAO project, which was coming to its end, to discuss what had been achieved and in turn INTA, who would take over the mantle from then on, wanted to know what the growers thought should be done. We debated for three days, and at the end I had the doubtful privilege of delivering the message to the assembled company, directed in fact to higher authority who were present in the form of the (National) Secretary of Agriculture. 'Before we can consider research and the application of new techniques,' I said, 'first you have to determine whether settlement of Patagonia is to continue or not. The conditions are already there which could bring about the emptying of the land.' We did not intend to be prophetic in any way, but there were already large areas of marginal country in Chubut and northern Santa Cruz where farming was being carried out at a loss. Neither the federal nor provincial authorities had seen fit to address the problem, which was economic rather than technical, so we tried to draw their attention to the situation. Sadly to no avail, and twenty years later over half the farms in Santa Cruz lay empty – of people and of sheep.

But problems much nearer home were brewing. The FAO sheep breeding team headed by Brian Jefferies and Luis Iwan had thought up a fine-wool project very similar to our Cormo Argentino and had prevailed upon our neighbour, John Fenton at Estancia Monte Dinero to carry it out. This, like ours, involved crossing their existing Corriedale ewes with Merino rams, and started a year later. The rams required were brought down from Chubut in May 1971, but unfortunately proper scab control measures were not adhered to, the rams were put straight out with the ewes and it was not until they were taken off several months later that the outbreak of scab was discovered. We were advised at the beginning of November and by that time the infestation had already leaked into our flocks.

Scab had not been seen south of Gallegos since the 1930s, and it was to be with us for five years. With efficient modern insecticides all you have to do is ensure that every single sheep goes through the dip twice, with a ten-day interval between each. This sounds easy enough but apart from the time involved it calls for a very high degree of planning and an even higher demand on supervision. Every one of the forty-four camps had to be first gathered, then, while the flock was being driven to the nearest dip for treatment, the camp was gathered again, a process known as 'clean gathering', in order to pick up any stragglers.

I had foremen and shepherd bosses to do the gathering, but only two assistants I could really trust to make sure it was done properly. Peter Robertson had returned to the Falklands with his family, and to replace him I had consulted Tim Paine, general manager of the ASL and so my opposite number in the group. He recommended Pancho Höbich who had spent a year in Australia and whose elder brother Jorge was a manager with the

ASL and married to Paine's daughter Angela. Pancho was with us for five years, but just as the scab broke out had been offered a manager's job back in his home stamping grounds. We had as second down in Gap one Robert Sinclair whose family had a farm considerably inland from San Julian, and his wife Ann was a daughter of Theo Lewis from Santa Cruz. Although lacking experience for the Condor job, he had the virtue, from having lived in the San Julian and Santa Cruz districts, of being able to recognise scab when he saw it (which few locals could) so I promoted him in Pancho's place. Either myself, Sinclair or Pablo Peñaloza would go out to every clean gather in a truck, ensure that the horsemen went into every last corner, and collect any weak animal that could not walk.

The control rules laid down by SELSA (11) obliged us to treat the entire farm even though the infestation was confined to one corner. It was not, of course, possible to tackle the whole farm at once; lamb-marking and shearing had to be attended to in due season. Suffice it to say that to clear the first attack took us the entire season, from November to the following June. Unfortunately it was not possible to avoid contact across the frontier and the camps adjoining us in Chile became infested. These included the former Estancia Punta Delgada which some years before had been expropriated under the land reform programme and was being run by a sort of cooperative of the former workers. They did not know how to run a control programme and the Marxist government vets were apparently incapable or non-existent, so before they knew where they were the scab had spread all along the frontier, some 150km inland. It was not until the 1972/73 season, when the Ministry of Agriculture of the new junta government could restore some order, that they were able to carry out a proper control programme. Although we cleared our own first outbreak, we were reinfested from Chile twice, with the whole laborious process to do all over again.

Cordoba Hills

The risks and worries arising from terrorism affected everybody in an executive or administrative position associated with a company which might be good for a few millions in ransom. Insurance policies were taken out, and it became a matter for one-upmanship in business circles in Buenos Aires how much your company had you insured for. I was perhaps not in this league, but visiting directors from England certainly were and there was no means of knowing whether you might join them without prior warning. Rules were changed for travelling: plans, dates and arrival times, having been arranged by letter, were never discussed on the phone, by cable or by telex. You could ring up to say you had arrived, but never mention where. It was not easy to keep your head down either, when articles appeared in the glossy magazines or in sensationalist newspapers saying that Condor belonged to the British Crown.

We had little alternative, if their overall education was not to be affected, than to continue sending the children to boarding school, even if it was hard to put them on a plane with a bright smile. Once we sent Alison off back to school, and the same flight the following week was hijacked and ended up in Cuba. St Hilda's was in Hurlingham, a wealthy suburb and prime kidnapping territory where Agar Lockwood, the Born brothers and other prominent businessmen were taken and later ransomed. The school, among whose pupils were the daughters of Hugo Banzer, President of Bolivia, had strict security measures in place and the girls had an evacuation drill, supposedly in case of fire (read bombs). To visit or collect your child was dramatic – first you had to satisfy the guard at the gate of your identity by showing your ID card which was checked against a list, then the child was sent for and only when she viewed you through the closed, barred gate and said 'Yes, that's my daddy' were you allowed in.

St Paul's up in the Cordoba Hills was more remote and little affected by all this. We noticed however that although the majority of the boys were from English-speaking families of British descent, either from the camp or from Buenos Aires, there were quite a number of non-British from Buenos Aires, almost without exception from leading Argentine families who were very glad to have their sons tucked safely away in the hills. We could seldom accompany the children back to school ourselves, but all possible arrangements were made. A known and trusted driver from Waldron & Co. would meet the incoming plane from Rio Gallegos and transport Alison to Hurlingham and the boys to the long-distance bus station (then at Constitución, near the railway station) where they would meet up with the other boys for the fifteen-hour overnight bus trip to La Cumbre.

Alison's guardian was Ann Cowan, who had been at school with Monica in Montevideo and whose daughter Helen was now in the same class. Ann's husband Peter was general manager of Liebig's (12) farming operations in Argentina, located mainly in Entre Rios. They lived in Hurlingham not far from the school, but at long weekends and mid-term breaks would often go out to one or other of the company estancias, taking Alison with them. St Paul's was too far away for much weekending by parents, but the school was run on a seven days per week basis with much camping and similar expeditions into the hills. Longer exeats occurred at mid-term, built around the long weekends of the 25 May and 12 October national holidays to get a break of four to five days. At the October exeat the annual athletic sports would be held, so most parents would go up to La Cumbre for this and many stayed on in the vicinity for the whole exeat.

We met the Kenneth McCallums on p287. Kenneth's father had been an engineer who came out from Scotland to build the pier for the port of Comodoro Rivadavia after oil was discovered there in 1913, and went on to a distinguished career in engineering, much of it concerned with the railways. He was very much a pillar of the British community, and was knighted for his services on both counts. Sir William had acquired a property near General Pico, La Pampa, known as Estancia 'La Gwenita' and a large house in La Cumbre called 'El Aljibe'. Here those of their family as had boys at St

The Rotary Club of Rio Gallegos, founded 1967, has provided welcome companionship and relaxation over the years. Here I had just won a sponsored *asado*-roasting contest.

Paul's would gather at exeats. Michael had been invited from his very first term, when he found himself in the same form as 'Tico', Kenneth's second son, and they became lifelong friends. Peter was a year older, and Edward and Andrew, sons of Kenneth's brother Colin, were older yet, but still at school at that time. So when Stephen joined them in 1972 he was also invited, writing home: 'We had a lovely time at the Aljibe, Uncle Kenneth is the funniest man. We caught a rattlesnake and put it in a bottle'. Full stop. The hills around were full of *bichos* (creatures) of all sorts, and Tico was a keen naturalist who later assembled quite a collection at school, but we never really discovered how, in fact, you set about putting a rattlesnake into a bottle!

That October we also went up to El Aljibe for the first of a number of holidays, which soon took on a pattern. The house party of twenty or more included Kenneth and Diana as hosts and Derek and Helen Chennell, whose sons David and Alan were the same age as ours, and other families some related and others not. Parents and sisters got rooms, boys slept in rows in the attic in their sleeping bags.

An advance party, usually ourselves and the Chennells, would be responsible for laying in supplies from an enormous list made out by Diana, most of which we bought at Roy's Store (13) where we could get discounts for quantity. I contributed some basic stuff on mass feeding derived from farm logistics, which caused Derek some amusement. Other parents arrived in the course of the afternoon, and the first evening, usually Friday, was the school play, concert or other performance. The Saturday was given over to the athletic sports inter-house meeting in which all the boys competed, and the rest of the long weekend was spent in picnics and expeditions to the hills.

Stuart by now was going to the Condor school, so we left him and Frances on the farm with Otilia and María. We had taken delivery of a new truck and extended our holiday after the exeat by continuing north to Cruz del Eje, then west across the desert to La Rioja and Catamarca. Here we took local advice, and continued west over some spectacular mountain roads to Andalgalá and Belén, hard up against the Andes. This was primitive farming and herding country, with very small plots cultivated by horses or mules in the valleys (we found a threshing floor just like those in the Bible) and sheep, goats and llamas herded in the mountains – Belén particularly is a centre for spinning and weaving hand-crafted ponchos. The poncho is an Andean invention, and looks like a blanket with a hole in the middle. Its close relative, the *ruana*, has the hole extended in a slit to the front edge, allowing the ends to be wrapped warmly round the neck.

We struck Route 40 (14) and turned north., well aware that there was nothing between us and the Pacific Ocean apart from the Andean mountains and the Atacama Desert in Chile. The road was not paved, and in pulling over to the side to take a photo we got stuck in pure, dry and loose sand, the only time in many a dicey experience that this has happened to me. Fortunately the truck was fitted with a self-locking differential for use in Patagonia, so we got out without difficulty. We continued up through the back-blocks of Salta and down to Jujuy, where we joined Route 9 which

Loading a shipment of ewes headed for Bolivia, a journey of over 5000 kilometres. The cable-tool drilling rig on the right was one used by contractor Garland Ford in the twenties to drill for water.

follows the Humahuaca Gorge to La Quiaca and Bolivia.

The previous year, Condor had participated with two other farms in a historic export of 2,000 ewes to Bolivia. They were trucked 5,000km from Rio Gallegos to San Pedro de Jujuy, where they were loaded onto a train for the rest of the journey. This had puzzled us at the time, as it seemed to add to the already considerable travel stress against which we had taken a number of precautions. Now we discovered why: some of the bends in the Humahuaca Gorge are too tight for articulated stock trucks to negotiate.

We did not go all the way to the Bolivian border at La Quiaca, as while visiting the pre-Columbian village of Tilcara, near Humahuaca, we felt a bit odd, which we attributed to the altitude, although it may have been the spirits of those long-departed people. So we returned south through Tucumán and Santiago del Estero, having visited nine provinces. When leaving Buenos Aires we had found both our driving licences to have expired, but there was nothing for it but to press on. Highway police checks on the main roads are the norm, and at every one they asked to see our personal identity cards, but it wasn't until the very last check that they asked for my licence and the fault was discovered. Fortunately the police sergeant had a sense of humour, as when I congratulated him and said that none of his other colleagues had spotted our expired licences, he roared with laughter and sent us on our way. It transpired that General Aramburu (page 302) had been kidnapped and the police everywhere were looking for people, not vehicles.

Letter to Perón

The biggest Condor myth of all, which one heard repeated time and time again, was that it belonged to the British Crown. I have never really been able to work out just why this should have been thought, but not only did tour guides point it out to their busload as 'the farm owned by the Queen' but quite senior officials really believed it. As a company registered in London it was of course an expatriate British asset, and in the event of unwelcome attentions by the host country the embassy would have had something official to say, but then the same would apply to any of the thirty or more British-owned lands companies operating in Argentina at that time. It is true that visiting directors tended to be whipped straight from the airport to the farm and vice versa, spending no time on public relations (which were left to us), and that the chairman of the board, Kenneth Suggett, was tall and fair-haired, so observers might have thought him royal, but no. Nor is it true that the royal gardener came out once a year to oversee the gardens. I once answered the front door to a quite serious young man who said he understood that royal residences in the UK were often shown to the public, so could he please see around? The family said afterwards that I should have shown him around with a straight face and charged an entrance fee, but it wasn't really funny.

Jorge Cepernic, whose father had been an immigrant from Croatia before the Great War, was a die-hard peronist who had spent several years in gaol for subversive activities in the 1970s, a privilege he shared with the future president, Carlos Menem. (15) When Cámpora came to power he had opened the gaols and released all the political prisoners, and the judicial system being what it was, it was not very clear just where the line was drawn between an activist who had been rounded up in the course of a demonstration, and convicted felons, murderers etc. In 1973 Cepernic ran for governor of Santa Cruz on the peronist ticket and got in on the backlash towards Perón which swept the country. I have since been told by old-guard peronists, good friends of ours and honourable men who had backed his nomination, 'we reckoned we could keep Jorge in order, but he was got at by the Montoneros [the left or terrorist wing] so we lost him'.

I was in London when the election results were published, and with them Cepernic's loudly announced intention of expropriating Estancia Condor. This was now a subsidiary of the ASL, and Kenneth Suggett was my boss, although Maurice Waldron was still on the board. They had retained Waldron & Co. (now Waldron SA) as representatives in Buenos Aires, where Eric Waldron had retired and the senior partners were now G.H. ('Willie') Van Deurs and Stelvio Barbieri. (16) I returned hot-foot to Buenos Aires, to find they had their finger adequately on the pulse of the federal government and the word was that Cepernic was talking out of turn. Condor being a foreign asset, only the federal government could take such a step – a province could not do so alone. So after taking advice as to what actions to take should truckloads of Montoneros actually turn up demanding to take over, I returned to Condor where Monica had all the children at home from school, it being the winter holidays.

Beyond packing up all our silver and valuables in a box which we left in safe keeping in the bank in Rio Gallegos (where they remained for three years), we took no further action. The children returned to school, and I continued to battle against scab. Cepernic issued declarations from time to time, in which he proclaimed his intentions to take over the assets of all the 'foreign-owned' farms in the province which it seemed came to the nice round figure of 500,000 hectares. Bulletins named them, with Condor top of the list as it belonged to the Queen and Coronel next because it was said to be owned by the San Julian Sheep Farming Company Ltd, another factual error since the latter had in fact ceased to exist some years back and the farm was no longer a foreign asset, being owned by Ganadera Coronel SA in Buenos Aires (see Chapter 17). We knew therefore that Cepernic's announced intentions were flawed, so it was a matter of riding the waves.

This did not stop local harassment, however, particularly by the media. The provincial government continued to announce its intentions to the world, which were repeated in the national press. We received visits from local and national journalists, and articles appeared in some of the glossy weeklies, profusely illustrated with misleading shots. One (taken without our knowledge) showed a sheepdog barking, and the low angle of the shot shows the dog behind wire netting. The caption gave the impression that the fierce dog was keeping out the innocent cameraman, but a second glance showed that the animal was in fact a half-grown pup, and he was not barking but laughing and probably wagging his tail. I did give a few interviews, partly so as not to be unwelcoming and partly in the hope that some of the more blatant untruths might be corrected, but after being misreported several times I gave it up.

The season ran its course and in the second week in March the Rio Gallegos British Community Council of which I was district chairman held its annual charity fundraising event known as the Gymkhana (see Chapter 19). The British consul general in Buenos Aires, John Shakespeare, was coming down for the occasion. As soon as I arrived at the venue I was advised by the local vice-consul, Jesse Aldridge, that the governor had let it be known that he wished to see Mr Shakespeare, and that he proposed a meeting, not at Government House, but out at Condor. The consul general advised that we should go along with this, as he in any case was coming to stay with us, so on the day following the gymkhana we awaited Don Jorge for tea. I was very tempted to bug the living room so as to record the proceedings but in the end decided not to.

He arrived alone carrying a briefcase, having left his chauffeur outside in the car, evidently confident that he was going to get either an agreement or a payoff. The Queen was not mentioned, but his arguments were that as 'nobody knew who the owners were', therefore the land should be farmed by more deserving people. We limited ourselves to stating the facts – namely that the owners were perfectly well known, and that all he or the Argentine embassy in London needed to do was to go and ask at Companies House in the City of London, where the names of shareholders are registered. We had in the meantime checked that the company's non-Argentine status, registered in Buenos Aires, entitled it to be handled by federal courts, not provincial ones. We had further prepared a number of statistics, showing that the present single-company operation was far more productive than, say twenty small farms; and it employed more personnel and maintained more families on and off the property than any land reform programme could possibly do. But we did not need to produce either of these arguments, then nor later. When the governor saw that he was not going to get anywhere, that neither the Queen (represented by the consul general) nor the company (represented by me) were going to offer him an emolument to get him off our backs, he took his departure.

As soon as I reported this to Waldron & Co. in Buenos Aires, it was decided to follow up by going right to the top, so a letter was prepared and sent to President Perón, knowing that he did not actually have any land reform plans in hand any more than he had in 1947. The results were spectacular. Cepernic was called up to Buenos Aires, and as soon

311

as the Aerolineas plane he was travelling on landed it was met at the end of the runway by official cars, so he could not contact the press. He was taken off to the official presidential residence at Olivos and hauled over the coals by the president. No more was heard of the expropriation project. It later appeared that the final straw had been when none other than the Rio Gallegos branch of the CGT, (17) who anybody would have thought to have been in favour of the takeover, discovered that the soon-to-be-subdivided Condor had in fact been pre-awarded on paper to a number of Cepernic political supporters, so there would in fact never be any 'land for the workers'! Sadly, we later learned that several of these supporters had British names and indeed were considered pillars of the community . . .

The Cepernic family had a farm, Estancia 'Josefina', near Lago Argentino, which was rather run down and needed restocking. Many years later, after Menem had become president and the state had money running out of its ears from the sale of the public utilities, he gave his old cell-mate a substantial sum by way of compensation for their former imprisonment. Although for some years Don Jorge and I had been greeting each other amicably enough, letting bygones be bygones, it was still a surprise when he quite seriously set about buying ewes from Condor, paying cash on the nail. It seemed a fitting way to round it off.

Notes

1 Andrew Merrick was an early sea captain and hunter of seals and penguins. (Chapter 2)

2 The ten original partners of the Patagonian Sheep Farming Company were James Lovegrove, Walter Brind (chairman), his son Walter George, Arthur, Stephen, Thomas and John Frederick (all Waldrons), Henry and Stanley Wood, and Thomas Greenshields. Board meetings were held at W.B.Waldron's residence at Peasemore, near Newbury.

3 John Hamilton with his partner Saunders, were the owners of Weddell, Saunders, Beaver and Passage Islands in the Falklands. Their Estancia Punta Loyola in Santa Cruz owned all the land on the Atlantic coast between Condor and the Gallegos River, and they went on to settle an important area of land near Rio Turbio, with estancias 'Little Hill' and 'Rincón de los Morros'. Local gossip relates that Hamilton 'always had scabby sheep'. Certainly the boundary between the two properties was the only stretch of double fencing, supposedly scab-proof, in the district.

4 The present Estancia 'Monte Dinero'. The Greenshields succession set up the Lucacho Sheep Farming Co. Ltd, which operated the farm until after the Second World War when John Fenton, returning from war service, bought out his relations and remained sole owner. Lionel Pickering (see Chapter 8, page 132) had been there as a cadet before the war.

5 There is a letter written in 1903 from the managing director, London, to Arthur Waldron at Condor, which says, 'now that you can get from Condor to Rio Gallegos in *two days* . . .' Today it takes less than an hour!

6 The entry of the sale to the Baker Company can be seen in the Condor stock book for January 1907. It lists 20,500 ewes, 850 rams, 200 wethers and 22 horses.

7 See *People's Prison* by G.H.S. Jackson, 1973. A graduate of Emmanuel College, Geoffrey Jackson described in this book, and in a moving account for the College magazine, his experience and how he drew on his background, religion and education for the moral strength with which to survive the ordeal.

8 Chile at that time did not have a 'ballotage' law, requiring a second vote to choose between the two presidential candidates who polled most the first time. Allende was elected in a three-way contest, the other two parties, not having been able to read the writing on the wall, putting up two candidates instead of agreeing on one single non-communist ticket.

9 *Ejercito Revolucionario del Pueblo:* Revolutionary Army of the People.

10 FIAS in turn is affiliated to the *Confederaciones Rurales Argentinas,* the body which in theory represents all sectors of farming on a national level. Its voice however is weakened by the presence of the *Sociedad Rural Argentina,*

which represents all the really powerful stock breeders, *Federación Agraria Argentina*, representing smallholders, and CONINAGRO which groups all the farming cooperatives. The four bodies often differ in approach, so there is no single voice to speak for farming interests.

11 *Servicio de Luchas Sanitarias*, the department of the National Secretariat of Agriculture which controlled all animal health problems throughout the country.

12 Liebig's Extract of Meat Co. Ltd was a British firm operating on both sides of the River Plate which marketed the Fray Bentos brand of corned beef. Like Bovril and Vestey's they produced much of the beef on their own estancias, many of very large size and including a number of showplaces.

13 Roy was a *turco* – i.e. he came from the eastern end of the Mediterranean, probably from Syria or the Lebanon. Like many of his compatriots he had come to Argentina with very little and had built his original small grocery shop into a moderate supermarket.

14 Route 40 is the longest road in the country, hugging the eastern side of the Andes all the way from Rio Turbio in the south to Jujuy in the north. Most of it has spectacular scenery, some bits are well used and have been macadamised, others have not.

15 Menem had money, supplied by his wealthy family in La Rioja, so could afford to live comfortably in the quarters reserved for political (as opposed to criminal) prisoners. Cepernic did not, so he did the cooking.

16 Willie van Deurs was a well-connected businessman in Buenos Aires with considerable interests of his own. He was related to the Ricketts and Lafone families in Uruguay and both he and his wife owned a number of camp properties. Stelvio Barbieri had joined the firm in the 1940s as head wool man, and continued to work closely with van Deurs for many years afterwards.

17 The *Confederación General de Trabajo* (General Confederation of Labour) represented organised labour throughout the country, and was very close to Perón, having been virtually created by him during his first term of office.

17

The Family's Farm

Ganadera Coronel SA

Estancia Coronel had been ticking over nicely under Lionel Pickering, assisted by his brother Tom, with Arthur travelling out every year after Christmas to supervise and generally direct operations. At an early stage he made a particular point of settling the Pickering family. Their father, Ernest, had come out from Lancashire with two brothers when their sister married Herbert Elbourne who had set up a general office in Rio Gallegos. Pickering later set up on his own in Deseado, where most of their children were born, although Tom was born in England. At the time of which I write Mrs Pickering was bedridden and being looked after by their only daughter, Dorothy. Forever matchmaking, Arthur arranged for them all to come and live at Coronel, so that Dorothy could marry Sandy Mann who after a period at Condor as cadet under Eric Davies and other farm posts in the district had come back to the farm where he had been born and brought up. Mrs Mann had died, and Don Alec, now retired but still active as a gardener, lived with Tom and Lydia.

This was the set-up I had found when I went out in 1952, and it worked very well. Lionel ran the farm, but all major decisions were taken by Arthur, either by letter or in person on his annual visits. While I was there we cautiously ventured towards new ideas, such as keeping Jersey cows for milk and sowing alfalfa on the pampa. By the time we removed to Condor in 1958, Coronel, like most Patagonian farms, had taken advantage of the current prosperity and tax-free imports and there were new vehicles, tractors and lighting plants, and a lot of rebuilding had been done. While I was second at Condor I clearly could not take time off to visit San Julian, but once I became manager my time was more my own and I started to make occasional trips to Coronel and gradually became involved in its operation, particularly the more technical aspects. It was a happy time in many respects, with all three Pickering/Mann families in residence, and a total of ten children between them. For a number of years the farm put a station wagon at their disposal, and the children were driven daily into San Julian to school. Following the success of our camp school at Condor, however, we applied to the provincial authorities for one at Coronel, which was granted. Escuela Provincial No. 33 was started in 1965, and it was heartwarming at the opening ceremony to be able to recall Millicent's contribution. The presence of two of her former pupils, Mary and Lydia, seemed wholly apt.

The sole presence of INTA in the province at that time was a small experiment station at Cañadón León (later 'Gobernador Gregores'), only 250km inland, and their new agronomist, Dalmiro Molina, was keen to get out to the farms and do some trials. When I returned from my trip to Australia in 1966 we started serious trials at Coronel under Molina's supervision, which led to the sowing of quite large areas with the help of government grants. Also at that time I was working on the selecting of rams by weighing the fleeces and bodies, and it was at Coronel that Jefferies, Iwan and I perfected

The old Big House was ideal for the school, providing quarters for the teacher, lodging during the week for children from the outlying shepherds' houses, and the classroom in the *galería*.

the charts that we used for this purpose for nearly twenty years, until the job was taken over by computers.

In the late 1960s, however, all the British land companies operating in Argentina began to be harassed, not as has often been suggested by Perón or other Argentine government agencies, but by the British Government in London. Up until then the Treasury had been very happy to have the proceeds of overseas farming activities flow into the City, to the extent of granting a number of tax concessions, even in the case of countries like Argentina with whom there was no formal reciprocal agreement. However, the Callaghan government began to clamp down on this and such companies found themselves in the position of first paying all their Argentine taxes, then remitting the profits to London where they were regarded as gross income and taxed all over again. With that, the withdrawal of British capital began – this had in fact begun as early as the 1950s, and Condor would be the last to go (see Chapter 21).

The board of the San Julian Sheep Farming Company Ltd consisted of Uncle Robert, Arthur Blake and Ted Mathews, with Hilary Jacomb and A.E. Bell (who were senior partners in the wool-broking firm of Jacomb Hoare and Company). They were all hard-headed, experienced businessmen, so they put their heads together and in 1962 set up an Argentine company in Buenos Aires, with Willie van Deurs as chairman and Arthur Blake as vice-chairman. The remaining directors were senior staff of Waldron SA. The land, livestock and general assets were transferred to the new company, which was called Ganadera Coronel SA, and the shares in the latter were wholly owned by the San Julian Sheep Farming Company Ltd, so that the UK shareholders were not affected.

This arrangement was only partly successful, as the parent company continued to pay UK tax, and this was exacerbated in 1968 when the British Government abolished Double Taxation relief. When I was on leave in 1969 there was much discussion among leading shareholders as to the future of sheep farming in Patagonia. Not all of them shared my optimism as to the possibilities now opening up for changes in farming methods and the development of more profitable sheep towards which the Condor board and the Waldrons had directed my steps. This was one approach – could there be others?

Arthur had continued to visit San Julian every year, until in 1971 he was left behind in Montevideo by BSAA (1) when returning to the UK. This traumatic experience quite put him off travelling, and in theory with a board in Buenos Aires and myself at Condor this did not seem to be so necessary. But the personal touch, to which the Pickering brothers were accustomed, was lacking, and I was too junior in their eyes to replace my father in anything except the technical aspects like breeding and the new sown pastures. In any case, my job at Condor did not allow me to spend much time at San Julian.

Three generations – Arthur, Michael and John – at Coronel in 1965.

Lionel and Mary had tragically lost their first born and only son Adrian, a fine upstanding young man who was completing his studies at an agro-technical school in the Buenos Aires Province, when he contracted *mal de los rastrojos*, a virus disease harboured in the stubbles (*rastrojo*) of the grain country, and it proved fatal. By now the younger children of both families had moved on to secondary school in San Julian, bringing about the closure of the school on the farm, there being no other families coming on. The moral support of Don Arturo's annual visits was keenly missed, and so a period of uncomfortable relations ensued, with the Pickerings holding sway on the farm and not much control being effected by the new board in Buenos Aires. It was a case of 'my rams' really (see page 273), with the major aspects of production (as had been taught by Arthur years ago) being meticulously attended to, but they had difficulty in adjusting to some of the newer requirements necessary to cope with the ever-rising costs of production and could not see that times had changed and so had the company's requirements. Maybe it was easier for me on a commercially-run place like Condor, where decisions came down the line and you had to hop to it, but at Coronel they had no experience of this way of working.

In 1973 I took a quick trip to England to see my father, who had had a mild stroke but was still living at Westfield under the loyal care of Mrs Gatehouse. It was, in fact, the onset of Alzheimer's disease, which gradually took its insidious hold until he had to go into a nursing home in Bristol, where he died in February 1976. However in 1973 we could still have serious conversations – I remember him expressing surprise at my confidence in the future of sheep production in Patagonia, and we looked at various possibilities for Coronel. I started to sound out some of the other UK shareholders (most of course one or more generations removed from the original people who had formed the company in 1900) to find out just who among the uncles and cousins and aunts was really interested in a sheep farming company in Argentina. This approach was followed up in Buenos Aires, until in 1974 after considerable negotiation all the UK equity was bought out by new shareholders in Buenos Aires. Somewhat to our surprise, the Braun Menéndez family, who owned 30 per cent, decided to pull out also, so new money was put up, mainly by bringing in the Siracusa interests – this was a family from Sicily who had come over after the war and set up important meat abattoirs at several ports down the Patagonian coast. We will meet them again later on.

The new board of Ganadera Coronel SA now had Willie van Deurs as chairman with 20 per cent of the shares, myself as vice-chairman with 20 per cent, Stelvio Barbieri with 20 per cent, Antonino Siracusa with 25 per cent and the remaining 15 per cent spread between the senior employees of Waldron SA. There were, in the end, no shareholders resident in the UK, no Brauns, and Uncle Robert's daughter Ann Wood and her family in Neuquén, the only other descendants of the founder resident in Argentina, also opted out. I was therefore the only Blake to continue in the business, but I reckoned there was a good future in finer wool and in lamb production for meat. The early years of the Cormo Argentino project at Condor were showing positive results, as we will see.

Both the outgoing UK board and the new one in Buenos Aires were much concerned with the forthcoming retirement of Lionel, who would be 60 in 1975 and have completed over thirty years service with the company. Tom was six years younger and had never worked anywhere else, but there was some doubt among the directors as to his personal stamina and ability – was he really capable of carrying out the top job? After much discussion, it was decided that as Lionel would be living in San Julian, and had been given a seat on the board, he could provide such local support as might be needed and so Tom was appointed manager. The outgoing London board, possibly overreacting to this situation, insisted on presenting the Pickering brothers with an extremely generous bonus, equivalent at the time to the value of a property fully stocked with 5,000 sheep. More cautious voices from Buenos Aires, including my own, tried to point out that actual on-farm performance over the past five years or so did not justify such a princely golden handshake, but we were overridden. Lionel retired from Coronel in 1975 and took up residence in San Julian while Tom continued running the farm, now as manager. The handshake was duly paid, and we heard they had invested it in a small farm but knew no further details.

Sadly, the cautious voices proved right. One night in November 1976 I received a call from Stelvio Barbieri, reporting that Tom had attempted unsuccessfully to take his own life. It transpired that in June of that year Tom had forgotten to send the returns of the mating of the pedigree flock to the register in Buenos Aires. With the arrival of lambing, this omission (not irretrievable) so preyed on his mind that he took the dreadful decision. He survived, albeit in an invalid state, and Lionel naturally had to go back and pick up the reins again as manager.

Summer holidays

Once the children started secondary school, it ceased to be possible to take, as it were, a summer holiday in winter, by going away to the northern hemisphere in the slack season from May to September. Being away at boarding school for most of the year, holidays at home were mostly spent happily with the horses and dogs, with Christmas along the way. But we all needed a break so in February, once shearing was over, we usually managed to get away for a few days with them and this meant camping.

For several years the farmers round Calafate, Lago Argentino, ran their own small local show which usually coincided with the end of shearing, which at that time lasted nearly two months, and it was great just to be able to down tools, pile the camping gear into the truck and get away for a long weekend. One farm quite near Calafate put a field at our disposal, and there could be half a dozen or more family groups doing just the same, with children much of the same age. They were not yet into dancing and parties, so I took my accordion, and somebody else might have a guitar, and we would have great singsongs round the camp-fire.

Other years the dates did not fit, so we would go off on our own. One trip, when Frances was about 3, found us camped near the Torres del Paine in Chile, later to become a national park, when a storm came down and we were very glad of our thick canvas lamb-marking tent into which we could all pack, and listen to the williwaws roaring down from the mountains. But the sun came out next day, and we made our way down to Punta Arenas, driving straight through and intending to camp in the wooded country south of the town. We passed a fishing village, where one hut had a *centolla* hanging up outside, indicating in the centuries-old manner that he had them for sale. I pulled up to enquire, and the man leaped into a dinghy and quickly sculled out a few metres and hauled up a cage, out of which he took a fine specimen which I paid for, put into a bucket and off we went in search of a campsite. The beast was alive, of course, and kept on trying to climb out of the bucket to the great consternation of little Frances. When we made camp, we found we did not have a pot or pan large enough to cook it in, so had to use the washing-up basin, weighting it down with a suitable rock. But it was delicious eating in the end . . .

The *centolla*, often wrongly called 'king crab', flourishes in the cold waters of the Humboldt current, round the Straits of Magellan and up as far as Comodoro. It is technically a 'sea spider', with eight equal legs so is not a crab at all. Another local delicacy were the mussels, which grew on the rocks off both the Straits and the Atlantic beaches. At normal low tides normal-sized mussels would be uncovered, quite as good as any found at Mar del Plata or Punta del Este which are larger than those found in European waters. However at certain places there were banks of *cholgas* or giant mussels 8-10cm long which are also specific to the Humboldt current, and these could only be reached at low Spring tides. One such bank was off the coast, near our Gap section although actually reached through Monte Dinero land, and another near Cape Virgins. At 'Cholga tides' people would come out from Rio Gallegos and camp out for two or three days, collecting the cholgas by the bagful. We often went for the day, always taking Otilia and Erasmo Davet for the outing, and usually ended up grilling the shellfish on hot stones by a driftwood fire. The children learned a lot of lore from the Davets, who would also take them off on picnics down to the beach on the Straits, a two-hour walk from Condor settlement, a great treat for all concerned.

The following year (1973) we were more ambitious and crossed over to Tierra del Fuego, first into Chile so as to take the car ferry operating at the First Narrows, then into the Argentine part of the island, through Rio Grande and on to Estancia 'Viamonte', home of the Bridges family (see Chapter 2, page 30). Don Lucas's younger sister, Clarita, had married John Goodall, sometime manager of the Rio Grande freezer, who was responsible for first introducing trout (brown, rainbow and brook) into the Fuegian rivers, which now provided some of the finest fly-fishing in the world. Their son, Adrian, was managing the farm, and his daughter Cristina later went to both school and university with Frances. From there we pottered on down through the *nothofagus* (southern beech) forests to Ushuaia, enjoying the thrill of catching our lunch in the Rio Ewan on the way, and spent several nights camping at Rio Pippo, between Ushuaia and Lapataia. Not very good fishing there, indeed Chacho managed to catch himself on his own hook in the back of the neck, we had to take him into the excellent clinic in Ushuaia to have it removed . . .

That was to be our last visit across the frontier for seven years. The peronist government which came into power in Argentina following the 1973 elections included a number of fringe factions and fellow-travellers, particularly in Santa Cruz Province where the Cepernic administration was controlled by the left-wing Montoneros, who welcomed any Chilean extremists who found it expedient to leave their own country. All the same, there were a number of cases of quite innocent travellers, of one country or the other, being arrested on various security charges , so it was no time to be sticking your neck out.

Even after the expropriation threat was quashed by Perón, we clearly had to keep a low profile and ourselves to ourselves. But there was always plenty to do on the farm during the holidays. As the children grew up, their horse-riding became second nature, and there were always dogs (Border collies) around. The earliest were Sandy and Mandy, who came from Coronel as puppies, their father being an imported pedigree dog and the mother a good working bitch of Tom's. Mandy never worked sheep (although she bred some very good working dogs), but being highly intelligent she made a very good guard dog. She had an incredible perception of people, and if she thought some visitor was not what they purported to be, she often had to be restrained in order to let him in – awkward if he was an important official . . . There were times when we slept better knowing Mandy was out there. I never had time to train a dog properly, to work like Glen or even Skip, but we always bred good dogs, they were such a joy to have around. I used to give them to the shepherds on the condition they never left the farm.

As the boys got bigger, they often used to go gathering with the shepherds, which in summer meant a crack-of-dawn start – i.e. 4 a.m. or so. Hence it became quite usual for them to ask to leave their mounts in the stable overnight, so as to gather such-and-such a camp on the morrow. Many years later, Michael and Stephen confessed to having climbed out of their bedroom windows so as to go riding in the moonlight. When there was no wind blowing and on a warm night the camp was unbelievably beautiful. . . The McCallum boys and other school friends would come to stay, and at the height of the scab problem it was handy to be able to count on an extra few horsemen to gather an unexpected paddock. Another time Derek and Helen Chennell came to stay, with their sons David and Alan. One evening they had all gone out for a walk, and when they got back Derek told me with a perfectly straight face that 'there was a penguin in the *paso libre*' (2) which of course I flatly refused to believe. However a solemn expedition set forth complete with box, and the penguin – which really was in the pit – was duly rescued. Quite how it got there remains a mystery to this day. 'Roaming' penguins do turn up from time to time – they seem to lose their ocean-related sense of direction, and just set off inland, being quite capable of walking considerable distances. I once collected one which had got mixed into a group of ewes and lambs being gathered for lamb-marking, and shut it into the pen, too.

Another summer activity was ringing wild geese. It seemed that crop farmers in the wheat belt in BA province had been trying to get the Ministry of Agriculture to declare the geese a national pest, as they would descend on the wheat fields in their hundreds and tread down the young crop. The

Michael raking hay, helping out during the summer holidays.

Ministry with due caution and knowing little about the migrating habits of geese, had first set up a study project under Maurice Rumboll, a leading ornithologist in the Museum of Natural Science who had been a master at St Paul's in Bob Thurn's early years. He was given a truck with driver and a small budget, with which he took himself off to Tierra del Fuego and spent the early part of the summer catching goslings before they could fly, and putting light aluminium bands on one leg. Then in the autumn when they started migrating he moved over to the mainland to observe where the banded ones went.

The first time he turned up at Condor in May, and camped 'under the flight path' [of the geese, that is. In fact it differs little to that of aircraft], just a few kilometres east of Condor. Like all naturalists, they put out nets in the bushes near their camp, and caught a particularly rare species of mouse, whose prized skin was sadly eaten by Frances' cat while put out to dry in the *galería*. His tiny budget did not allow of hiring any labour, so he used to enthuse schoolboys and undergraduates, mostly ex St Paul's, to come on a fun camping expedition to Patagonia and band goslings. Our boys went along on some of these expeditions, which later extended up the Gallegos and Coyle rivers, and it was Stephen who suggested the use of lamb-marking nets to 'sweep' the water and so corral the goslings. On that same expedition they reached the 'Laguna de Los Escarchados' up near Lago Argentino (3), where they made a rare discovery of a new species of bird. This was the *Macá Tobeano* or Hooded Grebe *(Podiceps gallardoi)* which only nests on water at high altitudes in Santa Cruz, where a particular water weed can be found.

At the end of 1974 Alison finished school. She had responded very well to St Hilda's under Norman Bissett's sensitive coaching, in spite of the tensions of the times. But these had left their mark nonetheless and she was most unwilling to pursue a university course in Argentina. (4) Her inclinations towards nursing as a career had been strengthened by the sound advice of the school matron, and we had ascertained that her academic qualifications (Argentine *bachillerato* plus three A levels) were sufficient to get into a teaching hospital. We had sent in applications to four of these, so in May 1975 I took her to England for the interviews.

Granfy now had to be under full-time professional care and had moved into the private nursing home in Bristol. Alison and I needed a base so we settled into Westfield for the time being, but the house that had been home to us all for so long, now seemed empty and characterless without the people who had made it welcoming for so many years. It had been decided to sell the house once our present visit was over, but it was of course full of contents and in between trips to London for Alison's interviews and visiting friends and relations we put in a lot off time sorting them out. Hugh, Eleanor and Rosemary all came down to decide who should have what (Alison wisely took herself off for the day) and in effect we got it all apportioned amicably. After a while we began to receive answers from Alison's hospitals, and to our great pride and satisfaction she was accepted by all of them. However, the number one choice was always St Thomas', the nursing school founded by Florence Nightingale in 1860, and so they arranged for her to start there in early September.

Diagonal Norte 547

While we were busy with all this a bombshell broke. The ASL, owners of the Patagonian Sheep Farming Company, received a takeover offer from a financial company registered in Luxembourg. I went haring up to London to see the chairman, Kenneth Suggett, and find out what was going on. Yes, indeed, negotiations were well under way to sell the group to Argentine interests, namely a partnership comprising the Menéndez Montes, Ochoa and Paz families. Neither Suggett nor my former boss, Maurice Waldron, who was still on the board, could give me any reassurance as to my personal future in spite of my contract and I felt obliged to take legal advice on the subject. Alison may have been embarking on her chosen profession, but there were four more children back home with many years of schooling still to come.

Tim Paine had retired as general manager of the ASL some years back, and somewhat to the surprise of many informed Patagonia-watchers I had not been promoted in his place. Don Luis (Tim) Paine was probably the most knowledgeable Merino breeder in the country, but had been less able to weld together the overall business of the company into an efficient whole.

Their running costs were astronomical and their technology lagging in spite of having the INTA/FAO project right there on their doorstep. Paine was simply not replaced – instead his functions were divided between a business manager and a farming manager, which as in the case of most dual commands, did not work well in practice. I always thought that the sale of the group had some element of snag-shifting about it. I am not sure if I ever really wanted the job, it was never offered to me and I was left in charge at Condor.

So leaving Alison rather forlornly in her new probationer's uniform, I flew back to Buenos Aires to meet my new employers. In 1974 the Patagonian scene had been staggered by the news that the Menéndez interests in general had been subdivided and apportioned among all the heirs up to and including the grandchildren of Don José Menéndez (the first). It is usual in Chile and common in Argentina to clarify relationships by using both the paternal and maternal surnames, and retaining the mother's maiden name. Thus the children of José Menéndez and María Behety de Menéndez were styled Menéndez Behety; the children of José Menéndez Behety, who married María Montes, were styled Menéndez Montes and so forth. One therefore heard of estancias up and down the country now belonging to the Menéndez Préndez, the Campos Menéndez, the Braun Lasala families and so on. The biggest farms, such as Estancia José Menéndez on Tierra del Fuego were divided, into four farms of 40,000 sheep apiece. One went to José Menéndez Montes and another to the Paz Menéndez family. Similarly, the elegant office building only half a block from the Plaza de Mayo at 547 Roque Sáenz Peña Avenue (otherwise known as 'Diagonal Norte') was divided by floors into the major family holdings. The first floor was Menéndez Behety, the second floor Braun Menéndez and so forth. I directed my steps to the fourth floor, the Menéndez Montes.

In 1952 Don 'Pepe' Menéndez Montes, his cousin (also Don Pepe) Paz Menéndez and their friend and partner Federico Ochoa, a wealthy cattle farmer of Basque descent with important holdings in Buenos Aires Province, had bought up the shares of the Tecka (Argentina) Lands Company, a British outfit who ran Merino sheep and cattle in Chubut, just south of Esquel. It was this group, composed of the Menéndez, Ochoa and Paz families (MOP for short) who were buying the ASL. One of my worries was that the Menéndez clan as a whole did not have a very good reputation as employers, but I need not have been concerned. I never met Pepe Menéndez, who had died by then, but he had married Carmen Hume, the daughter of a Scottish engineer who built most of the Southern Railway and, as well as being a good businessman (5) was extremely anglophile. Most of this had rubbed off on his son Eduardo Menéndez Hume, who turned out to be the person who really ran the MOP group, and so became my immediate boss.

In this way we started a new relationship that was to last for twenty years. I soon found that my fears were groundless – they were very happy to have an experienced man running the show in the south, and I was equally happy to find they would give me pay and fringe benefits accordingly. Eduardo knew perfectly well that I was equally at home on both sides of the boardroom table, but I was always careful to keep my place as the managerial employee when the other partners were around. Don Pepe Paz, in particular, considered that they had purchased the group for the sake of its Merino farms, and that Condor was just a white elephant tacked on at the end.

In point of fact, the fine wool project was starting to produce positive and convincing results, better than many had expected, and was in need of high-level board decisions. Five years of breeding had produced a type of sheep which we took, in effect, one look at and said, 'This is what we are looking for!' The hands-on breeder and his assistants are, of course, the first people to realise this, and it had to be followed up by trials and measurement to produce figures which could be reported to the board.

We still had at that time large flocks of Corriedale sheep of all levels of breeding, and should the project have proved a failure we could have backtracked in a few years and returned to a Corriedale-only operation. But the point had now been reached when the decision had to be taken, either to go forwards or to back track, otherwise it might be difficult to change direction at a later date. The MOP partners were clearly far more Merino-oriented than the former Patagonian Sheep Farming Company board, so once I produced all the facts and figures they saw the advantages and the decision was taken to go all-out with the Cormo breeding.

Most of the partners came to see the farm and its people that summer. This was a completely different style of visit to that of English directors who seldom came with more than their wives. Now the parties were larger, some with several children and a nanny in tow, the elder ones with a self-contained four for *Canasta* so that the women could play cards while the men went round the farm. Meals tended to be more flexible in timing, which Monica and her staff took in their stride, Otilia no doubt remembering how things were in the Punta Arenas mansions of her youth.

I found that working for MOP was in many ways easier than working for a board in London. One only had to pick up the telephone to contact a point of decision in Buenos Aires, rather than send cables to London, and as the MOP owners were all experienced Patagonian land operators you didn't have to write long reports explaining the local picture as they knew it already.

Frances was by now attending the Condor school regularly, and we would always make it to La Cumbre for the St Paul's October exeat. Michael and Tico were to leave school at the end of 1976, so the 'Aljibe' party that year was particularly boisterous. I took my accordion up and we had Scottish country dancing as well as sing-songs. The 'Aljibe' song (below) was written for this occasion.

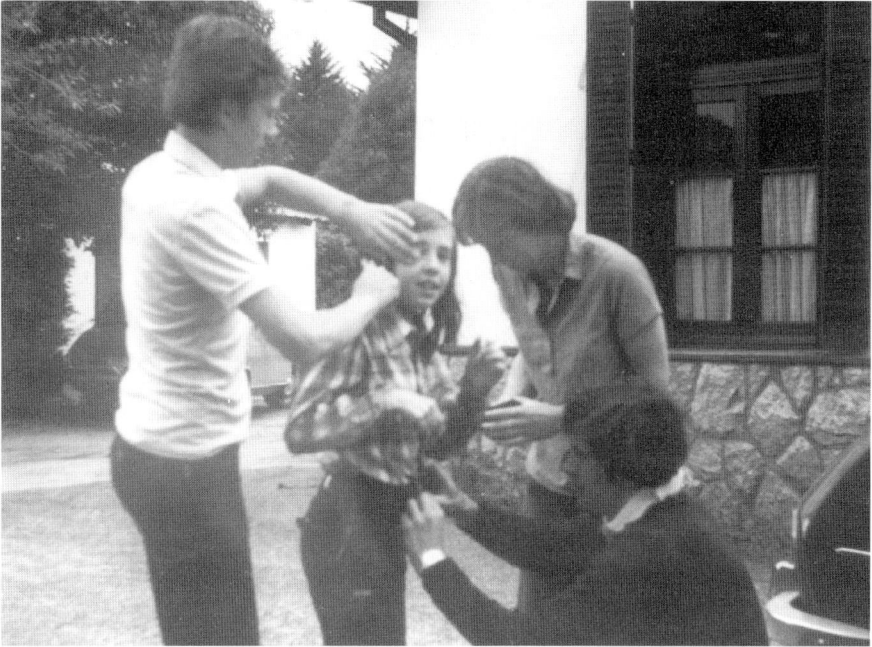

During the October exeat of 1979, Stuart, Alison and Michael tidy Frances at El Aljibe, before going to St Paul's for school prize-giving.

Aljibe Song

John Blake
Tune: original, calypso rhythm

Chorus:
For it's sports time, yes it's sports time, why, everybody likes sports time
To La Cumbre [Aljibe] come for our holiday so let's all be merry and gay.

Verses:
The clans are now all gathered – October exeat time:
McCallum sends us, McChennell bends us, McBlake he say it in rhyme.

Inhabitants of Aljibe, they come from far and near;
There's drivers of engines and finders of penguins and brewers of home-made beer.

La Cumbre weather uncertain, ain't always what it seems;
It makes you wonder when you hear the thunder – is it rain or is it the beans?

Loudspeaker fellah[1], talking, can't hear a word he said!
But that don't matter 'cause all that natter comes out the top of his head!

At Aljibe a big mystery, something to ponder on:
Let's ask Inspector Thomas[2], detector – where has all the ketchup gone?

Four hundred metre hurdles, there they pound along;
But they ain't a match for fleet-footed Chach[3] who wins by half a furlong.

Here come the mums a'racing, let's give them a cheer, my lads!
They seem to be puffing but that ain't nothing, just wait till you hear the
  dads!

Athletic sports now over, competed through thick and thin;
Close-finish races and hard-won places and Scott just managed to win !
[or, according to the results, 'Livingstone[4] did win' !]

A.H. Thurn on birthday list[5] of HBM QE –
So when we hear it we start to cheer it: 'Saint Paul's School, OBE!'

[1]Derek Chennell always announced the races and generally emceed the Sports.
[2] Stephen, later to become a Detective Sergeant in the West Midlands' Police,
once acted Inspector Thomas on stage, complete with pipe and deerstalker hat.
[3] Stuart later won this event for St Andrews' University, becoming Scottish Universities' Champion.
[4] 'Scott' and 'Livingstone' were the two competing houses at St Paul's.
[5] Headmaster 'Bob' Thurn was awarded the OBE in the 1975 Birthday
Honours.

Storm clouds

In March 1976, national affairs took a serious turn. Perón had died in 1974
and his widow as vice-president had succeeded to executive power, surrounded by a group of advisers which included some strange and mystical
characters such as José López Rega, but no competent statesmen. Although
still propped up economically by positive productivity in farming, whose
exports continued to finance the country, there were many sectors of society
who were not happy about the way the country was going. Terrorism and
extortion were rife and lawlessness on the increase. Although Chile seemed
to be putting its house in order there were real fears that Argentina might
slide into anarchy. So for the fourth time in fifty years a sizeable portion of
the electorate favoured the hard option and in a well-planned *coup d'état* a
junta composed of the heads of the Army, Navy and Air Force took over all
levels of government. They were supported by a great number of responsible and thinking people from all walks of society, who felt that as Argentines
up until then had not made a very good job of governing themselves dem-
ocratically, they might perhaps be better off being 'managed' by authority.
  In Patagonia, where the urban terrorist problems had not penetrated, life

went on much as usual. The first governors appointed to Santa Cruz were senior Air Force officers who made real efforts to go out and understand regional needs and put in train several worthwhile development pro-grammes.

All our boys being Argentine-born had to do military service at age 18. Michael having been born in February was not due for the regular call-up until 1978, but had found out that he could enlist as a volunteer in the coast-guards (*Prefectura Nacional Marítima*) in April 1977 and so gain a year before going on to university. So he joined them in Rio Gallegos, where the regional command headquarters was located in addition to the local port detachment.

We had some years previously purchased with our savings a small house in Rio Gallegos, which up until them we had rented out on short-term leases. This we now recovered and redecorated, and it became 'boys' cottage' for the next six years. It is only just up the road from the Prefectura HQ, so was very handy for Michael. His best friend, Eric Heesch, was doing service in the Army at the same time, so would often stay there when not required to sleep in barracks. They had a stock of eighteen plates, which it is said got washed up when one or other of the mums was due in from camp, and therefore the house had to be clean and ready for inspection. Eric's father, Carlos, had been a friend of mine since I was out in 1952, and had managed nearby Estancia 'Bellavista', one of the oldest farms in the district, for the Bitsch family. Carlos had sadly died of a brain tumour leaving a young family, and we always tried to give his widow Eileen and her children as much support as possible. When younger, the boys would often spend nights away at each other's homes.

One winter, when they were about 10 and staying at Bellavista, they had gone to bed as usual but were not yet asleep when they saw lights out of the window. Looking out, they saw the classic row of lights associated with an unidentified flying object, which seemed to move slowly without noise. After a while the lights went out. Discipline was firm in the Bitsch household, so the boys quietly crept back to bed and only told of their experience the next morning at breakfast. The men went out to see, and although the pampa in general was all frozen over solid to a depth of four inches or so, there was a large circular mark of soft, thawed ground as if *something* had landed there and emitted considerable heat. No sensible explanation has ever been offered.

On another occasion, also in winter, Monica and I were going to Rio Gallegos one evening for a social occasion. Monica was driving and I was snoozing after a day's work. Near the Frailes Hills she saw some lights approaching, coming towards us but too high to be an oncoming vehicle. Nudging me awake, she pulled over to the side and switched off our own lights and engine. There was no noise. The lights came slowly towards us and passed overhead, some distance up, on a course no aircraft would take. At that point we heard an aircraft coming from Tierra del Fuego, perfectly on course for Rio Gallegos with normal lights flashing. Our UFO seemed to react, as still without any noise it suddenly increased speed and disappeared out to sea in the general direction of the South Atlantic. The car engine started with no difficulty and we continued thoughtfully on our way.

We had already foregone UK leave for the sake of the children's education, but could otherwise arrange our movements and local holidays as we thought best. Monica had not been to England since 1969, so in 1977 it was her turn to go. Alison was now well installed at St Thomas', half way through her training, and they took a beach holiday on Ibiza together as well as watching Queen Elizabeth's Silver Jubilee. Monica had been in London for the coronation with her parents and knew the ropes, having camped out with them along the Mall – this time they found a good spot near Horse Guards' Parade to watch the jubilee procession.

It was eight years since we had last gone to England with our whole family. Westfield had been sold in 1976 and my parents' estates wound up. The other families were, like ours, going to school and growing up. Following the death of Chris, Eleanor had made a home in Crewkerne with Peter Hodge, but Peter had sadly died so we suggested that she come out and spend a month or two with us. She joined us in Buenos Aires just in time for the October exeat, the sports and El Aljibe. We had taken delivery of a pickup that year, fortunately with a fairly roomy cabin, so after the exeat the three of us plus Frances (now 8) set off on another road trip south. We headed up the Rio Negro Valley to Zapala, and visited Ann and Jim Wood, our only cousins in the country, at their estancia, 'Huechahue'. Ann was Uncle Robert's second daughter and Jim was the son of George Wood, sometime mastermind of the Waldron and Wood interests who had set up the firm in Buenos Aires which came to represent most of the British sheep farming companies in Patagonia. He retired to Newbury before the war and was on many company boards including the ASL. Jim and Ann had married after the war but Jim had opted out of the big company scene and bought his own farm in the foothills of the Andes. This was Manzanero country, from where the marauding bands of Indians used to mount raids across the pampas (6) and where the wild apples grew, said to have been planted by Jesuit missionaries. Jim used to make cider but was never able to market it commercially, although he sold a lot of nuts to the chocolate industry in Bariloche.

When we got to San Julian on Eleanor's first visit there since the age of 14, we were disappointed that we could not stay on the farm. For some years prior to retirement Mary had been unwilling to live in the Big House with its wooden structure and two storeys, so the second house built for them originally on their marriage had been considerably refurbished and a guest wing had been added. They had lived in it for a few years prior to retirement and had returned there afterwards. Tom had only partially recovered from his tragic action, and he and Lydia were now living in San Julian. Guest wing notwithstanding, we were not invited to stay even though I was by that time vice-president of the company and had reason to visit there on business.

Still, we went out to the farm for lunch and a look around before carrying on down to Rio Gallegos and Condor, where Eleanor stayed with us for a couple of weeks before returning to England. She had been corresponding with Rod Dixon, the Rights-of-way Officer in the Somerset County Council and Minister of Taunton Unitarian Chapel. They were married in July 1978 and bought a house at Chedzoy, on Sedgemoor not far from Bridgwater, which was also in Rod's ministry. Eleanor had always been active in the Unitarian chapel in Crewkerne where the Blake connection went back for many years. Our father Arthur had been President of the General Assembly of Unitarian and Free Christian Churches in 1960/61, and we all felt honoured when a few years later Eleanor was invited to follow in his footsteps, which she did in 1982/83, the only occasion when this august office has been filled by a daughter following her father. In 1989, now her children were grown up she took on more chapel work and in 1989 was appointed Lay Pastor of Crewkerne and she continued to look after the parish until her retirement in 2002.

The coastguards were very good to Michael, who after his year's service wanted to go to the university of Buenos Aires to study agronomy (i.e. to follow dad). Towards the end of his year's service they had him transferred to Buenos Aires to a desk job, which allowed him to study for the university entrance exam while seeing out his last few weeks with them, and in April 1978 he started in reading agronomy at the University of Buenos Aires.

That year the World Association Football Cup was being held in Argentina, and I had been lucky enough to win some tickets to all the matches, so in June I joined Michael in Buenos Aires and we started going to the games. The pressure mounted, and once Argentina qualified for the quarter finals we were not surprised to get an urgent phone call from Stephen, then in his last year at St Paul's, saying, 'Dad, if Argentina gets to the final, the "boss" [headmaster Bob Thurn] will give Chacho and me the weekend off to come down and see it!' So I rushed out and managed to get two tickets for the Gran Rex cinema, who had laid on wide screen direct TV coverage of the matches. These Michael and I used, leaving the boys our standing-room tickets for River Plate Stadium. The rest is history – Argentina beat Holland after extra time. This caused transport chaos because the extra trains laid on to take the fans away from River Plate had been timed to coincide with a normal match-ending time, and the schedules were completely thrown out by the extra half hour of play! The boys travelled stretched out in the luggage racks, and we all met up downtown to share the extraordinary scenes of celebration.

But rumblings were in the air in the south, where Argentina and Chile were arguing about the Beagle Channel. (7) In early October an Army staff car appeared at Condor, and the colonel explained that he might have to bring his regiment to the area. If so, where could he house them? Nothing was as yet known however, but next morning three *peons* were waiting outside the office to ask for their accounts. Not wishing to lose three men right at the beginning of the season, I persuaded them to stay on. A few weeks later however, when the 4th Infantry Regiment from Monte Caseros arrived and occupied the Frailes section, the three men just took off, without even waiting for their pay. We learned later that, rather than return to Chile, they had fled still further into Argentina for fear of their compatriots catching up with them.

Tension continued to mount, as unit after unit appeared in Rio Gallegos, and a battery of heavy artillery joined the regiment at Frailes. Monica had gone to La Cumbre to attend Stephen's *bachillerato* graduation, leaving Frances on the farm with me, but things looked serious so I sent her on her first air trip alone, to join her mother. In December, however, Monica was requested by MOP to return to the farm to support the families living there. Aerolineas was flying normally, but the cabin windows were blacked out so that passengers could not see anything they shouldn't at Comodoro Rivadavia.

Our shearing gang from Corrientes arrived as usual under Don Isabelino Giménez, who told me that before bringing his men south he had gone to his local army HQ to ask whether he should in fact take his group, some thirty-five strong, to this tricky area. 'By all means!' answered the general. 'Make sure they take their knives and when we go over into Chile make sure they follow us!' This was the fire-eating General Galtieri, at that time in command of the Second Army Corps (from where the 4th Infantry had come, as also the 12th Infantry who replaced them in January. Both these regiments later served with distinction in the Falklands.) Shearing duly started, and we had arranged not to use Frailes with its new shearing shed, as it was full of soldiers. I would go and visit them from time to time, and was fascinated to find that that many of the gunners, particularly the warrant officers and NCOs, were just the same sort of laid-back characters as those I had known in the Royal Artillery all those years ago. Discreet glances into the gun pits revealed directors (8) and artillery boards very similar to those we had used at Larkhill. I thought they had sited their 155mm guns on deep, peat-like soil into which they would sink if actually fired, but it was none of my business . . .

Term came to an end, the boys came back from school and we heard that the regimental chaplain was planning a Christmas service. We pricked up

The Beagle Channel crisis did not prevent Santa Claus (Stephen) from arriving on time. Stuart standing, third from right, Frances kneeling, fourth from left.

our ears and offered the big Condor shearing shed as a venue. An altar was rigged up from wool bales, and a well-lit and decorated Christmas tree set up as well as benches in the front for all the farm women and children. The soldiers came down from Frailes, and the chaplain was quite taken aback to find a community mostly consisting of Chileans. So he had to change his service and improvised a sermon on family values which had many of the homesick conscripts in tears. Stephen in the meantime did not waste his time and next day turned up as Santa Claus at the Boxing Day children's party in an army truck escorted by grinning soldiers.

Fortunately in January good sense started to prevail. Both countries appealed to the Vatican to intervene, and hostilities were averted. The troops were withdrawn and Frailes section was handed back to us, in impeccable condition: every item of farm equipment was in its place, any timber or firewood had been replaced, and the gun pits were filled in. But it had been a near thing.

Sale of Coronel

Three years had gone by since Condor started phasing out the Corriedale commercial (but not stud) flocks, and the reality of the Cormo breed was fully bearing out and even exceeding our planned expectations. While we still had large numbers of both breeds on the same property at the same time, production and commercial trials could be run and important statistics assembled. The three original premises on which the plan was based were being fulfilled – first, the weight of wool cut per head not only did not fall, but rather continued to rise slowly as the genetic gain set up by objective measurement took effect. Second, the average fibre diameter had dropped from 27–28 microns to about 24.5, bringing with it an improvement in value of between 35 and 50 per cent. Third, lambing rates (the basis of important sales of animals for meat) were also creeping up as other genetic aims took hold.

Furthermore, two other quite unexpected and unplanned gains had appeared: one was that the wool had inherited from its Merino past a brilliant white colour, highly desirable in the trade. The other was a very fast rate of growth from birth onwards – in other words high efficiency of conversion of feed into body mass. Coupled with high rates of lactation, which were actively and positively selected for, this meant first weaning heavier lambs at an earlier age and then making optimum use of the scanty and hard-won range forage. (9) I was naturally very keen to get these important commercial traits into the Coronel sheep at the earliest opportunity, but was quite unable to get the leading members of the board to agree – mainly van Deurs and Barbieri who had not yet seen that the Corriedale breed had its limitations. Ironically these gentlemen were later to buy Cullen Station from the Waldrons and run Merinos there, but that is another story.

Lamb-marking, new style, at Killik Aike Norte in 1990. Stephen on right. The equipment can also be assembled inside the shed.

In the meantime, changes had been happening in the freezer trade. During the war and after, the demand for sheep meats from Britain and the Continent was enormous. There were freezers at all the ports and the slaughtering season began in late January when seasonal labour (mostly Chilote) became available as the shearing gangs finished their engagements. The sheep were brought down from the farms by drovers, taking anything from two to three days for nearby farms like Condor to thirty or more from the foothills of the Andes. Wethers and surplus ewes made up the bulk of the kill, but south of the Santa Cruz lambings were better and large numbers of hoggetts were shipped as 'lamb'. This was fine for meat-starved Europe at first, but as domestic supplies gradually rose during the 1960s the freezing companies started looking for other products. The Swift plant in Rio Gallegos approached me at Condor, to see whether we would supply current-season's lambs in December, and for several years we carried out joint trial operations, the resulting high-priced 'spring lamb' being flown to Rome for the Christmas trade. Gradually the husbandry systems began to change as farmers realised that by running a greater portion of the farm under ewes they produced roughly the same amount of wool but more kilos of meat if most of this was in the form of lamb, which in any case could be sold for a better price per kilo.

Lamb-marking had always been a picturesque and down-to-earth operation requiring considerable expertise by all hands, involving considerable time and therefore cost. Arthur had streamlined the Coronel system by mechanising the transport of men and using portable yards, and we had done much the same at Condor in Peter Robertson's day. Now that we were starting to sell important quantities of lambs, virtually straight from their mothers, we began to question whether it was worth doing the conventional marking operation at all, if we were going to market virtually half of them (the males) at weaning. So after two or three years of trials we worked out a totally new system. The flocks were not touched at all in November, but in January when the ewes had to be gathered for shearing we marketed the surplus males, marked the females for retention as replacements, and in effect weaned the lot. The whole operation took just a *quarter* of the labour required for conventional marking.

Handling large lambs in January, weighing 25k or more, was of course far more exacting than lifting small lambs under 10kg in November. Here also we had moved on. Cradles of varying degrees of sophistication had been developed in Australia for ease of upturning and holding sheep for a variety of operations. Condor had adapted one of these for Patagonian use, where it could be made easily out of wood and set up at the end of any simple parting race. They had already proved invaluable for eyeclipping, cutting the labour requirement for this wearisome job by half, and so we started using them for lamb-marking as well. As lamb production became more intensified, profits from the ewe flocks became ever more important and the numbers of ewes run started to rise, from 30 to 50 per cent of the total number, and this was to grow to 65 per cent by the time I left Condor. When we planned the Cormo project in 1969, 20 per cent of farm income came from meat, and this was to rise to 40–45 per cent by the late 1970s.

These were some of the changes that were happening in the sheep business in its broadest sense, which perhaps were not so obvious to those not closely in contact with the production end. But Condor was doing fine. Its finer wool was fetching 35 per cent or so more than Corriedale wool and its annual offtake of 25,000 freezer lambs and 10,000 ewes and wethers were all produced by 65–70 per cent of the labour required in the 1950s. I did not see that other farms needed to put up with less.

Coronel, as we have seen, was being run by Lionel Pickering on a temporary basis, so some serious decisions had to be taken. Clearly the issue of the manager had to be addressed, and if we were going to go out and recruit somebody much would depend on the aims and intentions planned for ensuing years. Due to the Pickering family's problems the farm had been rather coasting along – some of the new methods described had been put into operation, others were waiting in the wings. I wanted to go all-out for Cormo, which I saw as ideal for the San Julian district, where Coronel supplied a lot of flock rams and was still very much a leader in breeding matters, but I was not prepared to get more deeply involved in supervising and training a new manager unless the farm's breeding and commercial aims coincided with my own ideas.

At this point a proposal was received from Antonino Siracusa whereby either he would sell his 25 per cent share to the rest of us, or he and his brothers would buy us all out. After due consideration the latter was accepted, and in 1978 the entire share capital of Ganadera Coronel SA was acquired by the Siracusas, so ending the Blake era at San Julian which had lasted for eighty-six years.

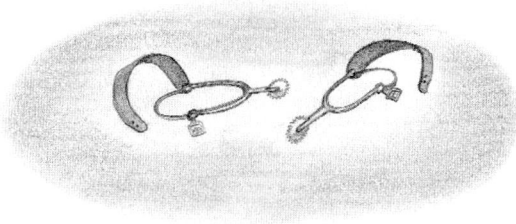

Notes

1 Arthur descended in transit in the usual way but failed to hear the reboarding announcement. The cabin crew unbelievably failed to count their first-class passengers when they reboarded, so he was left behind without a scrap of baggage or even personal documents. He never travelled abroad again.

2 A *paso libre* or *guardaganado* is a livestock barrier or grid on the road, made of bars or rails covering a pit, replacing a gate. Animals cannot walk over but vehicles can pass freely.

3 *Los Escarchados* is sited on uplands 800 metres above sea level. Its name ('The Frozen Ones') records the fate of some drovers in the early days who were caught in a snow storm and perished of cold.

4 Universities in Argentina at that time were hotbeds and recruiting grounds for the left-wing extremists – ERP, Montoneros, you name it. The 'Franja Morada' (Purple Band) student wing of the socialist Radical Party was little better. University education in Argentina is free to all, so it is easy for all sorts of social misfits to 'pursue their studies' for years and years as long as they have some form of modest financial support.

5 Pepe Menéndez, together with Don Carlos Braun Menéndez who headed up the Braun interests at that time and was a shareholder in the San Julian company, had been one of the quite small family group who had masterminded the division of the Menéndez family assets in 1974.

6 'Cerro Huechahue', just a few kilometres away from the Woods' estancia, was the site of the final and definitive battle between General Roca and the Mapuches in 1879.

7 The Beagle Channel runs between the Argentine part of Tierra del Fuego and Navarin Island, which belongs to Chile. The treaty of 1881 had not defined whether it then followed the shores of the former eastwards, or whether it curved round southwards following the latter. This had important theoretical bearings on both countries' sea projection towards, and theoretical claims to, Antartica.

8 A director is an artillery sighting instrument which ensures that all the guns point in the right direction.

9 Several years later (1991) we sent test animals to trials held by the *Sociedad Rural Argentina* comparing most of the sheep breeds found in the country. The Cormo had the highest rate of daily growth of all breeds which included mutton breeds such as Lincoln, Romney Marsh and Texel.

18

Our Own Farm

Last Christmas together

For Monica and me, the sale of Coronel was the second big milestone in our family life, the first having been the decision to leave Hill Cove and take up the job at Condor. The latter, although exacting, was well paid and we could look forward to giving all our children a university education and eventually retire with a satisfactory pension. We now had, in addition, a nice nest egg tucked away in Switzerland as a result of the sale of the family farm asset. Should we just keep this for our old age, or was it still good business to reinvest in sheep farming in Patagonia? I had just spent the best years of my life sharpening up both the technology and the business aspects of this activity, and firmly believed this to be so (and still do). In which case, should we give up the Condor job and go farming on our own, or could we find a property not too far away which could be run at the same time? On the whole we inclined to the latter, even if it might have to rather 'tick over' for a few years until we retired from Condor and would then have our own place to go to. Any farmer who has worked all his life for other people will understand the strong wish to have your own land. There were, after all, several hundred years of deep country roots pulling away there. So we started to cast around and look at the alternatives, visiting farms from San Julian to Tierra del Fuego, but hoping to find one not too far away from Condor.

We had plenty of time for all this, as for the first time we were alone without any of our children at home. Frances had attended the Condor

338

school up to fifth grade (age 9) but like the others the time had come for wider bilingual schooling in Buenos Aires. Since Alison had left, St Hilda's had ceased to take boarders, mainly because St George's College over the other side of the city in Quilmes had opened its doors to girls. This certainly solved the problems of many camp families who had both boys and girls, but we still had our reservations about the St George's work ethic. Still, Mr Henry the headmaster of the prep school where she would spend her first two years had a great reputation, and the senior school (known as 'college') would be starting International Baccalaureate in her year, so Frances started there in March 1979.

Alison graduated as a State Registered Nurse at St Thomas' in July 1979, and came out to Argentina for six months. Quite apart from seeing her brothers and sister after over four years away, she needed to work out the various possibilities for her career. On arrival in Buenos Aires, she made a few phone calls, one of which was to the Güemes Sanatorium, a well-known private clinic specialising at that time in neo-natal work, who said in effect, 'You're St Thomas' trained? Got your uniform? Come right round Monday morning!' They made her a good offer so she started in with them in a highly specialised area, operating new equipment and performing related tasks which at that time in Argentina were only handled by doctors. She worked there until Christmas, meanwhile looking at the employment scene for the future. It seemed that while jobs like that at the Güemes were well paid and easy to get, in the longer term she did not have an Argentine qualification and there was no way she could register or revalidate her St Thomas' certificate so as to be able to take up an administrative nursing post. (1) She had prudently put her name down for an accident course in London before leaving the UK, so decided to go back to it at the end of the summer.

That was a great Christmas all together at Condor – it was to be the last time we had all five children together at our own home, and we would not be able get them all together at any one place at the same time for another fifteen years. Frances, Stuart and Michael were home on vacation and Stephen had just been released from his military service. He had finished school at the end of 1978 and done the regular call-up, first in the 24th Infantry Regiment in Rio Gallegos and then in an office job at district HQ. While in training, he had interceded when some NCOs were bullying another conscript, one Guillermo Ávila, who always considered Steve had saved his life. The incident did Steve no harm, as he later got promoted to acting unpaid lance corporal, an unusual distinction for a conscript.

Among other local forms of relaxation I had got interested in road regularity trials. The Rio Gallegos Automobile Club ran regular speed races, but a few years back had organised events in which the competitors were given a route sheet and you had to complete a circuit on local roads, with stretches clearly marked and the different speeds at which you had to go. Points were deducted for failing to pass predetermined points unknown to the drivers at the correct time. It was a fascinating exercise calling for intense mental concentration and agility both by driver and navigator. I had done one as passenger in the back, and then two others with Stuart as navigator, both of which we won! This established us with a reputation to maintain, so when that summer a new regularity event was announced, we entered two cars, Chacho and I in one with Frances as passenger in the back, and Michael, Stephen and Alison in the other. The route both started and finished in Rio Gallegos, and we were car No.1 so went first, preceded by a police car with a radio commentator on board, who did not have a route sheet. Entering the town on the return trip, our calculated speed (as ordered by the sheet) was faster than the police car, so we found ourselves pushing them down the main street accompanied by suitable comment over the radio. But the route sheet (and we) were right, and we again won. The No.2 car came further down, having lost too much time arguing among the passengers.

By this time we were taking Cormo rams to shows further afield, i.e. into northern Santa Cruz and Chubut where fine wool was the rule, but many farmers were not happy with Merino alone and used to cross with Corriedale. Condor had always sold rams in this area. The Esquel show took place towards the end of January, while Condor was still shearing, followed the next week by Comodoro Rivadavia, the most important Merino show in the country. I sent the rams off on the farm stock truck, driven by

Alison with Grand Champion Cormo Argentino ram, at Comodoro Rivadavia, the principal show in Argentina for fine-wool breeds, in 1980.

a trusted driver, Eladio Aguilar (otherwise known as 'the Bear'), to deliver a sale lot to a farm near Comodoro, and continue to Esquel with a team of show rams. Meantime Alison, Michael, Stephen and Stuart went along in a large pickup. This allowed me to fly direct to Esquel on the Saturday, to find the show rams duly bedded down and titivated, ready to go into the ring! During the following week, while I flew back to Condor, they shifted the rams to Comodoro where I rejoined them for the show there the next weekend. We all had a great time and it was a grand bit of teamwork.

The World Corriedale Congress of 1980 was held in Punta Arenas in February, and this Monica and I attended. We had not crossed the frontier for ten years, mainly for security reasons, so it was good to meet so many good friends – not only neighbours in Chile but from all over the world. Quite a number of visiting breeders extended their visit by coming over to Rio Gallegos, and we hosted a field day at Condor for them.

All too soon it was time for Alison to return to the UK, accompanied by Stephen who wanted to become a policeman. He had had this ambition in mind for several years, and having achieved both the Argentine *bachillerato* and several O levels was keen to try to get into the Metropolitan Police in London. They travelled via Peru, visiting Monica's sister Pam and her husband Douglas Russell who lived in Arequipa. Douglas was a railway engineer who had had experience in India during World War II on mountain railways in India, and now held a key post on the Southern Peruvian Railway which links the port of Mollendo on the Pacific Coast with the uplands at 4,500 metres and eventually to La Paz, Bolivia, via Lake Titicaca. Like most South American railways, it had been built by the British and still kept some expatriate staff.

Michael was also on the move. The Rotary Club of Rio Gallegos (2) had received an invitation from the Rotary Student Fund of Georgia, USA, to send one undergraduate student for a year's scholarship, and the committee under the presidency of Simón Giubetich were good enough to put Michael up for it, and he was accepted. This could affect his university career as at that time such studies pursued outside Argentina would not be accepted in Buenos Aires. The University of Georgia, on the other hand, did accept his grades and matriculated him into his second, or sophomore year, starting in September 1980. We reckoned that one year of general farm-related studies in Georgia (where there are no sheep) would do him no harm, as long as he then went west to Wyoming or Montana to complete his studies.

Community relations

We have seen how over 5,000 young men and women of British descent had gone from Argentina to serve in the forces during the Second World War.

After the war, rather than put up some piece of statuary as a monument to them and in particular to the 200 or more who did not survive, it was thought more fitting to create a living monument in the form of the British Community War Memorial Fund (BCWF). This provided medical, social and (originally) financial assistance to Britons who were in needy circumstances. Most of those who had come out to work on contract had either returned home at the end of it, married and settled locally, received some form of pension or in other ways were looked after by their former employers. But there were some less fortunate, and up and down the country could be found English governesses, Irish engine drivers or Scottish shepherds who had nobody to care for them.

Two very fine institutions looked after some of these needs. The British Hospital of Buenos Aires was founded in 1843 and has always been in the forefront of the medical profession in Argentina. It is a self-financing private institution, run professionally under an overall board of governors appointed by the community, and operates a contributory scheme for people of British descent. Charity patients have to be paid for by somebody, and this aspect, from early post-war days, was looked after by the BCWF. For the elderly, the Devoto Old People's Home is run by the British American Benevolent Society, founded in 1880. This devoted body is entirely self-funded from donations, legacies, and contributions from the community, including British and American commercial firms.

Community matters in general, including fundraising for the BCWF was coordinated by the British Community Council, composed of a central committee and a number of district chairmen mostly representing the various suburbs of Buenos Aires. There were important groups of people of British descent in other parts of the country, such as Rosario, Cordoba (both city and hills) and the Rio Negro Valley, but the most numerous integrated group outside Buenos Aires was in southern Patagonia and these people were represented by the Rio Gallegos district. The latter was run by a committee closely integrated with the British Club. This had been founded in 1911, and was the physical centre of community activity in and around Rio Gallegos. There were 'town members' but the majority were 'camp members' who lived out on the farms. If you went into town for a day's business or shopping, the Club was where you gathered to meet others, leave parcels and meet up with the rest of the family in the evening for tea and the trip home, having first rung the farm on the magneto telephone to advise that you were leaving, especially when the tracks were at all bad.

Those long trips home over rough tracks in the early days with small children were a bit of a trial. Heating in the vehicles was not very good, so everyone bundled up with warm clothes, even hot water bottles. You always carried a potato in frosty weather, which if cut and rubbed on the windscreen would prevent it misting up. The last bend in the road before reaching home was called, with good reason, 'Hungry Corner'.

At the time when we first joined the local community in the late 1950s, the Club had changed little since the early days. The bar and billiards rooms were for men only, but there was a separate ladies' room (no men allowed) and the lounge was common ground. It was unquestionably the leading social body in town, and its dances and other social gatherings were well attended. Voting members had to be of British descent, but there were also a number of non-British associate members who had no say in the running of the Club but had full use of its facilities. People like the federal judge would not frequent the two or three other sporting and social clubs as they all had some political bias whereas the 'British' was socially impeccable. The Club committee spent most of its time organising social events, but was intimately integrated with the BCC district committee under a separate chairman, who when we first arrived was Eric Davies.

The BCC committee had two functions. First, to help any person of

P C Blake: Stephen as a newly-joined constable with the West Midlands Police Force.

British descent in need of medical or other assistance. At that time there were still a few old-timers around who lived quietly in a back room of a *boliche* or on a farm where they had worked, maybe doing some light chores for their keep. These arrangements were usually fine until some medical problem arose, whereupon someone would draw the committee's attention to the case, and arrangements would be made to transfer the patient to Buenos Aires, where the BCWF would take care of him, put him into the British Hospital, or whatever. This involved expenditure for fares and medical costs, so the second function of the BCC was fundraising. Most of the families of British descent, and the farming companies (of which at that time there were half a dozen) made regular donations to the fund, but an enormous amount of work was put in by community members in raising money from the non-British inhabitants.

This revolved around one single annual event, known as the gymkhana, which took place in early March. A lineal descendant of the various kermesses and fêtes organised during the war (3), the first gymkhana had been held at Estancia Güer Aike in the early 1950s and had included equestrian events. It was soon found that horses, a slap-up *asado* and a freely-frequented bar were not the safest of combinations so after a year or two the horse events were dropped, but the name stuck. The four farms nearest the town took it in turns to host the event, and a bus service ran all day. Stalls sold produce (meat, vegetables, flowers, crafts and fancy goods), there was a bar of course, and a full *asado* with all the trimmings for everyone who bought an entry ticket. In the afternoon there were foot races and children's events, usually a tug-of-war, raffles were drawn, tea was available with home-made cakes and in the evening the helpers and their families (probably fifty or sixty people) gathered for supper in the farmhouse where auctions of donated goods took place.

The organisation was admirable: each stall, including the bar, the *asado* and the teas, was run by a family group with a head organiser who recruited such extra assistance as required, usually the same people year after year. In addition to the chairman, who had to be free to look after visiting dignitaries, there was usually an organiser or steward to run the event, keep things flowing and disentangle glitches, and a treasurer to collect the cash.

Condor was one of three or four farms providing important logistical support, such as lorry transport and maybe some labour for putting it all up and taking it down. I found myself becoming assistant to John Fenton of Estancia 'Monte Dinero' in general organisation, and took this over when Eric Davies retired and John was elected district chairman in his place. During the 1960s it ceased to be practical to hold the event out on farms, so we transferred it to the *Sociedad Rural* showground in town, and *really* started to make money. The basic principles of any good fundraising event are simple – first you have to attract your public, and get them through the gates. The aroma of roasting twenty or more lambs and a couple of steers floating out over the town usually took care of that one. Then, having got your public in, you have to entertain them by providing things to do or to watch, or stalls selling goods at fair prices. While this is going on you quietly relieve them further of their money by selling raffle tickets and holding auctions. We always took good care to give a sizeable chunk of the takings (10,000 dollars or more most years) to local charities such as the district hospital, and saw to it that people knew this.

In 1970 John Fenton gave up the chairmanship, and there was some bickering between those who thought that the Club (without whose support the gymkhanas could not have been held) should benefit more from all this, and others who did not. At the annual general meeting I ventured to pour oil on these waters as the community could hardly support two separate bodies. This was successful, but perhaps inevitably I was elected district chairman, which post I was to hold for twelve years.

Killik Aike Norte

Nestling on the north bank of the Rio Gallegos estuary, just opposite the airport, lies Estancia Killik Aike Norte, one of the oldest farms in the district, having been founded in 1892 by Herbert Stanley Felton, the same year that Robert Blake had founded Coronel. A younger brother of J. J. Felton of Teal Inlet (p. 47) by some 15 years, Herbert had worked first as shepherd then foreman and finally manager for Bertrand and Felton at Roy Cove, West Falkland. He had been one of the first to come over in response to Moyano's representations, and at first leased land at Otern Aike, south of the Gallegos, in partnership with Clark in 1889. When Moyano started to offer land in freehold in 1890, rather than continue the partnership Felton bought the block just across the river from Otern Aike, known as Laguna Colorada, and in 1892 purchased Killik Aike Norte, a few kilometres further downriver on the estuary, separated from Laguna Colorada by Estancia Güer Aike.

Herbert Felton had married Emma Bartlett, of Port Stanley in 1882, and their daughter Emily ('Millie') was born in 1890 at Otern Aike, and their son Carlos Stanley at Killik Aike Norte in 1900. A crusty but hardworking entrepreneur, Herbert built a jetty (the only one on the Gallegos at that time) and ran his own schooner. The first one was called the *Malvina* and then came the *Priscilla* in partnership with the captains. (4) The Gallegos is a small river with shifting mud banks near the mouth, so ocean-going ships had to anchor out in the roads and all cargo was handled by lighters. Felton could tie up alongside, load up provisions and stores and run them up to Killik Aike, returning with cargoes of wool. They also carried cargoes to the Coyle for

Felton's ships *Malvina* and *Priscilla* tied up at the Killik Aike jetty, which was linked to the bale shed by a light rail track just like the Falkland farms.

other settlers and it was on one such trip that the *Priscilla* was lost with all hands. On at least one occasion, wool was loaded directly at Killik Aike. Hatcher (below) relates how in 1896 he witnessed a sailing ship, the *Bootle*, described as an ocean-going schooner, come upriver at high tide, tie up at the jetty and after two days loading bales of wool set sail for Liverpool, implying that she was of a fair size.

Herbert Felton died of a heart attack in 1920 while returning from a visit to the England, leaving his affairs in a rather parlous state. Carlos had gone to St George's College in Buenos Aires, and was only 20 when his father died. He found the first years very difficult. He had to sell Laguna Colorada in order to buy out his sister Millie who had married one Charles Henstock at an early age and lived there, but after her father's death they were happy to move to Vancouver. The early 1920s were not easy years anywhere. Carlos persuaded an old school friend, Errol Kennard, to come down and help him, and they worked together for some years until Kennard was offered the job of manager of neighbouring Estancia Güer Aike, a 20,000-sheep spread belonging to the French Bittencourt family, where he remained until retiring in the late 1960s. Carlos married 'Tommy' Rudd from Cape Fairweather, and Errol married her sister 'Biddy', and the two families were always very close. The Kennards' daughters Valerie and Naomi went to St Hilda's, and Naomi was head girl in Eleanor and Rosemary's time.

Killik Aike had been stocked with Falklands sheep and Herbert had set up a Romney Marsh stud flock, which won prizes at local shows, but Carlos came to realise that the sheep which his father had been happy to breed were perhaps not the best suited to the country, so decided to switch to Corriedales, and in 1937 imported his first pedigree animals. This was to

346

prove well timed, and by the time the Second World War ended the Killik Aike stud had established itself as a leading breeder of pedigree rams, which found a ready market not only in Patagonia but also at Palermo in Buenos Aires and at the 'Prado' show in Montevideo. The war had of course put a stop to imports from New Zealand, but wool was booming all over and good breeding stock were in demand.

With money pouring in from ram sales, Carlos and Tommy rebuilt the Big House in 1944. They never had children, which may have prompted Tommy's wistful greeting to my mother when she and Arthur paid them a visit in 1946: 'Welcome, Millicent, to the house without a soul'. Don Herbert had first replaced the original two-roomed shack put up in 1892 with a comfortable house built about 1897. He liked to do himself well, and in 1904 had replaced the latter with a fine timber mansion, equipping it with elegant acetylene gas lighting and very fine furnishings. Carlos, having been brought up in this house, could not bring himself to change it all that much and retained all the original internal walls and the chimneys while virtually rebuilding around them. He had installed 110-volt electric lighting before 1930, this was kept and is still running in 2002, as far as I know the oldest electric plant in Patagonia still in working order. Coal-fired central heating was also added. There was even a party room in the basement, known to local folklore as the 'Boite', although I believe only two parties were ever held there.

Killik Aike as a place exists because of the springs which rise there, and Herbert had laid out extensive gardens with channel irrigation, and the farm was renowned for its vegetables. Carlos used to run the vegetable stall at the gymkhanas and Tommy was a leading exhibitor (and winner) at the flower shows. They used to contribute generously to BCC funds, and in 1976 we put his name up to the British embassy for a decoration, and he was awarded an OBE. Tommy sadly died in 1977, and Carlos was left a widower with some twenty-four nephews and nieces as his heirs. He tried several times to install one or other of these as his manager, but it never worked out.

We in the meantime were casting around for a property. We had looked at staying at San Julian by keeping one of the sections, and visited other properties nearby. We had also looked across the water at the idea of a property on Tierra del Fuego, tucked away in the woods. And we had dropped a word in Carlos Felton's ear. Without any obvious heir to carry on, he was unwilling to have his beloved farm squabbled over and decided to sell outright and leave his heirs more liquid assets. So in early 1979 we started to work on it, and in the end set up an arrangement whereby we bought the whole farm with livestock, buildings and contents, but allowed him the usufruct of the Big House, supporting buildings and garden, for his lifetime. We also took over the installed manager, Eduardo Rushen, who lived with his wife Daisy in a separate manager's house and there was a small house down by the beach where we were happy to stay for weekends.

For we were not yet ready to leave Condor. I had a good job, the children were all at boarding school or university and the Cormo project was just starting to really bear fruit, the breed having been officially recognised by the *Sociedad Rural Argentina* in 1978. Although I never got to form part of the ASL administration, the Menéndez brothers were using me as technical adviser, both for their own farm on Tierra del Fuego and for some of the Merino farms. Eduardo Rushen ran Killik Aike without needing much overseeing – Carlos used to go away in early June to Vancouver and London (where he kept a room at the Kensington Palace Hotel) and return in November for lamb-marking. He once told me that in fifty years he had not spent a winter *anywhere*. Most Patagonian farms are sold on a 'closed gates' basis – i.e. all livestock included – and often the price is expressed as so much per sheep as opposed to per hectare or league. We bought Killik Aike Norte with 15,000 sheep, and these had to be properly counted. By now it was March 1980 and Michael was only just beginning his university term, so we brought him down to do this for us. He lived with Eduardo and Daisy while all the flocks were mustered, dipped and counted. Meanwhile Carlos disposed of the surplus. Finally in April we signed all the deeds and officially took over the farm and all responsibility for it as from 1 May 1980.

Michael later travelled to Griffin, Georgia, for his year at the University of Georgia in Atlanta, to start term in September 1980. He was one of about sixty students gathered from all over the world to spend one year at universities and high schools in Georgia, funded entirely by the Rotarians of that state. Each student was looked after by a local family. Michael's host was Sam Blake (no relation), and they participated fully in community events throughout the year. It was a wonderful chance for Michael to meet people from all over the world and broaden his experience. The academic side was no problem, and from Atlanta he was able to arrange his transfer to the University of Wyoming in Laramie, and started in there in September 1981.

Beach cottage

At Killik Aike we soon fell into a way of working. Eduardo continued to run the farm, and I found it possible to lay out a programme for several weeks and only come over from Condor from time to time. It was almost like having another section. For shearing we used the same gang as Condor, once they had finished there, so we could come over and settle down for two weeks or so, Condor in the meantime ticking over at low key under the sub-manager. When it was a matter of introducing new methods, then I had to come and supervise. In this way we quickly introduced tip spraying (I never used the plunge dip) and portable handling cradles for lamb-marking and

The original Killik Aike Norte house, built 1892, taken some years later. Note decauville track leading to the jetty.

The second house, built about 1897, after a fairly typical fall of snow.

The new house in 1904, with house number 2 behind.

The same in 1936, with the considerable gardens laid out.

later for eye-clipping. The senior men soon realised that all these new-fangled inventions were not just quirks of the new boss but were there to save them a lot of hard work, so they readily caught on.

We started to absorb 'north bank' lore. We knew that the estuary of the Gallegos has tides in excess of 13 metres, the third highest in the world after the Bay of Fundy and the Bristol Channel, but only now we learned that, like the Severn, it has a bore which appears at the highest tides. At these times, the volume of water entering the river (5) is far greater than that flowing out, so a sort of tidal wave is set up which travels slowly upstream. Behind it flows the incoming tide, setting up ugly whirlpools and cross-currents and filling the estuary, which is about 3km wide at this point, in a matter of twenty minutes or so. With the *Gaviota* days in the background, I had sometimes thought it might be nice to do a little boating, but after one look at the currents following a bore I never seriously thought about it again.

The river can be crossed either by the road bridge at Güer Aike, some 15km to the west, so in all it is 44km by road to Rio Gallegos, or else by boat from the town itself to Hill Station, the Halliday family's farm settlement. Carlos told us how it was also possible to ford the river from Killik Aike Norte to the 'Killik Aike Sud' farm on the south bank, which belonged to the Macdonald family, and how in the 'old' days the men would go off at weekends by first fording the river, from where it was just half an hour's gallop to town. But up on the headland there is a grave, where lies Charles Jefferies, the farm carpenter who left it a bit late when returning home one day and was overtaken by the tide. In horseback days it was usual for travellers riding down from Santa Cruz to avoid the long detour by Güer Aike and head directly to Hill Station, 12km east, i.e. downriver from Killik Aike Norte, just opposite the town. They could leave their horses there and going over by rowboat, and at least two *boliches* functioned there at one time, there were other buildings and the settlement was known for many years as 'North Gallegos'.

One weekend we were settling into our cottage when a big pickup loaded with camping gear drove up, and a large Canadian emerged (with family) asking permission to camp, and to go and visit 'where Hatcher found the fossils'. Well, we had heard of Hatcher and the Princeton expeditions, mostly from Chace, but we did not then know of his close connection with Killik Aike. (6) Fossils had been found in the Gallegos by Sulivan, on the first voyage of the *Beagle*, and in the wake of Darwin and his writings, which took many years to collate and publish, much theorising arose in the scientific world about the formation of mountains such as the Andes, and the significance of marine deposits being found on the tops of hills. The relationship between geology and the fauna which once inhabited the earth and/or the sea is clearly of primary importance. The eminent Argentine savant, Dr Florentino Ameghino, had put forward a number of hypotheses which were not in line with North American thinking and so Princeton University sent Professor John Bell Hatcher down to see. He was an eminent palaeontologist who had done a great deal of field work out in Nebraska and the Dakotas, at that time (1896) still Indian and bison country. He was therefore extremely experienced, not to say hard-boiled, thinking nothing of living off the land and shooting his own supper, be it moose or guanaco.

He and one companion travelled to Rio Gallegos early in 1896 on the *Villarino* (see Chapter 2 footnote 3), were welcomed by the governor of the territory, Edelmiro Mayer, and with some trouble managed to buy a cart and horses. By the time they got to Güer Aike and forded the river, Hatcher was getting impatient, so leaving his assistant Petersen to follow with the cart and camping gear, he forged ahead down to Killik Aike, where he was welcomed by Felton's foreman. He then describes how he walked down to the beach and in the bluffs which overlook the river he saw the skull of *Icochilus* – a small prehistoric ungulate. This was treasure trove indeed, and casting around further he found fossilised remains of dinosaur-like creatures, some as large as a small rhinoceros, such as *Nesodon, Astrapotherium, Diadiaphorus* and *Prothylacinus*. The bluffs on the north side of the Gallegos River were at one time, many millions of years ago, the end of the continent. The land to the south was below sea level and only rose later as a result of volcanic activity, and hence contains no fossils. Hatcher and Petersen spent the whole winter under canvas, working the river bluffs, and then moved on up the coast. For the second expedition at the end of 1897 he prudently took his own wagon, a 'light two-and-three-quarter-inch mountain wagon with a good pair of

John Bell Hatcher (seated, right) on the second Princeton Expedition, 1898. Camped on the Rio Gallegos in the valley near Killik Aike. Mrs Felton on left.

352

double harness' and purchased his horses in Punta Arenas where the locals where less voracious in the matter of price. This wagon can still be seen at Killik Aike, where he left it after his third expedition in 1889.

As well as extinct dinosaurs, Killik Aike harbours a fair amount of birds and other wild life. Buff-necked ibis or bandurrias *(Theristicus caudatus)* nest high up on the side of the bluffs, and every morning just after sunrise can be seen wending their way inland in search of breakfast – honking as they go if rain is pending, according to local lore. Peregrine and other falcons also nest there, and buzzard-eagles *(Aguila mora, Geranoaetus melanoleucus)* can be seen perching on the communications mast. The Feltons quite early on had started planting trees, and with abundant water set out a considerable park and garden, with fruit and other trees brought out from Britain, including the only specimens of English Oaks *(Quercus robur)* in Patagonia. This has created something of a bird sanctuary. Great horned owls *(Bubo virginianus)* nest in the trees as well as lesser owls and a whole host of smaller birds. Black-crowned night herons *(Nycticorax nycticorax)*, known in the Falklands as 'quarks' also nest there, and in latter years we have dammed the stream, issuing from the springs and a family of speckled teal *(Anas flavirostris)* have made it their home and every year hatch out a brood of five ducklings. Out on the pampa you can hear the drumming of snipe, and the rude shouting of the *tero-teros* (southern lapwing, *Vanellus resplendens)* to lead you away from their nest. Plovers and dotterels seem to shoot out from under your pickup's wheels, and with luck you might see crested partridge *(Martinetas, Eudomis elegans)* or the rarer uncrested Patagonian tinamou *(Tinamotis ingoufi)*. Sea birds come flocking in from the ocean, or crowd on to the mudbanks of the estuary waiting for the shoals of fish brought in by the rising tide.

In 1900 a young woman landed in Rio Gallegos, with her husband and little boy. This was Mary Gilmore, née Cameron, formerly schoolteacher at the Australian settlement at Cosmé, Paraguay, which had been founded by a group of social idealists in 1893 following the Queensland shearers' strike of 1891 which had been put down by the British Army amid a lot of ill feeling. Over 500 Australians had come over, led by one William Lane, to found an idyllic utopia in the Paraguayan Chaco. Like the Welsh in Chubut in 1865, the host country was only too glad to have them and awarded them generous grants of land. The enterprise cannot be said to have been a failure, as descendants of the settlers are still in Paraguay and Argentina, many having succeeded in farming or other professions. But there was some dissension in the early days and a number of the men went off to Argentina to ply their trade as shearers. Some, including Will Gilmore, went as far as Patagonia. Gilmore returned to fetch his family and they took ship for Rio Gallegos where he had secured a position for himself and his wife at Killik Aike with Herbert Felton. Mary became governess to Millie, and they lived in a small house built, it is thought, about 1895. The arrangement only lasted for about eight months, and Mary then spent a difficult time in Rio Gallegos, living and working for her keep at the Hotel Londres and giving English lessons while Gilmore worked out his time with Felton.

In Rio Gallegos she heard from Dr Fenton (7) that the Condor company was about to put in machine shearing equipment, the first to be installed in Patagonia. She at once wrote to her husband suggesting that with his experience with machine shears in Australia he might be useful in helping to install the equipment and training people to use it. This he seems to have done, earning credit for 'installing machine shears at Condor'. But they were not happy in Patagonia – Mary was ill much of the time, so in early 1902 they took ship, first to London and eventually back to Australia where Mary was able to put her literary talents to good use, becoming in time Australian Poet Laureate. In 1937 she was awarded the DBE (Dame of the British Empire). (8)

New Year's honours

Quite out of the blue I had received during 1980 a letter from the British consul in Buenos Aires, our old friend John Shakespeare, saying that my name had been put up for an OBE and if I accepted it would be announced in the New Year's honours list for 1981. This was a delightful surprise, especially as the citation read 'For services to the British community in Patagonia'. On acceptance, one is given the option of receiving the decoration from the ambassador, or of travelling to London to receive it from the Queen in person. We chose the latter, and were advised in due course that we could attend an investiture at Buckingham Palace on 28 October 1981.

I had not been to Britain for six years, Monica for four, so it seemed a

In the vehicle on the right: Herbert Felton (in hat), Emma behind holding baby Carlos. Millie standing in white dress. Mary Gilmore seated at left, husband Billy on horseback behind.

354

good time to travel. Frances was at boarding school and Stuart had left St Paul's and had joined the coastguards in April to do his National Service, living at our house in Rio Gallegos like his brothers had. The other three were overseas. Michael was in Wyoming, and Alison, on returning to England, had taken an accident course which she had prudently enrolled in before coming to Argentina, and had now taken up an appointment with the Birmingham Accident Hospital, soon becoming sister in the emergency ward. She was living with my Aunt Vida Worsley in Edgbaston. Uncle Edgar having died in 1975, Vida, who was still very active, wanted someone to live in. Stephen had had a difficult time: the Metropolitan Police would not accept him, so while his applications to other forces were being processed he had worked as a farm labourer and tractor driver, first for his cousin William Lawrence and then with Robin Worsley. Both Edgar and Vida had been justices of the peace in their day, so when Stephen's application reached the West Midlands force there were people who knew his background and he was accepted. He was now doing basic training at Ryton, near Coventry.

We first visited Michael in Wyoming, a long flight via Miami, where our flight arrived delayed and we missed our connection to Denver. Delta Airways rattled around and rerouted us, via Atlanta and Dallas but not until the next morning. So to Denver and finally by Rocky Mountain Airways, quite a small plane by now, to Laramie. Michael had been welcomed by my friend Paul Etchepare, who I had met in 1966 and whose Warren Livestock Co., with 15,000 sheep, was the largest sheep operation in Wyoming. Sheep were run all over the unfenced Rocky Mountains, tended by herders. These were traditionally Basques, indeed in 1966 I met one with Paul, and we had no common language: Etchepare spoke to the man in Basko, I to him in Spanish, and we two in English! By 1980 the Basque herders were being replaced by Peruvians from the Altiplano, so Michael as a Spanish speaker was welcome. Paul had taken him on as 'camp tender', providing a truck and a flat to live in. The job involved driving up to the sheep camps daily, taking stores and imparting instructions to the herders, while still leaving plenty of time for attending the university.

We put up at a nearby motel, and entered into the western way of life. Apart from having the university, Laramie was a major railway junction and depot for two of the main lines running through the Rockies from the West Coast to Chicago, but otherwise it was still very much a cow town, providing supplies and services for a considerable area. We found the whole scene almost unbelievably Patagonia-like, with one important exception – everything worked! Imagine Patagonia with paved roads everywhere, mains electricity and telephones laid on to every farm, school buses running even in winter, and that is rural Wyoming! American school buses are unique – of a distinct design and painted bright yellow, they run in all weathers and in most states have the right of way in many situations. There are strict penalties for interfering with school buses.

Several local families, faculty members and others including Paul and Hellen Etchepare who lived in Cheyenne, invited us to their homes and we found them all so friendly and homely. We went on several road trips with Michael, to places like Sundance, Medicine Bow and Horse Creek. It was a bit late in the season and by the time we got to Yellowstone Park it was snowing and all traffic had been halted. So we swung south past Jackson Hole and the Tetons down through Pinedale (population 300 but with a splendid general store selling jeans and roping gloves which I still have), and back across the desert through Rock Springs. The hardware stores in Laramie were starting to display snow ploughs (9) along with the lawnmowers, and the cashier at the supermarket said her husband drove a highway grader, that they had been called out and she had not seen him for three days. So we reckoned it was time to go – indeed the day we left it was snowing in Laramie.

Our fourteen-seater Rocky Mountain Airways plane picked us up all right, but by the time we approached Cheyenne the weather had closed in completely, and the pilot circled for an hour to use up fuel before trying a landing, just in case . . . He put her down all right, and we then waited around for several hours, first in the airport and then sitting in the plane at the end of the runway waiting for word of a 'clear gap' to allow us to nip across to Denver (half an hour away) and slide in before it closed down again. We still had minimum fuel on board so we sat huddled up with the heating turned off. The gap appeared, we took off, and made it to Denver – definitely one of our dicier trips, Patagonia included! Fortunately the bad weather had also delayed our connecting flight, so we caught this and set off non-stop to London. Some way out they announced we were flying over Winnipeg, so I said to myself 'What the hell are we doing up here?' but of course we were flying the great circle over the Arctic and in fact approached London via Scotland.

The great day for the investiture approached. We were allowed to invite two guests as well as spouses, so both Alison and Stephen could accompany Monica. Alison had bought a little car and we found an economical hotel near Victoria, where I changed into my morning suit and we set off for the Palace. Parking was in the inner courtyard, where a policeman asked Alison to 'Just open the boot, please miss, to let the dog sniff your sandwiches,' just in case we were carrying anything we should not. Then into the Palace and guests were drafted off to their seats in the banqueting hall where the chamber orchestra of the Grenadier Guards was playing suitable airs. Recipients were directed to the main picture gallery and marshalled by officers with lists into pens separated by silk ropes, according to decorations. We 'Os' milled around making polite conversation, and then we were instructed

356

in the procedure.

Finally our turn came and we were ushered into line and one by one stood before the Queen. I had not realised quite how petite Her Majesty is, and had certainly not experienced the powerful charm of her personality. She hung my medal onto its prepared hook, and asked what I had done. I said I had served the British community in Patagonia, and quick as a flash she said, 'Patagonia – that's in Argentina, isn't it ?' and went on to say that she did not remember having given a decoration to a Patagonian before. A smile, a quick bow, and on to the next . . . One followed the more or less marked trail, aides whipped the gong off its hook and put it into its box, and we followed round to join our family, who all said the queen had spoken to me longer than to the majority, and wanted to know what she had said.

Once the investiture was over, we all drifted through the picture gallery. It was rather an anticlimax, feeling we could at least have been given a glass of sherry. Then we made a visit to the royal loos (which we had been recommended to see – they were quite in keeping with the Palace ambience) and went out into the courtyard for photos. We then repaired to the 'Albert', a well-known pub near the Army and Navy Stores, for a restoring lunch.

Chacho in the meantime had been holding the fort in Rio Gallegos. He had followed Michael into the Coastguards, and had been appointed driver and batman to the zone (10) commander, Prefecto Mayor Williams, who had two small boys whose bicycles always seemed to need fixing. Condor was ticking over nicely during our absence under Pablo Peñaloza, who I had promoted to sub-manager a few years previously.

That spring the Vth Division (11) conducted extensive manoeuvres in the area, and tramped across the farms north of the river, including Killik Aike Norte. The chief of the general staff, General Leopoldo Fortunato Galtieri (soon to become president), came down to visit the exercises, and was served *mate* by Chacho when he called in. Eduardo Rushen managed to keep an eye on the gates and fences, but an inevitable number of sheep (mostly rams) disappeared. On my return, I duly put in a claim for damages. At that time we were (at Condor) on very good terms with the XI Brigade for public relations reasons on both sides, and I commented to the second in command, Lieutenant Colonel Sánchez, how odd that the foraging troops, living off the country in Napoleonic fashion, should catch rams rather than less strongly-flavoured sheep. 'Oh, that is easy,' he said, 'all these boys come from the north [of Argentina] and really want beef – i.e. a thick steak. They expect sheep to taste horrible anyway, so are quite happy to eat rams.' We were, in fact, able to collect reimbursement for damages and sheep 'lost'.

Looking back now, the tensions of 1982 were already starting to build up. Galtieri became president, and talks were being held at the United Nations about the Argentine claim to the Falklands. There was already trouble in South Georgia, where an Argentine company put in an appearance with an ostensible contract to dismantle the now derelict whaling station at Grytviken, once run by Salvesen & Co., Norwegian whalers. It has been suggested in Britain that this episode was an initial step by Argentina in their attempts to recover the Falklands, but in point of fact a joint venture of Norwegian and Argentine capital known as *Compañía Argentina de Pesca* had operated the whaling station in the 1950s so that legitimate Argentine commercial interests already existed, and the incident raised no eyebrows in South America.

In early March we held the gymkhana as usual, and this was graced with the presence of the British ambassador, Sir Anthony Williams, and his wife. Some of our members thought that the ambassador was remarkably quiet and perhaps poorly informed on the subject of the Falklands in general and any possible tensions between the two countries. Some rather acrimonious meetings had recently taken place at the United Nations in New York on the subject, but on the diplomatic and community front, at least, there were as yet no ripples.

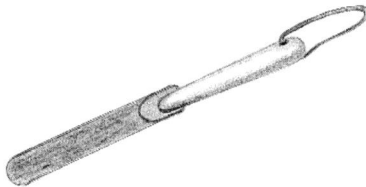

Notes

1 The rules for recognising overseas degrees in Argentina are quite archaic. In 1975, when I thought I might be out of a job and looking for a new one, I went into the matter of registering my Cambridge degree. I found that my MA was no problem, but having Chilean secondary education instead of Argentine I would have to sit three secondary-level exams. Fortunately it never became necessary.

2 I was a charter member of this club, founded in 1967, and the only one living in camp. At that time it was the only Rotary Club in Patagonia south of Comodoro Rivadavia although the much older club of Punta Arenas, Chile, was one of our sponsors.

3 The community was expert in organising events to which the non-British public was happy to go to, enjoy themselves and spend money for the relevant cause – during the war to buy Spitfires, after it to support charitable objectives.

4 The captain of the *Malvina* was one W. Blake, but we have not been able to find out any more about him.

5 We calculated that about one cubic kilometre (Km^3) or 1,000,000,000 cubic metres enters the estuary with normal tides of a nominal 10 metres in height, far more at spring tides, which could reach 13 or even 14 metres.

6 *Bone Hunters in Patagonia* by John Bell Hatcher has been described as 'one of the great exploration stories of all time' and the combination of science and adventure is comparable to Darwin's voyage on the *Beagle*.

7 The first doctor in Rio Gallegos, Arthur Fenton came from Ireland and his house can still be seen, now restored as a museum. See also page 294.

8 For further reading about the Australian colony in Paraguay, see *Paradise Mislaid* by Anne Whitehead.

9 The town or highway authority will clear the roads of snow, but the householder or rancher has to get himself from his house, to the garage, to the cleared road.

10 The area of Argentine waters from Bahía Blanca down to Ushuaia and eastwards including the Falklands is known as '*Zona Mar Argentino Sud*'. The coastguard HQ is in Rio Gallegos.

11 With HQ in Bahía Blanca, the Vth Division covers all Patagonia, and includes the XI Brigade, established in Rio Gallegos after the Beagle Channel crisis of 1978/9. In the light of later events, there is little doubt that the Army was rehearsing operations in Falklands-like terrain.

19

South Atlantic Tragedy

Vernet and the *gauchos*

The Falkland Islands situation exists because there is in the background a complex history with no simple answer. On the face of it, we have a *de facto* occupation by Britain, to which Argentina objects mainly on the grounds of usurpation of her own previous occupation. But if we start looking at the many aspects surrounding the sovereignty issue, we find that *neither* country has a clear *de jure* position based on historical facts, such as could be argued in any court. The only doctrine or concept which could, or even should be taken into account in these enlightened days of human rights and self-deter-mination, is that of the origins and wishes of the present inhabitants. So we might take a quick run here through the events which have given rise to the present dispute. For a fuller account of the discovery and earlier history of the islands, please turn to Appendix I.

The Spanish Crown had purchased the primitive settlement at Port Louis (*Puerto Soledad*) on the East Falkland (*Isla Soledad*) from the French in 1766, although the records of continued settlement there are incomplete. The coastal settlement at San Julian had been abandoned in 1783, but Puerto Deseado was still occupied and in theory depended from Puerto Soledad although the seat of government had been transferred to Deseado. There was certainly a governor there in 1806 – Second Lieutenant Juan Crisóstomo Martínez. Following the first 'English invasion' of the River Plate (see Chapter 1), in 1807 Martínez abandoned both settlements and returned to Buenos Aires, although according to Lenzi (1) it is understood that although Deseado was evacuated, a small military detachment remained at Puerto Soledad.

Following the Declaration of Independence in 1816, the United Provinces of the River Plate, as the new republic was first called, was made up of the former Spanish possessions which had hitherto depended from the vice-royalty of the River Plate. In spite of its other commitments to neighbouring countries such as Chile and Peru, who had not yet thrown off the Spanish yoke, (2) the new government found time in 1820 to contract and send down a ship to take possession of these outposts. This ship was the frigate *Heroina* under the command of Colonel Daniel Jewitt, who formally took possession of the archipelago in the name of Argentina. In 1823 Luis Vernet was granted land, cattle and fishery rights on the East Falkland. Vernet was an entrepreneur with capital and partners, and succeeded in establishing both cattle and settlers, although among the latter were a number of very rough citizens described today as *gauchos* which, indeed, they probably were. But many of them had been sent to the Islands as the result of having committed some crime back in the United Provinces – that is, Argentina proper, following the practice well-known to Spain, Britain and other colonial powers of the time. Cattle were taken over and multiplied and soon ran semi-wild just as they did on the pampas.

In 1829 Vernet was appointed governor by the United Provinces, and by 1831 there were some ninety successful settlers near Puerto Soledad. They cultivated the land and hunted the cattle in the true *gaucho* tradition, and were soon exporting dried beef and salt fish to Brazil. Captain Fitzroy visited the settlement in 1830 in the *Beagle*, and reported being invited to dinner by Vernet in his comfortable stone house, graced by Señora de Vernet and other ladies, with music and dancing to a 'grand pianoforte'.

From about the turn of the century, ships of several flags including British, Dutch and American had been visiting these shores, hunting seal and penguins. Whalers also appeared, although the bigger blue and finback whales of the South Atlantic were as yet beyond the capabilities of the 'Moby Dick' era of rowed whaleboats and hand-held harpoons. But there was an active trade in seal and penguin oil, and in the pelts of fur seal for the fashion trade, and of elephant seal for industrial leather.

In July 1831 Vernet managed to 'arrest' two American sealers, ostensibly for poaching fur seal on the West Falkland. They were taken to Buenos Aires. The Yankee skippers appealed to their consul there, George W. Slacum, and one of them escaped to an American corvette, the USS *Lexington* which happened to be in Montevideo at the time. Her commander, Silas Duncan, at once set sail for the Falklands and proceeded to sack Puerto Soledad and take off a number (but not all) of the inhabitants. Later events showed that a number of the *gauchos* escaped inland, to the camp.

361

Like Popham's expedition in 1806, it is not certain how much of this escapade was ordered, or otherwise authorised, by the US government back in Washington – in fact they probably authorised none of it, as there was hardly time for consultation. It certainly created a furore which has not yet abated. The immediate result was that the USA did in fact uphold its consul's action and, waiving the Monroe Doctrine of 'America for the Americans' and not having as yet sufficient naval forces to restore order in the South Atlantic, were very happy when the British, who did, stepped in. Consequently, when HMS *Clio* under the command of Captain Onslow put into Puerto Soledad in January 1833 and formally took possession of the Islands in the name of the British Crown, it did so with the full support of the USA.

The British seamen were welcomed with open arms by the few unfortunate remaining inhabitants of Puerto Soledad, where following the burning of the settlement by the *Lexington*, the *gauchos,* led by Antonio Rivero, a notorious outlaw, had revolted and committed a number of murders and other atrocities. *Pax Britannica* was therefore established to the satisfaction of all law-abiding parties concerned, and continued for almost 150 years.

In Buenos Aires, however, feelings ran very high. The British occupation was (and still is) considered a direct annexation or usurpation of existing sovereignty. The question really lies in whether such sovereignty (of Argentina) in fact existed. In general, following independence from the Spanish Crown, all lands in South America formerly occupied by Spain became, *ipso facto,* sovereign territory of the new countries, and it is on this doctrine that the Argentine position relies. But the infant republic had far too much to do to organise itself within its continental confines for most of the rest of the nineteenth century, so apart from firing off diplomatic protests from time to time, the colony was allowed to settle down and expand.

The inconvenient colony

So began a period of mixed relationships which was to last until broken for ever in 1982. On the positive side, the Falklands played a very important part in the settlement of southern Patagonia, from the early 1880s onwards. President Julio Roca was the first to realise the practical aspects of this, and actively encouraged settlement as we have seen in Chapter 2. There was much integration with Patagonia over the years, right up to the Second World War, but it was too much to expect Argentina to allow shipping under the British flag to trade between two 'Argentine' ports, so the *Fitzroy* and her predecessors, as we have seen, traded between Port Stanley, Montevideo and Punta Arenas. But that did not stop Argentine business interests selling

Stanley Harbour in about 1900, when much shipping came round Cape Horn or through Punta Arenas, before the Panama Canal was built.

goods and supplies to the Islands for good hard sterling, shipping them first over the river to Uruguay.

The value of the actual islands to Britain was mixed. Strategically, both as a naval base and as a coaling station, together with Simonstown in South Africa it allowed the British Navy to control both the South Atlantic and the South Pacific. The battles of the Falkland Islands and of the River Plate in two world wars point this up very clearly. On the other hand, however, the colony was always a financial drain on UK resources in spite of all the efforts of the Colonial Office, from Fred Cobb's time onwards, to make it live off its own resources such as sheep farming. It was not until serious pelagic whaling began in the inter-war years that this situation changed, and the Dependencies (3) as a group became a net earner.

In mainland Argentina in the meantime, British trade and investment had been on the increase since the early, turbulent post-colonial days. A number of important government bond issues were floated by the infant republic through British banks, and following the opening of the first railway in 1857, it was British engineering and enterprise which, pushing inland in the wake of the tracks, opened up the interior and allowed settlement and soon development of the camp. The real riches of Argentina – the still virgin pampas – started to create wealth, and the wealth was enormous. As we have seen in Chapters 1 and 2, Britain soon became a leading trading partner with Argentina – first an important source of government bonds and funding, then an early investor in land and produce, and then the main buyer of grain, beef, wool and sheep meats. People came too – to settle the land, to run the companies, to build the railways and drive the trains. Before long the British community in Argentina became the largest group of ethnic Anglo-Saxons in the world, outside the Commonwealth.

But the sovereignty issue refused to go away. At times it did not altogether suit Buenos Aires to pay more than occasional lip-service to it, but the protests and claims continued to be forwarded regularly and all Argentine children learned even before they could read that the Malvinas were Argentine. Between 1900 and 1940 the population of Argentina had been nearly doubled by the arrival of immigrants from Europe, second only in number to the USA. Most of these came from Italy and Spain, so that by the Second World War a second, Argentine-born generation had grown up who had little love for things European: their parents – having fled from poverty and misery – owed everything to their new homeland. Nationalist feelings became stronger, and when Perón came along in the mid-1940s his doctrines found fertile ground. After the war the peronist government nationalised the British-built railways and the sovereignty issue was taken to the United Nations. In general the annual claims became stronger and nastier.

There cannot fail to have been some elements in Whitehall who found this inconvenient (4) and would rather have done without the colony, which in the meantime was quietly ticking over, financed by the whaling and the high post-war prices paid for wool.. The idea arose that if the islanders could be persuaded to *wish* to become Argentine, then the Islands might be handed over without loss of face in the fullness of time, so shifting yet another snag at a time when 'giving control to the natives' was happening all over the former British Empire. There were after all large numbers of persons of Welsh, Scottish, English and Irish descent who had been living happily and prosperously for generations in Argentina, so what was so awful about the Falkland Islanders also becoming Argentine?

There had always been a group of informed people, including the Blakes and the Waldrons, who knew at first hand the problems on both sides and were not happy with the status quo. Once they got wind of this proposal, they were horrified at the idea of the Islanders being in any way 'sold down river' without much say in the matter, but at the same time they fully agreed that it was time some attempt was made to break out of the deadlock. A 'Falklands Committee', combining all interests both private and official began to meet in London. David Summerhayes was by then (1970) consul general in Buenos Aires, and word was got through, both to Whitehall and to the Foreign Ministry in Buenos Aires, that perhaps a new approach could be hammered out, seeking a new relationship but without either side altering their position on sovereignty – at least for the time being. It was soon agreed that a first requisite was for the Islanders to become acquainted with the people and customs of Argentina, as also for Argentines to get to know 'their' Malvinas. There had been a lot of integration with Patagonia prior to World War II, but little since. Hopefully, after a period (unspecified) of getting to know the other side, the time might come when some form of more permanent relationship could be worked out.

The result was the Communications Agreement of 1971 which opened up the Islands and got people travelling there. A landing strip was built at Stanley by the British, and an air service was set up, run by *Lineas Aereas del Estado (LADE)*. Operated by the Argentine Air Force, they flew Fokker F27 turboprop aircraft carrying twenty-odd passengers between Stanley and Comodoro Rivadavia. Fuel for this service was supplied by YPF (*Yacimientos Petrolíferos Fiscales*, the state oil company) and was delivered by Argentine ships, and other goods and supplies from the mainland began to appear in the Stanley shops. A special travel card was issued, used by citizens of both countries, to avoid any thorny sovereignty issues over who stamped whose passport. Islanders then started to come over, visit their relations in Patagonia, travel to Britain quicker via Buenos Aires, have their ailments attended to in the British Hospital and send their children to the bilingual British schools. Relatively few Argentines, however, took advantage of the arrangement to go over and see for themselves, in spite of the stalwart efforts of Wing Commander Rodolfo De La Colina, the officer sent over to run the Stanley end of the air link. He did a magnificent job of gaining the respect and understanding of the Islanders; of seeing and explaining both sides of the question not only in the Islands but also back in Argentina..

But the Kelpers were not, on the whole, all that keen on what they found in Argentina. The elder ones, who remembered or had been told about life in quasi-British Patagonia prior to the war, found it all Hispanicised and unfamiliar. Life on the Islands was quiet and well organised, and those who travelled to the British Isles found the same at the other end. Buenos Aires was brash and noisy, Comodoro a rough oil town. The younger ones who went to school got on better, but much depended on the school and the degree to which their parents had the vision to try to make it work. We, having children at the same schools, observed those who did and others who did not. It became obvious to informed observers that it would take quite a long time before the desired integration might gradually develop into an achievement. Tragically, there were others who were not prepared to wait.

Galtieri and the marines

At dawn on 2 April 1982 this tranquil, isolated and mainly rural community was rudely awakened. In a well-planned attack, helicopters carrying a force of very tough and well-trained assault troops flew into the barracks of the Royal Marines at Moody Brook, at the west end of Stanley, which they rapidly subdued, and took over the radio station. Meanwhile another group landed at York Bay just opposite the Mount Pleasant airstrip, taking possession of this with its communications set-up, thus effectively isolating the colony from the outside world. The eighty-strong force of British Marines had only had some twenty-four hours' notice of the impending attack and could do little to resist it. A few shots were fired, one Argentine officer killed but no British, and soon Government House was surrounded and the governor, Rex Hunt, obliged to surrender. Within hours the transports, which had reached Port William unobserved during the night, steamed into the harbour and started disembarking troops and equipment. Meanwhile strike aircraft from Comodoro Rivadavia, guided by the experienced pilots of the former Transport service started landing on the airstrip, soon to be followed by Lockheed Hercules heavy transports bringing further troops. The 'recovery of the Malvinas' was complete. (5)

Monica and I, together with Chacho, were in Comodoro Rivadavia, which we had reached the night before on our way down by road from Estancia Leleque, Chubut, with a load of stud rams we had gone to select. Going down to breakfast, we heard and read the astounding news, and got

A shepherd with a flock of Cormo Argentino rams at the main Killik Aike Norte settlement.

on the road as soon as possible to complete the journey back to Rio Gallegos and Condor. In the course of the twelve-hour run we picked up the radio bulletins throughout the day, and started to work out some of the almost unbelievable implications.

That an adventure of this sort should be undertaken at that particular moment in time was not, after the initial shock, so surprising. President Leopoldo Fortunato Galtieri was the latest in a succession of *de facto* presidents, which had started with Jorge Rafael Videla in 1976 when a military junta took over government and pulled the country back out of the chaos of Isabelita Perón's inept administration. Galtieri himself was a bit of a fire-eater – as commander of the II Army Corps we had seen him down at Condor haranguing the troops during the Beagle Channel crisis, and then as Army commander-in-chief he had come down again to oversee the Vth Division manoeuvres in November 1981.

The sovereignty claim had always been a useful political red herring which could be hauled out and spread over the media whenever the government of the day wished to direct public opinion away from embarrassing domestic issues. The Galtieri administration was not doing well – there was a lot of civic unrest and actual riots in Cordoba, so the ultimate red herring card was played by actually invading the lost islands. This move was entirely successful, bringing about an intense wave of patriotic enthusiasm. A few warning notes were sounded – we heard the second-in-command of the XI Infantry Brigade utter an audible aside on a public occasion: 'This will end badly', and died-in-the-wool peronist supporters long resident in Santa Cruz expressed the sentiment of 'what do they want those stupid islands for, if they [the federal government] do nothing for Patagonia?' But the bulk of the population promptly forgot its domestic woes and rallied in the wake of the recovered possession. Jewellery and family heirlooms were willingly given, and a fund was opened for providing cigarettes and other comforts for the troops.

The real villain of the piece was not however President Galtieri, but the foreign minister, Nicanor Costa Méndez. A prominent lawyer who had been to Oxford University, he had masqueraded as an Anglophile up to that point, to the extent of having his chambers in the same building as several British firms including Waldron SA. Now, however, he revealed his true colours and said in effect to Galtieri: 'You go ahead and invade the Islands, and I will then consolidate the *fait accompli* by diplomatic means'. In this he was to fail, mainly because he had not read the signs right and had underestimated the reactions not only of Britain but also of the USA. I have to admit that we ourselves also underestimated the British government, and thought at first that it was all a put-up job following lines of thought similar to those suggested earlier [p. 365] in this chapter; and that given the *fait accompli* of actual occupation, Whitehall would bow to the pressure and negotiate without loss of face. We had not reckoned on Margaret Thatcher and the 'Falklands factor'.

Our personal situation was not uncomplicated. I am British and a second lieutenant Royal Artillery (retired), and was managing a still technically British company sitting right on the Chilean border, covering 62km of frontier and 45km of open South Atlantic beach. The farm had operated a 'citizen's band' radio for several years to communicate with Waldrons in Buenos Aires. This had not been successful and we had given it up, but the masts and aerials were still in place. So it was no surprise when on D+3 day a car full of plain-clothes agents appeared 'to take away our transmitter'. I explained the absence of a transmitter, but agreed it would be a good thing to report to Army Intelligence in Rio Gallegos, which I did the next day. The colonel in charged received me cordially, and confirmed that yes, they did know all about us, the company and myself personally, and were very happy to have us looking after a sizeable stretch of frontier with Chile. (6) He was really more interested in finding out more about the local British community, and was surprised to hear that only about four of us actually had British nationality, all the rest being Argentine-born.

Technically the Patagonian Sheep Farming Company was still English, so not knowing just where we stood, personally or company-wise, the next item on the agenda was a flight to Buenos Aires, where I was greeted by Eduardo Menéndez with '*¡Hola, John, qué boludos que somos los Argentinos!*' ('Hi, John, look what fools we Argentines are!') and the latest copy of *Newsweek* on the office table. Eduardo's grandfather, after all, had been a Scot and the whole family was extremely Anglophile. Their general attitude was fairly typical of many of the leading families (socially and financially) and much of the business community: while in general holding to the overall concept of the

Argentine claim, in the meantime they were quite agreeable to continuing the status quo of the British colony. The Argentine owners of Condor had purchased the share capital of the English companies but had not wound them up, so like all other British assets they were placed under supervision. In the event this caused no difficulties and I was told to return to the farm. We had other things to think of down in the south.

Troops were being airlifted steadily to the Islands from Comodoro and Rio Gallegos air bases, and you could see the lines of conscripts flown straight down from Corrientes shivering on the tarmac waiting to board the Hercules transports. Other units were billeted in the vicinity by way of reserve and in the first week we had an engineer regiment encamped at Killik Aike. Carlos Felton had wisely left already, so we lodged the commanding officer in the Big House, two vacant houses were taken over for the officers and NCO's messes and the troops slept under canvas. We had to keep a very close watch to make sure they didn't chop the trees down for firewood.

Over at Condor the searches continued for the non-existent transmitter. I had got to know the intelligence colonel quite well by now, and by the third search it was quite obvious that somebody had laid information against us. I was then asked to provide lodging for an infantry platoon who would man a series of observation posts down on the coast – a logical precaution. We had the shearers' quarters empty and available so there was no problem. Monica and I drove out to see about this, arriving at Condor after dark, to be greeted by flashlights and armed plain-clothes men barring our entry, then after identifying ourselves we were escorted into our own home, where they promptly confiscated every firearm they could see and my shortwave broadcast receiver on the grounds that it might be a transmitter. (7) I was then asked to show them the shearers' quarters, so I did, and at every open door two armed men did a foot-first break-in as if we had SAS or marines hidden away there, which they probably thought we did! The platoon arrived during the night, and turned out to have been provided by our old friends the 24th Infantry, the home regiment of Rio Gallegos. It was commanded by a senior reservist lieutenant, recalled for the duration, who took one look at my venerable firearms and radio receiver, roared with laughter and promptly returned them.

We were very glad that Frances was tucked away boarding at St George's in Buenos Aires, and out of the active area. Monica went up to see her at Easter, and took her over to Montevideo for the long weekend, staying with Joan and Chub Coates. When I drove Monica in to catch the plane, we were intrigued to observe the bridge over the Rio Chico (south of Rio Gallegos) being mined against approach from the general direction of Punta Arenas..

Stuart, of course, was still in the coastguards, and his new zone commander, Prefecto Mayor Leyro, kept him very firmly as his driver and orderly, so avoiding any possibility of his being sent 'over there'. Monica and I were constantly on the move, maintaining contact between the two farms, with Stuart in the middle. Once we struck a road block on our way out to Killik Aike, and on showing my ID card, my British nationality was revealed, resulting in a search of the car and our weekend bag. When I reported this to my (by now) friend the intelligence colonel he said, 'Oh, we can't have that,' and issued me with a special pass. This served me well another time when I was caught out after curfew.

By this time we were into May, the cruiser *General Belgrano* had been sunk, the San Carlos landings had taken place and it was all much grimmer. Mirage fighters were flying sorties daily from the XI Air Brigade in Rio Gallegos, and people began to count how many returned and do the arithmetic. It was possible to keep up with what was going on via the BBC broadcasts, and at Condor we could pick up the transmissions from Punta Arenas of *Televisión Nacional de Chile* who had set up a well-informed war desk. The daily bulletins were mostly supplied by Reuters and they had some good correspondents.

The weather got colder and wetter, and the lines of soldiers waiting every morning for sick parade at the Medical Officer's tent in the Killik Aike front paddock got longer and longer, until the colonel decided he had better get them under cover, and so found other billets with sheds. They were replaced by a squadron of tanks, under a Major Dietrich, whose father had at one time been head of the National Telephone Company (ENTEL) and had once visited Condor. The tanks were not parked in neat lines, but scattered around the paddocks, hidden away between the calafate bushes and mostly near the beach, pointing towards the air base just across the river. About this time (after the sinking of HMS *Sheffield* and other ships by Exocet missiles) it became evident that the Argentines were afraid of special troops landing – SAS or similar – with the logical intention of 'nobbling' the air bases of Rio Gallegos and Rio Grande. The latter was a Navy air base, equipped with Super Etendard aircraft which carried the Exocets – probably the most effective weapon in the Argentine armoury.

There was the mysterious incident of a British Sea King helicopter, empty but for the flight crew, which made a forced landing in Chile (south of Punta Arenas, just where we had camped some years back). We saw it all on TV. There were rumours that flotsam had been found on the Atlantic coast not too far north of Cape Fairweather, suggesting SAS presence, but nothing definite ever emerged. Second in command of intelligence was one Major Eduardo Burgoa, and he always used to greet me or Monica with, 'I *do hope*, for your own sakes, that there are no "strange people" out there on your camps . . .' Burgoa later left the army to practise law in Rio Gallegos, and we became good friends.

One day I was out at Condor, when Monica, in town for a few days with

Prefectura Naval Argentina. Stuart (left) on parade, 25 May 1982.

Chacho, rang me up, basically to see if I was all right as she had read in that morning's local paper that one J. Blake had been arrested by the federal judge for espionage. As I had clearly not been arrested, perhaps I had better go and see the judge (who we knew personally) and find out what was going on. He came round to our house on San Martín street to explain that it was a false alarm, and he had ordered the paper to publish a retraction, although the item had already been picked up by the British press and we had to send off soothing messages to the children overseas. Several people had come to our house that morning: the Bishop of Rio Gallegos sent his secretary to see if they could intercede in any way; the chief of the federal police came to see why he did not know about it; a butcher client who supplied the army with a wide variety of goods came to see whether he could apply backstairs pressure and the wife of a doctor friend came with a basket of goodies 'for John in his cell'!

Hostilities continued, and National Day, on 25 May, always widely celebrated, was fast approaching. At the Condor school there was to be a ceremony, to which we had invited the lieutenant of the 24th and his men. About an hour before this a party of soldiers appeared at the Big House, headed by a very junior officer from brigade HQ, with a senior warrant officer technician, a sergeant and half a dozen privates carrying, in addition to their rifles, sledges with which (you guessed it) to smash the hidden transmitter once they found it! We solemnly showed them all around. Monica insisted on taking them up to the hen run to look in the laying boxes, while I explained to the WO technician that those mast things up on the hill were not for sending communications outwards but for receiving television inwards, and perhaps they might go and take a look at them while we went to the ceremony at the school. There we met our friend of the 24th, who told us with some amusement that the party had actually arrived much earlier, but he would not allow them to come and bother us before mid-morning.

This was the fifth transmitter search, so the next day I went to see the colonel and he finally showed me the full telex received from intelligence in Buenos Aires. I took one look at it, recognised the style and some of the events quoted, and said, 'This was either provided by a particular person [name supplied] who had been school teacher at Condor in certain years, or someone known to him or who was around at about that time.' I never heard any more about transmitters, so they must have been satisfied.

The fighting wound to its eventual conclusion and all of a sudden it was over. Major Dietrich at Killik Aike was utterly shattered – he could not believe that Argentine arms had suffered a reverse, even though he had earlier hinted privately to Monica that he was not the only one to have reservations about the conflict. Carlos' housekeeper Luz Maldonado cooked him a special supper to cheer him up. The tanks were pulled out within a few days, and the major was most meticulous in going round the settlement with Monica seeing that all was in order. Over in Stanley there were stories of food and cigarettes found hoarded in depots, and the Gurkhas had to exercise firm control to prevent break-ins by the disarmed Argentines. One also heard of the latter's amazement at observing British officers and NCOs giving orders in quiet, normal voices rather than shouting at their troops, who jumped to it just the same. Not much of this, however, got into the national press.

Other than the professional soldiers who made up the original shock troops, and other specialists, it became obvious that very few Buenos Aires based units containing conscripts (who might have talked freely to their friends and relations) had been sent over. Most of the regiments were drawn from the centre and north of the country. The 4th Infantry from Corrientes, which had been at Frailes in 1978, put up a stiff resistance during the final stages of the British advance on Stanley, and the 12th Infantry was also there, both regiments are cited in the British campaign accounts. The ripples of stories brought by the returning troops were less likely to spread in Corrientes than they were in Buenos Aires. The British took the most excellent step of sending the *Canberra* to Port Madryn with a large number of Argentine soldiers for repatriation, and one heard stories of their trooping down the gangplank clutching handfuls of P&O cruise literature and telling all who cared to listen that the food on board was better than anything they had had for months. Reporters were kept away from the quayside as much as possible, and the returned soldiers were quickly piled into buses and sent home. Many years later I met an Argentine war veteran who now has a shop near our flat in BA, and he confirms all this, adding quite spontaneously that 'they were very well treated by the *ingleses*'.

The forgotten community

During the seventy-five days that the conflict lasted, the British community in Argentina (8) had gone through some traumatic experiences. Many families, now into their third or fourth generation, were starting to feel more Argentine than British, especially if they had married into non-British families, and in spite of roots going way back they felt that their loyalty lay with their country of residence. This in some cases led to people whose fathers or other relations had served in the Second World War returning their medals as a sign of dissociation with the British. Some were worried that their business might suffer. Others were sufficiently well-established so as not to be concerned with this aspect, but were concerned about relations with their friends and neighbours. There were many variations. In Buenos Aires there are still a number of totally English-speaking families who circulate socially almost exclusively with others of similar background, and these were little affected. In the interior in general, and in Patagonia in particular, there had always been more integration with the non-British majority.

During the first weeks of occupation, before the fighting started, the Argentine government considered it had achieved a *fait accompli*, and was concerned with post-occupation civil government of the Islands. They wanted to send one or more Argentines of British descent over to Port Stanley to talk to the Islanders and point out the advantages of living in Argentina like the 11,000 or so people of British descent already there. To many this was a reasonable approach, it was only seasoned Falklands watchers who knew that it was a non-starter. The British embassy having been closed down, the government could only approach the British community through the BCC. While in Buenos Aires, as district chairman I attended several meetings of the central committee under the chairmanship of Billy Murchison, and I believe in the end a delegation was in fact sent, but with the resumption of hostilities these well-meant approaches were soon forgotten.

In the meantime the British task force was making its ponderous way south, and people began to wonder how it would end. I had returned to Rio Gallegos when I was rung up from Buenos Aires and asked whether I would be prepared to be one of a delegation of leading members of the community who proposed to travel to London and talk to the British Government. About what? Basically to ask Mrs Thatcher not to shoot! It seemed that people were concerned that in the event of actual fighting breaking out, their businesses and other assets might suffer. Personally I had already nailed my colours to the mast and had had a quiet talk with Billy (as well as my employers) before leaving Buenos Aires, so I declined this invitation, and a second one sent later by the Anglican bishop. To anyone familiar with the armed forces of both sides, once the composition of the British land force was known, the ultimate outcome was in little doubt.

Argentina had, of course, never been to war except for squabbling with its neighbours Paraguay and Brazil during the post-colonial period. Possibly because of this, to them we (the visible British within) were not the enemy – the enemy were those tough guys sent out by Mrs Thatcher in the task force. Until the shots began to fly, the latter were not taken seriously by the population in general – to them the paratroops and marine commandos were perhaps accepted as being 'real' soldiers but the Guards were portrayed as fancy soldiers only good for ceremonial parades in their red coats and bearskins and the Gurkhas of course were only mercenaries . . . The 'enemy' syndrome such as existed in Britain in two world wars, when people with Teutonic-sounding names were ostracised and dachshunds persecuted, did not happen in Argentina. On the contrary, people expressed sympathy with us personally as they felt we must be in a difficult position, as indeed we were, but not in the way our friends thought. I was local chairman of the BCC, and although this conferred no real position other than linking the local community with Buenos Aires in welfare matters, we found that others looked to us for example and, on occasion, advice. The British Club, the British School and the London Bank all continued to function. No patriotic graffiti were daubed on their walls, although the Club was sensitive enough as to take down for the duration the brass plate on the front door announcing its identity. I felt at first that I might not be welcome at the meetings of our Rotary Club, but after several weeks a delegation came to see me to invite me to resume regular attendance, which I did.

Two local weddings took place during the conflict. One was the son of the current president of the British Club, who rather than put on a big splash which might have been the case in normal times, got married quietly in his private house. But the other was held in the Club. This was the wedding of the son of a very long-established family of early Scottish settlers. An uncle of the bride was a Mirage pilot who was flying sorties daily, and there was some concern as to whether he had returned safely (he had). The wedding took place as planned, and the only concession to wartime discretion was to

Shearing board at Killike Aike Norte 2001. The first shearer (left-handed) won the National Shearing Championships.

suspend the festivities before 4.00 a.m. instead of the usual (Patagonian) all-night affair.

I cannot leave this unfortunate period without recording the story of Wing Commander Rodolfo De La Colina, a gallant officer who always tried to do his best for his country. We recall that he had been in charge of the LADE (Air Force transport) group in Stanley operating the passenger flights from there to Comodoro Rivadavia, and how he had gained the respect of both islanders and his own superiors for his understanding and discretion. Soon after the Beagle Channel crisis of 1978/9 the air base in Rio Gallegos had been upgraded to an air brigade and De La Colina was promoted in command. When the South Atlantic War began, Air Command in Buenos Aires clearly thought him an unsuitable person to command an operational wing, possibly due to his period in Stanley in close contact with 'the enemy', and replaced him. Although by now fairly senior, he was returned to flying duty and put in charge of an intelligence-gathering unit. He flew a number of sorties in a specialised aircraft, until this was shot down over Pebble Island and disappeared into a peat bog, crew and all, from which the remains were only recovered and repatriated by the British several years later. The civil airport of Mar del Plata has been named in his memory.

The after-effects of the conflict in Argentina were far-reaching. Once the reality of the debacle had sunk in, with the country still in a parlous state socially and economically, the military junta realised that it had shot its bolt and could hardly get out fast enough. Hurried preparations were made for returning to democracy, for which the citizenry were clamouring but for which they were still not really prepared. The peronist faction had not yet recovered from the murky currents left behind by the Peróns, and did not have a suitable figure to run for president, so the Radical party therefore had a fairly clear run and duly won. President Raúl Alfonsin has been credited with 'restoring democracy' to Argentina, but really it just happened naturally, the military regime fell by the weight of its own mistakes and he was the first elected president to follow. The Radicals hold to the same idealistic socialist doctrines that held sway in Europe immediately after World War II, but whereas both in France and in Britain these had been found wanting and by the early eighties had been outmoded, in Argentina this had not, and has still not yet, taken place.

But returning to democracy did not just mean holding elections. Argentina is a federal republic broadly similar to the USA, so that each of the twenty-two provinces has its own legislature (many with two chambers), cabinet, ministers, all of which need staff and advisers. Hundreds of thousands of new jobs were suddenly available, many of whom had at their disposal funds which could be allocated without much reference to any authority. All this had to be paid for out of government funding, national or provincial, in an already shaky economy. In the event, the Alfonsin administration was to prove unable to cope with this problem and could not finish their term of office, but in 1983, for the time being, the military were back in their barracks and freedom was available to all.

Post-war repercussions

The ripples took time to subside, and there were few people involved in the conflict whose lives were not affected in some way, including our son Stuart. The coastguards were among the forces sent over to the Islands, and one of their patrol vessels was on the receiving end of a gun action and sustained some casualties. Fortunately the zone commander, Leyro, kept Stuart in Rio Gallegos so the nearest he got to the action was to serve *mate* to visiting senior officers. He was not, however, released from service until early July, some three months later than his normal term of engagement.

I had always wanted Stuart to follow me into Emmanuel, where he would have been the fourth generation of the Worsley family to have matriculated. St Paul's had done their best for him, and he was able to sit some A-level exams, but they did not have the resources or the staff to cope with science at that level so he was going to have to sit the university entrance examinations in Cambridge. We had arranged for him to go to Britain after his coastguards service to do a course of intensive preparation at a crammers there, but the time available for this was cut to half so he did not in the end achieve the level of exam results required. On the advice of his coaching staff he had put St Andrew's University in Scotland as his second choice, and they accepted him. So in September 1983 he went there to begin a four-year honours course in natural sciences.

In Rio Gallegos, the future of the annual fundraising gymkhana was in doubt. It seemed to most of the senior members of the community that we should perhaps continue to keep our heads low. Personally, I had now been district chairman for twelve years and felt it was about time somebody else had a go, preferably a younger person who had been born locally and was hopefully more integrated with the non-British than the manager of a London-based company. (9) I called a meeting of all the family groups who ran the main stalls, and it was agreed that it would be unwise to hold such an event for a year or two. No person was proposed as district chairman, so the matter lapsed inconclusively. The following year, however, a local garden club put on a flower show in the gymkhana tradition, and gradually with the passage of years other events took its place. Nor did further cases appear of distressed Brits needing help, so the community had in fact outlived the need for raising money for this purpose. The British Community Welfare Fund continues to operate at a national level in Buenos Aires, and is now known as the Argentine-British Welfare Fund.

Over in the Islands, people were trying to get back to normal, with varying degrees of success according to their personal experiences. (Twenty years later, some of these continue to be vivid and unforgettable, even unforgivable.) In the camp, things were not helped by the slide in wool prices during the 1980s, which had already begun. Having my hands full at Condor, over the years I had only kept in general touch through my father, and later Bill. I had been followed to Hill Cove as Bill's assistant by our cousin Tim, Norman Blake's youngest son, who after spending a season with us at Condor, took over the management from Bill in 1965. Tim had married Sally Clements whose mother Babs (Luxton) was a sister of Beat Harding, and whose father Wickham Clements was a nephew of old Wickham Bertrand who founded Roy Cove. Bill and his second wife Susan retired to England where they lived in Richmond and Bill became active in the affairs of the FIC.

The West Falkland had been little affected by the conflict as all the serious fighting had taken place on the East Falkland. Port Howard and Fox Bay, being on the Falkland Sound, had seen something of the hostilities, particularly the operations in the air, but Hill Cove had not. The farming scene in general, however, was of some concern given its fairly rigid structure dictated by both climatic and geographical limitations and the fact that wool was the sole product, all attempts at developing a meat trade having come to naught. In 1984 when we were in England for Alison's wedding (see Chapter 20) I found Bill seriously worried about the viability of H&B as a business. For many years the income from wool sales had been insufficient to cover the running expenses, although it was still possible to make up the difference from reserves. In other words, the farm was operating at a loss even though the company was not, thanks to its prudent portfolio of investments.

Given our experience over on the coast in the matter of using the new genetic technology to breed more profitable sheep, it seemed to me that something similar could be done at Hill Cove, particularly as I had been in on the original Chevidale crossbreeding project. This did not seem to have been followed through to the best advantage as far as wool production was concerned, but had had the desired effect of improving both the lambing rates and general survivability – first essentials in any improvement scheme. There was some experience in the Islands, right next door at Roy Cove, in the use of Polwarth rams to grow finer wool, so it seemed something might be possible.

So I put together a scheme for Hill Cove embodying the existing state of the flocks as reported by Bill, applying the principles and experiences we had accumulated at Condor and Coronel over the years, modulated by my

Shorn fleeces are thrown over a slatted table, to have stained parts taken off before being bundled up and placed in bins (behind) prior to being pressed up into export bales.

own knowledge of camp conditions and the various limiting factors in the Islands. We had learned a lot in fifteen years about gene transfer, and in creating the Cormo breed had done just that – taken a fine fleece off one breed and grafted it onto another. There seemed no reason why one could not start with a Chevidale base with all its fertility and survivability and put a fine fleece on its back. Fine wool is always worth more per kilo than coarse, so if you can avoid the losses and hold the cut (kilos) per head by selection, you can hardly avoid making more money. Tim had come home to the UK on leave that year, so I was able to discuss all this with both of my cousins.

But others beside the farmers were concerned with the viability of the colony in the light of the war. Lives had been lost, ships sunk, aircraft downed and enormous sums expended on a tiny colony which many people in the UK had hardly heard of before April 1982. Whaling was in abeyance, offshore fishing had not yet become as important as it was to do a few years later, oil was a big question mark, so what about the sheep? Whitehall clearly needed the colony, recovered at such vast expense, to be viable for domestic (UK) political reasons. On an international level, too, it was necessary to be able to point to a stable and thriving population of genuine inhabitants who had been there for several generations, so a committee was set up under Lord Shackleton to study the matter.

The suggestion soon arose that the land might produce more efficiently if it were subdivided into smaller, owner-operated farms. Land reform, in other words, was being proposed by a Conservative Government! Now, in most other farming environments this concept, attractive as it sounds in theory, just does not work out in practice. The realities of scale (size) are absolute, and usually the subdivision is guided by political or social factors so that the new, smaller properties are in fact too small to be viable without new technology. Unless this is forthcoming, including the training of the new operators, after a period the subdivided properties start to coalesce until an economically viable size of property is once again reached. This has happened in the USA, Australia, the UK, Argentina and Chile. The only way to avoid it is to subsidise, which in this case Whitehall was clearly prepared to do, providing government support for wool production and farming in general, as well as substantial support for the colony as a whole, in order to keep the land occupied. So in addition to providing a massive garrison and a direct air service from the UK, it went ahead with its plans for subdivision and resettlement of the land.

I was a shareholder in Holmested Blake, and although in general terms we had kept up with the Shackleton report and its proposals, we were not aware that any specific changes were in sight. One day in 1987 however, again on a visit to the UK, I learned in the course of a telephone conversation with Tim's eldest brother Charles, that the Hill Cove property was on the point of being divided between the employees by decision of the board of directors. We were at first shocked and hurt at not having been told about this, much less consulted, and were not entirely in agreement with the proposed terms, which rather smacked of 'giving it away' for resettlement by the employees and others.

Having been very close to land reform projects in South America where 'expropriation' was a much feared concept akin to confiscation, our outlook was more hard-boiled than that of the well-wishers on the board. It seemed to us that if the UK government for its own domestic political reasons was wanting to resettle the land, it would in due course make a fair proposal to the company offering proper compensation and the deserving and faithful employees would be duly looked after. It was not necessary for the board to rush in with a scheme of its own. I spent a good deal of time visiting and talking to the directors, but without avail and the proposed sale duly took place in 1988. Holmested, Blake & Co. Ltd was wound up, and some 110 years of history created by Robert Blake came to an end in the Islands, just as it had at San Julian less than ten years before.

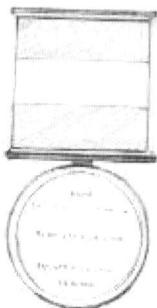

Notes

1 See *Historia de Santa Cruz* by Juan Hilarión Lenzi page 319.
2 Such as organising, recruiting and supplying the army which General José de San Martín led over the Andes in 1817 to achieve the final independence of Chile and Peru.
3 The group includes South Georgia and the South Shetland and South Orkney Islands, to all of which Argentina also lays claim in spite of having had no historical presence there.
4 Not for the first time. In 1848 Sir William Molesworth, MP for Southwark, had proposed in the House of Commons that the 'claims of Buenos Aires to the Falkland Islands' be acknowledged. See Appendix I.
5 For details of the landings, and of the subsequent recovery of the Islands, see the ample literature on the subject. I have used mainly *The Falklands War*, by the Sunday Express Insight Team.
6 Running like a thread through the whole South Atlantic campaign was the thought that Chile might invade Argentina while the latter was looking the other way. Pinochet had always made it his business to keep on good terms with Britain. Certainly no troops stationed on the western boundary were pulled out to go to the Falklands, not even the highly trained mountain troops, who were far more accustomed to the wet and cold than the conscripts from Corrientes.
7 I had assembled a collection of firearms, some historic with no ammunition, some the usual arms found in any camp, such as 12-bore shotguns and .22 rifles. In Argentina at that time, you were allowed to have weapons for personal defence, and although we seldom locked the doors of the house, it was usual to have weapons quietly tucked away at different points, including the master bedroom. In three generations I never heard of any being needed – it was better to have the dogs loose.
8 For a full account of how the British community evolved, and some idea of the importance it had achieved in the Argentine Republic, see *The Forgotten Colony* by Andrew Graham-Yooll, and *Argentina: La Gesta Británica* by Emilio Manuel Fernández-Gomez. '*Gesta*' here means 'achievement'.
9 The Menéndez, Ochoa and Paz owners in fact moved fairly fast, and by June 1983 had transferred all the assets of their former London companies to Argentina, setting up new Argentine companies, one for each farm. So the former Patagonian Sheep Farming Co. (1908) Ltd became Estancia Condor Rio Gallegos SA.

20

A New Day Dawns

Down to basics

But there are more to roots than just property, and the family roots which had been deeply planted in Patagonian soil were still very much there and had already born fruit in the form of our continued activity at Condor and Killik Aike Norte. So our own lives now returned to normal, or at least as normal as possible. Alison, as a nursing sister at the Birmingham Accident Hospital often had to deal with cases brought in by her brother Stephen, now a constable with the West Midlands Police. Stuart would start at St Andrew's in September, and in the meantime was working for Wool Testing Services in Wembley, the main laboratory of the International Wool Testing Organisation (IWTO) who set the standards for wool measurement and testing worldwide, under the aegis of the International Wool Secretariat. Michael's graduation from the University of Wyoming was coming up in June 1983, and we had always promised the children that one at least of us would be there. In the end only I went, partly because the date clashed with Frances' winter holidays and partly so that both Michael and I could continue on to Australia from Wyoming on a ram-buying expedition.

So together with Paul and Hellen Etchepare I attended Michael's graduation ceremony, and spent a few days with them in Laramie and Cheyenne. Then we flew from Denver via Honolulu to Sydney, and on to Adelaide where a concentrated tour of Merino stud breeders had been organised by Brian Jefferies, who had returned to Australia after his tour with the FAO project in Bariloche and now had an advisory job with the South Australian Department of Agriculture.

The reason for seeking new Merino blood was a strategic one. Condor had so far retained its Corriedale stud, not only the pedigree flock but also the selected ram breeding flocks controlled and inspected annually by the Argentine Corriedale Breeders' Association. These had been bred up to a high level of production over the past thirty years or more, using artificial insemination to make the most of the sires imported from New Zealand and Australia. A policy decision had been taken to phase out these flocks, but not before we had absorbed their valuable genetic potential into the Cormo gene pool by injecting new Merino blood while we still had a large number of Corriedales (some 7,000 ewes) into which to absorb it.

Now the Merino breed has more variation within it than any other, and at least four major sub-types can be found in Australia alone. Up to this point, all Merinos imported into Argentina (known as *'Merino Australiano'*) were the peppin type, characterised by very heavy fleeces of moderately fine wool, but with poor conformation for meat and not very good lambing performance. For these reasons we had based our Cormo project on the Corriedale, to correct these requirements. We now met for the first time the South Australian type of Merino, which has far better meat conformation, a heavy body and few skin wrinkles, and although on average their wool is stronger than other Australian types we could find fine-woolled rams among the variations offered. This type of sheep was hitherto unknown to us, and gave us furiously to think. By using these well-bodied rams, might we not reduce the time needed to create our new breed by one or even two generations?

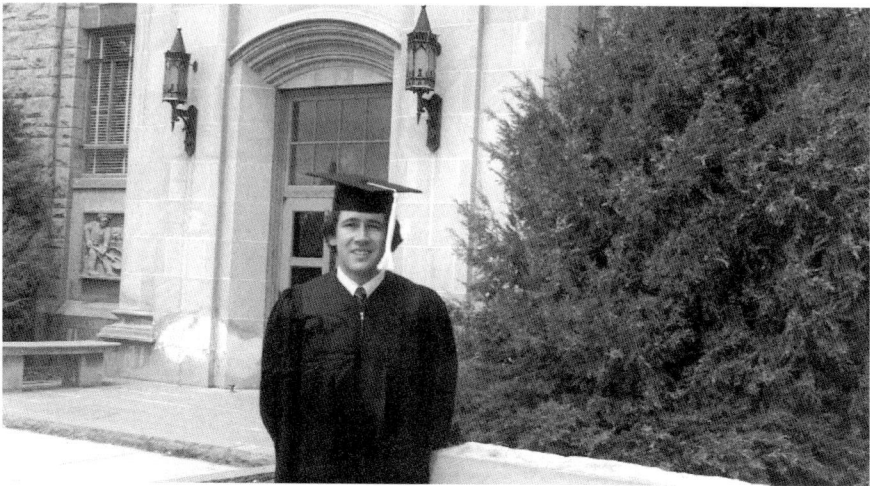

Michael graduated on 15 May 1983 with a BSc from the University of Wyoming, USA.

We were not content with the big-name studs like Collinsville, or the highly technified Anama, or the classic Haddon Rig. In November 1981 we had hosted a visit to Condor by the Australian Merino Society, a group of breeders mostly from Western Australia who had broken away from the sire-oriented breeding principles of the traditional studs and were using an integrated system of exchange of sires and dams between their members which was proving extremely powerful in creating new, more productive genotypes. Their leading thinker was Jim Shepherd, and so from Adelaide we flew to Perth and were driven out to his farm in the wheat belt. We soon got down to basics and talked breeding and genetics for half the night. It seemed that as well as creating new types of Merino, they had set up a new breed which they called Beddale, in which they had incorporated genes of several UK mutton breeds (1) with Merino. Now this is just what Little had done to form Corriedale over a hundred years previously, and what we were now doing with the Cormo – using British breeds of high meat, lambing, fertility and milking characteristics to cross onto the Merino, which provided the fine wool. Might not these genes also be of use to us?

With all these new ideas fizzing around, we boarded the 'red-eye special' (Australian for night flight) back to Sydney to take counsel with that fountain of genetic wisdom, Helen Newton Turner. Helen had been retired for some years, but invited us to her home for supper during which she confirmed absolutely the ideas we had been forming. Basically, the wider the genetic base the better, both in number of ewes and in variety of genotypes. Mix them all up together and let your selection process pick out the new and more productive combinations. This concept, which has become known as the 'genetic pot', is diametrically opposed to the 'pure breeding' concept of the show ring and the 'perfect' sire which has become a limiting factor to the development of many breeds of animals. I have a fond memory of Helen seeing us off in our taxi, making stirring motions with her hand and saying, 'Stir the pot, John, stir the pot!' With this encouragement, I set to and lined up a shipment of seventeen rams, of all the types mentioned, which was later confirmed by the board once we got back to Buenos Aires.

Michael had spent a very fruitful time in the USA, gathering a wide range of experience from both Georgia and Wyoming, but had been away from home for three years and was longing to return to Patagonia and 'follow dad' in some way. There might have been several avenues open to him, but Argentina was still in uncertain health and we felt it was too soon to commit himself, especially having an American degree which would afford him much wider possibilities. Given the long and strong family tradition we have described at some length, it was particularly hard to have to persuade your eldest son not, in effect, to follow in your footsteps. However we all agreed in the end to shelve the issue for two years by his returning to the University of Wyoming to study for his Master's degree. Once there he was given the excellent advice of studying economics and business rather than the scientific side.

Meantime over in England Alison also was moving on. She had become engaged to Trevor Jones, who we had met in 1981, and with Stephen had spent a pleasant weekend together at Llangollen. Trevor's father was Welsh, from Port Madoc in North Wales, on the Lleyn peninsula where the emigrants who settled the Welsh colony in Chubut mostly came from, although we have not established any family connection with them. Bob Jones had been a bank manager in Edinburgh and lately retired there, while his wife Hazel was Scottish. Trevor had graduated in medicine at St Andrew's and was currently specialising as a General Practitioner at Yeovil Hospital. Alison had followed her Accident experience with a course in Midwifery, and then specialised in the very exacting nursing involved in the Intensive Care of premature babies at the Taunton Hospital, founded originally by Dr Malachi Blake. With her team, she was involved in the first successful birth of 'Test-tube triplets', conceived 'in vitro'. . . She had found a little house there, and they were making plans for their wedding for which we and Frances travelled over in August 1984.

Michael had completed one year of his Master's degree, and was working temporarily with Prouvost Lefebvre & Co., a French wool firm with worldwide connections, at their wool-combing mill in Charleston, South Carolina. He could not leave the USA for his sister's wedding as his student's visa would have expired. So I took a swing that way, flew via Miami and spent a few days with him, during which we were able to look up some of the Rotarians in Georgia who had been so good to him during his time there.

We rented a house at Wellington, near Taunton, and installed ourselves there for the wedding. Alison and Trevor were married on 8 September 1984 at St Margaret's church in Taunton, where the vicar's wife was the sister of General Jeremy Moore who had commanded the ground troops in the Falklands campaign. The reception at the County Hotel was a great family getting together: no less than six 'Mrs Blakes' were present, and there was a strong River Plate presence in the form of Monica´s sister Joan and her husband John (Chub) Coates, Kenneth and Diana McCallum as well as Bill and Jean Waldron and Eric and Joan Davies, formerly of Condor. .

Ten days or so before the wedding came the news that Kenneth Suggett, former chairman of the ASL, had died at his home in Weybridge. Although the land and assets in Argentina had all been transferred to new companies set up by MOP, the London company was still in existence, albeit in the process of being closed down. Over the telephone from Buenos Aires, Eduardo Menéndez asked me to take over this task, so after the wedding we went and stayed at Joan and Chub's house, also in Weybridge, from where I commuted daily to the City. I found that the only serious commitment of the parent company was in fact to myself, as an original UK contract employee, so the situation allowed me to strengthen my position *vis-à-vis* MOP regarding my future arrangements for retirement, in theory now only five years away.

The lady friend

The trip to Australia was also memorable because it marked my introduction to computers. Mainframe machines had reached Rio Gallegos, but were only handled by experts in the field. While at Laramie I consulted people at the university as to possible uses for computing on farms and in small businesses, and was given good advice – so much so that I bought my own little home computer to learn on, the sort you plug into a TV set. We were by then using a fair amount of elementary formulae in the breeding work at Condor, first for grading the pedigree breeding ewes on their real-time production of lambs, and then for selecting male and female replacement progeny at all breeding levels by easily measured characteristics, known as objective measurement (See Appendix II for details). We worked these calculations out on paper using simple arithmetic, later assisted by hand-held calculators. There was nothing particularly difficult about all this, but it was very time-consuming. There were about 1,000 recorded ewes, with individual records in a card index, whose annual updating took several weeks of evening work, and to fully process the statistics of the charts used for grading ram and ewe hoggets off-shears took several days. It seemed that we could harness the number-crunching power of computers to do this work for us. There were also simple programmes available for office tasks like payrolling.

So I persuaded the board to buy a computer for the farm, justifying the expense in the man-hours to be saved by the office staff (two men) monthly in working out the payroll for a workforce of around a hundred people, and in 1984 we installed the first on-farm computer in Patagonia. This was entirely successful, although it was, perhaps, ahead of its time or at least of available software. The payroll programme was a package purchased in Buenos Aires, but I was unable to find software (worldwide) which would handle the statistical analysis of the 2,000-bale wool clip and the production records of the pedigree flock. So I had to get down to writing the programmes myself, often a matter of long hours of overtime. The computer lived in the farm office, so I would necessarily be delayed in coming home which gave rise to a family nickname for the computer: my *'querida'* or 'lady friend'. I found the mental exercise both relaxing (after a day's work coping with the routine administration work of a large farm) and creative, possibly taking the place of the music which had been a feature of my younger days.

Michael, Monica, Frances and Stuart with part of the Killik Aike Norte wool clip.

Professional matters continued to thrust themselves upon us. I had been intrigued to receive an invitation to a symposium to be held in Debrecen, Hungary, in August 1984 on 'Sheep Production on Large Farms'. Condor being definitely in this category, and the date suitable, I had flown from Atlanta to Budapest on the way, as it were, to Alison's wedding. Debrecen is a university city not too far from the Russian border and near the 'Hortobagy' – vast steppes where sheep raising has been going on for hundreds of years. The symposium had been organised, basically, to attract breeders and scientists from Australia and New Zealand in order to acquire much the same latter-day technology that I had been at some pains to travel to find out, so it was no surprise to meet up with a number of old friends from those countries, both farmers and scientists. There were also a number of eminent Europeans with newer technologies, particularly in artificial insemination. A lot of the work was concerned with milk and cheese production, very widely practised in Europe and rather out of my sphere, but generally interesting.

On the last day, wanting souvenirs to take to the family, I had asked the (English-speaking) girls at the hotel desk to direct me to a suitable shop where I could buy the exquisitely embroidered blouses they all wore, for my wife and daughters. I was duly directed, but found no English speaker in the shop. It was possible to point to the desired garments but the question of size arose so amid great giggles and no doubt earthy Hungarian I indicated approximate sizes and shapes by pointing at the various assistants round the shop . . .

The following year we went to another World Corriedale Congress (they happen every five years) which took place at Sant'Ana in Brazil, a town twinned with Rivera in north-eastern Uruguay. In the adjoining districts of both countries, sheep raising is a very important farming activity. Our relationships with the Corriedale world were somewhat mixed, particularly in Argentina. Condor by now was actively breeding Cormo and it was no secret that it had given up the Corriedale breed having found it wanting. On the other hand, both Condor and the Blake family had earlier in the century been prominent in getting Corriedales into Patagonia, and later in propagating the breed and spreading its influence. Also we had found in Punta Arenas that at a breed congresses of this sort one got together with avant-garde breeders from other countries with new ideas, all stimulating.

We enjoyed the congress, which was very well organised by our Brazilian hosts, but the last few days were marred by petty breed society politics. As is usual, there was a stock show going on at the same time, given world repute of course by the presence of delegates from all over. Due to some animal health regulation which had not been properly cleared beforehand, animals from Argentina were at the last minute not allowed into Brazil. The Argentine delegation to the congress withdrew in a huff, and tried to 'order' observers like ourselves to do the same. We reckoned it was not our business, and stayed on, as did one other couple, even though the huffees went to the length of leaving one of their members behind to see that we took no part in any of the official proceedings . . .

But we had other and much pleasanter things to do. The previous summer, a group of Uruguayan breeders had visited Rio Gallegos at show time and asked specifically for a visit to Condor in spite of it not having been included in their programme. We duly laid it on and they all came out, and to Monica's delight several of the party came from Salto and one, 'Chichín' Goncalves, had been at school with her there! Over the years we had never been able to get up there for her to pick up her childhood memories, so we had arranged first to meet him at the congress, and then after it was over we caught a Greyhound bus across Uruguay to Salto. There we spent several delightful days meeting all the families Monica had known in her youth. The Bank of London and South America no longer had a branch there, so we could only look at the front door from the street, but the tiny Anglican church where she was baptised is still there, cared for by the Grasso family among others. They are leading Merino sheep breeders with property in the district with whom we had become friendly at shows. Their grandmother was of a staunch Anglican family named Jones, so in spite of their mainly Italian extraction they have retained Church of England beliefs.

'Keoken'

Monica in the meantime had been branching out on her own. We had for a number of years been pursuing a public relations policy of trying to integrate Condor with the local community, in an attempt to counteract the negative image of Condor in the press and elsewhere – that it belonged to the Queen, that it was a foreign company exploiting Argentine assets (= territory). The ASL board had not been very interested in this, but we were the ones who had to live there and read the scurrilous write-ups in glossy magazines and tabloid newspapers about our spying for the British government and my having been decorated by the Queen for looking after her assets . . . So we tried to counter at a different level by hosting visits of all sorts including groups of schoolchildren; by getting alongside the church; by strongly supporting our on-farm school and its community relations; and by our own visibility, availability and 'joining in' local activities where the previous generation had rather tended to keep themselves to themselves.

Rotary was a good start, and through this excellent institution we participated in a number of town activities and social events. We were more or less *'ex-oficio'* on the visiting lists of government and the armed forces, whose invitations it was good policy to accept, even though dinner often started at 10 p.m. or later and often Monica would drive us out to the farm while I slept in the car. I had to be visible on the farm when shearing started a 6 a.m. the next morning . . . Our conduction of local BCC affairs during my district chairmanship had kept all these principles firmly in mind and well to the fore – indeed I like to think that a positive fruit of all this was lack of harassment to the local community during the South Atlantic War.

At the old gymkhanas, one of the leading stands was the fancy goods stall, run traditionally by the chairman's wife. Monica had taken it over from Pat Fenton and carried on, organising during the year the knitting, sewing and other hand-crafting of goods to be sold at the stand on the day. Most of this work was done by British ladies in the community, particularly those who lived in Santa Cruz or San Julian, or away inland on their farms. But latterly she had come into contact with a few craftswomen of humble origin, mostly Chileans of Mapuche descent, who could spin and weave or knit raw wool into garments, wall hangings and the like. The gymkhanas and the fancy stall had not been revived after the conflict, but Monica continued to encourage her craftsladies and we had taken a number of homespun cushion covers with us to England at the time of Alison's wedding, as gifts. On returning, Monica got together with a friend and they decided to open a craft shop for woollen goods. There were plenty of women living in the outlying parts of town who were only too glad to supplement their meagre income by spinning in their homes, while their husbands were working out in camp or otherwise not present.

Florita Rodríguez de Lofredo was born in Spain but came out at an early age with her parents. She is a well-known writer and poet, who had been secretary to the provincial governor among other administrative jobs. Now retired, she and Monica put their heads together and set up a crafts shop in our little house, now no longer required for our boys doing national service, and *Keoken Artesanias* opened for business in December 1984. 'Keoken' means the dawn, or break of day, in the Tehuelche language. We turned the front room into the shop and retained our bedroom for sleeping in. However, the shop ended up invading both the kitchen and the other front room. Initially the crafts were all wool-based, although other local crafts such as pottery and needlework were later added. But woollen goods continue to be the main line, knitted or woven from home-spun yarn. We got to know the poorer districts, and the farm white car in which Monica used to go round distributing fleeces and collecting the work became very well respected.

We also got a glimpse of the seamier side of their life. The red light district, credit cards and all, was round the corner and on occasion when visiting some craftswoman Monica might ask after the daughter, to be told '*me la llevaron*' (they took her away) – meaning that the girl had been taken away to be initiated into the oldest profession. The craftswomen were always paid

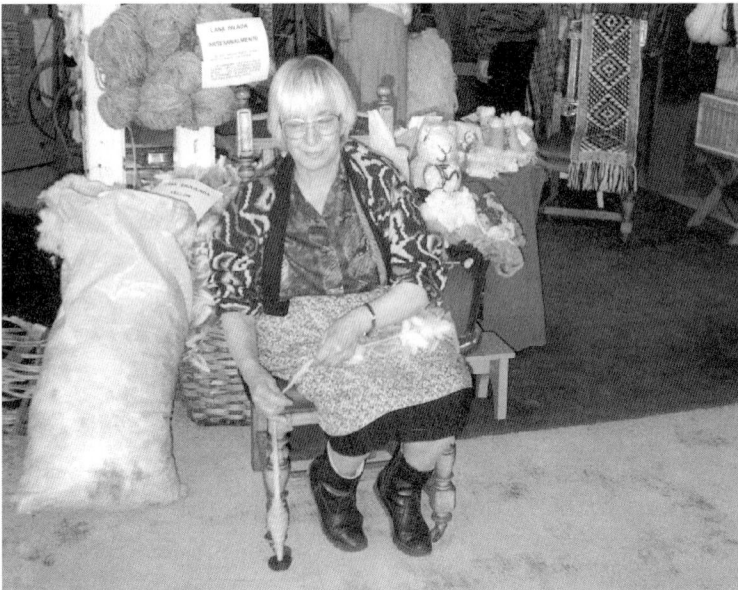

Elisa spinning at the Keoken stand at the Rio Gallegos Stock Show. The weighted spindle, or huso, is held in the right hand and the raw wool is fed in from the left.

in cash on the spot for their work, but soon took to bringing their spun wool or other products down town to the shop rather than have us collect it from their homes. In this way they could take the money to the shops nearby and buy food for the family, rather than have the husband come home and take it away for drink. If the shop was short of change they could be trusted to take a high denomination bill, go and make their purchases and bring the change back. Many a poor family has been fed in this way, especially in the winter when the men were out of work.

We also started to learn about wool. Although we had as a family been wool growers for three generations, on the farms it was a product to be baled up and sent off to Bradford or Japan and we had not really got to know it as a craft material. The spinners mostly use a hand-held spindle, imparting a twirl with the fingers and feeding the wool in from a bundle held under the arm. This is the most ancient form of spinning and allows the operator to move around, even suckle a child. A few use a wheel, always home-made. In both cases the wool is spun greasy, not washed, and the first result is hanks of disgusting looking grey yarn, smelling strongly of sheep, keds and frowsty hovel. The hanks are then washed, usually by another woman, but we have done our share of washing in the bath at home, and here one of nature's miracles occurs – you just swill it around in lukewarm water, maybe with a little soap or else without, and all that horrible dirt just falls away and you are left with a beautiful white, soft yarn.

Centenaries

The centenary of the foundation of Rio Gallegos was coming up in December 1985, and no sooner had the shop opened than Florita was asked by the mayor to chair a committee for the erection of a monument to the early settlers. The committee represented people of all the various ethnic groups which settled in the town and surrounding countryside: Spanish, British, Italian, Yugoslav, Chilean and so forth, and had to raise the funds, commission the artists and get it built. Monica was among the committee members, and this devoted band worked very hard all that year. The centenary was duly celebrated on 19 December 1985, and President Alfonsin came down for the occasion. The night beforehand bright lights and sparks could be seen issuing from the monument, and many thought that it was a preview of the fireworks display to be held the next night, but no, it was the welders frantically completing an artistic metal sculpture which forms part of the monument. It was all ready by the day, and the principal plaque commemorating the twenty families who first settled in Santa Cruz, Robert Blake the eighth name from the top, was duly unveiled by the president.

The following year would be the centenary of Estancia Condor, and we felt the occasion should be marked by doing something for Rio Gallegos. The district hospital was very much directed to charity or otherwise needy patients, and a devoted group of nuns of the St Vincent de Paul order did a great deal of the nursing. They held services in a back room, so the idea arose of building a chapel for the hospital. We had always kept in close touch with the Church, and the bishop at that time, Miguel Angel Aleman, came from a well-connected Hurlingham family of Irish descent and was among our supporters in town. He was delighted with the idea, and his only stipulation was that the altar be built of bricks and mortar so that it could not be moved or otherwise displaced. He also introduced us to a builder, Vicente Raciatti, and the foundation stone was laid by José Menéndez as part of the Rio Gallegos centenary programme. Building then proceeded throughout the year, and the building was duly inaugurated as part of the Condor centenary celebrations.

Eduardo Menéndez and Don Pepe Paz came down for the event, with several others of their families, and Monseñor Aleman did us proud with an inaugural Mass conducted in person, with the choir from the cathedral. In return he was presented with a rosary made from knitted wool and calafate wood by one of Monica's craftspeople. Out on the farm the next day there was a large *asado* for all the farm people, both present and as many past as could come. A special bus took people out from Rio Gallegos, and over 200 sat down to lunch in the bale shed, the only building large enough. Former employees came who had worked there as many as forty years before and some had travelled from Punta Arenas and elsewhere for the occasion. Every person currently on the books got a medal, and those with ten years' service or more (about 35 per cent of the workforce) received an engraved silver salver. It was a warm and friendly occasion which bore out the positive aspect of the personal, labour and social relationships which we and our predecessors had built up over so many years.

It was, perhaps, fitting that in Condor's centenary year we should set up a historical first – that of importing deep-frozen ram semen into Argentina. While in Australia with Michael in 1983 we had come across the trail of the Booroola Merino. Now the production of twins in sheep is very desirable, but hitherto twinning had been known to be inherited only through females as a function of their ovulation rate. (2) The Booroola genotype had first been discovered by CSIRO, and rams carrying a specific gene for twinning had been detected and tested. In New Zealand we had found a breeder, James Innes of Haldon Station, who was breeding Booroola rams and so in 1986 we arranged to import a shipment of frozen semen.

New techniques had been developed in order to inseminate with this material, which the reader will find described in the Appendix II. The existing Condor artificial insemination set-up had been developed over some twenty years with the technical guidance of our consultant veterinarian, Dr

Unveiled in December 1985 in honour of the settler communities, the centenary monument has a guard of honour provided by the Coastguards.

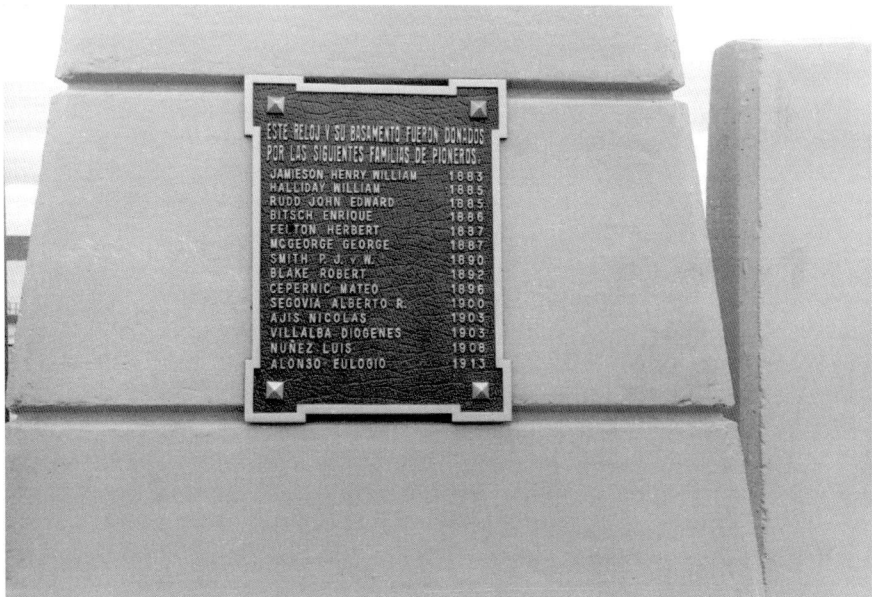

The plaque on the Centenary Monument, in memory of the earliest settlers.

Ben Griffin, grandson of George Macgeorge (see page 54). For the Booroola operation he and his son Benjie had got together with the Department of Veterinary Medicine of the University of Buenos Aires and come up with a simple technique, which Benjie had used with success that season, obtaining a very satisfactory rate of pregnancy, thus introducing the gene for twinning into the Condor stud flock.

Congresses

Further development of the Cormo Argentino breed at Condor had now reached the stage of producing statistical results. Each year that went by added a few more, and the original objectives had by now been fully achieved. The vital one – that of increasing the value of the wool clip, was successful in that Cormo wool was selling for around 35 per cent more than Corriedale. Lambing rates, once a matter of some concern, continued to rise, and the rate of food conversion into live-weight increased. We felt it was time to start to inform the outside world, and in March 1986 I had presented a paper on the breed at the Annual Congress of the Argentine Association for Animal Production at San Martin de Los Andes, Rio Negro. This was well received by the scientific fraternity, who paid me the compliment of referring to me as '*Ingeniero Agronomo*' even though I had never registered my Cambridge degree in Argentina. We had gone up by car, and the return trip was enlivened by the World football (soccer) Cup being played in Mexico, which Argentina was eventually to win after beating England in a hotly debated semi-final with some rather dodgy play (known in Argentina as 'the Hand of God') by star centre forward Diego Maradona. The matches were being televised in every hotel, and we were actually in Bariloche for this one.

We had not been home for long when the thrilling news came through that we would be grandparents – Alison was expecting a baby in November! After a few months it transpired that twins were on the way, and so on 23 November Richard and William arrived safely into this world. This made a visit to England highly desirable so feeling by now quite at home among the scientists, we put together a trip on which we first went to the Second World Merino Congress in Madrid, and from there we would carry on to the UK.

This was our first big international congress, and determined to get the most mileage out of it we had put our names down for a pre-congress tour into Estremadura, visiting areas not usually reached by the regular tours. We found ourselves on a bus with South Africans, Australians and New Zealanders and our old friend Clair Terrill from Dubois, Idaho (see page 275). We were the only Spanish speakers among the 180 passengers, and although the travel agency had provided a guide/interpreter on each of the four buses, these girls were not up to translating sheep jargon from Down Under. We were given a reception that first evening in the town of Zafra, and the head of each delegation felt obliged to express their thanks, so the translation of these speeches was rather wearying. I, as the sole Argentine delegate, delivered our thanks in Spanish, much to the relief of our hosts. We were fêted at every town, usually twice a day (lunch and evening) and after the first one I suggested that I express the thanks of everybody, and by the time we got back to Madrid had become official interpreter and was invited by the organisers to translate at the main reception given by the *alcalde* (mayor) of Madrid!

Quite early in the tour I was approached by the Australians on a matter of politics. The First World Merino Congress had been organised four years before in Australia, and the problem was where to hold the third one. There was known to be a strong bid by the communist bloc, and another by South Africa (still with apartheid), so the Aussies wanted to dodge both by proposing Argentina. I was very glad when we got back to Madrid to find that there was indeed an Argentine delegation (who had not gone on the tour) who agreed with me that we could not possibly invite such an important event without prior government support. So in the end the 1990 congress went to South Africa. I was later to be invited to give a keynote presentation, which I had regretfully to decline.

From Madrid we proceeded to Britain to see our grandchildren. Trevor had taken up the offer of a partnership in a practice in Worcester, so they had moved there from Taunton and were living in a rented house while looking around, indeed while we were there they found 'Green Roof' in Lower Broadheath, convenient to the surgery which was in St John's and also on the right bank of the river. Here they were to make their home for over ten years.

Perhaps it was inevitable that Stuart, in his second year at St Andrew's, should have enrolled in the first course in genetics there, as opposed to natural science, and to pursue computer science within it, winning the university computer prize as well. Now into his last year, he had been head-hunted by ICI for some rather special work requiring genetics with computer science. It was just the time when all the big agricultural chemical firms got the wind up over 'genetic engineering' – i.e. the creation of new species of crop plants, inherently resistant to pests and thus requiring few chemicals. Consequently they were busy buying up all the important seed firms worldwide. ICI required a system to be written to tie it all together. But first came his graduation to which we decided to take Frances who was on the point of finishing at St George's, being one of the first class to take the International Baccalaureate as well as the *Bachillerato Nacional*, and successfully completed both courses by the end of 1986. So we decided to give her a trip round the world before she continued her university studies.

Michael by now had also been moved on. While still at Charleston, he had been offered a job by Prouvost Lefebvre who were planning to start a wool-combing mill in Argentina and wanted a smart young Argentine graduate to work alongside the French technicians. He was given a three-month training period at their central plant in Tourcoing, Flanders, but before he finished this the Argentine government turned the project down - the Alfonsin Radical administration was very inward looking and not in favour of foreign investment in the country. Michael was sent instead first to Wellington in New Zealand, and then to Sydney. We therefore planned to go to first to Australia with Frances, see Michael and then carry on round the world to the UK in time for Stuart's graduation.

The family has always held that I set this trip up in order to be in Australia and New Zealand for the first Rugby World Cup. This is quite untrue – it was merely a happy coincidence! Frances went on ahead, to spend a few weeks on farms in Tasmania whose owners had visited us at Condor at various times, including the Downies of Dungrove, who had bred the original (Australian) Cormo sheep. Michael had obtained leave, so we all met up in Wellington. Then we went over to South Island and drove down to Christchurch, visiting farms and old friends in Canterbury and also in the Mackenzie country. Then we went to Sydney, and embarked on a similar tour of New South Wales. After this we went down to Adelaide to visit the South Australian Merino studs and justify the trip as far as my employers were concerned, as we set up the purchase of three important rams to be

Selecting rams for export in South Australia. Frances taking notes.

flown over to Buenos Aires. And yes, we did see some rugby matches, mostly on TV, but were fortunate in being at the Sydney cricket ground when France beat Australia – a real cliffhanger of a game. We were surrounded by French supporters and the tension was tremendous.

We continued on to Hong Kong and then via Gatwick to Edinburgh where Chacho met us and drove us to St Andrew's where we soon recovered from our jet lag in that ancient town, set on the windswept coast of the Kingdom of Fife (the kings of Scotland lived at Dunfermline prior to the union with England in 1603), at the same time the home of golf and of the oldest university in Scotland (est. 1411, the third oldest in Britain). We discovered that the university owns much of the town, where there are many forms of hostelries from bed-and-breakfast in private houses to large hotels, all catering for visitors to the golf. This generates a very important income whereby the university is able to keep its own character and a certain independence relative to the Ministry of Education. Cambridge and Oxford are less fortunate in this respect.

After the graduation ceremony we continued our tour up the east coast to John O'Groats, then across to Durness on the equally exposed north-west where we found a Highland games meet going on in spite of the rain, and Chacho ran in the 400 yard race. Then we headed on down through the Highlands in the general direction of Skye, and quite by chance the landlady of our overnight cottage near Ullapool knew Ethel Kennedy (see page 108) and told us where to find her. This we did, and she gave us coffee and was thrilled to talk about old times at San Julian.

Alison had found a house for us at Broad Green and we settled in for a month there with Stuart and Frances, and Stephen could come down from Birmingham for his days off. There is delightful country westwards up the Teme Valley towards Hereford and the Welsh border; the Malvern hills are just down the road and we took many a charming trip by way of relaxing after rugged Patagonia. We also made the usual forays to visit friends and relations, and it was while we were there that we first heard of the proposed sale of Hill Cove (page 379).

Arctic to Antarctic

My name was now on the mailing list of the world scientific community, so I received notice of the Sixth World Conference on Animal Production to be held in Helsinki, Finland, in July 1988. This seemed a good opportunity to present our new Cormo Argentino breed to the world, so I offered to contribute a paper and was accepted. The conference was preceded by another in Paris, the Third World Congress on Sheep and Beef Cattle Breeding, so that world savants visiting Europe could conveniently attend both events, and we decided to join their number.

Although cattle have been inseminated with frozen semen for many years, there are a number of difficulties which have limited its use in sheep. I had delivered a paper on the subject to a symposium at the University of Lomas de Zamora in December 1987, so now I wrote one specifically for the congress in Paris which was accepted. Hence in June 1988 we were back in Britain, and at Gatwick joined a group flying to Marseilles for a pre-congress tour of sheep-interest places in the Camargue, the Massif Central, Roquefort (cheese), Mazamet (sheepskins and rugby football) and across to Bordeaux (wine). We found breeds we never knew existed, learned much about sheep dairying and cheesemaking and more than we needed about artificial insemination. In France there is a far greater gap than there is in either Britain or in Argentina between growers and technicians, and we were struck by the lengths gone to by the latter to keep it that way. It was very much a case of 'Why do it simply when it can be so beautifully complicated?' – requiring the professional services of technicians and scientists. The relatively simple process of artificial insemination we had developed with Ben Griffin at Gap would never have done for the French.

In Paris we combined attending the conference with visiting Notre Dame and the Louvre, and exploring the lovely little restaurants on the Left Bank. Then we joined a post-conference tour to Munich to see yet other forms of beef and sheep growing, including totally stabled livestock behind closed doors in otherwise apparently built-up villages, not a blade of grass in sight. Munich was full of raucous Dutch football fans, only a few degrees less so than the English, so we kept close to the hotel. Most of our group then continued by bus to Hamburg and then by air to Helsinki.

The conference was extremely well organised, and the Finns were superlative in their hospitality. The whole world being in theory present, the sole official language was English but nearly all the staff attending the conference centre were students speaking some other language so as to make the visitors feel at home. My paper ['*Cormo Argentino: development of a new breed for wool and meat production in the higher latitudes*'] was presented in poster form, but the technical committee found it of sufficient interest (and merit) to be delivered to the conference verbally, which I duly did. I was also asked to moderate one of the sessions of paper presentations and the ensuing discussion. Another day we all separated by species, and the sheep people (about sixty) spent the day in session at the Finnish Sheep Centre. There are less than a million sheep in Finland, in spite of being the home of the 'Finnsheep' breed, which is noted for high lactation as well as being able to breed out of season (Colburn had used Finnsheep in his Colbred project for this reason). Before leaving Finland we took a post-congress tour up to Lapland, beyond the Arctic circle, to Rovaniemi and on to Ivalo in 68°N, passing a road junction saying 'To Murmansk' just in case we did not realise quite where we were. We saw reindeer, Lapps, Santa Claus village and giant mosquitoes. We panned for gold in streams and had our first sauna bath, all in company with eminent scientists like our old friend Clair Terrill and Professor Bradford from California. I have an imperishable memory of Clair in the sauna . . .

Thinking we should make the most of our visit to Scandinavia, from Helsinki we proceeded slowly westwards, first by the overnight ferry to Stockholm, which city we visited for a day, and then by train to Oslo. After another day to look around and take a trip round the harbour, we took the Norwegian train up over the mountains to Bergen, for an easy week relaxing after all our travels. This delightful port and cultural centre was full up, as the annual '*Nordliek*' or folk festival of the Nordic peoples was being held there. We enjoyed going to the concerts, and the grand finale was a folk dancing display by some 2,000 dancers, held at a sports arena.

Back at Condor, we found that Eduardo Menéndez had offered to host a visit of the 'Young Presidents' Organisation', a USA-inspired group of keen young executives whose members had to have become President of their company before age 40. They had organised a trip to 'search for the end of the world' which involved a day's visit to Condor and then a day trip to the Argentine Antarctic Base 'Comodoro Marambio'. This was the first time ever that civilian tourists were taken to Antarctica, and they had prevailed upon the Air Force to take the party on a regular supply flight of a Lockheed C-130 'Hercules'. We organised the day at Condor, which took place in April 1989, and they were kind enough as to invite us to go along on the flight, so within six months we had crossed both the Arctic and Antarctic circles!

The Rotary Club had come to play an important role in my life. Living in camp as we did, I found that by association one made real friends out of people

Visiting the Argentine Air Force Base *Comandante Marambio*. Monica third from right.

who otherwise one would have just known by sight. When travelling and visiting other lands it was good to be able to visit other clubs and get to know other ways. In 1989 I was elected club president, and took over on 1 July. Our club has a strong 'Inner Wheel' made up of members' wives, (3) and so Monica took charge of that for our year in office. The club had built its own premises and inaugurated them two years' previously, and it fell to me and my committee to finish off the property registration and lay down guidelines as to how it was to be used.

I was determined to attend every meeting during my presidency, having never yet been able to meet a personal target of 100 per cent attendance, but in October was laid low with a bout of pneumonia which sadly made me miss one week! On the other hand it produced a welcome visit from Alison who had had a little girl, Helen, on 1 January. This had been somewhat of a drama because the expected date being what it was, they were quite unable to find a sitter for the twins, now 3, so Stephen had stepped in to look after Richard and William. We had Frances (now at university) at home for the Christmas holidays, so it was a tremendous event when Stephen rang us up about 4 a.m. on the first (midnight Argentine time) with the glad news. By October Helen was a bouncing baby, who in fact took her first steps in our house at Condor.

The next event was Michael's wedding. We had met Jennifer Leighs in Sydney in 1987, and she had come with Michael to spend Christmas at Condor the following year, also joined by Chacho. We understand that Michael, in true Blake tradition, popped the question on the beach at Killik Aike. Jennifer's father, Tom Leighs, was a New Zealander and had been a representative of Saatchi & Saatchi in Christchurch, among other commercial activities. He had risen to the rank of brigadier in the Territorial Army, New Zealand having by then no other professional land force. Penny Leighs was Fijian, her maternal grandfather having been a tribal chief, and she together with her sister owned the island of Matagi, Fiji. Jen had graduated from the University of Christchurch and was working with McGraw-Hill Publishing in Sydney.

The wedding naturally took place in Christchurch, on which we all descended in April 1990 except for Alison, whose children were still rather small for such a long trip. We, with Frances, flew from Rio Gallegos on the so-called 'transpolar route' to Auckland and Christchurch, while Stephen and Stuart flew from London to Sydney and joined us with Michael after a notable stag party in Sydney. My old friend Chris Bonner, by now settled with Marguerite (see page 217) on his own farm near Christchurch, having sold his San Carlos property in the Falklands, proposed the health of the happy couple.

Our guest list had inevitably a strong Corriedale element and some were also members of the Christchurch Rugby Union. The day after the wedding there was a classic match: South Island versus North Island, with a number of All Blacks on both sides, so a male party headed by Tom Leighs hauled the brand-new bridegroom off to see it. After the game, and some discussion as we were not wearing ties, we were invited into the VIP lounge where we had the long-remembered experience of Alex Wylie (the All Blacks coach at the time) pouring the beer . . .

The rest of that winter we spent back at Condor, so that I could complete my presidency of Rotary at the end of June, although we did take time off to revisit Salto and the 'Termas del Arapey' hot springs near there that we had discovered in 1985 and visited frequently. So the following year we were ready for a more extended holiday and accepted the Leighs' invitation to Matagi, where they, or rather Penny's sister and family, ran a world-class scuba diving resort. Getting there involved a flight to Nandi (Fiji), then a fourteen-seater plane to Taveuni, one of the lesser islands, and down to the beach by Land Rover. There one took off one's shoes and socks to wade out to a motor boat, suitcases being ferried by boys, and there was an hour's run out to Matagi island, where the coral reefs were spectacular, although we felt it was all a bit remote – maybe we had enough remoteness in Patagonia.

Acadamy Recognition

In the meantime I had been invited by the National Academy of Agronomists and Veterinarians in Buenos Aires to submit my curriculum vitae and details of my professional work, to be considered for the Massey Ferguson Prize. This is awarded annually to a person or group of people who the Academy considers to have made some important contribution to the agricultural development of the country - a sort of farming Oscar or Pulitzer Prize, and like its counterpart in the UK is considered a great honour. We were therefore thrilled to be advised on our return to BA that it had been awarded to me! It was particularly pleasing and honouring in that not only was it the first time that a non-Argentine had been so distinguished, but it was also a recognition of sheep farming in Patagonia and the degree to which some of us had been successful in contributing modern technology to this ancient activity.

The actual ceremony took place in October, in Buenos Aires, at the Academy building on Avenida Alvear. Monica and Frances were there, and a number of invited guests as well as some who had read about it in that day's paper and came along to join us. I was required to give an address describing my work in depth, and had been tipped off that what the Academy really wanted to hear was how the Cormo Argentino breed had been created. But I was able to get in a good deal about Patagonian pioneering, indeed much of what the patient reader has been gleaning from these pages, and afterwards there were some very pleasing compliments paid.

But things in Patagonia had gone from bad to worse, this time due to natural causes rather than human ones, through the eruption of the Hudson Volcano. I wrote the following account in January 1992 from Condor, as a report to my family and other persons interested in Patagonia and San Julian.

This [the volcano] is situated in Chile, some 250km to the west of Los Antiguos, on the east face of the cordillera proper which is quite the wrong place for a volcano as most currently active ones are right on top, or on the western face. It was in eruption for 3-4 days, with a West to North-west wind blowing, and deposited ash all the way across to the Atlantic. This ash has since been analysed and seems to be non-radioactive and non-toxic chemically, being mostly 'primitive crystalline silicates' of all sizes of particles from marbles down to the finest powder. The primitive aspect means recently formed, with sharp edges and therefore highly abrasive. The other physical aspect which is of concern is its hygroscopícity (silica gel and all that). The ash cover varied in particle size and depth deposited, initially with the distance from the volcano and was later complicated by winds from other directions. In Chile proper, quite large particles fell, rendering farms completely useless. At Los Antiguos, sand-size ash fell to a depth of 10-15cm. This can be shovelled and is to big to be picked up by the wind, and we are told that the town has since been cleared of ash.

A triangle from Los Antiguos roughly to Deseado and San Julian recieved much lighter material, 5-10cm in depth, varying with the degree of drifting caused by the wind eddies. Clearly the area is not sharply defined; there is a grading off of the deposits on both sides and a appreciable amount reached the Santa Cruz river. All the land in between, an area of some 150,000 to 180,000 square kilometres, was of course covered also. There are countries in Europe smaller than this. After the eruption proper, the lighter particles started to blow anywhere, according to the winds. Ash has been blown as far as Buenos Aires, the Falklands and Ushuaia. Here at Condor, during September and October, a North wind would start bringing ash after about 10-12 hours,with a gradual reduction in visibility (you could not see the TV antenna on top of the Hill Paddock, from our house some 600 metres away). When I flew back from a trip to Buenos Aires, we were stuck in Rio Grande for 36 hours as the ash in Rio Gallegos was such that aircraft could not operate. The high abrasion factor does jet turbines little good. . . .!

Lots of people in the affected area had to move out, at least initially, because of respiratory problems, including several members of the Mann/Pickering family, I believe both Lydia and Lionel were in hospital at one stage. In the past 2-3 months, the problem of the very fine ash blowing around seems to have lessened. We no longer get it blown down here and I believe most people have returned home, or at least those whose living does not depend on the Camp, and here we come to the real human drama which is the economical one.

Most of the area described had never recovered from the bad winter of 1985 which wiped out large numbers of sheep which were already in poor order after the drought of 1984. The majority of farms in that area are marginal at the best of times and as a result were mostly overgrazed, although some kind of sheep production still continued, and the more efficient were still making a living off the land. The drama arises through the water situation - the hygroscopic silicates settle on the waterholes, springs and any streams not big enough to carry it away, and first form a sort of jelly or morass round the edges in which sheep get bogged and die. If wet it no longer gets blown away but the next wind brings more and so a build-up results which may end by absorbing all the water . . . End of story or at least end of possibility of running sheep in that area.

Some of the stories you hear from people in the less affected areas about getting their sheep out are quite dramatic. At a very early stage those who could set about finding available camp for rent or similar in the unaffected southern third of the Province and the problem was physically how to gather the sheep for trucking. With the slightest wind, zero visibility set in at once, and horses, men and vehicles all had their clogging-up problems. We sent our two stock trucks on one such operation, and the senior driver (the 'Bear') said that when that happened you just shut off the engine, closed the windows turned up the radio and lit the water heater for *mate*!

It is not surprising that it did not get much into the world Press, as it got little dice here. Oil-covered penguins off Peninsula Valdés got more column-inches, and at least some attention from ecological bodies. Ten million dollars was voted by the Nation as relief, in September; some of this is now [1992] being paid, in the form of a once-only payment of $12,000 US per farm, but no serious plan for relocation or similar has yet been mooted that we know of. Maybe a total evacuation is the best (and only) thing for the land, but quite what people are supposed to do, or live on, does not seem to have been considered.

Ten years later, most of the farms in the affected area are empty, of sheep and of people. The latter have migrated, most to the towns and a few still farm in other areas. Some farms are still viable on the coast, and further south where the ash fall was less there has been some recovery. No other active government measure came into effect, so that north of Santa Cruz river there are few properties in production today.

Notes

[1] 'B. E. D. Dale' combined the blood of Border Leicester, English Leicester, Dorset Horn and Dorset Down, all with differing characteristics. I was reminded of Oscar Colburn at Northleach using four different breeds to make his 'Colbred' sheep, using exactly the same principles.
2 Ewes can only produce one birth per mating, whereas a given ram can serve thirty to sixty ewes, several hundred if using artificial insemination. The males therefore are far more efficient in spreading any new character.
3 Rotary International later admitted women to full membership – a hotly debated topic worldwide – but at that time (1989) clubs in Argentina were still for men only.

21

Modern Patagonia

Retirement

The rules for retirement in Argentina for men were to have reached age 60 and have carried out thirty years of service in one or more forms of employment. I had reached both of these goals in 1988, and with the death of Carlos Felton that year we started giving the matter serious thought. Having as it were exchanged Coronel for Killik Aike Norte, we had settled into a comfortable routine with Carlos – he lived in his house while we lived mainly at Condor, and happily occupied the cottage at Killik Aike for weekends or periods of work such as shearing. But now we took over the Big House and started to look more seriously at living in it. We set in train a number of improvements and updates, such as rewiring the whole pre-war electric installation and insulating the roof space. When in 1944 they rebuilt the 1904 house, Carlos and Tommy had engaged the firm of Maples Ltd from Buenos Aires to do the internal decoration. All the doors and windows were purpose-built, and we found the drawings for them. Every room was planned separately with the furniture designed for it, and the light fittings, colour scheme, painting and wallpaper were all blended and balanced. A few choice pieces of furniture and light fittings were retained from Don Herbert's time, but otherwise it was all new. We later went to Maples and found old employees who remembered the 'Killik Aike job' as an outstanding order as indeed it was, and were able to produce the original designs for the furniture.

We had no objection to all this, except that many of the light fittings were rather art nouveau and not to our taste. Luckily Carlos had thrown little away, and in a store shed we found many of the old gas light fittings, used in Don Herbert's day with an acetylene generating plant.(1) It gave us much pleasure to be able to wire up many of these priceless old fittings, some of them still complete with their Edwardian draperies, fringes and all, for modern use! I had brought from Coronel a few pieces of furniture that we reckoned were 'Blake' and not 'Company', so we were able to put something of our own character into it all.

But one thing was lacking – a conservatory or *galería* to soak up the sun and sit in, particularly in mid-season when it gets a bit chilly outside. The Condor house had a good one which we had rather got used to, so by way of celebrating the centenary of both Coronel and Killik Aike Norte we decided to build one. It took the form of a 10- by 4-metre extension of an existing porch, with the entire north-facing wall made of glass, and a purpose-built barbecue grill at the end. We engaged our old friend Vicente Raciatti to build it, and he did a first-rate job, matching it in with the character of the main house (which has a tiled roof – rare in Patagonia). Work started in the Autumn (March–April) and finished in the spring of 1992, ready for Christmas.

There was no sign of the Condor owners wishing to move me on, or of engaging a potential replacement, much as I had been recruited to replace Eric Davies some thirty years before. There was still plenty to do there, so having ascertained that they would be glad to continue employing me even after receiving my actual pension, I applied for this and it was granted in February 1992. I was also entitled to a UK pension arising out of my original Patagonian Sheep Farming Company contract, but this was not due until age 65. In the meantime both the owners and myself were happy for me to go off the Argentine payroll and provide professional advice on a fee basis.

In August 1992, a hundred years after Robert Blake first set foot on the beach at San Julian, the Third World Sheep and Wool Congress was held in Buenos Aires, at the same time as the Palermo stock show. Held in a unique venue, where hundreds of thousands of people go daily just to see the animals, it seemed the ideal moment to introduce the Cormo Argentino breed to the Argentine farming community and general public by exhibiting live rams. Condor had never shown sheep there, but the Cormo Argentino breed was not totally unknown in Buenos Aires sheep circles. The previous year we had sent six ram hoggetts to a grazing trial run by the *Sociedad Rural Argentina* near Buenos Aires, where they had outshone all the participants which included specific mutton breeds, in terms of daily weight gain. We prepared a team of six rams, and reserved space for a stand for the Breed Society (*Asociación de Criadores de Cormo Argentino*) which we had set up

The Rio Gallegos Show. Left to right: handler Velazquez, Sociedad Rural President Cesar Fuatti, John, Frances, Chilean judge Daniel Rodriguez, Condor stud stockman Juan Vivar.

and which was properly affiliated to the *Sociedad Rural Argentina*. We also discovered that Michael Downie, the son of Ian Downie, the original breeder of the Australian Cormo breed in Tasmania, was planning to attend the congress so we prevailed upon him to judge the breed in the ring.

The Palermo show lasts for two weeks, and the *Sociedad Rural* required that the stand be manned twelve hours per day, so we took on a salaried assistant who with Frances and ourselves kept it going, the rams being looked after by Ricardo Pizarro, one of the cadets at Condor. After leaving St George's and returning from our trip round the world, Frances had enrolled in the University of Belgrano, and was nearing the end of a five-year course in Farm Economics. We had bought with our savings a flat in Palermo, near the botanic gardens and only ten minutes walk from the 'Rural' showground main entrance, and Frances lived in the flat while attending university. There was always plenty of room for us all to stay there while in Buenos Aires. The show was a great success – the breed created a lot of interest and all the rams were sold. One of them during the duration of the show was gaining weight at the rate of 456 grams per day, a respectable weight gain even for cattle!

Before the show, however, we went to the UK, where we had not been for four years. Alison was settled in at Broadheath with their young family. Stephen after some years in uniform was now a detective in the Criminal

Investigation Department (CID) attached to the Belgrave Road police station, whose district covered a wide variety of communities, socially and ethnically, including Edgbaston and Bournville and the red-light district on the southern side of Birmingham. He had bought a house in Redditch which was within easy commuting distance of his 'patch'.

Stuart had a flat in Petersfield, near the ICI complex at Fernhurst, half an hour's drive away out in the country. He had duly written their in-house executive information system for them and was now engaged in the process of getting a PC on to every managerial desk, where previously the computers tended to be tucked away in back rooms and handled only by specialists. He was however finding company politics irksome and was working his way towards easing out of employment and setting up his own IT firm. While staying with him we met his fiancée, Carla Jones. Her parents, Edward and Katherine Jones had lived for a number of years in Canada, where they had relations, but had returned to England when Carla, her sister Tessa and brother Matthew were still of school age and lived at Mellor, near Blackburn, Lancashire. Carla went on to Trinity College, Cambridge, from where she had graduated with a good degree and now had a responsible job with Ernst & Young, the well-known business advisory consultants.

Michael was also now in a big company. Prouvost Lefebvre had never been able to implement their plans for a mill in Argentina. Their chairman and prime mover, M. Albert Bruno Prouvost, had gone over and was looking very closely into putting up a plant in Chubut, to such effect that he and Charlie Fleury, the Buenos Aires manager, were on a small aircraft scouting round near Gaiman when they ran into a storm, the plane came down and they were both killed. The Prouvost family, somewhat in shock, accepted a takeover offer from Chargeurs, a French holding with vast interests in TV and cinema as well as textiles.

Michael and Jen were moved to France to be near the main base mill in Tourcoing, near Lille in Flanders, and had spent the previous Christmas with us on their way, and soon after they left us it transpired that they were expecting their first child. We flew first to stay with them in their charming house, not far from the Prouvost chateau, where we got to meet Madame Prouvost. Then we moved over to England where Alison had found us a *pied-à-terre* in Powick, near Worcester, and we made a base for all of them to come and go while we were there.

Emilie Dale was born in October, and Jen and Michael brought her out to join the family party at Condor for Christmas and New Year at Killik Aike, for which we were joined by Tom and Penny, Jen's parents, as well as Stephen, Chacho with his fiancée Carla Jones, and Frances with her fiancé Luis Alberto Barbero. The Barberos were farmers and Corriedale breeders with an estancia near Quemú-Quemú, La Pampa, and had been friends and clients for a number of years. During this visit it was arranged that Frances and Luis Alberto would, after their wedding the following year, come and live at Killik Aike and manage it for us. In the course of the gathering, so as to commemorate the centenary both of Robert Blake arriving at San Julian and Herbert Felton settling Killik Aike Norte, we planted a May tree in the garden.

Benetton

Although I had never been promoted or otherwise moved out of Condor to a more senior position, as the years went by I found myself being used more and more as a consultant, particularly by Eduardo Menéndez. I made several trips over to Tierra del Fuego to visit and report on their own farm, Estancia José Menéndez, and after Kenneth Suggett's death was asked for a confidential report on the operation of the ASL farms, (2) which was certainly an eye-opener to me. It was no surprise therefore when I was asked to organise the formation of a pedigree flock of polled (hornless) Merinos at Maitén.

The justly famous Estancia Leleque, probably the leading Merino stud flock in Argentina, bred horned Merinos of the peppin type, known in Argentina as *Merino Australiano*. As from 1983, Condor had invested in the

Presenting the Champion. From right: Provincial Governor Nestor Kirchner, leading breeder Juan Carlos Gomez, Secretary of Agriculture Felipe Sola (in light suit), Confederacion Rural Argentina President Arturo Navarro.

importation of some quite important sires from South Australia, all polled, which were used in fortifying the Cormo breed. The suggestion was now made to use this genetically valuable material to form a flock of polled Merinos which would be the first one of its type in Argentina. In addition to the Leleque stud, Estancia Maitén had its own Merino stud flock which was really rather superfluous as far as peppins were concerned, and I was asked to reorganise it as a polled flock. This called for maximum tact and diplomacy to avoid the ASL managers feeling that they were being super-seded in any way, but fortunately I had known the Leleque manager, Michael Weaver, since sharing holidays as schoolboys at La Quebrada, and I could not have wished for better cooperation.

But deep waters were moving. The MOP group were not happy about the returns on their investment, but differed among themselves as to the reasons. They reshuffled their holdings in the reformed Argentine companies so that, basically, the Menéndez family became majority owners of Condor while the other two families were mainly concerned with the ASL and Tecka (see page 325). Finally, Patagonia and its watchers were rocked by the news that the entire ASL had been sold to the Benetton family, owners of the world-wide textiles brand. The price has never been revealed, and the sale was all the more remarkable in that the ASL had been making a loss in recent years. (3) Many theories have naturally been suggested as to the motives for this purchase, but the Benettons keep their own counsel.

Even deeper waters were moving in Santa Cruz. Early in 1993 contact had been established between MOP and Saudi Arabia (which means the royal family of that country) in the matter of supplying that country with sheep meat, shipped on the hoof. This trade had been developed by Australia and to a lesser extent New Zealand, special ships had been built, and a few voyages carried out from Argentina and from Uruguay. The pro-posal now was to set up some form of joint venture with Saudi capital, to purchase farms in Patagonia and operate them with the primary objective of providing live sheep for shipping to Arabia. A glance at the map (or better still a globe) shows us that the sea distance from Patagonian ports to the mouth of the Red Sea is about the same as from Adelaide, so that the ship-ping costs would be similar.

In the South Atlantic, pelagic fishing using modern trawlers and factory ships, catching and freezing hake, mullet and squid for both European and Far Eastern markets had been spreading since the 70s, largely displacing whaling which had fallen into environmental disrepute. (4) Fishing licences were issued both by Britain and Argentina for their respective waters and became an important income both for the Falklands colony and for the province of Santa Cruz. The control of unauthorised fishing became a matter of serious naval patrolling involving both countries, and the need for cooperation was a major factor in healing breaches caused by the 1982 conflict. The supply and maintenance of the fishing fleets required ports and provided a welcome additional activity to sheep farming, and a port facility had been built in the 1980s at Punta Quilla at the mouth of the Santa Cruz river, where the water was deep enough for large, ocean-going vessels to operate alongside the jetty at any stage of the forty-foot tides which occur on the Atlantic coast.

I was first asked to visit this port, to see whether it could be used for the purpose of shipping out live sheep. The ships carry upwards of 50,000 sheep at a time, the bigger ones 100,000, so the logistical problems are first to assemble the sheep somewhere nearby and then to load them in an acceptably short time – say twenty-four hours, forty-eight maximum. In Adelaide and Fremantle, the main Australian ports for this trade, the first is partly covered by having good tarmac roads running way inland, but Patagonia is rather different. Still, we made a start and I put in a report and some video footage, and was then invited to join in the discussions in Buenos Aires. The contact had been made by Federico Del Puerto, an oil man with contacts in Saudi Arabia who also owned a farm on the Santa Cruz river, and I was asked to accompany him on a 'technical mission' to Jeddah to talk to the Saudis and generally further the project.

So in November 1993 Federico and I found ourselves on a British Airways flight to London. From our overnight hotel near Heathrow I phoned Alison and the boys, telling them what was going on, and next morning we were on our way to Jeddah. We were put up very handsomely at the Sheraton Hotel, and the next morning began our talks with Mr Mohammed Bawazeer, an urbane gentleman speaking perfect English who was the equivalent of a chief executive or managing director. Federico's English was adequate, but not really up to this sort of negotiation especially when it came to farming matters. Mr Bawazeer on the other hand had no knowledge of farming at all, so relied on a Syrian adviser who appeared from time to time but spoke neither English nor Spanish. Neither knew the first thing about Patagonia.

I had not been able to stitch together a plan as it was not clear to us in Buenos Aires what the Saudis really wanted, and we were short of a lot of detail including costs regarding the sea freight side of the operation. Once we got this, and some idea of how many animals were required within a timescale, we started to put it together. The initial target called for 100,000 lambs per year, something like five times the current output of Condor, so a number of other properties would have to be bought or otherwise brought in on a share basis. Quite a large area of land would be required near the port facility, plus considerable outlay in yards for holding the sheep pending loading, and other installations for handling the fodder for provisioning the ship. The animals would have to be fed while on board, and it is interesting to compare with the early shipments of live sheep on the *Rippling Wave* a century before (see page 61). Range-bred animals who have never seen a feeding trough have to be taught how to use one, itself an important but time-consuming operation requiring both lairage and fodder near the loading point. Argentina being a primary producer of grain and fodder in general could supply it easily enough, either by the ship putting in to Bahía Blanca or similar, or by trucking it down for loading at Santa Cruz.

We were well looked after, alternating talks with Mr Bawazeer and various advisers with visits to points of interest like their vast holding yards for the incoming sheep, and an experimental farm where we were regaled with a typical Arab feast of lamb cooked in a sort of below-ground oven, eye-balls and all. Finally we produced our scheme and showed them a video I had put together showing sheep raising in Santa Cruz. One of the problems was that I was quite unable to work out whether Bawazeer's translation into Arabic of the farming aspects expressed by us in English was in fact correct. Judging from some of the questions which came back down the same route, I had my doubts. However, a basic plan was put together, and the next stage agreed on, which would be the visit of a Saudi technical mission to Argentina.

On the return trip I had managed to squeeze in two days in England, for which in the meantime the boys had arranged, and carried out, a rapid trip to Worcester and back to London, via Stratford where Stephen was playing rugby. It was real foggy November, too, which I had not experienced since

In our flat in Buenos Aires just before Frances' wedding. Standing: Frances with Emilie, Michael, Alison, Stephen, Monica, John. Below: Stuart, Helen, Richard, William.

1951, so I was glad to get back to sunny Buenos Aires to rejoin first Frances in the flat, and then to Monica at Condor. Having graduated from the University of Belgrano, Frances was working part-time with Waldron SA, while in the meantime making arrangements for her wedding in April.

For this we at long last managed to gather the whole family together at one spot, the first time since 1980. Alison, Trevor and their children came early, in time to come down and spend time with us at Condor and Killik Aike. Stephen and Stuart came out alone, but Michael and Jen, now with Mathieu Robert Locke (born in January) in addition to Emilie, were in the process of being transferred back to Sydney so had arranged to travel via Argentina and spend time with us in the south after the wedding – meanwhile their goods and chattels were wending their way by sea. So Frances and Luis Alberto were married in St Saviour's church, Belgrano on 9 April 1994, and we held the reception in the Centro Italiano, a beautiful *fin de siècle* mansion in central Buenos Aires with gardens at the back. This was to be the only one of our weddings to be held in Buenos Aires, so it was pleasing to be able to invite all our friends to share in the occasion.

Frances and her husband settled into the manager's house at Killik Aike, formerly occupied by Eduardo and Daisy Rushen. Eduardo had retired with a terminal illness in 1985, and we had promoted the foreman, Americo Paredes, as overseer under my overall guidance, but the arrangement had not been not entirely satisfactory. We were in the process of introducing the new farming principles and working practices that had proved so successful at Condor, but which needed closer supervision and indeed training. We often went over to Killik Aike every week, maybe with a night in Rio Gallegos coming or going, so for quite long periods we never slept more than three nights consecutively in the same bed. A friend once asked Monica in which of her three houses she really lived, and the rueful answer was 'I live in the car!' An active hands-on manager, particularly if one of the family, would therefore be a great help. Frances had been operating the computer applications for several years, and Luis Alberto was *au fait* with much of the technology. We gave them a pickup for their own use and it was a great relief to be able to ease up on the constant travelling. I had managed to install a direct-dialling telephone as at Condor, (5) so I was in instant touch with Luis Alberto on the one hand and the Condor office and administration on the other.

Moving house

Killik Aike was even more attractive now with Frances and Luis Alberto there, so I had delicately raised the question of a successor for the Condor management with MOP, who did not seem unduly worried. Pablo Peñaloza had retired some years back, and I had promoted Errol O'Byrne in his place. Errol was the second son of Pat O'Byrne, (6) then manager of Cullen Station, and of Naomi Kennard (see page 346). His grandfather, Errol Kennard, had specifically asked me to take him on as a cadet some years back. I had got as far as suggesting that Errol might succeed me as hands-on manager, while I functioned as adviser from Killik Aike, much as Bill Waldron had guided me from Gap. Before any of this could happen, however, young Errol was offered a manager's job in the district and left, although a few years later he succeeded his father at Cullen which had been sold by the Waldrons to Willie van Deurs and Stelvio Barbieri. His successor as second, Leopoldo Henin, had joined as a 19-year-old cadet some five years before and although not yet managerial material, was quite competent enough to cover during the winter. So feeling more comfortable with the various local arrangements but shelving the question of retirement until our return, we took ourselves off in May for a holiday, first to sunny Spain and then on to Britain.

We made our base with Stephen in Redditch, from where we could easily nip over to Worcester and Broadheath to see Alison and family. While we were staying with him there, Eduardo Menéndez rang me to say that Benetton's man of affairs in BA, Diego Perazzo, had been asked by his principals to visit Condor and put in a report, so he, Eduardo, would be taking him down on a visit. That we were away did not matter really as the house staff were there, Frances and Luis Alberto could go over to host the visit and the farm staff could provide any other service required. So the visit took place, followed a few weeks later by another, accompanied this time by Carlo Benetton. Contact with the Saudis had been maintained all this time, but political events in the Middle East moved on and the proposed return mission never took place. It was therefore no surprise to us to hear before we returned to Buenos Aires at the end of August that the basis of an agreement had been reached for the sale of Condor to the Benetton group.

Then ensued an extremely stressful eight months. Once the sale agreement had been signed on 30 September 1994, the Menéndez family took little further part in the operation, all arrangements being conducted by their lawyer in Buenos Aires and the actual physical handing over by myself. Unusually, it was not the company that had been sold, involving merely an exchange of share certificates, but the farm itself, with its livestock and inventory, including all personnel. Everything had to be counted and signed for, and in the case of the latter the buyers had checked the payroll and identified a number of people whose services they did not wish to retain. These were mostly the older ones approaching pensionable age, headed by our cook Otilia with fifty years of service, most of whom were only too pleased to be paid off with full severance pay. I was already off the books, although it was initially suggested that Benetton might later engage me on an advisory basis.

Jennifer (right) and Frances with ewes and lambs in Killik Aike pens.

The big job was to count the livestock. The wool clip and surplus livestock belonged to the sellers, so nothing could start until after shearing, at the end of January. By this time they had recruited a manager, who appeared in February with an enormous suitcase, apparently intending to take up residence with us in the Big House for the duration. We entertained him as a guest for a few days but then shifted him down to the Comedor Chico, which was not a popular move. It seemed that Perazzo and the Benettons had assumed that to hand over the livestock it was just a matter of rounding them up for counting. This was true enough but it was necessary to explain that for over 100,000 sheep in forty-odd paddocks totalling 200,000 hectares this job would take well over a month, at considerable cost, and would further postpone the routine sheep work normally fitted in between shearing and the onset of winter. Their manager had not realised the implications either, but I had worked out an integrated programme whereby the removal of sales sheep off the property, the counting and the regular autumn work could all be carried out simultaneously, and after some discussion this plan was adopted. Luis Alberto was engaged by the selling party to do the counting on their behalf, as the on-farm staff headed by the second, Henin, became *ipso facto* employees of the buyers.

Some counting was done during February, but the process was interrupted by the World Corriedale Congress which took place in Calafate at the end of February, a great event and honour for Santa Cruz. Condor was still a Corriedale breeder, as were the Barberos, so the four of us attended and Frances in particular found a niche in operating the public address

415

system in both English and Spanish. Interestingly, I was approached during the congress by several former buyers of Condor rams (Cormo not Corriedale), asking in effect, 'Now that Condor has been sold, where can we get rams from?' Happily, I was able to tell them, 'From Killik Aike'.

The Cormo breed functioned round a nucleus of which the hub was the Condor pedigree stud flock, FBA [Flock Book Argentino] No. 1 from which depended all the other stud flocks. This system being officially registered with the *Sociedad Rural Argentina*, we had formally asked Benetton if they wished to continue with this arrangement. In accordance with their policy of not having anybody looking over their shoulder, the answer was 'No', so we transferred the nucleus formally to Killik Aike Norte – FBA No. 2. I rather naughtily spent a fair amount of time during the (Corriedale) congress working on this arrangement and the necessary restructuring of the Killik Aike flocks

Back at Condor, we got seriously down to the handing-over process, due to be completed by 30 March. This now included moving house. In forty years of married life we had really only moved house once, when we came to Condor from Hill Cove, as when we moved from the second's house to the Big House it was just a matter of trundling stuff up the road. Thirty-four years on it was a different story, but luckily we had good help. Nelson Hernández, our house boy, was coming to Killik Aike with us, and he and the two truck drivers, Eladio 'The Bear' Aguilar and Heriberto Silva worked marvels – nothing of any importance was broken and only one chair somehow failed to arrive. We officially vacated the Big House on 30 March 1995, thirty-four years to the day after taking over the management of Condor, thirty-eight in all there. The new manager, Marcelino Díaz, took over the running of the farm although the counting of sheep continued well into April, Luis Alberto driving over as required to monitor the process..

Quite early on in the proceedings I had found it necessary to ask Eduardo Menéndez to define what had actually been sold in terms of technology. The sheep were there, along with the pedigree inscription records, the fleece-weighing machines, the artificial insemination laboratory, but what about the know-how involved in using them? I had written three original computer programmes which were legally my property, and there was a computerised payrolling system in place as well as a whole lot of spreadsheet records and minor working tools. None of this, it seemed, had been asked for by the buyers so we emptied the computers and took the files away. At the final handover on 30 April 30 there was an awkward moment when an agronomist who Perazzo had brought down to advise them asked me for details of the sown pastures, of which there were nearly 10,000 hectares, half the area of cultivated land in Santa Cruz Province. I had to say that I had no instructions to provide them and Perazzo, who knew this quite well, had to confirm it. So finally I handed over the stock books, the pedigree registers and the manager's car, and drove back with Luis Alberto to Killik Aike Norte.

Here, at long last, we were really able to set up our own home. This was particularly important to Monica, as in common with Millicent, Edith and other women living with their husbands out on the job in company houses she could never feel the house in which she lived was really her own. Comfort and staff were provided, husbands came home to most meals and nights, and so a home was created and the family born and reared there. To the children it was indeed their home to which they returned from school at first daily, later for holidays, but for the parents there was always the demands of the job hovering over, farm guests to be lodged, fed and entertained. Now, at Killik Aike, we could at last make ourselves a real home without having to ask anybody's permission.

So we left Condor with rather mixed feelings. It had indeed been 'home' for thirty-eight years and four of the five children were born there. We had 'done' a great deal, both professionally on the farm and in creating a home and its surroundings, as well as establishing a lot of very warm personal relationships. But it was still a job with its obligations and responsibilities, and we were now looking forward to being our own bosses and not have to answer to anybody.

We had as far as possible 'personalised' the Company house at Condor with our own pictures and ornaments so that the 'look' of the rooms there was what both we and the children had lived with for over thirty years and was therefore 'home'. When we first took over the Killik Aike house in 1988 we had moved none of these things so now we could start to draw all our roots together. Our wedding presents, Millicent's desk and piano, other furniture and pictures from San Julian, watercolours from Rodney Lodge, some of them over 100 years old now, and heraldic shields from Bridge have all come together now in one place, together with our personal mementos collected over the years. At long last it is really home.

The snow of the century

Not that we did much about it just then, beyond hanging the pictures, as events continued to press upon us. Only the actual 'Estancia Condor' had been sold to Benetton, i.e. the land, livestock and inventory. The company '*Estancia Condor Sociedad Anónima*' remained in existence and there was still a lot of winding down to do. My book-keeper, Manuel García was on Benettons 'not wanted' list, so we transferred the farm books at the beginning of April to rented premises shared with Duncan Pickering (still the company's representative in Rio Gallegos) where it continued to function for a further six months, its main function being to provide work certificates for any ex-employee who might in the future require them to get a pension. There was also a certain amount of paper and other work to be done in Rio Gallegos concerning the sale and hand-over, but by the end of June we could drop everything and take ourselves off to Michael, Jen and their family for a well-earned holiday.

Sydney in winter is much like Buenos Aires, wet and often cold. So to get some sun we went to Queensland, first embarking at Townsville on the *Coral Princess* for a four-day cruise of the Great Barrier Reef. We did not go as far as scuba-diving, but I learned to use a snorkel and Monica enjoyed going out in a glass-bottomed boat for viewing the wonders of the deep. The other passengers were an agreeable lot, some very well-travelled. From Cairns we took various tours, including one day trip well inland into cattle and mining country, and then worked our way up the coast to Port Douglas, the sugar-cane fields and the rain forest, noting the various beaches and attached resorts for future reference! We returned from Cairns to Brisbane by train – twenty-four hours in an air-conditioned sleeper with a good restaurant car. We had provided ourselves with things to do and read, but I never thought I would just sit at the window, hour after hour, watching the ever-changing scenery go by, from the extensive cane plantations with their miles of narrow-gauge tracks through differing types of eucalypt forest and scrub (all known as 'bush'), to cultivated areas where irrigation was available and the small townships clustered, as in Argentina, close to the railway. As a local song says: 'Australia is a bi-i-i-ig land'.

While we were at Port Douglas, Michael had phoned us to say he had spoken to Luis Alberto and it had snowed heavily at Killik Aike. On arrival back at Sydney after a couple of nights in Brisbane, we rang through to Killik Aike Norte to find they had had a second heavy fall, it was white everywhere. We were due to fly back to BA at the end of the week, and before we left it had snowed a third time, in all three storms, two from the west and one from the east, leaving an aggregate of 6 feet (1.80 metres) of snow. Even after the falls the slightest breeze picked up the powdery snow and piled it up over the fences and eddied under *cañadon* rims forming deeper drifts. Sheep sheltering in such places from the freezing wind were buried. Such conditions had not occurred in most people's memories, certainly not at Killik Aike, and most records showed it to have been the heaviest fall in the district since 1904. There was little advice I could offer over the phone. There were no longer the troops of horses to be used as trail-breakers as at San Julian in 1935, and I was reluctant to order out the farm tractor which had no cabin, no aids to traction, and more particularly no experienced drivers. There were a few motor-driven sleighs or 'snowmobiles' in the district, and when we got to BA Luis Alberto asked me if I could find one, so they could get out to the drifted sheep. We found one and sent it down (the transport company took it for free). Once they had the means,

Frances and Luis Alberto spent days out on it, directing rescue operations. Over 500 breeding ewes were thus saved, worth far more than the cost of the snowmobile.

Thirty-five per cent of the Killik Aike Norte sheep stock were lost in that snow, in proportion far more than the dipping losses at Coronel reported by Chace in 1904 which probably amounted to about 8-10%. The heaviest loss I had ever had at Condor due to heavy snow was 13% in1973. Not all the losses were from being buried in drifts – sheep could and did walk over the fences, trailing downwind away from the weather and often ending up several farm properties away. The ones that did not, piled up against the fences and were drifted over. We later found sheep dead on *both* sides of fences, where the successive storms from different directions had driven them. Others carried on walking, so you did not know whether your missing animals were alive or dead on another property. The sorting-out process continued for the whole season – we recovered sheep from farms as far as the Coyle, but there were cases in the district of their getting as far as the Santa Cruz. We also spent months picking up wool. Most ewes were in almost-full fleece and well on in pregnancy, making their getting up and walking that much more difficult. After shearing we sent out a team with a tractor-drawn trailer to go from drift to drift plucking the wool which was in excellent condition, clean and long. The following year we sold over five tons of fleece collected in this way.

The effect of the snow was felt for five years at Killik Aike but longer on some other properties who were virtually driven out of business. It had hap-

The snow of the century. Drifted snow, several weeks after it had melted off the higher ground. Note dead sheep on both sides of the boundary fence, here four feet (1.2 metres) high.

pened at a time when farm production in Santa Cruz was at a low point, mostly due to political factors. The Alfonsín administration had ended ingloriously in hyper-inflation, and the Menem government which succeeded it, while controlling inflation and stabilising the country in many ways, had brought in a number of populist measures including statutory wage increases out of proportion to the activity involved. Added to a slump in wool prices due to over-stockpiling in Australia, the effect was that in terms of kilos of wool the cost of labour increased five times between 1989 and 1995. This was exacerbated by the fact that with the loss of livestock your tonnage of wool was sharply reduced and you had no sheep for sale either, due to having to retain all available animals for restocking. The situation was not helped by having an anti-farm government in power in Santa Cruz, which while it took immediate action during the snow such as clearing roads and sending helicopters out to rescue stranded settlers, all of which could be shown on TV, never attempted to support 'the camp'. The two principal money-spinners as far as the Kirchners (7) were concerned were oil and deep-sea fishing, although farming was still, in the aggregate, the major employer of labour.

Back in England, Chacho and Carla were preparing for their wedding, scheduled for the propitious date of 25 May 1996. We had hoped that Frances and Luis Alberto might come with us, but in February, after much of the aftermath of the snow had been dealt with, he received a job offer in the pampas which could hardly be ignored. The big money in the grain trade had rented land on which to grow large acreages using contracted equipment, and were offering good salaries for people to run the operations. It was a natural step for Luis Alberto, who could also help his father on their family property, so at the end of April he and Frances left for Quemú-Quemú. We decided to postpone our search for a replacement manager or overseer, and left the farm in the charge of the shepherd boss for the winter.

Stuart had left ICI and after a spell with a related company had taken the plunge of setting up on his own, offering his services freelance, and set up his own company, besides moving to the centre of the universe – i.e. London. It seemed that his work with ICI was sufficiently well-known in the IT world to enhance to his professional reputation, and from then on he seldom had long to wait between contracts.

Their wedding took place at Carla's home in Mellor, near Blackburn, Lancashire, and we were all there except Frances and Luis Alberto – Michael and his family having flown over from Australia for the event. It was Whitsun weekend, so Monday was Bank Holiday and, as Chub Coates put it, the celebrations lasted for four days! Many of the guests came from a considerable distance, so we virtually took over the Millstone Hotel. Among other notable features such as the glorious music (choral and brass), and a splendid reception at the Inn at Whitewell, Edward and Katherine Jones had nobly organised an *asado* at their home on the Sunday so that the far-flung members of both families, having travelled so far, could continue to make acquaintance. This amounted to some sixty-five people, requiring two lambs given by the local butcher which Stephen and I cooked (in the rain!) over a fire of beech wood for which Edward had cut down a tree, especially for the event.

Another notable feature was our first acquaintance with Stephen's fiancée, Liz. The past few years had greatly widened Stephen's experience. As a junior constable in the uniform branch he had been commended for a tricky chase and eventual disarming of a villain; then he went into the CID where we heard of some nasty murders being solved, and of a hands-on apprehension of an axe-bearing thief which earned him the Police Medal and the headline 'HERO PC' in the local paper. Fortunately a pocketful of loose change prevented the axe from doing any serious damage . . . Now a sergeant, he had joined the Special Branch and was posted to the security team at Birmingham Airport, where he met Elizabeth Powell, who was in charge of the ground staff of American Airlines. They became engaged, and it was at Chacho's wedding that poor Liz, an only child, had to go through the ordeal of meeting her formidable family-to-be. In fact she was delighted to be incorporated into the give-and-take of a large family, as both she and her parents assured us when we later met. John and Ann Powell live in Sutton Coldfield, from where Ann ran Millarde Fashion at Wilde Green, established by her mother. This had over the years made a particular niche for itself and well-to-do ladies came from near and far to be dressed for weddings and garden parties. Liz had by now left American Airlines and was helping her mother with the business, so Stephen sold his house in Redditch and they moved into a larger one in Sutton Coldfield, with the lovely idea of having room for the *viejos* (i.e. Monica and me), and indeed we have spent much time happily with them, ever since.

While casting around for a venue for their own wedding the following year, Steve and Liz found that suitable places were being booked a year ahead, so they settled on the same day and on 25 May 1997 they were married in the Sutton Coldfield parish church and the reception was held at Moor Hall nearby. Frances had been able to come over for the wedding, so we were again all seven together at one place. So were all four of my family, and the three Lawrence sisters with their husbands, as well as Jen's parents from New Zealand, so once again it was a great get-together.

Gathering the roots

Michael had hired a 'people carrier' and with him, Jen, Emilie and Matty we took a run round 'Blake country', i.e. Somerset, looking up Seymour

The fourth generation: Michael and Stuart discussing strategy over a snack, while out on a sheep gathering operation.

and Daphne and visiting all the places like Bridgwater and the Admiral Blake museum, South Petherton and its cemetery where so many (including my father) are buried, Old Bridge where we met my cousins John and Francis, Seymour's eldest sons. John had spent a season after leaving school, partly with Tim at Hill Cove and partly with us at Condor, indeed we still have his 'thornproof' coat at home. John had returned to farm the Old Bridge home farm together with Francis, and they had been among the pioneers in the growing of organic vegetables, driving their produce up to sell in Bristol and by 1997 Frances had become Secretary of the Soil Association, the leading British agency for the certification of organic produce. From South Petherton we found our way to Winscombe, looked at 'Westfield' from the road, and had a picnic on the recreation ground where Michael was delighted to find the swings and slide he had played on as a little boy were still there...

Later that summer we went to the Royal Show, whose permanent showground is an easy drive from Sutton. There I found Francis at the Soil Association stand, and began to learn about the organic movement. This is, basically, the growing of crops and the rearing of animals without the use of harmful chemicals but the philosophy is far wider than this as we will see below. At first I imagined that sheep rearing, where you have to dip and drench against parasites, would not qualify but Francis said that there were

422

acceptable ways and means of controlling these pests, at which I rather pricked my ears up. It also transpired that he would be going to the 12th Annual Congress of the International Federation of Organic Movements (IFOAM) to be held in Mar del Plata in November 1998.

Returning to Killik Aike after Chacho's wedding, we had to find a new overseer or bailiff for the farm. As I was living there and actively running it, we did not need a manager such as Carlos used to have, but it did require somebody capable of carrying out the day-to-day work and taking charge in our absence. Rather than look for somebody with previous experience, we decided to 'train up our own' and promoted Ciro Vargas, a smart young man working for us at the time as an outside shepherd or *puestero*. It took over a fortnight of Monica and I visiting him, drinking *mate* and talking it over, before he agreed, but in the end he said 'Count on me, Don Juan' and, in the time-honoured way of sealing an agreement which still survives in Patagonia, we solemnly shook hands on it and the arrangement has been extremely successful.

Life for us had now settled into a comfortable rhythm, more suited to our supposedly retired state. We had long since put into place the various technical and labour-saving practices which have appeared from time to time in these pages, so that the farm more or less ran itself with little hands-on activity on our part. As the various seasons rolled by I would monitor it all on my computer and generally direct operations. We would travel every winter, some years to Britain, other times to Australia, and there were few Christmases when one or other of our children did not come to stay with us. What with e-mail and the telephone we all kept very much in touch and momentous decisions like selling the wool were usually shared over the three continents.

In November 1998 I went to the IFOAM conference at Mar del Plata, attended by over 200 delegates from some 62 countries. I had no idea that the movement was so widespread, that it had so many eminent and competent people among its members, and in particular that it was so advanced in Argentina. Francis was there, and introduced me to a number of the English delegates, and he later came south and stayed with us at Killik Aike for a few days before returning to Somerset. It had all given me furiously to think, and Francis put me in touch with wholesale meat dealers in the UK, Messrs Lloyd Maunder of Devon, who were kind enough to give me an idea of prices. It seemed to me that the difference between what was being paid by local (Rio Gallegos) freezers for lambs for export and the sort of price that was paid in the UK was wide enough to cover the extra cost of organic certification and leave a good deal over. So with that encouragement I applied to Argencert, one of the Argentine certification agencies, for registration and we had our initial inspection in April 1999.

We found that, sure enough, it was not too difficult to adapt current farming practice to the simple norms laid down by the Organic Movement.

The animals roam the open range freely, grazing the unimproved native pastures all the year round, so are 'naturally' Organic to a very large extent. The treatment required to keep the very low incidence of sheep keds under control is easily carried out using approved products. SENASA (8) was still in the process of writing the regulations, some of which we were able to keep an eye on to make sure they were workable for Patagonian conditions, very different from the Province of Buenos Aires. One must undergo two years of supervision by the certifying agency before being allowed to market produce certified 'Organic', but it took us all that time to set up a system, find clients overseas and organise the slaughtering. Fortunately our old friends the Siracusa brothers to whom we had sold Coronel had also bought one of the Rio Gallegos plants and were putting a lot of money into it, so I persuaded them to have it certified for organically controlled slaughter and processing. This involved inspections of the plant not only by SENASA but also by technical advisers sent out from the UK by our potential clients. Finally, in early 2001 we were ready to start, and had sent quite important samples to London, when Foot-and-mouth Disease appeared in central Argentina and all meat exports to the European Union (and most other markets) were suspended. This restriction was however lifted for Patagonia south of parallel 42° in April 2002.

In September 2001 Port San Julian celebrated its centenary. I had been in touch with the organisers since the previous year, and had contributed an article about Robert Blake and the founding of Estancia Coronel, to be included in a Centenary publication, as well as information about the storage shed RB had built on the beach over100 years back, the first build- ing to be erected at the future port and which is still standing. So on 16 September Monica and I drove up to San Julian to attend the Centenary celebrations. The book was presented at a gathering which included the descendants of most of the settler families, and took place at the Cine 'Talía', which I was delighted to find little changed since our day, when among other events the British Community fêtes used to be held there. The committee had produced a well-written history of the town itself following its foundation in 1901, and had collected the history of over 200 families, being pretty well everybody whose forebears had arrived before 1930. By way of giving credit to the really early settlers, the descendants of those who arrived before the turn of the century were called up in order of arrival and presented with complimentary copies of the two volumes of the Centenary Book. Blake was sixth in order.

After the ceremony we started to meet people, some of whom we see all the time as they live in Rio Gallegos, others who I had not seen for anything from twenty to fifty years, and yet others who one knew by name but had never met. This process was to continue for the next two days, and it was amazing how many people now living in Buenos Aires or elsewhere had returned 'home' for the occasion. San Julian may have grown a bit, from 2000 in our day to about 8000, but is still very much a small town in which 'word gets around'. We were touched to find that the name Blake still meant something, as from the second day we started to meet people who said 'Oh yes, we heard you were here . . .' There was a Centenary Exhibition with stalls showing and selling goods from all over the province and elsewhere, and a big stage where in the afternoons local dance and folklore groups put on performances and at night there were professional entertainers, pop groups and the like.

We did not go out to Coronel, which had been bought by Benetton a couple of years back (9), but took a run out to Sholls's grave, the now derelict Swift Freezer and Potter's beach. The Centenary proper on the 17th was marked by an immense march past by every group active in the town, and it was good to see a strong 'camp' element, forty or more riders in their finery (both man and horse), and even a *chata* pulled by three horses with a family group of 'settlers' aboard. We returned home feeling that there were plenty of roots still there in San Julian, even if our own had got themselves well transplanted into Killik Aike.

Some months later they were to be consolidated even further. When we first bought the property from Carlos Felton back in 1980, I had taken in partners who put up 50 per cent of the capital, and we worked together comfortably for 15 years or so, I operating the farm without let or hindrance and splitting the dividends between us. When we retired from Condor, I had been able to buy out some of the partners and so achieve a majority of 64 per cent which was virtual ownership but not as yet full possession. In March 2002 we received an approach from the sole remaining partner who now wanted to sell out, so after considerable negotiation we reached an agreement, and the final settlement was made in May 2002. I had invested my share of the proceeds of the sale of Hill Cove with an eye to this possibility so it was from this source that we drew on to complete the purchase of Killik Aike Norte. It was particularly pleasing and fitting, therefore, that 130 years after Robert Blake first took ship from his native Somerset, that we could bring all our roots – Hill Cove, San Julian, Condor and Killik Aike – together in this way.

Meantime – what of Argentina? Following the return to democracy in 1983 the ensuing governments have done little to correct the real ills of the country, namely the top-heavy and inefficient public administration with its chronic fiscal overspending to say nothing of corruption. No country can withstand indefinitely its income from production being insufficient to pay for its outgoings. Argentina stood it for longer than most, but even the wealth of the pampas and the minerals under them had to run out some time. Perón started it fifty years ago, as we have pointed out, and it has still not been attended to.

This is not the place to review the unfortunate happenings and civic disturbances of 2001-2002 – far worse than anything yet seen. The series of events which brought about the fall of De la Rua and gave rise to the Duhalde administration was in effect a *coup d'état* with just the same results, except that the 'troops' involved wore no uniforms, other than taking off their shirts which clearly identified them as *descamisados*, successors and descendants of those who had supported Perón in his time. Wide-ranging and fundamental changes are necessary to overcome the deeply entrenched sectors of political self-interest, which are in turn reluctant to themselves initiate or much less put into effect any such change. There are serious, responsible people in Argentina who are concerned about all this, and new undercurrents can be detected. If they can mature and take hold then there is hope yet.

Patagonia nowadays is a very different place from a century ago. It has been settled by man to some degree but is still full of *mystique* and adventure, with new challenges added to or replacing those faced by the pioneers. We have described something of the development of Argentina, a process which is clearly still going on, and whereas the early pioneers had to cope with physical obstacles, and the difficulties they presented, today their descendants have other problems to deal with, arising out of the human elements which have taken the place of the challenges of nature.

It is a fascinating country.

Notes

1 Several of these acetylene gas generating plants had been installed on farms in pre-electricity days, including both Condor and Gap. When electricity came along it was often convenient to use the gas pipes as conduits in which to run the wall cables.

2 The Argentine Southern Land Co. comprised Estancias Leleque, Pilcañeu, Maitén and Alicura. To my Blake- and Waldron-trained eye they seemed unbelievably top-heavy in the use both of staff and of labour, and hence in running costs. It seemed that hitherto this expense had been offset by the high value of Merino wool, plus the fact that they could run important numbers of Hereford cattle.

3 Eduardo had also asked me to look into the profitability issue. While Condor at the same time was making a net profit of about 25–27 per cent over turnover, the only ASL farm making a profit was Leleque, due to its sale of stud rams and cattle.

4 In addition to the activities of Greenpeace and other conservationist bodies, it so happened that the demand for whale oils and by-products used for animal feeding had been greatly reduced in world markets by the spread of vegetable oils from cultivated crops like soy beans and ground nuts.

5 Telephone service by VHF radio link to farms where lines had not been installed was not readily available from the Argentine state telephone company (ENTEL). The Condor connection took four years to negotiate, Killik Aike a mere two years, and they were the first two camp subscribers to be connected to the Rio Gallegos automatic exchange.

6 Pat's father, Tom O'Byrne, had come to Patagonia at the age of 18 with 'The O'Mahoney', an Irish chieftain who emigrated to Deseado with his entire household. Tom was the coachman. He went on to work on Menéndez farms and became manager of Estancia 'Monte León', and one of their most respected stud breeders.

7 Nestor Carlos 'Lupín' Kirchner came from an old Rio Gallegos family of Swiss and Jewish origin. Both he and his wife Cristina Fernández had graduated from the University of La Plata in the early 1970s, a time when it was riddled with left-wing ideology. Highly intelligent, Kirchner restored the shaky finances of the province and in the process created a fiefdom wherein a substantial proportion of the populace dared not move counter to his wishes for fear of losing their jobs. Farming and other independent activities therefore received little or no support.

8 *Servicio Nacional de Salud Animal*, the department of the Secretariat of Agriculture dealing with Animal Health, include all aspects relating to the export of meat.

9 Following the purchase of Condor in 1995, Benetton had bought Coronel from the Siracusas in 1999 and further gone on to buy a number of smaller farms contiguous to both, until their total holding in Santa Cruz now exceeds 500,000 hectares. My former cadet and pupil, Leopoldo Henin, who had become second at Condor under Marcelino Díaz, was put in charge of Coronel.

Appendix 1

Early History of the Falkland Islands

Early reports of land and/or islands in the South Atlantic have been attributed to Amerigo Vespuccio (1502) and Magellan (1520) among others, but none of these sightings are very reliable given the primitive methods of navigation of the day, whereby the seafarers barely knew where they were when out of sight of a known mainland. The discovery of the islands proper is generally credited to John Davis, discoverer also of Davis Strait in the Arctic, who commanded the *Desire* on Sir Thomas Cavendish's second expedition in 1591. In May 1592 the *Desire* lost the flagship in a fog and spent three months trying to find it before finally heading for the Straits of Magellan. During this time they were driven by storms to 'certain isles never before discovered by any known relation, lying fiftie leagues or better from the shore east and northerly from the Streights'. The islands were given the name 'Davis' Southern Isles'.

In 1594 Sir Richard Hawkins made a reconnaissance of the northern shores of the islands although he did not land. He described them favourably and named them 'Hawkins' Maidenland' in honour of the Virgin Queen (Elizabeth I). In 1600 one of the early Dutch navigators, Sebald de Weert in the *Geloof* sighted three small islands which were thus known as the Sebaldines or Sebaldes and these were also reported by Schouten and Lemaire on their way to discover Cape Horn.

The first landing on the islands was made by John Strong, of the English ship *Welfare*, in 1690, although he made no claim to discovery as he refers to them as 'Hawkins Maiden Land'. He also named the sound separating the East and West islands 'Falkland Sound' after Lord Falkland, First Lord of the Admiralty. The name 'Falklands Land' was given to the islands by an English privateer, Captain Woodes Rogers in 1708. Lord Anson, writing after the incredible difficulties of his voyage into the Pacific of 1740-1744, recommended the Admiralty to have the islands surveyed as a possible 'place of refreshment' for ships heading for Cape Horn and the Pacific.

The French were not far behind the English when it came to exploring, and in 1701 Gouin de Beauchêne landed, and described the country including its lack of trees. He also discovered the island to the south of the archipelago which bears his name. Other French sighted the islands, and named them 'Isles Malouines' after St Malo, their home port. The name first appeared in a printed map in 1712, and from it the Spanish *Malvinas* is derived.

Following the loss of French Canada, Antoine Louis de Bougainville a young nobleman who had been at the Battle of Quebec, made a proposal to his government of setting up a colony with similar aims to those suggested by Anson. Bearing in mind the considerable French interests in the South Pacific, this made a lot of sense. He personally financed the expedition, for which two new ships were built in St Malo, from where in September 1763 they sailed with everything necessary for a new colony, including settlers from the former French settlement in Nova Scotia. After calling at Montevideo to pick up livestock they headed for the Falklands and after some searching found a 'commodious harbour' at Berkeley Sound, and there they built the first settlement, naming it Port Louis. Formal possession of the islands by France was taken on 5 April 1764.

The St Malo expedition had been prepared in great secrecy, but the British got wind of it just the same and in June 1764 HM ships *Dolphin* frigate and the sloop *Tamar* sailed from Plymouth. They were under the command of Commodore John (Foulweather Jack) Byron who had been specially chosen because of his experience with southern regions on Anson's expedition (p.5), and he was required to carry out a voyage of exploration first of the islands and then of the Straits of Magellan and surrounding waters. He entered the remarkably sheltered sound which would eventually bear his name, and dropped anchor off Saunders Island in 'one of the finest harbours in the world' which he named Port Egmont after the Earl of Egmont, First Lord of the Admiralty. On 23 January 1765 Byron took formal possession in the name of Great Britain. On their way to Port Famine[1] they sighted a strange sail which hoisted French colours, but such was the reserve on both sides that Byron did not discover that this was in fact Bougainville's *Eagle*.

The Admiralty, however, continued to hear rumours of a French landing, and in September 1765 sent out Captain John McBride with HM ships *Jason* and *Carcass* to carry out the long-delayed survey of the islands. It was McBride who named them the 'Falkland Islands' and renamed the Sebaldes the 'Jason Islands'. The sailors set up a settlement at Port Egmont, with a blockhouse and turf huts. Gardens were planted with vegetables, and goats, sheep and pigs which they had brought with them all thrived. The British were not long in discovering the French settlement at the other end of the islands, and McBride visited Port Louis where there were seventeen houses and some 130 inhabitants. He requested the French to leave, as his Admiralty Orders required, the French commandant predictably refused,

---

1 The site of Sarmiento de Gamboa's ill fated settlement on the Straits of Magellan. See p.3

and there the matter rested.

The Port Louis colony was quite openly getting supplies from Montevideo, which was part of the Spanish Vice-Royalty of the River Plate. Spain, fully aware of the strategic value of the islands' position regarding access to the Pacific, was not happy about the French presence there and after lengthy negotiations between Madrid and Paris the latter were persuaded to cede their right of possession to Spain, in return for a substantial sum of money. In 1766 the colonists sailed away and a Spanish detachment of troops took over. These were not very taken with their isolation and so called the settlement *Puerto Soledad* (Port Solitude) and the East Falkland *Isla Soledad*.

The departing French do not seem to have informed the Spaniards about the British presence at Port Egmont, and it was not until September 1769 that a surveying expedition under Captain Hunt in the *Tamar* met a Spanish schooner doing the same. Protests were exchanged, albeit with great courtesy, but the fat was in the fire. Actual hostilities were avoided on the spot as initially the British had three ships to the Spanish two, but soon five frigates were sent down from Buenos Aires and the British had to withdraw.

The resulting furore in Europe was considerable and Britain and Spain very nearly came to blows. Great diplomatic efforts were made by both sides, to the extent of history suggesting that a 'secret treaty' was drawn up, whereby to save face on both sides Spain would hand the islands back to the British, who would in turn undertake to vacate them a few years later. Whatever the arrangements were, in February 1771 Port Egmont was formally returned to Great Britain, represented by Captain Stott in the frigate *Juno* and the Union Jack duly hoisted. Stott reported that 'The transaction was effected with the greatest appearance of good faith, without the least claim of restitution being made by the Spanish officer on behalf of his Court'.

Whether or not there was in fact a secret treaty is now immaterial. It was certainly a time of government retrenchment, and there is a letter[2] quoting the intention of Lord North, then First Lord, 'in order to avoid the expense of keeping any seamen or marines in the Falkland Islands they should be brought away after leaving their proper marks of possession and of it belonging to the Crown of Britain.' Three years later, in May 1774, the British formally abandoned Port Egmont, but left a lead plaque nailed to the door of the blockhouse saying:-

---

2 Quoted in Cawkell et al, 'The Falkland Islands'

'Be it known to all nations that Falkland's Islands, with
this fort, the storehouse, wharfs, harbours, bays and creeks there-
unto belonging, are the sole property of His Most Sacred Majesty,
George the Third, King of Great Britain, France (sic) and Ireland,
Defender of the Faith. In witness whereof this plate is set up, and
His Britannic Majesty's colours left flying as a mark of possession
by S. W. Clayton, Commanding officer at Falkland's Islands,
A. D. 1774.'

The plaque was later removed to the archives in Buenos Aires, where it was discovered by General Beresford when he was briefly in control of the city during the English invasion of 1806 (p.9), and he took it back to England.

The Spanish settlement at *Puerto Soledad* continued in theory until 1810, but the records are incomplete. Certainly by 1784 there was a population of eighty-two including convicts, for whom a penal settlement had been set up at San Carlos. In 1785 the administration of *Puerto Soledad* was amalgamated with that of *Puerto Deseado* on the mainland. The latter was abandoned in 1807 but the former was still inhabited, certainly by convicts if not by troops guarding them, in 1810 when the citizens of Buenos Aires first declared their independence from Spain.

Appendix 2

Technical Aspects of Sheep Production

Artificial insemination

Technical Artificial Insemination (AI) includes a variety of techniques designed and developed to impregnate the ewe without the direct service of a live ram. Under natural paddock conditions it is usual to put about 3 per cent of rams or 1:30 ewes, although in small paddocks this can be raised to 1:50 or even 1:80 if closely controlled. If for any reason not enough rams of the desired type or quality are available, then AI must be used.

Much of the basic research was carried out at Cambridge by Sir John Hammond before the Second World War, and soon became widely used in dairy cattle. Its use in sheep came much later due to the fact that ewes on heat do not exhibit visible behaviour patterns like cows do, and because in Australia the highly developed Stud Ram industry could provide plenty of reasonably-priced sires to be used conventionally. By the late fifties, however, Uruguayan technicians had developed both techniques and equipment and all three appeared in Patagonia.

To detect ewes on heat, 'teaser rams' are used. These are usually vasectomised by removing a piece of the *vas deferens* so that they can behave like an entire ram in every way, except fertilise a female. They are turned out overnight with the ewe flock with their briskets heavily coloured, or wearing a harness carrying a crayon. They mount the ewes during the night so the latter are nicely marked next morning and can be parted off for insemination.

The sires proper are usually housed and fed, and are induced to mount a ewe but ejaculate into an artificial vagina, where the semen can be collected, examined, often diluted with a buffer solution and using a long glass pipette a drop is placed at the mouth of the cervix of a suitably restrained ewe. This is known as 'cervical insemination' and is the simplest method. More complicated, surgical systems have been developed using endoscopy, but they need not concern us here.

Breeding aspects A ram used for AI can easily impregnate 200-300 ewes, even 1000 or more in a season. This raises a whole lot of breeding questions,

as right away you have increased the risk of spreading undesirable characteristics unless you are very sure of the quality of the sires employed. It is
usual to carry out some sort of test-mating or progeny testing of potential
sires to make sure they are, in effect, desirable.

On the other hand, if the supply of rams is short or expensive, then AI is
the answer. The entire 'Cormo Argentino' project described below was
carried out using seven 'Cormo' and three Merino sires on an original ewe
base of some 3,500 CDL ewes, although this rose to over 7,000 by the end
of the initial period of back-crossing described below. At this point our
genetical adviser, Dr Helen Newton Turner (page 275) recommended drop-
ping AI for a period of years, to avoid the pitfalls of using untested sires. It
was not for another ten years, once we had a supply of home-bred outstanding sires coming forward, that we reverted to Insemination.

Booroola project

The inheritance of factors which lead to the production of twins is mostly
concerned with the hormonal balance and ovulation rates of females.
However a gene has been discovered which operates in the ram, and this has
been called the 'Booroola' Gene, found in the 'Booroola' strain of Merino.
It is a straightforward Mendelian character, which can be present in a single
dose (heterozygous) or double dose (homozygous). The latter will thus pass
the twinning character on to *all* its progeny, male and female.

In order to raise the twinning rate of our Cormo Argentino breed, we
wished to introduce this influence. The possibility of purchasing live
homozygous rams (which could be imported) was remote, but we found a
breeder in New Zealand who had such rams standing at stud, and was prepared to sell us semen from them.

The use of deep-frozen sheep semen presents a number of problems not
met with in cattle, in which it is widely used. Techniques have been developed whereby, using endoscopy, thawed sheep semen is placed directly into
the ova in a surgical operation via the abdominal cavity. This is clearly a
complex and expensive operation, consequently its use is justified only for
high-priced stud animals.

An alternative technique, using a buffer solution to absorb the thawed
semen and applied per the cervix like 'normal' AI described above, was
developed in Argentina and has been described in world scientific literature.

'Cormo Argentino' breed

This was basically a multiple cross-breeding project, carried out at several
centres, with the overall objective of creating a type of sheep carrying much

finer (and thereby more valuable) wool than the Corriedale breed being used all over southern Patagonia, but maintaining (or hopefully improving) its lambing and meat production aspects.

First of all, at 'Dungrove', Tasmania, Australia, Corriedale (CDL) was crossed with Merino, starting in 1963. The latter were of a super-fine-woolled type commonly grown in Tasmania, while the former were Australian in type, which differs from both the New Zealand and South American types of CDL. The resultant 'new breed' was called *Cormo* by its creators.

Next, on Estancia Condor in Argentina, Merino rams of the 'Peppin' type, fine-woolled but less so than the Tasmanian type, were crossed with Corriedale, and the first cross progeny were termed 'MX'. These were considered to be lacking in meat-production capabilities, especially when it was found that the Australian-bred Cormo had wool just as fine as the Peppin Merino in spite of being already half Corriedale.

Both imported Cormo and home-bred MX rams were mated in 1970 at Condor to CDL ewes, the resulting offspring therefore carried one quarter Merino and three quarters CDL blood and were termed 'CX'. We must note however at this point that two sources of Merino and two sources of CDL had been mixed together.

We liked the look of the CX type but tried a further step by crossing again, CX rams on CDL ewes to produce a one-eighth Merino/seven-eighths CDL which we termed 'CCX'. These were fine for meat and carcass quality, but we felt the wool could be finer. So by way of really 'stirring the pot' we back-crossed CX rams on CCX ewes and *vice versa*, and bingo – there was the answer! The resultant type was, to look at, different in phenotype to the Tasmanian Cormo, and quite different in genotype, so we registered it in Argentina as a breed in its own right, called 'CORMO ARGENTINO'.

Quadruple teats

The udder of domestic sheep comprises two mammary glands, normally each provided with one teat. (The cow has four 'quarters'.) Occasionally however females may be born with four or more teats, which may or may not be functional (i.e. produce milk), and genes for this character have been shown to be hereditable in several breeds. The commonest condition is known as '4x4', where four functional teats are present, two on each side.

The heredity of this condition has been shown to be hormone-oriented, along with high ovulation rates and milk production, all tending to increase lamb production and growth. The presence of multiple teats therefore allows the grower to select his replacements visually for higher reproduction rates.

Face Cover

When sheep are bred for wool rather than meat, it is not unusual for it to grow on all parts of the body, right down the legs and also on the face and down the nose. This can create a condition known as 'wool-blindness' where the vision is physically impaired by the presence of wool. The animal simply can not see to get around, and is, in effect, blind. Apart from the physical risk of falling into streams or over cliffs, even with reduced vision its well-being is affected, it spends too much time just getting around and less time in foraging, consequently it loses condition and grows less wool, and both males and females are less fecund.

At first glance the condition can easily be remedied by 'wigging' or 'eye-clipping' the wool away from the face, thus restoring full vision, and many flocks in Patagonia carry out this operation three or even four times in the year. But there is more to it than that, and it was soon found that animals with excessive face cover, even if clipped weekly so that it can always see clearly, still grow less wool, puts on weight less readily and weans less lambs than those with open (wool-less) faces.

During my time at Condor we followed up the research carried out on this subject in New Zealand, and proved all these points to our satisfaction. The characteristics involved are all directly inheritable, and today the desirability of 'open-faced sheep' is accepted by all the wool-growing breed societies.

Keds or 'ticks'

The sheep ked (*Melophagus Ovinus*) is a wingless fly specific to the sheep. It is often wrongly called 'tick' but should not be confused with the true ticks (*Ixodes spp, Boophilus spp*) of which some (*I. Ricinus*) do attack sheep but are not found in Patagonia. Keds suck blood and cause irritation, but not to the extent of scab. Heavy infestations cause loss of body condition, but more importantly stain the wool a greenish colour and give off a characteristic odour. The staining is difficult if not impossible to remove in the scouring process, and this aspect is really more serious to the farmer than the loss of condition which also occurs. If a visiting wool buyer detects a whiff of 'tick stain' in a shearing shed he may well lower his offering price.

Like scab, the pupa stage lasts ten days, so that to avoid re-infestation the insecticide used must retain its efficiency for at least this period and in fact most modern products last considerably longer.

Dipping in a swim or plunge bath was the traditional treatment until various types of spraying equipment started to be marketed after the Second World War. These were of two types, the first being a low pressure/high volume system known as a 'sheep shower', where the fleece was saturated to the skin. This had exactly the same effect as plunge dipping, but with far less stress to the animal and therefore quicker to carry out. A later development was 'tip-spraying', a high pressure/low volume system in which the sheep passes through a fine mist which merely wets the surface of the fleece, leaving it to the chemicals to do the rest. As many as 2000 sheep can be tip-sprayed per hour, as against 600 or so in a dip.

The products thus applied to the tip of the fleece mix with the 'yolk', the mixture of oils, waxes and lanolin which lubricates and nurtures the wool fibre, and so works its way down the latter to the skin. Some products do no more than that, others get incorporated into the body fluids and so become systemic. Either way the insecticidal drug is held on or in the skin where it kills the keds as and when they appear. The protective or residual effect varies from several weeks to three or more months.

More recently this principle was extended to adding excipients and emulsifiers to the product, which could then be applied to a single spot on the withers or a short line along the back, from where the insecticide is 'carried' into and all over the fleece with the same effect. This application is called 'back-lining' or in Spanish *'la gota'* (the drop) and while it needs no more equipment than a dosing pistol, it can take as much as 30 days for the last ked to be eliminated.

Nucleus system of breeding

Any breeding programme must be based on the availability of improving material. In its simplest form such a source would be one or more rams, bought in or imported to the stud, of a desirable breed or type within a breed, such as the Corriedale rams imported by the Blakes from New Zealand in 1909. To spread the improving effect of this new type over tens of thousands of less productive sheep required the design and setting up of a system.

First, a small flock of ewes is assembled, preferably of the same breed or type as the new rams, in most breeds this flock would be recorded in a pedigree register. Female offspring are retained for replacement and the male offspring used to sire a larger flock of maybe ten times the size, known as a General Stud or Ram Breeding Flock (RBF). The function of this flock is to produce rams, usually referred to as 'commercial' or 'flock' rams, for use on the general or commercial flocks which may, again, be ten times the size of the RBF. Flock rams may also be sold to 'commercial' growers who do not have their own RBF.

In the original nucleus system as described, all 'improvement' (change in type, increase in productivity etc.) can only come from the top, i.e. by spreading the influence of the very few sires imported into the pedigree flock.

Objective measurement

This means the selection of animals for breeding, on the basis of characteristics which can be weighed or measured (objectively) as opposed to those which can only be appreciated by looking at them (subjectively). The judge in the show ring, or the sheep classer examining visually, can only estimate the possible effect of the animal being judged or classed, whereas if we weigh the fleeces or the animals we can choose those which have actually produced more wool or reached a higher live weight.

All we then need to know is whether this advantage will be passed on to any offspring. This is called 'heritability' and has been thoroughly investigated by researchers in all the countries where sheep are reared commercially. Suffice it to say here that all the main commercial characters involved in sheep production have been proved to be selectable objectively.

Over the years on-farm practices have been developed for taking such measurements at convenient times such as shearing, and laboratory and support services set up to grade and rank the samples or measurements sent in by growers. 'Sheeplan' in New Zealand, 'Woolplan' in Australia and '*Provino*' in Argentina provide such services today.

Open Pedigree

The modern version of a nucleus system allows genetic material to flow in the opposite direction, via the female replacements. At 'flock' level a certain amount of recombination of productive genes occurs, and provided a suitable selection technique can be designed to detect the superior animals, a proportion of these, say 10 per cent of the total, are selected 'up', i.e. used as replacements in the RBF, from where a similar proportion are selected for replacements in the nucleus.

Where the nucleus is enclosed within a Pedigree Register, it is necessary for the Breed Society or other controlling body to provide the regulations admitting the registration and incorporation of such selected females. Usually this is done gradually, requiring initial registration in a separate list, often known as a Preliminary Register, from where only after two or more generations can the offspring be registered as full Pedigree. This is therefore known as an Open Pedigree.

Sheep scab

This is a serious condition caused by a mite, *Sarcoptes Scabei*, which has affected sheep for hundreds of years. The mite burrows into the skin, setting up severe itching and irritation so that the animal spends virtually all its time biting at the affected part and rubbing against gates, fences, trees etc. so as to relieve the itching. This causes great damage to the fleece with loss of wool, and severe loss of condition of the animal who is left with little time to spend grazing. It is highly contagious. The live mite cannot survive off the host sheep for very long, but its life cycle includes a pupa stage (known to shepherds as 'eggs') which take ten days to hatch out and can therefore last that long, more if the temperature is low, off the sheep. Unaffected animals can therefore pick up the infestation if they come into contact not only with other, affected, sheep but with fences, bushes etc. holding rubbed wool carrying pupae.

Traditionally the only way to treat scab was by dipping, i.e. submerging sheep in a bath or wash containing appropriate chemicals, described in Chapter 5, and this continued right up till the 1990s when the *ivermectins* were discovered, synthetic drugs which can be injected into sheep. They have a systemic effect, i.e. the body fluids become lethal to the scab mites. This avoids the enormous labour of dipping, and allows treatment at any tine and any place, with no harmful effects. Since the drug also kills internal parasites, it is in fact doubly beneficial.

'Stirring the pot'

The traditional breeding philosophy thought up first by Robert Bakewell and his followers in the eighteenth century, and still practised today by many stud breeders world-wide, is the search for 'the perfect sire'. If such an animal were to exist, then it would be bred from, but until such time the breeder is on the continuous lookout for a better sire than the ones he has. Excellence is usually judged on show-ring, subjective appreciation and is very much oriented towards the ram rather than the ewes he may service. Animals bred at this level are individually identified, and records are kept of their descent and family relationships, called 'Pedigree registration'. They are often no more than just that, with no other recorded information such as individual production.

Even when performance or production is recorded, pedigree breeding tends to minimise or reduce genetic variation between individuals not only in physical appearance (phenotype) but also in heritable characteristics (genotype). To produce new genotypes it is necessary to introduce new genes by crossing with other breeds. A simple cross between two different breeds can produce a stimulus to production known as 'hybrid vigour' or 'hetero-sis', which often out-produces both of the parent breeds, but this stimulus tends to fade out in successive generations.

If a number of crosses are made, using more than two genotypes, het-erosis as such disappears, but new combinations of genes can be formed which may or may not be advantageous. Provided adequate selection tech-niques are available, the breeder can pick out those combinations which carry and can reproduce in their offspring higher levels of production. This process has been likened to putting ingredients into a genetic pot (the flock or herd), stirring it well by crossing and re-crossing, and designing the selec-tion process which will select the most productive among the progeny. In theory, genotypes can be thrown up which are *more productive* than any of the parent ingredients.

Appendix 3

Bibliography

Apolant, Juan, *Operativo Patagonia*. Montevideo: Letras S.A., 1970.

Aloyz de Simonato, Camila Raquel, *Raigambres Sureñas*. Comodoro Rivadavia: Gráfica, 1984.

Barbería, Elsa Mabel, *Los Dueños de la Tierra en la Patagonia Austral.*1880–1920, Rio Gallegos: UNPA, 1982.

Barclay, W.S., *The Land of Magellan*. London: Methuen, 1926.

Barrett, Katherine and Robert, *A Yankee in Patagonia*. Cambridge: Heffer, 1931.

Bayer, Osvaldo, *Los Vengadores de la Patagonia Trágica*, 3 vols. Buenos Aires: Planeta, 1972–74.

Bennett, Hugh Hammond, *Soil Conservation*. New York: McGraw-Hill, 1939.

Blake, Christopher, *Times and Seasons*. Castle Cary: Mendip, 1989.

Borrero, José María, *La Patagonia Trágica*. Buenos Aires: Editorial Americana, 1967.

Boyson, V.F., *The Falkland Islands*. London: Clarendon Press, 1924.

Bridges, E.L., *Uttermost part of the Earth*. London: Hodder & Stoughton, 1948.

Braun, Menéndez, Armando, *Pequeña Historia Magallánica*, Buenos Aries: Planeta, 1945.

Castelli, Jorge, *El Delicado Umbral de la Tempestad*. Buenos Aires: Sudamericana,2001.

Cawkell, M.B., Maling, D.H. and Cawkell, E.M. *The Falkland Islands*. London: Macmillan, 1960.

Correa Falcón, Edelmiro, *La Patagonia Argentina*. Buenos Aires: Private publication, 1924

Craig, C.W. Thurlow, *A Rebel for a Horse*. London: Arthur Baker, 1934.

Crawford, Robert, *Cross the Pampas and the Andes*. London: Longmans, Green, 1884

Darwin, Charles, *Voyage of the Beagle*. London: Henry Colburn, 1839.

Dixie, Lady Florence, *Across Patagonia*. London: Bentley & Son, 1880.

Eddy, Paul and Linklater, Magnus, *The Falklands War*. London: André Deutsch, 1982.

Ferns, H.S., *La Argentina*. Buenos Aires, Sudamericana, 1983.

Fernández-Gomez, Emilio Manuel, *Argentina: La Gesta Británica*. Buenos Aires: L.O.L.A, 1998

Gibson, Herbert, *The history and present state of the Sheep-breeding Industry in the Argentine Republic*. Buenos Aires: Ravenscroft & Mills, 1893

Goebel, Julius, *The Struggle for the Falkland Islands*. New Haven: Yale University Press,1927.

Goring, Rosemary, *The Journeying I*. Lewes: New Times Press, 1993.

Graham-Yooll, Andrew, *The Forgotten Colony*. London: Hutchinson, 1981.

Hatcher, John Bell, *Bone Hunters in Patagonia*. (narrative to the Princeton University Expeditions to Patagonia, 1896–99), Woodbridge, Conn: Ox Bow Press, 1985.

Hosne, Roberto, *Barridos por el Viento: Historias de la Patagonia Desconocida*. Buenos Aires: Planeta, 1997.

Holdich, Col. Sir T.H., *The Countries of the King's Award*. London: Hurst & Blackett, 1904.

Hough, Richard, *The Blind Horn's Hate*. London: Hutchinson, 1971.

Hibbert, Christopher, *A soldier of the Seventy-first*. Moreton-in-marsh: Windrush Press, 1996

Hudson, W.H., *Idle Days in Patagonia*. London: Chapman & Hall, 1893.

Hudson, Thomas N, *The Honourable Warrior*. Bishop Auckland: Pentland Press, 2001

Jackson, Geoffrey H S , *People's Prison*. London, Faber, 1973

James, Lawrence, *The Rise and Fall of the British Empire*. London : Abacus, 1994.

Jones, Tom P., *Patagonian Panorama*. London: Outspoken Press, 1961.

Lawson-Clarke, Peter, *The Blakes of South Petherton*. South Petherton: Lawson-Clarke, 1998.

Lawrence, William, *A Dorset Soldier: Autobiography 1790–1869*, ed. Eileen Hathaway. Staplehurst: Spellmount, 1993.

Lenzi, Juan Hilarión, *Historia de Santa Cruz*. Rio Gallegos: Segovia.

Llewellyn, Richard, *Up into the Singing Mountain*. London: Michael Joseph, 1963.

Llewellyn, Richard, *Down where the moon is small*. London: Michael Joseph, 1966.

Longford, Elizabeth, Wellington: *The Years of the Sword*. London: World Books, 1971.

Luna, Felix, *Historia Integral de la Argentina*, 10 vols. Buenos Aires: Planeta, 1997.

Mainwaring, Michael, *From the Falklands to Patagonia*, London: Allison and Bushey, 1983.

Moorehead, Alan, *Darwin and the Beagle*. London: Hamish Hamilton, 1969.

Musters, George Chaworth, *At Home with the Patagonians*. London: John Murray,1871

Newbery, Diego, *Pampa Grass*. Buenos Aires: Guarania, 1953.

Owen, J.B., *Performance Recording in Sheep*, technical communication no. 20. Slough: Commonwealth Bureau of Animal Breeding and Genetics, 1971.

Pigafetta, Antonio, *Magellan's Voyage: A Narrative Account of First Navigation*. New Haven: Yale University Press.

Powell, J.R., *Robert Blake: General at Sea*. London: Collins, 1972.

Prichard, H. Hesketh, *Through the Heart of Patagonia*. London: Heinemann, 1902.

Robertson, R.B, *Of whales and men*. London: World Books, 1954

Skottsberg, Carl, *The Wilds of Patagonia*. London: Edward Arnold, 1911.

Slocum, Joshua, *Sailing Alone Around the World*. London: Rupert Hart-Davis, 1900.

Smith, Sir Harry, *Autobiography, 1787–1819*. London: Constable, 1999.

Thomas, Donald, *Cochrane: Britannia's Sea Wolf*. London: Cassell, 1978.

Tilman, H.W., *Mischief in Patagonia*. Cambridge: Cambridge University Press, 1957.

Topcic, D. Osvaldo, *Historia de la Provincia de Santa Cruz*. Cordoba: Centro de Estudios Históricos, 1998.

Trehearne, Mary, *Falkland Heritage*. Ilfracombe: Stockwell, 1978.

Trehearne, Mary, *Patagonian Harvest*. Private printing, 1989

Tschiffeley, A.F., *Southern Cross to Pole Star*. London: Heinemann, 1933.

Whitehead, Ann, *Paradise Mislaid*. St Lucia: University of Queensland Press.

Letter sources

Letters from Robert Blake to his younger brother, Edward Jarman Blake, 1884–93.

Letters from Robert Blake while at Hill Cove, Falkland Islands, 1892–1900.

Letters from Robert Blake while at Yeabridge, Somerset, 1898–1904.

Letters from Robert Blake to Robert Blake Junior at San Julian, 1909–11.

Letters from Robert Blake to Arthur Blake at San Julian, 1926–27.

Letters from Sydney Miller at Hill Cove to Robert Blake, 1901–35.

Diary sources

Diaries of Robert Blake Junior, 1909–24.

Appendix 4

Family Trees

Rev. William BLAKE ------ m. --- Malachi BLAKE 1813-1820 --- Edith M BLAKE 1845-1896
1773-1821, of Crewkerne

married Hannah (JARMAN) and
after her death married her sister
Elizabeth (JARMAN) ------ m.

Rev. William Blake of Crewkerne
was 2nd cousin (5 times removed)
of
Admiral RobertBlake 1598-1657

William BLAKE 1815-1901 m. --- William F BLAKE 1846-1927
of Bridge, South Petherton m. Eleanor (JONES) 1858-1890

--- Elizabeth (BLAKE) 1817-1881 --- Malachi L BLAKE 1848-1930
m. John ROBBERDS 1814-1892
--- Emily D (BLAKE) 1849-1934
--- Margaret (BLAKE) 1818-1860 m. Fred E COBB 1845-
m. William A JONES 1819-1873
Robert BLAKE 1851-1931 m.
--- Mary BLAKE 1820-1866 **of the Falkland Islands**

--- Edward J BLAKE 1853-1936
m. Alice (RICHMOND)1863-1944

William BROWNE ----------- m.
1791-1859
--- Fanny O (BLAKE) 1854-1911
m. Herbert FORDHAM 1852-

Fanny F O (BROWNE) ----- m.
1821-1917
--- Florence BLAKE 1856-194?

Mary (OSLER) 1785-1877 m.
sister of Thomas Osler 1783-1861
--- Arnold W BLAKE 1864-1949

Rev. William H HERFORD m. --- John E HERFORD
1820-1908
of Ladybarn House, Manchester --- Llewellyn HERFORD

"Dora" (HERFORD) -------- m.
1852-1923

Elizabeth (DAVIS) ----------- m.
1824-1880
--- Caroline (HERFORD)
m. Robert Blake after Dora's death

--- U. Vernon HERFORD
"Bishop-at-large"

--- Anna WORSLEY 1862-1862

Philip WORSLEY ----------- m. --- Alice Sarah WORSLEY 1833-
1802-1893 Watercolourist --- Mary T WORSLEY 1864-1943
of Regent's Park. London
Philip J WORSLEY ---------- m. --- Bertha (WORSLEY) 1865-1923
1834- m. Bryan JOHNSON
of Rodney Lodge, Bristol
Anne (TAYLOR) ----------- m. **Philip J WORSLEY** ----------- m.
1806-1877 --- Richard WORSLEY 1836- **1869-1946 of Winscombe, Som.**
daughter of John Taylor F.R.S. m, Frances (DOWSON)1867-
1779-1863, eminent mining --- Alice Worsley 1870-1940
entrepreneur and engineer, e.g. --- Honora (WORSLEY) 1838-1879
of Tavistock Canal, m. Richard ROSCOE --- Isabel WORSLEY 1872-1948
m. Anne (PRING)
--- Reginald WORSLEY 1844- --- Susan WORSLEY 1873-1952
m. Sarah (PERCY)
--- Katherine WORSLEY 1875-1952

Anna (TAYLOR) 1835- m. --- Arthur A WORSLEY 1876-1966
daughter of Thomas L TAYLOR m. A Laura (DECKER) -1977
Thomas OSLER of Starston, Norfolk
1763-1861 m.
brother of
Mary (OSLER) --- "Dora" S Smith 1873-
1785-1877 m. Cecil CROSSKEY 1859-

Thomas C
OSLER **Howard S SMITH 1842-1912** m. --- Harry SMITH 1874-1943
1811-1876 m. m. Edith (DEAR)

Fanny **Muriel A (SMITH)** ------------m.
(FOLLETT) m. **1878-1958**

Ann **Ellen F (OSLER) 1848-1914** m.
(HORNBLOWER) --- Gerald O SMITH 1879-
1820-1851 m. m. Gladys (MARTIN) 1899-

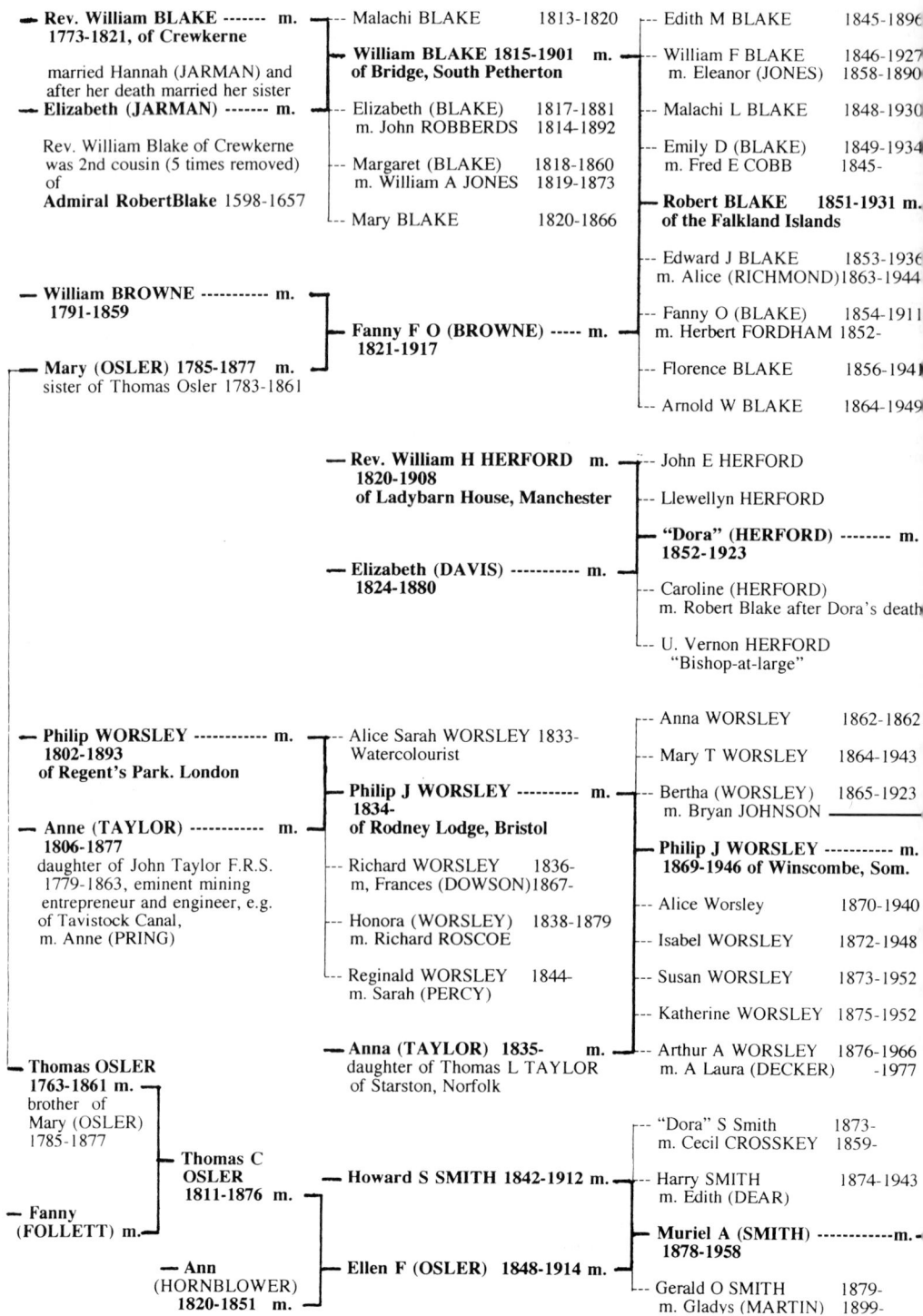

Family Tree of John Locke Blake

Elizabeth "Elsie" F (BLAKE)
1882- 1938
m. James E CURREY 1888-
(Canada)

Robert BLAKE   1884-1965
m. Edith (WEDDERBURN)
1884-1972

C E Bridget BLAKE   1886-

Violet BLAKE   1887-

E "Willy" H BLAKE   1889-
m. Lettice (MARRIOTT)

Dorothy F (BLAKE)   1892-
m. Wyndham CARLES 1892-

Arthur Locke BLAKE -------- m.
1895-1976

Norman D BLAKE   1896-1974
m. Alice (BOYLE)
m. M Wendy (GREENSTREET)
                        -2002

Hubert JOHNSON
m. Margon (JACKSON)   -2000

Anna M "Nancy" (JOHNSON)
m. Christopher SUMMERHAYES
1896-

Millicent Ellen (WORSLEY) m.
1901-1964

Philip H WORSLEY   1904-1969
  m. "Peggy" (SALE) 1911-1991

Edgar T WORSLEY   1907-1973
m. Vida (McCORMICK)
1909-1987

Francis "Sam" A WORSLEY
1910-1988
m. Mary (DIAMOND) 1911-1998

--- Hugh W BLAKE   1930-
    m. L Ruth (SLEEMAN) 1933-

--- Philip H BLAKE   1957-
    m. Nicola (MOORE)   1959-

--- Richard D BLAKE   1959-
    m. Lefoko (NOGA)   1963-

--- Thomas P BLAKE   1963-
    m. Anne (ROSENBROCK)
    1954-

--- Eleanor M (BLAKE)   1932-
    m. Christopher DAVIS 1932-1963
    m. Roderick N DIXON 1928-

--- "Penny" J (DAVIS)   1958-
    m. Charles WATTS div.
    m. Andrew JOYCE div.
    m. David JOHNS

--- John S B DAVIS   1959-
    m. Ann E (MILLER)

--- Robert C DAVIS   1963-
    m. Nicola J (DREW)

--- Stephen M DIXON   1961-

--- Rosemary J (BLAKE)   1935-
    m. J Jeremy GORING   1930-

--- "Charlie" R GORING   1960-
    m. Jackie (GLASS)

--- George W GORING   1962-
    m. Mercy (USIA)

--- Margaret E (GORING) 1964-
    m. José C G GONZALEZ

--- Daniel J GORING   1967-

— John Locke BLAKE ---------- m.
1928-

--- **Alison Jean (BLAKE) 1957-**
    m. Trevor JONES   1954-

--- **Michael Locke BLAKE**
    1959-
    m. Jennifer (LEIGHS)

--- **Stephen Colin L BLAKE**
    1961-
    m. Elizabeth (POWELL)

--- **(John) Stuart BLAKE 1963-**
    m. Carla (JONES)

--- **Frances Monica (BLAKE)**
    1969-
    m. Luis A BARBERO

— **Monica Beaven (LAWRENCE)**
1934-   m.
[Family Tree on adjoining pages]

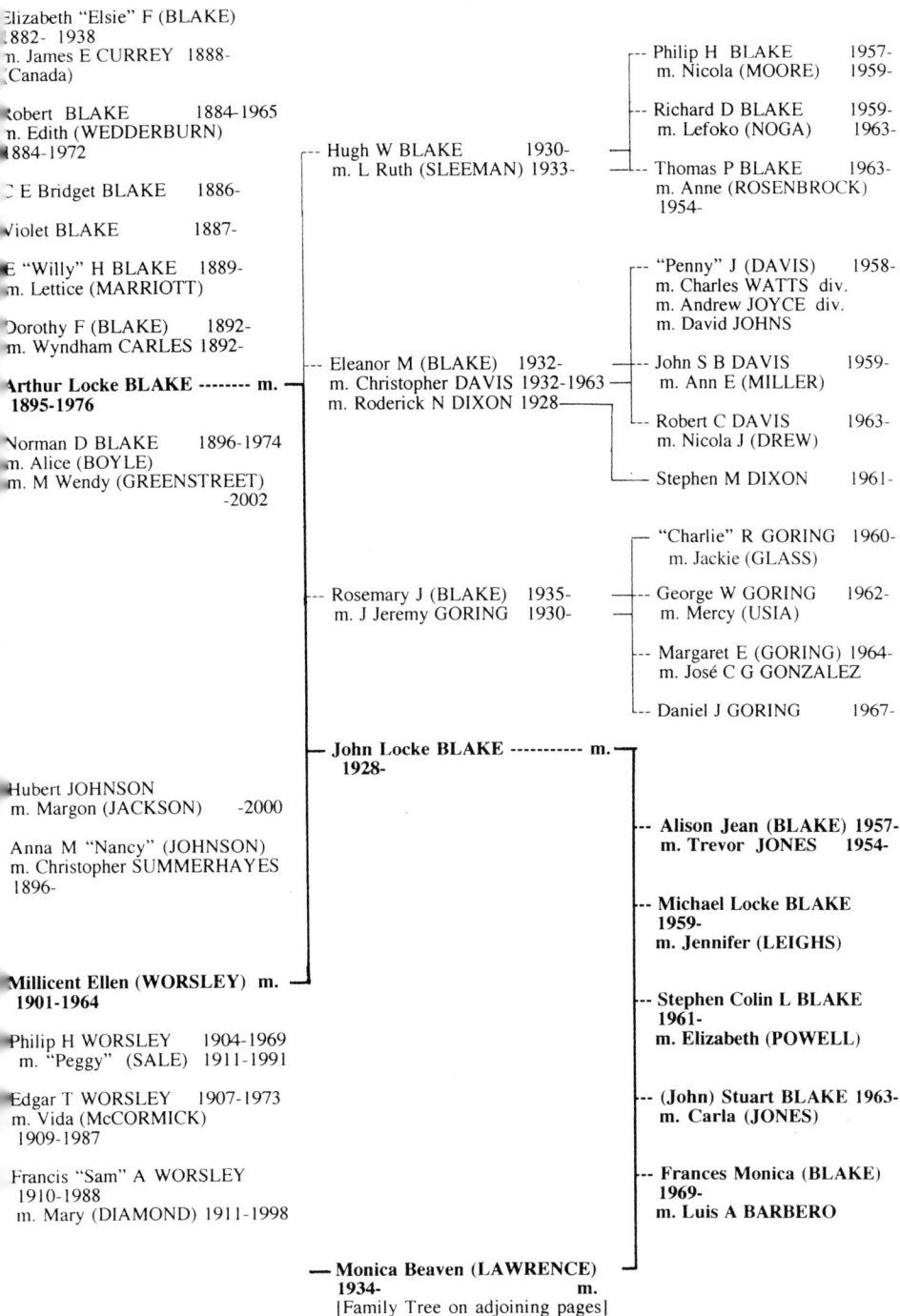

Family Tree of John Locke Blake

— George LAWRENCE 1630-1710
   m Ann (................)

   George Lawrence was Yeoman
   of Brignell or Beacon Hill Farm,
   Hilmarton, Wiltshire, and great-
   great-grandfather of

— James LAWRENCE ---------- m.
   1812-1892
   of Lower Farm, Idstone, Oxon.

— Jane (HULL) 1817-1906   m.

--- Richard LAWRENCE   1839-
   m. ....(GODWIN)

--- William LAWRENCE 1841-1912
   m. ....(CHISMAN)

— James LAWRENCE --------- m.
   1842-1933, of Common Farm,
   Uffington, Oxon, and later of
   Stall Pits Farm, Shrivenham,
   Oxon.

--- Sarah LAWRENCE   1844-1936

--- John LAWRENCE   1846-1909

--- Mary (LAWRENCE)   1849-1942
   m. .... (CHISMAN)

--- Frances LAWRENCE 1851-1937

--- Emma LAWRENCE   1853-1868

--- Matilda LAWRENCE 1855-1943

--- Herbert LAWRENCE 1857-1948
   m. ....(HEDGES)

— Martha(FROGLEY) ------- m.
   1866-1923

--- Edith LAWRENCE   1867-18
--- James LAWRENCE   1868-19
   m. Ada (LAWRENCE) his cou

— Sydney LAWRENCE --------
   1870-1952

--- Beatrice(LAWRENCE)1871-19
   m. .... HEDGES

--- Henry LAWRENCE   1873-19
   m. ....(POLLOCK)

--- Walter LAWRENCE   1873-19.
   m. ....(TAYLER)

--- Ethel (LAWRENCE)   1876-19
   m. ....COLEING

--- Isabel LAWRENCE   1878-18

--- Agnes (LAWRENCE   1880-19
   m. ....WHATLEY

--- "Dick" LAWRENCE   1882-19
   m. ....(SWANTON)

--- Francis LAWRENCE   1884-
   m. ....(ORLANDO)
   m. ....(HATTINGH)

--- Mabel LAWRENCE   1885-
--- Reginald LAWRENCE 1889-19
--- Ida LAWRENCE   1892-

--- James BEAVEN

— Charles BEAVEN 1822-1887 m.
   of Ivy House, Shepton Moyne,
   Glos.

--- Batten BEAVEN   -1886

--- Christopher BEAVEN   -1858

--- Mary Anne (BEAVEN)1818-1887
   m. .... AYRES

--- Susan A BEAVEN   1830-

--- Elizabeth H BEAVEN   -1888

— Elizabeth (WATSON) ------- m.

--- Charles BEAVEN
--- George BEAVEN   1859-
   m. ....(BRAILSFORD)

--- Herbert BEAVEN   1861-19
   m. ....(STACE)

--- Alfred BEAVEN   1864-
   m. ....(...................)

--- Elizabeth (BEAVEN)   1866-1
   m. .... WESTLAKE

— Frances (BEAVEN) ----------
   1868-1952

--- William BEAVEN   1871-
--- Frederick BEAVEN   1872-19
   m. .... (COLLIN)

— James ALMON   d. 1767
   A ship owner trading from
   Genoa, he came to New Jersey
   USA as a young man. His son

— William James ALMON M.D.
   1708-1817 m. Rebecca (BYLES).
   They moved to Nova Scotia at
   the American Revolution and
   had issue

--- 4 siblings

— Hon. Mather B ALMON ---- m.
   1796-1871

— Sophia (PRYOR) ------------ m.

--- 11 siblings
— Rev. Henry P Almon -------- m.
   1837-1880

— Sara F (DeWOLF) ----------- m.
   1842-1922

--- James M D Almon

— Capt. Henry C M ALMON   m
   1865-   of the "Loanda"

--- Sophia M (ALMON)   1866-19
   m. Hubert A HENSLEY

— ---------- WOODS

— Elizabeth Ann (   )

— Matilda (WOODS) ----------m.
   1883 -

— Mary Agnes (WOODS) 1885 -
   m. Robert H KIBBEY

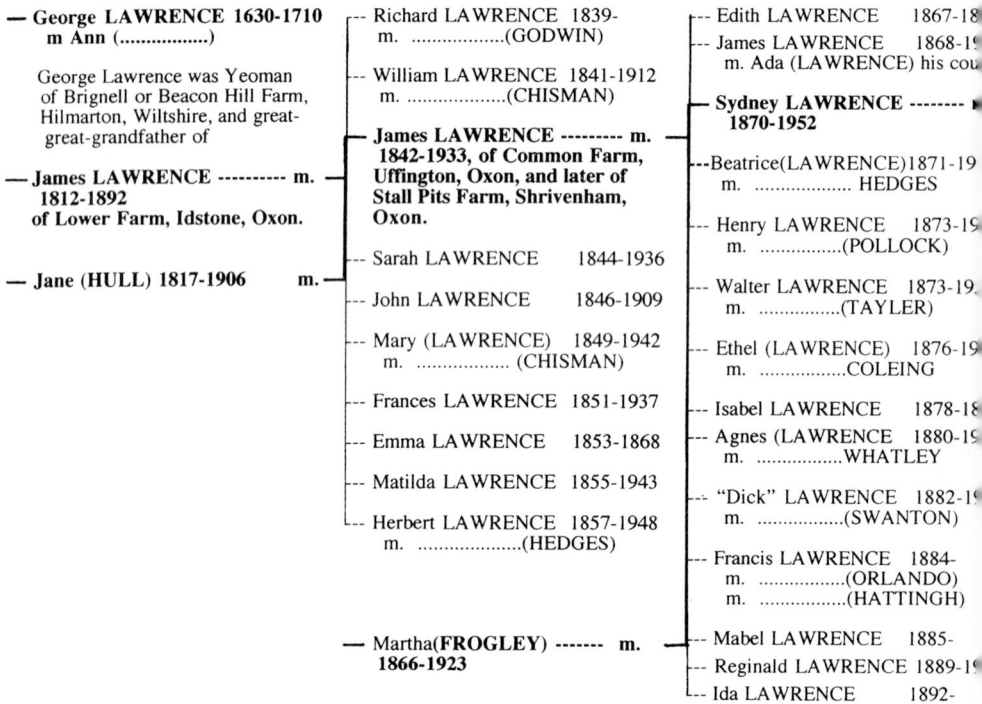

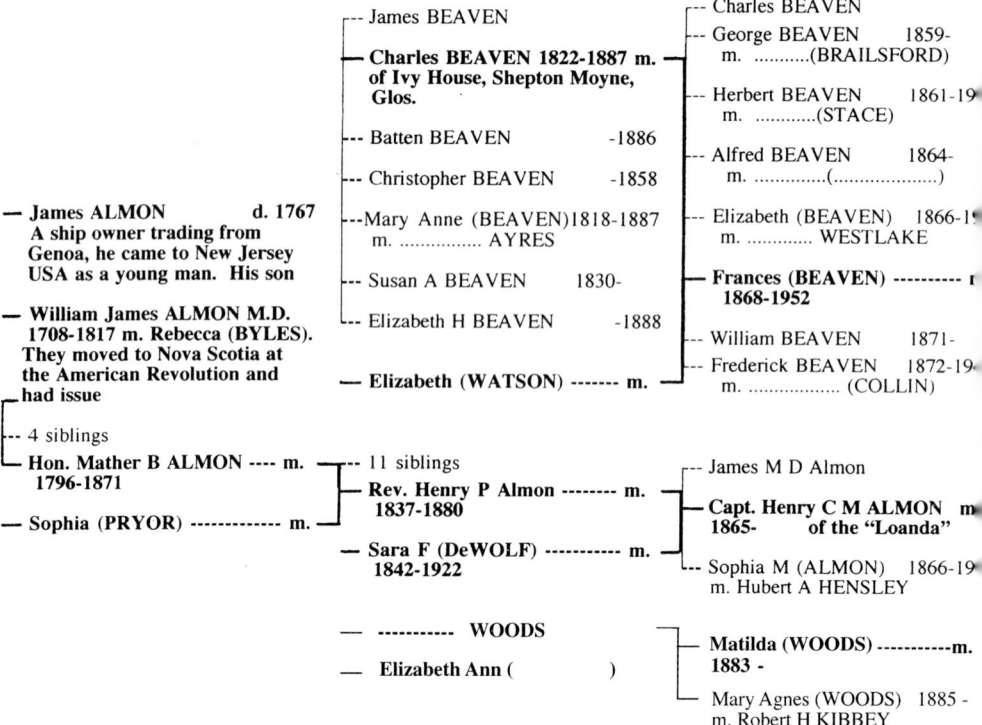

Family Tree of Monica Beaven (Lawrence)

[Family Tree on adjoining pages}

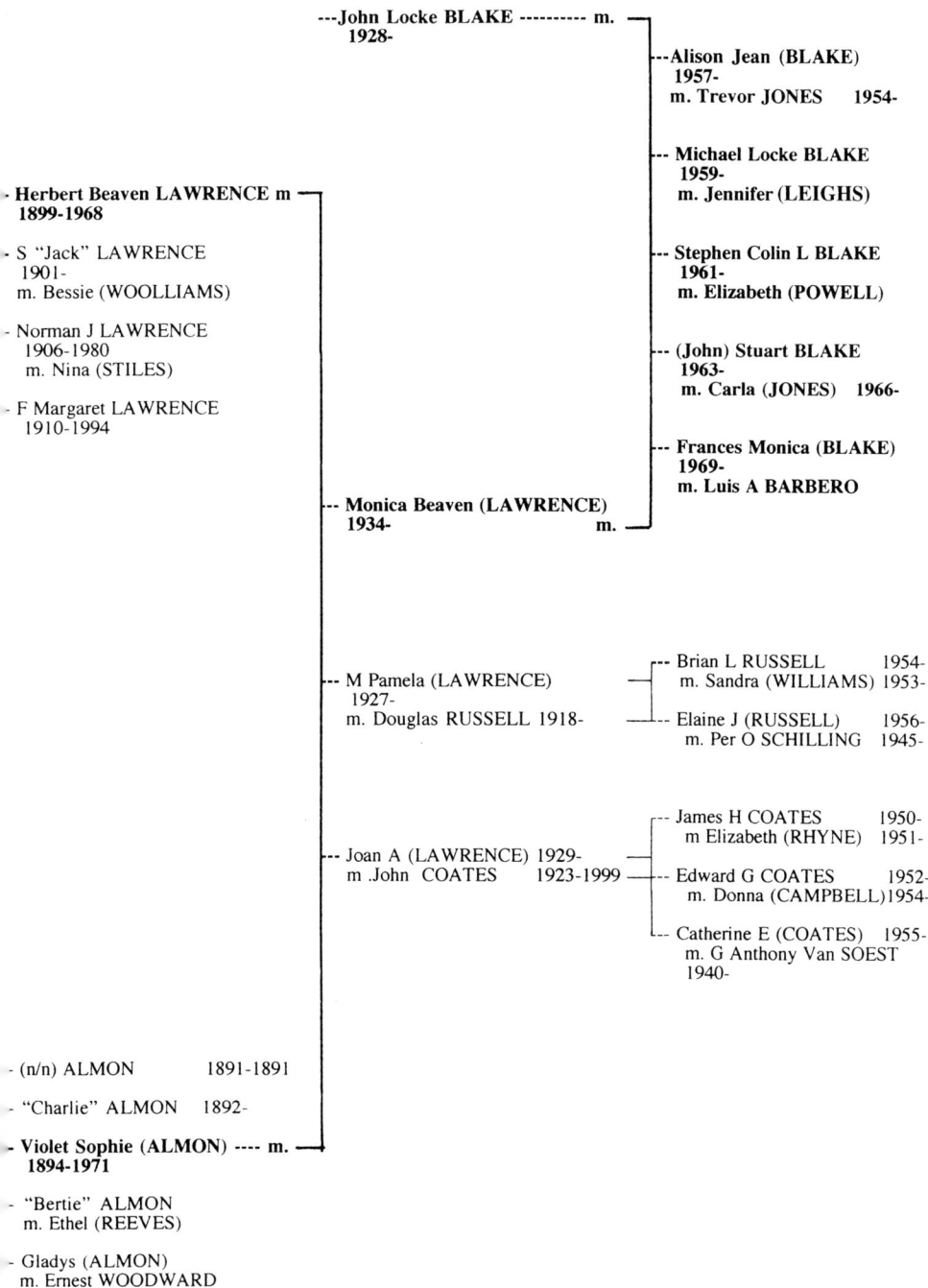

---John Locke BLAKE ---------- m.
    1928-

---Alison Jean (BLAKE)
   1957-
   m. Trevor JONES   1954-

--- Michael Locke BLAKE
    1959-
    m. Jennifer (LEIGHS)

- Herbert Beaven LAWRENCE m
  1899-1968

- S "Jack" LAWRENCE
  1901-
  m. Bessie (WOOLLIAMS)

--- Stephen Colin L BLAKE
    1961-
    m. Elizabeth (POWELL)

- Norman J LAWRENCE
  1906-1980
  m. Nina (STILES)

--- (John) Stuart BLAKE
    1963-
    m. Carla (JONES)   1966-

- F Margaret LAWRENCE
  1910-1994

--- Frances Monica (BLAKE)
    1969-
    m. Luis A BARBERO

--- Monica Beaven (LAWRENCE)
    1934-   m.

--- M Pamela (LAWRENCE)
    1927-
    m. Douglas RUSSELL 1918-

--- Brian L RUSSELL   1954-
    m. Sandra (WILLIAMS) 1953-

--- Elaine J (RUSSELL)   1956-
    m. Per O SCHILLING   1945-

--- Joan A (LAWRENCE) 1929-
    m .John COATES   1923-1999

-- James H COATES   1950-
   m Elizabeth (RHYNE)   1951-

--- Edward G COATES   1952-
    m. Donna (CAMPBELL)1954-

-- Catherine E (COATES)   1955-
   m. G Anthony Van SOEST
   1940-

- (n/n) ALMON   1891-1891

- "Charlie" ALMON   1892-

- Violet Sophie (ALMON) ---- m.
  1894-1971

- "Bertie" ALMON
  m. Ethel (REEVES)

- Gladys (ALMON)
  m. Ernest WOODWARD

Family Tree of Monica Beaven (Lawrence)

General Index

Family names (Blake, Lawrence etc) are indexed if they appear in the text, for others see Family trees.
Place names which appear in the text are indexed. For others see Maps.
References of both appearing frequently are limited to principal events.
Key references followed by much detail or several pages in **bold.**

Abrazo del Estrecho 32
Adam, Mount, FI 47, 201, 210
Acrolineas Argentinas 186, 246
Aeroposta Argentina 104, 110, 133
Affleck, Tommy 98, 132
Agrarian Reform 189, 379
Ajax Bay, FI 225
Alacaluf, people 15
Aldridge, Jesse and Pat 236
Alfonsín, President Raúl 376, 420
Allende, Salvador 300
Aljibe, El 306, 326
Almon, Capt. Henry Charles Moore 194
Almon, Violet (m. Lawrence) 194, 206, 300
Aloyz, Julio 81, 101, 118, 228
Aloyz, Raquel, de Simonato 101
Andes, mountains 32
Anita, Estancia 64, 87
Anson, Commodore George 5
Antarctica 399
Aónikenk (southern people) 15
Araucanians 1, 14
Argentine Republic **12**
Argentine Southern Land Company (ASL) 265, 324
Arrowsmith, Sir Edwin Porter 221
Arthur, Sir Raynor 204, 218, 221
Artilleros, mutiny 64
asado, asador 112
Asturiano, SS 83, 126, 165
Atacama desert 32
Auchmuty, Sir Samuel 9
Avila Star, SS 132
Aztecs 14

Baillon and Stickney 153
Baird, Sir David 7
Baker, river 107, 297
Balfour, Graham 135
Bank, London & South America 100, 104, 193, 261
Bank, London & Tarapacá 104, 234
Banks, Sir Joseph, FRS 27
Barbero, Luis Alberto 408, 420
Barbieri, Stelvio 310, 319, 334
Baring Brothers, bankers 24
Beagle Channel 27, 32, 331
Beagle, HMS, brig 25, 361
Bedatou, Peter & Sara 102
Behm, Ernest 64
Bell, A.E. 65, 317
Bellows, Fellowship of 142
Benetton, family and group 410, 414
Beresford, Col. William Carr 7, 10
Bertrand, Wickham 47, 153, 160, 377
Bío-Bío, river 1, 13
Bishops Hull 42
Blair, Peter Hunter 174
Blake, (Edward) William 77
Blake, (John) Humphrey 77, 122
Blake, (William) Seymour 108, 422
Blake, Admiral Robert 4, 41
Blake, Alison Jean (m. Jones) **219**, 233, 261, 263, 268, 281, 306, 323, 339, 385, 394, 400, 408
Blake, Arthur Locke **77**, 79, 83, 92, 95, 99, 116, 124, 132, 146, 165, 182, 186, 315
Blake, Bridget 74
Blake, Dorothea (née Herford) 47, 69
Blake, Dorothy (m. Carles) 95, 99, 173
Blake, Dr. Malachi (1771-1843) 41, 385

Blake, Edith (née Wedderburn) 74, 80, 120, 182, 217
Blake, Edward Jarman 49
Blake, Eleanor Muriel (m. Davis, Dixon) **110**, 149, 165, 214, 330
Blake, Fanny Follett Osler (née Browne) 43, 95
Blake, Frances Monica (m. Barbero) **284**, 308, 326, 338, 395, 408, 413
Blake, Hugh Worsley, and Ruth **102**, 119, 132, 138, 142, 145, 165, 169, 171, 214, 244
Blake, John 'The Elder' 40
Blake, John Locke **100**, 119, 136, 138, 146, 157, 168, 185, 191, 202, 228, 250, 354, 371, 400, 405
Blake, John Stuart Beaven ('Chacho') **263**, 308, 357, 369, 376, 395, 408, 420
Blake, Malachi Locke 44
Blake, Mary (m. Trehearne) 84
Blake, Michael Locke **236**, 267, 283, 307, 328, 341, 347, 355, 382, 396, 400, 408, 421
Blake, Millicent (née Worsley) 95, 98, 206, 235, 267
Blake, Monica (née Lawrence) **192**, 205, 216, 219, 236, 300, 330, 332, 389
Blake, Norman 77, 159, 377
Blake, Robert (1851-1931) 30, 44, 47, 58, 61, 63, 80, 95, 99, 152, 158, 217, 237
Blake, Robert Jr (Uncle Robert) **67**, 69, 73, 79, 83, 87, 116, 182, 317
Blake, Robert III (Bob) 119, 131, 265
Blake, Rosemary Joy (m. Goring) **115**, 149, 165, 244
Blake, Stephen Colin Lawrence **249**, 307, 331, 341, 355, 408, 421
Blake, Violet 69, 74, 123
Blake, William (1815-1901) 43
Blake, William Wedderburn 119, 182, 198, 377
Bolas, use of 147
Bolivar, Simón 12
Bonaparte, Napoleon & José 12
Bonner, Christopher 150, 174, 176, 180, 217, 400
Borrelli, Dr Pablo Jacinto 235, 284
Bougainville, Louis de 6
Bovril, beef producers 24
Bowen, Godfrey 255
Braun & Blanchard 61, 66, 72
Braun, Elías 72

Braun, Moritz 38, 65, 73
Braun, Sara 73
Bridge House 43
Bridges, David 120, 134
Bridges, Jannette 110
Bridges, Lucas 29, 107, 120, 297
Bridges, Thomas 28, 160
Bristol 28, 97, 121, 179
Britannia, HMS 217
British Antarctic Survey 217
British Club, Rio Gallegos 235, 259, 342
British Community in Argentina 18, 117, 144, 146, 206, 306, 311, 342, 376, 424
British Hospital, Buenos Aires 25, 110, 115, 342, 365
British Schools, Montevideo 195, 206
Buena Esperanza, Estancia 187
Buenos Aires Herald, newspaper 185
Buenos Aires 1, 7, 12, 16
Byron Sound 5, 48
Byron, Admiral John 5

Cable and Wireless 152, 195
Cadbury, family 97
Cadbury, Sir Adrian 178
Cadbury, Veronica 173
Cameron, A.A. 67
Campos Torreblanca, Francisco 104
Cañadon de las Vacas, Estancia 30
Canal, Grand Union 180
Canal, Kennet & Avon 180
Canning, George 11
Cape Fairweather, Estancia 54, 346
Cape Virgins 2, 29, 243, 294
Carles, Alan 173
Carmen de Patagones 6, 13
Casa Rosada 132
Cassidy, Butch 104
Castlereagh, Lord 11
Cerro Redondo, oil field 288
Cepernic, Jorge 310, 312
Chace, Edward (Ned) 36, 64, 70, 90, 229
Challenger, HMS 26
Charles II, King 4, 173
Chartres, River and farm, FI 47, 160
chatas (wagons) 106
Chennell, Derek and Helen 307, 322
Chilote people 15, 85, 238
Chubut, Territory/Province 30
Clark, William 34, 345
Clements, Babs (née Luxton) 160
Clifford, Sir Miles 197, 204

Clio, HMS 362
Coates, John (Chub) 196, 268
Cobb, Frederick Edward 44
Cochrane, Lord Alexander 13
Colburn, Oscar 277, 286
Collett, Sir Christopher 178
Colonia del Sacramento 10
Colorado, Rio (river) 104
Communist Party 300
Condor, Estancia 38, 67, 107, 143, 186, 215, **227**, 293, 310, 392, 414, 417
Cook, Bessie 120, 108, 110
Cook, Captain James 25, 27
Cooper, William & Nephews 92, 146
Coronel, Estancia 64, 86, 98, 132, 186, 315, 336, 425
Corrientes, *correntinos* 256, 332
Costa Mendez, Nicanor 368
Coy Inlet, Estancia 56, 251
Coyle, River 56
Craig, C. Thurlow 172, 207
Craufurd, General Robert 10
Crawford, Robert 24
Croft, Kemble 171
Cromwell, Oliver 4
Cross Owen, brig 62, 72
CSIRO (Commonwealth Scientific and Industrial Research Organisation) 276
Cullen Station (Estancia) 143, 297, 334
Curumalán, Estancia 73

Darwin Station, FI 46, 54
Darwin, Charles 27
Darwin, RMS 220
Davet, Otilia, and Erasmo 247, 283
Davies, Eric, and Joan 186, 216, 228, 237, 248, 272, 297
Davies, Richard 186
Davis, Chris 214, 244, 265
Davis, John 3, 6
De la Colina, Rodolfo 366, 375
Denholm, Alexander 54
Desaparecidos ('missing people') 302
Descamisados ('the shirtless') 189, 426
Deseado, Port/Puerto 6
Desire, ship 3
Despard, Rev. George Packenham 28
Dinosaurs 353
Dipping **89**, 164, 256
Dixon, Roderick 331
Donald, Mount, FI 46

Douglas DC3 aircraft 137, 143, 186
Drake, Sir Francis 3

Eberhardt, Capt Herman 38
Emmanuel College, Cambridge 146, 173, 376
Engledow, Sir F.S. 174
English School, San Julian 118
Esquel, town 32
Etchepare, Paul 275, 355, 382
Evans, Douglas and Mary 160
Evans, Dr R. 174
Evans, Orissa 160
Evans, Pole 160
Explotadora de Tierra del Fuego, Sociedad 231, 261, 296
Eyeclipping 239, 255

Falkland Islands Co (FIC) 45, 151, 220
Falkland Islands Government Air Service (FIGAS) 197, 220
FAO (Food and Agriculture Organisation of the United Nations) 274, 276, 280, 304
Farewell family 42
Felton, Carlos 345
Felton, Bet (m. Miller) 153
Felton, Henry 47
Felton, Herbert Stanley 38, 345, 353
Felton, John James 47
Felton, Kate (m. Bertrand) 47
Ferrero, *cacique* 64, 70
Fitzroy SS 151, 159, 214, 220
Fitzroy, Captain Robert 27
Florida, street 126
Floridablanca, San Julian 6
Football, Association 25, 331, 394
Football, Rugby 136, 175, 396, 400
Forbes, Archie 120
Fox Bay, FI 153
Fray Bentos, Uruguay 24
Frazer, Jack 56
Frazer, Ronnie and Nora 132
Fresno Star, SS 165

Galicia, *gallegos* 2, 142
Gallegos, river 2, 295
Galtieri, General Leopoldo Fortunato 332, 357, 367
Ganadera Coronel S.A. 317, 319
Gardiner, Allen 28
Gath y Chaves, store 112, 114, 126

Gauchos, Argentine 18, 172, 188, 241, 258
Gauchos, Falklands 46, 50, 204, 361
Gaviota, cabin cruiser **179**
Gebhard, Mateo 88
General Belgrano, ARA, cruiser 370
Gente Grande, Estancia 30
Gibson family 17
Gilmore, Dame Mary, and Will 353
Giménez, Isabelino 256, 332
Goats 109
Goodall, George 192
Goring, Jeremy 244
Government House, Stanley 163, 197, 204, 366
Grange School, The 133
Great Britain, SS 152
Greenaway, Dr Geoffrey 216
Greenshields, Thomas 294
Guanaco 15
Guards, Brigade of 10, 374
Guevara, Ernesto 'Ché' 302
Gurkhas 372, 374
Gymkhana, The 344, 358, 389

Halliday, William 38, 53
Hamilton, John 38, 54, 295
Hammond, Sir John 174
Harding, Hugh and Beat 153, 158, 182, 210, 219
Hatcher, John Bell 346, 351
Hawkins, Sir Richard 3
Hell's Kitchen 158
Hembury Fort Cross 120, 122
Herford, Rev. William H. 45
Hewlett, John 242, 251
Highland Brigade, RMS 123, 185
Highland Chieftain, RMS 126, 192
Hill Cove, FI 30, 48, 50, 56, 198, 213, 379
Hill Station, Estancia 53, 351
Hobbs, Ernest 30, 67, 147, 262, 293
Hobbs, Olive 134
Holdich, Col. Thomas Hungerford 32
Holmested, Blake & Co Ltd 49, 191, 214, 378, 380
Holmested, Ernest 30, 46
Hope, Annie 55
Hope, William 55
Hudson, William Henry 17
Hudson Volcano 401
Huincas (palefaces) 18
Hunt, Sir Rex 366

Immigration 21, 88
Incas 14
Independence, Decl (Argentina) 12, 360
Independence, Decl of (USA) 6
Industrial Revolution 21, 46
INTA (*Instituto Nacional de Tecnología Agropecuaria)* 273, 304, 316
Isla Pavón 34

Jackson, John, A. S. 135, 146
Jackson, Sir Geoffrey 300
Jacomb, Hilary, W. 66, 317
Jacomb, Hoare & Co 66, 253
Jamieson, Henry 54
Jarman, Hannah and Elizabeth 43
Johnson, Eric 159, 198
Johnson, Ted 159
Johnson's Harbour, FI 56
Jones, Carla 408, 420
Jones, Trevor 385
José Menéndez, SS 110, 115

Kelpers 154
Kennedy, Alec, and Ethel 81, 108, 132, 397
Keoken Artesanías 390
Keppel Island, FI 29, 54, 210
Killik Aike Norte, Estancia **345**, 369, 372, 405, 413, 418
Kimiri Aike, Estancia 249, 260, 295
King Edward VII, award 32, 294
King, Lieutenant Parker 26
Kirchner, Nestor Carlos 420
Kyle, Andrew 56, 66

La Anónima (Sociedad Anónima Importadora y Exportadora de la Patagonia) 73, 126
La Colmena, Estancia 55
La Quebrada, Estancia 149
Lafone, Samuel Fisher 18, 46, 206
Lafonia, FI 46
Lafonia, SS 163
Lago Argentino 28, 320, 323
Lamb marking 154, 238, 254, 335
Lambrook, school 120
Lapland 398
Lawrence, Joan (m. Coates) 194, 196, 268
Lawrence, Monica (m. Blake) **192**, 205, 216
Lawrence, Norman, and Nina 178, 214, 244
Lawrence, Pam (m. Russell) 194, 341
Lawrence, (Herbert) Beaven 193, 205, 214, 243, 281

Leach, Stephen 174, 180
Leighs, Jennifer 400, 408
Leleque, Estancia 265, 409
Lewin's Mead Meeting 97, 122
Lewis, Frank 160
Lewis, Maurice 161
Lexington, USS 361
Liebig Extract of Meat Co 24, 306
Liniers, Santiago 9
Lippert & Munro 66
Little, James 68
Llangollen 172
Loanda, barque 194
Locke, John of Pitminster 42
Los Machos, Estancia 67
Los Yngleses, Estancia 17, 73
Luxton, Connie (née Miller) 160, 219
Luxton, Keith 160

Macdonald, Archie 132, 149
MacGeorge, George 54, 394
Mackay, Dave and Rosie 156, 198
Mackay, John 98, 116, 132
MacLagan-Wedderburn, Dr 74
MacLean, Jack 55
Macleod, 'Chico' 81
Magellan, Ferdinand 2
Magellan, Straits of 3, 30, 268, 293
Maldonado, Uruguay 7, 9
Malvina House, Stanley 163, 219
Malvinas/Malouines 6, 366
Mann, Alec 98, 132, 140, 149, 229
Mann, Lydia m. Pickering 149, 186
Mann, Mary m. Pickering 149, 186
Manzaneros, people 6, 15
Mapuche people 6, 15, 389
Mark's Barn 95
Massey Ferguson Prize 401
Masters, Percival 249
Mata Grande, Estancia 66
Mate, beverage 35, **187**
Mathews, E, G, (Ted) 69, 161, 215, 317
Mathews, Edmund ,J. 66
Mathews, Jack 69, 79
Mayflower, ship 40
McAskill, John 56, 61
McCallum, Kenneth and Diana 287, 306
Menem, President Carlos 310, 420
Menéndez, Eduardo 325, 368, 385, 392, 399, 409
Menéndez, José 38, 62, 73, 104, 126, 250, 262

Menéndez, Ochoa & Paz (MOP) 325, 332, 410, 413
Mesopotamia campaign 79
Middleton, Mary (m. Augustin) 108
Miller, Barney 176, 180
Miller, Gen. William 13
Miller, John 16
Miller, Syd (Jr) 153
Miller, Sydney 67, 153, 201
Mimosa, ship 33
Miramar, Hotel 56, 81, 88, 102
Misioneros, Cañadon de los 35
Missionaries 6, 28
Monte Dinero, Estancia 294
Montevideo 194, 205
Montoneros 302, 310
Moreno, Dr Francisco P. 53
Morgan, Sir Henry 4
Moyano, Capitán Carlos Maria 35, 38, 53, 345
Munro, Donald 56, 61, 64, 79

Narborough, John 5
Navarino, SS 238
Newton, Richard Blake 18
Newton Turner, Helen 275, 287, 384
Northlands, school 149

O'Higgins, Bernardo 13
Odgers, William Blake, KC 177
Old Bridge 43
Olympian, SS 231
Ona people 15
Order of the British Empire 347, 354
Oren Aike, Estancia 66
Organic Movement 423
Oswestry 170

Pacific Steam Navigation Co 22
Pack, Colonel Denys 7, 10
Paine, Tim (Luis) 266, 324
Palermo Show 115, 346, 406
Paraná, gunboat 29
Pardo Darwin, Estancia 56, 66
Parish Robertson brothers 17
Paso Ibáñez 35, 56
Pasture improvement 278
Patagones, Carmen de 53
Patagonian Sheep Farming Co (1908) Ltd 215, 227, 265, 294, 368
Patterson, Robert 66, 69
Patterson, Bob (Jr) 132

Peat (fuel) 158, 161
Pehuenche people 15
Peñaloza, Pablo 253, 413
Perkins, Henry 88
Perón, Eva Duarte de (Evita) 188, 241
Perón, Juan Domingo 188, 241, 301, 311, 328
Perón, María Estela Martínez de (Isabelita) 188, 301, 367
Peronism **188**
Philip, Duke of Edinburgh 216
Philomel, SS 159, 220
Phoenix Hotel, Buenos Aires 82, 126, 161
Pickering, Duncan 228, 417
Pickering, Lionel 87, 132, 149, 165, 186, 319
Pickering, Tom 132, 149, 186, 319
Piedra Buena, Comandante Luis 29, 34, 53
Piedra Buena, town 35
Pilcañeu, Estancia 265
Pinkerton Detective Agency 104
Pinochet, Gen. Augusto 189, 301
Popham, Admiral Sir Home 7, 10
Port Egmont, FI 5, 9
Port Famine 4
Port Howard, FI 47, 66, 160, 213
Port Louis (*Puerto Soledad*), FI 6, 45, 360
Port Madryn 33
Port Stanley, FI 45, 152, 196
Posadas, Lago 107
Potter, family 81
Powell, Elizabeth 421
Prefectura Nacional (Coastguards) 328, 357
Princeton University 352
Punta Arenas 4, 30, 250, 260, 297
Punta Delgada, Estancia 258, 293
Punta Loyola 295

Quambone Station, NSW 68
Queen Elizabeth I 3
Queen Elizabeth II 229, 309, 357, 389
Queen Mother, The 74
Quichua people 14
Quigley, Agnes (m. Rodríguez) 104
Quigley, Tommy 102

Railway, BA Pacific 24, 134
Railways, Argentine 22
Rawson, Minister Guillermo 33
Red Cross 144
Regiment, 17th Training, RA 168, 170
Regiment, 68th Training, RA 170

Regiment, 71st Highland 7, 11
Regiments, other 7, 9
Reid, Tony 175
Reynard, Henry 30, 293
Rhea darwini (ostrich) 15, 117, 138
Riachuelo, river 10
Richards, family 41
Richmond, Don Juan 35
Rio Gallegos, town 29, 35, 53, 228, 391
Rippling Wave, schooner 57, 61, 73
River Plate 1, 7, 144, 165, 194, 360, 364
Rivero, Juan 87
Robertson, Charlie and Anne 154
Robertson, James 154
Robertson, Peter, and Ann 253, 304
Roca, Gen. Julio Argentino 31, 32, 36, 37, 362
Rocquaud, Ernesto 35
Rodney Lodge, Clifton 97, 123
Rodríguez de Lofredo, Florita 390
Roedean, school 95, 165
Rolfe, Bob 98
Rosas, Gen. Juan Manuel de 19
Rotary Club 268, 341, 399
Roy Cove, FI 47
Royal Artillery 168, 332
Rudd, Jack & William 38, 54
Rumboll, Maurice 323

Saint Exupery, Antoine de 110
Salto, Uruguay 194, 207, 388
San Julian Sheep Farming Co Ltd 65, 80, 116, 124, 142, 310
San Julian, Bay 2, 6, 60
San Julian, Port 57, 72, 87, 89, 101, 128, 424
San Martín, Gen. José de 12
Santa Cruz, Port/Puerto 35
Santa Cruz, river 2, 28, 34, 53, 411
Santa Cruz, Territory/Prov 31, 53, 321, 410
Santiago, Chile 133, 145
Sarmiento de Gamboa, Pedro 3
Sarmiento, Domingo Faustino 24
Saucemelú, Estancia 187
Saudi Arabia 410
Saunders, William 54
Saxby, Sydney 102
Schaer, gardener 109
School of Agriculture, Cambridge 174, 273, 285
School, Condor 264, 371

Scott, Evelyn 102
Scott, John 67, 102
Sedbergh, school 67
Shallow Bay, FI 47
Shearing 159, 184, 200, 255
Sheep breeds, Cheviot 183, 225
Sheep breeds, Cormo Argentino **288**, 304, 326, 333, 340, 348, 382, 394, 406, 416
Sheep breeds, Corriedale 68, 73, 100, 116, 183, 186, 225, 271, 285, 341, 346, 382
Sheep breeds, Merino 55, 73, 265, 271, 286, 382, 409
Sheep breeds, Polwarth 225, 378
Sheep breeds, Romney Marsh 52, 73, 225, 270, 346
Sheep keds ('tick') 164
Shields, Captain and Mrs, 121
Sholl, Lieutenant 26
Simplicity, barque 18
Siracusa, Antonino 319, 336, 424
Slocum, Joshua 30
Smith, John and Peter 38, 56
Smith, Sir Harry 9, 11, 16
Sociedad Rural Argentina 116, 279, 348, 406
Soil Association 422
Solís, Uruguay 222
Somerset Light Infantry 77, 168
Soto, Antonio 85
South American Missionary Society 28
Spanish Armada 3
Speake, Ernest 229, 252
Spearing and Waldron 62, 227
Sports Meeting (Races) 162, 213
Spurr, Captain Federico 29
St Andrews Scots School 25
St Andrews University 377
St George's College 132, 149, 176, 282, 339, 346
St Hilda's College 149, 251, 281, 306
St Paul's School 282, 306, 323
Stirling, Bishop Whait 29
Stokes, Captain Pringle 25
Stone runs 201
Stronach, Bettye 49
Stubenrauch, Hobbs and 31
Suggett, Kenneth 265, 324, 385
Sulivan House, Stanley 163
Summerhayes, David 166, 173, 365
Summerhayes, Nancy (née Johnson) 166
Summerhayes, Robert (Bobs) 166, 173, 180
Summerhayes, Sir Christopher 173
Sundance, Wyoming, USA 104

Swift & Co, freezers 100, 144, 149, 253, 298, 335
Sword, Bob 187
Sword, Donald 174 , 187

Taylor, John 96
Teal Inlet, FI 46
Teal River 156
Tehuelche people 2, 15, 33
Terrorism 299, 305
The Point Rincon, Hill Cove 158, 204, 210
Thompson, Basil 185
Thurn, A.H. (Bob) 282
Tierra del Fuego 2, 30
Top Settlement, Hill Cove 158, 210
Tordesillas, Treaty of 1
Torrey, family 41
Treaty 1881 32
Trelew 33
Trevelin, town 32
Tupamaros, terrorists 299, 302
Turner, Ethel, de Moyano 38
Tussac grass 61

University of New South Wales 274, 280
Uppingham, school 77
Ushuaia 29
Uspallata Pass 134, 137

Van Deurs, G.H. ('Willie') 310, 317, 319, 334
Vernet, Luis 361
Vernham, Miss 119
Viamonte, Estancia 30, 321
Viedma, Antonio de 6
Villarino, transport 29
Viñas, Dr Ismael P, 80

Wadham College, Oxon 41, 146
Wager, HMS 5
Waldron, Arthur 294
Waldron and Wood 81, 142, 227, 310
Waldron, Bill and Jean 186, 225, 249, 297
Waldron, Fay and Pamela 186
Waldron, James Lovegrove 47
Waldron, Maurice 227, 249, 310
Waldron family 38, 293
Wallace, William 56
War, 'Dirty' 87, **302**
War, English Civil 4
War, Peninsular 10, 12
War, South Atlantic 1982 10, **366**, 375

War, World I (1914-18) 77, 144
War, World II (1939-45) 92, 121, 123, 142, 189, 241, 299, 346
Ward-Best, Lieut. Dick 171
Weaver, Michael 150
Welbourne, Edward 146, 173
Welsh, colony 15, 31
Westfield, Winscombe 100, 166, 244, 265, 277, 285, 318, 324
Wheelwright, William 22
Whitelocke, General 10
Williams, Captain Juan 30
Williams, Sir David G.T. 178
Wolcott, family 41
Wood, Henry Pye 38
Wood, Mount 5

Wood, Philip Worsley 173
Woodman, Dr H.E. 174
Woods, Matilde (m. Almon) 194
Worsley, Edgar, and Vida 146, 173, 180, 355
Worsley, Francis, and Mary 173, 180
Worsley, Muriel (née Howard Smith) 97
Worsley, Philip (Rodney Lodge) 97, 121
Worsley, Philip Howard, and Peggy 95, 178
Worsley, Philip John 95, 113, 120, 173
Worsley, Sir Edward 173

Yaghans 15, 27
Yeabridge 67, 73
YPF (*Yacimientos Petrolíferos Fiscales*) 288, 365

Oxalis squamoso
radicosa Steud
Scurvy grass

Schinus dependens Ortega

Suaeda patagonica

Verbena ligustrina

Sympyosticum
narcissoides Mais
Pale Maidens

Sisyrinchium
junceum Mey

Sisyrinchium
F. S. chilegovolum

Lepidophyllum cupressiforme
A small bush